NINTH EDITION

FINANCIAL INSTITUTIONS, MARKETS, AND MONEY

David S. Kidwell
University of Minnesota

David W. Blackwell
Texas A&M University

David A. Whidbee
Washington State University

Richard L. Peterson
Texas Tech University

WILEY

John Wiley & Sons, Inc.

ASSOCIATE PUBLISHER   Judith R. Joseph

PROJECT EDITOR   Cindy Rhoads

EDITORIAL ASSISTANT   Brigeth Rivera

MARKETING MANAGER   Heather King

SENIOR PRODUCTION EDITOR   Patricia McFadden

SENIOR DESIGNER   Kevin Murphy

PHOTO EDITOR   Ellinor Wagner

PRODUCTION MANAGEMENT SERVICES   Hermitage Publishing Services

COVER DESIGN   David Levy

COVER PHOTO   ©Greg Pease/The Image Bank/Getty Images

This book was set in 10.5/12 Janson Text by Hermitage Publishing Services and printed and bound by Von Hoffmann Corporation. The cover was printed by Von Hoffmann Corporation.

This book is printed on acid-free paper. ∞

Library of Congress Cataloging-in-Publication Data

Financial institutions, markets, and money / David S. Kidwell . . . [et al.].–9th ed.
     p. cm.
  Includes bibliographical references and index.
  ISBN 0-471-69757-5 (cloth)
   1. Finance–United States. 2. Financial institutions–United States. 3. Banks and banking–United States. 4. Monetary policy–United States. I. Kidwell, David S.

HG181.K48 2005
332.1'0973–dc22   2004059087

Printed in the United States of America

10 9 8 7 6 5 4 3

PREFACE

TO THE STUDENT

We hope you are as excited about taking a course on financial institutions and
markets as we were about writing the book. The core topics covered in the book
are at the heart of what happens every day in the financial sector of the economy.
When you have finished the course, reading the *Wall Street Journal*, *The Financial
Times*, or the business section of the *New York Times* will be a piece of cake. Your
friends, family, and future colleagues will marvel at your insights!

As an introductory book, we stress fundamental concepts with an emphasis
on understanding how things really work. At the same time, the vibrancy and ex-
citement created by the dramatic changes taking place in the U.S. financial system are also an integral part of the text. Our goal is to provide a book that can
guide you to a confident mastery and understanding of the U.S. financial system
in an interesting and, hopefully, entertaining manner. The book is your passport
to linking your classroom experience to what is happening in the real world.
What you learn will be applicable to your business career or in managing your
personal financial affairs.

TO THE FACULTY

The focus of the ninth edition of *Financial Institutions, Markets, and Money* is the
same as the previous editions: to provide a balanced introduction to the operation, mechanics, and structure of the U.S. financial system, emphasizing its institutions, markets, and financial instruments. The Federal Reserve System
and its conduct of monetary policy are given special attention. We stress the
impact of monetary policy on interest rates and the way financial institutions
adjust their operations to reduce risk caused by changes to the interest rate environment.

Throughout the book we also stress the risks that financial institutions face
and how they can manage those risks in financial markets. These risks include
interest rate risk, credit risk, liquidity risk, foreign exchange risk, and political
(or regulatory) risk. Further, throughout the book, we recognize the impact that
technology and globalization are having on the operations and structure of the
financial system.

The book is written with a strong historical perspective. Throughout the
book we give attention to the historical development of financial institutions and
markets and discuss important historical events. We believe that relating historical events to the book's fundamental concepts gives the students a richer understanding of the material and a better perspective from which to evaluate current

developments. As with the first edition, we continue our free market approach to the analysis of economic, market and regulatory issues.

Teacher-Friendly.   In revising the book, we are mindful of the demands on faculty who are asked to do more with less. We want to help make your course on financial institutions and markets as successful as possible. To that end, we have worked hard to write in a clear and understandable manner. Also, we have put much effort into updating and improving the chapter learning features: chapter previews, boxed items, and chapter "take-aways." Finally, we provide first-rate teaching and learning aids such as the instructor's manual, test bank, study guide, and PowerPoint presentations that accompany each chapter.

The Book's Evolution.   Our book, like the financial system, has had to adapt to the rapidly changing economic environment. When we published our first edition, the existing textbooks were primarily descriptive, merely describing the activities of financial institutions, or they were *de facto* money and banking texts, primarily focused on the banking system and monetary policy. In our first edition, we broke new ground by emphasizing both financial institutions and markets, and how monetary policy affected financial institutions. At that time, our "free market" approach to regulation, which emphasized market-oriented rather than government-imposed solutions to problems was not mainstream and, to some, was considered controversial.

   As technology, regulation, and financial innovation changed the financial landscape, our book has had to evolve. In subsequent editions, we increased our emphasis on how interest rates are determined and on the structure of interest rates. We also increased our emphasis on the risks faced by financial institutions and on how institutions manage these risks using the financial markets. Over the years, we expanded our coverage of financial markets and, now for example, the book has separate chapters on mortgage markets, derivatives markets, and international markets.

The Competitive Edge.   Our approach to the topic made our book very successful in the early editions and it continues to be successful today. Imitation is the sincerest form of flattery, and we have seen a number of imitators of our approach, which apart from the wide use of this book, is the best evidence of its appeal both to students and faculty.

   Our *competitive edge*, however, comes from our adherence to the approach for the book that was set in the first edition. First, we stress the mastery of fundamental material, placing an emphasis on how things really work in a market context. Second, we have a balanced coverage of the U.S. financial system with strong emphasis on both institutions *and* markets. Third, we continually update the book to reflect major new developments in the financial system or to highlight changing trends. Finally, we focus on writing a book *for the students*, our most important audience, which facilitates learning and makes the study of financial institutions and markets an enjoyable experience.

Let Us Hear from You.   We thank the faculty that have adopted our book and the students that have purchased our book. As you go through your course, we hope that we have lived up to our promise of providing a clear, concise, well-written, and academically sound text on the U.S. financial system. If you have found a mistake or have concerns about a particular section, we would like to hear from you. Contact us via our e-mail addresses, which are listed at the end of the preface.

Apart from the customary updating of facts and exhibits throughout the book, we have worked painstakingly to improve the readability and the chapter features in this edition to better facilitate student learning. Consequently, we believe this edition of the book is better than the eighth edition for a number of reasons, which we discuss below.

KEEPING THE ATTIC CLEAN

Like an old house, a book entering its ninth edition accumulates clutter. In the ninth edition, we started the process of thoughtfully "cleaning out the attic." With help from many of you, we continue to review all materials and retain only what we believed essential for students. We appreciate your comments and suggestions.

EMPHASIS ON "REAL-WORLD" DATA

In this edition, especially in the chapters on financial markets, we continue our emphasis on how to read and interpret actual financial data, such as that reported in the Wall Street Journal or the Financial Times. For example, where allowed by copyright laws and availability, the data used to create exhibits will be made available so that it can be used for class projects or assignments.

MORE EFFECTIVE LEARNING

We continue to refine the chapter pedagogical features. Each chapter begins with a list of "Learning Objectives" that highlight for students the most important concepts. At the end of the chapter is a section called "Chapter Take-Aways" that provides a brief explanation of each of the important concepts highlighted in the Learning Objectives. To make learning easy, there is a one-to-one correspondence between the Learning Objectives and the corresponding numbered Chapter Take-Aways.

BETTER EXHIBITS

We have updated and revised all of the book's exhibits as necessary, but we have also simplified and streamlined many of the tables, charts, and graphs to allow the student to better understand the point of the exhibit. We have also expanded discussion of the exhibits in the text to better explain to the student what it is he/she should be taking away from the exhibits. There is a descriptive legend included with each exhibit, as appropriate, that gives a brief statement of what the student should be learning from the exhibit.

WHY IS THIS EDITION BETTER THAN THE PREVIOUS ONE?

The ninth edition has a number of features to motivate the interest of students and to help them learn the material. As we discussed above, each chapter begins with a Chapter Preview to motivate student interest in the chapter. Each chapter includes "Do You Understand?" questions, which appear several times in each chapter. These questions check student understanding of critical concepts in the material just covered or ask students to apply what they have just read to real-

PEDAGOGICAL FEATURES

world situations. To give students feedback on the "Do You Understand?" questions, we include the answers on the book's website, which is described below. The answers are also included in the Instructor's Manual. We provide captions for the exhibits to inform students of the main point they should draw from the exhibit. Learning Objectives appear at the beginning of each chapter and corresponding Chapter Take-Aways at the end of the chapter, as described above. We include a list of key terms and concepts at the end of each chapter. The terms appearing in the list are printed in boldface the first time they appear in the chapter. The definitions of all key terms and concepts appear in the glossary at the end of the book. Each chapter ends with questions and problems. The answers to these questions and problems are in the Instructor's Manual. Finally, we have provided an Internet Exercise at the end of each chapter. These exercises direct students to websites from which they can obtain additional information about the chapter's topic or analyze data that illustrate key points from the chapter.

ORGANIZATION OF THE BOOK

MAJOR CHANGES TO THE BOOK

Here we summarize the major changes to the book from the eighth edition. For those wanting to know more, see the detailed table of contents, which lists the major sections of a chapter.

Chapter 9, Mortgage Markets, has been completely rewritten. Because most students will eventually borrow money to buy a house, we make the material more meaningful to the student by discussing the mortgage lending process and underwriting criteria (e.g., credit scoring, loan-to-value ratios, payment-to-income ratios) while retaining the coverage of important institutional concepts.

Chapter 11, Derivative Securities, has been rewritten to include more real world examples and less institutional detail. One of the goals in revising this chapter is to pique the interest of students by applying the concepts in the chapter to realistic (but relatively straightforward) examples. Another goal is to focus on basic principles about how derivative securities work so that students gain some economic intuition about how to use them. Finally, we have deemphasized some of the institutional details found in previous editions.

Chapters 13 and 14, which cover commercial bank operations, performance, and management, retain the discussion of the industry as a whole, but we have made available, via the text's web site, a discussion of a specific bank's current situation as an example of the concepts discussed in the two chapters. In addition, the web site will provide up to date versions of selected exhibits from these two chapters.

POSSIBLE COURSE OUTLINES

We have organized this book to reflect a balanced approach to both financial markets and institutions, which reflects a typical course outline. However, depending on individual preference and course emphasis, there are alternative ways to organize the course and our book is written to allow for a reorganization of the chapters for professors who wish to give primary focus either to institutions or markets. The only constraint in our flexible design is that Parts 1 and 2 should be assigned first, because they provide the conceptual foundation and vocabulary for the financial system regardless of subsequent topic emphasis. The diagram below shows the balanced approach and an alternative sequence that emphasizes financial institutions:

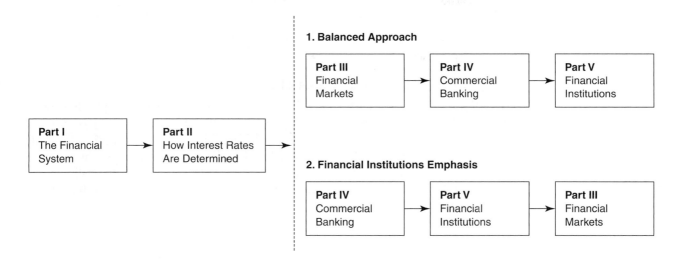

For this edition of the book, we offer updated, ancillary materials that should help both the students and the instructors who use this book.

ANCILLARY PACKAGE

INSTRUCTOR'S MANUAL WITH TEST QUESTIONS

Written by Babu G. Baradwaj at Towson University and Lanny Martindale at Texas A&M University, this volume contains a wealth of useful teaching aids, including chapter-by-chapter learning objectives, key points and concepts, answers to end-of-chapter questions and problems, and an outline of changes from the previous edition. Finally, the Test Bank, which includes at least 75 examination questions per chapter, has been updated to reflect the textbook's greater emphasis on numerical problems. It consists of True/False, Multiple Choice, and Essay type questions.

COMPUTERIZED TEST BANK

A computerized version of the Test Bank is available for use on an IBM PC computer (or compatible) running on MS-Windows. It contains content from the test bank provided within a Test Generating Program that allows instructors to customize their exams

STUDY GUIDE

Babu G. Baradwaj and Lanny Martindale have revised the Study Guide to reflect the revisions made to this ninth edition. Students will find this tool to be a valuable part of the learning package as they learn using this text. Each chapter provides a detailed chapter overview and list of learning objectives, topic outline, key terms review, completion, true/false and multiple-choice questions, problems, and annotated solutions. Each chapter also includes a short "Career Planning" section designed to encourage students to begin thinking about their careers. There is a special "Supplementary Material" section that expands and applies each chapter's concepts to the real world by providing library references and assignments and flow-of-funds data analysis assignments. In addition, each of the early chapters features a "How to Use *The Wall Street Journal*" section intended to acquaint students with the organization of the *WSJ*. In later chapters, specific sections, data tables, and other features that pertain to specific chapters, such as futures and options, are discussed in the appropriate chapters.

POWERPOINT® PRESENTATIONS

The PowerPoint® Presentations have been updated by Babu G. Baradwaj and Lanny Martindale so they reflect the updates within this revision. These chapter presentations are available on the companion web site. The presentation for each chapter provides bulleted lecture notes and figures, tables, and graphs selected from the text, ready for classroom presentation. Instructors with the full version of PowerPoint® on their computers can customize the lectures to reflect their personal course notes.

WEBSITE MATERIALS

A companion web site also accompanies this revision. It is located at www.wiley.com/college/kidwell and provides resources such as answers to the "Do You Understand?" questions found in each of the chapters of the text. The answers are accessible to both faculty and students. In addition, faculty adopting the book will be able to access an electronic version of the Instructor's Manual and Test Bank on the web site in addition to the Computerized Test Bank and PowerPoint Presentations. Students will also be able to access the PowerPoint lecture notes on the website.

There will be additional supplemental materials available on the companion web site. First, will be a chapter titled "History of the Financial System," which long-time users of the book will recall from previous editions. Second, the web site will contain a technical note on the deposit expansion process for instructors who wish to go into more detail about how to measure changes in the money supply resulting from Fed policy actions.

ACKNOWL-EDGMENTS

As with any textbook, we, the authors, owe an enormous debt of gratitude to many people. First, we thank the reviewers who have contributed valuable suggestions for this ninth edition:

Dean Baim, Pepperdine University
Rita Biswas, University of Albany
M.E. Bond, The University of Memphis
Myles J. Callan, University of Virginia
James M. Felton, Central Michigan University
Jann C. Howell, Iowa State University
Forrest Huffman, Temple University

Robert W. McLeod, University of Alabama
Rose M. Prasad, Central Michigan University
Robert Schweitzer, University of Delaware
Joseph F. Sinkey, Jr, The University of Georgia
John C. Yeoman, North Georgia College & State University

We also appreciate the many thoughtful reviews we have received over the previous eight editions. While their names are too numerous to list here, we are nonetheless grateful for their efforts and credit them with helping the book to remain a success.

At John Wiley & Sons, we are grateful to Judith R. Joseph, Associate Publisher, and Cindy Rhoads, Project Editor, who provided many helpful suggestions and much support, guidance, and motivation. We also applaud the efforts of editorial assistant, Brigeth Rivera, for her diligence in guiding the manuscript through the production process. The persistence and patience of Cindy and Brigeth are greatly appreciated. We would also like to thank Cindy Rhoads, for her coordination of the supplement package to accompany this revision. In addition, we appreciate the efforts of the other members of the Wiley team: Kevin Murphy, who coordinated the design of the stunning cover and layout of the book, and Patricia McFadden who performed superbly as production editor.

We gratefully acknowledge Mike McNamara of Washington State University who assisted us in the revision of Chapter 18, "Insurance Companies and Pension Funds." We also thank Lauren Dyal for valuable research assistance on Chapters 19 and 20.

Finally, we would like to thank our families for their encouragement and for putting up with our many hours at the writing table. To all, thank you for your support and help.

David S. Kidwell
Washington, D.C.
david@dskidwell.com

David W. Blackwell
College Station, Texas
dblackwell@cgsb.tamu.edu

David A. Whidbee
Pullman, Washington
whidbee@wsu.edu

Richard L. Peterson
Lubbock, Texas
chippete@aol.com

ABOUT THE AUTHORS

DAVID S. KIDWELL

Dr. David S. Kidwell is Professor of Finance and Dean Emeritus at the Curtis L. Carlson School of Management at the University of Minnesota. He holds an undergraduate degree in mechanical engineering from California State University at San Diego, an MBA from California State University at San Francisco, and a Ph.D. in finance from the University of Oregon.

Before joining the University of Minnesota, Dr. Kidwell was Dean of the School of Business Administration at the University of Connecticut. Prior to joining the University of Connecticut, he held endowed chairs in banking and finance at Tulane University, the University of Tennessee, and Texas Tech University. He was also on the faculty at the Krannert Graduate School of Management, Purdue University, where he was twice voted the outstanding undergraduate teacher of the year. Dr. Kidwell has published research in the leading journals, including *Journal of Finance, Journal of Financial Economics, Journal of Financial and Quantitative Analysis, Financial Management,* and *Journal of Money, Credit, and Banking.*

Dr. Kidwell has been a management consultant for Coopers & Lybrand and a sales engineer for Bethlehem Steel Corporation. He is an expert on the U.S. financial system and is the author of over 80 articles dealing with the U.S. financial system and capital markets. Dr. Kidwell has participated in a number of research grants funded by the National Science Foundation to study the efficiency of U.S. capital markets, and to study the impact of government regulations upon the delivery of consumer financial services.

Dr. Kidwell currently serves on the Boards of Schwan's Sales Enterprises, and Minnesota Life Insurance Company. He is the past Secretary-Treasurer of the Board of Directors of AACSB, the International Association for Management Education. He is a past member of the Boards of the Minnesota Council for Quality, the Stonier Graduate School of Banking, and the Minnesota Center for Corporate Responsibility. He has also served as an Examiner for the 1995 Malcolm Baldrige National Quality Award and is on the Board of Directors of the Juran Center for Leadership in Quality.

DAVID W. BLACKWELL

Dr. David W. Blackwell is the James W. Aston/RepublicBank Professor of Finance and Head of the Department of Finance at Texas A&M University's Mays Business School. Prior to joining Texas A&M, Dr. Blackwell worked several years as a consultant with PricewaterhouseCoopers LLP and KPMG LLP. Before his stint in the Big 4, Dr. Blackwell served on the faculties of the University of Georgia, the University of Houston, and Emory University. He was also a visiting professor at the University of Rochester.

Dr. Blackwell's areas of expertise include corporate finance, commercial bank management, and executive compensation. His publications have appeared in the leading scholarly journals of finance and accounting such as *Journal of Finance*, *Journal of Financial Economics*, *Journal of Financial and Quantitative Analysis*, *Financial Management*, *Journal of Financial Research*, *Journal of Accounting Research*, and *Journal of Accounting and Economics*.

While in the Big 4, Dr. Blackwell consulted on a broad range of litigation matters including securities, breach of contract, and intellectual property infringement cases. He also consulted on matters involving securities and business valuation, corporate governance, and executive compensation.

In addition, Dr. Blackwell has delivered executive education seminars in corporate finance and management of financial institutions for IBM, Kaiser Permanente, Chemical Bank, Southwire Company, Georgia Bankers Association, Warsaw Institute of Banking, Bratislava Institute of Banking, and the People's Construction Bank of China (PRC).

Dr. Blackwell earned his Ph.D. in Finance in 1986 and his BS in Economics in 1981, both from the University of Tennessee, Knoxville. He is a past president of the Southern Finance Association and a former Associate Editor of the *Journal of Financial Research*.

DAVID A. WHIDBEE

Dr. David A. Whidbee is an Associate Professor of Finance at Washington State University. He received his Ph.D. in Finance from the University of Georgia and his MBA and B.Sc. in Finance from Auburn University. After receiving his MBA, he worked as a financial analyst in the Chief Economist's Office at the Federal Home Loan Bank Board and, subsequently, the Office of Thrift Supervision. While on the staff at these regulatory agencies, he performed research and analysis on the thrift industry and prepared congressional testimony concerning the problems the industry faced in the late 1980s.

In 1990, Dr. Whidbee left the OTS to begin the Ph.D. program in Finance at the University of Georgia where he wrote his dissertation on corporate governance in the banking industry and began teaching financial markets and institutions. His other teaching interests are in the areas of commercial banking, financial institutions, and corporate finance. Upon completing the Ph.D. program, he joined the faculty at California State University, Sacramento, where he taught commercial banking and financial markets and institutions. In 1997, he left Cal State Sacramento to join the faculty at Washington State University, where he continues to teach commercial banking and financial markets and institutions.

Dr. Whidbee's research interests are in the areas of financial institutions and corporate governance. His work has been published in several outlets, including the *Journal of Business*, the *Journal of Accounting and Economics*, the *Journal of Banking and Finance*, the *Journal of Corporate Finance*, *Financial Management*, and the *Journal of Financial Services Research*. In addition, he has presented his research at numerous academic and regulatory conferences.

RICHARD L. PETERSON

Dr. Richard L. Peterson is Professor of Finance Emeritus at Texas Tech University. Dr. Peterson was the "High Scholarship Graduate in Economics" from Iowa

State University in 1962, and received a Ph.D. in Economics from the University of Michigan in 1966. Subsequently, he taught economics at Southern Methodist University, was a financial economist on the staff of the Board of Governors of the Federal Reserve System, and served as the Associate Director of Purdue University's Credit Research Center before joining Texas Tech University in 1982 as a Professor of Finance and holder of the I. Wylie and Elizabeth Briscoe Chair of Bank Management. He has taught at numerous schools in the United States and abroad for domestic and international financial institution executives and has consulted for Dun and Bradstreet, Chemical Bank, Citicorp, and the National Second Mortgage Association. He has served as an expert witness for law firms representing the FDIC in savings and loan litigation, in New York Stock Exchange arbitration hearings, and in other matters.

Dr. Peterson has also written a book titled *The REAL Social Security Problem* and has published numerous papers. His papers have appeared in the *Journal of Money, Credit, and Banking; Journal of Finance; Journal of Financial and Quantitative Analysis; Journal of Financial Research; Journal of Financial Services Research; Journal of Futures Markets; Bell Journal of Economics; Quarterly Journal of Economics; Journal of Macroeconomics; American Banker; Banker's Magazine;* and numerous other publications. He also has presented papers at numerous academic meetings and at conferences sponsored by Federal Reserve Banks and Federal Home Loan Banks, and he participated in the American Assembly's comprehensive study of the U.S. financial system and its regulation.

He received Texas Tech's President's Excellence in Teaching Award in 1989 and its Academic Achievement Award in 1992. Dr. Peterson remains active in practical finance as a writer of tracts on financial and economic policy issues and as an investor in real estate, stocks, bonds, futures, and options.

BRIEF TABLE OF CONTENTS

Contents

HOW INTEREST RATES ARE DETERMINED   83

PART II

FINANCIAL MARKETS 165

PART IV

COMMERCIAL BANKING   367

THE FINANCIAL SYSTEM

1

An Overview of Financial Markets and Institutions

CHAPTER PREVIEW

This chapter is about the U.S. financial system, which consists of financial markets and institutions. Some of the players in the financial system are household words like the New York Stock Exchange, Bank of America, Wells Fargo Bank, and GE Capital. Others are lesser-known firms with characteristics that vary widely, such as size, reputation, product line, and international presence.

The role of the financial system is to gather money from people and businesses that have more money than they need right now and route those funds to those that can use them for either business or consumer expenditures. The flow of funds through financial markets and institutions in the U.S. economy is huge—trillions of dollars—and the flow impacts business profits, the rate of inflation, interest rates, and the production of goods and services. In general, the larger the flow of funds and the more efficient the financial system works, the greater the economic output and welfare in the economy. It is not possible to have a modern, complex industrial economy like that in the United States without an efficient and sound financial system.

The financial system also affects your everyday life. For example, Bob is a business major and receives an $8,000 student loan for college at the beginning of the school year, but he needs only $3,000 of it right away. Bob deposits the $8,000 in the bank near campus but is surprised to learn that even at this amount his checking account pays no interest because his balance is below the bank's minimum balance requirement. The bank manager suggests that Bob buy a $5,000 certificate of deposit (CD) that pays 5 percent interest and matures just as the winter semester begins. Bob buys the CD because the interest rate is very competitive and the timing of the funds matches his need to buy books and pay tuition for the winter semester.

At the same time that the bank received Bob's $8,000, it was reviewing an application from the local pizza shop for a $25,000 loan to expand its home delivery service. The loan interest rate is 9 percent, payable in five years, and money from Bob's CD is pooled with the money from other CDs the bank recently sold. Consistent with the bank's goal of profit maximization, the bank ultimately decided to make the pizza shop loan because of the project's favorable rate of return and the owner's high credit standing. Other loans were rejected because the applicant had a poor credit rating and/or the project's rates of returns were not as favorable as the pizza shop loan. The bank is happy with the pizza shop loan at 9 percent because it has borrowed the money for 5 percent, earning a tidy 4 percent (9 – 5) gross profit margin.

In the bigger picture, the financial system works properly when consumers receive the highest possible interest rates for their CDs and deposits and only projects with favorable rates of return and good credit standing are financed. The more efficient and competitive the financial system, the more likely this is to happen. ∎

The financial system is like a huge money maze—funds flow to borrowers from lenders through many different routes at warp speed. The larger and more efficient the flow, the greater the economic output and welfare of the economy.

This chapter presents an overview of the financial system and how it facilitates the allocation of funds throughout the economy. The chapter begins by describing the role of the financial system, defining surplus and deficit spending units, and describing characteristics of financial claims. It then explains how surplus and deficit spending units are brought together in financial markets, either directly or with the help of financial intermediaries. Next, the chapter identifies the types of financial institutions and markets that exist in the United States and the benefits they provide to the economy. Finally, the chapter provides a unifying framework for the book by discussing the five key risks faced by financial institutions and participants in financial markets: interest rate risk, credit risk, liquidity risk, foreign exchange risk, and political risk. ∎

LEARNING OBJECTIVES

The objectives of this chapter are to:

1 Explain the role of the financial system and why it is important to individuals and to the economy as a whole.

2 Explain the function of direct and indirect financial markets and the role of financial institutions.

3 Describe a financial claim and identify the characteristics that make various financial claims unique.

4 Describe the economic services provided by financial institutions.

5 Explain the economic function of the money markets and identify the most important money market securities.

6 Explain the economic function of the capital markets and identify the most important capital market securities.

7 Identify the key risks that financial institutions face and describe how financial institutions manage these risks.

ROLE OF THE FINANCIAL SYSTEM

The financial system consists of financial markets and institutions. Financial markets are just like any kind of market you have seen before: people buy and sell, haggle and argue, win and lose, and, yes, some may become rich playing in financial markets and others may lose it all. Markets can be informal like a flea market in your community or highly organized and structured like the gold markets in London or Zurich. The only difference is that in financial markets, people buy and sell financial instruments like stocks, bonds, futures contracts, or mortgage-backed securities. **Financial institutions**, as part of the financial system, also facilitate the flow of funds from savers to borrowers. They are firms such as commercial banks, credit unions, life insurance companies, and finance companies. Financial institutions are called by a special name: **financial intermediaries**. These firms dominate the financial scene worldwide and are the firms that most consumers transact with when they seek financial services. We now turn to a discussion of how economic units and financial intermediaries transact in the financial markets.

All economic units can be classified into one of the following groups:

1. Households
2. Business firms
3. Governments (local, state, and federal)

Each economic unit must operate within a budget constraint imposed by its total income for the period. Households, like the one you may have grown up in, typically receive income in the form of wages and then make frequent expenditures for food, clothing, medical expenses, entertainment, education of children, taxes, and housing expenses either as rent or home mortgage payments. Businesses sell a variety of goods and services to households and other businesses for revenues and spend their money to pay wages, buy inventory, and for expenses necessary for production. Occasionally, businesses make capital expenditures in the form of new buildings and equipment. Governmental units obtain income by collecting taxes and fees and make expenditures for myriad services, such as health, welfare, education, police and fire protection, and, in the case of the federal government, military protection.

BUDGET POSITION

Just like you, for a given budget period, any economic unit can have one of three possible budget positions: (1) a balanced budget position: income and planned expenditures are equal; (2) a surplus position: income for the period exceeds planned expenditures; or (3) a deficit position: expenditures for the period exceed receipts. The financial system is concerned with funneling money—and with it purchasing power—from **surplus spending units (SSUs)** to **deficit spending units (DSUs)**. DSUs include some households, some state and local governments, the federal government in most periods, and a large number of businesses. Other economic units may be SSUs. Taken as groups, however, business firms and governments are typically DSUs. Somewhat surprisingly, overall, households are SSUs.

SSU → lenders
DSU → borrowers

What makes a household an SSU or a DSU? There is a strong correlation between a person's age and whether that person is a DSU or SSU. People typically start out life as "big time" DSUs (child rearing is expensive) and remain that way, more or less, until they graduate from college. There is typically a brief flirtation with being an SSU as a young single or married couple. Then, once child rearing is undertaken, one gains a greater appreciation for their parents as they rejoin the ranks of the DSUs. At some point in time, children graduate from college, the house is paid for, the dog dies, and family units become SSUs. Of course if you are rich, you may spend most of your life as an SSU—not a bad situation. Remember that the only difference between the rich and the poor is that the rich have more money!

FINANCIAL CLAIMS

The problem facing the financial system is how to transfer the SSUs' excess purchasing power to the DSUs that wish to borrow to finance current expenditures.

The transfer can be accomplished by an SSU lending money to and accepting an IOU from a DSU. An IOU is a written promise to pay a specific sum of money (the principal) plus a fee (an interest rate) for the privilege of borrowing the money over a period of time (maturity of the loan). IOUs are called **financial claims**. They are claims against someone else's money at a future date.

To a DSU, a financial claim is a liability, and the interest payments are the penalty for consuming before income is earned. To the SSU, the financial claim is an asset, and the interest earned is the reward for postponing consumption. The fact that financial claims (IOUs) are liabilities for borrowers (DSUs) and are simultaneously an asset for lenders (SSUs) illustrates the two faces of debt. That is, total financial liabilities outstanding in the economy must equal total financial assets.

Once a financial claim is outstanding, the lender (SSU) may hold the claim until it matures. Alternatively, the SSU may sell the financial claim to someone else before it matures. The DSU continues to have use of the funds even though the lender is now a different party.

The ability to resell financial claims is important because it allows SSUs to purchase financial claims with maturities that do not exactly match their investment horizon. If an SSU purchases a financial claim with maturity longer than the planned investment period, the claim can be resold to another SSU at the appropriate time. Likewise, an SSU can purchase a financial claim with maturity shorter than its time horizon if additional claims, either new or outstanding, can be easily purchased. The ease with which a financial claim can be resold is called its **marketability**.

There are a wide variety of financial claims that trade in the financial markets, all designed to meet the preferences of both SSUs and DSUs. Financial claims differ according to their maturity, risk of default, marketability, tax treatment, and other special features that may be attached to them such as options or convertibility into another type of financial claim. How these characteristics interact to determine the interest rate on a financial claim is the topic of Chapter 5.

TRANSFERRING FUNDS FROM SSUs TO DSUs

The purpose of the financial system is to transfer funds from SSUs to DSUs in the most efficient manner possible. The job of bringing DSUs and SSUs together can be done by (1) **direct financing** or by (2) **indirect financing**, or, as it is more commonly called, **financial intermediation**. Regardless of the financing method, the goal is to bring the parties together at the least possible cost and with the least inconvenience. An efficient financial system is important because it ensures adequate capital formation for economic growth. Thus, if the system works properly, firms with the most promising investment opportunities will receive funds, and those with inferior opportunities will not receive funding. In a similar manner, consumers who are willing and able to pay the current market rate of interest can purchase cars, boats, vacations, and homes on credit—and thus have them now rather than waiting until they have the money.

DIRECT FINANCING

In direct financing, DSUs and SSUs exchange money and financial claims directly. DSUs issue financial claims on themselves and sell them directly to SSUs for money. The SSUs hold the financial claims in their portfolios as interest-bearing assets. The financial claims are bought and sold in **financial markets**. The transactions appear as changes in the balance sheets (asset and liability holdings) of the two parties as follows:

SSU		DSU	
Assets	**Liabilities**	**Assets**	**Liabilities**
−Money to DSU		+Money from SSU	+Direct claims sold to SSU
+Direct claims bought from DSU			

The claims issued by the DSU are called **direct claims** and are typically sold in direct credit markets, such as the money or capital markets. Direct financing gives SSUs an outlet for their savings, which provides an expected return, and DSUs no longer need to postpone current consumption or forgo promising investment opportunities for lack of funds. Thus, direct credit markets increase the efficiency of the financial system.

In simplified form, the upper portion of Exhibit 1.1 illustrates the flow of funds from SSUs to DSUs by way of direct financing in financial markets. An important characteristic of the direct financial market is that it is a wholesale market, where the minimum transaction or financial claim denomination is $1 million or more. We shall now discuss some of the institutional arrangements that facilitate the transfer of funds in the direct credit markets.

direct financial market
⇒ wholesale market
(denomination ⇒ 1 million)

EXHIBIT 1.1
Transfer of Funds from Surplus to Deficit Spending Units

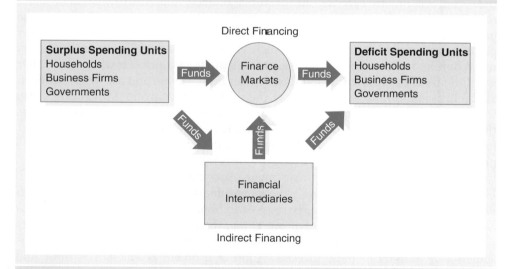

The role of the financial system—financial institutions and markets—is to facilitate the flow and efficient allocation of funds throughout the economy. The greater the flow of funds, the greater the accommodation of individuals' preferences for spending and saving. An efficient and sound financial system is a necessary condition to having a highly advanced economy like the one in the United States.

Private Placements.   The simplest method of transferring funds between SSUs and DSUs is a **private placement**. Here a DSU, such as a corporation, sells an entire security issue to a single institutional investor or small group of such investors. The advantage of a private placement is the speed with which funds can be committed and the low transaction cost of bringing the securities to market. An investment banker usually assists in private placements and charges a fee for helping to design and place the securities.

Investment Bankers.   Another direct method of bringing financial claims to market is with the services of an **investment banker**. Investment bankers help DSUs market newly created financial claims, often called IPOs (initial public offerings). To do this, the investment banker purchases an entire issue of stocks or bonds from the DSU at a guaranteed price and then resells the securities individually to investors at a higher price, a process known as **underwriting**. Investment bankers provide other services for their clients, such as helping prepare the prospectus, selecting the sale date, and providing general financial advice to the issuer. Issuers who enter the direct financial markets infrequently or have complicated financial deals find these services valuable. Investment bankers are compensated for underwriting services through what is called an **underwriting spread**, which is the difference between the investment banker's purchase price and sale price.

Brokers and Dealers.   Once financial claims have been issued, they may be resold to other investors. To aid in the search process of bringing buyers and sellers together, a number of market specialists exist. **Brokers** do not actually buy or sell securities; they only execute their clients' transactions at the best possible price. Thus, brokers provide only a search service in that they act as "matchmakers," bringing SSUs and DSUs together. Brokers are compensated for their services with a commission fee. **Dealers**, on the other hand, "make markets" for securities. They do this by carrying an inventory of securities from which they stand ready either to buy or sell particular securities at quoted prices. Dealers make profits by selling from their inventory and, on average, sell securities for a higher price than they paid for them. The dealer's **bid price** is the highest price it offers when purchasing a security. The **ask price** is the lowest price at which the dealer is willing to sell a security. The difference between the bid and ask price is known as the **bid-ask spread** and represents the dealer's gross profit. Most dealers also function as brokers and typically specialize in a particular type of market, such as the commercial paper market, bond market, or equity market.

INDIRECT FINANCING

Until now we have considered only the flow of funds from SSUs to DSUs through direct credit markets—the upper portion of Exhibit 1.1. There are some problems with direct financing, however. For one thing, the denominations of the securities sold in direct credit markets are very large ($1 million or more), and thus few consumers can transact in these markets. Another problem is that DSUs must find SSUs that want direct claims with precisely the characteristics they can and will sell.

As an example, Bob, the student featured in the chapter preview, needs the proceeds from his student loan to pay for tuition and books at the beginning of the spring semester in 3 months. Therefore, he probably would not want to invest his funds in a 30-year corporate bond because it has a longer maturity than he needs. In addition, Bob's CD is risk free because the Federal Deposit Insurance

Corporation insures the bank's deposits. The corporate bond market is much more risky, and Bob may not want to risk having the price of the bonds go down, thereby jeopardizing his ability to pay his tuition. In sum, the CD gives Bob a safe place to store his money until he needs it and at the same time earn interest.

As shown in the lower portion of Exhibit 1.1, if financial intermediaries are involved, the flow of funds from SSUs to DSUs can be indirect. Financial intermediaries transform financial claims in ways that make them more attractive to the ultimate investor. Financial intermediaries include commercial banks, mutual savings banks, credit unions, life insurance companies, and pension funds, to name a few. These and other financial intermediaries emerged because of inefficiencies found in direct financing. For direct financing to take place, the DSU must be willing to issue a security with a denomination, maturity, and other security characteristics that match exactly the desires of the SSU. Unless both the SSU and DSU are satisfied simultaneously, the transfer of money will probably not take place. For example, Bob, with his limited funds, cannot purchase 3-month commercial paper, which would have a higher yield than his bank CD, because the minimum transaction in the commercial paper market is a cool, but large, $1 million.

To overcome these problems, financial intermediaries intervene between the borrower (DSU) and the ultimate lender (SSU). Financial intermediaries purchase direct claims (IOUs) with one set of characteristics (e.g., term to maturity, denomination) from DSUs and transform them into indirect claims (IOUs) with a different set of characteristics, which they sell to the SSU. This transformation process is called financial intermediation. Firms that specialize in intermediation are called financial intermediaries or financial institutions; these two terms are interchangeable. And to no one's surprise, **disintermediation** is the reverse: SSUs take their funds out of financial institutions and invest in direct claims in the direct financial markets. The changes in balance sheets describing financial intermediation are as follows:

financial intermediation

SSU		Financial Intermediary		DSU	
Assets	Liabilities	Assets	Liabilities	Assets	Liabilities
−Money to financial intermediary		+Money from SSU	+Indirect claim to SSU	+Money from financial intermediary	+Direct claim to financial intermediary
		−Money to DSU			
+Indirect claim from financial intermediary		+Direct claim from DSU			

Notice that the balance sheet of the financial intermediary consists entirely of financial claims—indirect claims as a source of funds (liabilities) and direct claims as a use of funds (assets). Furthermore, notice that in the financial intermediation market, the SSU's claim is against the financial intermediary rather than the DSU, as is the case with direct financing. The financial intermediation market is typically a retail market, and the indirect financial claims issued by financial intermediaries are often given names such as checking accounts, savings accounts, or money market fund shares.

DO YOU UNDERSTAND?

1. What is the role of the financial system and why is it important to the economy?
2. What is a financial claim? How can a financial claim be both an asset and a liability at the same time?
3. What are some problems with direct financing that make indirect financing a more attractive alternative?
4. Explain what is meant by the term "financial intermediation."
5. What are investment banks and what role do they play in the financial system?

THE BENEFITS OF FINANCIAL INTERMEDIATION

Financial intermediaries are firms that operate to make a profit. They buy and sell specialized financial products. More specifically, they buy financial claims (held as assets of the intermediary) like business loans, consumer installment loans, corporate bonds, corporate common stock, and government bonds from DSUs. These financial claims have characteristics designed to meet the needs of particular DSUs. Financial intermediaries finance the purchase of these financial claims by selling financial claims on themselves (held as liabilities of the intermediary) like checking accounts, savings accounts, life insurance policies, and mutual fund shares to SSUs. These financial claims have characteristics that are attractive to SSUs.

To earn profits, financial intermediaries buy financial claims from DSUs whenever the income generated by the financial claim is expected to cover all of their borrowing and production costs. Let us explain. In the example about Bob in the preview to this chapter, the local bank might charge the pizza shop owner 9 percent for the business loan, and the bank's cost of funds for time deposits might average 5 percent. Thus, the banker's gross interest margin is 4 percent, from which the bank has to cover its cost of manufacturing the loan, its overhead expenses, and the risk of not getting paid back. This is an application of the banking axiom of "lend high and borrow low!" Sounds like a good business as long as everyone pays you back.

3 sources of benefits

Financial intermediaries enjoy three sources of comparative advantage over others who may try to produce similar services. First, financial intermediaries can achieve economies of scale because of their specialization. Because they handle large numbers of transactions, they are able to spread out their fixed costs. Second, financial intermediaries can reduce the transaction costs involved in searching for credit information. A consumer who wishes to lend directly can also search for information, but usually at a higher cost. Finally, financial intermediaries may be able to obtain important but sensitive information about a borrower's financial condition because they have a history of exercising discretion with this type of information. Furthermore, the intermediary may be able to reduce the problem of unreliable information because of its intimate knowledge of the borrower's operations, personal history, and character.

For the reasons mentioned above, financial intermediaries are often able to produce financial services at a lower cost than individual consumers. If they did not, individuals would "manufacture" their own financial services and thus would transact in the direct credit markets. Financial intermediaries exist, therefore, because of the high transaction costs involved in producing many financial services in small quantities.

Finally, it is worth noting that competition among financial intermediaries tends to force interest rates to the lowest level compatible with their cost structures, which means, for the reason given above, lower interest rates in the overall economy. A high rate of economic growth requires a substantial amount of business expenditures (investments). The lower interest rates, the more willing businesses are to make expenditures on real investments.

The lower the interest rate, the higher rate of economic growth (by Investment)

PEOPLE & EVENTS

Japanese Financial System: The Great Economic Snooze

The Japanese economy, once the envy of the world, went into a 13-year economic slump following the stock market crash of 1989. During the 1990s, the economy struggled to stay afloat, and by the end of 2002 industrial production was 10 percent below its 1989 level. The once "power economy" of the 1980s become the undisputed "snooze" champion of the industrial world.

Unfortunately for the people of Japan, the country became a case study of the importance of a well-functioning financial system. Many of the country's economic woes can be attributed to troubled financial institutions, especially commercial banks. Banks were so loaded with bad loans they were reluctant to make any new loans. Compounding the problem was the weak capital position of many large Japanese banks. It took years for Japanese authorities to recognize and admit to the scale of the problem. They had hoped that the economy would "grow" its way out of trouble, but it never did. As a result, the economy continued to sputter, bad loans piled up at banks, and bank lending continued to decline. Some banks failed, were nationalized, or had to merge. The crisis cost more than mere money, as some senior bank officials took their own lives.

When banks and other financial institutions are unwilling to make loans, businesses must seek financ-

ing in the direct credit markets or forgo promising investment opportunities. However, when the economy is struggling, investors lack confidence in government policies and typically are unwilling to buy stocks or debt sold by businesses in the credit markets. As a result, promising investment opportunities are passed over and the economy languishes, as was the case in Japan.

On the bright side, during 2002 the Japanese government announced a new plan to foster economic growth by calling on banks to make more loans, introduced new measures to support the stock market, pledged to forestall any financial crisis by bailing out failing banks, and loosened up monetary policy at the central bank. Since then, Japanese banks have made serious inroads into their nonperforming loans, Japanese exports have done especially well, and the economy is growing for the first time in years (real gross domestic product [GDP] was up 6.4 percent in the fourth quarter of 2003). On the other hand, some economists see the government plan as too timid and weak to drive a significant economic recovery.

As a follow-up, you might want to check the *Wall Street Journal* to see how the Japanese economy is faring. Regardless of what you find, the Japanese case illustrates the importance of the financial system to the overall economic well-being of a country's economy.

INTERMEDIATION SERVICES

In "transforming" direct financial claims into indirect ones, financial intermediaries perform five basic services:

Denomination Divisibility. Financial intermediaries are able to produce a wide range of denominations—from $1 to many millions. They can do this by pooling the funds of many individuals and investing them in direct securities of varying sizes. Of particular importance is their acceptance of deposits from individuals who typically do not have money balances large enough to engage in the wholesale transactions ($1 million or more) found in direct financial markets.

Currency Transformation. Many U.S. companies export goods and services to other countries, but few individuals living in the United States are willing to finance the overseas activities of these companies by buying direct financial claims denominated in a foreign currency. Financial intermediaries help to finance the global expansion of U.S. companies by buying financial claims denominated in one currency and selling financial claims denominated in other currencies.

Maturity Flexibility. Financial intermediaries are able to create securities with a wide range of maturities—from 1 day to more than 30 years. Thus, they are able to buy direct claims issued by DSUs and issue indirect securities with precisely the maturities (usually shorter) desired by SSUs. For example, savings and loan associations obtain funds by issuing passbook accounts and savings certificates and invest the funds in long-term consumer mortgages.

Credit Risk Diversification. By purchasing a wide variety of securities, financial intermediaries are able to spread risk. If the securities purchased are less than perfectly correlated with each other, the intermediary is able to reduce the fluctuation in the principal value of the portfolio. Portfolio diversification is an application of not putting "all of your eggs into one basket," where they might be "broken" simultaneously.

Liquidity. For most consumers, the timing of revenues and expenses rarely coincides. Because of this, most economic units prefer to hold some assets that have low transaction costs associated with converting them into money. Many of the financial commodities produced by intermediaries are highly liquid. For example, a checking account permits consumers to purchase an asset or repay a debt with minimal transaction cost.

5 types of intermediation

Financial intermediaries, therefore, tailor the characteristics of the indirect securities they issue to the desires of SSUs. They engage in one or more distinct types of intermediation: (1) denomination intermediation, (2) currency intermediation, (3) risk intermediation, (4) maturity intermediation, and (5) liquidity intermediation. They provide these and other services to earn a profit. SSUs and DSUs use these services as long as the cost of doing so is less than providing the services for themselves through the direct credit markets.

SSUs' or DSUs' choice between the direct credit market and the intermediation market depends on which market best meets their needs. Typically, consumers whose transactions are small in dollar amount (retail transactions) find that the intermediation market is most cost-effective. In contrast, economic units that deal in large dollar amounts (wholesale transactions) can switch back and forth between the two markets, selecting the market that offers the most favorable interest rate. For example, many large businesses take out loans from commercial banks, an intermediation transaction, and also raise money by selling commercial paper in the direct credit market.

DO YOU UNDERSTAND?

1. Why is denomination divisibility an important intermediation service from the perspective of the typical household?
2. What are the three sources of comparative advantage that financial institutions have over others in producing financial products?
3. What would be the implications for investment in physical assets such as oil refineries or long-distance telephone cable if financial intermediaries were not willing to invest money for long periods of time?
4. Why are economies of scale important to the viability and profitability of financial intermediaries?

TYPES OF FINANCIAL INTERMEDIARIES

Many types of financial intermediaries coexist in our economy. Though different, financial intermediaries all have one function in common: they purchase financial claims with one set of characteristics from DSUs and sell financial claims with different characteristics to SSUs.

Exhibit 1.2 shows the major financial intermediaries in our economy and their growth rates between 1980 and 2003. During this period, the assets of all financial intermediaries totaled $32.1 trillion and their assets grew at a compound annual rate of 9.2 percent. This rate of growth was faster than the economy as a whole, which grew at a 6.1 percent annual rate. The largest financial intermediaries in the U.S. economy are commercial banks, but the fastest growing intermediaries are mutual funds (20.7 percent annual growth rate) and money market funds (15.3 percent annual growth rate). The rapid growth rate of financial intermediaries reflects the growth in indirect securities issued, the increase in the proportion of funds being channeled through the intermediation market, and the tremendous wealth created by the U.S. economy in recent years, especially over the last decade.

Financial intermediaries are classified as (1) deposit-type institutions, (2) contractual savings institutions, (3) investment funds, or (4) other types of intermediaries. Exhibit 1.3 lists the major types of financial institutions and the primary assets and liabilities they hold on their balance sheets. Notice that both their assets and liabilities are financial claims. A nonfinancial firm like Ford Motor Company also holds financial liabilities (e.g., long-term debt), but the primary assets held are real assets like plant and equipment. As you read through this section, you should carefully follow along and note the asset and liability holdings of each institution as shown in Exhibit 1.3.

EXHIBIT 1.2
Size and Growth of Major Financial Intermediaries

Intermediary	Rank	2003 Total Assets ($billion)	% of Total	1980 Total Assets ($billion)	% of Total	Annual Growth Rate%
Commercial banks	1	7,812.2	24.3	1,482	35.0	7.5
Mutual funds	2	4,664.9	14.5	513	12.1	20.7
Private pension funds	3	4,194.0	13.1	62	1.5	9.6
Life insurance companies	4	3,823.4	11.9	464	11.0	9.6
Government-sponsored enterprises	5	2,819.4	8.8	195	4.6	12.3
State and local government pension funds	6	2,284.2	7.1	76	1.8	11.3
Money market funds	7	2,016.0	6.3	197	4.7	15.3
Savings institutions	8	1,475.1	4.6	792	18.7	2.7
Finance companies	9	1,380.6	4.3	197	4.7	8.8
Casualty insurance companies	10	1,043.3	3.2	182	4.3	7.9
Credit unions	11	617.3	1.9	68	1.6	10.1
Total		32,130.4	100.0	4,228	100.0	9.2
GDP		10,985.5		2,796		6.1

Commercial banks are the largest and most important financial intermediaries in the U.S. economy. Mutual funds and money market funds, however, are the fastest growing. The rapid growth of financial intermediaries, especially those involved in investment, reflects the tremendous wealth generated by the U.S. economy, the growing proportion of funds being channeled into the intermediation market, and the interest in wealth accumulation.

Source: Board of Governors, Federal Reserve System.

DEPOSIT-TYPE INSTITUTIONS

Deposit-type financial institutions are the most commonly recognized intermediaries because most people use their services on a daily basis. Typically, deposit institutions issue a variety of checking or savings accounts and time deposits, and they use the funds to make consumer, business, and real estate loans. The interest paid on deposit accounts is usually insured by one of several federally sponsored insurance agencies. Thus, for practical purposes, the deposits are devoid of any risk of loss of principal. Also, these deposits are highly liquid because they can be withdrawn on very short notice, usually on demand.

Commercial Banks. Commercial banks are the largest and most diversified intermediaries on the basis of range of assets held and liabilities issued. At the end of 2003, commercial banks held almost $7.8 trillion in financial assets. Their liabilities are in the form of checking accounts, savings accounts, and various time deposits. The Federal Deposit Insurance Corporation (FDIC) insures bank deposits up to a maximum of $100,000. On the asset side, commercial banks make a wide variety of loans in all denominations to consumers, businesses, and state and local governments. In addition, many commercial banks have trust depart-

EXHIBIT 1.3
Primary Assets and Liabilities of Financial Intermediaries

Type of Intermediary	Assets (Direct Securities Purchased)	Liabilities (Indirect Securities Sold)
Deposit-type institutions		
Commercial banks	Business loans	Checkable deposits
	Consumer loans	Time and savings deposits
	Mortgages	Borrowed funds
Thrift institutions	Mortgages	Now accounts and savings deposits
Credit unions	Consumer loans	Share accounts
		Time and savings deposits
Contractual savings institutions		
Life insurance companies	Corporate bonds	Life insurance policies
	Corporate stock	
Casualty insurance companies	Municipal bonds	Casualty insurance policies
	Corporate bonds	
	Corporate stock	
Private pension funds	Corporate stock	Pension fund reserves
	Government securities	
	Corporate bonds	
State and local government pension funds	Corporate stock	Pension fund reserves
	Government securities	
	Corporate bonds	
Investment funds		
Mutual funds	Corporate stock	Shares in fund
	Government securities	
	Corporate bonds	
Money market funds	Money market securities	Shares in fund
Other financial institutions		
Finance companies	Consumer loans	Commercial paper
	Business loans	Bonds
Federal agencies	Government loans	Agency securities

This exhibit presents a summary of the most important assets and liabilities issued by the financial institutions discussed in this book. Notice that deposit-type institutions hold liability accounts that are payable upon demand. This makes liquidity management a high priority for these firms.

Source: Board of Governors, The Federal Reserve System, Flow of Funds Accounts.

ments and leasing operations, and may underwrite certain classes of securities. Because of their vital role in the nation's monetary system and the effect they have on the economic well-being of the communities in which they are located, commercial banks are among the most highly regulated of all financial institutions.

Thrift Institutions.   Savings and loan associations and mutual savings banks are commonly called thrift institutions. They obtain most of their funds by issuing checking accounts, savings accounts, and a variety of consumer time deposits. They use these funds to purchase real estate loans consisting primarily of longterm mortgages. They are the largest providers of residential mortgage loans to consumers. In addition, they are now allowed to make a limited number of consumer and business loans. In effect, thrifts specialize in maturity and denomination intermediation, because they borrow small amounts of money short term with checking and savings accounts and lend long term on real estate collateral. The FDIC insures deposits in thrifts in amounts up to $100,000.

Credit Unions.   Credit unions are small, nonprofit, cooperative, consumer-organized institutions owned entirely by their member-customers. The primary liabilities of credit unions are checking accounts (called share drafts) and savings accounts (called share accounts); their investments are primarily devoted to short-term installment consumer loans. Credit union share accounts are federally insured to a maximum of $100,000. Credit unions are organized by consumers having a common bond, such as employees of a given firm or union. To use any service of a credit union, an individual must be a member. The major regulatory differences between credit unions and other depository institutions are the common bond requirement, the restriction that most loans are to consumers, and their exemption from federal income tax because of their cooperative nature.

CONTRACTUAL SAVINGS INSTITUTIONS

Contractual savings institutions obtain funds under long-term contractual arrangements and invest the funds in the capital markets. Firms in this category are insurance companies and pension funds. These institutions are characterized by a relatively steady inflow of funds from contractual commitments with their insurance policyholders and pension fund participants. Thus, liquidity is usually not a problem in the management of these institutions. They are able to invest in long-term securities, such as bonds, and in some cases in common stock.

Life Insurance Companies.   Life insurance companies obtain funds by selling insurance policies that protect against loss of income from premature death or retirement. In the event of death, the policyholder's beneficiaries receive the insurance benefits, and with retirement the policyholder receives the benefits. In addition to risk protection, many life insurance policies provide some savings. Because life insurance companies have a predictable inflow of funds and their outflows are actuarially predictable, they are able to invest primarily in higher-yielding, long-term assets, such as corporate bonds and stocks. Life insurance companies are regulated by the states in which they operate and, compared to deposit-type institutions, their regulation is less strict.

Casualty Insurance Companies.   Casualty insurance companies sell protection against loss of property from fire, theft, accident, negligence, and other causes that can be actuarially predicted. Their major source of funds is premiums charged on insurance policies. Casualty insurance policies are pure risk-protection policies; as a result, they have no cash surrender value and thus provide no liquidity to the policyholders. As might be expected, the cash outflows from claims on policies are not as predictable as those of life insurance companies. Consequently, a greater proportion of these companies' assets are in short-term, highly marketable securities. To offset the lower return typically generated by these investments, casualty companies have substantial holdings of equity securities. Casualty insurance companies also hold municipal bonds to reduce their taxes.

Pension Funds.   Pension funds obtain their funds from employer and employee contributions during the employees' working years and provide monthly payments upon retirement. Pension funds invest these monies in corporate bonds and equity obligations. The purpose of pension funds is to help workers plan for their retirement years in an orderly and systematic manner. The need for retirement income, combined with the success of organized labor in negotiating for increased pension benefits, has led to a remarkable growth of both private pensions and state and local government pension funds since World War II. Because the inflow into pension funds is long term, and the outflow is highly predictable, pension funds are able to invest in higher-yielding long-term securities.

INVESTMENT FUNDS

Investment funds sell shares to investors and use these funds to purchase direct financial claims. They offer investors the benefit of both denomination flexibility and default-risk intermediation. The uses of funds attracted by investment funds are shown in Exhibit 1.3.

Mutual Funds.   Mutual funds sell equity shares to investors and use these funds to purchase stocks or bonds. The advantage of a mutual fund over direct investment is that it provides small investors access to reduced investment risk that results from diversification, economies of scale in transaction costs, and professional financial managers. The value of a share of a mutual fund is not fixed; it fluctuates as the prices of the stocks in its investment portfolio change. Most mutual funds specialize within particular sectors of the market. For example, some invest only in equities or debt, others in a particular industry (such as energy or electronics), others in growth or income stocks, and still others in foreign investments.

Money Market Mutual Funds.   A money market mutual fund (MMMF) is simply a mutual fund that invests in money market securities, which are short-term securities with low default risk. These securities sell in denominations of $1 million or more, so most investors are unable to purchase them. Thus, MMMFs provide investors with small money balances the opportunity to earn the market rate of interest without incurring a great deal of financial risk. Most MMMFs offer check-writing privileges, which make them close substitutes for the interest-bearing checking accounts and savings accounts offered at most depository institutions. This advantage is limited, however, in that most MMMFs restrict the amount or frequency of withdrawals, and the federal government does not insure the funds.

OTHER TYPES OF FINANCIAL INTERMEDIARIES

There are several other types of financial intermediaries that purchase direct securities from DSUs and sell indirect claims to SSUs.

Finance Companies.   Finance companies make loans to consumers and small businesses. Unlike commercial banks, they do not accept savings deposits from consumers. They obtain the majority of their funds by selling short-term IOUs, called **commercial paper**, to investors. The balance of their funds comes from the sale of equity capital and long-term debt obligations. There are three basic types of finance companies: (1) consumer finance companies specializing in installment loans to households, (2) business finance companies specializing in loans and leases to businesses, and (3) sales finance companies that finance the products sold by retail dealers. Finance companies are regulated by the states in which they operate and are also subject to many federal regulations. These regulations focus primarily on consumer transactions and deal with loan terms, conditions, rates charged, and collection practices.

Federal Agencies.   The U.S. government acts as a major financial intermediary through the borrowing and lending activities of its agencies. Since the 1960s, federal agencies have been among the most rapidly growing of all financial institutions. The primary purposes of federal agencies are to reduce the cost of funds and increase the availability of funds to targeted sectors of the economy. The agencies do this by selling debt instruments (called agency securities) in the direct credit markets at or near the government borrowing rate, then lending those funds to economic participants in the sectors they serve. Most of the funds provided by the federal agencies support agriculture and housing because of the importance of these sectors to the nation's well-being. It is argued that these and other target sectors in the economy would not receive adequate credit at reasonable cost without direct intervention by the federal government.

DO YOU UNDERSTAND?

1. Why do casualty insurance companies devote a greater percentage of their investments to liquid U.S. government securities than do life insurance companies?
2. What are credit unions and how do they differ from a commercial bank?
3. Why have mutual funds grown so fast as compared to commercial banks?
4. For a consumer, what is the difference between holding a checking account at a commercial bank and holding a money market mutual fund?

TYPES OF FINANCIAL MARKETS

Financial intermediaries buy the financial claims of others and sell their own claims in financial markets. As one would expect, there are many different types of financial claims issued in the primary markets by financial intermediaries and other economic units such as the federal government and large corporations. And, to no one's surprise, there are a large number of markets in which these claims are bought and sold. In this and the following sections, we shall briefly describe the different types of financial markets and the more important financial instruments.

PRIMARY AND SECONDARY MARKETS

Financial claims are initially sold by DSUs in **primary financial markets**. All financial claims have primary markets. An example of a primary market transaction is IBM Corporation raising external funds through the sale of new stock or bonds.

People are more likely to purchase a primary financial claim if they believe they will not have to hold it forever (in the case of most common stock) or until its maturity date (in the case of bonds). **Secondary financial markets** are like used-car markets; they let people exchange "used" or previously issued financial claims for cash at will. Secondary markets provide liquidity for investors who own primary claims. Securities can only be sold once in a primary market; all subsequent transactions take place in secondary markets. The New York Stock Exchange (NYSE) is an example of a well-known secondary market.

ORGANIZED AND OVER-THE-COUNTER MARKETS

Once issued, a financial claim (security) can be traded in the secondary market on an organized security exchange (such as the NYSE). Trades made through an exchange are usually made on the floor of the exchange or through its computer system. Organized security exchanges provide a physical meeting place and communication facilities for members to conduct their transactions under a specific set of rules and regulations. Only members of the exchange may use the facilities, and only securities listed on the exchange may be traded. The NYSE is the largest securities exchange for stocks. The Chicago Board of Trade (CBOT) and the Chicago Mercantile Exchange (CME) are the largest futures exchanges.

Financial claims also can be traded "over the counter" by visiting or phoning an over-the-counter dealer or by using a computer system, such as that operated by the National Association of Securities Dealers (NASD), that links over-the-counter dealers. **Over-the-counter markets** have no central location. Usually, however, they have strict rules that must be followed by dealers in the market. The National Association of Securities Dealers regulates trading in U.S. securities markets and may penalize or deny trading privileges to members who do not abide by the rules.

FUTURES MARKET

A **futures market** is a market in which people trade contracts for future delivery of securities (such as government bonds), commodities (such as a kilo of gold or a barrel of oil), or the value of securities (such as the value of the S&P 500 stock index) sold in the cash (or spot) market. The **futures contract** "delivery" date is the future time when the contract is scheduled to be settled by the exchange of cash for the contracted "goods." Futures contracts trade on organized exchanges, such as the Chicago Board of Trade, and each contract is standardized in terms of delivery amounts, instruments, and dates. The futures exchange guarantees contracts negotiated through its auspices.

OPTION MARKETS

Option markets trade **option contracts** that call for conditional future delivery of a security, a commodity, or a futures contract. Option contracts call for one party (the *option writer*) to perform a specific act if called upon by the option buyer or owner (such as buy 100 shares of AT&T stock at a price of $80 per share on the third Friday in January 2005). Option contracts on securities are traded on major organized exchanges such as the Chicago Board Options Exchange (CBOE), the Philadelphia Stock Exchange (PHLX), and the American Stock Exchange (AMEX).

FOREIGN EXCHANGE MARKET

The foreign exchange market is the market in which foreign currencies are bought and sold. Foreign currencies such as the British pound, the Japanese yen, the euro, or the Swiss franc are traded against the U.S. dollar or are traded against other foreign currencies. Foreign currencies are traded either for spot or forward delivery over the counter at large commercial banks or investment banking firms. Futures contracts for foreign currencies are traded on organized exchanges such as the Chicago Mercantile Exchange.

INTERNATIONAL AND DOMESTIC MARKETS

Financial markets can be classified as either domestic or international markets depending on where they are located. The most important international financial markets for U.S. firms are the short-term **Eurodollar market** and the long-term **Eurobond market**. In these markets, domestic or overseas firms can borrow or lend large amounts of U.S. dollars that have been deposited in overseas banks. These markets are closely linked to the U.S. money and capital markets. Large financial institutions, business firms, and institutional investors, both in the United States and overseas, conduct daily transactions between the U.S. domestic markets and the international markets.

THE MONEY MARKETS

Money markets are markets in which commercial banks and other businesses adjust their liquidity position by borrowing, lending, or investing for short periods of time. The Federal Reserve System conducts monetary policy in the money markets, and the U.S. Treasury uses them to finance its day-to-day operations. Also, in the money markets, businesses, governments, and, sometimes, individuals borrow or lend funds for short periods of time—from 1 to 120 days. Exhibit 1.4 shows the amount of various money market securities outstanding.

The money market consists of a collection of markets, each trading a distinctly different financial instrument. In the simplest terms, the money markets are a wholesale market ($1 million) for financial claims that have characteristics very similar to money. Money market instruments typically have short maturities (usually 90 days or less), are highly liquid (active secondary markets), and have low risk of default. There is no formal organized exchange, such as the New York Stock Exchange, for the equity markets. Central to the activity of the money markets are the dealers and brokers who specialize in one or more money market instruments. The major money market instruments are discussed below.

EXHIBIT 1.4
Major Money Market Instruments Outstanding (December 2003)

Instrument	$Billions
U.S. government securities	
Treasury bills	985
Other marketable short-term securities	531
Short-term municipal securities	101
Large, negotiable CDs	1,234
Commercial paper	1,289
Federal funds and security repurchase agreements	1,663

Money market instruments have maturities less than 1 year, have active secondary markets, and have low default risk. Business firms and wealthy individuals use money market instruments to adjust their liquidity positions.

Source: Board of Governors, Federal Reserve System, Flow of Funds Accounts.

TREASURY BILLS

Treasury bills are direct obligations of the U.S. government and thus are considered to have no default risk. They are sold weekly and have maturities that range from 3 months to 1 year. Financial institutions, corporations, and individuals buy these securities for their liquidity and safety of principal.

NEGOTIABLE CERTIFICATES OF DEPOSIT

Negotiable certificates of deposit (NCDs) are large-denomination time deposits of the nation's largest commercial banks. Unlike other time deposits of most commercial banks, NCDs may be sold in the secondary market before their maturity. Only a handful of banks sell NCDs.

COMMERCIAL PAPER

Commercial paper is the unsecured promissory note (IOU) of a large business. Commercial paper typically has maturities ranging from a few days to 120 days and does not have an active secondary market. Corporations and finance companies are the major issuers of commercial paper.

FEDERAL FUNDS

Technically, **federal funds** are bank deposits held with the Federal Reserve bank. Banks with deposits in excess of required reserves may lend those excess reserves—called fed funds—to other banks. The bank that acquires the fed funds may use them to cover a deficit reserve position or can use the funds to make consumer or business loans. Fed funds loans are typically for 1 day or for over a weekend. At a more practical level, you may think of the **fed funds market** as the market in which banks make short-term unsecured loans to one another and the fed funds interest rate is the interbank lending rate. Though somewhat confusing, the fed funds market has no connection with the U.S. Treasury.

THE CAPITAL MARKETS

Individuals own real assets to produce income and wealth. Thus the owner of a machine hopes to profit from the sale of products from the machine shop, and the owner of a factory hopes to earn a return from the goods produced there. Similarly, owners of apartments, office buildings, warehouses, and other tangible assets hope to earn a stream of future income by using their resources to provide services directly to consumers or to other businesses. These assets are called capital goods; they are the stock of assets used in production. **Capital markets** are where capital goods are financed with stock or long-term debt instruments. Compared to money market instruments, capital market instruments are less marketable; default risk levels vary widely between issuers and have maturities ranging from 5 to 30 years.

remind: marketability p. 6

Financial institutions are the connecting link between the short-term money markets and the longer-term capital markets. These institutions, especially those that accept deposits, typically borrow short term and then invest in longer-term capital projects either indirectly through business loans or directly into capital market instruments. We will now briefly describe the major capital instruments. Exhibit 1.5 shows the amounts outstanding for selected capital market instruments.

COMMON STOCK

Common stock represents an ownership claim on a firm's assets. Also referred to as equity securities, stock differs from debt obligations in that equity holders have

---

EXHIBIT 1.5
Selected Capital Market Instruments Outstanding (December 2003)

Instrument	$Billions
U.S. government securities	
Treasury notes	1,983
Treasury bonds	564
Inflation-indexed notes and bonds	188
State and local government bonds	1,450
Corporate bonds	6,840
Corporate stock (at market value)	15,498
Mortgages	9,465

Capital market instruments are used to finance real assets that produce income and wealth. They are bought and sold in the direct credit markets and typically have maturities greater than 1 year.

Source: Board of Governors, Federal Reserve System, Flow of Funds Accounts.

the right to share in the firm's profits. The higher the firm's net income, the higher the return to stockholders. On the other hand, stockholders must share in any of the losses that the company may incur. And, in the event of bankruptcy, creditors and debt holders have first claim on the firm's assets. Most stock market transactions take place in the secondary markets.

CORPORATE BONDS

When large corporations need money for capital expenditures, they may issue bonds. **Corporate bonds** are, thus, long-term IOUs that represent a claim against the firm's assets. Unlike equityholders' returns, bondholders' returns are fixed; they receive only the amount of interest that is promised plus the repayment of the principal at the end of the loan contract. Even if the corporation turns in unexpectedly phenomenal performance, the bondholders will only receive the fixed amount of interest agreed to at the bonds' issue. Corporate bonds typically have maturities from 5 to 30 years, and their secondary market is not as active as for equity securities.

MUNICIPAL BONDS

Municipal bonds are the long-term debt obligations of state and local governments. They are used to finance capital expenditures for things such as schools, highways, and airports. The most distinguishing feature of municipal bonds is that their coupon income is exempt from federal income taxes. As a result, individuals or companies that are in the highest income tax brackets purchase municipal bonds. Although the bonds of large municipalities have secondary markets, most municipal bonds have limited secondary markets and, thus, are not considered liquid investments.

MORTGAGES

Mortgages are long-term loans secured by real estate. They are the largest segment in the capital markets in terms of the amount outstanding. More than half of the mortgage funds go into financing family homes, with the remainder financing business property, apartments, buildings, and farm construction. Mortgages by themselves do not have good secondary markets. However, a large number of mortgages can be pooled together to form new securities called mortgaged-backed securities, which have an active secondary market.

mortgaged-backed securities

As you have probably figured out from reading the chapter so far, financial markets facilitate economic growth and make society better off in various ways. This section discusses how different aspects of financial market efficiency affect the efficiency and growth of the economy. We discuss three forms of market efficiency: allocational efficiency, informational efficiency, and operational efficiency.

FINANCIAL MARKET EFFICIENCY

ALLOCATIONAL EFFICIENCY

Allocational efficiency is a form of economic efficiency that implies that funds will be allocated to (i.e., invested in) their highest valued use. This means that the funds could not have been allocated in any other way that would have made society better off. The practical implication is that business firms invest in the projects offering the highest risk-adjusted rates of return and that households invest in direct or indirect financial claims offering the highest yields for given levels of risk.

INFORMATIONAL EFFICIENCY

Of critical importance is the ability of investors to obtain accurate information about the relative values of different financial claims (or securities). In an informationally efficient market, securities' prices are the best indicators of relative value because market prices reflect all relevant information about the securities. When new information about a security arrives in an efficient market, market prices adjust very quickly. Price adjustments occur quickly because there are potentially thousands of analysts and millions of investors gathering information about securities in a quest for quick profits. Large profits can be earned by identifying overpriced securities before the price begins to rise. The actions of analysts and investors ensure that market prices reflect all information relevant to their values at any point in time.

Why is it important that market prices reflect all relevant information about securities? With accurate price information, investors can determine which investments are the most valuable—providing the highest expected return for a given level of risk—and invest accordingly. Thus, informational efficiency ensures that the financial markets are allocationally efficient because households or business firms can get the information they need to make intelligent investment decisions.

informational efficiency ensure allocative efficiency

OPERATIONAL EFFICIENCY

A market is operationally efficient if the costs of conducting transactions are as low as possible. These transaction costs, which we have discussed earlier in the chapter, include broker commissions, bid-ask spreads, and underwriter spreads. Why is operational efficiency important? If transaction costs are high, fewer financial transactions will take place, and a greater number of otherwise valuable investment projects will be passed up. Thus, high transaction costs can prevent firms from investing in all desirable projects. The forgone investment opportunities mean that fewer people are employed and economic growth slows or declines. Society becomes worse off.

RISKS FACED BY FINANCIAL INSTITUTIONS

Now let's turn our attention back to financial institutions, which, in providing financial intermediation services to consumers and businesses, must transact in the financial markets. Financial institutions intermediate between SSUs and DSUs in the hope of earning a profit by acquiring funds at interest rates that are lower than they charge when they sell their financial products. But there is no free lunch here. The differences in the characteristics of the financial claims financial institutions buy and sell expose them to a variety of risks in the financial markets.

As moot testimony to the importance of successfully managing these risks, the decade of the 1980s was a battleground now littered with the corpses of financial institutions that failed to adequately manage these risks. Managing these risks does not mean eliminating them—there is a trade-off between risk and higher profits. Managers who take too few risks sleep well at night but eat poorly—their slumber reaps a reward of declining earnings and stock prices that their shareholders will not tolerate for long. On the other hand, excess risk taking—betting the bank and losing—is also bad news. It will place you in the ranks of the unemployed with an armada of expensive Wall Street lawyers defending you.

In their search for higher long-term earnings and stock values, financial institutions must manage and balance five basic risks: credit risk, interest rate risk, liquidity risk, foreign exchange risk, and political risk. Each of these risks is related to the characteristics of the financial claim (e.g., term to maturity) or to the issuer (e.g., default risk). Each must be managed carefully to balance the trade-off between future profitability and potential failure. For now, we summarize the five risks and briefly discuss how they affect the management of financial institutions to provide a frame of reference for other topics in the book.

CREDIT RISK

When a financial institution makes a loan or invests in a bond or other debt security, the institution bears **credit risk** (or default risk) because it is accepting the possibility that the borrower will fail to make either interest or principal payments in the amount and at the time promised. To manage the credit risk of loans or investments in debt securities, financial institutions should (1) diversify their portfolios, (2) conduct a careful credit analysis of the borrower to measure default risk exposure, and (3) monitor the borrower over the life of the loan or investment to detect any critical changes in financial health, which is just another way of expressing the borrower's ability to repay the loan.

INTEREST RATE RISK

Interest rate risk is the risk of fluctuations in a security's price or reinvestment income caused by changes in market interest rates. The concept of interest rate risk is applicable not only to bonds but also to a financial institution's balance sheet. The savings and loan association industry (S&Ls) is the prime example of how interest rate risk adversely affects a financial institution's earnings. In the volatile interest rate environment of the late 1970s and early 1980s, many S&Ls failed because the interest rates they paid on deposits (liabilities) increased faster than the yields they earned on their mortgage loans (assets), causing earnings to decline.

LIQUIDITY RISK

Liquidity risk is the risk that a financial institution will be unable to generate sufficient cash inflow to meet required cash outflows. Liquidity is critical to financial institutions: banks and thrifts need liquidity to meet deposit withdrawals and pay off other liabilities as they come due; pension funds need liquidity to meet contractual pension payments; and life insurance companies need liquidity to pay death benefits. Liquidity also means that an institution need not pass up a profitable loan or investment opportunity because of a lack of cash. If a financial institution is unable to meet its short-term obligations because of inadequate liquidity, the firm will fail even though over the long run the firm may be profitable.

FOREIGN EXCHANGE RISK

Foreign exchange risk is the fluctuation in the earnings or value of a financial institution that arises from fluctuations in exchange rates. Many financial institutions deal in foreign currencies either for their own account or they buy or sell currencies for their customers. Also, financial institutions invest in the direct credit markets of other countries, or they may sell indirect financial claims overseas. Because of changing international economic conditions and the relative supply and demand of U.S. and foreign currencies, the rate at which foreign currencies can be converted into U.S. dollars fluctuates. These fluctuations can cause gains or losses in the currency positions of financial institutions, and they cause the U.S. dollar values of non-U.S. financial investments to change.

POLITICAL RISK

Political risk is the fluctuation in value of a financial institution resulting from the actions of the U.S. or foreign governments. Domestically, if the government changes the regulations faced by financial institutions, their earnings or values are affected. For example, if the Federal Deposit Insurance Corporation (FDIC), which insures deposits at banks and thrift institutions, decided to increase the premium charged for deposit insurance, earnings at the affected institutions would likely decline. It is important for managers of financial institutions to monitor and predict as best as possible changes in the regulatory environment. Managers must be prepared to react quickly when regulatory changes occur.

Internationally, the concerns are much more dramatic, especially when institutions consider lending in developing countries without stable governments or well-developed legal systems. Governments can repudiate (i.e., cancel) foreign debt obligations. Repudiations are rare, but less rare are debt reschedulings in which foreign governments declare a moratorium on debt payments and then attempt to renegotiate more favorable terms with the foreign lenders. In either case, the lending institution is left "holding the bag." To grow and be successful in the international arena, managers of financial institutions must understand how to measure and manage these risks.

CHAPTER TAKE-AWAYS

1 The role of the financial system is to gather money from SSUs and transfer it to DSUs in the most efficient manner possible. The larger the flow and the more efficiently the funds are allocated, the greater the accommodation of individual preferences for current spending and savings and the ability of businesspeople to invest in their firms.

2 There are two basic ways the transfer of funds takes place in the economy: direct financing (financial markets) and indirect financing (inter-

mediation market). The direct credit market is a wholesale market for financial claims where DSUs and SSUs trade financial claims among themselves; brokers, dealers, and investment bankers facilitate these transactions. In the indirect credit markets, financial institutions intermediate, or stand between, transactions between DSUs and SSUs. Financial intermediaries such as commercial banks, life insurance companies, pension funds, and mutual funds facilitate indirect financing.

3 A financial claim is a promise of one party, say a DSU, to pay a certain amount of money at a certain time with a given interest rate to another party, say an SSU. Financial claims differ according to maturity, risk of default, marketability, tax treatment, and other special features that may be attached to them, such as options or convertibility into another type of financial claim.

4 Financial institutions provide five fundamental services: (1) denomination divisibility—which means producing financial claims of varying dollar amounts; (2) currency transformation—buying financial claims denominated in one currency and selling financial claims denominated in another; (3) maturity flexibility—creating financial claims with a wide range of maturities; (4) credit risk diversification—diversifying risk more efficiently than individual SSUs might be able to on their own; and (5) liquidity—buying direct financial claims with low liquidity and issuing indirect financial claims with more liquidity.

5 The money markets are a collection of markets in which commercial banks and businesses adjust their liquidity positions by borrowing or lending for short periods of time. The Federal Reserve System conducts monetary policy in the money markets, and the U.S. Treasury uses the market to finance the day-to-day operations of the federal government. The most important money market securities are Treasury bills, negotiable certificates of deposit, and commercial paper.

6 The capital markets are where business firms obtain funding for long-term investments or where consumers finance purchases of long-term assets. Capital market securities are long term and typically involve more risk than money market securities. The most important capital market securities are corporate stock, Treasury bonds, and residential mortgages.

7 Financial institutions are profit-maximizing businesses that earn profits by acquiring funds at interest rates lower than they earn on their assets. The nature and characteristics of the financial claims they hold expose them to a variety of risks. The major risks that financial institutions face are credit risk, interest rate risk, liquidity risk, foreign exchange risk, and political risk.

KEY TERMS

Financial intermediary
  (or financial institution)
Surplus spending unit
  (SSU)
Deficit spending unit
  (DSU)
Financial claim
Marketability
Direct financing
Financial intermediation
  (or indirect financing)
Financial market
Direct claim

Private placement
Investment banker
Underwriting
Underwriting spread
Broker
Dealer
Bid price
Ask price
Bid-ask spread
Disintermediation
Commercial paper
Primary financial
  market

Secondary financial
  market
Over-the-counter market
Futures market
Futures contract
Option market
Option contract
Eurodollar market
Eurobond market
Money markets
Treasury bills
Negotiable certificates of
  deposit

Federal funds
Fed funds market
Capital markets
Common stock
Corporate bonds
Municipal bonds
Mortgages
Credit risk
Interest rate risk
Liquidity risk
Foreign exchange risk
Political risk

QUESTIONS AND PROBLEMS

1. Does it make sense that the typical household is a surplus spending unit (SSU) while the typical business firm is a deficit spending unit (DSU)? Explain.

2. Explain the economic role of brokers, dealers, and investment bankers. How does each make a profit?

3. Why are direct financing transactions more costly or inconvenient than intermediated transactions?

4. Explain how you believe economic activity would be affected if we did not have financial markets and institutions.

5. Explain the concept of financial intermediation. How does the possibility of financial intermediation increase the efficiency of the financial system?

6. How do financial intermediaries generate profits?

7. Explain the differences between the money markets and the capital markets. Which market would General Motors use to finance a new vehicle assembly plant? Why?

8. Compaq Computer needs $1 million for 2 months. Using T-accounts, explain how Compaq might obtain the money through a transaction in the direct credit market and in the intermediation market.

9. Metropolitan Nashville and Davidson County issues $25 million of municipal revenue bonds to finance a new domed stadium for the Tennessee Titans football team. The bonds have a face value of $10,000 each, are somewhat risky, and have a maturity of 20 years. Enterprise Bank of Nashville purchases one of the bonds using the $5,000 received from Sarah Levien and Ted Hawkins, who each purchased a 6-month certificate of deposit from the bank. Explain the intermediation services provided by Enterprise Bank in this transaction. Illustrate with T-accounts.

10. Explain the statement, "A financial claim is someone's asset and someone else's liability."

INTERNET EXERCISE

The government agencies that regulate financial institutions provide an array of statistics on their Web sites. Much of the data is available as downloadable files, making it easy for students, analysts, and researchers to learn about financial intermediaries by examining current and historical data on the different types of intermediaries. For example, several of the exhibits in this chapter were derived from data available from the Board of Governors of the Federal Reserve System (http://www.federalreserve.gov/releases/). The Federal Reserve Board's Z.1 statistical release *(Flow of Funds Accounts of the United States)* contains current and historical flow-of-funds accounts data. Your task in this Internet Exercise is to find data on the level of financial assets held by commercial banks. You will be looking for current and historical data from Table L.109.

1. Once you have located the data, enter them into a spreadsheet. The Web site provides instructions for downloading the data into a spreadsheet file, such as an Excel file. Create a chart using the following categories of financial assets: government securities, municipal bonds, corporate and foreign bonds, consumer loans, business loans, real estate loans, and other assets. Consider making the chart a 100 percent stacked-area chart. On the chart, show the percentage of assets in each category for the previous 3 to 5 years. This will show you the percentage of commercial banks' portfolios devoted to the various types of financial assets. You will notice some short-term trends and some long-term trends.

2. Also make a standard stacked-area chart showing the dollar amounts. It will show the aggregate increase in banks' lending and investing activities.

3. Using the two charts, identify the short-term trends in banks' lending and investment activities. What are the long-term trends?

4. Can you relate any of the long-term trends in banks' lending and investing activities to any long-term economic or societal trends? Can you relate any of the short-term fluctuations in banks' lending and investing activities to fluctuations in economic activity? To answer these questions, you might need to get some economic data such as GDP (gross domestic product) from the Federal Reserve Bank of St. Louis's FRED database (http://www.stls.frb.org/fred/).

2

The Federal Reserve and Its Powers

CHAPTER PREVIEW

This chapter is about the Federal Reserve System (the Fed) and its impact on interest rates and the economy. It is often said that the chairman of the Federal Reserve Board is the second most powerful person in the United States. Only the president, who is commander in chief of our armed forces, is more powerful. Where does all this power come from? It comes from the Fed's role as the nation's central bank and its responsibilities and powers to conduct monetary policy. The Fed's monetary policy actions have a direct effect on the level of interest rates, the availability of credit, and the supply of money, all of which have a direct impact on financial markets and institutions and, more importantly, on the level of economic activity and the rate of inflation in the economy.

To make the story even more interesting, with all of this awesome power, the Fed is "privately" owned by the banks that are members of the Federal Reserve System. As a result, the Fed is not a government agency and is remarkably free from presidential and congressional pressure. As you can tell, we have a lot of important issues to work through and explain in this chapter, so let's get down to business—the business of money. That's what the Fed is really all about! ∎

You're looking at over $2 million in foreign gold that was being counted by "sitters" in the bottom most vault (76 feet below the busy financial district) of the Federal Reserve Bank of New York. Each gold bar weighed between 27 and 28 pounds and was worth $14,000. Over one quarter of all the official monetary gold of the free world—about $13.4 billion worth—is stored in 120 compartments held by over 70 countries and watched constantly by "sitters." Sales require frequent transfers and gold is shifted bar by bar from one to another of the compartments.

The purpose of this chapter is to explain what the Federal Reserve is, what it does, and why it is so powerful. The Federal Reserve System is the most important financial institution in our country. As our nation's central bank, it regulates our major financial institutions and controls the nation's money supply. The Fed has three basic tools to conduct monetary policy, which are implemented by controlling key accounts on its balance sheet. In Chapter 3, we will examine in detail the Fed's ability to affect the level of interest rates and how monetary policy impacts various sectors in the economy. ∎

LEARNING OBJECTIVES

The objectives of this chapter are to:

1 Explain the problems leading to the establishment of the Federal Reserve bank in 1914.

2 Explain the Fed's primary responsibilities as a central bank.

3 Identify the most powerful policy group within the Fed and discuss its powers.

4 Explain how the Fed conducts monetary policy and the necessary policy tools.

5 Explain why open market operations are the Fed's primary tool to conduct monetary policy.

ORIGINS OF THE FEDERAL RESERVE SYSTEM

A central bank regulates a nation's money supply and financial institutions in an attempt to provide the nation with a stable economic environment and an effective payment system. Early in its history, the United States had two central banks that operated reasonably well by the standards of the day. However, American politics has always feared centralization of power and economic concentration, and central banks were a prominent symbol of these fears. Both of these early central banks engaged in some minor political peccadilloes and lost their charters. The First Bank of the United States was disbanded in 1811 and the Second Bank of the United States died a quiet death after its charter was renewed but vetoed by President Andrew Jackson in 1832. Jackson's veto rendered a consummate political message which denounced the bank as unconstitutional, detailed the dangers of concentrated economic power that the bank posed, and denounced the bank as a menace and threat to American democracy. Jackson's powerful veto message was widely circulated as it was the death knell for central banking in the United States for over 80 years.

Between 1832 and 1914, the United States operated without a central bank. During this time, individual banks issued deposit liabilities and banknotes that served as the nation's money supply. Banknotes were IOUs of individual banks that looked and functioned like our present-day currency. Exhibit 2.1 shows a banknote issued by Canal Bank in New Orleans. The banknotes served as money to people who borrowed from banks or deposited money with them. Since banknotes were IOUs of individual banks, they carried the default risk of the bank that issued them. If a bank was viewed as too risky, its banknotes were exchanged in the market at a discount to their face value—so people would have to offer more money if they wanted to buy goods with risky banknotes. For example, if you had a banknote from a sound and well-managed bank like Wells Fargo Bank, an item priced at a dollar cost a dollar. But if you tried to make a purchase with banknotes issued by a bank that dealt in risky real estate developments, it might take $1.25 worth of that bank's notes to make the same purchase. And if you presented banknotes from a bank that was rumored to be about to fail, no one would take that bank's notes for purchases, unless they did not know any better. No wonder people preferred hard currency—gold or silver coins—over paper money. At one time in the United States, there were more than 15,000 different banks issuing their own banknotes. You can see the obstacles this made for commerce because it was difficult to know the good players from the bad.

Furthermore, from 1836 until the mid-1860s, the quantity of money varied widely in the United States as banks made more loans and issued more money during economic booms and contracted their lending and the money supply during recessions. Also, private banks failed with some regularity during recessions, further contracting the money supply. Thus, the nation's money supply not only was of varying credit quality but also expanded and contracted during economic cycles, thereby exaggerating the cycles.

EXHIBIT 2.1
Banknote Issued by Canal Bank, New Orleans, Louisiana

Historically, individual bank liabilities (called banknotes) served as money. The fact that so many different monies existed made commerce difficult. A person never knew if the banknote was from a sound bank or from a failed or disreputable bank. It's no wonder that banknotes from lesser-known banks were heavily discounted.

NATIONAL BANKING ACTS

In the mid-1860s, the United States passed a series of national banking acts that tried to improve the soundness of the nation's money supply and to help finance the Civil War by allowing the sale of U.S. government bonds. State-chartered banks that issued banknotes were assessed a 10 percent annual tax on them—thereby making them prohibitively expensive to issue. However, banks were allowed to obtain charters as national banks and issue banknotes provided that they met certain conditions and agreed to be regulated by the newly authorized Comptroller of the Currency. Among the conditions necessary for issuing banknotes were (1) the requirement that each bank have its banknotes printed by the U.S. Mint to cut the risk of counterfeiting and (2) the requirement that each bank back its banknotes with holdings of U.S. government bonds that slightly exceeded the value of each banknote issued. In that way, each banknote could always be redeemed at face value even if the bank failed.

State banks were allowed to continue to operate after the National Banking Acts were passed. Federal bank regulators had expected the numbers of state banks to dwindle because the 10 percent tax on their banknotes would make it difficult for them to compete against national banks. However, they could issue demand deposit liabilities (checking accounts) instead of banknotes. To the surprise of federal bank regulators, checking accounts quickly became popular with the public. National banks also could issue checking accounts. Since demand deposits weren't insured and banks had some risk of failure, demand deposit liabilities, like individual banknotes before them, were often discounted when they were used to finance transactions. Furthermore, banks were still subject to failure if they issued too many demand deposits relative to the amount of "reserves" in the form of cash or deposits they held at other banks that were available to meet deposit withdrawals.

This problem was aggravated by the fact that the National Banking Acts let some banks count deposits held at other banks as part of their reserves. This "pyramiding of reserves" meant that many banks could run short of reserves simultaneously. This happened because as a bank ran short of cash to meet withdrawals, the bank would draw down its deposits at other banks to get cash, thereby making the other bank run short of cash. Because the nation's banknote currency supply was limited by the amount of government bonds outstanding, when the public demanded more cash, the banking system often ran short of cash and the economy experienced problems—called "bank panics."

The scenarios preceding financial panics were similar. First the economy would enter a period of rapid expansion, creating heavy demand for bank credit. Banks would then issue more and more banknotes to satisfy their loan demand; this would increase the money supply, further stimulate the economy, and lead to inflation and higher interest rates. At some point, some banks had overextended themselves by issuing too many banknotes relative to their reserve holdings. A slight downturn in economic activity would cause overextended banks to fail and, then, people would panic! Why? The public knew that banks had small amounts of reserves relative to the amount of banknotes outstanding. When large numbers of people simultaneously demanded the conversion of their paper money into hard currency, banks were forced to "call" in loans from their customers. At that time, most bank loans were **call loans**, which are loans that are due when the bank calls and asks for repayment. When business loans were called unexpectedly, many businesses failed because they had purchased with their loan money inventory and capital equipment that could not quickly be converted to cash to pay the bank. Bank panics would spread, leading to large numbers of bank failures, which precipitated a large number of business failures as banks called more and more loans. The result was that the country would descend into a recession. The public and politicians began to suspect that there was some relationship between bank failures and the onset of a recession.

From the mid-1860s until the early 1900s, the economy suffered a number of serious recessions and financial "panics," culminating in the crash of 1907. The 1907 panic resulted in widespread bank failures, substantial losses to depositors, and a crippling economic recession. The public and politicians were now convinced that a central bank was needed to prevent widespread bank failures and the resulting recessions. However, creating a structure for the new central bank that would be politically acceptable to the public was a challenge. The western and agricultural states, in particular, feared that the eastern industrial complex would control the central bank. These states preferred an "easy money" policy, which meant it was easy for banks to issue banknotes when businesses wanted loans (easy credit) and low interest rates. The eastern states preferred a stronger central bank that had the power to rein in inflation and put an end to the financial panic which led to the economic recessions that periodically crippled the country. As you will see, establishing our third central bank was not an easy task.

PEOPLE & EVENTS

Wildcat Banks: Red Dogs and Cow Chips

The 26-year period from 1837 to 1863 is known as the Free Banking era in U.S. history. Banks operated with fewer laws and regulations than in any other period, and anyone who could meet minimum requirements could open a bank. Allowing such freedoms did not work very well; many free banks failed and their banknotes became worthless.

One of the most disastrous experiences with free banking occurred in Michigan. Early in 1837, the state legislature passed the first free banking law to encourage banking and promote economic stability. Unfortunately, it did not. Because banks created money by issuing banknotes, people found banking an excellent way to "raise" money by printing banknotes to finance speculative or dishonest business ventures.

By the end of 1839, most free banks had failed and the public was left with worthless banknotes.

Many of the financial shenanigans pulled by banks in Michigan were carried out by "wildcat banks." Wildcat banks were opened by dishonest bankers who intended to defraud the public by issuing banknotes far in excess of their reserves (gold or silver). The scam could work as follows: to discourage the public from redeeming banknotes, bank offices were set up in remote places "where only wildcats would dare tread." The bank would put the bogus banknotes into circulation by investing in assets that could be sold easily for hard currency or for the banknotes of a sound bank. As soon as the bank had the notes in circulation, it would close. The bank officers would then hop the stagecoach with all the assets they could carry and ride off with a tidy profit. Bank creditors were left with an empty vault and worthless banknotes.

Because many people had at one time or another "got taken" with worthless banknotes, the American vernacular developed many colorful names for paper money. Today, with strict bank regulation and federal deposit insurance, people no longer refer to paper currency as "shinplaster," "stump rails," "red dogs," or "cow chips."

FORMING THE FEDERAL RESERVE SYSTEM

The passage of the Federal Reserve Act in 1913 was meant to correct some of the shortcomings of the national banking system that became apparent during the severe financial crisis of 1907. The goals of the legislation were to establish (1) a monetary authority that would expand and contract the nation's money supply according to the needs of the economy, (2) a **lender of last resort** that could furnish additional funds to banks in times of financial crisis, (3) an efficient payment system for clearing and collecting checks at par (face value) throughout the country, and (4) a more vigorous bank supervision system to reduce the risk of bank failures.

The Federal Reserve System's ability to provide currency was established to eliminate the financial panics that had plagued the country when the public feared currency would not be available on demand. An **elastic money supply** was achieved by authorizing the Federal Reserve banks to issue a new type of banknote—the Federal Reserve note. Member banks of the Federal Reserve System could obtain Federal Reserve notes whenever they needed extra currency. Today Federal Reserve notes are the principal form of currency in circulation.

Because people were wary of centralized power, the Federal Reserve Act provided for 12 largely autonomous regional Federal Reserve banks coordinated by a Board of Governors in Washington, D.C. As originally conceived, each regional bank was responsible for the economic needs of a particular geographic area of the country and was "owned" by member commercial banks in each district that bought stock in the local Federal Reserve bank.

Over the years, the goals and role of the Federal Reserve System have changed with the changing political and economic environment. Originally, the structure of the Federal Reserve System was designed to diffuse power along regional lines, between the private and government sectors, and among bankers, businesspeople, and the public at large. This structure can still be seen today in the geographic boundaries of the district banks shown in Exhibit 2.2. Today, most authority in the system resides with the Board of Governors in Washington, D.C., rather than with the regional Federal Reserve banks, and the primary function of the Federal Reserve is economic stabilization through the management of the nation's money supply.

THE CURRENT STRUCTURE OF THE FED

The modern-day Federal Reserve System consists of a seven-member Board of Governors, 12 regional Federal Reserve banks (and their branches) located throughout the country, approximately 3,000 member commercial banks, and a series of advisory committees. The structure also includes the powerful Federal Open Market Committee (FOMC), which conducts the nation's monetary policy. We will now discuss each of the major players in the Federal Reserve System and their responsibilities and powers. You might want to follow along with Exhibit 2.3, which shows the modern structure and policy organization of the Fed.

FEDERAL RESERVE DISTRICT BANKS

The 12 Federal Reserve banks in each region assist in clearing and processing checks and certain electronic funds payments in their respective areas of the country. They also issue Federal Reserve notes, act as a depository for banks in their

EXHIBIT 2.2
The Federal Reserve System

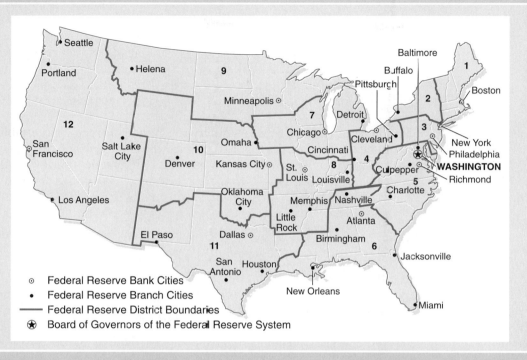

- ⊙   Federal Reserve Bank Cities
- •   Federal Reserve Branch Cities
- ───   Federal Reserve District Boundaries
- ✪   Board of Governors of the Federal Reserve System

The Federal Reserve System consists of the Board of Governors and 12 Federal Reserve districts. Each district is served by a Federal Reserve bank that is named after its headquarters city. Historically, this unusual structure was necessary to calm the public's fear of concentration of political and economic power.

Note: Hawaii and Alaska are in the Twelfth Federal Reserve District.
Source: Federal Reserve Bulletin.

respective districts, monitor local economic conditions, provide advice to the Federal Reserve Board, and participate in the making of monetary policy.

When first established, Federal Reserve district banks were intended to represent regional interests in Washington and to provide for the credit needs of their regions. Thus, they were given power to issue currency and establish discount rates applicable to all institutions in their regions that wished to borrow from them. Historically, discount rates have occasionally varied from one Federal Reserve bank to another. In recent years, however, the Federal Reserve Board has used its power to review discount rates to enforce uniformity.

Over time the regional banks have relinquished powers to the Board of Governors. Not only can the board review and disapprove the banks' discount rates, thereby causing the district banks to change their discount rates to satisfy the board, but the board also appoints the top officers of each district bank and determines their salaries. Nonetheless, through their periodic representation on the Federal Open Market Committee (11 banks rotate four FOMC memberships, while the Federal Reserve Bank of New York has a permanent representative), Federal Reserve bank presidents help establish monetary policy.

EXHIBIT 2.3
The Formal Structure and Policy Organization of the FED

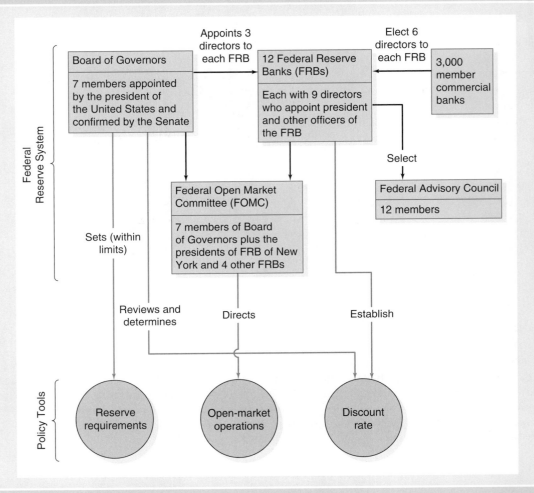

The Federal Reserve System has overlapping lines of authority. All members of the Board of Governors and 5 of the 12 Federal Reserve bank presidents vote equally on monetary policy decisions made by the FOMC.

MEMBER BANKS

Member banks include all nationally chartered commercial banks, plus approximately 17 percent of all state-chartered commercial banks, which joined the Fed voluntarily. Member banks buy stock in their regional Federal Reserve banks and help elect each regional bank's board of directors. The "stock" member banks pay a modest 6 percent dividend but do not carry the traditional powers of ownership, such as sharing in the profits and voting on important management decisions. Prior to 1980, only member banks had unrestricted access to the Federal Reserve's free check-clearing services. In 1980 Congress gave access to Federal Reserve services to all depository institutions, but it required that the Federal Reserve impose service charges. About 36 percent of all banks are members of the Federal Reserve System, and they hold about 76 percent of all banking deposits.

THE BOARD OF GOVERNORS

At the head of the Federal Reserve System is the seven-member Board of Governors headquartered in Washington, D.C. Because the Board of Governors sets the nation's monetary policy, the Board is among the most powerful of all governmental bodies. It is financially and administratively independent of both Congress and the president.

To preserve the Fed's political independence, Congress established 14-year overlapping terms for Federal Reserve Board members, with one 14-year term expiring every 2 years. The governors, who are appointed by the president, are required to come from different Federal Reserve districts to prevent a concentration of power in one region of the country. The Senate confirms all presidential appointments.

The Chairman of the Board of Governors is chosen by the president from among the existing governors and serves a 4-year term. Also, it is expected that if a new chairman is chosen, the old chairman resigns from the board, regardless of the time remaining in the appointment.

THE FOMC

The **Federal Open Market Committee (FOMC)** consists of the seven members of the Board of Governors of the Federal Reserve System plus five presidents of Federal Reserve banks. The president of the Federal Reserve Bank of New York is a permanent member. This apparent "inequity" exists because the Federal Reserve Bank of New York implements monetary policy on a day-to-day basis. The FOMC is extremely important because it is this group of people that actually determines monetary policy. The FOMC monetary actions directly affect the reserve balances of depository institutions and, ultimately, the country's level of economic activity.

The Board of Governors controls monetary policy because it controls the FOMC, which determines monetary policy. The reason is that there are only 12 voting members on the FOMC—7 governors and 5 district bank presidents—and, simply put, the board has the majority votes. The board also sets reserve requirements (within limits set by legislation) and effectively sets the discount rate. The board chairman advises the president on economic policy, testifies on the state of the economy before Congress, and may, from time to time, represent the U.S. government in negotiations with foreign countries on economic matters. The board has a large staff of well-trained economists that advises it on economic policy matters and researches important economic questions. In recent years, many of the board members—and usually the chairman—have been trained economists.

MONETARY POWERS OF THE BOARD OF GOVERNORS

REALITIES OF MONETARY POWER

The reality of power at the Fed is that the Chairman of the Board of Governors is the dominant figure in the formulation and execution of monetary policy (see Exhibit 2.4). Because of this power, the chairman is often called the second most

EXHIBIT 2.4
The Power Structure of the Fed

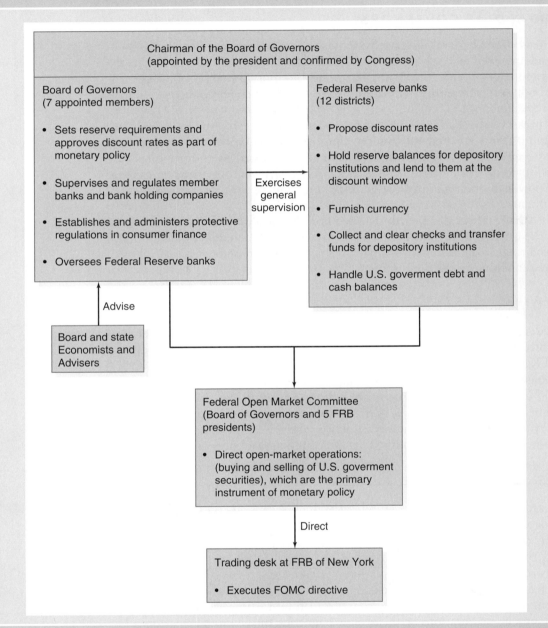

Chairman of the Board of Governors
(appointed by the president and confirmed by Congress)

Board of Governors
(7 appointed members)

- Sets reserve requirements and approves discount rates as part of monetary policy

- Supervises and regulates member banks and bank holding companies

- Establishes and administers protective regulations in consumer finance

- Oversees Federal Reserve banks

Exercises general supervision

Federal Reserve banks
(12 districts)

- Propose discount rates

- Hold reserve balances for depository institutions and lend to them at the discount window

- Furnish currency

- Collect and clear checks and transfer funds for depository institutions

- Handle U.S. goverment debt and cash balances

Advise

Board and state Economists and Advisers

Federal Open Market Committee
(Board of Governors and 5 FRB presidents)

- Direct open-market operations: (buying and selling of U.S. goverment securities), which are the primary instrument of monetary policy

Direct

Trading desk at FRB of New York

- Executes FOMC directive

The dominant person in the formation and execution of monetary policy is the Chairman of the Board of Governors. The chairman sets the agenda and chairs meetings of both the Board of Governor's and the FOMC.

powerful person in the United States. The chairman controls the agenda and chairs the meetings of both the Board of Governors and the FOMC. The chairman is the most prominent member of the board and is the official spokesperson for the board to Congress and the national press. Though not always the case in the past, today the chairman is a trained economist with significant academic and/or practical experience on Wall Street or in the Federal Reserve System.

To lead the Federal Reserve System, the chairman must have the leadership skills and intellectual credentials to gain the respect of his colleagues. If he does not, senior officials are less willing to defer to his judgment when the board or FOMC votes on important monetary or policy issues. These situations manifest themselves publicly when the board's votes are split rather than the normal consensus vote. However, there are times when board members or voting regional bank presidents have legitimate policy differences with the chairman and want to express those differences publicly and demonstrate their independence. However, if the truth be known, if you have a powerful chairman in the mold of Alan Greenspan or Paul Volcker, and you rack up too many votes contrary to those of chairman, you will quickly find yourself shut out of the corridors of power. Split votes also begin to occur near the time when the chairman is expected to step down and other board members begin to position themselves for the position of the chairman. As an example, at the September 24, 2003, board meeting, two board members openly broke with Chairman Greenspan's decision to hold monetary policy steady, the first time in 4 years there had been such dissent.

The board's professional staff of economic experts and advisers is a significant source of informal power within the Fed. Many of these staff have a long tenure in the Federal Reserve System, have in-depth knowledge of its operation and practices, and have a significant power base because of their expertise in some facet of monetary analysis. Furthermore, they interact daily with the Board of Governors, providing them with situational briefings, giving them access to and interpretation of research done at the Fed, and advising them on important decisions. Thus, the professional staff exerts an indefinable but significant influence on policy issues and in the decision-making process at the Fed.

THE FED'S REGULATORY POWERS

Over the years, the Fed has been given a multitude of regulatory powers over commercial banks. Historically, many regulatory powers were granted following a major financial crisis, such as the Great Depression in 1929. More recently, the Fed has gained regulatory powers to protect consumers, to deal with discrimination in the marketplace, and to adjust to the changing structure of the financial system. To give you a feel for the scope of the Fed's regulatory powers, we will discuss some of the more important regulations of the Fed. Exhibit 2.5, though admittedly dry, does a nice job of summarizing important regulatory powers of the Fed. The overall regulation of banks and other financial institutions will be covered in detail in Chapter 16.

The Banking Act of 1933 (often called the Glass-Steagall Act) gave the Fed the power to regulate the maximum interest rate that banks could pay to depositors under **Regulation Q**. The Fed was given this power to prevent excessive and destructive competition among banks to attract funds from depositors. At the time, it was believed that excessive competition for deposits contributed to bank failures and the Great Depression, which began in 1929.

Over time, however, regulators discovered that Regulation Q periodically had adverse effects on banks and other depository institutions. The reason was that banks found it difficult to attract or retain deposits when the market rate of interest was higher than the maximum rate banks could pay for funds under

EXHIBIT 2.5
Important Federal Reserve Regulatory Powers

Regulation	Topics of Regulations	Institutions Affected
A	Establishes Fed discount window policy	Borrowers from discount window
D	Establishes reserve requirements	All depository institutions
E	Regulates electronic funds transfer	All financial institutions
J	Regulates check collection and wire transfers of funds	All institutions using Fed facilities
K	Regulates international banking in United States and by U.S. banks abroad	Domestic and foreign banks
M	Regulates consumer leasing transactions	Institutions leasing consumer goods
G, U, T, X	Establishes securities margin requirements	Brokers, dealers, banks, and individuals
Y	Sets rules applicable to bank holding companies	Banks and their affiliates
Z, B, BB, C	Regulates consumer and mortgage credit transactions according to the following Acts: Z = Truth-in-Lending and Fair Credit Billing Acts B = Equal Credit Opportunity Act BB = Community Reinvestment Act C = Home Mortgage Disclosure Act	Institutions offering consumer and mortgage credit
Q	Prohibits interest on demand deposits; formerly set interest rate ceilings on savings and time deposits	All commercial banks
DD	Regulates interest rate disclosures on deposits	All depository institutions offering interest-bearing deposits

Regulation Q. During these periods of time, banks would face disintermediation as depositors withdrew their funds from banks and reinvested their money in financial instruments that paid the market rate. In fact, money market mutual funds emerged in the early 1970s to provide an investment medium that paid the market rate of interest to consumers and investors with small dollar balances. Ultimately, Regulation Q was phased out by the Depository Institutions Deregulation and Monetary Control Act (DIDMCA) of 1980 and the Depository Institutions Act of 1982.

During the depression that followed the 1929 stock market crash, the Fed was given the power to regulate the purchase of stock on "margin," which means using borrowed funds to purchase stock, which is then used as collateral for the loan. Under Regulations G, T, U, and X the Fed could regulate stock market "margin" credit requirements (or **margin requirements**), which determine the proportion of the stock's value that can be used as loan collateral. The Fed used these regulations to prevent what was then viewed as excessive speculation in the stock market. Prior to the crash, people could finance 90 percent or more of their stock purchases with the stock as collateral. Thus, if stock prices fell only by 10 percent, they might be unable to repay their debt. As a result, they had to sell quickly when stock prices started to fall, and their selling aggravated the stock price decline. By raising margin requirements, panic selling could be reduced or eliminated. At present, stock margin requirements are 50 percent.

Since the early 1940s, the Fed has been given expanded powers to protect consumers from the vagaries of the market. For example, during World War II and the Korean War the Fed was given temporary powers to regulate down payment percentages and maximum payment terms on many types of consumer loans under Regulation W (currently lapsed). Further, with the passage of the Truth-in-Lending Act in 1968, the Fed acquired the power to mandate and regulate the disclosure of interest rates on consumer credit offered by banks, savings institutions, credit unions, retailers, finance companies, and other consumer lenders under Regulation Z. The Fed has also been given the power to write regulations mandating that financial institutions meet the requirements of the Equal Credit Opportunity Act (Regulation B), the Community Reinvestment Act (Regulation BB), the Fair Credit Billing Act (Regulation Z again), and many other consumer protection or "antidiscrimination" acts passed by Congress in the 1960s, 1970s, and 1980s.

In the Depository Institutions Deregulation and Monetary Control Act (DIDMCA) of 1980, the Fed was given the power to assess reserve requirements on the transaction deposits of nonbank depository institutions (under Regulation D) and to allow all such institutions to borrow from its discount window (under Regulation A). Besides its domestic responsibilities, the Fed conducts U.S. interventions in foreign currency markets and is the primary regulator of foreign banks operating in the United States and U.S. banks operating overseas.

Over time, then, the Fed's powers have increased greatly. The Fed has gained power over banks, bank holding companies, nonbank depository institutions, consumer lenders, securities market participants, foreign banking institutions operating in the United States, and many other entities. Furthermore, through its monetary policy, it is fair to say that it can affect every borrower and lender and all other people who use the U.S. dollar to conduct transactions in the United States and elsewhere.

INDEPENDENCE OF THE FED

One of the controversial aspects of the organization of the Federal Reserve System is the issue of its independence. Although the Fed is the key player in the management of the nation's economy through the conduct of monetary policy, it is not directly under the authority of Congress or the president. The Fed's independence is a result of the historical legacy of how it was founded and organized. The term "Fed independence" means that the Fed is free from political and bureaucratic pressures when it formulates and executes monetary policy.

In the short run, the Fed has a substantial degree of independence because it operates as a bank—in fact, a very profitable bank. Thus, unlike other government agencies, the Fed does not rely on Congress for funding. For example, in recent years the Fed's net earnings after expenses have been around $20 billion per year. The Fed makes the lion's share of its earnings, about 85 percent, from its large portfolio of government securities. The balance of its earnings comes from loans to banks and nonbanks that borrow at the discount window and from miscellaneous fees it charges for services such as check clearing. Further adding to Fed independence is the long 14-year terms of the governors, which insulate them from day-to-day political pressures. Assuming no resignations, an incoming president can appoint only two governors in his first 4-year term and a majority of the board late in his second term.

Over the longer run, the Federal Reserve banks' independence is constrained. The Fed is well aware that it is our nation's third central bank. The two previous central banks lost their charters. The Fed is fully aware that Congress created the Federal Reserve System and that its charter can always be modified or terminated by Congress. Also, if the truth be known, it is unlikely that Congress would want the responsibility of setting monetary policy: Who would they have to blame when the economy performs poorly? Finally, the Fed is subject to the laws of the United States, including the Employment Act of 1946 and the Full Employment and Balanced Growth Act of 1978, which come close to spelling out the economic responsibilities of the federal government. As a result, the Fed is keenly aware of political pressures and of secular changes in economic policy. A study of monetary policy after World War II indicates shifts in Fed economic policy whenever the presidency has changed hands. These shifts have brought the Fed's policies more in line with the views of the new president, regardless of the personal views of the chairman or the president who originally appointed him.

In summary, overall the Fed has an extraordinary degree of independence for a government agency and is one of the most independent central banks in the world. And most interested parties agree that the Fed and, particularly, monetary policy should be insulated from short-run partisan politics. However, like the Supreme Court, the Fed recognizes the power of the political process and is not immune from the desires of the electorate. Thus, the Federal Reserve System is independent within, rather than independent of, the federal government.

IS INDEPENDENCE IMPORTANT?

Advocates of *independent* central banks believe that independence from day-to-day political pressure allows central banks to better manage their countries' national economies. By "better" we mean that the central bank can take short-run policy actions that may be politically unpopular but in the longer run benefit the economy's overall macroeconomic performance. For example, this is often the case when inflationary pressures begin to build up in an economy during a period of rapid economic expansion. To dampen the inflation, a central bank will raise interest rates to slow the rate of economic growth and, thus, dampen inflationary expectations. Needless to say, raising interest rates to slow down an economy rarely wins political applause.

Research supports the benefits of an independent central bank. When central banks for different countries are rank-ordered as to their degree of independence on a scale of 1 to 4 (1 the least and 4 the most independent), performance in controlling inflation is found to be best in countries with the most independent central banks. As can be seen in Exhibit 2.6, the countries with the least independent central banks, Spain and New Zealand, had average annual inflation rates for the study period of around 12 percent. In contrast, the two countries with the most independent central banks, Switzerland and Germany, had average annual inflation rates around 3 percent. In the United States, whose central bank independence index was a 3, the average inflation rate was slightly more than 6 percent. Most economists agree that low rates of inflation

EXHIBIT 2.6
Central Bank Independence and a Country's Rate of Inflation

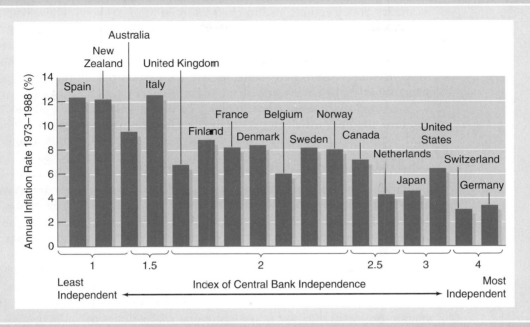

Countries with independent central banks have lower rates of inflation than countries with less independent central banks.

Source: Alberto Alesina and Lawrence Summers, "Central Bank Independence and Macroeconomic Performance, Some Comparative Evidence," *Journal of Money, Credit, and Banking* 25 (1993): 151–162.

are generally good for an economy. It is important to note that the study found that countries with independent central banks were no more likely to have high unemployment or greater fluctuation in national income than countries with less independent central banks.

independence → both low inflation rate and low unemployment rate

DO YOU UNDERSTAND?

1. What were the objectives of the National Banking Acts and what problems existed in the U.S. banking system before those acts were passed in the 1860s?

2. What were the problems posed by the National Banking Acts?

3. Why was the Fed initially established?

4. How did the Federal Reserve System try to solve problems from the National Banking Act period?

5. Why is the Fed chairman called the second most powerful person in the country?

THE FED'S BALANCE SHEET

To gain an understanding of what the Fed does and how it implements monetary policy, it is useful to examine the Fed's balance sheet. As we will see, the Fed's monetary policy actions lead to changes in its balance sheet. These balance sheet changes ultimately result in changes to the nation's money supply. Thus, our first task is to understand the major accounts on the Fed's balance sheet. Fortunately, the Fed's balance sheet is not that complicated. Keep in mind that the Federal Reserve bank is just like any bank, in that it accepts deposits and makes loans. The difficulty arises because some of the balance sheet items have special names such as "reserves" or "discount borrowing." Exhibit 2.7 presents a simplified balance sheet for the Fed, which you should use to follow our discussion.

LIABILITIES AND CAPITAL OF THE FED

Operationally, the Fed conducts monetary policy by changing the nation's **monetary base**. The monetary base equals the sum of the currency in circulation plus the deposits of financial institutions at the Fed. Holding everything constant, an increase in the monetary base will lead to an increase in the money supply. As a practical matter, the Fed issues most of the currency in circulation, but the U.S. Treasury Department does issue some currency, which accounts for a small percentage of the monetary base. However, we can ignore the monetary liabilities of the Treasury because the Treasury is not allowed to engage in monetary policy actions. Let's examine in more detail the most important monetary liabilities of the Fed.

Federal Reserve Notes.   As shown in Exhibit 2.7, by far the largest single liability of the Fed consists of Federal Reserve notes in circulation. Look at the bills (if any) in your pocket. You will find that each has a seal of the Federal Reserve. You can take the bill to the Fed and ask for lawful money in exchange, but you will get back only another Federal Reserve note. You will not get gold or any other precious metal. Federal Reserve notes are lawful money, because they are "legal tender for all debts public and private." That means you can repay any debt in this country by offering the proper amount of Federal Reserve notes.

Depository Institution Reserves.   All banks and other depository institutions by law must hold deposits at the Federal Reserve banks, and these deposits are given the special name "reserves." Reserves consist of all deposits held at the Fed and cash which is physically held in the bank's vault (called vault cash). These deposits are useful because they can be transferred from one institution to another when checks and wire transfers are "cleared" from one institution to another. The Fed pays no interest on deposits (reserves) held at the Fed, which is of course a good deal for the Fed.

Reserves are also useful to the Fed for controlling the nation's money supply. Depository institutions are required to hold a certain amount of reserves at the Federal Reserve bank determined by the amount of transaction deposits their customers hold at their bank. Depository institutions can withdraw cash (Federal Reserve notes) from their reserve accounts at the Fed when they need it. As we will explain, any time there is an increase in reserves at the Fed, there will be an increase in the money supply.

It is important to note, that the **total reserves** *(TR)* held by a bank can be divided into two components: (1) reserves that the bank is required to hold by law,

EXHIBIT 2.7
Fed Balance Sheet (December 2002)

	Millions	% of Total
Assets		
Gold certificates	$11,039	1.5%
Loans to depository institutions	40	0.0
U.S. government and agency securities	629,416	85.8
Securities purchased under agreements to resell	39,500	5.4
Cash items in process of collection (CIPC)	11,498	1.6
Other assets	41,756	5.7
Total	$733,249	100.0%
Liabilities and capital		
Federal Reserve notes	$654,273	89.2%
Securities sold under agreements to repurchase	21,091	2.9
Deposits		
Depository institution reserves	22,541	3.1
U.S. Treasury	4,420	0.6
Other	1,292	0.2
Deferred availability cash items (DACI)	10,666	1.5
Other liabilities	2,206	0.3
Capital	16,760	2.3
Total	$733,249	100.0%

In implementing monetary policy, the Fed takes policy actions that change its balance sheet. These changes ultimately lead to changes in the nation's money supply.

Source: Board of Governors, Federal Reserve System. *89th Annual Report, 2002.*

called **required reserves** *(RR)*, and (2) reserves in excess of those required, called **excess reserves** *(ER)*. Thus,

$$TR = RR + ER. \qquad (2.1)$$

As we mentioned previously, a bank must hold required reserves that are a specified percent (fraction) of the total deposits at the bank. This fraction is called the required reserve ratio or reserve requirement, expressed as a percent. For example, if the reserve requirement is 10 percent and the bank has $10,000 in deposits, the bank's required reserves are $1,000. Thus, the formula for required reserves is:

$$RR = k \times DEP \text{ or } k = RR/DEP. \qquad (2.2)$$

where k is the required reserve ratio and *DEP* is the total deposits held at the bank. Using Equation 2.1, if the bank has total reserves of $1,500, the bank has excess reserves of $500 ($1,500 – $1,000).

What will the bank do with the $500 in excess reserves? The bank could leave the funds at the Fed; however, there is an opportunity cost since reserves do not earn any interest. To put the money to work and earn some interest, the bank could use the reserves to make commercial loans, loans to consumers, or the bank can lend the reserves to other banks in the fed funds market. The point here is that the bank has some options regarding what to do with its excess reserves and, being a profit-maximizing firm, it is unlikely the bank will allow the excess to sit at the Fed.

Treasury Deposits.   Another important class of Federal Reserve deposits consists of U.S. Treasury deposits. The Federal Reserve acts as the "fiscal agent" for the U.S. Treasury Department. That simply means that the Fed acts as a bank for the Treasury, which can pay its bills by writing checks from its account at the Fed. If you ever get a check from the federal government, read the fine print and you will find that the check was written on a deposit at a Federal Reserve bank. The Fed pays no interest on its checking accounts and rarely provides free coffee and doughnuts for its depositors.

Deferred Availability Cash Items.   **Deferred availability cash items (DACI)** represent the value of checks deposited at the Fed by depository institutions that have not yet been credited to the institutions' accounts. For instance, if a bank in New York deposits a $200 check written on a bank in California, it will get a $200 deferred availability cash item for 2 days. At the end of that time, the New York bank's reserve deposit will be increased by $200. The Fed does not give the New York bank instant credit because it takes time to ship the check to California and collect on it from the California bank. If all goes well, the Fed expects to collect the check in 2 days, and usually it is cheaper and more desirable to transfer the funds to the New York bank's account automatically than to wait for a message saying the check was finally collected from the California bank.

Capital.   Fed "capital" primarily represents money paid in by banks that are members of the Federal Reserve System (member banks) to purchase stock. The Fed pays a 6 percent dividend on that stock regardless of its earnings and returns the remainder (over $25 billion a year) to the U.S. Treasury each year. As we mentioned previously, stock in the Fed does not carry the typical rights of ownership as does stock in a corporation.

ASSETS OF THE FED

There are two important assets on the Fed balance sheet we need to discuss. First, the Fed's loan accounts: changes in the loan accounts lead to changes in the reserve account and, hence, changes in the money supply. Second, the Fed's portfolio of government securities: the Fed earns billions of dollars every year on its large portfolio of government securities. Though most of these net profits are returned to the Treasury, they provide part of the foundation for the Fed's political independence from the president and Congress.

Loans.   Like any bank, the Fed can make loans, but it only makes loans to banks and other depository institutions. Loans from the Fed are for short periods of time, and the rate charged is referred to as the **discount rate**. When first established, the **discount window**, which is where banks borrow from the Fed, was designed to provide loans as a lender of "last resort." Thus, when a bank was unable to attract the funds it needed in the market, it could borrow from the Fed. In case you're wondering, there is no physical discount window; it's just an expression. Historically, however, when banks wanted to borrow from the Fed, they had to provide bank loans as collateral for their borrowing. When the loans were brought to the "teller's" window at the Fed, the loans were collateralized at less than their face value, or discounted—hence, the term "discount window."

Government Securities.   The Federal Reserve bank's largest asset category is its portfolio of U.S. Treasury and U.S. government agency securities. The Fed can buy and sell government securities in the market at will through its **open-market operations**. When the Fed buys government securities, it pays for them by providing the bank with additional reserves, thereby increasing the money supply.

Cash Items in Process of Collection.   **Cash items in process of collection (CIPC)** are items the Federal Reserve is clearing but for which it has not yet obtained funds. In our earlier example, the $200 check deposited by the New York bank is a CIPC item until it is actually subtracted from the account of the California bank on which it was written. Because the Fed clears many checks, the number of CIPC items is large.

Float.   Float represents a net extension of credit from the Fed to depository institutions. It is the difference between CIPC and DACI. For instance, if it took the Fed 3 days to collect the check from the California bank instead of the 2 days assumed by the deferred availability credit schedule, the New York bank would receive a $200 deposit to its reserve account at the Fed the day before the money was withdrawn from the California bank's reserve account—so, DACI would fall but CIPC would not; as a result "float" would rise by $200.

Float = CIPC − DACI

Many checks and electronic transfers are "cleared" by local banks exchanging them through local clearinghouse associations. Those clearinghouses net out the value of checks and transfers drawn on or received by each depository institution in the association and make only net payments of the net balances due among members in the association. This saves much time and expense since payments do not have to be made for each transaction individually.

   The Fed also plays a major role in check clearing, particularly in clearing checks drawn on depository institutions located in other market areas or different parts of the country. The Fed clearing process is facilitated by the fact that most depository institutions either directly or indirectly hold reserve deposits or clearing deposit balances with the Fed. These deposits can then be easily transferred from one institution to another by making appropriate entries on the Fed's books.

   It is important to remember that reserve balances are transferred from one bank to another when checks are cleared between them. They do not disappear

THE FED'S ROLE IN CHECK CLEARING

from the banking system, only from the account of the bank on which the check was drawn. The total level of reserves at the Fed remains unchanged.

FEDERAL RESERVE TOOLS OF MONETARY POLICY

As noted earlier, the Federal Reserve is the most important financial institution in the economy because it controls the nation's money supply. The Fed has three major tools to either increase or decease the money supply: (1) open-market operations, (2) changing the discount rate, and (3) changing the reserve requirement ratio.

OPEN-MARKET OPERATIONS

Open-market operations involve the buying and selling of government securities through the trading desk at the Federal Reserve Bank of New York. It is the most important policy tool the Fed has for controlling the money supply. The FOMC is the focal point for setting monetary policy at the Fed; it meets eight times per year in the main building of the Board of Governors in Washington, D.C. The purpose of the meeting is to set the target growth rate for the money supply, given past, current, and expected economic conditions.

The FOMC meeting starts at 9:00 A.M. sharp with the 7 members of the Board of Governors and the 12 regional bank presidents, along with assorted senior staff from the regional banks, the Board of Governors, and officers in direct charge of domestic and international securities operations. The board and the regional bank presidents (and a few key board staff members) sit around a large conference table. Other attendees are relegated to sitting around the sides of the room and, according to tradition, remain silent. Also, although only 5 of the regional bank presidents can vote, all are allowed to participate in the discussions.

The meetings have a predictable schedule. After housekeeping chores like approving the minutes of the last meeting, the first substantive report is a presentation on domestic open-market operations and foreign currency market operations since the FOMC's last meeting. Next is a briefing that is prepared by the board's economists on past and current economic conditions and then a 2-year national economic forecast. This report is often called the "green book forecast" because of the color the folder it is bound in. Then regional bank presidents present their views of economic conditions in their districts. The information, contained in a report called the "beige book" (the cover color is beige), is derived from regional statistical data and extensive interviews with regional business and political leaders. The beige book is the only Fed briefing book distributed publicly and frequently receives considerable press coverage. The final formal presentation, contained in the "blue book," is made by the board's Director of Monetary Affairs. The presentation usually contains three alternative scenarios for monetary policy, given current and expected economic conditions.

After a discussion, the Chairman of the Board of Governors presents his view on the state of the economy and what monetary policy actions are warranted. Then FOMC members and nonvoting regional bank presidents express their views on the appropriate monetary action. At some point, the chairman summarizes the discussion and proposes a specific wording for the monetary policy directive that will be given to the open-market desk to execute. The

Alan Greenspan: Fed Chairman and National Icon

At the time of this writing (the spring of 2004), Alan Greenspan has been in the national spotlight for 16 years as the Chairman of the Federal Reserve System. His influence over monetary policy makes him among the most powerful persons in Washington. During his tenure as chairman, the nation has enjoyed unprecedented economic growth, low inflation, and low unemployment—all of which are good news. The 76-year-old chairman is now in his fourth 4-year term, which ends just months before the 2004 presidential election. To avoid enmeshing his successor in election-year politics, he is expected to step down within a year or 2 following the election. Along with former Fed Chairman Paul Volcker, many believe that Greenspan is destined to be enshrined in the pantheon of Fed chairmen. Among Greenspan's most admired achievements are the following:

- He presided over the longest peacetime expansion of the U.S. economy, which saw unemployment fall to 4.6 percent, the lowest level in a generation.

- He brought inflation under control, achieving the Fed's long-term goal of stable prices and, at the same time, encouraged economic growth. Inflation declined from 3.5 to 1.8 percent.

- He correctly foresaw that information technology was spurring increases in productivity, which enabled the economy to grow faster without rekindling inflation. On his watch, industrial productivity increased from 2.2 to 2.7 percent.

- He managed the economy through numerous crises by smoothing the impact of negative shocks, such as the stock market crash of 1987, the 1997 Asian financial crisis, the 1998 Russian debt default, and the terrorist attacks of 2001.

Greenspan's detractors concede his many accomplishments but believe he got it wrong when he allowed the stock market speculative bubble in the late 1990s to take hold, brought on by investor exuberance rather than sound fundamental information about value. Speculative bubbles can lead to economic instability, with hard-to-control deflationary consequences. These Greenspan critics believe the Fed should have been more aggressive in increasing interest rates and, thus, reined in the excesses in asset markets much more quickly. In terms of policy, this means a central bank that is much quicker to raise interest rates once the economy has picked up steam and one that is less likely to let unemployment decline to such low levels as 3.9 percent, which risks igniting inflation. Thus, a good deal of the economic suffering experienced during the prolonged post-bubble recession that began in 2000 could have been avoided.

On the other side of the ledger, if the U.S. economy has a robust recovery in 2004—the stock market picks up, unemployment continues to decline, and inflation remains in check—then the Greenspan wizardry of monetary policy will have been confirmed. If this happens, which many economist expect, Chairman Greenspan may go down in history as the best central banker ever. You might want to check and see how the economy has done since the 2004 election to see in which direction Greenspan's reputation is headed.

FOMC secretary then reads the proposed directive, and the 12 voting members vote. The policy directive is delivered to the Manager of the Open-Market Account at the New York Fed, who uses it as a guideline to instruct traders at the open-market desk to buy or sell government securities. All of this is usually done by lunchtime.

In the afternoon of the same day, the Fed makes a public announcement of the outcome of the meeting: whether the Federal Reserve discount rate and target Fed funds rate will be lowered, raised, or left unchanged. Historically, the Fed did not make public announcements after the meeting and the markets had to guess what policy actions were taken. This led to intense speculation and, over time, a whole industry developed on Wall Street called "Fed watching." The policy directives were published with a lag of 90 days. In 1994, however, the Fed decided to post meeting announcements to reduce the intense speculation and rumors that followed each meeting.

The Trading Desk.   Located in the heart of New York City's financial district, the trading desk at the Federal Reserve Bank of New York has the day-to-day responsibility of conducting open-market operations in accordance with the directive from the FOMC. The desk buys or sells specific dollar amounts of government securities from government securities dealers. The amount of securities bought or sold in any one day depends on current market conditions, the technical factors mentioned previously, the Fed's monetary policy objectives, and the price of securities across various maturities (the term structure). The Fed trades with firms from an approved list of government securities dealers, which are either large commercial banks such as Citibank or part of a large securities firm like Goldman Sachs.

Changes to the Money Supply.   The Fed changes the amount of reserves in the banking system on a day-to-day basis through the purchase or sale of government securities on the open market. The Fed is the only institution in the country that can expand or contract its liabilities at will. To expand them, it need only issue Federal Reserve notes or write a check on itself. The Fed can "print" up money whenever it needs it!

Let's do a simple example with T-accounts to see what happens when the Fed buys or sells government securities. Let's say the Fed decides to buy $1,000 in government bonds from Citibank in New York City. The T-accounts for Citibank and the Fed after the transaction are as follows (see upper portion of T-accounts):

Citibank		The Fed	
−$1,000 Gov. bonds +$1,000 Reserves at FRB		+$1,000 Gov. bonds	+$1,000 Reserve deposit of Citibank
+$1,000 Gov. bonds −$1,000 Reserves at FRB		−$1,000 Gov. bonds	−$1,000 Reserves at Citibank

Notice that the Citibank balance sheet shows a reduction of $1,000 from its bond portfolio and an increase of $1,000 in its reserve deposit with the Federal Reserve bank (FRB). Essentially, the Fed has paid the bank $1,000 in reserves for the government bonds. As you can see in the upper portion of the T-accounts, the banking system as a whole now has an additional $1,000 in reserves because of the Fed's purchase of government bonds and, hence, there is an expansion of the money supply.

Using similar reasoning, the sale of securities by the Fed leads to a contraction of the money supply. The lower portion of the T-accounts above illustrates what happens when desk traders at the Fed are instructed to sell government securities, with Citibank buying $1,000 of the bonds. Citibank pays for the bonds using its funds (reserves) at the Fed. As a result, the banking system has fewer reserves and, hence, the money supply has decreased.

DISCOUNT WINDOW BORROWING

The discount rate is the rate of interest that financial institutions must pay to borrow reserve deposits from the Fed. When the discount rate is low, financial institutions have an inexpensive source of funds for reserve requirement obligations, provided they don't mind the "discount window scrutiny." That is, banks that frequently borrow from the discount window signal that they may have serious financial problems since they are not able to obtain funds in the market. Thus, when the discount rate is low, financial institutions will prudently expand their assets and deposits more readily, because it will not cost them as much to obtain the reserves required to back their new deposit or asset holdings. When the discount rate is high, the institutions are more reluctant to borrow reserves and are therefore more careful about expanding asset and deposit holdings if they must borrow from the Fed.

When banks borrow from the discount window, the funds they borrow are paid in reserves by the Fed. For example, suppose that Citibank borrows $1,000 at the discount window, resulting in the following T-account transaction:

Citibank		The Fed	
+$1,000 Reserves at the FRB	+$1,000 Discount loan	+$1,000 Loan to Citibank	+$1,000 Reserve deposits of Citicorp

Thus, when banks borrow at the discount window, there is an increase in reserves in the banking system and, hence, an increase in the money supply. The bank can hold the reserves if it is short of required reserves; it can make loans to businesses or consumers; or it can lend the reserves to other banks in the federal funds market. Similar reasoning suggests that when banks pay back loans at the discount window, the payment is made in reserves, thus decreasing the reserves in the banking system and resulting in a corresponding decline in the money supply.

The Fed can influence the extent of money supply expansion by changing the discount rate. All else being equal, if the Fed raises the discount rate, banks will be inclined to borrow less at the discount window. Thus, banks will make fewer loans or reduce their investments so they can repay their loans from the Fed, reducing the amount of reserves in the banking system and, hence, the money supply.

If the Fed cuts the discount rate, the opposite effect will occur. Banks that can do so will take advantage of the lower borrowing rate, especially banks with seasonal borrowing privileges at the Fed. The Fed's seasonal borrowing privilege plan allows smaller banks with large seasonal fluctuations in loan demand, such as banks in agricultural areas, to borrow at the Fed's discount window. By borrowing cheap funds at the discount window and lending them out at a higher rate, these banks can make more profits when the discount rate is low.

In the early days of the Fed, changing the discount rate was the primary way in which the Fed attempted to affect national monetary policy. Changing the rate affected a bank's willingness to borrow from the Fed, the total amount of Federal Reserve credit outstanding, and the nation's money supply. However, it is difficult to predict how much bank discount window borrowing will increase or decrease when the discount rate is changed. Also, such changes may be misinterpreted by "Fed watchers," who believe they foretell alterations in Fed policy. Thus, in recent years, the Federal Reserve has relied mainly on open-market operations to implement monetary policy. Today, changes in the discount rate are undertaken either in response to changes in other market interest rates or to send a "message" to the market of a change in Fed policy. If the Fed wants to have a psychological effect on the financial markets to show that it is serious about wanting to ease (or tighten) its policy, it will often lower (or raise) the discount rate to make sure its policy intent is not misunderstood.

RESERVE REQUIREMENTS

The Federal Reserve can establish reserve requirements within limits set by Congress. These requirements are important because they determine the amount of funds financial institutions must hold at the Fed in order to back their deposits. The Monetary Control Act of 1980 simplified the reserve process by bringing all depository institutions' reserve requirements under the control of the Fed, subject to the same reserve requirements. For instance, a depository institution that is subject to a reserve requirement of 10 percent on its transactions deposits must back every dollar of those deposits with 10 cents of reserve assets.

Exhibit 2.8 shows the reserve requirements for different types of deposit accounts. In addition to reserves on their transactions accounts, financial institu-

EXHIBIT 2.8
Reserve Requirements for Depository Institutions

Type of Deposit	Deposit Amount	Reserve Requirement (%)	Allowable Range (minimum/maximum %)
Transaction deposits	Under $6.6 million	0	0
	Between $6.6 million and $45.4 million	3	3/3
	Over $45.4 million	10	3/14
Nonpersonal time deposits (CDs)		0	0/9
Consumer savings deposits (under $100,000)		0	
Eurodollar deposits		0	

Source: Board of Governors, Federal Reserve System.

tions may be required to hold small reserves, either in vault cash or deposits at the Fed, against their holdings of short-maturity, nonpersonal time and savings deposits. Also, at the discretion of the Federal Reserve, banks may be required to hold reserves against certain other liabilities—such as Eurodollar borrowings from overseas branches or certain liabilities issued by bank holding companies.

The power to establish reserve requirements is one of the tools the Fed has to control the nation's money supply. Only the Fed can change reserve requirements for depository institutions. To show how changes in reserve requirements change the money supply, let's work through an example. Assume a bank has $5,000 in demand deposits *(DD)* and the reserve requirement for the bank is 20 percent ($k = 0.20$). Suppose the bank is fully loaned up, meaning it has no excess reserves *(ER = 0)*. Also, for our example, *DD* is the money supply.

The top frame in Exhibit 2.9 (Initial Condition) shows the T-account for the bank's initial situation. Notice the bank's required reserves *(RR)* are $1,000 (0.20 × $5,000) and the bank has no excess reserves *(ER)*; that is $ER = TR - RR = \$1,000 - \$1,000 = 0$. Also notice that $1,000 of reserves can support $5,000 in deposits and that the bank is fully loaned up with $4,000 in loans. If you're feeling a little confused, you may want to review Equations 2.1 and 2.2.

Now suppose that the Fed decides to reduce reserve requirement on demand deposits from 20 percent to 10 percent. The mechanics of the process involves two steps. First, the reduction in the reserve requirement on the bank's existing deposits lowers the amount of required reserves to $500 and increases excess reserves by $500. That is, $RR = 0.10 \times \$5,000 = \$500$ and $ER = \$1,000 - \$500 = \$500$, as can be seen in the middle frame of Exhibit 2.9.

The second step is deciding what the bank should do with the $500 in excess reserves. It could just hold them at the Fed, but deposits at the Fed do not pay interest. More than likely, the bank will make loans and expand deposits to the point where all of the excess reserves are again absorbed as required reserves. At the reserve requirement level, $k = 10$ percent, the bank can support $10,000 of deposits ($DEP = RR/k = \$1,000/0.10 = \$10,000$). Thus, the Fed can expand the dollar amount of bank deposits by lowering reserve requirements on deposits, thereby increasing the money supply (see the lower frame of Exhibit 2.9). Similar reasoning indicates that when the Fed increases reserve requirements, the banking system will contract the amount of bank deposits and, hence, decrease the money supply.

COMPARING THE MONETARY TOOLS

Exhibit 2.10 summarizes how each of the three monetary policy tools—open-market operations, adjustments to the discount rate, and reserve requirement changes—affect the money supply. As you will see, the Fed does not use all three tools to conduct monetary policy on a regular basis and, as a practical matter, each plays a different and important role in the Fed's monetary policy arsenal.

Open-market operations are the primary tool used by the Fed to conduct monetary policy on a day-to-day basis. The advantages are that open-market operations can be done easily, almost instantaneously, and with no announcement effect. In addition, any change to the money supply can also be easily reversed without an announcement effect. This is particularly important because one of the Fed's responsibilities is to ensure that the Treasury Department can sell and retire its debt in an orderly manner. This means that on a short-term basis, the Fed will

EXHIBIT 2.9
How Changes in Reserve Requirements Change the Money Supply (Demand Deposits)

Initial Condition

Assets		Liabilities	
Reserves	$1,000	Demand Deposits	$5,000
Required	1,000		
Excess	0		
Loans	4,000		
Total	$5,000	Total	$5,000

Reduction in Reserve Requirements

Assets		Liabilities	
Reserves	$1,000	Demand Deposits	$5,000
Required	500		
Excess	500		
Loans	4,000		
Total	$5,000	Total	$5,000

New Equilibrium

Assets		Liabilities	
Reserves	$1,000	Demand Deposits	$10,000
Required	1,000		
Excess	0		
Loans	9,000		
Total	$10,000	Total	$10,000

EXHIBIT 2.10
How Tools of Monetary Policy Affect the Money Supply

Monetary Policy Tool	Increase in Money Supply	Decrease in Money Supply
Open-market operations	FOMC directs the trading desk to purchase Treasury securities in the secondary market	FOMC directs the trading desk to sell Treasury securities in the secondary market
Adjust the discount rate	Board of Governors lowers the discount rate	Board of Governors raises the discount rate
Adjust bank reserve requirements	Board of Governors lowers the reserve ratio (within limits) to cause a higher money multiplier	Board of Governors raises the reserve ratio (within limits) to cause a lower money multiplier

intervene in the Treasury market to "smooth" interest rates (i.e., reduce interest rate volatility).

Adjustments to the discount rate have a number of shortcomings as a tool for monetary policy. First, changes to the discount rate will affect the money supply only if banks are willing to respond. As we mentioned previously, the Fed closely scrutinizes borrowing at the discount window; therefore banks are reluctant to overuse this privilege. Furthermore, borrowing at the discount window is short term, and it is difficult to gauge the impact on the money supply for a given change in the discount rate. Thus, as a practical matter, changing the discount rate is not a viable tool for conducting monetary policy.

Finally, changes to reserve requirements are not used as a tool of monetary policy. The reason is that it is difficult to make a number of small adjustments to reserve requirements, as frequent changes are disruptive to the banking system. When the Fed does change reserve requirements, however, it is typically done to deal with a structural problem in the banking system.

CHAPTER TAKE-AWAYS

1 Prior to the establishment of the Fed in 1914, pyramiding of reserves and lax state banking regulations allowed banks to issue too many banknotes (and other bank liabilities) relative to their reserve holdings. Then any downturn in the economy caused large numbers of depositors to simultaneously redeem their deposits or banknotes for hard currency, which was in short supply. The result was a large number of bank failures and business failures as banks called in business loans, which led to economic recession.

2 The Federal Reserve System was established to provide an elastic money supply, be a lender of last resort, improve bank regulation, and improve the performance of the nation's payment system.

3 The most powerful policy group within the Fed is the Board of Governors. They set reserve requirements, set the discount rate, and control the FOMC because they have the majority of the votes.

4 The Fed's most important duty is to establish the nation's monetary policy by changing reserve requirements, the discount rate, and its open-market operations that affect the amount of reserves in the banking system and, hence, the money supply.

5 Over the years the Fed has come to rely more on open-market operations (directed by the FOMC) rather than the discount rate policy of individual district Federal Reserve banks when it wants to change monetary policy. Open-market operations can be implemented almost instantaneously with a great deal of precision, with no announcement effect, and can be easily reversed.

KEY TERMS

Call loans
Lender of last resort
Elastic money supply
Federal Open Market
  Committee (FOMC)

Regulation Q
Margin requirements
Monetary base
Total reserves
Required reserves

Excess reserves
Deferred availability cash
  items (DACI)
Discount rate
Discount window

Open-market operations
Cash items in process of
  collection (CIPC)

QUESTIONS AND PROBLEMS

1. Explain why the banking system was so unstable prior to the establishment of the Federal Reserve System in 1914.

2. What is a "call loan" and how did call loans contribute to economic recessions?

3. What were the four goals of the legislation that established the Federal Reserve System? Have they been met today?

4. Explain why the Board of Governors of the Federal Reserve System is considered so powerful. What are its major powers and which is the most important?

5. Explain why the FOMC is the key policy group within the Fed.

6. Explain why Regulation Q caused difficulties for banks and other depository institutions, especially during periods of rising interest rates.

7. Explain the sense in which the Fed is independent of the federal government. How independent is the Fed in reality? What is your opinion about the importance of the Fed's independence for the U.S. economy?

8. A bank has $3,000 in reserves, $9,000 in bank loans, and $12,000 of deposits. If the reserve requirement is 20 percent, what is the bank's reserve position? What is the maximum dollar amount of loans the bank could make? What would happen to the nation's money supply if the Fed lowered the reserve requirement for banks to 10 percent? Demonstrate your results with a numerical example and T-accounts.

9. Why does the Fed not use the discount rate to conduct monetary policy? How does the Fed use the discount rate?

10. Explain how the Fed changes the money supply with an open-market purchase of Treasury securities.

INTERNET EXERCISE

The Federal Reserve Board Web site contains valuable information and useful links to other Web sites. All the following questions can be answered by going to the Federal Reserve Board's Web site (http://www.federalreserve.gov) or to one of the sites linked to it.

1. First, go to the Federal Reserve Board's Web site, click on the monetary policy link and then the Federal Open Market Committee link. Identify when the most recent FOMC meeting occurred. Read the *Statement* issued after the meeting. What did the FOMC decide concerning the target fed funds rate? Briefly, what was the justification for that decision?

2. Next, while you are still on the monetary policy page, click on the beige book link. Then click on the *Report* link for the most recent FOMC meeting. Read the national summary page and the page for your Fed district. Discuss how the economy in your Fed district is performing. Is it faring better or worse than other districts? What sector of the economy in your district is driving your conclusions?

3. Finally, comment on whether you think the most recent FOMC decision will benefit your Fed district more or less than other Fed districts.

3

The Fed and Interest Rates

CHAPTER PREVIEW

Following a Federal Open Market Committee (FOMC) meeting, it is very common for newscasters to report something like "the Federal Reserve lowered the fed funds interest rate today in an effort to stimulate the lagging economy." Though it's a great sound bite, in truth, there are a number of things wrong with this statement.

First, the Fed does not "set" the fed funds rate. The fed funds rate is a market-determined rate negotiated between borrowers and lenders in the fed funds market. The fed funds rate is the rate that banks charge to lend overnight funds to one another. The reason why the newscaster may have made the statement is that the Fed, through open-market operations, is able to expand or contract the total reserves in the banking system, which in the short term, has an impact on the fed funds rate and other interest rates in the economy. However, on any given day there are many factors that affect interest rates. For the Fed to "lower" interest rates, it may have to persist in injecting additional reserves into the banking system.

Second, the only interest rate the Fed can "set" is the discount rate, which is the interest rate that the Fed charges banks that want to borrow from the Fed. The discount rate is often lowered (or raised) to "signal" the Fed's intent for monetary policy.

Finally, what the newscaster may have been reporting are comments contained in public releases by the Fed following an FOMC meeting. Given what the newscaster said, the statement may have contained language like, "The Federal Open Market Committee decided to lower its target for the Fed funds rate." This means that the fed will be increasing the amount of reserves in the banking system with the goal of increasing the money supply, which should put downward pressure on interest rates, and ultimately stimulating business and consumer spending, and increasing real gross domestic product (GDP). Overall, the newscaster's statement is incomplete and misleading. After you finish this chapter, you will be able to dissect the above statement or similar statements with the precision of a financial surgeon. ∎

U.S. Chairman of the Federal Reserve, Alan Greenspan, testifies before the Senate Banking, Housing and Urban Affairs Committee on Capitol Hill, February 13, 2001. Greenspan attended the hearing to present the Federal Reserve's monetary policy report.

In Chapter 2, we explained what the Federal Reserve is and how it controls the total reserves in the banking system by initiating changes to its balance sheet. The purpose of this chapter is to explain how the Fed conducts monetary policy, which affects the money supply, the level of interest rates, the rate of inflation, and the level of economic activity. Finally, to better understand why the Fed makes some of its monetary policy decisions, we discuss a number of policy goals, which the Fed, as the nation's central bank, is responsible for achieving. ■

LEARNING OBJECTIVES

The objectives of this chapter are to:

1 Explain how the Fed measures and manages the money supply.

2 Explain how the Fed influences the level of interest rates in the economy.

3 Describe the transmission process for monetary policy.

4 Discuss the goals of the Fed in conducting monetary policy.

5 Explain how the Fed's policies affect economic activity.

FEDERAL RESERVE CONTROL OF THE MONEY SUPPLY

As we discussed in Chapter 2, one of the most important powers of the Fed is its ability to control the monetary base. By controlling the monetary base, the Fed is able to control the money supply. The components of the monetary base—vault cash and reserve balances—are the only assets that financial institutions can use to satisfy reserve requirements. By controlling the monetary base, the Federal Reserve can control the total amount of assets that financial institutions can use to meet their reserve requirements. The Federal Reserve uses its power over these reserves to control the amount of money outstanding in the country.

MEASURES OF THE MONEY SUPPLY

Up to this point, we have used the term "money supply" conceptually without providing a specific definition or measure. The reason for this is that there are many different definitions of money, and each measure has a role in monetary policy. Some of the definitions of money are based on theoretical arguments over the definition of money—is money primarily transactional or is money primarily a safe haven to store purchasing power? Putting theory aside, inside the Fed things are more practical; that is, what the Fed really wants to know is that when it increases or decreases the money supply, what definition of money has the greatest impact on interest rates, unemployment, and inflation.

The most widely used definitions of money are summarized in Exhibit 3.1. **M1** is the definition that focuses on money as a "medium of exchange." M1 con-

---

EXHIBIT 3.1
Money Supply Measures

M1 = currency + checking deposits

M2 = M1 + savings deposits, money market deposit accounts, overnight repurchase agreements, Eurodollars, noninstitutional money market mutual funds, and small time deposits

M3 = M2 + institutional money market mutual funds, large time deposits, and repurchase agreements and Eurodollars lasting more than 1 day

MZM = M2 – small denomination time deposits + institutional money market mutual funds

---

sists of financial assets that people hold to buy things with—transaction balances. Thus, the definition of M1 includes financial assets such as currency and checking accounts at depository institutions.

M2 and **M3** are the definitions of money that emphasize the role that money plays as a "store of value." This means that if you hold these balances, your purchasing power will be protected to some extent if there is inflation. Recall that the value of money is its purchasing power—what you can buy with it. When there is inflation, you can buy less with a given amount of money; hence, there is a loss of purchasing power. Thus, M2 includes everything in M1 plus savings accounts, money market accounts, small time deposits, and some overnight money loans. M3 goes even further toward the store of value notion and adds to M2, large time deposits, large money market fund balances, and longer-term money market loans.

Another group of definitions of money are known as **MZM** and **divisia money**. Since people can temporarily store purchasing power in many types of accounts and financial assets before they spend it, many definitions of money are possible. One definition that appeals to many is MZM (or "zero maturity money"). MZM includes all financial assets that can be converted into cash immediately if the owner wishes to spend it. As Exhibit 3.1 shows, MZM includes most of M2 and some of M3. Other economists use a concept called divisia money, which weights various types of financial assets according to their degree of "moneyness" and sums them up to try to determine how much money people think they have when it comes time to spend it

MONETARY BASE AND MONEY SUPPLY CHANGES

When the Fed changes either the monetary base or reserve requirements, the money supply will usually change in a predictable manner. The reason is that banks are economically motivated to minimize their holdings of **excess reserves**, which pay no interest. They do this by making additional loans or buying investment securities. Let's work through some examples to see how this mechanism works for the banking system as individual banks pursue their own economic self-interest.

Our example begins in the top frame of Exhibit 3.2, which shows our initial condition for the banking system. Assume that the reserve requirement is 10 per-

EXHIBIT 3.2
Fed's Impact on the Money Supply with an Open-Market Purchase of Treasury Securities ($billions)

Initial Condition

Assets		Liabilities	
Reserves	$60	Transaction Deposits	$600
Loans and Investments	540		
	$600	$600	

Fed Injects $30 Billion of Reserves into Banking System

Assets		Liabilities	
Reserves	$90	Transaction Deposits	$600
Loans and Investments	510		
	$600	$600	

Banking System Loaned/Invested Up

Assets		Liabilities	
Reserves	$90	Transaction Deposits	$900
Loans and Investments	810		
	$900	$900	

cent and that total reserves (**actual reserves**) in the banking system are $60 billion. Banks hold $540 billion in loans and investments, and demand deposits are $600 billion. Recalling our discussion in Chapter 2 (Equations 2.1 and 2.2), we see that the amount of **required reserves** is $60 billion ($RR = k \times DD = 0.10 \times \$600$ billion = $60 billion) and, hence, excess reserves equal zero ($ER = TR - RR = \$60$ billion – $60 billion = 0). Thus, the banking system is fully "loaned" up—it cannot make any additional loans or investments because there are no excess reserves available. Banks are motivated to keep their excess reserves near zero because the Fed does not pay interest on reserves held at the Fed.

Now suppose the Fed buys $30 billion in government securities in an open-market transaction and pays for them by giving banks $30 billion more in reserve deposits at the Fed (see center frame of Exhibit 3.2). Thus, the total reserves held in the banking system increase from $60 billion to $90 billion, investments are reduced by $30 billion and, initially, banks now hold $30 billion in excess reserves ($90 billion – $60 billion = $30 billion), since deposits are $600 billion. Being profit maximizers, banks try to "spend" any excess reserves they hold by making more loans and buying investments that pay an interest return. When a bank makes a loan, it gives a transaction deposit to the borrower or gives the borrower a check. When the check is cashed, either the borrower's transaction deposits increase or the transaction deposits of the person the borrower gave the check to increase. In all cases, total transaction deposits in the banking system increase when a bank uses some of its excess reserves to make a loan. Conversely, if a loan is repaid, the checking account of the person who repays the debt decreases when the bank cashes the check, and so will total transaction deposits unless the bank makes more loans.

When a bank uses excess reserves to expand investments, a similar process occurs. When a bank buys investments for its own account, it pays with a check or a wire transfer. When the check or wire transfer clears, the demand deposit of the person who sold the investment securities will increase, and so will total deposits in the banking system. Conversely, when the bank sells some of its investment securities to the public in exchange for a check, when the check clears, the public's transaction deposits will decrease along with the bank's holdings of investment securities.

Therefore, banks expand their loans and investments so they can earn extra income. At the same time, by making more loans and by acquiring investments, they expand the public's holdings of transaction deposits. This process continues until they reach the state depicted in the lower panel of Exhibit 3.2. As shown, the banking system holds $900 billion in transaction deposits. Therefore, required reserves in the banking system are $90 billion, which equals total reserves and leaves no excess reserves with which to make additional loans or purchase additional investment securities. Thus, the deposit expansion stops at $900 billion. At that point, banks back their $900 billion in deposits with $90 billion in reserves and $810 billion in loans and investments. Note that the Fed's control of the money supply, as discussed here, depends on its ability to control the level of reserves and set reserve requirements.

The fed funds interest rate is one of the most closely watched interest rates in the economy. The market for fed funds consists of the borrowing and lending of overnight reserves among large banks and financial institutions on an unsecured basis. In simple terms, the **fed funds rate** is the "interbank lending rate" and represents the primary cost of short-term loanable funds. The rate on these overnight interbank loans is highly volatile, as it is not unusual for the rate to fluctuate more than 25 basis points (0.25 percent) on either side of the average level in a day. The fed funds rate is of particular interest because (1) it measures the return on the most liquid of all financial assets (bank reserves), (2) it is closely related to monetary policy, and (3) it directly measures the available reserves in the banking system, which in turn influences commercial banks' decisions on making loans to consumers, businesses, or other borrowers.

THE FED'S CONTROL OVER INTEREST RATES

MARKET EQUILIBRIUM INTEREST RATE

To give you an initial understanding of how the fed funds rate is determined, look at Frame A of Exhibit 3.3. The demand curve for reserves is primarily influenced by the demand for excess reserves that are sensitive to interest rate changes. Thus, holding all other things constant, if the fed funds (FF) rate increases, the opportunity cost of holding excess reserves increases and the quantity of reserves demanded declines. As a result, the demand curve for bank reserves (D_{RES}) is downward sloping.

The Federal Reserve bank controls the quantity of reserves in the banking system. However, as we discussed in Chapter 2, when the Fed lowers the discount

EXHIBIT 3.3
Impact of Monetary Policy on the Fed Funds Rate

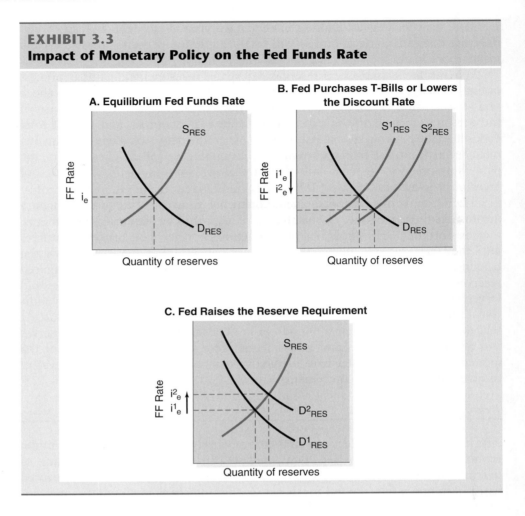

A. Equilibrium Fed Funds Rate

B. Fed Purchases T-Bills or Lowers the Discount Rate

C. Fed Raises the Reserve Requirement

rate, banks are more likely to borrow reserves from the discount window. The reason banks borrow these funds is to loan them out as commercial loans or, more likely, to lend to other banks in the fed funds market. Thus, holding all other things constant, if the fed funds rate increases, banks borrow more from the Fed, increasing the quantity of reserves in the banking system. Thus, the supply curve for reserves (S_{RES}) slopes upward, as shown in Exhibit 3.3, Frame A.

The market equilibrium rate of interest occurs when the quantity of reserves demanded by depository institutions is equal to the quantity supplied ($D_{RES} = S_{RES}$).

MONETARY POLICY AND THE FED FUNDS RATE

Now that we understand how the fed funds rate is determined, we want to see what impact the fed can have on the fed funds rate when it exercises the three tools of monetary policy: open-market operations, adjustments to the discount rate, and changes to the reserve requirement.

Open-Market Operations. Given our previous discussions, the analysis is straightforward. Let's say the Fed plans to increase the amount of reserves in the banking system through open-market operations. To do this, the Fed instructs the trading desk at the Federal Reserve Bank of New York to purchase Treasury securities, thereby increasing the amount of reserves in the banking system. Thus, the open-market purchase shifts the supply curve to the right (S^1_{RES} to S^2_{RES}), as shown in Frame B of Exhibit 3.3, and, as a result, the market rate of interest declines from i^1_e to i^2_e. The same reasoning explains why interest rates rise when the Fed sells Treasury securities; a sale of Treasury securities shifts the supply curve to the left, causing the interest rate to rise. We conclude that an open-market purchase causes the fed funds rate to decline and an open-market sale causes the fed funds rate to increase. These changes can be seen in Frame B of Exhibit 3.3.

Adjusting the Discount Rate.   If the Fed decides to cut the discount rate, profit-maximizing banks may increase their borrowing from the Fed to make loans. Since banks borrow reserves when they borrow at the discount window, the supply curve for the quantity of reserves in the banking system shifts to the right (S^1_{RES} to S^2_{RES}), as seen in Frame B of Exhibit 3.3, and, as a result, the market rate of interest declines from i^1_e to i^2_e. We conclude that, all other factors held constant, when the Fed lowers the discount rate, the fed funds rate will fall; and when the Fed raises the discount rate, the fed funds rate will rise.

Adjusting the Reserve Requirement.   Let's say the Fed decides to increase the reserve requirement. When this occurs, required reserves held by banks increase and the quantity of reserves demanded therefore must increase at any given interest rate. Thus, the demand curve for reserves must shift to the right (D^1_{RES} to D^2_{RES}), as seen in Frame C of Exhibit 3.3, causing the fed funds rate to increase from i^1_e to i^2_e. Similarly, if the reserve requirement is decreased, the amount of excess reserves in the banking system is increased, causing the fed funds rate to decline. Thus, we conclude that when the Fed raises the reserve requirement, the fed funds rate increases and, similarly, when the Fed decreases the reserve requirement, the fed funds rate declines.

THE MARKET ENVIRONMENT

Many people believe that the Fed implements monetary policy by changing the fed funds rate. However, as we discussed, the fed funds rate is determined by negotiation between the private borrowers and lenders of reserves. In the fed funds market, banks and other institutions with immediately available excess reserves lend to other institutions that need reserve balances on an overnight basis only if the price—the fed funds rate—is agreeable to both the borrower and the lender of the funds.

The Fed can influence the fed funds rate only in the very short run by using its monetary policy to expand or contract the monetary base. For instance, if the Fed buys a large amount of government securities through its open-market operations, when it pays for them many banks will find they have additional excess reserves. As they lend those reserves out to earn interest as quickly as possible, they may accept lower fed funds rates offered by borrowers, and the fed funds rate will fall on an overnight basis. Conversely, if the Fed sells a large amount of government securities, when the buyers pay for those securities many banks and other depository institutions will find that they have fewer reserves and excess reserves than they expected. To meet their reserve requirements, they may bid aggressively to borrow additional reserves in the fed funds market, and the fed funds rate will rise. Thus, the Fed always has the power to drive the overnight fed funds rate up or down.

The Fed, however, does *not* have the power to set the fed funds rate in the long run. To see that this is true, let's do a "thought experiment." Assume that the Fed tries to keep the fed funds rate at 2 percent when the rate of inflation is 8 percent. This means that people can borrow money, invest in goods, and expect the price of goods to rise so fast that they can later sell them, repay their loan, and still make a profit. The real rate of return is negative, so they can expect to make money if they borrow. Thus, the demand for loans will be very high. Banks might borrow in the fed funds market at 2 percent and lend the money out at 5 percent, while the bank's borrowers borrow at 5 percent and expect to make a sure positive return just by buying and hoarding goods (such as gold or other metals that don't deteriorate over time). As banks lend out more and more money to eager borrowers who want to borrow cheaply to buy goods, they will start to run short of excess reserves. Some may try to borrow extra reserves in the fed funds market by offering a higher rate. However, if the Fed really wants the fed funds rate to stay at 2 percent, it will buy more government securities so that depository institutions will have more reserves and the fed funds rate won't rise. As the Fed buys more government securities and banks and other depository institutions make more loans, the monetary base and the money supply will increase. This will make people fear even more inflation, so they will want to borrow more before interest rates rise. This process will continue with ever-increasing rates of growth in loans, reserves, the monetary base, and the money supply until the Fed gives up and lets the fed funds rate rise.

The Fed will also experience long-run problems if it tries to keep the fed funds rate too high. If the rate is too high, few people will want to borrow, and so the fed funds rate will fall, unless the Fed sells government securities and reduces bank reserves. As bank reserves fall, however, the monetary base and the money supply will contract, and fewer people will want to borrow in such a deflationary environment. Thus, if the Fed persists in keeping the fed funds rate too high, the process of contraction will continue—as in the Great Depression of the 1930s.

Clearly, then, the Fed cannot control the fed funds rate in the long run—and if it tries to do so it may generate either excess inflation or a depression. The best the Fed can do in the long run is to try to run its monetary policy so people will expect very little change in the price level. Then interest rates will not fluctuate widely in response to changing inflationary expectations (via the Fisher effect you will read about in Chapter 4) and the value of the dollar will be relatively stable over time.

THE IMPORTANCE OF THE FED FUNDS RATE

One may ask why the financial markets pay so much attention to changes in the fed funds rate if the Fed really can't control that rate in the long run. It is mainly because changes in the fed funds rate provide a clue to short-run changes in the Fed's monetary policy, because, on any given day, the Fed's actions can cause the fed funds rate to rise or fall. When the Fed is decreasing the growth rate of the monetary base and bank reserves, the fed funds rate will tend to rise as more banks and other depository institutions find themselves short of reserves at the end of the day and rush to borrow their required reserves. Conversely, when the Fed is trying to encourage depository institutions to lend so the economy will expand, it will make reserves readily available, so the fed funds rate will tend to fall.

The main reason the Fed tries to change the monetary base and, in the short run, interest rates is to affect the level of economic activity in the economy. *Monetarist economists* believe that when people have more money relative to their needs, they will spend more freely and, thus, will stimulate the economy directly **(Monetary theory)**. Conversely, if people have less money than they need given their income and expenditure levels, they will spend less so they can accumulate more cash. Thus for monetarists, the key variable that drives changes in economic activity in the economy is the money supply as measured by the monetary base. The fed funds rate and other short-term interest rates serve primarily as a signal as to how monetary policy is proceeding.

Keynesian economists, who follow theories first developed during the Great Depression by John Maynard Keynes **(Keynesian theory)**, tend to disregard the direct effects of changes in the money supply on purchases of goods and services. Instead, they focus on the impact that changes in the level of interest rates have upon spending in the economy. They note that when people and banks have more money, they will tend to buy more securities and make more loans, thereby driving down interest rates and increasing credit availability. Thus, in the Keynesian view, "expansive" monetary policy usually stimulates the economy by reducing interest rates and increasing credit availability so people and businesses can borrow more inexpensively and, thus, spend more freely. Conversely, Keynesian economists say that the reduction in bank reserves will cause banks to ration credit and increase interest rates; as a result, people will borrow less and, therefore, spend less.

In the Keynesian world, monetary policy always works unless the economy is in a **"liquidity trap,"** such as during the Great Depression of the 1930s, when Keynes thought people already had so much money relative to their needs that any extra money would be hoarded and would no longer drive down interest rates. However, since liquidity traps are rare and arguably only occur during major depressions, Keynesian theorists believe an "expansive" monetary policy will stimulate the economy by driving down interest rates and increasing credit availability.

MANAGING RISK: THE FED'S IMPACT ON STOCK AND BOND MARKETS

In the interest rate chapters that follow, you will learn that when there is an increase in market interest rates, the value of fixed-income securities (e.g., bonds, notes, and bills), which promise to pay predetermined fixed amounts in the future, will decline. Conversely, if market interest rates decline, the value of all fixed-income securities will rise. There is a similar, albeit weaker and less precise inverse relation between interest rates and stock prices.

Edson Gould, a famous stock market analyst, has formulated two rules that provide useful insights. One rule is "three steps and a stumble." That rule says that when the Fed takes three serious steps in succession to restrain money and credit growth, such as raising the discount rate or, possibly, raising reserve requirements, the stock market will have a great fall. The second rule is "two tumbles and a jump." That rule says that the second time that the Fed takes a serious public step to encourage money and credit growth to stimulate the economy, the stock market will leap upward.

Starting in late 1990, the Fed adopted an easy monetary policy, which became obvious to all when, in December of 1991, the Fed cut the discount rate by a full 1 percent. The stock market had bottomed in October 1990, and after the discount rate was cut by 1 percent it leapt upward, rising more than 200 points in a month. Even more dramatically, when the Fed cut both the discount rate and the fed funds rate (the second fed funds rate cut in a month) on October 15, 1998, the Dow Jones average leaped over 300 points *the same day.*

On the other side of the ledger, after the Fed took its third step to tighten monetary policy in 1965, 1968, 1973, and 1980, the Dow Jones average subsequently dropped (18.8 percent in 1980–1982 and 39.4 percent in 1973–1974).

While we are certainly not advocating Edson Gould's "rules," the important point here is that Fed policy changes do have a direct impact on bond and stock market prices. As illustrated above, at times these price changes can be large and dramatic. Thus, almost all participants in financial markets constantly monitor Fed policy actions so they won't be blindsided by Fed actions that increase their risk.

DO YOU UNDERSTAND?

1. What is likely to happen to the monetary base if (a) the Treasury Department sends out Social Security checks payable from its account at the Fed, (b) the Fed buys more government securities, (c) banks in general borrow less from the Fed's discount window and repay their past borrowings?
2. What is likely to happen to the fed funds rate under the scenarios in the previous question?
3. What is likely to happen to the fed funds rate if the Fed increases the reserve requirement? Explain.
4. Why do the financial markets pay so much attention to the fed funds rate given that the Fed can't really control that interest rate in the long run?

OBJECTIVES OF MONETARY POLICY

In Western democracies, governments are charged with the responsibility to achieve certain social, political, and economic goals. Politically and socially, these goals center around preserving individual rights, freedom of choice, equality of opportunity, equitable distribution of wealth, individual health and welfare, and the safety of individuals and society as a whole. Economically, the goals typically center on obtaining the highest overall level of material wealth for society as a whole and for each of its members. For the U.S. government, the responsibility for achieving economic goals is spelled out in the Employment Act of 1946 and the Full Employment and Balanced Growth Act of 1978 (commonly called the **Humphrey-Hawkins Act**). The centerpiece of these two bills commits the federal government to promoting high employment consistent with a stable price level. For the Fed, the two acts translate into six basic goals:

1. Full employment
2. Economic growth
3. Stable prices
4. Interest rate stability
5. Stability of financial system
6. Stability of foreign exchange markets

We will briefly look at these six goals and identify, where appropriate, some key measures.

FULL EMPLOYMENT

Full employment implies that every person of working age who wishes to work can find employment. Though most would agree that full employment is a desirable goal, in practice it is difficult to achieve. For example, a certain amount of unemployment in the economy is **frictional unemployment**, which means that a portion of those that are unemployed are in transition between jobs. Another reason for people not working is **structural unemployment**, meaning that there is a mismatch between a person's skill levels and available jobs or there are jobs in one region of the country but few in another region. Thus, a policy issue is whether workers should be required to move across the country for jobs or whether they should stay where their family and friends are located. As a result, government policy makers are willing to tolerate a certain level of unemployment—the **natural rate of unemployment**—a sort of "full employment unemployment rate." But even this rate is subject to debate and change. For example, in the 1960s, full employment was considered to be 4 percent unemployment but the comparable unemployment rate by 1980 was at least 5 percent.

Exhibit 3.4 illustrates the point that the acceptable rate of unemployment depends largely on the actual unemployment rate. The actual unemployment rate in the early 1980s was above 10 percent at times. Therefore, the politically acceptable rate of unemployment was also high. Today the acceptable rate of unemployment is around 5 percent, though unemployment did briefly dip below 4 percent in the late 1990s. During the recession that began in 2001, unemployment spiked upward to 6 percent; as the recovery picked up steam in 2004, unemployment is declining.

ECONOMIC GROWTH

Economic growth is a fancy name that economists use for a rising standard of living, as measured by output per unit of input. Economic growth means you are living materially better today than in the past or better than your parents were even though you are working the same hours per week they did. Economic growth is made possible through increased productivity of labor and capital. Typically, labor becomes more productive through education and training, and capital through the application of better technologies. Increases in economic growth may not always be desirable or benefit everyone. For example, it may not be desirable to have an increase in economic output if it results in significant degradation of the environment or our social infrastructure.

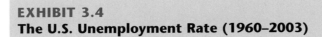

EXHIBIT 3.4
The U.S. Unemployment Rate (1960–2003)

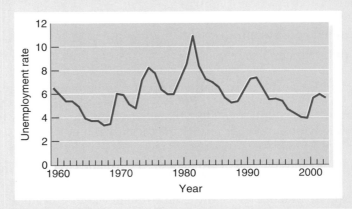

Full employment doesn't mean zero unemployment. A certain amount of unemployment is acceptable because some people will be unemployed as they transition from one job to another and other people will not have the skills required for the available jobs. In addition, it is common for regional differences in the demand for labor to cause some unemployment. The acceptable rate of unemployment tends to fluctuate but is currently around 5 percent.

Source: U.S. Department of Labor, Bureau of Labor Statistics.

In recent years there has been some concern about the rate of economic growth in the United States. In the 1950s and 1960s the real gross domestic product grew at an annual rate in excess of $3^1/_2$ percent. Since the early 1970s, real GDP has slowed down and has grown at only 2 to $2^1/_2$ percent. This means the standard of living for American families was increasing at a slower rate of growth than in the past. What has puzzled economists during this dry spell is that there did not seem to be any payoff in increased productivity from the extensive investment made by American businesses in technology. In the late 1990s and very early 2000s, however, economic growth rebounded to the $3^1/_2$ percent annual growth rate levels and Alan Greenspan, Chairman of the Federal Reserve Board, attributed the return to application of technology, especially computers and other digital technologies. Whether the return to the growth level of $3^1/_2$ percent is temporary or structural it is too early to tell. However, to the surprise of some economists, productivity remained around $3^1/_2$ percent through the recession beginning in 2001 and the sluggish recovery in 2004. Maybe Greenspan was right. You might want to check the current productivity numbers on the Fed's Web site given in the end-of-chapter Internet Exercise.

PRICE STABILITY

Price stability refers to the stability in the average price of all goods and services in the economy. Price stability does not refer to the price of individual goods. In a market economy, like in the United States, consumers have a free choice to buy or not buy whatever goods or services they want. Price movements—up or down—signal to producers what consumers want by reflecting changes in demand. Thus, for example, if the price of a product rises, the product is more profitable, and producers increase production to gain the additional profits. Price stability, then, means that for some large market basket of goods, the average price change of all the products is near zero. Within the market basket, however, the prices of individual products can rise or fall, depending on supply and demand conditions.

Inflation is defined as the continuous rise in the average price level. Because the value of money is its purchasing power, inflation affects a person's economic welfare. That is, when you have an inflationary economy, over time you have less and less purchasing power—your money buys less than it did before. Let's look at an example. Assume for instance that you have a rich grandmother who has promised to give you $40,000 to buy a new car 2 years from now when you graduate. You immediately go shopping and find that the car of your dreams is a BMW roadster, which happens to cost $40,000. However, you won't get the money until you graduate. If you graduate in 2 years and inflation has been nonexistent, the car should still cost $40,000. However, if during the 2 years all prices in the economy rise by 9 percent per year, could you still buy the car? Of course, the answer is no. In such an inflationary environment, the car would now cost $40,000 × (1.09) × (1.09) = $47,524. Therefore, with only $40,000 in hand, you would have to buy a less desirable car upon graduation.

Thus the value of money is determined by the prices of a broad range of goods and services it will buy in the economy. Changes in prices of goods and services that money can buy are measured by price indexes such as the Consumer Price Index (CPI) that are based on a market basket of goods or services purchased by consumers. There is an inverse relationship between price levels and the purchasing power of money. If prices rise, fewer goods can be purchased with the same amount of money; thus the purchasing power of money has declined. Conversely, if the prices of goods fall, one can buy more commodities with the same amount of money, so the purchasing power of money rises when prices fall.

The major problem with inflation is that it causes unintended transfers of purchasing power between parties of financial contracts if the inflation is unanticipated or if the parties are unable to adjust to the anticipated inflation. For instance, people on fixed incomes may anticipate inflation but cannot alter their income stream if prices rise. Retired people on pensions are particularly likely to experience such difficulties. On the other hand, if inflation is anticipated correctly and the appropriate adjustments are made, no unintended transfer of purchasing power occurs and inflation has no economic effect. Unfortunately, in the real world, this is rarely the case.

As can be seen in Exhibit 3.5, during the 1970s and early 1980s inflation was historically high and it was thought to be a disruptive economic influence. Specifically, prices accelerated in 1973–1974, and in 1979 the rate of inflation was 13.3 percent, the highest rate in U.S. peacetime history. Then two back-to-back recessions (1980 and 1982), caused primarily by restrictive monetary policy aimed at controlling inflation, reduced inflation to the 4 percent range by the mid-1980s. Inflation then began to creep upward in the late 1980s and was dampened by the recession in the early 1990s. The 1990s and early 2000s were notable in that they were marked by the nation's longest period of economic expansion, 10 years, and very modest rates of inflation.

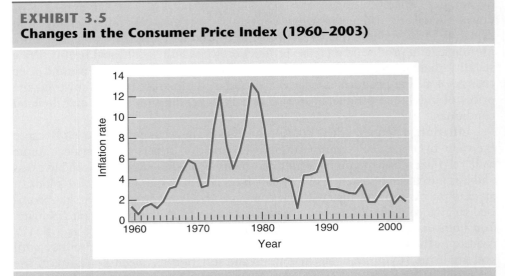

EXHIBIT 3.5
Changes in the Consumer Price Index (1960–2003)

The mid-1990s through the mid-2000s were unique because of long periods of economic growth accompanied by low inflation.

Source: U.S. Department of Labor, Bureau of Labor Statistics.

INTEREST RATE STABILITY

Interest rate stability refers to the swings or volatility of interest rates over time. Large interest rate fluctuations introduce additional uncertainty into the economy and make it harder to plan for the future. Furthermore, periods of high interest rates inhibit consumer and business spending. In particular, purchases of big-ticket items that tend to drive and support economic expansions are highly sensitive to interest rates. For business, these are capital expenditures like plant and equipment purchases, and for consumers, the purchase of a home. In a similar manner, the extremely low interest rates in the 2001–2002 recession stimulated record housing sales and renovation work and, in part, contributed to the mildness of the recession or "economic slowdown" as some economists preferred to call it. The movement of interest rates over time can be seen in Exhibit 3.6.

STABILITY OF THE FINANCIAL SYSTEM

One of the major responsibilities of the Federal Reserve is to stabilize the financial system. Disruptions in the financial system can inhibit the ability of financial markets to efficiently channel funds between surplus spending units and deficit spending units. Any reduction in the flow of funds will reduce consumer spending and business investment, which will lead to slower economic growth. Also, individuals may find it more difficult or expensive to borrow and, thus, may have to postpone certain purchases such as buying a new car.

Another major responsibility of the Fed is the stabilization of the banking system—primarily depository institutions. Widespread failure of banks and other depository institutions can have a debilitating effect on the economy. Without

EXHIBIT 3.6
Ten-Year Treasury Rates (1960–2003)

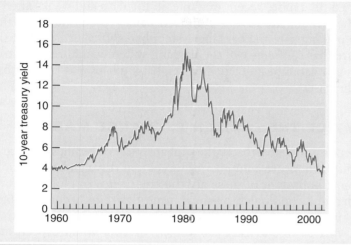

Periods of high interest rates tend to inhibit business and consumer spending. Therefore, it is not surprising that many of the recessions in the past few decades have coincided with periods of relatively high interest rates.

Source: Federal Reserve Board of Governors, H.15 Statistical Release.

going into detail, the 1929 stock market crash was followed by widespread bank failures and a devastating depression. Using the best analysis of the day, economists and politicians coalesced around the notion that somehow the Great Depression was caused by the misbehavior of Wall Street and the nation's banks. The Glass-Steagall Act of 1933 and other banking legislation of the period separated investment banking from commercial banking to remove various conflicts of interest, regulated margin requirements to reduce speculative investing, and introduced a number of anticompetitive measures in banking, such as Regulation Q, to reduce competition and, hence, bank failures. As one might expect, the number of bank failures dropped dramatically after this legislation and the country has not had a depression since.

Today, the Fed tries to strike a balance between keeping the banking system competitive without risking widespread bank failures. One important way the Fed stabilizes the banking system is in its role as the "lender of last resort." The Fed accomplishes this by providing massive amounts of liquidity (bank reserves) to depository institutions when any economic or political issue threatens the integrity or safety of the banking system. For example, during the "Black Monday" stock market crash of 1987 that will go down in history as the largest 1-day decline in stock prices, the Dow Jones Industrial index declined by more than 500 points. The meltdown had the potential of unraveling the financial sector of the economy and leading to a cataclysmic decline in economic activity—another 1929 crash. In 1987 Fed Chairman Alan Greenspan and New York Federal Reserve bank president Gerald Corrigan had grave concerns about the integrity of the banking system and Wall Street security firms. On October 20, the Fed stood ready to provide a massive amount of liquidity to the financial system, both to banks and securities firms. Because of this decisive action, a potential and real crisis was averted. In a more recent example, in the days and weeks after September 11, 2001, the Federal Reserve encouraged banks to borrow from the discount window. By making sure the banking system had sufficient liquidity, the Fed was able to ensure that confidence in the banking system would remain strong. Other than situations related to individual banks, bank panics and runs on banks are an artifact of the past.

STABILITY OF THE FOREIGN EXCHANGE MARKETS

Barring a major political setback, the globalization of business will continue well into the future. There are a number of forces that drive global economic integration. The most important of these are the emergence of global communications and other digital technologies, business firms' desire to become global suppliers, increasingly uniform business practices and standards, and the continued movement worldwide to free-market economies. As you would expect, international

---

PEOPLE & EVENTS

The Fed as Lender of Last Resort: Preventing a Financial Panic

In the days that followed September 11, 2001, the Federal Reserve played an important part in preventing a financial panic. The federal government essentially shut down after planes crashed into the World Trade Center and Pentagon, but the Federal Reserve System remained open. In fact, the Fed was very busy trying to forestall a financial meltdown.

The Fed has learned from previous crises that providing liquidity is the best way to calm financial markets and instill confidence in the banking system. By September 12, the Fed had added $38.25 billion to the banking system using repurchase agreements. The typical size of such operations is $2 billion to $6 billion. In addition, discount window borrowing far exceeded normal levels.

There are several reasons why banks demanded liquidity in the days after September 11. One reason is that many uncleared checks were stuck on grounded airplanes. Therefore, many banks borrowed at the discount window to finance the uncleared checks. A second reason is that the demand for cash by banks' customers surged. For example, the Chicago Fed reported that cash requirements were 10 to 15 percent above normal for banks in that district. Wells Fargo and other banks went so far as to impose limits on the size of cash withdrawals. Fortunately, the Fed's actions calmed fears of a panic and the financial system stabilized quickly.

These actions by the Fed are similar to its actions during other crises. For example, after the stock market crash on October 19, 1987, the Fed stepped in to provide liquidity to the financial system. Before the Fed's involvement, however, there was fear of a market meltdown as many brokerage houses and dealers were unable to find additional credit during the crisis. Without additional funding, many brokers and dealers would have had to liquidate their positions. Fortunately, the Fed stepped in to provide discount loans to banks that were willing to lend to the securities industry.

The result of both these actions by the Fed was that a financial panic was averted and markets were able to continue functioning.

trade is an increasingly important sector of the U.S. economy and, as a result, stability of exchange rates is a major concern at the Fed.

Exchange rates determine the value of the dollar relative to foreign currencies. (You will read about exchange rates in Chapter 12.) A rising value of the dollar means that U.S. dollars buy more foreign goods abroad but foreign currency buys fewer goods in the United States. The rising value of the dollar makes American firms less competitive abroad and, thus, reduces exports. At the same time, the rising dollar stimulates imports, because imports become less expensive. Clearly, widely fluctuating exchange rates introduce uncertainty into the economy and make it harder to plan and make international transactions in the future. Similarly, stabilizing exchange rates makes it easier for firms and individuals to purchase or sell goods abroad. Thus, stabilizing extreme fluctuations in the value of the dollar relative to other currencies is an important goal for the Fed.

POSSIBLE CONFLICTS AMONG GOALS

Fortunately, most of the goals of the Fed are relatively consistent with one another. The goals that have often been perceived in conflict are full employment and stable prices, at least in the short run. It is not the only conflict, but it is the one that has historically gained more attention from academic journals, policy makers, and the popular financial press.

The conflict revolves around the perception that, as unemployment decreases, inflation usually increases. The argument goes like this. At high levels of unemployment there is substantial unused industrial capacity; and one would tend to believe that the most productive workers and most efficient manufacturing facilities are being utilized. As the economy begins to expand, unemployment starts to decline as workers are called back to work, and capacity utilization increases as more goods and services are produced. As the expansion continues, less efficient workers are called back to work and wages begin to rise as labor becomes scarce. also, less efficient manufacturing facilities are brought on line, and raw materials supplies become scarce, leading to an increase in the rate of inflation that ultimately reaches the consumer.

Exhibit 3.7 shows a graph of this perceived trade-off between unemployment and inflation over time and how adjustments may take place. In the early to mid-1960s, the relationship between unemployment and inflation was fairly predictable and stable. But in the 1970s, the economy experienced periods of both high inflation and high unemployment, and since then, the relationship between unemployment and inflation has not been stable or predictable. Thus, curves such as those shown in Exhibit 3.7 are currently not believed to be useful as policy tools. Nonetheless, some public policy makers and members of the press continue to be concerned about the so-called "trade-off" between inflation and unemployment. Through the 1990s and the 2000s the U.S. economy has experienced both moderate inflation and moderate unemployment, and no trade-off has been apparent.

Turning to Exhibit 3.7, curve AB illustrates the possible trade-off between unemployment and inflation. Notice that as unemployment declines, the rate of inflation increases. Curve CD in the exhibit shows the trade-off curve that might exist if inflation is prolonged in the economy. In other words, after a prolonged period of inflation, inflation expectations become imbedded in the economy. Thus, as unemployment decreases, inflation only declines to point D, which then forms a new unemployment–inflation trade-off curve CD.

EXHIBIT 3.7
Possible Trade-Off between Unemployment and Inflation

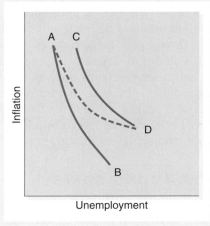

THE FED AND THE ECONOMY

Monetary policy is thought to affect the economy through three basic expenditure channels: (1) business investment, (2) consumer spending, and (3) net exports. Businesses spend for investment in plant, equipment, new buildings, and inventory accumulation. Consumer spending is typically divided into two categories: (1) consumer spending on durable goods such as automobiles, boats, appliances, and electronic equipment, and (2) consumer spending on housing, which tends to be very sensitive to interest rates. Net exports are the difference between goods and services imported into the country and those exported. Clearly, imports and exports will be sensitive to the exchange rate between the dollar and the currencies of foreign countries.

To better understand how monetary policy affects interest rates and the various sectors of the economy, we will examine the transmission process for monetary policy. By examining the transmission process, you will be able to trace changes in the money supply and see how the changes affect interest rates in financial markets and at financial institutions, the impact of money on spending in four sectors of the economy, and ultimately its impact on the GDP and inflation.

Let's assume that the economy has begun to slow down and the FOMC has met and decided that now is the appropriate time to stimulate the economy by easing monetary policy. Thus, the FOMC's decision is to increase the rate of growth of the money supply by purchasing Treasury securities through open-market operations. Following the meeting, the FOMC will issue a carefully worded statement in diplomatic economic language that has fairly precise meaning to experienced Wall Street economists and little or no meaning to people on the street or newscasters who report on the Fed. Typically the statement will have some wording conveying the state of the economy such as "in the context of the Committee's long-run objectives for price stability and sustainable economic growth, information that has become available since the last meeting suggests the economy is beginning to slow." The FOMC also will probably specify a lower target for the fed funds rate with a statement such as "the FOMC decided to reduce the fed funds target rate to $6\frac{1}{4}$ percent from $6\frac{1}{2}$ percent," and on occasion it may make a statement about the expected rate of growth of the money supply such as "contemplated reserve conditions are expected to be consistent with moderate to slightly faster growth in M2 and M3 over the coming months."

Turning to Exhibit 3.8, the process starts with the open-market purchase of Treasury securities at the trading desk at the New York Fed. The open-market

EXHIBIT 3.8
How Monetary Policy Affects Economic Variables

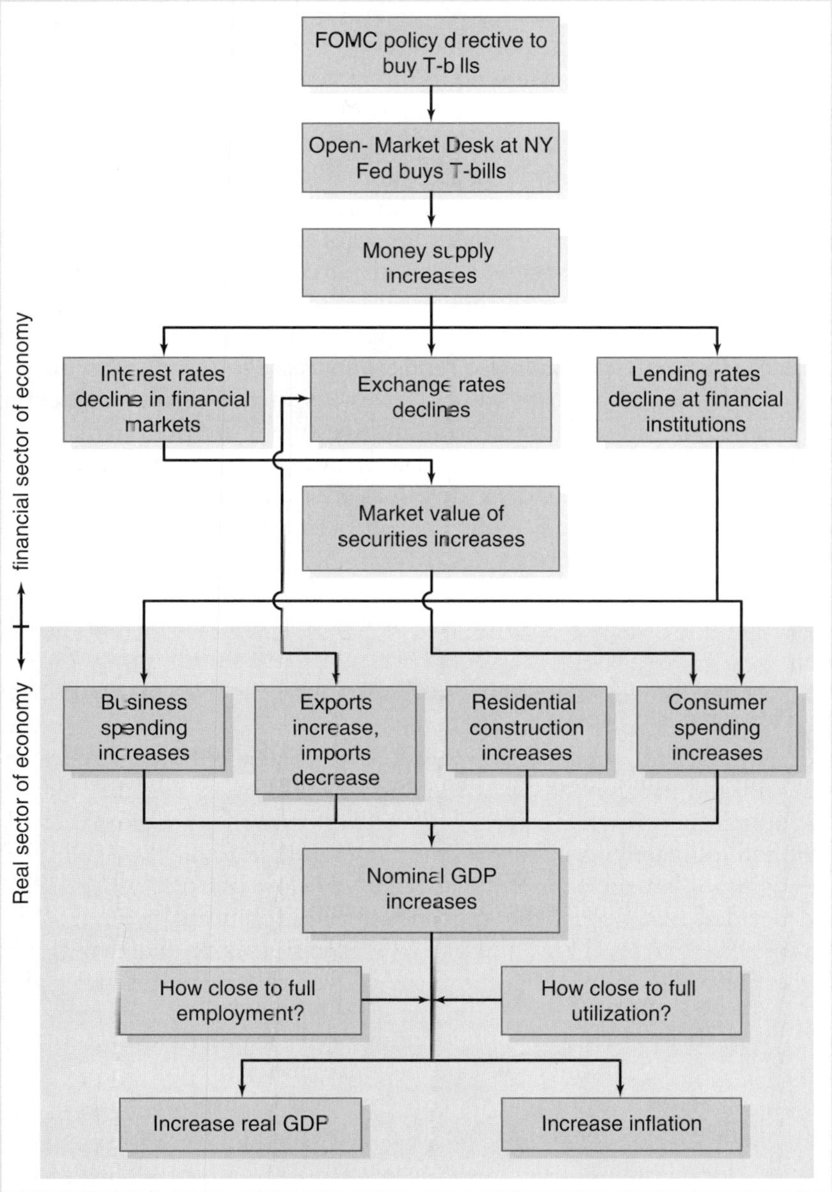

The real and financial sectors of the economy are closely related. The Fed attempts to manage the relation by controlling the monetary base and the money supply.

purchase injects additional reserves in the banking system and, hence, will lead to an increase in the money supply. As you recall, this happens because banks expand their deposits (money supply) until they have no excess reserves by making loans or purchasing securities.

An increase in the money supply also means an increase in the quantity of funds available to lend. All else the same, an increase in the supply of loanable funds causes a decline in interest rates in financial markets as well as a decline in lending rates at financial institutions. A decline in interest rates in financial markets increases the market value of fixed income securities like corporate bonds, mortgages, and mortgage-backed securities. This increase in the value of investment securities adds to the wealth of investors. At the same time, the reduced lending rate at financial institutions encourages borrowing by consumers. Consequently, consumer spending will tend to increase in response to an increase in the money supply. There are several channels through which an increase in the money supply can cause an increase in consumption expenditures. First, greater (or lesser) holdings of money can cause the public to spend more (or less) freely. Second, when credit becomes more readily available and interest rates decline, consumers may borrow more readily to buy cars and other durable goods. Third, when consumers perceive that their current purchasing power has increased (or decreased) because of changes in their wealth holdings or in the market value of their stocks or other securities, they may spend more (or less) on durable goods.

Similarly, business spending also tends to increase in response to lower interest rates and increased security values. Investors in new plants and equipment always consider the potential return on an investment and its financing costs. If costs decline or credit becomes more readily available (a particularly important consideration for small firms), these investors are more likely to undertake investment projects. When monetary policy becomes tighter, on the other hand, credit availability tightens and interest rates increase, so fewer investment projects will be undertaken. Thus, investment spending on plants and equipment is sensitive to changes in financial market conditions brought on by changes in monetary policy. Business investment in inventory is also sensitive to the cost and availability of credit. When interest rates are low, firms and retailers are more likely to acquire additional inventory.

A decline in interest rates combined with the expectations of increased inflation that typically coincide with an increase in the money supply will tend to make the U.S. dollar less desirable relative to foreign currencies. Therefore, an increase in the money supply will also tend to cause a decline in the value of the U.S. dollar against foreign currencies. As the relative value of the U.S. dollar declines, the cost of imported goods increases for U.S. consumers and the demand for imports declines. Conversely, the cost of U.S. goods declines for foreign consumers and the demand for exports increases. As exports increase relative to imports, the U.S. economy will be stimulated and domestic production, as measured by GDP, and income will rise. If the rising production level causes inflation to increase, however, U.S. goods will no longer be cheaper relative to foreign goods. If inflation in the United States is sufficiently great, the flow of exports and imports may reverse their direction unless the U.S. dollar's exchange rate continues to fall.

Housing investment is particularly sensitive to interest rate changes because of the large size and long maturity of mortgage debt obligations. A relatively small change in interest rates can substantially alter monthly payments and amounts due on mortgage loans. Hence, if interest rates decline, large numbers of people will

The Federal Reserve Bank Squashes Y2K Bug

Around the world, government officials, computer programmers, business leaders, and hundred of millions of revelers heaved a collective sigh of relief as the year 2000 arrived with few problems, technological or otherwise. What had many people concerned was the prediction by so-called experts of widespread global computer crashes with consequences ranging from massive power outages, to disruptions to the financial system, to the outright collapse of civilization.

What concerned people at the Federal Reserve was a potential year-end rush of cash withdrawals by depositors fearful that ATM machines, the credit card system, and even the check-clearing system might fail. If such a rush occurred, only people with a hoard of cash could buy basic necessities. In a worst-case scenario, as people were unable to get all cash they wanted, rumors could spread that banks lacked adequate reserves to pay depositors. The resulting "cash shortages" could result in runs on banks, bank failures, and economic disruption. The resulting currency drain could cause a contraction in the money supply, which, left unchecked, could have serious recessionary consequences.

No one was predicting a massive run on the U.S. banking system and the collapse of the economy as happened during the crash of 1929, which led to the Great Depression (1929–1933). There were some concerns, however, about the stability of some of the large Asian financial systems and their ability to withstand a large Y2K shock. Thus, the cash buildup by central banks around the world was done to boost consumer confidence in their respective financial systems.

How did the Fed handle this problem in the United States? Beginning early in 1999, the Federal Reserve had piles of extra money printed and shipped to U.S. banks here and abroad. On a normal day, about $150 billion in cash sits in the Federal Reserve banks and the vaults of U.S. banks. For Y2K, the Fed dispatched an additional $75 billion, which amounts to $255 for each man, women, and child in the United States.

When the clock struck midnight, marking the new millennium, the famous Y2K bug was remarkably benign, with no major computer-related incidents occurring. Most problems that did occur were detected quickly and corrected. In the United States, the Federal Reserve reported that no banks suffered any Y2K computer-related problems. Neither the New York Stock Exchange nor Nasdaq reported problems, and in the first five minutes of the new year AT&T handled 1.2 million calls, far above the normal volume, with no problems. Furthermore, large money centers and regional banks reported that they had not experienced any unusual demand for cash at their branches or at ATM machines. In fact, by January 7, 2000 just 10 "small" banks out of 9,000 banks in the United States reported to the Fed that they needed extra cash.

As it turns out, the Fed and other central bankers worldwide had prepared for a crisis that had become the biggest nonevent of the century. On the other hand, for the thousands of people who spent New Year's Eve in Y2K emergency centers, it was not "apocalypse now," but relief, laughter, and a great New Year's party.

---

find it easier to finance a new home mortgage. This, in turn, increases the demand for housing and the rate of housing investment. The reverse occurs when rates increase.

As business spending increases, exports increase, imports decrease, consumer spending increases, and residential construction increases, and we observe an increase in nominal GDP. Whether or not real GDP increases or inflation increases depends largely on how close the economy is to full utilization of production capacity and how close employment levels are to full employment. Recognize that GDP equals the quantity of goods and services produced times the price of goods and services produced. GDP can increase if the quantity increases or if the price increases. Real GDP growth occurs when the quantity of goods and services increases. If monetary policy is overly expansive and the economy nears full employment and full utilization, inflation may increase to the point that it dominates the nominal increase in GDP. In other words, the price level has increased faster than the quantity of goods and services. An extreme example of this effect would be if the quantity of goods and services decreased while prices were increasing rapidly. It would then be possible to observe an increase in nominal GDP from the price level increase, even though the quantity of goods and services went down. An overly restrictive monetary policy, on the other hand, can limit both the real and nominal GDP growth.

COMPLICATIONS OF MONETARY POLICY

The Fed's job of controlling the money supply is not easy. For one thing, there are a number of so-called **technical factors** that affect the monetary base. For example, while the Fed supplies the monetary base to the banking system, it cannot control cash drains. Cash drains cause a "leakage" between the change in the monetary base and the change in banks' holdings of actual reserves. In particular, cash holdings by the public "use up" the monetary base so it is not available to banks as actual reserves. Because cash drains from the banking system reduce actual reserves held by banks, the Fed must try to anticipate when people are likely to withdraw cash from banks. The Fed then tries to expand the monetary base to offset the cash drains so depository institutions' reserves will not fall and their loans, investments, and deposits will not contract as cash leaves the banking system. Conversely, the Fed must anticipate when people will put cash back in depository institutions and offset that addition to reserves, lest depository institutions expand their loans, investments, and deposits in an inflationary manner. Because seasonal fluctuations in cash flows are large, particularly around holidays, the Fed often must engage in open-market operations to offset these flows.

Similarly, the Fed must engage in open-market operations to offset the effects of float. Recall that float represents the difference between deferred availability cash items (DACI) and cash items in process of collection (CIPC). By its very nature, the level of float at the Fed changes on a daily basis.

A third technical factor is changes in Treasury deposits at the Fed. Large payments into or out of Treasury deposits at the Fed will cause large shifts in depository institutions' reserves as the checks are deposited and collected. Thus, the Treasury tries to minimize fluctuations in its deposits at the Fed. It also tries to coordinate any large fluctuations in its deposits with the Fed so that depository institutions' reserve deposits will not fluctuate violently.

A final factor that, while not a technical factor, complicates the Fed's ability to influence the level of economic activity is the **velocity** of money, which is the relationship between the money supply and economic activity. Velocity (V) is computed as the ratio of national income (or GDP), Y, to the money supply, M:

$$M \times V = Y \quad \text{or} \quad V = Y/M. \tag{3.1}$$

By knowing V, the Fed could predict by how much GDP would change for a given change in the money supply, M. Unfortunately for the Fed, the velocity of money changes over time and is difficult to predict. Therefore, even though the money supply and the level of economic activity tend to be correlated, the correlation may be sufficiently variable that it is difficult to use changes in the money supply to influence the economy in the short run. As you saw in Exhibit 3.8, the transmission process of monetary policy is extremely complex; therefore, it is difficult to predict exactly how a given monetary policy will impact the economy by using a simple concept like velocity.

The trading desk at the New York Fed makes permanent adjustments to the monetary base by buying or selling Treasury securities. To offset the effects of technical factors, however, the trading desk uses repurchase agreements and reverse repurchase agreements. A repurchase agreement consists of the sale of a short-term security (collateral) with the condition that, after a period of time, the original seller will buy it back at a predetermined price. The collateral used most frequently is U.S. Treasury or agency securities. However, it is possible to use any of the better known money market instruments. By using these agreements, the Fed can make very short-term, temporary adjustments to the monetary base. You will read more about repurchase agreements in Chapter 6, which covers money market instruments in detail.

DO YOU UNDERSTAND?

1. Describe the likely consequences for GDP growth when the FOMC directs the trading desk at the New York Fed to sell Treasury securities.

2. What defensive actions do you suppose the Fed takes during periods when cash holdings by the public increase? In other words, how does the Fed offset these cash drains?

3. As a college student who will be entering the workforce soon, if not already, which of the objectives of monetary policy would you like the Fed to focus on in the coming years?

CHAPTER TAKE-AWAYS

1 The Fed has different measures of the monetary base (M1, M2, M3, and MZM), which reflect the continuum between a transactional view of the money supply and the view that money is primarily a store of value. The Fed attempts to manage the monetary supply primarily through open-market operations. When the Fed wants to increase the money supply, it purchases Treasury securities on the open market through the trading desk at the New York Fed. When it desires a decrease in the money supply, the Fed sells Treasury securities on the open market.

2 To influence monetary policy, the Fed targets changes to the fed funds rate, which is the interest rate on overnight loans of reserves among banks. Through its open-market operations, the

Fed influences the amount of reserves in the banking system. When the Fed purchases Treasury securities on the open market, reserves tend to increase. A greater supply of reserves puts downward pressure on the fed funds rate. When the Fed sells Treasury securities, the opposite occurs.

3 When the Fed increases the money supply by purchasing Treasury securities on the open market, there is downward pressure on interest rates. Lower interest rates make it more attractive for businesses to spend money on long-term investments and for consumers to spend on durable goods and housing. Increases in business and consumer spending lead to increases in GDP. How close the economy is to full capacity utilization and full employment determines whether a portion of the increase in nominal GDP is due to increases in the average price level (or inflation).

4 The six objectives of the Fed in conducting monetary policy are full employment, economic growth, stable prices, interest rate stability, stability of the financial system, and stability of foreign exchange markets.

5 The financial sector of the economy and the real sector of the economy are closely related. The Fed attempts to influence both by controlling the monetary base through reserve requirements and open-market operations. The Fed's ability to control the monetary base is limited by technical factors that cause fluctuations in the level of bank reserves. The Fed uses repurchase agreements to help offset the effects of these technical factors.

KEY TERMS

M1	Actual reserves	Humphrey-Hawkins Act	Price stability
M2	Required reserves	Full employment	Inflation
M3	Fed funds rate	Frictional unemployment	Technical factors
MZM	Monetary theory	Structural unemployment	Velocity
Divisia money	Keynesian theory	Natural rate of	
Excess reserves	Liquidity trap	unemployment	

QUESTIONS AND PROBLEMS

1. What are the differences between M1, M2, M3, and MZM? Why are there different measures of money?

2. What would happen to the monetary base if the U.S. Treasury collected $4 billion in taxes, which it deposited in its account at the Fed, and the Fed bought $2.5 billion in government securities? Do you now know why the Fed and Treasury try to coordinate their operations in order to have minimal effects on the financial markets?

3. If the Fed bought $3.5 billion in government securities and the public withdrew $2.0 billion from their transaction deposits in the form of cash, by how much would the monetary base change? By how much would financial institutions' reserves change? By how much would financial institutions' required reserves change if all proceeds from bond sales and all withdrawals from transaction accounts were deposited in or taken from accounts subject to a 10 percent reserve requirement?

By how much would depository institutions' net excess reserves change?

4. If a country named Lower Slobovia decided to use U.S. dollars as a medium of exchange and therefore withdrew $10 billion in cash from its transaction deposits in the United States, what would happen to the U.S. monetary base? What would happen to depository institutions' actual reserve holdings? What would happen to U.S. financial institutions' net excess reserves if the Lower Slobovians withdrew their money from bank deposits subject to a 10 percent reserve requirement? What would probably happen to the U.S. money supply?

5. Assume a depository institution holds vault cash of $3 million, reserve deposits at the Fed of $25 million, and has borrowed $2 million from the Fed's discount window. If that institution holds $300 million in transactions deposits and is subject to a 3 percent reserve requirement on the first $50 million of those deposits and to a reserve requirement of 10 percent on all transactions deposits over $50 million, what are its required reserves? What are its excess reserves?

6. What is the essential difference between the Keynesian and the monetarist view of how money affects the economy?

7. What effects are decreases in reserve requirements likely to have on (a) bank reserves, (b) Federal Funds rates, (c) bank lending, (d) Treasury bill rates, and (e) the bank prime rate? Explain your answers.

8. Given your answers to the previous question, what, if anything, would you expect to happen to (a) housing investment, (b) plant and equipment investment, (c) intended inventory investment, (d) government expenditures, (e) consumption, (f) exports, and (g) imports? Why?

9. Explain the concepts of frictional unemployment, structural unemployment, and the natural rate of unemployment. How do these affect what is considered full employment?

10. What are some of the potential conflicts between goals of monetary policy? Explain.

11. What are technical factors? How do they affect the implementation of monetary policy?

INTERNET EXERCISE

The Federal Reserve Board Web site contains valuable information and useful links to other Web sites. All of the following questions can be answered by going to the Federal Reserve Board's Web site (http://www.federalreserve.gov) or to one of the sites linked to it. This is a long, but interesting, exercise. Get to work and you will learn a lot about the Fed!

1. As you know from this chapter, the Fed controls bank reserves, which are part of the monetary base. At the Federal Reserve Board Web site, go to its *Statistical Releases* and find release H.3. From that release, obtain the data needed to calculate the ratio of bank reserves to the monetary base for the most recent reporting period. Compute the ratio as a percentage and subtract it from 100 percent to find the portion of the monetary base that is held outside financial institutions. That is the end of your assignment, but here are some additional thought questions. *(a)* Can you see now why it is hard for the Fed to control the money supply precisely? *(b)* Where do you think the rest of the monetary base is, and under what conditions might it return to the banking system?

2. Find the most recent press release of the Federal Open Market Committee (FOMC) from the Web site (see Chapter 2's Internet Exercise). What action did the FOMC take with respect to the target Fed Funds rate? What is the FOMC's current thinking about the state of the economy? Find an article from the *Wall Street Journal*, the *New York Times*, or your local newspaper that discusses the outcome of the recent FOMC meeting. How does the discussion in the article compare to the FOMC press release? Did the reporters get it right? Did the articles mention any impact of the announcement on the stock market or bond market? If so, what was the impact and how did the article explain it? Again, did the reporter get it right?

3. Find the Fed's Monetary Policy Report to the Congress. Read Section 1, "Monetary Policy and the Economic Outlook." What was the Fed trying to do with monetary policy from 2000 to 2002? What was the economic basis for the Fed policy actions? What impact did the policy actions have on the Fed Funds rate, the 2-year Treasury rate, and the 10-year Treasury rate? Did the Fed change the discount rate during this period? What was the justification?

4

The Level of Interest Rates

If you read the *Wall Street Journal* or watch CNBC on a regular basis, you will see that interest rates are consistently in the news. During the 1980s, the cry was that interest rates were too high and volatile. Twenty years later, during the 2002 recession, there were fears that interest rates had become so low that the Fed's monetary powers and its ability to stimulate the economy had become ineffective. Then, as the nation's economy was finally showing signs of a strong recovery during 2004, journalists sounded the alarm to the public that higher interest rates were coming.

Why is there so much angst over interest rates? Interest rates are important because of how they affect business and consumer spending and the growth of the economy. The interest rate is the cost of borrowing someone else's money, which must be returned to the lender at a later date, for its purchasing power. The total cost of any purchase on credit is the price of the product plus the interest cost related to financing the purchase. Thus, when interest rates go up, the total cost of a purchase is higher. As we discussed in Chapter 3, as interest rates increase rapidly or are high, purchases become too expensive, spending slows down, and economic expansion is choked off. On the other hand, lower interest rates tend to stimulate spending and to increase the rate of economic expansion.

Let's illustrate how the interest rate affects one's ability to make a purchase. Suppose you have just graduated from college and decide to buy a brand new BMW M3 convertible costing $50,000—you figure you have worked hard to get through school and you deserve it! If you put $5,000 down and finance the remaining $45,000 for 3 years at 15 percent interest, your monthly payments will be $1,560. Wow, that's steep—especially since your apartment rent is $740 and your monthly take-home pay is only $2,300. Better head to the Chevrolet dealership. If, however, you could finance the car at 5 percent interest, your monthly payments would only be $1,349. What a difference a few percent make! Your payments would be lower by $211 per month or $2,532 per year. With your take-home pay *and* a 5 percent interest rate, you could keep your apartment, drive a shiny new car, *and* have a little money left over for necessities like food.

As you can see, borrowing is a mixed blessing. If we borrow money, we can have the things we want *now*—but at a price, the interest we must pay. If we choose not to borrow, we must *wait* until we save enough money to make the desired purchase. In the case of a house or an expensive car like a BMW, this could take years. The ability to borrow and lend in the financial markets allows individuals and businesses to adjust their consumption and spending patterns over time to better meet their preferences. ∎

Even though we understand the factors that cause interest rate to change, only people that have a crystal ball can predict interest movements well enough to make consistent profits. The gutters of Wall Street are littered with failed interest rate prediction models.

The purpose of this chapter is to explain the factors that cause interest rates to rise and fall. Our treatment of interest rates begins with an examination of the forces that establish the level of interest rates in the economy. We then highlight the effect of inflation on the level of interest rates. Finally, we describe how investors and financial institutions forecast interest rate movements. As you will see in later chapters, it is critical that managers of financial institutions understand the forces that cause interest rates to change. ■

LEARNING OBJECTIVES

The objectives of this chapter are to:

1 Define the concept of an interest rate and explain the role of interest rates in the economy.

2 Define the concept of the real interest rate and explain what causes the real interest rate to rise and fall.

3 Explain how inflation affects interest rates.

4 Calculate the realized real rate of return on an investment.

5 Explain how economists and financial decision makers forecast interest rates.

WHAT ARE INTEREST RATES?

For thousands of years, people have been lending goods to other people, and on occasion they have asked for some compensation for this service. This compensation is called *rent*—the price of borrowing another person's property. Similarly, money is often loaned, or rented, for its purchasing power. The rental price of money is called the **interest rate** and is usually expressed as an annual percentage of the nominal amount of money borrowed. Thus, an interest rate is the price of borrowing money for the use of its purchasing power.

To a person borrowing money, interest is the penalty paid for consuming income before it is earned. To a lender, interest is the reward for postponing current consumption until the maturity of the loan. During the life of a loan contract, borrowers typically make periodic interest payments to the lender. Upon maturity of the loan, the borrower repays the same amount of money borrowed (the principal) to the lender.

Like other prices, interest rates serve an **allocative function** in our economy. They allocate funds between surplus spending units (SSUs) and deficit spending units (DSUs) and among financial markets. For SSUs, the higher the rate of interest, the greater the reward for postponing current consumption and the greater the amount of saving in the economy. For DSUs, the higher the yield paid on a particular security, the greater the demand for that security by SSUs but the less willing they will be to supply the security. Therefore, SSUs want to buy financial claims with the highest returns whereas DSUs want to sell financial claims at the lowest possible interest rate.

The fundamental determinant of interest rates is the interaction of the production opportunities facing society and the individual's time preference for consumption. Let's examine how producers (investors in capital projects) and savers interact to determine the market rate of interest. Businesspeople and other producers have the opportunity to invest in capital projects that are productive in the sense that they yield additional real output in the future. By more *real output* we mean more automobiles, housing high-definition flat-panel TV sets, and so on. The extra output generated constitutes the **return on investment**. The higher the return on investment, the more likely producers are to undertake a particular investment project.

THE REAL RATE OF INTEREST

Individuals have different preferences for consumption over time. All other things being equal, most people prefer to consume goods today rather than tomorrow. This is called a **positive time preference** for consumption. For example, most people prefer to go on a vacation or purchase a stereo or new car now. People consume today, however, realizing that their future consumption may be less because they have forgone the opportunity to save and earn interest on their savings.

Given people's positive time preference, the interest rate offered to savers will determine how thrifty those persons are. At low interest rates, most people will postpone very little consumption for the sake of saving. To coax people to postpone additional current consumption and to save more, higher interest rates, or rewards, must be offered. However, as the interest rate rises, fewer business projects can earn an expected return high enough to cover the added interest expense related to financing the project. As a result, at higher interest rates fewer investment projects are undertaken.

Therefore, the interest rate paid on savings basically depends on (1) the rate of return producers can expect to earn on investment capital and (2) savers' time preference for current versus future consumption. The expected return on investment projects sets an upper limit on the interest rate producers can pay to savers, whereas consumer time preference for consumption establishes how much consumption consumers are willing to forgo (save) at the different levels of interest rates offered by producers.

Exhibit 4.1 shows the determination of the market equilibrium interest rate for the economy in a supply and demand framework. Aggregate savings for the economy represent the desired amount of savings by consumers at various rates of interest. Similarly, the aggregate investment schedule represents the amount of desired investment by producers at various interest rates. The two curves show that consumers will save more if producers offer higher interest rates on savings, and producers will borrow more if consumers will accept a lower return on their savings. The market equilibrium rate of interest (r^*) is achieved when desired savings (S^*) of savers equals desired investment (I^*) by producers across all economic units. At this point, funds are allocated overtime in a manner that fits people's preference between current and future consumption.

The equilibrium rate of interest is called the **real rate of interest**. The real rate of interest is the fundamental long-run interest rate in the economy. It is called the "real" rate of interest because it is determined by the real output of the economy. The real rate of interest is estimated to be on average about 3 percent

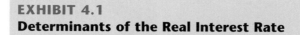

EXHIBIT 4.1
Determinants of the Real Interest Rate

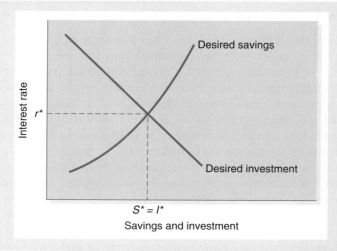

The real rate of interest is the base interest rate for the economy and usually varies between 2 and 4 percent. It is determined by the interaction of people who postpone consumption (savers) and businesspeople who invest in capital projects. The real rate of interest occurs at the intersection of the desired savings and desired investment curves.

for the U.S. economy, and it varies between 2 and 4 percent because of changes in economic conditions.

Using the supply–demand framework in Exhibit 4.1, you can see how changing economic forces cause interest rates to change. For example, a major breakthrough in technology would cause the investment schedule to shift to the right and thus increase r^*. Other demand factors that could shift the investment schedule to the right and increase r^* are an increase in productivity of existing capital, an increase in expected business product demand, reduction in taxes affecting corporations, or reduction in the expected risk on a particular class of investment projects. Likewise, economic factors can affect the supply of savings. For example, consumer attitudes toward savings can change so that they become thriftier. If this occurs, the savings schedule will shift to the right and the real rate of interest will decline. Other supply-side factors that could decrease r^* would be a reduction in the personal income tax rate and increases in personal income, both of which would tend to increase the amount of savings.

LOANABLE FUNDS THEORY OF INTEREST

Although the trade-off between productivity and thrift is the underlying force that determines interest rates, it is difficult to use this framework to explain short-run changes in the level of interest rates observed in a monetary economy (where money is the medium of exchange) such as ours. Interest rates can be viewed as being determined by the demand for and supply of direct and indirect financial claims during a particular time period. Thus, in the short run, interest rates depend on the supply of and the demand for loanable funds, which in turn depend

Irving Fisher (1867–1947): Economist and Social Reformer

Irving Fisher was one of America's best-known economists. A man of exceptional talents and diverse interests, he was an economist, a statistician, a businessman, and a social reformer. The son of a Congregational minister, Fisher entered Yale University in 1884 and studied widely in the physical and social sciences throughout his academic career. His doctoral dissertation combined his love of mathematics and economics and is considered a classic today. Upon receiving his Ph.D., Fisher taught mathematics at Yale for 4 years and then switched to economics, the field in which he spent the rest of his academic career.

As an economist, Fisher is most acclaimed for his theory of the real rate of interest (presented in this chapter) and his analysis of the quantity theory of money. Regarding interest rates, Fisher articulated that two basic forces determine the real rate of interest in a market economy: (1) subjective forces reflecting the preference of individuals for present consumption over future consumption and (2) objective forces depending on available investment opportunities and productivity of capital. Fisher also recognized the distinction between the nominal and the real rate of interest—the nominal rate of interest being composed of a real component and an inflation premium that compensates lenders for losses in purchasing power caused by inflation. Fisher's classic treatise on interest, *The Theory of Interest Rates*, was first published in the 1930s and is still reprinted today. Fisher's views on interest are the foundation for contemporary interest rate theory.

Outside the academic realm, Fisher had his share of crackpot ideas, but he also met with some successes. One of his major achievements was a card index system he invented and sold; the company he formed merged in 1926 with other companies to form Remington Rand Corporation.

Perhaps one of Fisher's most interesting endeavors came after an attack of tuberculosis in 1898. Following his recovery, he became an ardent advocate of eugenics and public health. His zeal went so far that he wrote a book advocating a temperate and healthful lifestyle. The book, *How to Live: Rules for Healthful Living Based on Modern Science*, was enormously successful, going through more than 90 editions. Though bizarre by today's standards, the book extolled the virtues of good posture, proper shoe fit, and complete chewing of food—all as a means to a long and healthy life.

on productivity and thrift. The loanable funds framework is widely used by financial analysts and economists because of its intuitive appeal and because it is easily employed as a basis for interest rate forecasting models.

DSUs issue financial claims to finance expenditures in excess of their current income. The need to sell these financial claims constitutes the demand for loanable funds. On the other side of the market, SSUs supply loanable funds to the market. SSUs purchase financial claims to earn interest on their excess funds. Exhibit 4.2 shows the major sources of the demand for and supply of loanable funds in the economy.

The scheme outlined in Exhibit 4.2 is, for the most part, disaggregated—it shows the sources of the gross supplies of and demands for loanable funds in the economy. Households, businesses, and governmental units operate on both sides of the market. For example, consumer personal savings are a major source of funds and, simultaneously, most households are demanders of funds as they

---

EXHIBIT 4.2
Sources of Supply of and Demand for Loanable Funds

Supply of Loanable Funds (SSU)

Consumer savings

Business savings (depreciation and retained earnings)

State and local government budget surpluses

Federal government budget surplus (if any)

Federal Reserve increases in the money supply (ΔM)

Demand for Loanable Funds (DSU)

Consumer credit purchases

Business investment

Federal government budget deficits

State and local government budget deficits

Notice that households, businesses, and governmental units are both suppliers and demanders of loanable funds. During most periods, households are net suppliers of funds, whereas the business sector is almost always a net demander of funds.

---

engage in a wide variety of consumer credit purchases. Similarly, business firms supply loanable funds through depreciation and retained earnings, and they demand loanable funds to invest in plant, equipment, and inventories. State and local governments can run surplus budgets (tax revenues exceed expenditures) that act as a supply of funds, whereas budget deficits (expenditures exceed tax revenues) create a demand for loanable funds as governmental units issue debt to cover the shortfall in revenues. The federal government historically has been a demander of loanable funds because it typically runs a deficit budget. In several recent years, however, the federal government has operated at a budget surplus.

The Federal Reserve is shown as a source of loanable funds. The supply of loanable funds is increased whenever the Federal Reserve increases the money supply (ΔM is positive). As we discussed in Chapters 2 and 3, money is created through central bank policy actions and changes in bank reserves and currency. The supply of loanable funds can be decreased if the Federal Reserve decides to contract the money supply (ΔM is negative). The supply of loanable funds also can be affected by the public desire to hold money balances.

The supply of loanable funds schedule is shown in Exhibit 4.3, Frame A. The aggregate schedule shown is a composite of all suppliers of loanable funds in the economy, and it is drawn sloping upward to the right. Hence, at higher interest rates, SSUs are willing to provide greater amounts of loanable funds. However, not all suppliers of loanable funds are equally sensitive to changes in interest rates.

In general, consumers will save more as interest rates rise. Higher interest rates will also stimulate business to finance investments out of internal sources (retained earnings and depreciation) rather than by issuing new debt or equity. This can be accomplished by reducing dividend payments to increase retained earnings or by switching to an accelerated depreciation method. Furthermore, at higher interest rates there will be a decrease in the demand to hold money bal-

EXHIBIT 4.3
Interest Rate Determination in a Loanable Funds Framework

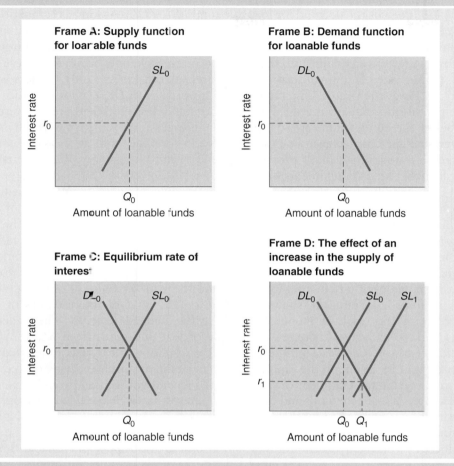

Frame A: Supply function for loanable funds

SL_0

Interest rate

r_0

Q_0

Amount of loanable funds

Frame B: Demand function for loanable funds

DL_0

Interest rate

r_0

Q_0

Amount of loanable funds

Frame C: Equilibrium rate of interest

DL_0 SL_0

Interest rate

r_0

Q_0

Amount of loanable funds

Frame D: The effect of an increase in the supply of loanable funds

DL_0 SL_0 SL_1

Interest rate

r_0

r_1

Q_0 Q_1

Amount of loanable funds

In the loanable funds framework, the equilibrium interest rate occurs at the intersection of the supply of loanable funds function and the demand for loanable funds function. At the intersection point, the supply equals the demand for loanable funds. All else equal, an increase in demand results in a higher interest rate. An increase in supply reduces the interest rate, as can be seen in Frame D.

ances because of the greater opportunity cost of holding non-interest-bearing money. Thus, as interest rates rise, the quantity of loanable funds supplied to the market increases.

The aggregate demand schedule for loanable funds is shown in Exhibit 4.3, Frame B. It is drawn as a downward-sloping function of interest rates. In general, the higher the interest rate, the smaller the quantity of loanable funds demanded by DSUs. Higher borrowing costs will reduce the level of business investments in plant and equipment, cause state and local governments to postpone capital expenditures, and reduce consumer installment purchases. The federal government's borrowing is not influenced much by higher interest rates.

The equilibrium rate of interest (r_0) is shown in Exhibit 4.3, Frame C, by the intersection of the aggregate demand for loanable funds schedule and the aggregate supply of loanable funds schedule at r_0. In equilibrium, the supply of loanable funds equals the demand for loanable funds ($SL = DL$). As long as competitive forces are allowed to operate in the financial sector, the forces of supply and demand will always bring the interest rate to this point (r_0). For example, if interest rates are above equilibrium, there will be an excess supply of funds because of the higher rate. To entice borrowers to purchase the excess funds, lenders will have to lower their rates. The rates will be lowered until $DL = SL$ at r_0, which is the equilibrium rate of interest. On the other hand, if the market rate of interest is below the equilibrium rate, there will be an excess demand for funds. Higher interest rates will decrease borrowers' demand for funds and at the same time increase the supply of funds provided by lenders until the supply of and demand for loanable funds is again equal at r_0.

The equilibrium rate (r_0) in Exhibit 4.3, Frame C, is only a temporary equilibrium point. Any force that provides a shift in positions of the supply of or demand for loanable funds will produce a change in the equilibrium rate of interest. Specifically, an increase in the level of interest rates may be accomplished by either an increase in the demand for or a decrease in the supply of loanable funds. Similarly, a decline in the level of interest rates can be caused by either an increase in the supply of or a reduction in the demand for loanable funds.

Exhibit 4.3, Frame D, shows the effect on the level of interest rates of an increase in the stock of money ($+ \Delta M$) by the Federal Reserve. The Federal Reserve's policy action increases the supply of loanable funds from SL_0 to SL_1, which results in a decrease in interest rates from r_0 to r_1. Of course, other factors can account for a shift on the supply side. An increase in consumer saving caused by more favorable tax treatment of savings by the federal government would increase the supply of loanable funds and bring down interest rates. So would an increase in business saving as a result of high business profits. A change in state or federal government policy from a deficit budget to a surplus budget position because of reduced government expenditures would also shift the supply of loanable funds schedule to the right. On the demand side, downward pressure on interest rates would result from a decline in expectations about future business activities. This would result in a shift to the left in the demand schedule because of both reduced business investments and consumer credit purchases. Likewise, an increase in taxes would reduce government deficits and the government's demand for loanable funds.

DO YOU UNDERSTAND?

1. Explain why the interest rate depends on the rate of return business firms expect to earn on real investment projects.

2. How does a consumer's time preference for consumption affect the level of savings and consumption? How does the interest rate affect the consumer's decision to spend or save?

3. How do you think an increase in personal tax rates would affect the supply of loanable funds, holding other things equal? Why? How would the equilibrium interest rate be affected?

In our discussion of interest rates so far we have not mentioned the influence of price level changes (inflation or deflation) on the level of interest rates. We assumed that price levels remained constant over the life of the loan or investment in securities. However, price level changes affect both the realized return that lenders receive on their loans and the cost that borrowers must pay for them. If borrower and lenders do not adjust the loan contract to address the impact of expected price level changes, there can be unwarranted transfers of purchasing power between borrowers and lenders. For example, if prices rise during the life of a loan contract, the purchasing power of the money will decrease and borrowers will be repaying lenders in inflated dollars—dollars with less purchasing power. If prices decrease, the purchasing power of the money will increase, and lenders will receive a windfall gain of more purchasing power at the expense of borrowers.

Protection against changes in purchasing power can be incorporated into the interest rate on a loan contract. Suppose that two individuals, an SSU and a DSU, plan to exchange money and financial claims for a period of 1 year. Both parties agree that a fair rental price for the money (i.e., the real rate of interest) is 5 percent, and both anticipate a 7 percent inflation rate for the year. In the spirit of fair play, a contract fair to both the borrower and lender would be as follows:

Items to be Paid	Calculation	Amount
1. Principal		$1,000.00
2. Rent for 1 year on money loaned	$1,000 × 5%	50.00
3. Compensation for expected loss of purchasing power on the loan amount	$1,000 × 7%	70.00
Total Compensation to Lender		$1,120.00

For the use of $1,000 for 1 year, the loan contract calls for the payment of three items at maturity: (1) $1,000, which is the repayment of the amount borrowed; (2) $50, which is the interest, or rent, for the use of the money's purchasing power for 1 year; and (3) $70, which is the compensation to the lender for the loss of purchasing because of the 7 percent inflation expected during the 1-year period. It is clear from the example that the actual "interest" charged is *not* 7 percent, but 12 percent ($120): 5 percent ($50) compensation for forgoing current consumption and 7 percent ($70) for the anticipated loss of purchasing power due to inflation.

THE FISHER EQUATION

The preceding example suggests that protection against price-level changes is achieved when the nominal rate of interest is divided into two parts: (1) the real rate of interest, which is the rate of interest that exists in the absence of price level changes and (2) the anticipated percent change in price levels over the life of the loan contract. This can be written as follows:

$$i = r + \Delta P_e \tag{4.1}$$

where
   i = the observed nominal rate of interest (the contract rate)
   r = the real rate of interest

ΔP_e = the expected annual percentage change in the average price level in the economy (expected inflation)

For our "fair" contract example:

$i = 0.05 + 0.07 = 0.12 = 12.00\%$

Equation 4.1 is commonly referred to as the **Fisher equation**. It is named after economist Irving Fisher, who is credited with first developing the concept.

There are a couple of important points we should note about the Fisher equation. First, notice that the equation uses the *anticipated* (or *expected*) percentage price level changes, not the observed or reported rate of inflation (or deflation). This way the lender is compensated for expected inflation (deflation) during the loan contract. Thus, to properly determine nominal interest rates, it is necessary to predict price-level changes over the life of the contract. Second, notice that ΔP_e is the expected change in *price levels:* price-level changes may be inflationary (rising prices) or they may be deflationary (declining prices). Most economies generally experience some rate of inflation most of the time. Deflation is not common; and, when it does occur, it is usually during a deep or prolonged recession.

Third, notice that the **nominal interest rate** is defined as the rate of interest actually observed in financial markets—the market rate of interest. For real and nominal rates to be equal, the expected rate of price-level changes (inflation or deflation) must be zero ($\Delta P_e = 0$). Finally, as with all expectations or predictions, the actual rate of inflation, which can only be determined at the end of the loan contract, may be different from the expected rate of inflation, which is estimated by the market at the beginning of the loan contract.

A RESTATEMENT OF THE FISHER EQUATION

Our "derivation" of the Fisher equation above was an intuitive approach. Technically, if we want to adjust the real rate of interest (r) for changes in anticipated price levels (ΔP_e), we must multiply the real rate by ΔP_e. Thus, the proper mathematical expression for the Fisher equation is:

$$(1 + i) = (1 + r)(1 + \Delta P_e), \tag{4.2}$$

Solving the Fisher equation for i, we obtain the following equation:

$$i = r + \Delta P_e + (r\,\Delta P_e). \tag{4.3}$$

where $r\Delta P_e$ is the adjustment to the interest rate payment for loss of purchasing power due to inflation. If either r or ΔP_e is small, $r\Delta P_e$ is very small and is approximately equal to zero. Returning to the loan example, Equation 4.3 shows that the two parties should agree to the following contract rate:

$$i = 0.05 + 0.07 + (0.05 \times 0.07) = 0.1235, \text{ or } 12.35\%.$$

Thus, for the 1-year loan for $1,000, the contract interest rate is 12.35 percent. The difference in the contract loan rate between the two variations of the Fisher equation (Equations 4.1 and 4.3) is 0.35 percent (12.35 – 12.00), less than a 3 percent error (0.35/12.35 = 2.83%). Thus, dropping $r\Delta P_e$ makes the insights from the

Can Interest Rates Be Negative?

Can interest rates be negative? The answer is yes, but as a practical matter they are rarely observed in global financial markets. A negative interest rate means that you would pay someone to take your money! For example, if the prevailing interest rate was a negative 2 percent and you decided to purchase a $1,000 certificate of deposit with a 1-year maturity from a bank, at the end of the year the bank would pay you $980. You would have effectively paid the bank $20 to keep your money. Under what circumstance would such tomfoolery occur?

The Fischer equation suggests that a negative interest rate could occur when the expected rate of deflation (a negative term) exceeds the real rate of interest. The real rate of interest is always positive because we assume that human nature is such that nearly all market participants have a positive time preference for consumption. Practically speaking, negative interest rates might occur when a country is in a deep and prolonged recession. During such a time, the real rate of interest should be low and the economy could suffer falling asset prices (deflation).

In November 1998, the interest rate on Japanese Treasury bills declined to a negative interest rate. At that time the Japanese economy was in the depths of

a 10-year recession, which ended in 2004. The Treasury rate became negative because large investors did not want to buy bank liabilities because of their concerns over the stability of Japan's fragile banking system; there were persistent rumors that some large Japanese banks were about to fail even though the government and bank regulators denied this was the case. Furthermore, investors were skeptical about the government's current economic recovery plans, since a number of previous plans had failed. On the other hand, these investors did not want to hold cash because of negative inflation (falling asset prices). Thus, the safest course of action for investors was to purchase government securities. At the November 1988 Treasury auction, investors bid the price of 6-month Japanese Treasury bills to yield a negative 0.004 percent!

Finally, we should stress that interest rates are normally positive. Negative interest rates are extremely rare. No country in the world has observed them since the Great Depression (1929–33) in the United States. At that time, the negative yield for U.S. Treasury securities was observed amid concerns over the stability of the U.S. banking system.

Fisher equation easier to understand without creating a significant computational error.

THE REALIZED REAL RATE

The Fisher equation (Equation 4.1) expresses that the nominal interest rate is affected by inflation expectations. As with all expectations, however, the actual rate of inflation more than likely will not equal what was expected. Hence, the realized rate of return on a loan contract (i.e., the actual rate of return to the lender at the conclusion of the loan) will differ from the nominal rate that was agreed on at the time the loan was made. Equation 4.1 can be modified so that the realized real rate of return can be expressed as:

$$r = i - \Delta P_a, \qquad (4.4)$$

EXHIBIT 4.4
Realized Real Rates of Return (1969–2003)

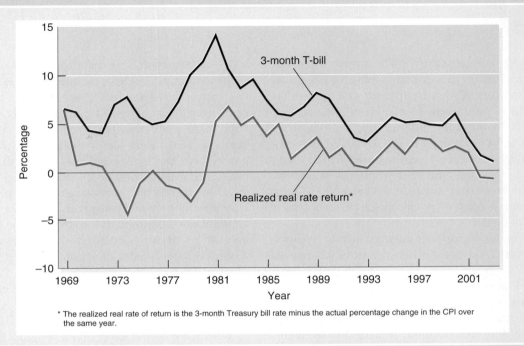

* The realized real rate of return is the 3-month Treasury bill rate minus the actual percentage change in the CPI over the same year.

The realized real rate of return can be positive or negative, depending on the extent to which the actual inflation rate exceeds the expected inflation rate. There is no evidence that lenders or borrowers and able to outpredict each other.

Source: Board of Governors, Federal Reserve System, and Federal Reserve Bank of St. Louis.

where r is the **realized real rate of return** and ΔP_a is the *actual rate of inflation* during the loan contract period. If actual inflation at the end of the loan turns out to have been higher than expected inflation at the beginning of the loan, then the lender will have a lower realized real rate of return, which means that there was an unintended transfer of purchasing power to the borrower from the lender. Conversely, if actual inflation turns out to be less than expected, then there would be an unintended transfer of purchasing power to the lender from the borrower. As can be seen from Equation 4.4, if actual inflation exceeds the nominal interest rate, i, the realized real rate of return is negative.

Exhibit 4.4 shows the nominal interest rate for 3-month Treasury bills plotted since 1969; also shown is the realized real rate of return on the 3-month bills for the same time period. As can be seen, the realized real rate was negative during most of the 1970s. Lenders underpredicted the rise in price levels and, in retrospect, charged too low a nominal rate of interest. Thus, unanticipated inflation caused unintended wealth transfers from lender to borrowers. In the 1980s and 1990s the opposite was true. The realized real rate was quite high because actual inflation was lower than was anticipated. However, there is no evidence that, as a group, borrowers or lenders are able to outpredict each other consistently.

EXHIBIT 4.5
Movements in Interest Rates and Inflation (1969–2003)

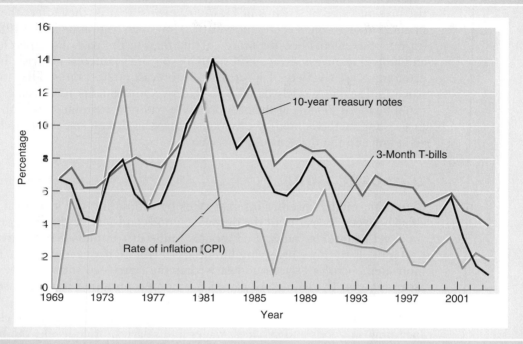

Interest rates change in response to changes in inflation, as predicted by the Fisher equation. Notice that short-term rates are more responsive to changes in inflation than long-term rates.

Source: Board of Governors, Federal Reserve System, and Federal Reserve Bank of St. Louis.

INTEREST RATE MOVEMENTS AND INFLATION

The movements in short-term and long-term interest rates since 1969 are plotted in Exhibit 4.5. Plotted along with the interest rates is the rate of inflation calculated from the Consumer Price Index (CPI). The exhibit shows that interest rates tend to change with changes in the rate of inflation, which is what we should expect, given the Fisher equation (Equation 4.1 or 4.3) Exhibit 4.5 also shows that short-term rates are more responsive to changes in inflation than long-term rates.

DO YOU UNDERSTAND?

1. If you believe that the real rate of interest is 4 percent and the expected inflation rate is 3 percent, what is the nominal interest rate?
2. If actual inflation turns out to be less than expected inflation, would you rather have been a borrower or a lender? Why?
3. During what period in the last 30 years were realized real rates of return negative? What causes negative realized real rates of return?
4. Explain why interest rates move with changes in inflation.

FORECASTING INTEREST RATES

There has always been considerable interest in forecasting interest rate movements. The reason, of course, is that changes in the level of interest rates affect the present value of streams of future payments; that is, they affect the prices of financial assets—one's economic wealth! Moreover, beginning in the 1980s, interest rate movements became more volatile than in the past, and, therefore, firms and individual investors faced substantial exposure to interest rate risk. In general, economists use a variety of approaches to forecast interest rates. They range from naive forecasting models based on subjective adjustments to extremely complicated financial models of the economy. We will now examine two of the popular forecasting methods used by economists on Wall Street: statistical models of the economy and the flow-of-funds approach.

ECONOMIC MODELS

Economic models predict interest rates by estimating the statistical relationships between measures of the output of goods and services in the economy and the level of interest rates. The models range in complexity from single-equation models to those involving hundreds of simultaneous equations. The common element of all such models is that they produce interest rate forecasts assuming that the pattern of causality among economic variables is stable into the future.

Some of the larger economic models simultaneously forecast changes in spending on goods and services, wages and salaries, price levels, the balance of international trade, credit demand, supply of securities, capital goods, the money supply, the fiscal policy of the federal government, and interest rates. Once the relationships among these variables are modeled, expected *changes* in key economic variables are entered into the model; then changes in interest rates and output in various sectors of the economy are forecasted. For example, in the agricultural sector of the economy, changes in the prices of farm produce affect the balance of payments, farm machinery sales, the sales of capital goods used to produce farm machinery, personal income of farmers and other workers whose livelihood is tied to agriculture, and retail food prices. Increases in these factors ultimately lead to higher national income and rising price levels (inflation), which cause higher interest rates. Many of these models are difficult to use and employ hundreds of different financial and economic variables.

A more modest model is one developed by the Federal Reserve Bank of St. Louis. This model consists of only eight basic equations and generates quarterly forecasts for a number of key economic variables, such as the change in nominal and real GDP, the change in the price level (inflation), the unemployment rate, and the market rate of interest. The key input variables into the model are the change in the nation's money supply, the change in federal government expenditures, the potential full-employment output of goods and services in the economy, and past changes in price levels. At the very heart of the Federal Reserve Bank of St. Louis model is the effect of changes in the money supply on national income (GDP), unemployment, and the rate of inflation. In case you have not guessed by now, the Fed of St. Louis model is a monetarist model of the economy. Exhibit 4.6 shows the linkage scheme for the model, with the key input variables shown on the left side of the exhibit.

EXHIBIT 4.6
The Federal Reserve Bank of St. Louis Interest Rate Forecasting Model

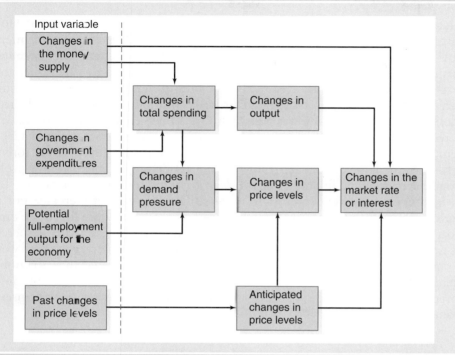

In the St. Louis Fed model, as in most sophisticated interest rate forecasting models, changes in the money supply, government spending, economic activity, and inflation determine the interest rate.

FLOW-OF-FUNDS ACCOUNT FORECASTING

One of the most widely used interest rate forecasting techniques makes use of the flow-of-funds framework embedded within the loanable funds theory of interest rates. The flow-of-funds data show the movement of savings—the sources and uses of funds—through the economy in a structured and comprehensive manner. The flow-of-funds accounts are companion data to the national income accounts, which provide information about the flow of goods and services in the real economy. Since 1955 the Board of Governors of the Federal Reserve System have published quarterly and annual data on the flow-of-funds accounts.

In forecasting interest rates, analysts look for pressure points at which the demand for funds in a particular market exceeds the supply of funds, which should cause interest rates in that market to rise and ultimately spill over into other financial markets that are closely linked. Conversely, a low demand for funds relative to supply should drive interest rates down in a sector. The projections of changes in supply and demand factors are based in part on projections of changes in monetary policy, changes in fiscal policy, expected inflation, and other relevant economic variables.

HOW GOOD ARE THE FORECASTERS?

Clearly, a great deal of analysis, judgment, and luck are necessary for a good forecast. A number of studies over the years have assessed the accuracy of interest rate forecasts. Most of these studies conclude that interest rate forecasters perform poorly. A study by Stephen McNees reports that forecasts by professional forecasters of the 3-month Treasury rate 6 months into the future were within 2 percentage points of the actual rate 67 percent of the time.[1] Thus, in January, if the 3-month Treasury rate was forecast to be 10 percent in July, there was a 67 percent chance that the actual rate would be somewhere between 8 and 12 percent. Other studies show that as the forecast period is lengthened, the forecast errors will be larger.[2] Another study by Michael Belongia looked at how professional forecasters did in predicting the *direction* of interest rate movements.[3] That is, if interest rates were forecast to increase, did they in fact increase? For the period 1982 to 1986, nine professional forecasters correctly predicted the direction of change of the 3-month Treasury rate 6 months into the future 42 percent of the time. If interest rate movements were random, a 50 percent record would be expected. Sadly, only one of the nine forecasters predicted the direction of change more than 50 percent of the time, predicting correctly on six of the ten forecasting opportunities. The worst prediction record was two correct predictions in ten chances.

IN PRACTICE

The 1980s Savings and Loan Crisis

One of the important take-aways in this chapter is that the nominal rate of interest equals the real rate of interest plus the expected rate of inflation over the life of the loan contract—see the Fisher equation. The size of inflation premiums depends on economic conditions within the economy and how the Federal Reserve manages the money supply. For example, if the Fed is successful in controlling inflation, inflation premiums can be relatively small,

such as 1 or 2 percent; or, if the Fed overstimulates the economy (too much money), inflation premiums can be very large—10 to 15 percent or even larger. Historically, changes in inflationary expectations (inflation premiums) are the primary cause of large changes in the nominal level of interest rates over time.

The collapse of the savings and loan (S&L) industry during the 1980s was caused in part by a failure of

[1] Stephen K. McNees, "Forecasting Accuracy of Alternative Techniques: A Comparison of U.S. Macroeconomic Forecasts," *Journal of Business Statistics*, January 1986, pp. 5–15.

[2] Victor Zarnowitz, "Rational Expectations and Macroeconomic Forecasts," NBER Working Paper No. 1070, January 1983.

[3] Michael T. Belongia, "Predicting Interest Rates: A Comparison of Professional and Market-Based Forecasts," *Economic Review*, Federal Reserve Bank of St. Louis, March 1987, pp. 9–15.

industry leaders to fully appreciate the relationship between inflation and interest rates and the risk caused by changes in the core rate of inflation. The root of the S&L problem was the relatively high inflation rates of the 1970s compared to prior periods. Let's briefly review how S&Ls operate and see why a shift in the inflation premium could cause problems.

As we discussed in Chapter 1, the primary role of S&Ls is to provide mortgages for single-family dwellings. S&Ls do this by taking in short-term deposits from consumers (savings accounts) and then using these funds to make long-term mortgage loans. Prior to the 1970s, the typical mortgage from an S&L was a 30-year fixed-rate loan. One reason that S&Ls were willing to make fixed-rate loans prior to the 1970s was that inflation rates were low and stable for a considerable period of time. Accordingly, the S&Ls were confident, though unwittingly that they would be adequately compensated in a fixed-rate loan contract with a relatively low premium for expected inflation. For example, the typical consumer savings rate might be 4 percent and the mortgage rate 7 percent; thus, an S&L would have earned a gross profit spread of 3 percent. The gross profit margin provided compensation for the cost of operating the firm, risk bearing, and profit.

Then in the 1970s, lax monetary policy brought double-digit inflation rates. The high rates of inflation caused the market to readjust the inflation premium upward and the prevailing market interest rates to increase dramatically. For example, the three-month Treasury bill yield was 3.91 percent in June 1972, but had increased to 8.92 percent by September 1973, about a 5 percent increase. Thus the cost of savings deposits for a S&L rose from 4 to 9 percent (4 + 5); and a corresponding increase in the mortgage rate put the cost of borrowing for a home at 12 per-

cent (7 + 5). The dramatic increase in inflation premiums and the corresponding increase in interest rates caused severe problems for S&Ls because they had to pay high interest rates for their deposits while earning a low fixed rate on their existing mortgage portfolios.

Continuing our example, for S&Ls the cost of savings deposits quickly rose from 4 to 9 percent. The reason is that savings deposits are a short-term source of funds and the S&L must pay the prevailing market rate of interest to retain these deposits. If they don't, consumers will simply withdraw their funds and deposit them in another S&L that pays a higher interest rate. On the other hand, as the cost of deposits skyrocketed for S&Ls, the average earnings on their loan portfolio remained fairly constant – rising from 7 to 7.1 percent. Mathematically, with a base of a large number of 7 percent loans, the average returns increased slowly as new higher interest rate loans were added to the portfolio. The result of this story is easy to predict: you cannot stay in business vary long paying more for your liabilities than you earn on assets. The situation is a recipe for a disaster. In fact, it led to the eventual collapse of the S&L industry and a subsequent bailout by the federal government.

So, what can we learn from the S&L crisis? The main lesson is that you don't want to bet the farm or the economic health of a financial institution on your ability to predict inflation rates. However, given that inflation is one of the main components in nominal (contract) interest rates, how can financial institutions avoid the need to predict inflation rates? One answer is to make variable-rate loans. This allows the loan rate to adjust to changes in inflation. We will discuss variable rate mortgage loan and their impact on business risk in Chapter 9 which covers the mortgage markets.

CHAPTER TAKE-AWAYS

1 The interest rate is the price of "renting" an amount of money over a given period of time. Interest rates are similar to other prices in the economy in that they allocate funds between SSUs and DSUs and between financial markets.

2 The real rate of interest is the fundamental lon-grun interest rate in the economy. It is the market equilibrium interest rate at which desired savings by savers equals desired investment by producers. It is the rate of interest that prevails under the assumption that there is no inflation in the economy.

3 To protect borrowers and lenders from unwarranted transfers in purchasing power, the nominal (or stated) interest rate on a loan equals the real rate of interest plus compensation for changes in purchasing power of money caused by price level changes. This relationship is shown in the Fisher equation, which states that

the nominal interest rate equals the real rate of interest plus the expected inflation rate. The return from a loan stated in terms of purchasing power of money is the realized real rate of return, which equals the nominal interest rate minus the actual rate of inflation. The realized real rate of return can be positive, zero, or negative, depending on how different actual inflation is from expected inflation.

4 Investors and financial institutions have a keen interest in forecasting the movements of interest rates because of the potential impact on their wealth. Interest rate forecasting models use expected economic activity and inflation expectations to predict interest rates. While models used to forecast interest rates are technically sophisticated and complex, the track record of forecasters in predicting the magnitude or direction of interest rate changes is weak.

KEY TERMS

Interest rate
Allocative function

Return on investment
Positive time preference

Real rate of interest
Fisher equation

Nominal interest rate

QUESTIONS AND PROBLEMS

1. What factors determine the real rate of interest?

2. If the money supply is increased, what happens to the level of interest rates?

3. What is the Fisher effect? How does it affect the nominal rate of interest?

4. The 1-year real rate of interest is currently estimated to be 4 percent. The current annual rate of inflation is 6 percent, and market forecasts predict the annual rate of inflation to be 8 percent. What is the current 1-year nominal rate of interest?

5. The following annual inflation rates have been forecast for the next 5 years:

year 1	3%
year 2	4%
year 3	5%
year 4	5%
year 5	4%

Use the average annual inflation rate and a 3 percent real rate to calculate the appropriate contract rate for a 1-year and a 5-year loan. How would your contract rates change if the year-1 inflation forecast increased to 5 percent? Discuss the difference in the impact on the contract rates from the change in inflation.

6. Under what conditions is the loss of purchasing power on interest in the Fisher effect an important consideration?

7. What is the track record of professional interest rate forecasters? What do you think explains their performance?

8. Explain how forecasters use the flow-of-funds approach to determine future interest rate movements.

9. An investor purchased a 1-year Treasury security with a promised yield of 10 percent. The investor expected the annual rate of inflation to be 6 percent; however, the actual rate turned out to be 10 percent. What were the expected and the realized real rates of return for the investor?

10. If the realized real rate of return turns out to be positive, would you rather have been a borrower or a lender? Explain in terms of the purchasing power of the money used to repay a loan.

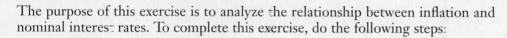

INTERNET EXERCISE

The purpose of this exercise is to analyze the relationship between inflation and nominal interest rates. To complete this exercise, do the following steps:

1. Access the Web site of the Federal Reserve Bank of St. Louis at http://www.stls.frb.org/.
2. From the bottom of the home page, select FRED.
3. Then select Consumer Price Indexes.
4. Then select the nonseasonally adjusted Consumer Price Index (CPI) for All Urban Consumers and copy the most recent 3 years of data to a spreadsheet.
5. Calculate the monthly percentage change in the CPI.
6. Now, from FRED access Interest Rates.
7. Select 1-Year Treasury Constant Maturity Rate and copy the most recent 3 years of data to your spreadsheet.
8. Select 20-Year Treasury Constant Maturity Rate and copy the most recent 3 years of data to your spreadsheet.
9. Graph the Treasury rates and the monthly changes in CPI.
10. Use the graph to assess the impact of changes in inflation on short-term and long-term interest rates.

5

Bond Prices and Interest Rate Risk

CHAPTER PREVIEW

Merrill Lynch is one of the largest and best-known financial services firms in the world, providing retail brokerage and investment banking services. During 1987, when Merrill was driving to become a top-tier investment bank, one of its bond traders, trading in long-term bonds, sustained losses of $250 million during a 1-week period! The loss today in current

dollars would be more than $420 million! As you might guess, Merrill fired the bond trader, several of his colleagues, and his supervisor.

The burning question is how a single bond trader could lose so much money in such a short period. Aren't bonds supposed to be safer than stock?

The answer is that during the 1980s, interest rates were very volatile—they took large and unpre-

dictable swings. Our bond trader had a strong conviction that he could read the economic tea leaves of interest rate movements and believed they were going to fall. Instead, interest rates went up.

As we will explain in this chapter, bond prices move *inversely* to interest rates. When interest rates go up, bond prices go down and vice versa, a phenomenon known as *price risk*. The bad news for our trader at Merrill Lynch was that interest rates shot up in April 1987, causing the bonds he purchased to drop in value.

This chapter will explain how bonds are priced and how their prices respond to interest rate changes. ∎

This building is the headquarters of the Federal Reserve System. Not much of a building by Washington D.C. standards, but the decisions made here affect interest rates, stock prices, bond prices, and the risk in financial markets.

The purpose of this chapter is to explain how interest rate movements affect the prices of assets and liabilities of investors and financial institutions. We focus on bonds because their behavior in the face of interest rate changes is similar to that of other financial instruments. Once you understand the mechanics of bond prices and how interest rates affect them, you can apply these concepts to understanding the critical management problems faced by individual investors and financial institutions.

We begin our treatment of bond pricing and interest rate risk with an examination of the concepts of future and present value. Next, we apply those concepts to develop a formula for pricing bonds and explain how to calculate various yield measures. We then discuss the characteristics of a bond that influence its price volatility and develop the concept of interest rate risk. Finally, we discuss how financial institutions measure and manage interest rate risk and how the concept of duration is used to manage this risk. ∎

 LEARNING OBJECTIVES

The objectives of this chapter are to:

1 Explain the time value of money and its application to the pricing of bonds.

2 Explain the different measures of yield that are important for analyzing a bond's performance:
   a. Yield-to-maturity
   b. Realized yield
   c. Expected yield

3 Explain how changes in interest rates cause bond prices to change.

4 Describe interest rate risk and its two components, price risk and reinvestment risk.

5 Explain how interest rate risk can be measured.

6 Describe how investors and financial institutions manage interest rate risk.

THE TIME VALUE OF MONEY

Before we can understand how bonds are priced, we need to review the concept of the time value of money. The **time value of money** is based on the belief that people have a positive time preference for consumption; that is, people prefer to consume goods today rather than consume similar goods in the future. Thus, the time value of money can be simply stated as *a dollar today is worth more than a dollar received at some future date.* This makes sense, because if you had the dollar today, you could invest it and earn interest. In contrast, the further the dollar is in the future, the less it is worth because people prefer to consume today, all else equal. Let's now examine how to place a value both on dollars today and dollars in the future.

FUTURE VALUE

Future value is the value of a given amount of money invested today (**present value**) at a given point in the future (**future value**) at a given rate of interest. The formula for calculating future value (**compounding**) is:

$$FV = PV(1 + i)^n,\tag{5.1}$$

where:

FV = future value of an investment n periods in the future
PV = present value of an amount of money (the value of money today)
i = interest rate
n = number of interest rate compounding periods

To illustrate, suppose you have $100 and put it in a savings account at a local bank, expecting to keep it there for 5 years. The bank pays 4 percent interest on savings accounts and compounds interest annually. Applying Equation 5.1, the future value is:

$$
\begin{aligned}
FV &= \$100(1 + 0.04)^5 \\
&= \$100(1.2167) \\
&= \$121.67.
\end{aligned}
$$

Thus, at the end of 5 years, the account will have $121.67, which consists of the $100 original deposit plus $21.67 of interest.

If the bank decided to pay interest quarterly, the number of compounding periods increases to 20 periods (5 years × 4 quarters) and the annual interest rate converted to a quarterly interest rate is 1.00 percent (4 percent/4 quarters). Applying Equation 5.1 to the new situation, the future value is:

$$
\begin{aligned}
FV &= \$100(1 + 0.01)^{20} \\
&= \$100(1.2202) \\
&= \$122.02.
\end{aligned}
$$

Notice that the dollar amount is slightly larger because we have increased the number of compounding periods and are now earning more interest on interest. For a given interest rate, the more frequent the compounding, the larger the future value. This explains why banks like to advertise daily compounding rather than annual or quarterly compounding.

If you have a calculator available, it is easy to calculate the interest factor, $(1 + i)^n$, with just the touch of a few buttons. Also, tables have been constructed for values of $(1 + i)^n$ for a wide range of values of i and n. Exhibit 5.1 is illustrative. The calculations are also made easily with financial calculators or spreadsheet software.

We define the term "future value *interest factor*," *IF*, as being equal to $(1 + i)^n$. Then Equation 5.1 can be rewritten as:

$$FV = PV(IF).\tag{5.1a}$$

Now it is only necessary to look up the appropriate *IF* value from Exhibit 5.1 rather than calculate it by hand. Turning to our original example, the correct

interest factor *(IF)* for the 5-year bank deposit earning 4 percent is found by looking down the "number of periods" column to 5, then across this row to the "4 percent" column to find the interest factor of 1.2167. Using this factor, the future
value of $100 after 5 years at 4 percent is:

$$FV = PV(IF)$$
$$= \$100(1.2167)$$
$$= \$121.67,$$

which is identical to our hand-calculated value using Equation 5.1.

PRESENT VALUE

Present value is the value today of a given sum of money to be received at a given
point in the future. For example, suppose that you could buy a financial claim that

---

EXHIBIT 5.1
Future Value of $1 at the End of *n* Periods: $IF = (1 + i)^n$
Future value is the amount to which a dollar amount will grow when compounded by a given interest rate.

Number of Periods	1%	2%	3%	4%	5%	6%	7%	8%	9%	10%	12%	14%	15%
1	1.0100	1.0200	1.0300	1.0400	1.0500	1.0600	1.0700	1.0800	1.0900	1.1000	1.1200	1.1400	1.1500
2	1.0201	1.0404	1.0609	1.0816	1.1025	1.1236	1.1449	1.1664	1.1881	1.2100	1.2544	1.2996	1.3225
3	1.0303	1.0612	1.0927	1.1249	1.1576	1.1910	1.2250	1.2597	1.2950	1.3310	1.4049	1.4815	1.5209
4	1.0406	1.0824	1.1255	1.1699	1.2155	1.2625	1.3108	1.3605	1.4116	1.4641	1.5735	1.6890	1.7490
5	1.0510	1.1041	1.1593	1.2167	1.2763	1.3382	1.4026	1.4693	1.5386	1.6105	1.7623	1.9254	2.0114
6	1.0615	1.1262	1.1941	1.2653	1.3401	1.4185	1.5007	1.5869	1.6771	1.7716	1.9738	2.1950	2.3131
7	1.0721	1.1487	1.2299	1.3159	1.4071	1.5036	1.6058	1.7138	1.8280	1.9487	2.2107	2.5023	2.6600
8	1.0829	1.1717	1.2668	1.3686	1.4775	1.5938	1.7182	1.8509	1.9926	2.1436	2.4760	2.8526	3.0590
9	1.0937	1.1951	1.3048	1.4233	1.5513	1.6895	1.8385	1.9990	2.1719	2.3579	2.7731	3.2519	3.5179
10	1.1046	1.2190	1.3439	1.4802	1.6289	1.7908	1.9672	2.1589	2.3674	2.5937	3.1058	3.7072	4.0456
11	1.1157	1.2434	1.3842	1.5395	1.7103	1.8983	2.1049	2.3316	2.5804	2.8531	3.4785	4.2262	4.6524
12	1.1268	1.2682	1.4258	1.6010	1.7959	2.0122	2.2522	2.5182	2.8127	3.1384	3.8960	4.8179	5.3503
13	1.1381	1.2936	1.4685	1.6651	1.8856	2.1329	2.4098	2.7196	3.0658	3.4523	4.3635	5.4924	6.1528
14	1.1495	1.3195	1.5126	1.7317	1.9799	2.2609	2.5785	2.9372	3.3417	3.7975	4.8871	6.2613	7.0757
15	1.1610	1.3459	1.5580	1.8009	2.0789	2.3966	2.7590	3.1722	3.6425	4.1772	5.4736	7.1379	8.1371
16	1.1726	1.3728	1.6047	1.8730	2.1829	2.5404	2.9522	3.4259	3.9703	4.5950	6.1304	8.1372	9.3576
17	1.1843	1.4002	1.6528	1.9479	2.2920	2.6928	3.1588	3.7000	4.3276	5.0545	6.8660	9.2765	10.761
18	1.1961	1.4282	1.7024	2.0258	2.4066	2.8543	3.3799	3.9960	4.7171	5.5599	7.6900	10.575	12.375
19	1.2081	1.4568	1.7535	2.1068	2.5270	3.0256	3.6165	4.3157	5.1417	6.1159	8.6128	12.056	14.232
20	1.2202	1.4859	1.3061	2.1911	2.6533	3.2071	3.8697	4.6610	5.6044	6.7275	9.6463	13.743	16.367

Source: Copyright © 1984 The Dryden Press. A division of CBS College Publishing.

would pay $121.67 in 5 years and there is no doubt the amount will be paid (i.e., a risk-free cash flow). Furthermore, assume that your only other investment opportunity is to put your money in the bank at a risk-free interest rate of 4 percent. (Is this starting to sound familiar?) How much would you pay for this financial claim today? You know from the previous example that $100 deposited in the bank for 5 years at 4 percent will be worth $121.67—the same amount as the 5-year financial claim. Therefore, in a strictly financial sense, you would be indifferent to a choice between $100 today or $121.67 at the end of 5 years. In our example, the $100 amount is the *present value (PV)* of $121.67 to be received 5 years in the future.

Finding the present value of some future sum of money (called **discounting**) is simply the reverse of compounding. To illustrate this point we can use Equation 5.1:

$$FV = PV(1 + i)^n.$$

The equation as it now stands allows us to solve for the future value *(FV)* of a given sum of money today (its present value). To solve for the present value *(PV)*, we solve Equation 5.1 by dividing both sides of the equation by the interest factor, $(1 + i)^n$, which results in the following equation:

$$PV = FV\left[\frac{1}{(1+i)^n}\right] \tag{5.2}$$

Going back to our original question, how much would we pay for $121.67 to be received 5 years in the future, if the interest rate on our next best alternative investment (i.e., your **opportunity cost**) were 4 percent? Using Equation 5.2, we compute the present value of $121.67 received in 5 years as:

$$PV = FV\left[\frac{1}{(1+i)^n}\right]$$
$$= \$121.67(0.8219)$$
$$= \$100.00.$$

The term in brackets in Equation 5.2 is called the *discount factor, DF,* and it is equal to the reciprocal of the interest factor (1/*IF*). Just as with the interest factor, tables have been constructed for various values of *i* and *n*, where $DF = 1/(1 + i)^n$. A table of discount factors is shown in Exhibit 5.2.

Exhibit 5.2 shows the present value of $1 paid at the end of various future years at different rates of interest. For example, at a market rate of interest of 10 percent, the present value (price) of a dollar not received until 1, 2, 3, 5, and 10 years from now is $0.9091, $0.8264, $0.7513, $0.6209, and $0.3855, respectively. Notice that the value of the amount becomes smaller the further into the future the money is to be received. Of course, that is the whole idea of the time value of money.

Using the discount factor *(DF)*, Equation 5.2 can be written in modified form as:

$$PV = FV(DF). \qquad (5.2a)$$

Again, how much would we pay for $121.67, to be received 5 years in the future, if our opportunity cost were 4 percent? Using Exhibit 5.2, we can find the discount factor by looking down the "number of periods" column to 5 and then across this row to the "4 percent" column to find the discount factor, 0.8219. We then compute the present value of $121.67 received in 5 years as:

$$
\begin{aligned}
PV &= FV(DF) \\
&= \$121.67(0.8219) \\
&= \$100.00.
\end{aligned}
$$

To no surprise, the answers agree. We now turn to how bonds are priced, a process that is merely an application of the present value formula.

EXHIBIT 5.2
Present Value of a Dollar Due at the End of n Periods: $DF = 1/(1 + i)^n$
The present value table illustrates the principle of the time value of money. A dollar today is worth more than a dollar in the future.

Number of Periods	1%	2%	3%	4%	5%	6%	7%	8%	9%	10%	12%	14%	15%
1	.9901	.9804	.9709	.9615	.9524	.9434	.9346	.9259	.9174	.9091	.8929	.8772	.8696
2	.9803	.9612	.9426	.9246	.9070	.8900	.8734	.8573	.8417	.8264	.7972	.7695	.7561
3	.9706	.9423	.9151	.8890	.8638	.8396	.8163	.7938	.7722	.7513	.7118	.6750	.6575
4	.9610	.9238	.8885	.8548	.8227	.7921	.7629	.7350	.7034	.6830	.6355	.5921	.5718
5	.9515	.9057	.8626	.8219	.7835	.7473	.7130	.6806	.6499	.6209	.5674	.5194	.4972
6	.9420	.8880	.8375	.7903	.7462	.7050	.6663	.6302	.5963	.5645	.5066	.4556	.4323
7	.9327	.8706	.8131	.7599	.7107	.6651	.6227	.5835	.5470	.5132	.4523	.3996	.3759
8	.9235	.8535	.7894	.7307	.6768	.6274	.5820	.5403	.5019	.4665	.4039	.3506	.3269
9	.9143	.8368	.7664	.7026	.6446	.5919	.5439	.5002	.4604	.4241	.3606	.3075	.2843
10	.9053	.8203	.7441	.6756	.6139	.5584	.5083	.4632	.4224	.3855	.3220	.2697	.2472
11	.8963	.8043	.7224	.6496	.5847	.5268	.4751	.4289	.3875	.3505	.2875	.2366	.2149
12	.8874	.7885	.7014	.6246	.5568	.4970	.4440	.3971	.3555	.3186	.2567	.2076	.1869
13	.8787	.7730	.6810	.6006	.5303	.4688	.4150	.3677	.3262	.2897	.2292	.1821	.1625
14	.8700	.7579	.6611	.5775	.5051	.4423	.3878	.3405	.2992	.2633	.2046	.1597	.1413
15	.8613	.7430	.6419	.5553	.4810	.4173	.3624	.3152	.2745	.2394	.1827	.1401	.1229
16	.8528	.7284	.6232	.5339	.4581	.3936	.3387	.2919	.2519	.2176	.1631	.1229	.1069
17	.8444	.7142	.6050	.5134	.4363	.3714	.3166	.2703	.2311	.1978	.1456	.1078	.0929
18	.8360	.7002	.5874	.4936	.4155	.3503	.2959	.2502	.2120	.1799	.1300	.0946	.0808
19	.8277	.6864	.5703	.4746	.3957	.3305	.2765	.2317	.1945	.1635	.1161	.0829	.0703
20	.8195	.6730	.5537	.4564	.3769	.3118	.2584	.2145	.1784	.1486	.1037	.0728	.0611

Source: Copyright © 1982 The Dryden Press. A division of CBS College Publishing.

DO YOU UNDERSTAND?

1. Why is a dollar today worth more to most people than a dollar received at a future date?
2. If you were to invest $100 in a savings account offering 6 percent interest compounded quarterly, how much money would be in the account after 3 years?
3. Your rich uncle promises to give you $10,000 when you graduate from college. What is the value of this gift if you plan to graduate in 5 years and interest rates are 10 percent?

BOND PRICING

This section focuses on how investors and financial institutions price bonds. The method employed involves the application of the present value formula. To find the present value, or price, of any financial instrument we must first identify the timing and the magnitude of all cash flows we expect to receive from that instrument. These characteristics of the cash flows are determined by the terms of a bond contract, which we now define.

TERMS OF THE BOND CONTRACT

A **bond** is a contractual obligation of a borrower to make periodic cash payments to a lender over a given number of years. A bond constitutes debt; so there is a borrower and a lender. In the parlance of Wall Street, the borrower is referred to as the **issuer** of the bond. The lender is referred to as the investor or the **bondholder**.

borrower – issuer
lender – bondholder

The bond consists of two types of contractual cash flows. First, upon maturity, the lender is paid the original sum borrowed, which is called the **principal, face value,** or **par value** of the bond. Note that these three terms are interchangeable. Second, the borrower or issuer must make periodic interest payments to the bondholders. These interest payments are called the **coupon payments** (C). The magnitude of the coupon payments is determined by the **coupon rate** (c), which is the amount of coupon payments received in a year stated as a percentage of the face value (F). For example, if a bond pays $80 of coupon interest annually and the face value is $1,000, the coupon rate is:

$$c = C/F$$
$$= \$80/\$1,000$$
$$= 8\%$$

To determine the timing of the cash flows we need to know the **term-to-maturity** (or maturity) of the bond, which is the number of years over which the bond contract extends. For example, a bond with 3 years to maturity and paying annual coupon payments will have three coupon payments. The principal amount will be repaid at maturity. Thus, a bond with a coupon rate of 8 percent and a face value of $1,000 will have $80 coupon payments at the end of each of the 3 years

College Student Wins $100 Million Lottery!

A basic problem in business is determining the value or price to pay for cash flows expected in the future. As you know from this chapter, such problems are an application of the time value of money. Conceptually, the time value of money states that *a dollar in hand today is worth more than a dollar received at some time in the future*. This makes sense, because if you had the dollar today, you could buy something with it, or you could invest it and earn interest. The concept of the time value of money is operationalized in the various present and future value equations developed in this chapter (for example, see Equation 5.1 or 5.3)

An illustration of the time value of money arises in the popular lottery game PowerBall™. In Power-Ball, a weekly number is drawn. There is a jackpot winner if a person purchased a PowerBall ticket that week with the winning number. For most weeks, there is usually no winner and the jackpot continues to grow until some lucky person buys a winning ticket. The winner gets the entire jackpot, and some jackpots exceed $100 million. If you won such an amount, headlines in the *New York Post* would read "Lucky College Student Wins $100 Million Jackpot!"

Does this mean that your winning ticket is worth $100 million? The answer is no, even though the newspaper headline reports that you have "won" $100 million! The problem is that the jackpot is paid out over a 20-year period—$5 million per year.* How much is your ticket worth? Its value or market price depends on the time value of money and the timing of the cash flows to be received. Applying the present value and assuming a 8 percent interest rate:

$$\text{Present value} = \$5/(1 + .08)^1 + \$5/(1 + .08)^2 + \$5/(1 + .08)^3 + \dots \\ \$5/(1 + .08)^{20} = \$49.09.$$

The value or market price of the winning ticket is $49 million, not the $100 million touted in the newspaper. As you can see, the actual value of the lottery payout is a long way from $100 million. On the other hand—let's be honest—$49 million is not chump change.

* (The winner has the option to be paid a lump sum; but, of course, the payment will be less than the advertised $100 million jackpot.)

---

and a principal payment of $1,000 at maturity. Note that for most bonds, it is assumed that the coupon and principal payments are received at the *end* of the year. In addition, many bonds pay coupon interest semiannually (or every 6 months) instead of once per year at the end of the year. We will discuss how to deal with this type of bond a little later in the chapter.

It is important to keep in mind that for most bonds the coupon rate, the par value, and the term to maturity are fixed over the life of the bond contract. Most bonds are first issued in $1,000 or $5,000 denominations. Coupon rates are typically set at or near the market rate of interest or yield on similar bonds available in the market. A similar bond is one that is a close substitute, nearly identical in maturity and risk.

Also, note that the coupon rate and the market rate of interest may differ. The coupon rate is fixed throughout the life of a bond. The yield on a bond varies with changes in the supply and demand for credit or with changes in the issuer's risk. We will discuss how to calculate a bond's yield later in this chapter. Since we now understand how the magnitude and timing of a bond's cash flows are determined, we can turn to a discussion of how to apply the present value formula to pricing bonds.

Difference between c and i.

THE BOND PRICE FORMULA

Because a bond is a borrower's contractual promise to make future cash payments, the pricing of a bond is an application of the present value formula. Thus, the price of a bond is the present value of the future cash flows (coupon payments and principal amount) discounted by the interest rate, which represents the time value of money. The formula for the present value, or price, of a fixed-coupon-rate bond with n periods to maturity, is:

$$PB = \frac{C_1}{(1+i)^1} + \frac{C_2}{(1+i)^2} + \cdots + \frac{C_n + F_n}{(1+i)^n}, \tag{5.3}$$

where:

market interest rate (i) and coupon rate (c):

{ i > c → discount bond
i < c → premium bond

PB = the price of the bond or present value of the stream of cash payments
C_t = the coupon payment in period t, where t = 1, 2, 3,..., n
F_n = par value or face value (principal amount) to be paid at maturity
i = market interest rate (discount rate or market yield)
n = number of periods to maturity

In words, the formula says that the present value, or market price, of a bond is the sum of the discounted values of all future cash flows (coupon payments and principal). Also, note that in applying the bond-pricing equation, there are five unknowns, and if we know any four of the variables, we can solve for the fifth.

Consider a 3-year bond with a face value of $1,000 and a coupon rate of 8 percent. The coupon payments are $80 per year. If coupon payments are made annually and the current market rate of interest on similar bonds is 10 percent, the price of the bond, using Equation 5.3, is:

$$PB = \frac{\$80}{(1.10)^1} + \frac{\$80}{(1.10)^2} + \frac{\$1,080}{(1.10)^3}$$

$$= \$72.37 + \$66.12 + \$811.42$$

$$= \$950.27.$$

Notice that to obtain the final cash payment, we have combined the final coupon payment ($80) and the face value of the bond ($1,000) to obtain $1,080. Note that the price of this bond is *below* its face value. This bond is said to sell at a discount from face value and is known as a **discount bond**. In the next section, we will discuss why bonds sell at prices other than their face values.

PAR, PREMIUM, AND DISCOUNT BONDS

One of the properties of the bond formula is that whenever a bond's coupon rate is equal to the market rate of interest on similar bonds (the bond's yield), the bond will *always* sell at par. We call such bonds **par bonds** because they sell at par value. For example, consider a 3-year bond with a face value of $1,000 and an annual coupon rate of 5 percent when the yield or market rate of interest on similar bonds is 5 percent. The price of the bond, using Equation 5.3, is:

$$PB = \frac{\$50}{(1.05)^1} + \frac{\$50}{(1.05)^2} + \frac{\$1,050}{(1.05)^3}$$
$$= \$47.62 + \$45.35 + \$907.03$$
$$= \$1,000.$$

As predicted, the bond's price equals its par value.

Now assume that the market rate of interest immediately rises to 8 percent. What will be the price of the bond? Will it be below, above, or at par? For i to equal to 8 percent, the price of the bond declines to $922.69. The bond sells below par; such bonds are called discount bonds. Whenever the market rate of interest on similar bonds is above a bond's coupon rate, a bond will sell at a discount. The reason is the fixed nature of a bond's coupon. If bonds with similar characteristics are yielding 8 percent and our bond is paying 5 percent (the coupon rate), no one will buy our bond at par since its yield is only 5 percent. To increase the bond's yield, the seller must reduce the price of the bond to $922.69. At this price, the bond's yield will be precisely 8 percent, which is competitive with similar bonds. Through the price reduction of $77.31 ($1,000 − $922.69), the seller provides the new owner with additional return in the form of a capital gain.

If the interest rate on similar bonds were to fall to 2 percent, the price of our bond would rise to $1,086.52. The bond sells above par; such bonds are called **premium bonds**. Whenever the market rate of interest is below a bond's coupon rate, a bond will sell at a premium. The premium price adjusts the bond's yield to 2 percent, which is the market yield that similar bonds are offering.

SEMIANNUAL COMPOUNDING

If coupon payments are made more than once a year, we modify Equation 5.3 as follows:

$$PB = \frac{\$C_1/m}{(1+i/m)^1} + \frac{C_2/m}{(1+i/m)^2} + \frac{C_3/m}{(1+i/m)^3} + \cdots + \frac{C_{mn}/m + F_{mn}}{(1+i/m)^{mn}}, \quad (5.4)$$

where m is the number of times coupon payments are made each year and the other terms are as previously defined. In the case of a bond with semiannual coupon payments (i.e., twice per year), $m = 2$. For example, if our 3-year, 5 percent coupon bond pays interest semiannually and the current market yield is 6 percent, the price of the bond would be:

$$PB = \frac{\$25}{(1.03)^1} + \frac{\$25}{(1.03)^2} + \cdots + \frac{\$1,025}{(1.03)^6}$$
$$= \$972.91.$$

Note that the market yield is 3 percent semiannually (6 percent yearly), the coupon payment is $25 semiannually ($50 per year), and the total number of interest payments is 6 (two per year for 3 years). Quarterly and monthly compounding periods are computed in a similar manner.

ZERO COUPON BONDS

Zero coupon bonds have no coupon payment but promise a single payment at maturity. The interest paid to the holder is the difference between the price paid for the security and the amount received upon maturity (or price received when sold). Common examples of zero coupon securities are U.S. Treasury bills and U.S. savings bonds. Generally, most money market instruments (securities with maturities of less than 1 year) are sold on a discount basis (issued at a price less than face value), meaning that the entire return on the security comes from the difference between the purchase price and the face value. In addition, some corporations have issued zero coupon bonds.

The price (or yield) of a zero coupon bond is simply a special case of Equation 5.4, in that all the coupon payments are set equal to zero. Hence the pricing equation is:

$$PB = \frac{F_{mn}}{\left(1+\dfrac{i}{m}\right)^{mn}}, \tag{5.5}$$

where:

PB = the price of the bond
F_n = the amount of cash payments at maturity (face value)
i = the interest rate (yield) for n periods
n = number of years until the payment is due
m = number of times interest is compounded each year

For example, the price of a zero coupon bond with a $1,000 face value, 10-year maturity, and assuming semiannual compounding, when the market interest rate is 12 percent is calculated as follows:

$$PB = \frac{\$1,000}{(1.06)^{20}} = \$311.80.$$

Notice that our calculation is based on semiannual compounding because most U.S. bonds pay coupon interest semiannually.

BOND YIELDS

The coupon rate on a bond reflects only the annual cash flow promised by the borrower to the lender. The actual rate of return the lender earns, however, depends on several key risks. First is the chance that the borrower fails to make coupon or principal payments in the amount or at the time promised. This is called **credit** or **default risk**.[1] Second, market interest rates may change, causing the lender to have to reinvest coupon payments at interest rates different from the

[1] We will thoroughly discuss the effect to default risk on bond returns in Chapter 6. For the remainder of this chapter we will assume that borrowers make all cash flows as promised so that we can focus our attention on interest rate risk.

interest rate at the time the bond was purchased. This is called **reinvestment risk**. Finally, interest rate changes cause the market value of a bond to rise or fall, resulting in capital gains or losses to the investor.[2] This is called **price risk**.

The purpose of this section is to explain various ways to measure bond returns or yields. In general, a yield on any investment, such as a bond, is the interest rate that equates the market price of an investment with the discounted sum of all cash flows from the investment. The ideal yield measure should capture all three potential sources of cash flow from a bond: (1) coupon payments, (2) interest income from reinvesting coupon payments, and (3) any capital gain or loss. We now discuss three yield measures: yield to maturity, realized yield, and expected yield.

YIELD-TO-MATURITY

If a bond's purchase price is known, the bond-pricing formulas (Equations 5.3 and 5.4) can be used to find the yield of a bond. A yield calculated in this manner is called the **yield-to-maturity** or **promised yield**. It is the yield promised the bondholder on the assumption that the bond will be held to maturity, all coupon and principal payments will be made as promised, and the coupon payments will be reinvested at the bond's promised yield for the remaining term-to-maturity. If the coupon payments are reinvested at a lower rate, the bondholder's actual yield will be less than the promised yield (reinvestment risk).

An example of a yield-to-maturity calculation follows. If a person purchased a 3-year, 5 percent coupon (semiannual payments) bond for $951.90, the yield to maturity is found by solving the following equation for the interest rate (*i*):

$$\$951.90 = \frac{\$25}{(1+i/2)^1} + \frac{\$25}{(1+i/2)^2} + \cdots + \frac{\$1,025}{(1+i/2)^6}.$$

Unfortunately, the yield to maturity (*i*) cannot be determined algebraically but must be found by trial and error. That is, the calculation is done by selecting different values of *i* until the present value of the cash flows on the right-hand side of the equation equals $951.90. Solving the preceding equation in this manner results in a yield of 3.4 percent semiannually, or 6.8 percent annually. The calculation of the final value of *i* (the yield) is cumbersome and difficult to make by hand because several iterations usually are required. Most financial calculators and spreadsheet programs provide the answer at the touch of a button.

REALIZED YIELD

The yield-to-maturity tells us what return we will earn on a bond if the borrower makes all cash payments as promised, if interest rates do not change over the bond's maturity, and if the investor holds the bond to maturity. Quite frequently, however, one or more of these events will not occur. For example, an investor may sell a bond before maturity at a price below the purchase price, or the bond issuer

---

[2] More technically, a capital gain (or loss) is the difference between the purchase price and the principal if the bond is held to maturity or the difference between the purchase price and the sale price if the bond is sold prior to maturity.

may default. In any event, the return actually earned on a bond will likely be different from the promised yield.

The **realized yield** is the return earned on a bond given the cash flows actually received by the investor and assuming that the coupon payments are reinvested at the promised yield. We now illustrate the calculation of realized yield with an example. Suppose you purchased a 10-year, 8 percent coupon (annual payments) bond at par. Recall that because the bond is selling at par, the yield to maturity (promised yield) equals the coupon rate. Three years later, you decide to take a vacation to Cancun and sell the bond to acquire the necessary funds. At the time you sell the bond, 7-year bonds with similar characteristics (e.g., default risk) sell at yields of 10 percent.

In this case, the realized yield will be different from the promised yield of 8 percent because market yields on similar bonds increased to 10 percent. We calculate the yield actually earned on the investment by solving for the interest rate that equates the price you originally paid for the bond with the discounted sum of the cash flows you actually received.

The first step is to calculate the current price of the bond (i.e., the market price of the bond on the date you sell it). In the example, you paid $1,000 for the bond. You held the bond for 3 years and received three annual coupon payments of $80 each. The market price of the bond on the day you sell it is equal to the present value of the remaining seven coupon payments and final principal repayment:

$$PB = \$902.63 = \frac{\$80}{(1.10)^1} + \frac{\$80}{(1.10)^2} + \cdots + \frac{\$1,080}{(1.10)^7}.$$

The next step is to set the original purchase price of $1,000 equal to the present value of the cash flows *actually received* (three coupon payments of $80 and the sale price of $902.63) and solve for the interest rate:

$$\$1,000 = \frac{\$80}{(1+i)^1} + \frac{\$80}{(1+i)^2} + \cdots + \frac{\$80 + \$902.63}{(1+i)^3}.$$

Solving the preceding equation either by trial and error or with a financial calculator results in a realized yield of 4.91 percent annually. The difference between the realized yield and the promised yield in this case is accounted for by the capital loss of $97.37 ($1,000 – $902.63) suffered when the bond was sold before maturity. In sum, realized yield is useful because it allows an individual investor or financial institution to evaluate the return on a bond *ex-post* (*after* the end of the holding period or investment horizon).

EXPECTED YIELD

Investors and financial institutions that plan to sell their bonds before maturity would like to know the potential impact of interest rate changes on the returns of their bond investments *ex-ante* (*before* the fact). They can use various forecasting techniques to estimate future interest rates based on information about the money supply, inflation rates, economic activity, and the past behavior of interest rates. Once armed with an interest rate forecast, an investor can predict the market price of a bond at the end of a relevant holding period. Given the prediction of the future price, the investor can calculate an **expected yield** that reflects the expected sale price.

Suppose when you purchased the bond in the preceding example (a 10-year, 8 percent coupon bond), you planned to sell it at the end of 2 years at the prevailing market price. When you purchased the bond, your investment adviser predicted that similar bonds with 8 years to maturity would yield 6 percent at the end of 2 years. Your interest rate forecast implies that the bond's expected price is $1,124.20:

$$PB = \$1,124.20 = \frac{\$80}{(1.06)^1} + \frac{\$80}{(1.06)^2} + \cdots + \frac{\$1,080}{(1.06)^8}.$$

Notice there are eight coupon payments and the principal payment remaining at the time of the planned sale.

To calculate the expected yield over your 2-year holding period, you solve for the interest rate that equates the original purchase price (par, or $1,000 in this example) with the discounted sum of the cash flows you expect to receive (coupon payments and the *expected* sale price):

$$\$1,000 = \frac{\$80}{(1+i)^1} + \frac{\$80 + \$1,124.20}{(1+i)^2}.$$

Solving the preceding equation, either by trial and error or with a financial calculator, results in an expected yield of 13.81. In this case, the difference between the promised yield and the expected yield is accounted for by the expected capital gain of $124.20 received from selling the bond before maturity.

DO YOU UNDERSTAND?

1. When a bond's coupon rate is less than the prevailing market rate of interest on similar bonds, will the bond sell at par, a discount, or a premium? Explain.

2. Under what conditions will the realized yield on a bond equal the promised yield?

3. Using the trial-and-error method, find the yield-to-maturity of a bond with 5 years to maturity, par value of $1,000, and a coupon rate of 8 percent (annual payments). The bond currently sells at 98.5 percent of par value.

4. An investor purchases a $1,000 par value bond with 5 years to maturity at $985. The bond pays $80 of interest annually. The investor plans to hold the bond for 2 years and expects to sell it at the end of the holding period for 94 percent of its face value. What is this investor's expected yield? Use the trial-and-error method.

BOND THEOREMS

There are three bond theorems that explain the relationship between bond prices and changes in the level of interest rates. These relationships are fundamental to understanding how to manage a bond portfolio. The bond theorems apply not only to bonds but also to all fixed-income securities. Recall that fixed-income securities are financial contracts whose interest or coupon payments are fixed for the life of the contracts. Typical fixed-rate contracts are most corporate, municipal, and Treasury bonds, as well as automobile loans and conventional home mortgage loans.

BOND PRICES AND YIELD

Bond prices and yields vary inversely. Specifically, as the market rate of interest (or yield) rises, a bond's market price declines; or as the market rate of interest (or yield) declines, a bond's market price rises. This inverse relationship exists because the coupon rate or interest rate on a bond is fixed at the time the bond is issued. For example, when market interest rates rise, the only way to increase a bond's yield to be equal to the market rate of interest is to reduce the bond's price because the rate of interest the bond pays is fixed for the life of the bond contract. The investor in such a bond is "paid" the additional interest as a capital gain. Likewise, if market interest rates decline, the only way to reduce a bond's yield to the market rate is to increase the bond's price. For some numerical examples of the inverse relationship between bond price and yield, see the previous section of this chapter dealing with premium and discount bonds. The inverse relationship, one of the most important concepts discussed in this book, applies to bonds or any financial contract whose interest rate payments are fixed for the life of the contract.

BOND PRICE VOLATILITY AND MATURITY

The mathematics of the present value formula have some interesting implications for the relationship between bond price volatility and maturity. Specifically, long-term bonds have greater price volatility than short-term bonds, holding other bond characteristics constant. **Bond price volatility** can be measured as the percent change in bond prices for a given change in interest rates.

Exhibit 5.3 demonstrates the relationship between bond price changes and maturity. The exhibit shows the price of a $1,000, 5 percent coupon bond when the market interest rate is 5 percent (column 2). The market rate of interest is then allowed to rise from 5 to 6 percent (column 3) and to fall from 5 to 4 percent (column 6). For both cases, the dollar price changes resulting from the given yield changes are recorded in columns 4 and 7. The percentage price changes (price volatilities) are recorded in columns 5 and 8.

As Exhibit 5.3 shows, when the market yield rises to 6 percent, a 1-year, 5 percent coupon bond falls to $990.57—a price decline of $9.43, or a price volatility of –0.94 percent. In contrast, the 20-year, 5 percent coupon bond sells at $885.30—a price decline of $114.70, or a price volatility of –11.47 percent. The 100-basis-point increase in interest rates causes a capital loss more than 12 times larger on the long-term bond than on the short-term bond.[3] Likewise, the price

---

[3] From now on, we will discuss changes in bond yields in terms of what investors and institutions on Wall Street call basis points. A basis point is 1/100 of 1 percent; that is, 100 basis points equal 1 percent. A change in yield of 25 basis points, for example, is equal to a change of 0.25 percent.

EXHIBIT 5.3
Relationship among Price, Maturity, Market Yield, and Price Volatility for a $1,000, 5%
Coupon Bond (Annual Payments)

(1) Maturity (years)	(2) Bond Price at 5% Yield ($)	Price Change if Yield Changes to 6%			Price Change if Yield Changes to 4%		
		(3) Bond Price ($)	(4) Loss from Increase in Yield ($)	(5) Price Volatility (%)	(6) Bond Price ($)	(7) Gain from Decrease in Yield ($)	(8) Price Volatility (%)
1	$1,000	$990.57	$ 9.43	−0.94	$1,009.62	$ 9.62	0.96%
5	1,000	957.88	42.12	−4.21	1,044.52	44.52	4.45
10	1,000	926.40	73.60	−7.36	1,081.11	81.11	8.11
20	1,000	885.30	114.70	−11.47	1,135.90	135.90	13.59
40	1,000	849.54	150.46	−15.05	1,197.93	197.93	19.79
100	1,000	833.82	166.18	−16.62	1,245.05	245.05	24.50

This exhibit shows that the longer the maturity of a bond, the greater the bond's price volatility. Thus, long-term bonds have greater interest rate risk than short-term bonds.

volatility of the long-term bond is 12 times greater than that of the short-term bond. Similar results are shown for an interest rate decrease in columns 7 and 8. In sum, the longer the term to maturity, the greater the price volatility; hence, long-term bonds have greater interest rate risk than similar short-term bonds.

Calculating Bond Price Volatility. As discussed above, a simple measure of bond price volatility is the percentage change in bond price for a given change in yield. More formally, the percentage change in a bond's price (price volatility) is calculated as:

$$\%\Delta PB = \frac{P_t - P_{t-1}}{P_{t-1}} \times 100, \qquad (5.6)$$

where:
$\%\Delta PB$ = the percentage change in price
P_t = the new price in period t
P_{t-1} = the bond's price one period earlier

For example, consider a bond selling at par with an 8 percent annual coupon. Suppose that yields on similar bonds increase by 25 basis points to 8.25 percent. In terms of dollars, the price of the bond falls from $1,000 to $983.41, a decline of $16.59. Applying Equation 5.6, the bond's price volatility is: $\%\Delta PB$ = ($983.41 − $1,000)/$1,000 = $16.59/$1,000 = −16.6 percent. Thus, a bond's price volatility is a measure of how sensitive a bond's price is to changes in yields.

EXHIBIT 5.4
Relationship among Price, Coupon Rate, Market Yield, and Price Volatility for a $1,000, 10-Year Bond (Annual Payments)

(1) Coupon Rate %	(2) Bond Price at 5% Yield ($)	Price Change if Yield Changes to 6%			Price Change if Yield Changes to 4%		
		(3) Bond Price ($)	(4) Loss from Increase in Yield ($)	(5) Price Volatility (%)	(6) Bond Price ($)	(7) Gain from Decrease in Yield ($)	(8) Price Volatility (%)
0%	$ 613.91	$ 558.39	$55.52	−9.04%	$ 675.56	$ 61.65	10.04%
5	1,000.00	926.40	73.60	−7.36	1,081.11	81.11	8.11
10	1,386.09	1,294.40	91.69	−6.62	1,486.65	−100.56	7.25

This exhibit shows that the lower the coupon rate of a bond, the greater the bond's price volatility. Thus, low-coupon bonds have greater interest rate risk than high-coupon bonds.

BOND PRICE VOLATILITY AND COUPON RATE

Another important factor that affects the price volatility of a bond is the bond's coupon rate. Specifically, the lower a bond's coupon rate, the greater the percentage price change (price volatility) for a given change in yield. This mathematical property of the bond-pricing formula is illustrated in Exhibit 5.4, which shows the prices of three 10-year bonds: a zero coupon bond, a 5 percent coupon bond, and a 10 percent coupon bond. Initially, the bonds are priced to yield 5 percent (see column 2). The bonds are then priced at yields of 6 and 4 percent (see columns 3 and 6). The dollar price changes for each bond given the appropriate interest rate changes are recorded in columns 4 and 7, and percentage price changes (price volatilities) are shown in columns 5 and 8. As column 5 shows, when interest rates increase from 5 to 6 percent, the zero coupon bond experiences the greatest percentage price decline, and the 10 percent bond experiences the smallest percentage price decline. Similar results are shown in column 8 for interest rate decreases. In sum, the lower a bond's coupon rate, the greater a bond's price volatility, hence, lower-coupon bonds have greater interest rate risk.

You can also see the effect of the coupon rate on bond price volatility using a price–yield profile. Exhibit 5.5 plots the percentage change in the bond's price (y-axis) versus the market yield (x-axis) for the zero and 10 percent coupon bonds in Exhibit 5.4. The exhibit shows that low-coupon bonds will have a greater percentage change in price from par value than will high-coupon bonds when market interest rates change.

SUMMARY OF BOND THEOREMS

You should remember three important properties of the relationship between bond prices and yields:

1. Bond prices are inversely related to bond yields.

EXHIBIT 5.5
The Relationship between Bond Price Volatility and the Coupon Rate

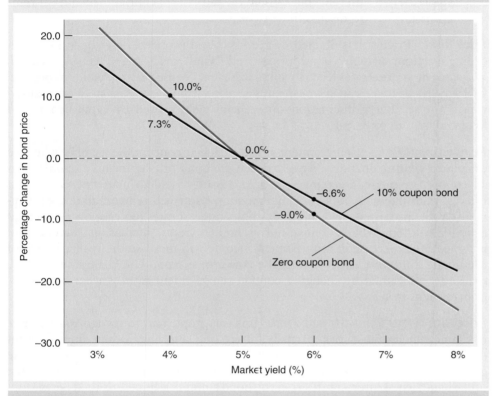

For two bonds with the same maturity, the bond with the lower coupon rate (0%) exhibits a larger percentage change in price for a given change in market yield and thus has more interest rate risk.

2. The price volatility of a long-term bond is greater than that of a short-term bond, holding the coupon rate constant.
3. The price volatility of a low-coupon bond is greater than that of a high-coupon bond, holding maturity constant.

We will call on these relationships to help us explain interest rate risk in the next section, and later in the book they will also help us explain how interest rate risk affects financial institutions.

By now, you should be catching on that investing in bonds could be risky. Market yields on bonds fluctuate on a daily basis, and these fluctuations cause bond prices to change through the mechanics of the bond-pricing formula (Equation 5.3). In this section, we formally present the concept of interest rate risk and show how investors and financial institutions attempt to manage it using a risk measure called duration.

INTEREST RATE RISK AND DURATION

INTEREST RATE RISK

Interest rate risk is the risk related to changes in interest rates that cause a bond's realized yield to differ from the promised yield or yield-to-maturity. Interest rate risk comprises two different, but closely related risks: (1) price risk and (2) reinvestment risk. We now discuss these two risks.

Price Risk. Price risk is defined by the first bond property described in the preceding section; namely, bond prices and bond yields are inversely related. Increases in interest rates lead to capital losses that cause realized yields to decline. Conversely, decreases in interest rates lead to capital gains that cause realized yields to rise. These fluctuations in realized yield caused by capital gains and losses constitute price risk.

Reinvestment Risk. Reinvestment risk is a trickier concept. Remember when we calculated yield-to-maturity, we noted that the bond pricing formula assumes that all coupon payments are reinvested at the bond's yield-to-maturity. Given that interest rates fluctuate, it is unlikely that an investor will reinvest all coupon payments at the promised yield. If, for example, interest rates increase over the life of a bond, coupons will be reinvested at higher yields, increasing reinvestment income.[4] The increase in reinvestment income will increase the realized yield of the bond. If interest rates decline, the converse is true. The change in a bond's realized yield caused by changing coupon reinvestment rates is what constitutes reinvestment risk.

Price Risk versus Reinvestment Risk. It is very important to recognize that price risk and reinvestment risk partially offset one another. When interest rates decline, a bond's price increases, resulting in a capital gain (good news!), but the gain is partially offset by lower coupon reinvestment income (bad news!). On the other hand, when interest rates rise, the bond suffers a capital loss (bad news!), but the loss is partially offset by higher coupon reinvestment income (good news!).

DURATION AND BOND PROPERTIES

It is important for investors and financial institutions to be able to evaluate the effect of interest rate risk on their bond investments. How can we measure interest rate risk? The problem we have is that bond price volatility varies directly with maturity and inversely with coupon rate. A good measure of interest rate risk should account for both effects simultaneously. A measure of interest rate risk (or bond price volatility) that considers both coupon rate and maturity is **duration**. Duration is a weighted average of the number of years until each of the bond's cash flows is received. Using annual compounding, the formula for duration is:

$$D = \frac{\sum_{t=1}^{n} \dfrac{CF_t(t)}{(1+i)^t}}{\sum_{t=1}^{n} \dfrac{CF_t}{(1+i)^t}} = \frac{\sum_{t=1}^{n} \dfrac{CF_t(t)}{(1+i)^t}}{PB} \tag{5.7}$$

---

[4] We use future value mathematics to calculate reinvestment income, which is really just the interest-on-interest from a bond. Future values behave just the opposite of present values when interest rates change. When interest rates increase, future value increases. When they decrease, future value also decreases.

where:

D = duration of the bond
CF_t = interest or principal payment at time t
t = time period in which principal or coupon interest is paid
n = number of periods to maturity
i = the yield to maturity (interest rate)

The denominator is the price of the bond *(PB)* and is just another form of the bond-pricing formula presented earlier (Equation 5.3). The numerator is the present value of all cash flows weighted according to the length of time to receipt. Admittedly, the formula for duration looks formidable. However, we will work through some examples and use them to illustrate the important properties of duration. We will be using the concept of duration throughout the book, so it is important that you grasp it now.

To illustrate the calculation of duration using Equation 5.7, suppose that we have a bond with a 3-year maturity, an 8 percent coupon rate paid annually, and a market yield of 10 percent. The duration of the bond is:

$$D = \frac{\dfrac{\$80(1)}{(1.10)^1} + \dfrac{\$80(2)}{(1.10)^2} + \dfrac{\$1,080(3)}{(1.10)^3}}{\dfrac{\$80}{(1.10)^1} + \dfrac{\$80}{(1.10)^2} + \dfrac{\$1,080}{(1.10)^3}} = 2.78 \text{ years.}$$

If the market rate of interest (yield) increases from 10 percent to 15 percent, the bond's duration would be:

$$D = \frac{\dfrac{\$80(1)}{(1.15)^1} + \dfrac{\$80(2)}{(1.15)^2} + \dfrac{\$1,080(3)}{(1.15)^3}}{\dfrac{\$80}{(1.15)^1} + \dfrac{\$80}{(1.15)^2} + \dfrac{\$1,080}{(1.15)^3}} = 2.76 \text{ years.}$$

Notice that duration gets smaller with the interest rate increase.

To give you a chance to practice calculating duration, Exhibit 5.6 shows the duration for a group of bonds with different coupon rates (zero, 4 percent, and 8 percent) and different maturities (1 to 5 years); in all cases the bonds are priced to yield 10 percent, and coupon payments are paid annually. Now get your pad, pencil, and calculator and see if you can use the duration formula to obtain the durations in Exhibit 5.6. Alternatively, if you are good with the computer, it is relatively easy to set up the duration calculation in a spreadsheet.

Exhibit 5.6 and our previous examples illustrate some important properties of duration:

1. Bonds with higher coupon rates have shorter durations than bonds with smaller coupons of the same maturity. This is true because the higher coupon bonds receive more of the total cash flow earlier in the form of larger coupon payments. For example, for any given maturity, the 8 percent coupon bonds in Exhibit 5.6 always have a shorter duration than the 4 percent or zero coupon bonds.

EXHIBIT 5.6
Duration for Bonds Yielding 10% (Annual Compounding)

Duration in Years			
Maturity (Years)	Zero Coupon	4% Coupon	8% Coupon
1	1.00	1.00	1.00
2	2.00	1.96	1.92
3	3.00	2.88	2.78
4	4.00	3.75	3.56
5	5.00	4.57	4.28

Duration is a measure of bond price volatility that considers both the coupon rate and term to maturity.

2. There is generally a positive relationship between term-to-maturity and duration. The longer the maturity of a bond, the higher the bond's duration.[5] This is true because the bond's cash flow is received further out in time. Among the bonds in Exhibit 5.6 with the same coupon rate, you can see that those with longer maturities have longer durations.

3. For bonds with a single payment (principal with or without a coupon payment), duration is equal to term-to-maturity. Thus, for zero coupon bonds (the single payment is the principal), duration equals final maturity. Likewise, the 1-year bonds in Exhibit 5.6 have duration equal to 1 year because they pay coupon interest annually. Bonds with interim payments always have durations less than their final maturity.

4. All other factors held constant, the higher the market rate of interest, the shorter the duration of the bond. This stands to reason because the higher the market rate of interest, the faster coupon reinvestment income accumulates.

One property of duration that is particularly important to managers of financial institutions is the direct relationship between bond price volatility and duration. The greater a bond's duration, the greater the percentage change in a bond's price for a given change in interest rates. Thus, duration is a good measure of interest rate risk because, as noted above, duration is positively related to maturity and inversely related to coupon rate.

USING DURATION TO CALCULATE BOND PRICE VOLATILITY

We have demonstrated that a direct relationship exists between bond price volatility and duration. In this section, we show how to use duration to estimate the per-

---

[5] For bonds selling at a discount (below par), duration increases at a decreasing rate up to a very long maturity, such as 50 years, and then declines. Since most bonds have maturities of 30 years or less, duration increases with maturity for most bonds we observe in the marketplace.

centage change in a bond's price resulting from a change in market interest rates using the following formula, which gives the relationship between bond price changes and duration:

$$\%\Delta PB \cong -D\left[\frac{\Delta_i}{(1+i)}\right]\times100. \tag{5.8}$$

Using the 3-year, 4 percent coupon bond in Exhibit 5.6, if the market interest rate increases 25 basis points from 10 percent to 10.25 percent, the percentage change in the value of the bond would be approximately:

$$\%\Delta PB \cong -2.88\left[\frac{0.0025}{1.10}\right]\times100 = -0.65\%.$$

For this bond, the actual price change is from \$850.79 to \$845.25, which results in a percentage change in price of –0.65 percent.[6] Therefore, we see that for this small change in the market rate Equation 5.3 works well for estimating the change in value of the bond. However, this equation may not work as well for large changes in interest rates. Using the same bond, let's see what happens if interest rates increase from 10 percent to 12 percent, an increase of 200 basis points. Equation 5.8 suggests the following change in value:

$$\%\Delta PB \cong -2.88\left[\frac{0.02}{1.10}\right]\times100 = -5.24\%.$$

The *actual* price change is from \$850.79 to \$807.85, which is a 5.05 percent drop in the bond price.[7]

Our examples show that Equation 5.8 works well for small changes in interest rates but not for large changes. The shortcoming of Equation 5.8 is demonstrated in Exhibit 5.7. The curve, which is a representation of a price–yield profile, shows the relationship between a bond's price and the prevailing market yield (or market's required yield), and the straight line represents the price–yield relationship estimated by Equation 5.8. We see that for small changes in market yields around the tangent point, the straight line is a good estimate of changes along the price–yield profile. However, for large changes in market yields, the straight line is not a good estimate. Thus, Equation 5.8 requires a correction for the error in using the straight line to estimate the curve. Bond traders refer to the correction factor as **convexity** because the curve in Exhibit 5.7 is convex, which means that it curves away from the origin of the *x-y* axes. There is a complicated formula for convexity, which we will not present here, but most bond traders have a good instinct for how bond prices will change given the maturity and the coupon rate of the bond.

---

[6] To calculate \$850.79, use Equation 5.3 with an interest rate of 10 percent. Similarly, you can obtain \$845.25. To arrive at –0.65 percent, use Equation 5.6 with P_t = \$845.25 and $P_t–1$ = \$850.79.

[7] To calculate 5.05 percent, use Equation 5.3 to obtain the bond prices at 10 percent and 12 percent and then substitute the prices into Equation 5.6.

EXHIBIT 5.7
The Typical Price–Yield Relationship

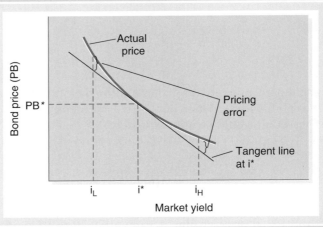

The tangent line to the price-yield profile can be used to estimate changes in bond prices due to changes in interest rates.

While the formulas for duration and convexity are daunting, you should know that bond traders use these measures frequently to assess the interest rate risk of bonds and to estimate price changes. The computer screens that bond traders use to track the bond markets automatically calculate duration and convexity and feature them prominently.

USING DURATION AS A MEASURE OF INTEREST RATE RISK

From the bond properties, we know that (1) long-term bonds have more interest rate risk than short-term bonds and (2) low-coupon bonds have more interest rate risk than high-coupon bonds. These properties, however, do not allow us to rank all possible pairs of bonds on interest rate risk. For example, if we want to know whether a 10-year, 7 percent coupon bond or an 8-year, 5 percent coupon bond is exposed to more interest rate risk, the bond properties do not directly help because it is difficult to "eyeball" the relative impact of the bonds' maturities and coupon rates on the their price volatilities.

Duration solves the problem because it provides a rank ordering of bonds on the dimension of interest-rate-risk exposure. Lower-duration bonds are exposed to less interest rate risk and higher-duration bonds are exposed to more. Duration is related to the slope of the price–yield profile for a given bond. The steeper the price–yield profile, the greater the bond's duration and the greater the exposure to interest rate risk.

Given the two bonds described above, assume a current market yield of 5 percent. At the 5 percent yield, the duration of the 10-year, 7 percent bond is 7.71 years and the duration of the 8-year, 5 percent bond is 6.79 years. The 8-year, 5 percent bond has a shorter duration and thus is exposed to less interest rate risk. To test our conclusion, let's assume that the market yield increases from 5 percent to 5.5 percent, or an increase of 50 basis points. For this change in yield, the price of the 10-year, 7 percent bond falls 3.58 percent while the price of the 8-year, 5 percent bond falls 3.17 percent. Thus, we see that duration properly ranked the bonds for their exposure to changes in interest rates.

DURATION OF BOND PORTFOLIOS

From the example above, we see that duration ranks individual bonds based on their exposure to interest rate risk. We know, however, that investors seldom hold individual assets and today, investors often buy investment funds instead of individual securities. So, can duration help with understanding the interest-rate-risk exposure of a bond portfolio or a bond mutual fund? The answer is yes. In fact, portfolio duration provides a rank ordering of portfolios by their exposure to changes in interest rates, just as it does for individual bonds.

To calculate duration of bond portfolios, we need only recognize that the duration of a bond portfolio is a weighted average of the individual bond durations. Each bond's duration is weighted according to the proportion of portfolio value accounted for by each bond. The formula for portfolio duration is

$$\text{Portfolio Duration} = \sum_{i=1}^{n} w_i D_i, \tag{5.9}$$

where w_i is the proportion of bond i in the portfolio and D_i is the duration of bond i. In later chapters, you will read how financial institutions use portfolio duration to manage their exposures to interest rate changes.

Let's work through a brief example to show how Equation 5.9 works. Suppose a bond portfolio contains four bonds, A, B, C, and D. Bond A has duration of 15.7 years and makes up 20 percent of the portfolio. Bond B has duration of 22.3 years and makes up 40 percent of the portfolio. Bond C has duration of 10.2 years and makes up 15 percent of the portfolio. Finally, Bond D has duration of 7.6 years and makes up 25 percent of the portfolio. You can calculate the duration of the bond portfolio with Equation 5.9:

$$
\begin{aligned}
D_{Portfolio} &= D_A w_A + D_B w_B + D_C w_C + D_D w_D \\
&= 15.7(0.20) + 22.3(0.40) + 10.2(0.15) + 7.6(0.25) \\
&= 15.49 \text{ years.}
\end{aligned}
$$

You can see from the above example that financial institutions are able to change the durations of their bond portfolios by changing the proportions of bonds in the portfolios. For example, to make the duration of the above portfolio longer, a portfolio manager could decrease the proportion invested in Bond D and increase the proportion invested in Bond B.

USING DURATION TO MEASURE AND MANAGE INTEREST RATE RISK

Probably the most important use of duration is as a tool for reducing or eliminating interest rate risk over a given holding period. For example, suppose that you are in the beginning of your junior year in college and wish to plan for a well-deserved vacation 2 years from now. You have a 2-year investment horizon over which you must accumulate enough funds to take your vacation. You consider investing in bonds, but you are concerned about the potential impact of interest rate risk on the returns to your investment and, hence, your ability to afford the vacation. We now discuss the relative merits of three possible approaches to dealing with interest rate risk.

The Zero Coupon Approach. The simplest way to avoid the interest rate risk in this situation is to invest in a zero coupon bond that matures in 2 years. This strategy eliminates price risk because the bond is held to maturity, and it eliminates reinvestment risk because there are no coupon payments to reinvest. The entire return from the zero coupon bond comes from the difference between the purchase price and the maturity value. Assuming default-free bonds, there will be no risk in this strategy.

The Maturity-Matching Approach. A more naive alternative is to invest in a coupon bond with a maturity equal to the 2-year holding period. With this strategy, you eliminate the price risk because you hold the bond to maturity, but there is still reinvestment risk because coupons are received. Consequently, interest rate changes could potentially wreak havoc with your vacation plans should interest rates decline dramatically over the 2 years.

The Duration-Matching Approach. A "surefire" way of eliminating both price risk and reinvestment risk is to structure your bond investment such that the *duration* of the bond or a bond portfolio equals your holding period.[8] What happens with the duration-matching strategy that results in the elimination of both price and reinvestment risks? By matching duration with your holding period, you set up a situation in which capital gains or losses from interest rate changes are exactly offset by changes in reinvestment income. You are able to lock in on a given target return to your investment and thus ensure that you will have enough money at the end of 2 years to take your vacation.

EXAMPLE OF THE DURATION MATCHING STRATEGY AT WORK

Let's work through the example above with some real numbers, so you can see exactly how duration can protect you from interest rate risk. Since you want to go on vacation to Cancun 2 years from now, your holding period or investment horizon (the period of time over which you invest) is 2 years. Assume that you expect the vacation to cost you approximately $1,210 2 years from now and the current market yield is 10 percent. If you purchase a zero coupon bond costing $1,000 with a maturity of 2 years and a maturity value of $1,210, you will receive $1,210 2 years from now regardless of how interest rates move, assuming the issuer of the bond does not default.[9] For purposes of this example, we will assume no risk of

---

[8] Technically, this is true only when the term structure of interest rates is flat and moves in parallel shifts. Interest rates, unfortunately, do not usually behave this way in the real world. As a result, it is usually not possible to eliminate interest rate risk from a bond investment with this strategy, although many academic studies show that it is possible to obtain substantial *reduction* in interest rate risk. We discuss the term structure of interest rates in Chapter 6.

[9] The idea for this example and the numbers in it come from James C. Van Horne, *Financial Market Rates and Flows*, 6th ed., Upper Saddle River, NJ: Prentice Hall, 2001, pp. 109–110.

Junk Bonds: A Really Bad Month

April 1990 was a tough month for Peter A. Cohen, former chief executive officer at American Express (AMEX) Company's investment banking subsidiary, Shearson Lehman Hutton. Security analysts say his miscalculations and lack of judgment caused AMEX to lose $115 million! For this, he was unceremoniously fired from his job—no surprise here. And his faithful dog, Rex, was reported to have bit him during the month. Now, that's a bad month.

Forgetting about the dog story, how did Cohen accomplish all of this in a month? Let's turn the clock back to early 1989, when the junk bond market was the "hot" market for investors willing to bear high risk. In case you don't know, junk bonds are bonds with a credit rating of BB or lower from rating agencies. They are issued by firms with poor earnings records and/or questionable credit standing. Because of their risky nature, junk bonds have much higher yields and price volatility than investment-grade bonds, which have credit ratings above BB.

Cohen and his colleagues at Shearson took a huge bet on the direction of interest rate movements and lost. Specifically, they plunked down $290 million to buy shares in seven junk bond mutual funds and another $190 million to buy individual junk bonds, for a whopping investment of $480 million. The promised yield on their high-risk bond portfolio of long-term bonds was in excess of 12 percent. Their junk bond spending spree was financed by having AMEX sell short-term floating-rate paper whose average yields were less than 9 percent. Cohen and other executives at Shearson reasoned that if they could earn 12 percent on their investments and pay 9 percent for money, the firm would earn a 3 percent spread, or 300 basis points, which is a huge return on investment. Furthermore, over time they expected interest rates to decline and then to be able to sell their junk bond portfolio for a substantial gain. Recall our first bond theorem: if interest rates decline, bond prices increase.

Of course, the 300 basis points are not free; they are the premium paid to investors for bearing risk. The Shearson junk bond portfolio of long-term bonds was a bet on interest rate movements with a portfolio that had a ton of interest rate risk. Recall our second bond theorem: for a given change in interest rates, long-term bonds have greater price swings than short-term bonds.

In the case of Shearson, its market timing—both the buying and selling of bonds—could not have been worse. The firm purchased the long-term junk bonds believing the "high" interest rates they saw in the market place would eventually decline. Instead, after they invested, interest rates spiraled upward, causing bond prices to decline precipitously. Compounding Shearson's problems was the fact that the interest cost on the floating-rate paper rose relative to long-term interest rates and, thus, reduced the firm's interest rate spread. In early April 1990, with the price of junk bonds falling and the cost of funding rising, Shearson decided to throw in the towel and bailed out of its junk bond holdings. The firm's losses totaled $115 million!

But again, the firm's market timing was off! Soon after bailing out, interest rates began to decline, as Cohen and his colleagues had expected. As one Wall Street analyst said, "They may not have hit the bottom with their selling, but they could not have done much worse."

What's the moral of the story? Simply put, long-term bonds have lots of interest rate risk compared to short-term bonds, especially high-risk junk bonds, whose price volatility is much greater than that of bonds of similar maturity with higher credit ratings. More important, no one can predict interest rate movements consistently, including the Fed—and it controls the money supply.

default. Now suppose that there are three possible interest rate scenarios: (1) the interest rate falls to 8 percent at the end of 1 year from now and remains at that level until the end of the second year; (2) the interest rate remains at 10 percent over the entire 2 years; or (3) the interest rate increases to 12 percent 1 year from now and remains there until the end of the second year. The maturity-matching strategy, which involves purchasing a 2-year bond with a 10 percent coupon rate, gives you the cash flows and the realized compound yields shown below:

Cash Flows from the Maturity-Matching Strategy			
	Interest Rate Scenario		
Cash Flows 2 Years from Now	**8%**	**10%**	**12%**
(1) Principal	$1,000	$1,000	$1,000
(2) Proceeds from Reinvesting the First Coupon Payment from the End of First Year to the End of Second Year[10]	108	110	112
(3) Second Coupon Payment	100	100	100
Total Cash Flow	$1,208	$1,210	$1,212
Realized Compound Yield	9.9%	10.0%	10.1%

The principal amount and the second coupon payment are fixed, regardless of which interest rate scenario occurs. What are affected by the interest rate change, however, are the proceeds from reinvesting the first coupon. When the level of interest rates remains the same at 10 percent, the total cash flow at the end of the second year is $1,210, exactly the amount you need to take your trip to Cancun. The bad news occurs when the interest rate falls to 8 percent. If that happens, the total cash flow falls short of what you need for your trip because you wouldn't be able to reinvest the intermediate coupon payment at the original yield-to-maturity of the bond, which is 10 percent. At a 12 percent market yield, you will have enough for your trip and a little left over to buy a margarita on the airplane. You are exposed to interest rate risk, because over your investment horizon of 2 years, your total cash flow and your realized compound yield will change as the market yield changes.

On the other hand, if you match the duration of your investment to the length of your holding period, you will be protected from interest rate risk. Suppose you are able to find a bond that will pay a 10 percent annual coupon payment and has 2.1 years to maturity.[11] Using the bond pricing formula, the value of this bond today would be

$$PB_{2.1} = \frac{\$100}{(1.10)} + \frac{\$100}{(1.10)^2} + \frac{\$1,010}{(1.10)^{2.1}} = \$1,000.$$

---

[10] The calculation is just a simple application of the future value formula. For example, assume you invest $100 for 1 year at 8 percent interest you will receive $100 × (1 + 0.08) = $108 at the end of the second year. The coupon reinvestment proceeds are calculated similarly for the other scenarios.

Notice that the last coupon payment is only $10 because the bond is held only one-tenth of a year. Let's see what happens to your cash flows at the end of 2 years if you buy this bond. The cash flows are shown below:

Cash Flows from Buying the 2.1-Year Bond

Cash Flows 2 Years from Now	Interest Rate Scenario		
	8%	10%	12%
(1) Proceeds from Selling the 2.1-Year Bond after 2 Years	$1,002	$1,000	$998
(2) Proceeds from Reinvesting the First Coupon Payment from the End of First Year to the End of Second Year[12]	108	110	112
(3) Second Coupon Payment	100	100	100
Total Cash Flow	$1,210	$1,210	$1,210
Realized Compound Yield	10.0%	10.0%	10.0%

Notice that the strategy above requires you to sell the 2.1-year bond 2 years from now, one-tenth of a year before it matures. At that point, the only cash flows remaining from the bond will be one-tenth of a coupon payment and the principal repayment, both occurring in one-tenth of a year. Therefore, anyone purchasing the bond will be willing to pay the present value of the remaining cash flows. For example, if rates fall to 8 percent, the bond will be worth $1,002 at the end of 2 years, when the bond has one-tenth of a year remaining to maturity:

$$PB_{0.1} = \frac{\$1,010}{(1.08)^{0.1}} = \$1,002.$$

You can do a similar calculation, which is just an application of the bond price formula, for the scenario in which rates increase to 12 percent.

There are several important observations in the preceding table. First, the cash flow at the end of 2 years is the same, regardless of which interest rate scenario occurs. This means that you have eliminated the interest rate risk from your position. Second, the realized compound yield is the same for each scenario, another indication that you have eliminated the interest rate risk. Finally, the strategy is structured such that the effects of price risk and reinvestment risk offset each other exactly. Notice that if interest rates rise to 12 percent, there is a price decrease of $2 on the bond (from $1,000 to $998) but an increase in reinvestment income of $2 (from $110 to $112). The bottom line is that you will have enough money for your trip to Cancun, regardless of how interest rates change.

---

[11] There aren't too many 2.1-year bonds out there that pay one-tenth of a coupon payment at maturity. Recognize that this bond is hypothetical and contrived for purposes of the illustration.

[12] The calculation is just a simple application of the future value formula. For example, assume you invest $100 for 1 year at 8 percent interest you will receive $100 × (1 + 0.08) = $108 at the end of the second year. The coupon reinvestment proceeds are calculated similarly for the other scenarios.

As it turns out, the *duration* of the 2.1-year bond is 2 years, so what you have really done is to match the duration of your bond investment with the length of your holding period or investment horizon. You can see the calculation of the bond's duration below:

$$D = \frac{\dfrac{\$100}{(1.10)} + \dfrac{\$100(2)}{(1.10)^2} + \dfrac{\$1,010(2.1)}{(1.10)^{2.1}}}{\dfrac{\$100}{(1.10)} + \dfrac{\$100}{(1.10)^2} + \dfrac{\$1,010}{(1.10)^{2.1}}} = 2.0.$$

Thus, the above example demonstrates that it is possible to eliminate interest rate risk by matching the duration of your investment with your holding period.

This example is admittedly somewhat contrived to make a teaching point, but the reality is that it is difficult to identify single bonds, such as the 2.1-year bond above, whose durations will equal a given holding period. What financial institutions do is to form bond portfolios that have a given duration. They accomplish this by using Equation 5.9, the formula for portfolio duration, and varying the proportions (i.e., w_i) until they achieve the desired duration. Further, the example above works because we assumed that interest rates change at the end of the first year and then remain at that level until the bond is sold. After studying the duration formula, you should recognize that the duration of a bond also depends on the market yield. Every time the market yield changes, the duration changes. This means that real-world financial institutions must periodically adjust the duration of their bond investments to match the remaining holding period to keep the interest-rate-risk protection working.

HOW FINANCIAL INSTITUTIONS USE DURATION

The duration-matching strategy has many real-world applications. Managers of pension funds use the strategy to protect from interest rate risk the value of bond portfolios used to provide workers with retirement income in the distant future. By using duration combined with a strategy of "dedicating" a bond portfolio's assets to paying a particular stream of pension fund obligations, fund managers can ensure that they will be able to pay retirees the contracted amount regardless of interest rate changes. Later in the book, we will show how managers of commercial banks and thrift institutions can use duration to reduce fluctuations in net interest income (the difference between the average return of the assets minus the average cost of liabilities) resulting from interest rate changes. In addition, you will see that banks can protect their net worth from interest rate risk by matching the average duration of the assets with the average duration of the liabilities.

DO YOU UNDERSTAND?

1. Consider a 4-year bond selling at par with a 7 percent annual coupon. Suppose that yields on similar bonds increase by 50 basis points. Use duration (Equation 5.8) to estimate the percent change in the bond price. Check your answer by calculating the new bond price.

2. Define "price risk" and "reinvestment risk." Explain how the two risks offset each other.

3. What is the duration of a bond portfolio made up of two bonds: 37 percent of a bond with duration of 7.7 years and 63 percent of a bond with duration of 16.4 years?

4. How can duration be used as a way to rank bonds on their interest rate risk?

5. To eliminate interest rate risk, should you match the maturity or the duration of your bond investment to your holding period? Explain.

CHAPTER TAKE-AWAYS

1 A given amount of money received today is worth more than the same amount of money received in the future in part because people prefer to consume goods today rather than consume similar goods in the future. Present value calculations determine how much a future cash flow is worth in today's dollars, given the rate of interest, which reflects the preference for current over future cash flow. Pricing a bond is a straightforward application of the present value formula. To price a bond, identify the timing and magnitude of its cash flows (principal and coupon payments) and use the market yield on similar bonds as the discount rate in the present value formula.

2 Bond yield measures tell investors the rate of return on bonds under different assumptions. Yield-to-maturity is the rate of return assuming the bond is held to maturity and that all coupon payments are reinvested to earn the yield-to-maturity. However, many bonds are sold before maturity, and the reinvested coupon may not earn the yield-to-maturity due to interest rate changes. To determine the actual rate of return that was earned on a bond investment in the past, investors use realized compound yield, which accounts for the actual holding period and actual reinvestment income. Most investors will want some idea of how a bond investment will perform in the future. Expected yield is the rate of return that reflects the anticipated holding period and the anticipated coupon reinvestment income.

3 Bond prices and bond yields move inversely. When market yields increase, bond prices decrease and vice versa. This effect is a mathematical property of the bond-pricing formula. The change in bond prices for a given change in market yield, also known as bond price volatility, is greater for bonds with longer maturities and lower-coupon rates, all other factors equal.

4 Interest rate risk is the change in the value of a bond given a change in market yields. Changes in interest rates affect the price of the bond and the coupon reinvestment income. Therefore, there are two types of interest rate risk: price risk and reinvestment risk. Price risk refers to changes in the market price resulting from changes in the market yield. Reinvestment risk is the variation in reinvestment income resulting from changes in the market yield. Price risk and reinvestment risk offset each other. When interest rates increase, bond prices fall, but coupon reinvestment income increases. The opposite occurs when market yields fall. Both types of risk can cause the realized compound yield to differ from the expected yield or the yield-to-maturity.

5 Investors and financial institutions can measure interest rate risk using duration. Bonds with more interest rate risk have larger durations and those with less interest rate risk have smaller durations.

6 Investors and financial institutions can manage interest rate risk using duration. By matching the duration of a bond investment with the length of the desired investment horizon or holding period, price risk and reinvestment risk offset each other. This strategy can eliminate the fluctuations in cash flow or realized compound yield over a given holding period.

KEY TERMS

Time value of money
Present value
Future value
Compounding
Discounting
Opportunity cost
Bond
Bond issuer

Bondholder
Par value (principal, face value)
Coupon payment
Coupon rate
Term-to-maturity
Discount bond
Par bond

Premium bond
Zero coupon bond
Credit risk (default risk)
Reinvestment risk
Price risk
Yield-to-maturity (promised yield)
Realized yield

Expected yield
Bond price volatility
Price–yield profile
Interest rate risk
Duration
Convexity

QUESTIONS AND PROBLEMS

1. Brennan Alston deposits $2,000 in a savings account offering 6.25 percent compounded daily. After 4 years, assuming he makes no further deposits, what will be the balance in his account?

2. Write the equation expressing the present value (or price) of a bond that has an 8 percent coupon (annual payments), a 4-year maturity, and a principal of $1,000 if yields on similar securities are 10 percent. Compute the price using a calculator.

3. Find the price of a corporate bond maturing in 5 years that has a 5 percent coupon (annual payments), a $1,000 face value, and an Aa rating. A local newspaper's financial section reports that the yields on 5-year bonds are: Aaa, 6 percent; Aa, 7 percent; and A, 8 percent.

4. What is the yield-to-maturity of a corporate bond with a 3-year maturity, 5 percent coupon (semiannual payments), and $1,000 face value if the bond sold for $978.30?

5. Explain why yields and prices of fixed-income securities are inversely related.

6. What is the relationship between bond price volatility and term-to-maturity? Between bond price volatility and the coupon rate?

7. Carol Chastain purchases a 1-year discount bond with a $1,000 face value for $862.07. What is the yield of the bond?

8. David Hoffman purchases a $1,000 20-year bond with an 8 percent coupon rate (annual payments). Yields on comparable bonds are 10 percent. David expects that 2 years from now, yields on comparable bonds will have declined to 9 percent. Find his expected yield, assuming the bond is sold in 2 years.

9. Calculate the duration of a $1,000 4-year bond with an 8 percent coupon rate (annual payments) that is currently selling at par.

10. Calculate the duration of a $1,000, 8-year zero coupon bond using annual compounding and a current market rate of 7 percent.

11. Define "interest rate risk." Explain the two types of interest rate risk. How can an investor with a given holding period use duration to reduce interest rate risk?

12. Calculate the duration for a $1,000, 4-year bond with a 4.5 percent annual coupon, currently selling at par. Use the bond's duration to estimate the percentage change in the bond's price for a decrease in the market interest rate to 3.5 percent. How different is your answer from the actual price change calculated using Equation 5.6?

INTERNET EXERCISE

This exercise asks you to assess the volatility of interest rates in recent times by performing the following steps on the Internet:

1. Access the Web site of the Federal Reserve Bank of St. Louis at www.stls.frb.org.
2. Select FRED (see button of Web page).
3. Select Interest Rates.
4. Select 1-year Treasury Constant Maturity Rates and copy the data for the most recent 10 years to a spreadsheet.
5. Select 20-year Treasury Constant Maturity Rates and copy the data for the same period as the 1-year rates.
6. Graph the data.
7. Calculate the mean and the standard deviation of the two data series.

Using the graphs and the calculations, assess the interest rate risk that bondholders of 1- and 20-year bonds were exposed to over the 10-year period.

6

The Structure of Interest Rates

CHAPTER PREVIEW

Armed with a basic understanding of the determinants of the general level of interest rates, we can now explore the reasons interest rates vary among financial products. The variation can seem overwhelming. To get an idea of how extensively rates differ across products, take a close look at the financial section of any major newspaper. On any given day, newspapers report yields on thousands of financial instruments, and almost every product has a different market rate of interest.

In the accompanying table you can see the diversity of interest rates that existed during May 2004. For example, why did 3-month Treasury bills yield 1.11 percent and 5-year Treasury notes yield 3.71 percent when both had the same issuer (the U.S. Treasury Department)? Or, why

Selected Interest Rates, May 2004	
Financial Instrument	**Interest Rate (%)**
3-month commercial paper	1.09
3-month certificate of deposit	1.11
U.S. government securities:	
3-month Treasury bills	0.97
1-year Treasury bills	1.56
5-year Treasury notes	3.71
10-year Treasury bonds	4.61
State and local bonds (municipal bonds)	4.89
Aaa corporate bonds	5.91
Baa corporate bonds	6.66

Source: Federal Reserve Statistical Release H.15 and Dow Jones Market Data.

do municipal bonds yield 4.89 percent and corporate bonds yield from 5.91 to 6.66 percent? If you read this chapter carefully, you will be able to explain how securities' characteristics, such as maturity, default risk, and tax treatment, cause their interest rates to differ. ∎

State and local governments issue tax-exempt municipal securities, often called "munis," to finance a multitude of capital projects. For example, "munis" finance athletic stadiums, bridges, college dormitories, parking facilities, and water and sewer treatment facilities.

Market analysts have identified five major characteristics that are responsible for most of the differences in interest rates among securities: (1) term-to-maturity, (2) default risk, (3) tax treatment, (4) marketability, and (5) special features such as call and put options. This chapter examines these factors separately and explains how each influences a security's yield. ∎

 ## LEARNING OBJECTIVES

The objectives of this chapter are to:

1 Describe and explain the relationship between interest rates and the term-to-maturity of a financial instrument.

2 Explain the meaning and the measurement of default risk premiums.

3 Describe how tax treatment affects yield differences across different types of securities.

4 Explain the relationship between the marketability of a security and its yield.

5 Explain how special characteristics such as call provisions, put options, and conversion options affect a security's yield.

THE TERM STRUCTURE OF INTEREST RATES
利率期限结构.

The **term-to-maturity** of a financial claim is the length of time until the principal amount borrowed becomes payable. The relationship between yield and term-to-maturity on securities that differ only in length of time to maturity is known as the **term structure of interest rates**. For term–structure relationships to be meaningful, other factors that affect interest rates, such as default risk and tax treatment, must be held constant. The term structure may be approximated by graphically plotting yield and maturity for equivalent-grade securities at a point in time. The term–structure relationship can best be seen by examining yields on U.S. Treasury securities because they have similar default risk (nearly none), tax treatment, and marketability.

Exhibit 6.1 shows some yield curves for Treasury securities during the 2000s. Yield curves such as those displayed are constructed by plotting the terms-to-maturity on the horizontal axis and the securities' yields on the vertical axis. The plots are then connected in a smooth line called the **yield curve**. Thus a yield curve shows the relationship between maturity and a security's yield at a point in time. From the chapter preview you can see that in February 2004 1-year securities yielded about 1.56 percent; 5-year securities, 3.71 percent; and 10-year securities, 4.61 percent. From this data, it appears that longer-term securities have higher yields. Thus, we say that the yield curve in February 2004 is upward sloping or ascending.

As you can see in Exhibit 6.1, the shape and level of yield curves do not remain constant over time. As the general level of interest rates rises and falls, yield curves

EXHIBIT 6.1
Yield Curves on Treasury Securities in the 2000s

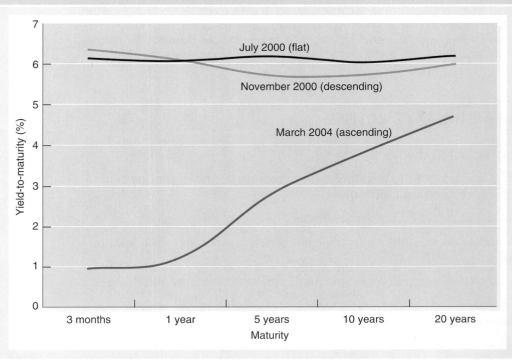

Although yield curves can be upward or downward sloping, they are typically upward sloping. There are also noticeable humps in the yield curves.

Source: Federal Reserve Board of Governors, H.15 Statistical Release.

correspondingly shift up and down and have different slopes. The exhibit shows the more common types of yield curves. An ascending yield curve is formed when interest rates are lowest on short-term securities, and it rises at a diminishing rate until the rates begin to level out on the longer maturities. The ascending yield curve is the most commonly observed yield curve. Flat yield curves are not common, but they do occur from time to time. Descending yield curves occur periodically, usually at or near the beginning of an economic recession. At this point you might be wondering what economic forces explain both the shape of the yield curve and its movement over time. You may also be asking yourself, "Why is it important that I understand yield curves?" We now discuss several theories that explain changes in the term structure. By studying these theories, you will come to a better understanding of how securities markets work and why prices and yields change.

THE EXPECTATION THEORY

The expectation theory holds that the shape of the yield curve is determined by the investors' expectations of future interest rate movements and that changes in these expectations change the shape of the yield curve.[1] The expectation theory is "idealized" because it assumes that investors are profit maximizers and that they have no preference between holding a long-term security and holding a series of short-term securities; that is, they are indifferent toward interest rate risk (or "risk neutral"). Nonetheless, economists believe the theory explains the basic force that alters the shape of the yield curve.

To see how changing expectations of interest rate movements can alter the slope of the yield curve, let's look at an example. Suppose that an investor has a 2-year investment horizon and that only 1-year bonds and 2-year bonds are available for purchase. Since both types of securities currently yield 6 percent, the prevailing term structure is flat, as indicated by the yield curve shown below. Now suppose that new economic information becomes available and investors *expect* interest rates on 1-year securities to rise to 12 percent within a year. This information, for example, might be an announcement by the Fed that it is targeting higher interest rates. Note that the 12 percent rate is a **forward rate** in that it is the interest that will exist 1 year in the future. Given this new information, what portfolio of bonds should profit-maximizing, risk-neutral investors hold?

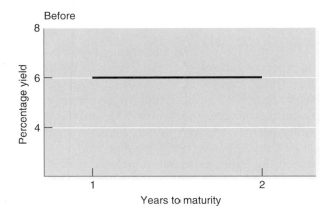

Under such circumstances, investors would want to buy 1-year bonds and sell any 2-year bonds they might own. Why? First of all, who would want to invest in long-term bonds and lock in the prevailing 6 percent yield when interest rates are expected to rise to 12 percent in the future? Most investors would prefer to buy short-term securities, wait for interest rates to rise, and then buy long-term bonds and lock in the higher interest rate.

To invest over a 2-year investment horizon, a profit-maximizing investor in our example would examine the alternatives of (1) buying a 2-year bond or (2) buying two successive 1-year bonds. The investor would then select the alternative with the highest yield over the 2-year holding period. Specifically, if an investor buys a 1-year bond that currently yields 6 percent and at the end of the year buys another 1-year bond expected to yield 12 percent, the average expected holding-period yield for the 2-year period is 9 percent $[\frac{1}{2}(6 + 12)]$.[2] Alternatively, if the investor purchases a 2-year security, the 2-year holding-period yield is only

---

[1] The expectation theory was first stated by Irving Fisher (see Chapter 4, People & Events) and was further developed by the British Nobel laureate in economics, Sir John Hicks.

[2] To keep things simple, we ignore interest-on-interest in the second year.

6 percent. Naturally, profit-maximizing investors begin to buy 1-year bonds, driving their price up and yield down. Simultaneously, investors sell 2-year bonds, driving their price down and yield up. The net effect of this portfolio adjustment is to shift the prevailing yield curve from flat to ascending, as shown in the following yield curve.

bond purchase → price up and yield down

bond sale → price down and yield up

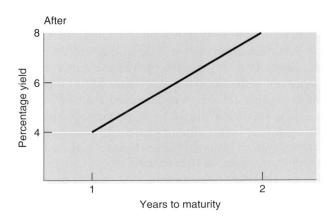

The process of buying 1-year bonds and selling 2-year bonds continues until any differential in expected returns over the 2-year investment period is eliminated. That condition *could* occur when the yields on 1-year securities equal 4 percent, the 2-year securities yield 8 percent, and the 1-year forward rate remains 12 percent. With this term structure, an investor who purchases a 2-year bond will have a 2-year holding-period yield of 8 percent. This is identical to the investor who purchases a 4 percent 1-year security and then reinvests the proceeds at the end of the first year in the bonds expected to yield 12 percent [$^1/_2(4 + 12)$]. This is an equilibrium condition because under either alternative the investor's average holding-period return is the same. That is, investors are indifferent between the yield on a 2-year security and the average holding-period yield they can earn when investing in two successive 1-year securities.

THE TERM–STRUCTURE FORMULA

Although simplified, the example in the preceding section illustrates that investors can trade among securities of different maturities and, if they are profit maximizers, obtain an equilibrium return across the entire spectrum of maturities. This implies a formal relationship between long- and short-term interest rates. Specifically, the long-term rate of interest is a geometric average of the current short-term interest rate and a series of expected short-term forward rates. More formally, the yield on a bond maturing n years from now is

$$(1 + {}_tR_n) = [(1 + {}_tR_1)(1 + {}_{t+1}f_1)(1 + {}_{t+2}f_1) \ . \ . \ . \ (1 + {}_{t+n-1}f_1)]^{1/n}, \qquad (6.1)$$

where:

     R = the observed (spot or actual) market interest rate
     f = the forward, or future, interest rate
     t = time period for which the rate is applicable
     n = maturity of the bond

The postscript identifies the maturity (*n*) of the security, and the prescript represents the time period in which the security originates (*t*). Thus, $_tR_1$ is the actual market rate of interest on a 1-year security today (time *t*), also called the **spot rate**; similarly, $_tR_{10}$ is the current market rate of interest for a 10-year security. For the forward rates, the prescript still identifies the time period in which the security originates, but now it represents the number of years in the future; thus $_{t+1}f_1$ refers to the 1-year interest rate 1 year in the future; likewise, $_{t+2}f_1$ is the 1-year interest rate 2 years from now, and so on.

Do not panic—the geometric average is not as difficult to apply as it looks. Let's consider an example. Suppose the current 1-year rate is 6 percent. Further, the market expects the 1-year rate a year from now to be 8 percent and the 1-year rate 2 years from now to be 10 percent. Using our notation,

$$_tR_1 = 6 \text{ percent};$$
$$_{t+1}f_1 = 8 \text{ percent; and}$$
$$_{t+2}f_1 = 10 \text{ percent.}$$

Given the market's expectation of future interest rates, we can calculate the current 3-year rate of interest by applying Equation 6.1:

$$(1 + {}_tR_3) = [(1.06)(1.08)(1.10)]^{1/3}$$
$$_tR_3 = 1.08 - 1$$
$$_tR_3 = 0.08 \text{ or } 8.0\%.$$

Notice that an investor with a 3-year investment horizon will be indifferent between buying a 3-year security yielding 8 percent and buying three successive 1-year securities that will also yield, on average, 8 percent.[3]

The reason for developing Equation 6.1 was not to dazzle you with mathematical footwork but to show how investors' expectations of future interest rates determine the shape of the yield curve. For example, when short-term interest rates are expected to rise in the future (as in our previous example), the yield curve will be upward sloping. This must be true, since the long-term interest rate is an average of the current and the future expected short-term interest rates. Likewise, if the market expects future short-term interest rates to decrease, the yield curve will be downward sloping. If no change is expected in future short-term rates, the yield curve will be flat. The behavioral implications of the yield curve from the expectation theory are as follows:

Expected Interest Rate Movement	Observed Yield Curve
Market expects interest rates to increase	Upward sloping
Market expects interest rates to decline	Downward sloping
Market expects interest rates to stay the same	Flat

---

[3] For students who have difficulty understanding the behavioral implications of Equation 6.1, the geometric mean can be approximated with the following simpler arithmetic mean formula:

$$_tR_n = \frac{1}{n} [{}_tR_1 + {}_{t+1}f_1 + {}_{t+2}f_1 \cdots {}_{t+n-1}f_1]$$

For our example,

$$_tR_3 = \frac{1}{3} [6 + 8 + 10] = 8.0\%.$$

But keep in mind that this approximation ignores the interest-on-interest.

USING THE TERM STRUCTURE FORMULA TO CALCULATE IMPLIED FORWARD RATES

Under the expectations hypothesis it is possible to calculate the forward interest rates implied by a set of spot interest rates. Suppose, for example, we know that the 1-year spot rate ($_tR_1$) is 6 percent, the 2-year spot rate ($_tR_2$) is 8 percent, and the 3-year spot rate ($_tR_3$) is 10 percent. Using this information, we can calculate the forward rates on a 1-year bond originating 1 year from now ($_{t+1}f_1$) and a 1-year bond originating 2 years from now ($_{t+2}f_1$). All we need to remember is that Equation 6.1 holds when the bond market is in equilibrium.

To find the **implied forward rate** on a 1-year bond originating 1 year in the future, set up Equation 6.1 as follows:

$$(1 + {_tR_2})^2 = (1 + {_tR_1})(1 + {_{t+1}f_1}).$$

Substituting the known information, we obtain

$$(1.08)^2 = (1.06)(1 + {_{t+1}f_1}).$$

Simplify and solve for $_{t+1}f_1$:

$$_{t+1}f_1 = (1.17/1.06) - 1 = 0.10 \ (10\%).$$

Thus, the set of spot rates implies that investors expect the 1-year interest rate 1 year from now to be 10 percent.

Similarly, we can solve for the implied forward rate on a 1-year bond originating 2 years from now using the information in the 2- and 3-year spot rates:

$$(1.10)^3 = (1.08)^2(1 + {_{t+1}f_1}).$$

Solving for $_{t+2}f_1$, we obtain 14 percent. Thus, you can see the relationship between spot rates and forward rates.

In general, we can find the forward rate implied by two spot rates of adjacent maturities with the following formula, which is a straightforward simplification of Equation 6.1:

$$[(1 + {_tR_n})^n/(1 + {_tR_{n-1}})^{n-1}] - 1 = {_{t+n-1}f_1}. \tag{6.2}$$

TERM STRUCTURE AND LIQUIDITY PREMIUMS

We have seen that the expectation theory assumes that investors are indifferent between purchasing long-term or short-term securities. However, this usually is not true. Investors know from experience that short-term securities provide greater marketability (more active secondary markets) and have smaller price fluctuations (price risk) than do long-term securities. As a result, borrowers who seek long-term funds to finance capital projects must pay lenders a **liquidity premium** to purchase riskier long-term securities. Thus the yield curve must have a liquidity premium added to it. The liquidity premium increases as maturity increases, because the longer the maturity of a security, the greater its price risk and the less marketable the security. The liquidity premium therefore causes the observed

---

EXHIBIT 6.2
The Effect of Liquidity Premiums on the Yield Curve

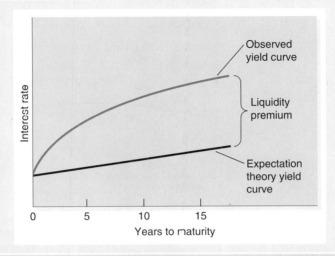

Liquidity premiums increase as maturity increases. Thus liquidity premiums cause an upward slope in market yield curves

---

yield curve to be more upward sloping than that predicted by the expectation theory. Exhibit 6.2 illustrates this effect.

THE MARKET SEGMENTATION AND PREFERRED-HABITAT THEORIES

The **market segmentation** theory, which differs sharply from the expectation approach, maintains that market participants have strong preferences for securities of a particular maturity and that they buy and sell securities consistent with these maturity preferences. As a result, the yield curve is determined by the supply of and the demand for securities at or near a particular maturity. Investors, such as commercial banks, who desire short-term securities determine the short-term yield curve; investors with preferences for intermediate maturities determine the intermediate-term yield curve; and investors who prefer long-term securities, such as pension funds and life insurance companies, determine the long-term yield curve. On the supply side, security issuers tailor the maturities of their security offerings to the length of time they need the borrowed funds (see Exhibit 6.3). Thus the market segmentation theory assumes that both issuers and investors have a preference for securities with a narrow maturity range. Changes in interest rates in one segment of the yield curve, therefore, will have little effect on interest rates in other maturities. Under the segmentation theory, discontinuities in the yield curve are possible. The segmentation theory is extreme in that it assumes that certain investors are almost completely risk averse, which means that they will not shift the maturity of their holdings in exchange for higher yields.

The preferred-habitat theory extends the segmentation theory and explains why we do not observe discontinuities in the yield curve. The **preferred-habitat**

EXHIBIT 6.3
Market Segmentation Yield Curve

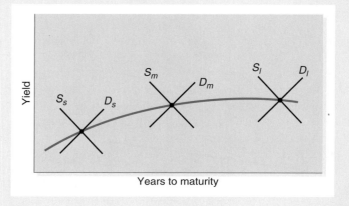

Market segmentation theory suggests that borrowers and lenders have strong preferences for securities of a particular maturity. As a result, the supply and demand for securities at or near a particular maturity determine the yield for that maturity.

Note: Supply *(S)* and demand *(D)* for *s* = short-term maturities, *m* = intermediate-term maturities, and *l* = long-term maturities.

---

theory asserts that investors will not hold debt securities outside of their preferred habitat (maturity preference) without an additional reward in the form of a risk premium. Holding longer-term assets than desired exposes the investor to price risk and holding shorter-term assets than desired exposes the investor to reinvestment risk; thus, leaving one's preferred habitat requires compensation for the additional risk. Unlike market segmentation theory, the preferred-habitat theory does not assume that investors are completely risk averse; instead it allows investors to reallocate their portfolios in response to expected yield premiums. The preferred-habitat theory can explain humps or twists in the yield curve but does not allow for discontinuities in the yield curve as would be possible under the segmentation theory.

WHICH THEORY IS RIGHT?

Available evidence is not sufficiently persuasive to establish any one theory as being totally correct in explaining the term structure of interest rates. Market participants tend to favor the preferred-habitat theory, whereas economists tend to favor the expectation and liquidity premium approaches. Day-to-day changes in the term structure reveal patterns that are most consistent with the preferred-habitat theory. Changes in interest rates in one segment of the maturity spectrum appear not to be immediately transmitted to other segments. Furthermore, yield curves are not always smooth. For longer periods of time, such as month to month, interest rate changes in one maturity segment appear to be transmitted throughout the yield curve and yield curves appear relatively smooth. These observations are consistent with most published studies on the term structure that support the role of liquidity premiums and expectations of interest rates as important components of any interpretation of the term structure.

YIELD CURVES AND THE BUSINESS CYCLE

The yield curve is an analytical tool widely employed by financial analysts and managers of financial institutions. As we previously discussed, the term structure of interest rates provides information about the market's expectations of future business activity. If the yield curve is upward sloping, the consensus of market participants is that interest rates will increase in the future. Since interest rates and the business cycle are procyclical, increasing interest rates imply that market participants expect a period of economic expansion.

Similarly, if the yield curve is downward sloping, the market expects interest rates to decline in the future and, therefore, slower economic growth. In fact, descending yield curves are common near the final phase of a period of economic expansion. This fact has led many practitioners to believe that inverted yield curves predict a recession. While it is true that inverted yield curves have preceded many recessions during the postwar period, it can also be said that inverted yield curves have predicted more recessions than have actually occurred. In other words, this rule of thumb is not infallible. The relationship between the yield curve and the business cycle is summarized in Exhibit 6.4.

EXHIBIT 6.4
Interest Rate and Yield Curve Patterns over the Business Cycle

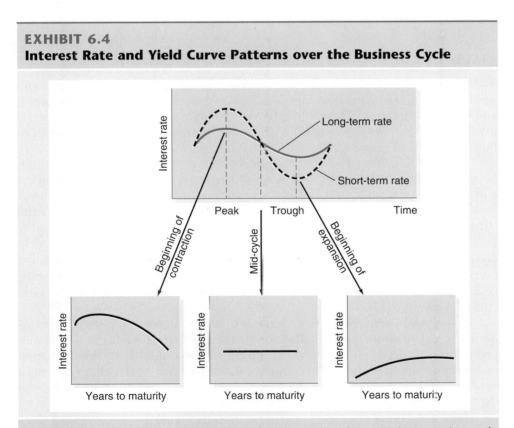

Yield curves are typically upward sloping during periods of economic expansion and turn downward when the economy begins to contract.

In financial markets, the most commonly observed yield curve is upward sloping. This comes as no surprise because upward-sloping yield curves are typically observed during period of business expansion and, postwar, the *average* period of expansion has been around 4 years. However, not every business cycle conforms to the average. For example, the last period of economic expansion lasted 10 years (1990–2000)!

Downward-sloping and level yield curves are seen less frequently and are typically viewed briefly near the end of a period of expansion. Periods of economic contraction tend to be short and, since the postwar period, the average has been about 9 months. Again, 9 months is an average value and actual periods of economic contraction can be much longer or shorter.

Predicting Interest Rates.   Everyone wants to predict the future. Some practitioners believe that the shape of the yield curve, which contains implicit consensus forecasts of future interest rates, can be used to predict the direction of interest rate movements and, hence, future economic activity. This subject is highly technical and controversial, with little agreement among practitioners.

To put the yield curve "prediction" issue in perspective, yield curves do provide information about market expectations of future interest rate movements or business activity. However, as with any expectations, they may not be realized. The yield curve observed at any point in time represents the market's best interpretation of the economic data available. As new information becomes available, expectations are revised.

YIELD CURVES AND FINANCIAL INTERMEDIARIES

The slope of the yield curve is important in managing financial intermediaries such as commercial banks, savings and loan associations, mutual savings banks, and finance companies. These and other intermediaries borrow funds in financial markets from surplus spending units and, after intermediation, lend the funds to businesses and consumers.

An upward-sloping yield curve is generally favorable for these institutions because they borrow most of their funds in the short term (transaction accounts and time deposits) and lend the funds at longer maturities, such as consumer loans, automobile loans, and home mortgages. For example, a bank borrows from consumers at 3 percent and makes 5-year automobile loans for 5 percent; the bank's gross profit margin is 2 percent (5 − 3). Clearly, the more steeply the yield curve slopes upward, the wider the *spread* between the borrowing and lending rates and the greater the profit for the financial intermediaries. At the beginning of a period of economic expansion, interest rates tend to be low and the yield curve is upward sloping.

When yield curves begin to flatten out or slope downward, different portfolio management strategies are called for. As the yield curve begins to flatten out, profits are squeezed and management must institute a number of cost reduction measures to rein in costs to help restore profitability. Typical tactics are to reduce headcount, shorten "banking" hours, increase fee-based income, and eliminate the "free" coffee and doughnuts to customers in the lobby.

If the yield curve is near the top of the business cycle and is downward sloping, financial institutions will typically try to shorten the maturity of their liabilities (sources of funds), thereby avoiding locking in relatively expensive sources of funds for a longer period of time; simultaneously, financial institutions will try to lengthen the maturity of their loans. The key strategy here is to get borrowers to lock in relatively high borrowing rates for long periods of time in anticipation that interest rates will decline in the future.

Continuing our example, assume that we are now at the top of the business cycle: interest rates are higher and the yield curve is inverted. Say, consumer deposit rates are now at $6\frac{1}{2}$ percent and 5-year auto loans are at 6 percent; the bank's gross margin is now a negative $\frac{1}{2}$ percent $(6 - 6\frac{1}{2})$. This is bad news. However, if bank management believes that in the short run interest rates will return to their normal level (our original rate structure), they should continue to make auto loans at 6 percent. Then, when interest rates decline as expected, consumer funds will cost the bank 3 percent, and the bank's gross profit margin on its portfolio of auto loans will be close to 3 percent $(6 - 3)$. On the other hand, if interest rates do not decline or, worse, rise even higher, the bank could be in serious financial trouble. Our discussion of how the management of financial intermediaries reacts to changes in the yield curve over the business cycles is summarized below:

Business Cycle	Yield Curve Slope	Interest Rates	Strategy
Beginning of expansion	Upward	Low	Borrow short term Lend Long term
Mid-cycle	Flat	High	Profits squeeze and cost reduction strategies
Beginning of contraction	Downward	Higher	Shorten maturity of liabilities Lengthen maturity of loans

DO YOU UNDERSTAND?

1. If you know interest rates are going to rise in the future, would you rather own a long- or a short-term bond? Explain.

2. Suppose the spot rate on 4-year bonds is 11 percent and the spot rate on 5-year bonds is 12 percent. What forward rate is implied on a 1-year bond delivered 4 years from now?

3. What bond portfolio adjustments would investors make if interest rates are expected to decline in the future? How do these adjustments cause the yield curve to change?

4. How does the existence of a liquidity premium affect the shape of the yield curve?

5. Why, under the market segmentation theory, do investors not shift their holdings into the securities with the highest returns? Under the preferred-habitat theory, what is necessary for investors to shift their holdings away from their preferred maturities?

DEFAULT RISK

A debt security includes a formal promise by the borrower to pay the lender coupon payments and principal payments according to a predetermined schedule. Failure on the part of the borrower to meet any condition of the bond contract constitutes **default**. **Default risk** refers to the possibility of not collecting the promised amount of interest or principal at the agreed time.

It is believed that most investors are risk averse in that if the expected returns from two investments are identical except for risk, the investors will prefer the security whose return is most certain. Therefore, to induce investors to purchase securities that possess default risk, borrowers must compensate lenders for the potential financial injury they may incur by purchasing risky securities. A security's default risk can be measured as the difference between the rate paid on a risky security and the rate paid on a default-free security, with all factors other than default risk being held constant.

The **default risk premium** may be expressed as

$$DRP = i - i_{rf}, \tag{6.3}$$

where DRP is the default risk premium, i is the promised yield to maturity on the security, and i_{rf} is the yield on a comparable default-free security. Yields on U.S. Treasury securities are the best estimates for the default-free rate. The larger the default risk premium, the higher the probability of default and the higher the security's market yield.

Market default risk premiums can be computed by comparing Treasury securities with risky securities of similar term to maturity and other issue characteristics. Exhibit 6.5 shows some typical risk premiums for selected securities. For example, the 90-basis-point default risk premium on Aaa-rated corporate bonds represents the market consensus of the amount of compensation that investors must be paid to induce them to buy risky bonds instead of default-free bonds (100 basis points = 1 percent). Also notice that as credit quality declines, the default risk premium increases.

Default risk premiums are not abstract notions, as can be attested by those who owned Penn Central debt securities when that company declared bankruptcy

---

EXHIBIT 6.5
Risk Premiums for Selected Securities (May 2004)

Security	Security Yield (%)	Equivalent Risk-Free Rate[a] (%)	Risk Premium (%)
Corporate bonds: Aaa	5.85	4.81	1.04
Corporate bonds: Aa	6.13	4.81	1.32
Corporate bonds: A	6.33	4.81	1.52
Corporate bonds: Baa	6.79	4.81	1.98

Notice that as bond-rating quality declines, the default risk premium increases.

[a] 10-year Treasury note yield.
Source: Federal Reserve Statistical Release H. 15 and Dow Jones Market Data.

in June 1970, precipitating the largest corporate failure in American financial history at that time, which has been recently eclipsed by the Enron failure. Other well-publicized defaults include that of New York City on its municipal bonds in 1975, the Braniff Airlines default in 1982, the failure of the Washington Public Power Supply System ("Whoops") in 1983 (the largest municipal default in history), the LTV Steel Company default in 1986, and the Texaco default in 1987. The year 2001 was the pits when it came to bond defaults—four of the largest defaults, in U.S. history occurred: Southern California Edison ($12 billion), Pacific Gas & Electric ($8 billion), Finova ($6 billion), and Enron (potentially $15 billion). Three of these four defaults were in the energy industry.

DEFAULT RISK AND THE BUSINESS CYCLE

Default risk premiums, as shown in Exhibit 6.6, vary systematically over the business cycle. They tend to widen during periods of economic decline and narrow during periods of economic expansion.

EXHIBIT 6.6
Default Risk Premiums (Yield Spreads between Corporate and U.S. Treasury Notes)

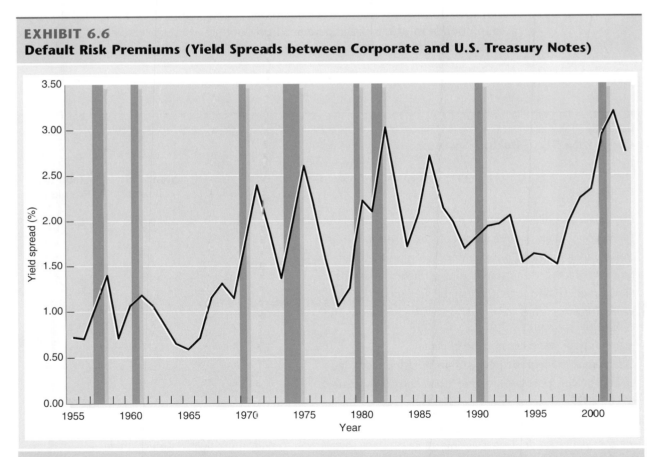

Notice that the default risk premium increases during periods of economic contraction and decreases during periods of economic expansion.

Note: Shaded areas indicate periods of economic recession. Corporate bonds are Baa rated. Treasury securities are 10-year Notes.
Source: Federal Reserve Board of Governors, H. 15 Statistical Release.

The pattern of behavior for default risk premiums is attributable to changes in investor willingness to own bonds of different credit ratings over the business cycle—the so-called *flight-to-quality* argument. Specifically, during periods of economic prosperity, investors are willing to hold bonds with low credit ratings in their portfolios because there is little chance of default and these bonds normally have higher yields. During such times, investors tend to seek out the highest-yielding investments. On the other hand, during a recession, the prime concern of investors becomes safety. As a result, there is a flight to quality as investors adjust their portfolios—buying bonds with high credit ratings (low default risk) and selling from their portfolios bonds with low credit ratings. The increase in demand for high-grade bonds drives their price up and their yield down; correspondingly, a decrease in demand for bonds with low credit ratings drives their price down and their yield up. The result is the increase in default risk premiums during periods of economic recession.

BOND RATINGS

Investors typically do not formulate the probability of default themselves but employ **bond ratings**, which are credit ratings assigned by rating agencies, principally Moody's Investors Service (Moody's) and Standard & Poor's (S&P). Both rank bonds in order of the perceived probability of their default and publish the ratings as letter grades. The rating schemes they use are shown in Exhibit 6.7.

EXHIBIT 6.7
Corporate Bond Rating Systems

Explanation	Moody's	Standard & Poor's	Default Risk Premium
Best quality, smallest degree of risk	Aaa	AAA	Lowest
High quality, slightly more long-term risk than top rating	Aa	AA	—
Upper-medium grade, possible impairment in the future	A	A	—
Medium grade, lack outstanding investment characteristics	Baa	BBB	—
Speculative issues, protection may be very moderate	Ba	BB	—
Very speculative, may have small assurance of interest and principal payments	B	B	—
Issues in poor standing, may be in default	Caa	CCC	—
Speculative in a high degree, with marked shortcomings	Ca	CC	—
Lowest quality, poor prospects of attaining real investment standing	C	C	Highest

Investment-grade bonds are those rated Baa or above by Moody's (or BBB by Standard & Poor's). Bonds below Baa are speculative grade. Financial institutions are typically allowed to purchase only investment grade.

Note: Moody's applies the modifiers 1, 2, and 3 to the ratings Aa to Caa, with a 1 indicating the issue is in the higher end of its rating, a 2 indicating it is in the mid-range, and a 3 indicating it is in the lower end. Similarly, Standard & Poor's modifies its ratings AA to CCC with a + or – to indicate when an issue is in the higher or lower end of its rating category.

The highest-grade bonds, those with the lowest default risk, are rated Aaa (AAA). The default risk premium on corporate bonds increases as the bond rating becomes lower.

Bonds rated in the top four rating categories—Aaa to Baa for Moody's and AAA to BBB for Standard & Poor's—are called **investment-grade bonds**. Bonds rated below Baa (or BBB) are called **speculative-grade bonds** or **junk bonds**. The distinction between investment grade and speculative grade is important because state and federal laws frequently require commercial banks, insurance companies, pension funds, and other financial institutions to purchase only securities rated as investment grade.

Important questions to ask are how bond credit ratings do as a measure of default risk and whether investment-grade bonds have fewer defaults than bonds ranked below investment grade. Shown below is the percentage of bond issues that defaulted over the last 15 years as rated by Standard & Poor's.[4] The first column shows the bond rating at the time the bond issue was sold. Notice that as bond credit quality decreases, the percent of bonds defaulting increases monotonically. That is, 0.52 percent of the AAA-rated bonds defaulted over the 15-year period, 1.31 percent of the AA-rated bonds defaulted, 2.32 percent of the A-rated bonds defaulted, and so on. We conclude that bond credit ratings do a reasonable job of ranking bonds with respect to their underlying credit quality.

Rating at Time of Issue	Default Rate (%)
AAA	0.52
AA	1.31
A	2.32
BBB	6.64
BB	19.52
B	35.76
CCC	54.38

The default rates for investment-grade bonds—those ranked BBB or better—were significantly lower than for any of the non-investment-grade categories. For example, the default rate on BBB-rated bonds was 6.64 percent, the default rate on BB-rated bonds—one ranking notch lower—was 19.52 percent, and the default rate for CCC-rated bonds was 54.38 percent. Overall, we conclude that bond ratings are a reasonable measure of default risk.

HOW CREDIT RATINGS ARE DETERMINED

Moody's Investors Services (Moody's) and Standard & Poor's (S&P) are the two main credit-rating agencies. Collectively, they provide more than 92 percent of all corporate and municipal debt credit ratings each year. The credit rating of a firm's

[4] Data from Standard & Poor's Corporation, 2004.

debt is a measure of the firm's default risk in the opinion of the rating agency. In making this determination, bond-rating agencies consider a number of factors when assigning a bond rating. Among the most important are (1) the firm's expected cash flow; (2) the amount of the firm's fixed contractual cash payments, such as interest and principal payments or lease payments; (3) the length of time the firm has been profitable; and (4) the variability of the firm's earnings. Once a bond rating is assigned to a particular issue, the rating is periodically reviewed by the rating agency and is subject to change.

To give you an idea of how bond ratings work, we briefly describe the credit-rating process of Moody's. A first-time rating begins with a request from the debt issuer. The process starts with an introductory meeting in which Moody's discusses its procedures and the specific types of data most useful in understanding the credit quality of the issuer. Moody's does not do an exhaustive analysis of the issuer; instead, it focuses on elements relevant to the long-term and short-term credit risk of the issuer. An analytical meeting with the issuer's senior management follows the initial meeting.

The analytical meeting takes place at the issuer's headquarters and often takes as long as 2 days. Moody's focuses the meeting on five key subjects:

1. Background and history of the company
2. Corporate strategy and philosophy
3. Operating position—including competitive position, manufacturing capacity, distribution and supply networks, and marketing
4. Financial management and accounting policies
5. Other topics—derivatives usage, regulatory developments, investment opportunities, and major litigation

Through the discussion of these topics with senior management, Moody's develops an understanding of management's philosophy and plans for the future, which is considered a critical element of credit quality. The discussions also give senior management the chance to discuss the risks and opportunities of the firm that affect credit quality and outline their plans to address them.

The rating decision usually takes 4 to 6 weeks from the time of the analytical meeting, and the decision is made by a rating committee that analyzes all the information collected about the issuer. The committee generally has four or more members, including the lead industry analyst. When the committee makes its decision, it notifies the issuer of the rating and Moody's rationale for the rating. The rating is also distributed worldwide through the major financial media.

Obviously, the firm's default risk and, thus, its credit rating change over time. Because things change, Moody's continuously gathers information on all debt issuers that it has rated. When new information about an issuer suggests a possible change in default risk, Moody's forms a rating committee to review the issuer's credit rating. If the committee decides to change a credit rating, it notifies the issuer and the financial press.

From this process, it is obvious that there is not a right answer. Instead, credit rating requires expert analysts to reach an informed opinion about the default risk of the issuer. Also, for a rating to change, the new information about the issuer must be sufficient for the experts to change their opinion about the default risk of the issuer.

Following the Enron bankruptcy on December 2, 2001, credit-rating agencies found themselves under attack by investors and the target of congressional ire. What attracted all of the attention was the failure of the credit-rating agencies to recognize the extent of Enron's financial problems and the slow pace at which they downgraded the energy trader in its final months. Despite growing questions about its partnerships and other irregular deals, the rating agencies still had Enron at an investment-grade credit rating just 4 days before its final implosion!

As it turns out, only three credit-rating agencies are authorized by federal banking regulators and the Securities and Exchange Commission (SEC) to appraise the creditworthiness of corporate and government bond issues, creating a troika that wields enormous influence over the investment decisions of financial institutions and individual investors. How did this cozy arrangement come about and what problems has it created?

The three credit-rating agencies—Moody's, Standard & Poor's, and Fitch—owe their elite status to two regulatory decrees. In 1936, the Comptroller of the Currency decreed that banks could hold only investment-grade securities and the responsibility to assess default risk was delegated to credit-rating agencies. Other regulatory agencies followed suit, and soon insurance companies, mutual funds, and other financial institutions had to pay attention to bond ratings. The upshot was that any company, municipality, or government unit that wanted access to the U.S. capital markets needed a credit rating, preferably an investment-grade rating, which is BBB or above. Further strengthening the position of the three rating agencies was a ruling in 1975 by the SEC that brokerage firms had to discount below-investment-grade bonds when calculating their assets and that the bond rating had to come from an approved "nationally recognized statistical rating organization."

Criticism of the credit-rating agencies runs deep, and it is not new. Critics charge that the rating agencies are slow to downgrade a firm's credit standing and often fail to recognize firms that are in serious financial trouble before they default. Over the years, the demise of many large business firms has played out in a pattern of events similar to that of Enron, and some firms even retained their investment-grade status on the day they declared bankruptcy. Not helping matters politically have been the exceptionally high profits that the three franchise players have been able to extract from the market. Moody's recently released its earnings for the first time ever, and its 50 percent operating margin left little doubt why other firms would like to get into the rating business.

Critics argue that allowing additional credit-rating firms to expand the troika would increase competition, resulting in better, more accurate, and more timely credit ratings. The jolt of competition, they claim, would also stimulate more innovative solutions to problems. Other critics have suggested that the special status of rating agencies should be abolished altogether. They would put the responsibility of determining the creditworthiness of a bank's bond portfolio back on banks and bank regulators. Individual investors would then purchase bond credit ratings, if they desired, from any crediting agency they deemed to be reputable. Some suggest that ratings could be replaced by *credit spreads*—the difference between a yield on the security being evaluated and the yield on a risk-free security of similar maturity, such as a Treasury security.

Despite all the carping, it is probably unlikely that bank regulators or the SEC will dismantle the current regulatory structure and open up the gates to all comers. Regulators' biggest fear is that issuers would shop around for the highest credit rating. Furthermore, to gain the status and reputation to rate firms would require a substantial amount of capital and time. Small niche players would have little impact on the credit-rating market and are also vulnerable to market pressures. However, the threat of potential competition, bad publicity, and pressure from regulators has stimulated some changes by the major credit-rating agencies. More recently, they have been much more aggressive and quicker to down rate companies with deteriorating financial conditions. They also have begun using more sophisticated quantitative risk models that estimate the probability of default and that can be updated as new data become available.

TAX TREATMENT

The interest rate most relevant to investors is the rate of return earned *after taxes*. Thus, the lower the taxes on the income from a security, the greater the demand for the security and the lower its before-tax yield. It is no surprise, therefore, that tax-exempt securities have lower market yields than similar taxable securities. Federal, state, and local governments impose a variety of taxes on income from securities, the most important of which is the federal income tax. Let us consider the effect that the tax structure has on the market yield of a security.

COUPON INCOME

All coupon income earned on state and local government debt is exempt from federal taxes. Thus securities issued by state and local governments (called **municipal securities**) sell for lower market yields than comparable securities issued by the U.S. Treasury or private corporations. The exemption of coupon income from federal taxes stems from the separation of federal and state powers, and its primary purpose is to help state and local governments borrow at lower interest rates than would otherwise be possible.[5]

The decision by an investor to purchase either a taxable or a tax-exempt security depends on the relative yields between the two securities and the investor's marginal tax rate. To see how investors make this decision, consider the following example. Assume that the current yield-to-maturity on a taxable corporate bond is 10 percent, whereas the current tax-exempt yield on a municipal bond of comparable maturity and bond rating is 7 percent. The after-tax yield on the two securities can be compared using the following formula:

$$i_{at} = i_{bt}(1 - t), \tag{6.4}$$

where i_{at} is the after-tax yield on the security, i_{bt} is the before-tax yield, and t is the marginal tax rate of the investor. The equation assumes that the return on the securities is composed entirely of coupon income, with no capital gains. The after-tax yields on the two bonds are as follows for investors in a variety of different tax brackets:

Investors' Marginal Tax Rate	Municipal Yield	Corporate After-Tax Yield
0%	7%	10 (1 − 0.00) = 10.0%
10	7	10 (1 − 0.10) = 9.0
20	7	10 (1 − 0.20) = 8.0
30	7	10 (1 − 0.30) = 7.0
40	7	10 (1 − 0.40) = 6.0
50	7	10 (1 − 0.50) = 5.0

[5] During April 1988, the Supreme Court ruled that Congress is free to tax all coupon interest on state and local government bonds. Overturning a major 1895 precedent, the court held that the Constitution does not protect state and local governments against federal taxation of interest received by a holder of municipal bonds. Currently, there is no movement in Congress to tax municipal bonds, but the potential to do so is now there. If the federal government were to tax municipal securities, it would most likely apply only to new bond issues and not to outstanding bonds.

For example, an investor in the 20 percent tax bracket would buy a corporate security, because the after-tax return is 8 percent versus 7 percent for the municipal security. However, as the investor's marginal tax rate increases, the return on municipal securities becomes more favorable compared to the after-tax return on corporate bonds. An investor in the 40 percent tax bracket would prefer a tax-exempt security yielding 7 percent to the corporate security, for which the after-tax return is only 6 percent. The rule that emerges is that investors in high tax brackets, such as wealthy and fully taxed corporations (e.g., commercial banks), usually hold portfolios of municipal securities because of their higher after-tax yield compared to taxable securities of the same risk and maturity. In contrast, investors in lower tax brackets, such as persons with low incomes and tax-exempt institutions (e.g., pension funds), receive high after-tax yields from taxable securities because they pay fewer taxes. On a personal note, discussing your municipal bond portfolio at a cocktail party subtly identifies you as an upper-income person without your actually saying so.

Exhibit 6.8 illustrates how the differential tax treatment of long-term municipal bonds affects their yields relative to long-term corporate and Treasury bonds. As you can see from the exhibit, Aaa-rated municipal bonds have

EXHIBIT 6.8
Tax-Exempt and Taxable Yields

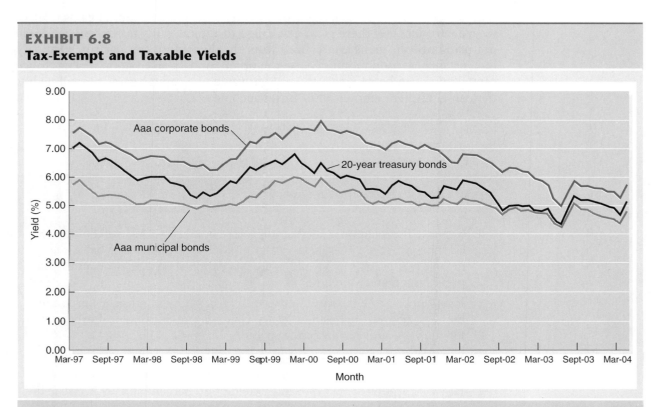

Because their coupon payments are tax exempt, the yield on municipal bonds is lower than the yield on similar securities.

Source: Federal Reserve Board of Governors, H.15 Statistical Release.

lower yields than either corporate bonds or Treasury bonds. It might seem odd that Aaa-rated municipal bonds have *lower* yields than those of Treasury bonds because municipal bonds have default risk and Treasury bonds do not. Don't forget, however, that the coupon income on Treasury bonds is subject to income tax, whereas municipal bonds are tax exempt. Apparently the tax benefit of owning the municipal bond offsets its increased default risk compared to the Treasury bond. Similarly, Aaa-rated municipal bonds have lower yields than Aaa corporate bonds because of the tax treatment of municipal bond income.

CAPITAL GAINS INCOME

From 1921 through 1986, long-term capital gains were taxed at substantially lower rates than ordinary income. For example, in 1986, long-term capital gains were taxed at 40 percent of the tax rate on ordinary income. During this period, taxable bonds trading at a discount from their par value had lower market yields than comparable bonds with coupon rates selling at or above par. The reason was that part of the income to the investor on the discounted bonds—the capital gain—was subject to the lower capital-gains tax rate. The tax law change that took effect in 1987 eliminated the tax differential, and thus capital-gains income was taxed as ordinary income. However, with the Taxpayer Relief Act of 1997 and the Reform Act of 1998, capital gains are once again taxed at a lower rate than ordinary income. Regardless of how the tax law treats capital gains relative to ordinary income, there is an advantage to capital gains in that the taxes are not paid until the gains are realized from the disposal of the security. Ordinary income such as coupon interest, on the other hand, is taxed upon receipt. Since capital gains can be deferred, the present value of a capital-gains tax will be less than an equivalent amount of ordinary income tax.

DO YOU UNDERSTAND?

1. Suppose the yield on a 30-year corporate bond rated Aaa is 8.86 percent and the yield on a 30-year Treasury bond is 8.27 percent. What is the default risk premium? Would you expect a higher or lower default risk premium on an A-rated bond?

2. How does the yield spread between Treasury bonds and risky corporate bonds vary over the business cycle? Can you provide a logical explanation for the cyclical behavior of the spread?

3. What factors do rating agencies consider when assigning bond ratings?

4. At what marginal tax rate would you be indifferent between an A-rated, 10-year corporate bond offering a yield of 10 percent and an A-rated, 10-year municipal bond offering a yield of 6 percent? Why does the municipal bond offer a lower rate if it has the same bond rating and maturity as the corporate bond?

The interest rate on securities also varies with the degree of marketability. **Marketability** refers to the cost and quickness with which investors can resell a security. The greater the marketability of a security, the greater the demand for it and the lower its yield, all other characteristics, such as maturity, default risk, and tax treatment, held constant. Marketability depends on the costs of trade, physical transfer, search, and information. The lower these costs, the greater the security's marketability.

Marketability is often gauged by the volume of a security's secondary market. For example, short-term Treasury bills have the largest and most active secondary market and are considered to be the most marketable of all securities. Investors are able to sell virtually any dollar amount of Treasury securities quickly and without disrupting the market. Similarly, the securities of many other large, well-known issuers enjoy a high degree of marketability, especially those actively traded on the New York and American exchanges. For thousands of other securities not traded actively each day, however, marketability can pose a problem. The market for these may be confined to a region or a community. As a result, trading in them may occur infrequently, and it may be difficult to establish the securities' fair market price.

Many bonds contain options that permit the borrower or lender to change the nature of the bond contract before maturity. More specifically, an option is a contract that gives the holder the right, but not the obligation, to buy or sell an asset at some specified price and date in the future. If the holder of the option has the right to buy the underlying security, the option is called a **call option (call provision)**; if the holder has the right to sell the underlying security, the option is called a **put option**; and if the option holder has the right to convert the security into another type of security, the option is called a **conversion option**. Options that are traded separately from the underlying security are discussed in Chapter 11.

CALL OPTIONS

Most corporate and municipal bonds and some U.S. government bonds contain in their contracts a call option, or as it is often referred to, a call provision. A call option (or call provision) gives the bond issuer the option to buy back the bond at a specified price in advance of the maturity date. The price is known as the **call price**, and it is usually set at the bond's par value or slightly above par (usually 1 year's interest payment above).

Bonds that contain a call option sell at a higher market yield than otherwise comparable noncallable bonds. The reason for the penalty yield on callable bonds is that the call option works to the benefit of the issuer (borrower) and to the detriment of investors. For example, if interest rates decline significantly below the coupon rate on a callable bond, the issuer can call (retire) the old bond issue and refinance it with a new one at a lower interest rate. The result of this action is that the issuer achieves an interest cost savings, but the investor is now forced to reinvest funds at the current lower market rate of interest, suffering a loss of interest income.

The difference in interest rates between callable and otherwise comparable noncallable bonds is known as the **call interest premium** and can be written as follows:

$$CIP = i_c - i_{nc} > 0, \tag{6.5}$$

where CIP is the call interest premium, i_c is the yield on a callable bond, and i_{nc} is the yield on a similar, noncallable bond. For proper comparison, the two bonds should be of similar default risk, term-to-maturity, tax treatment, and marketability. The call interest premium, therefore, is compensation paid to investors who own callable bonds for potential financial injury in the event their bonds are called. The greater the probability a particular bond will be called, the greater the call interest premium and the higher the bond's market yield. The call option is more likely to be exercised when interest rates are declining. Thus, the lower interest rates are expected to fall, the more valuable the option and, hence, the greater the CIP.

PUT OPTIONS

A put option allows an investor to sell a bond back (*put* the bond) to the issuer before maturity at a predetermined price. Investors typically exercise put options during periods when interest rates are rising and bond prices are declining. A put option sets a "floor" or minimum price of a bond at the exercise price, which is generally at or below par value.

Because the put option is an advantage to investors, bonds that contain a put option sell at lower yields than comparable nonputable bonds. The reason for the lower yield is that investors can protect themselves against capital losses due to unexpected rises in interest rates. For example, if interest rates rise significantly above the coupon rate on a putable bond, the investor can sell (put) the bond back to the issuer at the exercise price (par or near par), then buy a new bond at the current market yield. The difference in yield between putable and similar nonputable bonds is called the **put interest discount** and can be expressed as follows:

$$PID = i_p - i_{np} < 0, \tag{6.6}$$

where PID is the put interest discount, i_p is the yield on a putable bond, and i_{np} is the yield on a similar nonputable bond. The value of the put option depends upon interest rate expectations; the higher interest rates are expected to rise, the more valuable the option and, hence, the greater the interest discount.

CONVERSION OPTION

Another factor that affects the yields on different securities is a conversion option. A conversion option allows the investor to convert a security into another type of security at a predetermined price. The most common type of conversion feature is the option to convert a bond into an issuer's stock; another popular option in volatile interest rate periods is the conversion of a variable-coupon bond into a fixed-coupon bond. The timing of the conversion is at the option of the investor. However, the terms under which the conversion may take place are agreed upon when the security is purchased.

If you're at a Starbucks in the Wall Street area and you ask for a hot cocoa, you may get a hot chocolate latte or you may get a CoCo put option. *Contingent convertible bonds*, better known as CoCos, have taken Wall Street by storm over the last couple of years as the stock market began to recover from the 2001 recession.

A CoCo is similar to the convertible bonds we discussed earlier in the chapter—a bond that is convertible into a company's stock. An important feature of convertible bonds is that they allow investors to earn interest from the bond while waiting for the company's stock to increase in value. CoCos are slightly different from "plain vanilla" convertible bonds in that they can't be converted into stock until the stock price reaches a certain level.

Large business firms that can issue investment-grade bonds have issued over $40 billion worth of CoCos since they first appeared on the scene in late 2000. Issuers like CoCos because they can raise funds and pay 0 percent interest but at the same time take tax deductions on the equivalent amount of coupon interest that they would have paid on plain vanilla fixed-rate bonds.* Investors, on the other hand, must pay taxes on the equivalent amount of interest that they would have earned on the issuer's similar vanilla bonds.

You can see why issuers love CoCos. They pay 0 percent interest and get a big tax deduction to boot! Kind of like having your hot cocoa and your marshmallows, too! Believe it or not, in May 2002, the IRS blessed the arrangement. It sounds almost too good to be true if you are a corporate treasurer.

* On Wall Street, the term "vanilla" means the most common type security with no special features. For example, a vanilla bond is a bond with a fixed-coupon rate with no other special features. Likewise, the most common type of ice cream with no special features is "plain vanilla."

What about the investors? For them, the deal sounds like hot cocoa without the chocolate and the marshmallow. Depending on the structure of the CoCo, there may be "upside contingencies" or "downside contingencies" that benefit investors. For example, if the stock pays dividends, investors in CoCos may convert the bonds to stock early to reap the dividends from the stock. To prevent the early conversion of the bonds, the upside contingency will pay the holders of CoCo bonds interest equivalent to the dividends on the stock if the bond's value rises to a certain level. On the other hand, if the stock price falls, investors would have an incentive to put the bonds back to the issuer. To prevent this, the downside contingency will begin paying higher coupon interest to make the bond trade above the put price, making exercise of the put unattractive. Thus, investors get most of their return from the conversion and contingency features that kick in later.

CoCos, however, are not a free cup of cappuccino for issuers. They come with their own set of risks. They work great for issuers in bull markets when the company's stock price is increasing. While the securities can't be converted into stock until the share price hits a certain level, the investor has a put option on the bond that allows selling the bonds back to the issuer after a certain date, usually only a year or two after the issue. On the other hand, when a company's stock isn't doing well, its bonds usually aren't either. That means in a bear market, nervous investors could exercise their put options and possibly sell the bonds back to the issuer at a price higher than the original issue price. If a lot of CoCo investors decided to exercise their put options at the same time, corporations would have to scramble for cash to redeem the bonds, a situation that would send the corporate treasurers to Starbucks for a relaxing hot cocoa latte with extra sugar.

Because a conversion option is an advantage to investors, they pay higher prices (or require lower yields) for convertible securities. Thus convertible bonds have lower yields than similar bonds without this option. This difference in yield is called the **conversion yield discount** and can be expressed as follows:

$$CYD = i_{con} - i_{ncon} < 0, \qquad (6.7)$$

where CYD is the conversion yield discount, i_{con} is the yield on a convertible bond, and i_{ncon} is the yield on a similar nonconvertible bond. The conversion yield discount is the price investors are willing to pay for the conversion option.

Convertible bonds have lower yields than similar nonconvertible bonds because the investor holding a convertible bond is granted a hedge against future risk. For example, if an investor owns a bond that is convertible into common stock and the stock price falls, the investor earns a fixed rate of return in the form of interest income from the bond. If the stock price rises sufficiently, the investor can exercise the option and earn a capital gain as the stock's current market price rises above the option's exercise price. Thus the conversion option is most valuable during periods when stock market prices are rising and bond prices are declining.

For another example, suppose an investor owns a variable-coupon bond convertible into a fixed-coupon bond. If interest rates are rising, the investor would hold the variable-coupon bond and earn higher interest income as the coupon rates are adjusted upward in concert with the market rate of interest. Then, if the investor believes that interest rates are near their peak, the investor would exercise the option to convert into a fixed-coupon bond and, thus, lock in the higher rate of interest. The value of this conversion option depends on interest rate expectations; the higher interest rates are expected to rise, the more valuable the option and, hence, the greater the yield discount.

DO YOU UNDERSTAND?

1. Which securities tend to have higher yields, those that are more marketable or those that are less marketable? Why?

2. At what stage of the business cycle would you expect issuers to call in bonds? At what stage of the business cycle would you expect the call interest premium to be the highest? Explain.

3. Why do you think investors are willing to accept lower yields on putable bonds? Explain.

4. Holding the price of the firm's stock constant, would you be more likely to convert bonds into stock when interest rates are rising or falling? Explain.

CHAPTER TAKE-AWAYS

1 Yield curves represent the relationship between yield and term-to-maturity of financial instruments. Yield curves may be upward sloping, downward sloping, flat, or humped. The shapes of the yield curve are explained by several theories:

   a. The expectations theory suggests that if interest rates are expected to increase in the future, long-term rates will be higher than short-term rates, and the yield curve will slope upward. A downward-sloping curve occurs if market participants expect interest rates to decline.

   b. Liquidity premium theory suggests that risk-averse investors require yield premiums to hold longer-term securities because of greater price or liquidity risk. These yield premiums cause an upward bias in the slope of the yield curve.

   c. The market segmentation theory suggests that the shape of the yield curve is determined by the supply of and demand for securities within narrow maturity ranges.

   d. The preferred-habitat theory suggests that investors will leave their preferred maturity range if they are adequately compensated for the additional risk.

2 The greater a security's default risk, the higher the interest rate that must be paid to investors as compensation for potential financial loss and risk bearing. Risk premiums can be measured as the difference between the yield on a risky security and that of a risk-free security with the same term-to-maturity. Yields on U.S. Treasury securities are the best proxies for risk-free interest rates.

3 Most investors are concerned with after-tax yields on securities. Thus, investors require higher before-tax yields on securities whose income is taxed at higher rates. We see lower before-tax yields on securities whose income is subject to lower tax rates.

4 Marketability is the ease and quickness with which investors can resell a security. The greater the marketability of a security, the lower its interest rate.

5 A number of special options, including call provisions, put options, and conversion features, cause yields to vary across otherwise similar securities:

   a. A call provision allows an issuer to retire a security before its maturity date. Because the exercise of call options can injure investors, bonds with call options must offer higher interest rates than similar noncallable bonds.

   b. A put option allows an investor to sell a bond back to the issuer before maturity at a predetermined price. Because put options protect investors against capital losses caused by rising interest rates, putable bonds offer lower yields than similar non-putable bonds.

   c. A conversion feature allows the investor to convert a security into another type of security, allowing investors to hedge risk. Thus, convertible bonds offer lower yields than similar nonconvertible bonds.

KEY TERMS

Term-to-maturity	Liquidity premium	Investment-grade bonds	Put option
Term structure of interest rates	Market segmentation	Speculative-grade (junk) bonds	Conversion option
Yield curve	Preferred habitat	Municipal securities	Call price
Forward rate	Default	Marketability	Call interest premium
Spot rate	Default risk	Call option (call provision)	Put interest discount
Implied forward rate	Default risk premium		Conversion yield discount
	Bond ratings		

QUESTIONS AND PROBLEMS

1. Using the *Federal Reserve Bulletin* or the Federal Reserve Bank of St. Louis Web site (FRED) or the *Wall Street Journal*, plot the yield curve for U.S. Treasury securities on a quarterly basis for this year. Given your knowledge of the term structure of interest rates, what would be your economic forecast for next year?

2. Summarize the expectation theory and the preferred-habitat theory of the term structure of interest rates. Are these theories in any way related, or are they alternative explanations of the term structure?

3. A commercial bank made a 3-year term loan at 10 percent. The bank's economics department forecasts that 1 and 2 years in the future, the 1-year interest rate will be 10 percent and 14 percent, respectively. The current 1-year rate is 8 percent. Given that the bank's forecasts are reliable, has the bank set the 3-year rate correctly?

4. Define "default risk." How does the default risk premium vary over the business cycle? Explain your answer.

5. What do bond ratings measure? Explain some of the important factors in determining a security's bond rating.

6. Why do most commercial banks hold portfolios of municipal bonds and relatively few corporate bonds?

7. Explain the importance of a call provision to investors. Do callable bonds have higher or lower yields than similar noncallable bonds? Why?

8. Define "marketability". Explain why marketability of a security is important to both investor and issuer.

9. A new-issue municipal bond rated Aaa by Moody's Investors Service is priced to yield 8 percent. If you are in the 33 percent tax bracket, what yield would you need to earn on a taxable bond to be indifferent?

10. Historically, the yield curve typically has been upward sloping. Why would you expect this to be the case? (Hint: Historically, economic recessions typically last 9 to 12 months; expansions typically last 3 to 4 years.)

11. Under which scenario, rising interest rates or falling interest rates, would a bond investor be most likely to exercise a put option on a bond? Explain.

12. Suppose the 7-year spot interest rate is 9 percent and the 5-year spot rate is 6 percent. What is the implied forward rate on a 2-year bond originating 5 years from now? (Hint: Under the expectations hypothesis, in equilibrium an investor with a 7-year holding period will be indifferent between investing in a 7-year bond or a 5-year bond followed by a 2-year bond.)

13. Suppose you hold a corporate bond that is convertible into the firm's stock. Stock prices are falling and interest rates are also falling. Would it be a good idea to exercise your conversion option under these conditions? Why or why not?

14. Suppose you expect interest rates to increase in the future. You are not indifferent toward interest rate risk and desire to maximize expected return. If you hold a portfolio consisting of 50 percent short-term bonds (<1 year to maturity) and 50 percent long-term bonds, how might you adjust your portfolio to maximize your profit? Explain carefully.

15. You are the holder of a variable-coupon bond that is convertible to a fixed-coupon bond. If you expect interest rates to rise, should you exercise your conversion option? Explain. What if you expect interest rates to fall?

16. Assume that the term structure of Treasury securities includes the following rates:

Security	Annual Yield (in %)
3-month bill	4.50
6-month bill	4.57
1-year note	4.52
2-year note	4.51
3-year note	4.48

Using this information calculate: (a) the 6-month annualized yield expected in the second half of the current year, and (b) the 1-year yield expected for year 3 [Hint: To answer (a) you will need to adjust the term–structure formula for semiannual compounding.]

INTERNET EXERCISE

This exercise will allow you to observe how the yield curve has changed over the past several years and to examine how changes in the yield curve are correlated with changes in the stock market.

1. Go to StockCharts.Com Dynamic Yield Curve at http://www.stockcharts.com/charts/YieldCurve.html. You will see the yield curve and the S&P 500 plotted as seen below:

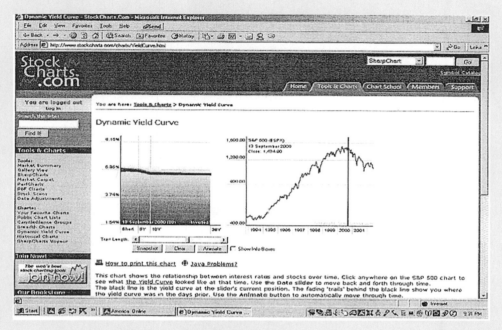

2. By moving the red bar on the S&P chart or clicking the "Animate" button, you can see how the yield curve changed over time. At approximately what date does the yield curve first slope downward?
3. Do you see any relationship between when the stock market peaks and when the slope of the yield curve changes? Based on the discussion in this chapter, can you come up with an explanation of why the yield curve began to slope down?
4. What happened to the yield curve between December 2000 and January 2002?

FINANCIAL MARKETS

7

Money Markets

CHAPTER PREVIEW

Every Monday at 1:30 P.M. EST a hand in the biggest and most lucrative (if you win) poker game in America is played. A typical hand may play for $200 billion, $300 billion, or more. The game is the Treasury Department's weekly auction of Treasury securities to finance the federal government.

One of the real "no-nos" in the public securities markets is trading on insider or privileged information.

An interesting situation occurred in a confidential meeting in October 31, 2001, when Treasury officials made a surprise announcement that they were ending the sale of 30-year Treasury bonds. At the meeting was Peter Davis, president of Davis Capital Ideas in Washington, D.C. When the meeting ended, he called several clients, one of which was Goldman Sachs.

Goldman Sachs traded on the information and, as a result, the Securities and Exchange Commission (SEC) charged Goldman with a securities violation for trading on confidential information ahead of an announcement; trading on nonpublic information is illegal, whether the securities are stocks or bonds.

Why was the information so valuable? Once market participants became aware of the new policy,

they reasoned that 30-year bonds would become scarce, driving their price up and their yields down. On the day in question, yields plunged in a single day from 5.20 percent to 4.23 percent.

Obviously, the first investor to trade on this information could earn a very handsome return. For example, if an investor purchased $100 million of 30-year par bonds when the market was at 5.20 percent and the yield plunged to 4.87 percent, the 1-day gain for the portfolio would be $16.88 million ($116.88 million – $100.00 million), or a cool 16.88 percent return, for just answering the phone! ■

Billions of dollars are traded at warp speed in the money markets as businesses, governments, and financial institutions adjust their liquidity positions. Money market participants borrow or lend large amounts of cash in transactions that are completed in the blink of an eye and that are for short periods of time.

The purpose of this chapter is to explain how money markets work and to describe how businesses, governmental units, and individuals use and participate in these important markets. The **money markets** are where depository institutions and other businesses adjust their liquidity positions by borrowing or investing for short periods of time. In addition, the Federal Reserve Bank conducts money policy in the money markets and U.S. Treasury finances the day-to-day operations of the federal government in the money markets. The instruments traded in the money markets typically have short-term maturities, low default risk, and active secondary markets. The name "money markets" comes from the fact that money market instruments have characteristics very similar to money. Exhibit 7.1 lists the major money market instruments and the dollar amounts of each outstanding: U.S. Treasury securities are the dominant money market instrument. As we shall see, it is the close substitutability of market instruments that links these markets. ■

LEARNING OBJECTIVES

1 Explain the economic role of the money markets.

2 Explain the characteristics of money market instruments.

3 Describe the market for Treasury bills.

4 Describe the market for short-term federal agency securities.

5 Describe the fed funds market.

6 Describe the market for repurchase agreements.

(continued)

EXHIBIT 7.1
Major Money Market Instruments Outstanding (December 2003)

Instrument	$ Billions
U.S. government securities	
Treasury bills	985
Other marketable short-term securities	531
Short-term municipal securities	101
Large, negotiable CDs	1,234
Commercial paper	1,289
Federal funds and security repurchase agreements	1,663

Federal funds and repurchase agreements dominate the money market, with over $1.6 trillion outstanding.

Source: Board of Governors, Federal Reserve System, Flow of Funds Accounts.

7 Describe the market for commercial paper.

8 Describe the market for negotiable certificates of deposit.

9 Describe the market for banker's acceptances.

10 Discuss the various participants of the money markets.

11 Describe the relationship among yields on the various money market instruments.

HOW THE MONEY MARKETS WORK

The money market consists of a collection of markets, each trading a distinctly different financial instrument. There is no formal organization for money markets, such as the New York Stock Exchange for the equity markets. Central to the activity of the money markets are the dealers and brokers who specialize in one or more money market instruments. Dealers buy securities for their own positions and sell from their security inventories when a trade takes place. Transactions, particularly in the secondary market, are almost always completed by telephone. The market is centered in New York City in downtown Manhattan because of the concentration of financial firms in that area. The major dealers and brokers are tied to each other and to their customers by direct phone lines all over the United States and in major European and Asian financial centers. Other communication devices, such as computers, link large banks, some big corporations, and other participants in the money markets.

The money markets are also distinct from other financial markets in that they are wholesale markets because of the large transactions involved. Although some small transactions do take place, most involve $1 million or more. Money market transactions are called open-market transactions because of their impersonal and competitive nature. There are no established customer relationships. For example, a bank trading in federal funds will ask for bids from a number of brokers, selling at the highest price and buying at the lowest. However, not all money market transactions are as open as the federal funds market. For example, money market banks often "accommodate" dealers who are good customers of the bank by selling them negotiable certificates of deposit even though the bank is not actively seeking funds at the prevailing market interest rate. Thus in the money markets we find some "give," not so much in the form of price concessions but in the form of accommodations.

The hubs of money market transactions are the trading rooms of dealers and brokers. When the market is open, these rooms are characterized by tension and a frenzy of activity. Each trader sits in front of a battery of phones that link the dealer to other dealers and their major customers. Phones never ring. Instead, incoming calls are signaled by what appears to be a continuous stream of blinking lights. Huge transactions—$5 million, $100 million, $500 million, or more—take place in conversations that average 10 seconds. Business is conducted in a shorthand jargon discernible only to traders.

Because billions of dollars worth of business is conducted over the phone, the motto of the money markets is "My word is my bond." Participants who renege on their word or make too many errors soon find themselves unable to transact with other brokers and dealers and must seek employment in another profession. Of course, mistakes do occur, and they are typically worked out over lunch in what is agreed to be the fairest way to all concerned.

Payment for securities traded in the money market is as simple as making the transaction over the telephone. Most transactions are settled in federal funds, with parties involved instructing the Federal Reserve to transfer funds from the account of one customer's bank to the other party's bank. The physical transfer of securities is also simplified by the availability of safekeeping facilities in New York City banks. Securities are rarely physically shipped between buyer and seller.

ECONOMIC ROLE OF THE MONEY MARKET

The most important economic function of the money market is to provide an efficient means for economic units to adjust their liquidity positions. Almost every economic unit—financial institution, business, or governmental body—has a recurring problem of liquidity management. The problem occurs because rarely is the timing of cash receipts and cash expenditures perfectly synchronized. Money market instruments allow economic units to bridge the gap between cash receipts and cash expenditures, thereby solving their liquidity problems.

Exhibit 7.2 illustrates this concept. For example, a business firm has a temporary surplus of cash. Rather than leaving the funds idle in a checking account and earning no interest, the firm can invest in the money markets safely for a period of 1 to 30 days, or longer if needed, and earn the market rate of interest. In another situation, if a bank is temporarily short of reserves in its account at the Fed it can go to the money markets to purchase (borrow) federal funds from

---

EXHIBIT 7.2
Money Markets Bridge the Gap between Intermittent Cash Flows

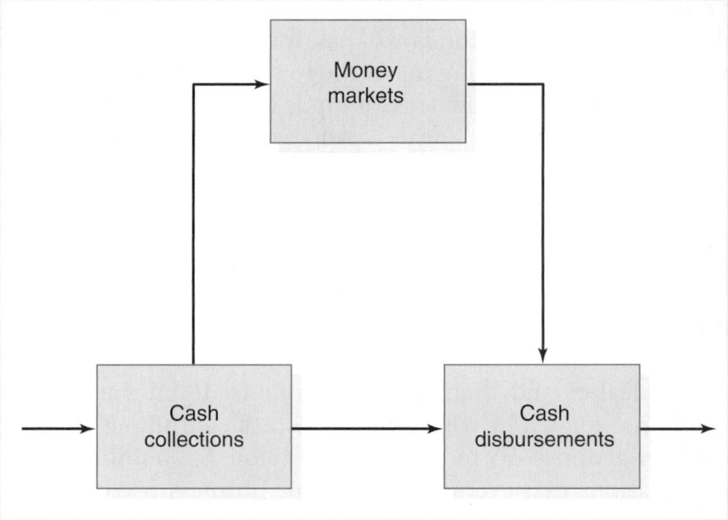

Money markets help governments, businesses, and individuals manage their liquidity by temporarily bridging the gap between cash receipts and cash expenditures.

another institution to deposit in its Federal Reserve account overnight and meet its temporary reserve need. The key notion here is that participants are adjusting their liquidity in these markets—they are lending idle cash or are borrowing for short periods of time.

CHARACTERISTICS OF MONEY MARKET INSTRUMENTS

Given the economic role of money markets—to provide liquidity adjustments—it is not difficult to determine the characteristics of the "ideal" money market instrument and the types of firms that could issue them. Specifically, people who invest in money market instruments want to take as little risk as possible. Thus, these instruments (1) have low default risk, (2) have low price risk (short term-to-maturity), (3) are highly marketable (i.e., they can be bought or sold quickly), and (4) are sold in large denominations so the per-dollar cost for executing transactions is very low. Let us examine in more detail why money market instruments have these characteristics.

First, if you have money to invest temporarily, you would want to purchase financial claims only of firms having the highest credit standing and minimize any loss of principal due to default. Thus, money market instruments are issued by economic units of the highest credit standing (i.e., the lowest default risk).

Second, you would not want to hold long-term securities because they have greater price fluctuations (interest rate risk) compared to short-term securities if interest rates change. Furthermore, if interest rates do change significantly, maturity is not far away for short-term securities, when they can be redeemed for their face value.

Third, temporary investments need to be highly marketable in the event that the funds are unexpectedly needed before maturity. Thus, most money market instruments have active secondary markets. To be highly marketable, money market instruments must have standardized features (no surprises). Further, the issuers must be well known in the market and have good reputations. Finally, the transaction costs need to be low. Thus, money market instruments are generally sold in large wholesale denominations—usually in units of $1 million to $10 million. For example, it costs between 50¢ and $1 to trade $1 million worth of Treasury securities. Exhibit 7.3 summarizes the characteristics of the most important money market instruments. We will now discuss in detail the individual money market instruments and the characteristic of their market.

TREASURY BILLS

To finance the operations of the federal government, the U.S. Treasury Department issues various types of debt. The most important of these are **Treasury bills** (T-bills), which are issued by the federal government to cover current deficits (i.e., expenses exceed revenues) and to refinance maturing government debt. Treasury bills are sold weekly through an auction process (described below) and have original maturities of 91 days (13 weeks), 182 days (26 weeks), or 12 months (52 weeks). They are typically issued in denominations of $10 million, $15 million, $50 million, $100 million, and $500 million. The minimum denomination is $1,000. The reason for the small denomination of $1,000 is a political concession by the federal government to individual investors. Individuals can purchase small-denomination T-bills directly from the Treasury or they can purchase them from

EXHIBIT 7.3
Characteristics of Money Market Instruments

Instrument	Typical Maturity	Marketability	Default Risk
U.S. Treasury bills	13 to 52 weeks	Excellent	None
Federal agency securities, maturing within a year	Up to 1 year	Good	Very Low
Commercial paper	1 to 270 days	Limited	Low
Negotiable certificates of deposit	14 to 180 days	Good	Low
Banker's acceptances	30 to 180 days	Good	Low
Federal funds	1 to 7 days	Excellent	Low
Repurchase agreements	1 to 15 days	Good	Low

Money market instruments are typically characterized by short maturities, high marketability, and low default risk.

dealers in the secondary market. Overall, however, the market for Treasury securities is a wholesale market; a round lot in the interdealer market is $5 million.

Because the U.S. government backs Treasury bills, they have virtually no default risk. In fact, the yield on Treasury bills is often referred to as the "risk-free rate." Of course, in reality, there is no risk-free rate, but T-bill yields are the best proxy available. Treasury bills also have little price risk because of their short maturity; and they can be readily converted into cash at very low transaction costs because of their large and active secondary market. Thus, Treasury securities are considered the ideal money market instrument.

AUCTIONING NEW T-BILLS

The Treasury Department has a systematic procedure for auctioning and redeeming Treasury bills. Each Thursday, the regular weekly offering of 91-day and 182-day bills is announced. The 52-week bills are sold similarly but are offered once a month. Bids, or tenders, must be received by a Federal Reserve bank on the following Monday by 1:30 P.M., New York time. Historically, bidders are apprised of awards the next morning. With advances in computer and telecommunications technology the time from bid to award has become shorter and shorter. For example, in 1995 the time to award was about 45 minutes and in 2000 the time to award had dropped to only 27 minutes on average. One reason the time to award was not shorter was that Treasury officials would check with dealers whose bids appeared to have a mistake such as the wrong name, bidder identification number, or even the wrong price.

In April 2002, the Treasury announced the "your bid is your bid" policy with the goal of shortening the time to award to 2 minutes. No more Mr. Nice Guy at the Treasury Department. If you make a mistake in your bid, you now must live with the consequences. The shorter release time will reduce the amount of time that bidders are exposed to uncertainty with respect to changes in interest rates. The reduced uncertainty favors both investors and dealers and, thus, will lower the government's borrowing cost.

Competitive Bids. Bids can be submitted either as competitive or noncompetitive bids. Competitive bids are usually made by large investors who actively participate in money markets on a regular basis, such as Wall Street brokerage firms and large commercial banks. In making a competitive bid, the investor states the quantity of bills desired and the bid price. An investor can enter more than one competitive bid, but the total of the bids cannot exceed 35 percent of the Treasury bills auctioned that week. In awarding the Treasury bills, the highest bidder (i.e., the bid with the *lowest* interest rate) receives the first allocation of T-bills, and subsequent bids are filled in decreasing order of price until all of the bills auctioned that week are distributed. Thus, the auction is a "price discrimination auction" in that different bidders pay different prices. The reason for the "35 percent rule" is to prevent any single bidder from "squeezing" the market. That is, if a single dealer controls a significant portion of a particular maturity, the dealer may be able to sell the bills at prices higher than otherwise would be the case in competitive markets.

Exhibit 7.4 shows the weekly results of the 4-week, 13-week, and 26-week Treasury bill auction for May 10–11, 2004. For the 13-week bills, competitive bids for over $39.1 billion of T-bills were tendered and the Treasury Department accepted $16.3 billion of the bids. Over $1.38 billion of noncompetitive bids were tendered and accepted. All successful bidders, competitive and noncompetitive, were awarded T-bills at a median yield of 1.050 percent.

Noncompetitive Bids. In making a noncompetitive bid, the investor indicates the quantity of bills desired and agrees to pay the weighted average price of the competitive bids that are accepted. Noncompetitive bids are given a preferential allocation in that all noncompetitive bids are accepted before the award of any competitive bids. The maximum bid limit on noncompetitive bids is $1 million, and individuals and small commercial banks usually enter them. Noncompetitive bids allow small investors who are not familiar with money market interest rate movements to purchase Treasury securities to avoid the risks of (1) bidding a price

---

EXHIBIT 7.4
**Department of the Treasury's T-Bill Auction Results,
May 10–11, 2004 ($Millions)**

	4-Week T-Bills	13-Week T-Bills	26-Week T-Bills
Competitive bids tendered	$55,432.5	$39,107.6	$27,570.7
Competitive bids accepted	$18,953.8	$16,317.1	$13,964.6
Noncompetitive bids accepted	$47.2	$1,383.6	$860.6
High yield	0.895%	1.060%	1.340%
Median yield	0.890%	1.050%	1.320%
Low yield	0.870%	1.030%	1.300%

T-bills are sold in weekly auctions by competitive and noncompetitive bids.

Source: Department of the Treasury, Office of Public Affairs, *Treasury News,* May 10–11, 2004.

too low to receive any bills or (2) bidding a price substantially above the market equilibrium.

To bid, an individual must submit a bid form and, if necessary, information needed to open an account with the "Treasury Direct" securities purchase program along with a certified check or other acceptable money transfer sufficient to pay for the securities bid upon. A copy of a form that can be used to submit bids ("tenders") for Treasury securities is shown in Exhibit 7.5. The form contains the information needed to place the securities in the proper Treasury Direct account. Those accounts are "book-entry" accounts that record the owners of the securities purchased and credit the owners with interest or principal as the securities mature. The Treasury will also reinvest the proceeds from maturing securities in new issues of similar securities if the buyer requests that the investment be rolled over automatically.

BOOK-ENTRY SECURITIES

An interesting innovation in the Treasury bill market occurred in 1976 when the Treasury announced that it would begin switching the entire marketable portion of the federal debt over to book-entry securities in lieu of engraved pieces of paper. Thus Treasury securities owned or held by banks that are members of the Federal Reserve System would exist only in the Fed's computer. All marketable government securities (Treasury and agency) may be held in book-entry form, and the bulk of the Treasury's marketable debt is now held in this form.

For example, in New York City, the major banks are linked by wire, and all securities transactions among them are by wire. Thus, if Chase Bank were to sell securities to Wells Fargo, it would make delivery by instructing the Fed to debit its Treasury bill account for the amount sold and to simultaneously credit Wells Fargo's account for the same amount. In that way, securities can be quickly "transferred" by electronic impulses over the "Fed wire," rather than by cumbersome physical transfers.

PRICING TREASURY BILLS

Zero-coupon bond

Treasury bills are sold to investors on a discount basis. The reason is that T-bills pay no coupon interest; thus, the interest income to the investors is the difference between the purchase price and face value of the bill at maturity. Exhibit 7.6 shows the Treasury bill rates as quoted in the *Wall Street Journal* on May 14, 2004. Column 1 lists the maturity dates for the bills. Column 2 specifies the number of days until a particular T-bill matures. For example, at the close of the trading day on May 14, 2004, the T-bills maturing on May 27, 2004, would trade for 10 more days before they would be retired by the Treasury Department. Note that the securities all have maturities of less than 1 year. Column 3 is the discount yield (defined below) on T-bills and reflects the price at which dealers are willing to buy T-bills from investors. Column 4 is the discount yield set by dealers and reflects the price at which dealers are willing to sell T-bills to investors. The difference between the bid yield and the asked yield is the spread. The spread is the dealer profit for buying and selling T-bills and represents the transaction costs incurred by investors for trading. Column 5 is the change in the ask yield from the previous day's close. Finally, column 6 is the asked discount yield converted to a bond equivalent yield, which we will discuss below.

EXHIBIT 7.5
Treasury Bill, Note, and Bond Auction Tender Form

PD F 5381 (I)
Department of the Treasury
Bureau of the Public Debt
(Revised October 1998)

www.treasurydirect.gov

OMB No 1535-0069

TREASURY DIRECT®

TREASURY BILL, NOTE & BOND TENDER
For Tender Instructions, See PD F 5382

TYPE OR PRINT IN INK ONLY – TENDERS WILL NOT BE ACCEPTED WITH ALTERATIONS OR CORRECTIONS

1. BID INFORMATION *(Must Be Completed)*

Par Amount:

$ _____
(Sold in units of $1,000)

Bid Type: *(Fill in One)*
○ Noncompetitive
○ Competitive at |__|__|.|__|__|__| %
(Bill bids must end in 0 or 5.)

DEPARTMENT USE
TENDER NO.

RECEIVED BY/DATE

2. TreasuryDirect ACCOUNT NUMBER
(If NOT furnished, a new account will be opened.)

|__|__|__|__|__| - |__|__|__|__| - |__|__|__|

3. TAXPAYER ID NUMBER *(Must Be Completed)*

|__|__|__| - |__|__| - |__|__|__|__| **OR** |__|__| - |__|__|__|__|__|__|__|
Social Security Number (First-Named Owner)   Employer ID Number

ENTERED BY

APPROVED BY

4. TERM SELECTION *(Fill in One)*
(Must Be Completed)

Treasury Bill
$1,000 Minimum   Circle the Number of Reinvestments
○ 13-Week..........0 1 2 3 4
                    5 6 7 8
○ 26-Week..........0 1 2 3 4
○ 52-Week..........0 1 2

Treasury Note/Bond
$1,000 Minimum
○ 2-Year Note
○ 5-Year Note
○ 10-Year Note
○ 30-Year Bond
○ Inflation-Indexed _____
                     Term

5. ACCOUNT NAME Please Type or Print! *(Must Be Completed)*

6. ADDRESS *(For new account or if changed.)* ○ New Address?

City   State   ZIP Code

ISSUE DATE

CUSIP 912795-

CUSIP 912827-

CUSIP 912810-

FOREIGN ☐

BACKUP ☐

REVIEW ☐

7. TELEPHONE NUMBERS *(For new account or if changed.)* ○ New Phone Number?

Work (___) ___ - _____   Home (___) ___ - _____

8. PAYMENT INFORMATION *(For new account only.)*   Changes? Submit PD F 5178.

Routing Number |__|__|__|__|__|__|__|__|__|

Financial Institution Name _____

Account Number |__|__|__|__|__|__|__|__|__|__|__|__|__|__|__|__|__|

Name on Account _____

Account Type: *(Fill in One)* ○ Checking   ○ Savings

9. PURCHASE METHOD
(Must Be Completed)

○ *Pay Direct*
(Existing *TreasuryDirect* Account Only)

○ Checks: $ _____
          $ _____
○ Securities: $ _____
○ Other $ _____

Total Payment Attached: $ _____
CHECKS ARE DEPOSITED IMMEDIATELY

CHECK #

10. AUTHORIZATION *(Must Be Completed – Original Signature Required)*

Tender Submission: I submit this tender pursuant to the provisions of Department of the Treasury Circulars, Public Debt Series Nos. 2-86 (31 CFR Part 357) and 1-93 (31 CFR Part 356), and the applicable offering announcement. As the first-named owner and under penalties of perjury, I certify that: 1) The number shown on this form is my correct taxpayer identification number (or I am waiting for a number to be issued to me), and 2) I am not subject to backup withholding because: (a) I am exempt from backup withholding, or (b) I have not been notified by the Internal Revenue Service (IRS) that I am subject to backup withholding as a result of a failure to report all interest or dividends, or (c) the IRS has notified me that I am no longer subject to backup withholding. I further certify that all other information provided on this form is true, correct and complete.

Pay Direct: (If using this purchase method.) I authorize a debit to my account at the financial institution I designated in *TreasuryDirect* to pay for this security. I understand that the purchase price will be charged to my account on or after the settlement date. I also understand that if this transaction cannot be successfully completed, my tender can be rejected and the transaction canceled. If there is a dispute, a copy of this authorization may be provided to my financial institution.

_____   _____
Signature(s)   Date

Individuals can bid at weekly Treasury security auctions by submitting a completed "tender" form prior to the auction. People who place a noncompetitive bid will receive the average price granted at the auction. The maximum size for a noncompetitive bid is $1 million.

EXHIBIT 7.6
Treasury Bill Quotations

(1)	(2)	(3)	(4)	(5)	(6)
Maturity	Days to Maturity	Bid	Asked	Change	Asked Yield
May 27, 2004	10	0.85	0.84	+0.01	0.85
June 17, 2004	31	0.82	0.81	+0.01	0.82
July 15, 2004	59	0.86	0.85	−0.01	0.86
August 12, 2004	87	0.97	0.96	−0.01	0.98
September 09, 2004	115	1.07	1.06	0.00	1.08
October 14, 2004	150	1.17	1.16	−0.01	1.18

Treasury bill bid and ask prices can be computed from the bid and ask yields and the days to maturity number reported in the *Wall Street Journal*. The discount rate understates the true rate of return on a T-bill. The *Wall Street Journal* also prints the bond equivalent yield, based on the ask yield, so people can better compare T-bill and bond returns.

Source: Wall Street Journal Online, Treasury Quotes, Friday, May 14, 2004.

The discount yield (y_d) on a Treasury bill is computed by multiplying the percentage price discount on the Treasury bill's face value (P_f) by 360 and dividing by the number of days (n) to the T-bill's maturity. Thus, the formula for calculating the discount rate (y_d) is given in Equation 7.1:

$$y_d = \frac{P_f - P_0}{P_f} \times \frac{360}{n} \times 100\%,$$ (7.1)

where

y_d = discount yield on an annualized basis
P_f = face value (amount paid to the investor at maturity)
P_0 = purchase price of the T-bill
n = number of days to maturity

Let's work an example with Equation 7.1. Say that you decide to purchase a 91-day Treasury bill with a face value of $10,000 at a price of $9,800 (it is purchased at a 2 percent discount). What is the T-bill's annualized yield?

The bill's annualized yield is 7.91 percent, calculated as follows:

$$y_d = \frac{\$10,000 - \$9,800}{\$10,000} \times \frac{360}{91} \times 100\%$$

$$= 7.91\%$$

The discount rate understates the true rate of return on a Treasury bill for several reasons. First, it assumes that the full face value was paid for the T-bill instead of a discounted price. This overstates the investment required to buy the T-bill and, thus, understates the discount as a percentage of the amount of money actually invested. Second, as everyone should know, there are either 365 or 366 days in a year. By understating the length of the year, the formula ignores the fact that if interest were earned for the full year, a higher rate of return would be obtained. Thus, interest can be earned on the interest received on the T-bill. Consequently, when T-bill yields are reported in financial publications such as the *Wall Street Journal*, the publications often publish a "bond equivalent yield," as well as the discount yield (see Exhibit 7.6).

The bond equivalent yield assumes that there is a 365-day year and that the price rather than the face value is invested in the T-bill. Because of these assumptions, the bond equivalent yield on a T-bill is always higher than the bank discount rate (see Exhibit 7.6). The formula for the bond equivalent yield y_{be} is:

$$y_{be} = \frac{P_f - P_0}{P_0} \times \frac{365}{n} \times 100\%. \tag{7.2}$$

Below you can see the calculation of the bond equivalent yield from our previous example:

$$y_{be} = \frac{\$10,000 - \$9,800}{\$9,800} \times \frac{365}{91} \times 100\%$$

$$= 8.19\%.$$

Notice that the bond equivalent yield is greater than the discount yield.

A Treasury bill's price can be computed from data in the financial press (e.g., see Exhibit 7.6) by taking Equation 7.1 or 7.2 and solving for the price (P_0). Using the discount yield, the equation to solve for the price is

$$P_0 = P_f - \left[y_d \times \frac{n}{360} \times P_f \right]. \tag{7.3}$$

Using the bond equivalent yield, the price is

$$P_0 = \frac{P_f}{\left[1 + \left(y_{be} \times \frac{n}{365} \right) \right]}. \tag{7.4}$$

You can see how these two formulas work by taking an example from Exhibit 7.6. Let's look at the T-bill maturing on October 14, 2004 as of the date of the *Wall Street Journal* listing, May 14, 2004 (see the last row of the exhibit). We have the following information, which we substitute into Equation 7.3 to obtain the price:

$P_f = \$10,000$
$y_d = 1.16\%$ (see column 4 of Exhibit 7.6)
$n = 150$ days (see column 2 of Exhibit 7.6)

Thus,

$$P_0 = P_f - \left[y_d \times \frac{n}{360} \times P_f \right]$$

$$= \$10{,}000 - \left[0.0116 \times \frac{150}{360} \times 10{,}000 \right]$$

$$= \$10{,}000 - \$48.33$$

$$= \$9{,}951.67$$

DO YOU UNDERSTAND?

1. Given the economic role of the money market, explain the importance of the typical characteristics of money market securities.

2. Using the information in Exhibit 7.4, calculate the *price* of a 13-week T-bill and express it as a percentage of face value.

3. Refer to Exhibit 7.6. On May 14, 2004, what is the price of the T-bill maturing on September 9, 2004? Calculate the price two ways, using both the asked yield and the bid yield. Assume a face value of $10,000.

4. Assuming a face value of $10,000, what is the price of a T-bill with 161 days to maturity if its bond equivalent yield is 1.99 percent?

5. Why is the bond equivalent yield of a T-bill higher than the yield calculated on a discount basis?

FEDERAL AGENCY SECURITIES

Since the mid-1960s, federal agency securities have been important in the money markets. They have features that make them attractive to a wide variety of investors. They have low default risk and, in many cases, well-developed secondary markets. All agency securities qualify as legal investments for financial institutions, and they are acceptable as collateral for commercial bank tax and loan accounts and as security for public deposits. They can also be used as collateral by banks for borrowing at the Federal Reserve discount window. Thus, federal agency securities offer many of the advantages of regular Treasury securities and usually provide slightly higher yield, because they are less marketable than Treasury debt and often have slightly higher risk of default.

A **federal agency** is an independent federal department or federally chartered corporation established by Congress and owned or underwritten by the U.S. government. Federal agency securities result from selected government lending programs. Initially these programs were designed to attract private capital to sectors of the economy where credit flows were considered to be insufficient. Housing and agriculture were traditionally the principal beneficiaries of federal credit programs. In recent years, the objectives of federal credit programs have expanded to include social and economic goals and to promote conservation and resource utilization.

TYPES OF FEDERAL AGENCIES

Exhibit 7.7 provides a list of the major government agencies authorized to issue debt. Many of them issue only long-term debt; however, as these issues approach maturity, they are traded in the money markets. With regard to short-term issues, about 25 percent of all new agency issues have an original maturity of 1 year or less. We shall now discuss three of the important federal agencies.

The Farm Credit System. The farm credit system (FCS) is a cooperatively owned system of banks and associations that provides credit and related services to farmers and agricultural cooperatives. The system holds about one-fourth of total farm debt in the United States. The oldest government debt-issuing agency in the system is the Federal Land Bank (FLB), created by the Federal Farm Loan Act of 1916. Today there are 12 FLBs throughout the country that make credit available to farmers to purchase and develop land and to buy farm equipment and livestock. In addition, farmers can obtain credit from Federal Intermediate Credit Banks (FICB), established in 1923, and from Banks for Cooperatives (Co-ops), organized in 1933.

The financial crisis in the farm sector during the 1980s raised concern over the riskiness of debt issued by farm credit agencies. This led to the passage of the 1985 Farm Bill, which allows Congress to provide direct federal aid to the FCS through a line of credit with the Treasury as well as direct borrowing by the Farm Credit Bank. Thus the act strengthened the market's perception of an implicit federal guarantee of agency debt in the event of default.

EXHIBIT 7.7
Selected Federal Agencies Authorized to Issue Debt

Farm Credit Bank
Federal Financing Bank
Federal National Mortgage Association
Government National Mortgage Association
Export-Import Bank of the United States
Federal Home Loan Mortgage Corporation
Small Business Administration
Federal Housing Administration
Student Loan Marketing Association
Tennessee Valley Authority
Veterans Administration

Historically, most federal agencies were involved in directing capital flows into farming or housing. Recently, the number of agencies directing capital to farming has declined, but federal agency credit programs have expanded into several other areas.

Housing Credit Agencies.   Another major group of federal agencies is involved in financing home construction. Foremost among these agencies is the Federal National Mortgage Association (FNMA, also called "Fannie Mae"), chartered by the federal government in 1938 initially to buy federally insured mortgage loans. FNMA is now privately owned, but it retains its government credit line. FNMA's objective is to provide a secondary market for home mortgages. The Federal Home Loan Mortgage Corporation (FHLMC, also called "Freddie Mac") is similar to FNMA except it was initially established to buy conventional (not federally insured) mortgage loans.

Federal Financing Bank.   In the past, most agency securities were sold through financial specialists known as fiscal agents. Each agency had one, usually located in New York City, whose job was to assemble a group of investment banking firms to distribute the agency's securities to retail buyers. Today this method of selling new issues is used primarily by federally sponsored agencies that issue large amounts of securities, such as the housing and farm credit agencies. Other government agencies now acquire most of their funds directly from the Treasury or from the Federal Financing Bank (FFB), established in 1973 to coordinate and consolidate the federal financing activities of agencies that issue small amounts of debt or infrequently enter the money and capital markets. The goal of the FFB is to lower the borrowing cost of participating agencies. The FFB purchases the securities of participating agencies and, in turn, issues its own obligations.

CHARACTERISTICS OF AGENCY DEBT

Except for GNMA (Government National Mortgage Association), Eximbank, and FHA (Federal Housing Administration) debentures, agency securities are *not* guaranteed by the federal government against default. These agency securities are often referred to as **nonguaranteed agency debt**. However, some form of federal backing is implied. First, it is unlikely that the federal government would allow one of its own sponsored agencies to default. Furthermore, for some issues the Treasury Department and the Federal Reserve are authorized to purchase securities in the event that market support is needed. For other issues, the agency can borrow from the Treasury up to certain limits.

The marketability of agency securities varies with each type of security. The securities of the Federal Land Banks, the Federal Intermediate Credit Banks, Banks for Cooperatives, the Federal Home Loan Banks, and Federal National Mortgage Association have well-established secondary markets. In recent years, the yield on agency securities has been 3 to 20 basis points above the yield on similar Treasury securities (100 basis points equal 1 percent). Though some of the yield spread difference results from the agency securities' higher default risk, most is attributable to their lower marketability. Exhibit 7.8 shows a list of federal agencies most active in issuing short-term debt and the characteristics of that debt.

FEDERAL FUNDS

The market for **federal funds** (typically called fed funds) is one of the most important financial markets in the United States. It provides the means by which commercial banks and a limited number of other financial institutions trade large amounts of liquid funds with one another, usually for a period of 1 day. The fed

EXHIBIT 7.8
Characteristics of Short-term Agency Securities

Issuer	Type	Maturities	Offering Schedule	Minimum Denomination ($)
Farm Credit Banks	Bonds	3 and 6 months	Monthly	5,000
	Discount notes	1 to 365 days	Daily	5,000
Federal Home Loan Banks	Discount notes	1 to 360 days	Twice Weekly	100,000
Federal National Mortgage Association	Benchmark bills	3 and 6 months	Weekly	1,000
	Discount notes	1 to 360 days	Daily	1,000

The majority of the federal agencies most active in issuing short-term debt offer securities daily with maturities typically in the 3- to 6-month range.

funds rate is of particular interest because (1) it measures the return on the most liquid of all financial assets; (2) it is closely related to the conduct of monetary policy; and (3) it measures directly the availability of excess reserves within the banking system, which, in turn, influences commercial banks' decisions concerning loans to businesses, consumers, and other borrowers.

Traditionally, the federal funds market has been described as one in which commercial banks borrow and lend excess reserve balances held at the Federal Reserve. The institution that borrows the funds incurs a liability on its balance sheet, called "fed funds purchased," and the institution that lends the fed funds records an asset, "fed funds sold." The overnight (or 1-day) interest rate to borrow the funds is called the fed funds rate. Also note that the name federal funds or "fed funds" is misleading. Federal funds have nothing to do with the federal government. When the market for fed funds originated in the 1920, the interest rate was close to the rate paid when borrowing from the Federal Reserve Bank; hence, the term "fed" funds.

Interbank borrowing and lending make up the majority of all federal funds transactions. They are essentially 1-day unsecured loans between banks. The typical unit of trade is $1 million or more. It is possible to borrow longer than 1 day, up to 7 days; however, "longer-term" borrowing makes up a very small part of the overall fed funds market. With respect to transaction size, some banks will trade smaller amounts, but trades of less than $500,000 are infrequent. In most cases, the only step necessary to arrange a fed funds transaction is a telephone call and wire transfer. No physical transfer of funds occurs.

The quoted yield on fed funds, y_{ff}, assumes a 360-day year. To compare yields in the fed funds market with those of other money market instruments, the fed funds rate must be converted into a bond equivalent yield, y_{be}. For example, if the overnight fed funds rate is 2.00 percent, the bond equivalent funds rate is calculated as follows:

$$y_{be} = y_{ff}(365/360)$$
$$= 2.00\% \ (365/360) = 2.028\%.$$

GROWTH IN FED FUNDS MARKET

The recent growth and change in the fed funds market makes the traditional description of the market overly simplified. Today, many active participants in the fed funds market do not hold balances at the Federal Reserve, such as commercial banks that are not members of the Federal Reserve.

A more appropriate definition of a federal funds transaction is that of an overnight loan (1 day) that is settled in **immediately available funds**. Immediately available funds are defined as (1) deposit liabilities of Federal Reserve banks and (2) liabilities of commercial banks that may be transferred or withdrawn during a business day. A growing portion of the fed funds market has consisted of large regional and money-center banks borrowing correspondent balances from smaller banks. At one time, these correspondent balances earned no interest and were held as payment for services. Today, small banks intentionally accumulate large balances in order to sell the excess to the correspondent for investment in the fed funds market. The unit amounts are usually somewhat less than needed for open-market transactions. However, the large bank accumulates these balances from its various smaller respondent banks to reach trading-lot size. The correspondent earns a fee for this service.

Nonbank financial institutions have also become increasingly active in the market for immediately available funds. These institutions may engage in certain types of immediate fund transactions because of federal regulations governing commercial bank funds that are subject to reserve requirements. They include federal agencies, savings and loan associations, mutual savings banks, branches of foreign banks, and government securities dealers. For example, a savings and loan association may lend federal funds to a foreign bank, or a commercial bank can borrow federal funds from an array of institutions, rather than just reallocating reserves among member banks.

REPURCHASE AGREEMENTS

Closely associated with the functioning of the federal funds market is the negotiation of **repurchase agreements** (RPs). A repurchase agreement consists of the sale of a short-term security (collateral) with the condition that, after a period of time, the original seller will buy it back at a predetermined price. The collateral used most frequently is U.S. Treasury securities such as T-bills or agency securities. However, it is possible to use any of the better-known money market instruments. This dual transaction, which in market jargon is called a **repo**, has developed into a meaningful money market instrument in its own right.

Repurchase agreements are most commonly made for 1 day or for very short terms. In recent years, however, the market has expanded to include a substantial volume of 1- to 3-month (and even longer) transactions. The smallest customary denomination for a repo is $1 million. As with other money market instruments, repurchase agreement transactions are settled in federal funds. A reverse repurchase agreement (reverse repo) involves the purchase of short-term securities with the promise to sell the securities back to the original seller at a predetermined price at a given date in the future.

A REPO TRANSACTION

The definition of a repo in the preceding section may seem a little mind-boggling. However, repos are really very simple transactions. A repo is just a loan to a firm or individual that is *secured* by a money market instrument of the same dollar value. Thus, if the borrower defaults on the loan, the lender keeps the collateral, usually a short-term Treasury security. Repos are considered very-low-risk investments because the collateral is of equivalent dollar value and is a short-term security, meaning it has little price risk. Let's work through an example so you can see how repos work. Suppose that a corporate treasurer has $1 million of excess cash for a 2-day period. The treasurer, wishing to earn interest on the funds, arranges to purchase $1 million worth of government securities from a bank with an accompanying agreement that the bank will repurchase the securities in 2 days. The interest paid to the corporation is the difference between the purchase price and repurchase price of the collateralized securities. The transactions for both the bank and the corporation (T-account entries) are as follows:

	Bank	Corporate Customer	
Before RP	$1 million deposit	$1 million deposit	
Creation of RP	−$1 million deposit	−$1 million deposit	
	+$1 million RP borrowing	+$1 million collateralized loan (RP)	
Completion of RP agreement	+$1 million deposit	+$1 million deposit	
	−$1 million RP borrowing	−$1 million loan (RP)	

Notice that, from the standpoint of the temporary seller of securities, repurchase agreements represent a source of funds; for the buyer, they represent an interest-earning investment. As our example illustrates, a commercial bank may buy idle funds from a corporate customer by selling Treasury securities on a repurchase basis. Or a commercial bank can sell immediately available funds to a dealer in U.S. government securities by purchasing the securities through a repurchase agreement. The dealer thereby finances its security inventory with funds purchased by the bank, and the bank receives interest income from the dealer at money market rates of return.

The unique feature that distinguishes repurchase agreements from other money market instruments is that they may be used to shorten the actual maturity of a security to meet the needs of the borrower and lender. For example, an investor may wish to invest funds for a very short period of time, say for 3 days. A Treasury bill maturing in 3 days could be purchased, but often a 3-day bill is not available. A longer-maturity bill could be purchased, held for 3 days, and then resold in the secondary market. However, this alternative involves price risk. If interest rates should rise during the 3-day interval, the investor would suffer a capital loss. A 3-day repo provides the investor with a money market instrument with the precisely needed maturity, thus eliminating all price risk on the repo.

PEOPLE & EVENTS

The Collapse of ESM: Life in the Fast Lane

When federal regulators confiscated the assets of Ronnie R. Ewton in March 1985, besides his luxury home with gold-plated bathroom fixtures, they seized a yacht worth $1 million+, two airplanes, three Mercedes, two Jaguars, and a dozen polo ponies. With all that loot, was Ronnie some kind of bank robber? No—better yet, he was one of three owners of ESM, a small government securities dealer that opened it doors for business in October 1976.*

ESM, located in Fort Lauderdale, bought and sold securities and repurchase agreements, doing business with banks, municipalities, high-net-worth individuals, and other securities firms. To the casual observer, the boys were doing pretty good, drawing salaries in the $500,000 range, but the real money was in the way they conducted their repo businesses.

From reading this chapter, you know that repos are normally considered to be very-low-risk investments. In a repo, an investor buys a security from a dealer who agrees to repurchase it a few days later at a higher price. The key to investor safety is that the dealer pledges a dollar-equivalent money market

security as collateral. Then, if the dealer defaults on its promise, the investors become the owner of the collateral and, thus, suffer no financial loss.

Investors who purchased repos from ESM earned above-market returns and, as is standard practice, the collateral was held by a third party. However, Ronnie and the other ESM partners were using unorthodox procedures to "cook the books." SEC investigators discovered that ESM had pledged the same security to a number of different customers and, in some cases, had created fictitious securities. Thus, the customer loans to ESM were not secured not by collateral but by "thin air."

As the truth emerged, investigators learned that ESM had been losing money for years but had kept afloat by increasing the dollar volume of its repurchase agreements to generate new cash. By the time ESM was shut down, the firm had accumulated red ink of more than $200 million. ESM had been able to get away with this scheme for so many years because of the lack of regulation of government securities dealers. After a few more highly visible defaults by small government security dealers, life in the fast lane was shut down when Congress passed the Government Securities Act of 1986.

* ESM was named after the three owners: Ronnie R. Ewton, Robert C. Seneca, and George Meade.

CALCULATION OF THE YIELD ON A REPO

The rate charged in repurchase agreements is negotiated between the buyers and sellers of funds, but it must be competitive with other money market rates. Transactions are arranged by telephone either directly between the two parties supplying and acquiring funds or through a small group of market specialists, usually government securities dealers.

The credit risk (default) on repos is very low because repo transactions are collateralized by T-bills. As a result, the 1-day repo rate is less than the 1-day fed funds rate, which is an uncollateralized loan. The spread between the two rates is typically 20 to 25 basis points. The yield on a repo is calculated as the annualized difference between the initial selling price and repurchase price, which includes the interest paid, using a 360-day year. The formula for the repo yield or interest rate is

$$y_{\text{repo}} = \frac{P_{\text{repo}} - P_0}{P_0} \times \frac{360}{n}, \tag{7.5}$$

where

P_{repo} = repurchase price of the security, which equals the selling price plus interest

P_0 = sale price of the security

n = number of days to maturity

For example, a commercial bank does a **reverse repurchase agreement** (or "reverse repo") with one of corporate customers who needs funds for 3 days. The bank agrees to buy Treasury securities from the corporation at a price of $1,000,000 and promises to sell the securities back to the corporate customer for $1,000,145 (includes $145 of interest) after 3 days. The yield on the reverse repo is calculated as follows using Equation 7.5:

$$y_{repo} = \frac{\$1,000,145 - \$1,000,000}{\$1,000,000} \times \frac{360}{3}$$
$$= 1.74\%.$$

Note that the bank corporate customer was able to borrow $1 million for 3 days for $145, not a bad deal! Also notice that repos and reverse repos are just opposite sides of the same deal. For the bank, the transaction was a reverse repo and for the corporate customer the deal was a repo.

COMMERCIAL PAPER

Commercial paper is a short-term, unsecured promissory note typically issued by large corporations to finance short-term working capital needs. In recent years, some firms have also used commercial paper as a source of interim financing for major construction projects. The basic reason firms issue commercial paper is to achieve interest rate savings as an alternative to bank borrowing. Because commercial paper is an unsecured promissory note, the issuer pledges no assets to protect the investor in the event of default. As a result, only large, well-known firms of the highest credit standing (lowest default risk) can issue commercial paper.

The commercial paper market is almost entirely a wholesale money market. Most commercial paper is sold in denominations of $100,000, $250,000, $500,000, and $1 million. Maturities on commercial paper range from 1 to 270 days, but most commercial paper has maturities of 20 to 60 days. Longer maturities are infrequent because issues with maturities greater than 270 days must comply with the costly and time-consuming SEC registration and prospectus requirements.

HISTORY OF COMMERCIAL PAPER

Commercial paper is one of the oldest money market instruments; its use can be traced back to the early 1800s. Early issuers were mainly nonfinancial business firms, such as textile mills, railroads, and tobacco companies. The principal buyers were commercial banks. Beginning in the 1920s, the nature of the commercial paper market began to change. The introduction of the automobile and other consumer durables created a demand by consumers for short-term personal loans. This led to the rapid growth of consumer finance companies that needed funds to finance consumer purchases. The first large consumer finance company to issue commercial paper was General Motors Acceptance Corporation (GMAC), which was established to finance the purchase of General Motors' automobiles. An innovation by GMAC was to sell its paper directly to investors rather than placing it through commercial paper dealers.

THE COMMERCIAL PAPER MARKET

Historically, commercial banks were the major purchasers of commercial paper. In the early 1950s, many other firms began purchasing commercial paper because of its combination of low default risk, short maturity, and relatively high yields. Today the major investors in commercial paper are large insurance companies, nonfinancial business firms, bank trust departments, and state and local government pension funds. Commercial banks still purchase commercial paper for their own accounts, but they are not a dominant force in the market. Commercial banks remain important to the operation of the commercial paper market, however, because they act as agents in issuing paper, hold it for safekeeping, and facilitate payment in federal funds. They also provide backup lines of credit to corporate issuers of commercial paper.

Currently, 600 to 800 firms issue significant quantities of commercial paper. The precise amount issued varies, depending on economic and market conditions, the number being smaller during high-interest periods and greater when money is more readily available. Most of these firms sell their paper through dealers. There are about 30 commercial paper dealers, most of whom are located in New York City. In addition, in recent years large money-center banks have gained expanded powers and are now allowed to underwrite and trade in commercial paper.

Dealers maintain an inventory of the commercial paper they sell and stand ready to buy paper back from their customers at the going market rate plus a one-eighth of 1 percent commission fee. Also, issuing firms will repurchase their own commercial paper within limits. Thus there is a secondary market for commercial paper, but it is not nearly as liquid as that for negotiable bank CDs. Dealers report that only about 2 percent of all commercial paper is redeemed prior to maturity.

CREDIT RATINGS IN THE COMMERCIAL PAPER MARKET

Both Moody's Investors Service and Standard & Poor's (S&P) rate commercial paper. From highest to lowest, paper ratings run P-1, P-2, and P-3 for Moody's, and A-1, A-2, and A-3 for S&P. Nearly all firms that issue commercial paper obtain credit ratings, and most obtain ratings from both Moody's and S&P. In addition, firms that buy significant amounts of commercial paper have their own credit analysts who assess the risks of purchasing a particular firm's commercial paper. Most commercial paper receives the highest rating. It is extremely difficult to sell commercial paper with the lowest rating, especially during hard economic times.

THE ROLE OF BACKUP LINES OF CREDIT

In most cases, issuers back up their commercial paper issue with a line of credit from a commercial bank, since there is always the risk that an issuer might not be able to pay off or roll over the maturing paper. Rolling over paper means that the issuer sells new commercial paper to get the funds to retire maturing paper. Therefore, backup credit lines ensure a source of funds in the event that the firm experiences a cash-flow problem or if credit market conditions become tight. Most investors will not buy commercial paper unless it is backed by a bank credit line. Banks receive a fee for providing backup lines.

ISSUING COMMERCIAL PAPER

Firms issuing commercial paper can sell it either directly to investors using their own sales force or indirectly using commercial paper dealers. At present, about 80 firms sell their commercial paper through direct placement. Most of these are large finance companies and bank holding companies, their volume accounting for about 60 percent of all commercial paper sold. Some of the major finance companies issuing paper directly are General Motors Acceptance Corporation, Sears, Ford Motor Credit, and Household International.

The major incentive for direct placement is that the issuer is able to save approximately one-tenth to one-eighth of a percent for the dealer's underwriting commission. For the commission, dealers can perform a number of services. First, dealers will price the securities, given current market conditions, and will also guarantee the sale of the entire issue. Dealers are able to do this because they are transacting in and monitoring the commercial paper market on a daily basis, maintain contact with a large number of firms, and have a sales force in place. They also provide all of the legal work and administrative assistance to bring a new issue to market. Unless a firm is a regular participant in the market, most firms find it less expensive to issue their commercial paper through a dealer.

For example, if a firm places $100 million in commercial paper through a dealer, the commission cost would be $125,000. However, to achieve the $125,000 savings, the issuer must maintain a small sales force—usually three to six employees plus a manager. Thus, most firms find that it pays to deal directly when the average annual amount outstanding is somewhere around $200 million.

Terms on directly placed commercial paper are negotiated directly between the borrower and the supplier of funds. When an agreement is reached as to the rate, maturity date, and amount to be borrowed, the borrower prints the agreement (often over a direct computer linkage to the supplier of funds), and the supplier of funds wires the money to the borrower's bank account.

COMMERCIAL PAPER YIELDS

Like Treasury bills, commercial paper is sold on a discount basis (i.e., it pays no coupon interest) using a 360-day year. Thus, Equation 7.1 can be used to compute the discount yield on commercial paper:

$$y_{cp} = \frac{P_f - P_0}{P_f} \times \frac{360}{n} \times 100\%, \tag{7.6}$$

where

y_{cp} = commercial paper yield on a discount basis
P_f = face value of commercial paper
P_0 = purchase price
n = number of days to maturity

The Perils of Commercial Paper— Being Kicked Out of the Club

Over the last decade, the commercial paper market has been a borrowing bonanza for American firms of the highest credit standing, which have been able to raise cheap money at a moment's notice. Commercial paper is *unsecured*, short-term borrowing, typically from overnight to 30 days. Many financial managers at these firms began to believe that commercial paper could be rolled over forever, creating, in effect, a low-cost machine for borrowing money.

They were rudely awakened beginning in the second quarter of 2001, when the market began to unravel. By the end of March 2002, the value of commercial paper issued by nonfinancial corporations declined by a third, the largest single contraction in 40 years. As a result, corporate issuers found themselves scrambling for financing because they were unable to refinance their commercial paper.

Why the sudden and dramatic meltdown of the commercial paper market? A number of factors contributed: an economic recession during 2001, the sudden bankruptcy of Enron, worries by investors over the lack of transparency in complex disclosures in financial statements, and the continued fallout of September 11. However, at the heart of the reluctance to lend was the greater uncertainty in the marketplace and greater credit risk of individual firms.

Usually in markets, as credit conditions deteriorate, lenders express their concerns by charging higher borrowing costs. However, lenders will do this only up to a point.

The commercial paper market works like an exclusive private club that has very tough admission standards, especially with respect to one's credit standing. The lenders—mutual funds and corporate investor with excess cash—want no surprises and absolutely no defaults in their portfolios. Thus, when any ill wind starts to blow, they start a "flight to quality," shifting their portfolios to Treasury securities or repo transactions that are secured and bail out of more risky commercial paper, which is unsecured.

A dramatic case in point was General Electric, one of the few corporate issuers with an AAA bond rating, which was squeezed out of the commercial market. Other venerable firms that have had their credit ratings downgraded and their access to the commercial paper market denied were AT&T, Daimler Chrysler, Eastman Kodak, The Gap, Motorola, Hertz, General Motors, and Disney. Over the previous decade, these and many other U.S. firms had improved their return on capital partly by their ability to raise funds cheaply in the commercial paper market. But, at least for now, these firms are out of the cheap-money club.

Equation 7.2 can be similarly modified to compute the bond equivalent yield for commercial paper:

$$y_{\text{cpbe}} = \frac{P_f - P_0}{P_0} \times \frac{365}{n} \times 100\%, \tag{7.7}$$

where the terms are as defined above.

Let's work through examples using Equations 7.6 and 7.7. Suppose a company purchases $1 million of 45-day commercial paper issued by GE Capital, a large finance company, for a price of $994,000. The discount yield on the commercial paper is calculated as follows:

$$y_{cp} = \frac{\$1,000,000 - \$994,000}{\$1,000,000} \times \frac{360}{45} \times 100\%$$
$$= 4.80\%.$$

On a bond equivalent basis, the yield is

$$y_{cpbe} = \frac{\$1,000,000 - \$994,000}{\$994,000} \times \frac{365}{45} \times 100\%$$
$$= 4.90\%.$$

As is the case with T-bills, note that the bond equivalent yield is higher than the discount yield.

A negotiable certificate of deposit (CD) is simply a bank time deposit that is negotiable. Because the receipt is negotiable, it can be traded any number of times in the secondary market before its maturity. The denominations of CDs range from $100,000 to $10 million. However, few negotiable CDs are denominated in less than $1 million because smaller denominations, although technically negotiable, are not as marketable and sell at concession prices. The normal round-lot trading unit among dealers is $1 million.

Negotiable CDs typically have maturities of 1 to 4 months. There is also a market for 6-month CDs, but beyond that maturity the volume is small and there is not an active secondary market. Most negotiable CDs, regardless of where the issuer is located, are payable in New York City in federal funds. This eliminates the problem of customers having to ship securities out of New York City to be presented to the issuing bank for payment. A sample negotiable CD is shown in Exhibit 7.9.

NEGOTIABLE CERTIFICATES OF DEPOSIT

BACKGROUND OF THE CD MARKET

The idea of a certificate of deposit is not really new. CDs, in one form or another, were sold by banks early in the 1900s to attract consumer and business deposits. However, before 1960, CDs were rarely issued in negotiable form. In February 1961, Citibank announced that it would issue negotiable CDs in large denominations and that major government security dealers had agreed to make a secondary market in them. Other money-center banks and dealers quickly followed Citibank's lead, paving the way for what proved to be a major innovation in the manner in which today's large banks manage their liquidity.

One reason for the development of negotiable CDs was the long-term trend of declining demand for business demand deposits at large banks. Banks are prohibited from paying interest on these accounts. Corporate treasurers in managing their cash balances were minimizing demand deposit balances and investing these funds in safe, income-generating money market instruments, such as Treasury bills and commercial paper. Large New York City banks, which are the principal banks for most large corporations, experienced substantial reductions in deposits. Negotiable CDs were designed to recapture lost corporate deposits

EXHIBIT 7.9
Negotiable Certificate of Deposit

CHEMICAL BANK   Negotiable Certificate of deposit

New York, N.Y   July 1, 1992   No. 159109 J1-12
                                                          210

This certifies that there has been deposited with this Bank the sum of

2,000,000.00   dollars

payable on July 31, 1992

to the order of XYZ Corporation

together with interest thereon at the rate of   10.25   per cent per annum (calculated on the basis of a 360 day year) from the date
hereof to maturity only, upon return of this certificate, properly endorsed

                                                Textbook Sample

No interest will be paid on this deposit after its maturity   Authorized signature

Chemical Bank of New York, now merged with Chase, was one of the nation's largest
money-center banks at the time this CD was issued. CDs are attractive to investors
because of their safety and high marketability.

by allowing commercial banks to pay competitive interest rates for short-term
funds.

The primary purchasers of CDs are corporate treasurers interested in maximizing the return of their firms' excess funds while maintaining the liquidity and
safety of their principal. The existence of a large secondary market is one of the
major reasons prime-name banks can attract a large quantity of corporate funds.
The secondary market allows corporate treasurers to enter the market at any time
and on either side—selling when they want to raise cash quickly or realize profits
(capital gains), or buying when they want maturities shorter than can be acquired
in the primary market. Surveys by the Federal Reserve System indicate that
between 70 and 80 percent of CDs are purchased by corporate customers.

NEGOTIABLE CD YIELDS

The rate paid on a CD is negotiated between the issuing bank and the buyer.
The underlying factors that determine the rate are current money market conditions, rates paid by competing banks on their CDs, yield on other similar
short-term instruments, and the characteristics of the issue, such as the default
risk and marketability of the CD. Banks post an "official" CD rate that serves as
an approximate guide to their actual rate. A bank will sell its CDs to any buyer
at the posted rate, which is typically a bit below the rate charged in the secondary market. The implication for this apparent anomaly between the posted and
actual rate charged is that commercial banks write CDs for their preferred customers at rates above those posted. However, if a bank is eager to attract funds,
it may adjust its posted rate above that of other banks and, in fact, a bit above
the secondary market.

Large prime-name banks, mostly located in New York City, are usually able to issue CDs at lower interest rates than smaller regional banks. The reason for this tiering of interest rates is the lower default risk and greater marketability of prime-name banks' CDs. This difference is also justified by past handling of failing banks by bank regulators. For example, the Federal Deposit Insurance Corporation (FDIC) has typically not allowed large banks to fail (most failures are small banks). A failing large bank is usually merged with another bank, and uninsured depositors rarely lose any money. In general, regional banks pay a premium of 5 to 25 basis points to sell their CDs.

The yield on a negotiable CD is an "add-on" rate paid over and above the principal balance using a 360-day year. As a result, CD yields will always be above T-bill discount rates for instruments with the same maturity—and the difference will be greater for higher levels of rates. Nonetheless, to make CD interest rates comparable to bond equivalent rates, adjustments need to be made to allow for a 365-day year.

BANKER'S ACCEPTANCE

A **banker's acceptance** is a time draft drawn on and accepted by a commercial bank. Time drafts are orders to pay a specified amount of money to the bearer on a given date. When drafts are accepted, a bank unconditionally promises to pay to the holder the face amount of the draft at maturity, even if the bank encounters difficulty collecting from its customers. It is the act of the bank substituting its creditworthiness for that of the issuer that makes banker's acceptances marketable instruments. Exhibit 7.10 shows a banker's acceptance.

EXHIBIT 7.10
Banker's Acceptance

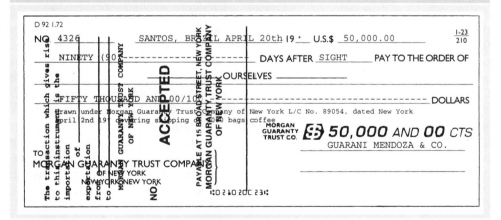

A time draft does not become a banker's acceptance until it is stamped "accepted" by a bank. The acceptance means that the draft is now a liability of the accepting bank when it comes due.

Source: Financing of Exports and Imports (New York: Morgan Guaranty Trust Company of New York, 1980).

Most banker's acceptances arise in international transactions between exporters and importers of different countries. In these transactions the accepting bank can be either a U.S. or a foreign bank, and the transaction can be denominated in any currency. However, the U.S. secondary market consists primarily of dollar acceptance financing in which the acceptor is a U.S. bank and the draft is denominated in dollars.

HISTORY OF BANKER'S ACCEPTANCES

The history of banker's acceptances dates back as far as the 12th century. Early acceptances were used primarily in Europe to finance international trade. In the United States, they were not widely used until after the establishment of the Federal Reserve System in 1913. At that time the Federal Reserve wanted to develop a dollar-based acceptance market to enhance the role of New York City as a center for international trade and finance.

Until the 1960s, banker's acceptances were not a major money market instrument. Their use depended on world economic conditions and the extent of U.S. foreign trade. Beginning in the 1960s, with the tremendous expansion of international trade, the volume of acceptances grew rapidly. Today foreign banks and nonbank financial institutions are the most important investors in the banker's acceptance market, regarding banker's acceptances as a safe and liquid investment. For some foreign holders, the income from acceptances is not subject to federal income tax, and thus foreign investors realize high yields. The next largest investors in acceptances are the issuing banks themselves. Typically, banks hold about 30 percent of all acceptances and about 85 percent of their holdings consist of acceptances drawn on themselves.

CREATING A BANKER'S ACCEPTANCE

To illustrate how banker's acceptances are created, the following example will be helpful. The sequence of events for our transaction can be followed in Exhibit 7.11. Assume that a U.S. importer wishes to finance the importation of Colombian coffee. Furthermore, the American importer wishes to pay for the coffee in 90 days. To obtain financing, the importer has an American bank write an irrevocable **letter of credit** for the amount of the sale, which is sent to the Colombian exporter. The letter specifies the details of the shipment and authorizes the Colombian exporter to draw a time draft for the sale price on the importer's bank. When the coffee is shipped, the exporter draws the draft on the American bank and then transfers the draft at a discount to its local bank, thereby receiving immediate cash payment for the coffee. The exporter's bank then sends the time draft, along with the proper shipping documents, to the American bank. The American bank accepts the draft by stamping "accepted" on its face and signs the instrument. The bank either returns the stamped time draft (acceptance) to the exporter's bank or immediately pays the exporter's bank for it at a discounted price reflecting the time value of money during the waiting period. If the American bank pays the exporter's bank for the acceptance, it can then either hold the accepted draft as an investment or sell it in the open market as a source of funds. When the draft matures, the American importer is responsible for paying the accepting bank. If for some reason the importer fails to pay, the accepting bank has legal recourse to collect from the Colombian exporter.

EXHIBIT 7.11
The Sequence of a Banker's Acceptance Transaction

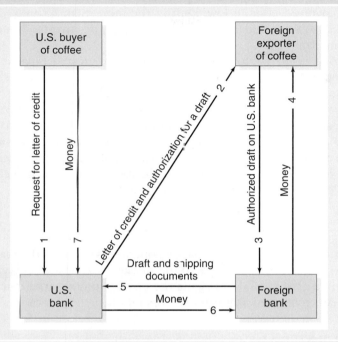

This exhibit shows a possible sequence for creating a banker's acceptance. However, there are many ways to create acceptances, and to do so requires a great deal of specialized knowledge on the part of the accepting bank.

The advantages of banker's acceptances in international trade are apparent from our simplified example. First, the exporter receives money promptly and avoids delays that could arise in international shipping. Second, the exporter is shielded from foreign exchange risk because a local bank pays in domestic funds. Third, the exporter does not have to examine the creditworthiness of the American firm because a large, well-known bank has guaranteed payment for the merchandise. Thus, it is not surprising that banker's acceptances are used primarily for international transactions.

MARKET FOR BANKER'S ACCEPTANCES

Creating a banker's acceptance requires a great deal of specialized knowledge on the part of the accepting bank. Consequently, there are less than 200 institutions worldwide that have specialized staff members who are knowledgeable about the banker's acceptance market. Domestically, the majority of all acceptances originate in New York City, Chicago, and San Francisco. The denomination of banker's acceptances depends on the originating transaction, which may be large or small. However, banker's acceptances trade in round lots, with $100,000 and $500,000 being the most common transaction sizes. Banks asked to finance large transactions will generally divide the amount into several drafts of $500,000. For small transactions, the bank may combine various drafts into a large, single, marketable draft. The maturities of acceptances are commonly 30, 60, or 90 days, but drafts may be acquired for any number of days up to a legal maximum of 180. The default risk involved is quite low. During the more than 65 years that banker's acceptances have been traded in the United States, no investor has ever suffered a loss of principal.

The secondary market for banker's acceptances is created as banks sell accepted drafts. Currently, there are roughly a dozen primary dealers in banker's acceptances who make an ongoing market in this instrument. The major dealers include most of the major Treasury securities dealers, some firms that specialize in banker's acceptances, and several large banks. In addition, there are a number of other banks and nonbank dealers that trade banker's acceptances on a less active basis. All dealers trade the acceptances generated by the major banks, and some specialize in making markets for selected groups of regional banks. Banker's acceptances are at least as marketable as commercial paper or bank-negotiable CDs.

MONEY MARKET PARTICIPANTS

To explain more fully how money markets operate, we discuss the major "players" in the money market, why they are in the market, and what their typical balance sheet position is. Exhibit 7.12 presents the major money market participants and the instruments most important to their operation.

COMMERCIAL BANKS

Commercial banks are by far the most important class of buyers and sellers of money market instruments. As Exhibit 7.12 shows, banks engage actively in almost all the money markets. They are continuously in the process of adjusting

EXHIBIT 7.12
Money Market Balance Sheet Position of Major Participants

Instrument	Commercial Banks A	L	Federal Reserve System A	L	Treasury Department A	L	Dealers and Brokers A	L	Corporations A	L
Treasury bills	■		■			■	■		■	
Agency securities	■		■				■		■	
Negotiable CDs		■					■		■	
Commercial paper		■					■		■	■
Banker's acceptances	■	■	■				■		■	
Federal funds	■	■								
Repurchase agreements	■	■	■				■	■	■	

Commercial banks are both important investors in and issuers of money market instruments.

Note: A = Assets, L = Liabilities.

their liquidity because of the short-term nature of their liabilities, wide variations in loan demand, and legal reserve requirements imposed on banks by regulations. During periods of cyclical boom, banks are typically faced with the problem of reserve deficiencies because of heavy loan demand. Needed reserves can be obtained by selling securities, such as short-term Treasury securities, from their investment portfolio; or banks can borrow reserves from other banks (federal funds), sell negotiable certificates of deposit, sell commercial paper, or borrow in the Eurodollar market. At other times, particularly during recessions, a major bank problem is that of investing excess reserves. During such periods, banks typically build up their secondary reserves by purchasing Treasury and government agency securities.

{economic boom – reserve deficiency
{recession → excess reserve

THE FEDERAL RESERVE SYSTEM

Although commercial banks are the largest class of participants in the money markets, the Federal Reserve is ultimately the most important participant because of its position as manager of the nation's money supply. The Federal Reserve System has no liquidity problems because of its ability to create money—its monetary power. Monetary policy is implemented by controlling the amount of reserve balances that member banks hold at the Federal Reserve. Changes in reserve balances are usually accomplished by open-market operations—the sale or purchase of Treasury securities by the Federal Reserve Bank. Thus direct intervention by the Federal Reserve in the Treasury securities market affects the liquidity of the nation's banking system by altering banks' reserve positions, which indirectly affects the liquidity of all economic units in the economy by its impact on general business conditions.

The Federal Reserve System also influences money markets through its discount window operation. Banks may borrow temporary reserves from the Federal Reserve System as an alternative to selling asset holdings or borrowing federal funds to cover legal reserve deficiencies. Thus, the discount window is part of the mechanism for adjusting short-term reserve deficiencies.

THE U.S. TREASURY AND TREASURY SECURITY DEALERS

Unlike the Federal Reserve System, the Treasury Department has a major liquidity problem. Tax receipts tend to be concentrated around the scheduled tax payment dates, but government expenditures tend to be more evenly distributed throughout the year. Furthermore, total government expenditures rarely equal and often exceed total receipts. The Treasury Department is given the job of financing the federal government's large debt; thus it issues both long- and short-term securities.

The economic function of primary government security dealers is to "make a market" for Treasury securities by maintaining an active position in most of the maturities issued. That is, dealers maintain an inventory of these securities at their own risk and stand ready to buy or sell from these inventories virtually any quantity of Treasury securities at their quoted bid or offer price. Making a market greatly increases the liquidity of Treasury securities, because the brokerage function of matching buyers and sellers in multimillion-dollar transactions would prove to be difficult, if not impossible, without it.

Most large dealers also trade in other money and capital market instruments. For example, some large dealers make markets in federal agency securities, banker's acceptances, negotiable certificates of deposit, and state and local government bonds. Still others specialize in commercial paper, corporate debt obligations, and over-the-counter stocks. Many securities dealers finance their holdings of securities by borrowing in the "repurchase agreement" or fed funds markets. Thus dealers help link together the nation's money and capital markets.

The lure of becoming a bond market dealer is based in the immense leverage available in the government securities market. Of course, high leverage means higher risk, and unfavorable interest rate swings of only a few basis points can mean catastrophic losses. On the other hand, favorable interest rate movements can mean substantial profits.

There have been a number of highly publicized failures of government securities firms, such as Drysdale (1982), Lombard-Wall (1982), ESM Government Securities (1985), and Bevill Bressler and Schulman (1985). These and other failures resulted in losses to investors of more than $700 million between 1980 and 1985. Prior to 1987, there were no federal regulations on firms that did business in the government securities market as long as they restricted their activities to being a broker or dealer in exempt securities, principally U.S. government securities. Thus, many large, well-known, and prudently operated government securities firms were unregulated, including the 30 to 40 primary dealers who report their financing and securities positions to the Federal Reserve Bank of New York. The center of the controversy was not these firms, however, but the questionable practices and sometimes outright fraud on the part of other unregulated government securities dealers, most of whom were small firms.

As a result of these and other abuses, Congress passed the Government Securities Act of 1986. The act standardized custody arrangements in repurchase agreements involving government securities. It also brought previously unregulated government securities firms under capital adequacy, financial recordkeeping, and customer protection standards similar to those that already apply to brokers and dealers in other securities.

CORPORATIONS

Although not as severe as the liquidity problems facing commercial banks, liquidity management problems also plague corporations. For corporations, the inflow of cash usually comes from the collection of accounts receivable that have been generated from sales. Corporate cash disbursements take place in various forms, such as expenditures for tax obligations, payrolls, inventory purchases, and services necessary to do business.

Because cash flows rarely balance, corporate treasuries are constantly juggling their cash positions. The focal point of corporate cash management strategy is the relationship with commercial banks. Some cash balances are held at commercial banks for liquidity needs and others are held as compensating balances as payment for bank services. Because compensating balance service contracts are usually based on monthly averages, corporate treasuries can use these bank balances as a day-to-day buffer for small, unexpected variations in cash flows. For larger, more persistent cash demands, corporate treasuries arrange for lines of credit or seasonal bank loans. If the corporation is large enough, it may find that commercial paper is a less expensive source of short-term credit than borrowing from a bank.

Although the various money market instruments have their individual differences, they serve as close substitutes for each other in investment portfolios. For this reason, the interest rates on different money market instruments tend to fluctuate closely together over time, as can be seen in Exhibit 7.13. For short periods, the traditional spreads between some money market instruments may get out of line. However, these temporary divergences set off forces that restore the rates to their normal spread. For example, if circumstances are such that corporations issue unusually large amounts of commercial paper, the commercial paper rate may rise relative to other money market rates. Sophisticated traders, noting the abnormal differential, will adjust their portfolios by selling other money market instruments, such as Treasury bills, and purchasing commercial paper. This action will cause commercial paper rates to fall and Treasury bill rates to rise until the normal or usual rate relationship is restored.

THE INTERRELATIONSHIP OF MONEY MARKET INTEREST RATES

EXHIBIT 7.13
The Comovement of Money Market Yields

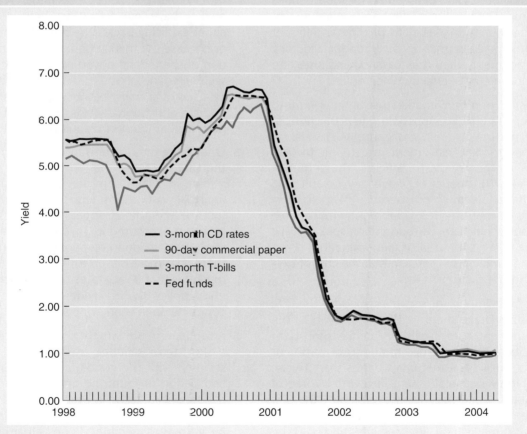

Yields in the money markets fluctuate together closely because the instruments are viewed as close substitutes.

Source: Federal Reserve Board of Governors, H.15 Statistical Release.

DO YOU UNDERSTAND?

1. Why do issues of securities by U.S. government agencies tend to have higher interest rates than similar issues of debt by the U.S. Treasury?
2. Why would you never observe a U.S. Treasury bill paying the same quoted rate of interest as a negotiable CD with the same maturity?
3. Why is a repo like a secured loan?
4. How and why do banker's acceptances frequently arise in international trade transactions?

CHAPTER TAKE-AWAYS

1 The money markets are where financial and non-financial businesses adjust their liquidity positions by borrowing or investing for short periods of time. The most important economic function of the money market is to provide an efficient means for economic units to conduct liquidity management when their cash expenditures and receipts are not perfectly synchronized.

2 Investors in money market instruments want to take as little risk as possible given the temporary nature of their cash surplus. Issuers of money market instruments are trying to deal with temporary cash deficits. Thus, money market instruments (1) have low default risk, (2) have low price risk because of their short terms-to-maturity, (3) are highly marketable because they can be bought or sold quickly, and (4) are sold in large denominations, typically $1 million or more, so that the cost of executing transactions is low.

3 The most important security issued by the U.S. Treasury Department is the Treasury bill. The government uses T-bills to finance short-term deficits and to refinance maturing government debt. T-bills have maturities of less than 1 year, are highly marketable, and are virtually free of default risk because they are backed by the U.S. government. T-bills have the most active secondary market of any security and can be bought and sold at very low transaction costs. T-bills are considered to be the ideal money market instrument.

4 Government-sponsored enterprises and federal agencies also issue short-term debt in the money markets. Agency securities are considered to have low default risk because they are either explicitly backed by the U.S. government or because the market perceives a moral obligation of the federal government to back agency securities. They trade in active secondary markets and offer many of the advantages of T-bills, but at slightly higher yields, because of the small perceived amount of default risk.

5 One of the most important financial markets in the United States, the fed funds market is the market in which commercial banks and other financial institutions lend each other excess funds overnight. Essentially, fed funds transactions are unsecured loans between banks for 1 to 7 days, in denominations of $1 million or more. The most important role of the fed funds market is that it facilitates the conduct of monetary policy by the Federal Reserve when it conducts open-market operations.

6 A repurchase agreement consists of the sale of a short-term security, usually a U.S. Treasury security, with the condition that after a specified period of time, the original seller will buy the security back at a predetermined price. In effect, a repo is a short-term loan collateralized by a Treasury security. Repos are made for 1 day to 3 months, or longer, with a minimum denomination of $1 million.

7 Commercial paper is a short-term promissory note issued by a large corporation to finance short-term working capital needs. Commercial paper is viewed as an open-market alternative to bank borrowing, and firms use the commercial paper market to achieve interest savings over otherwise similar bank loans. Commercial paper maturities range from 1 day to 270 days and it is sold in denominations from $100,000 to $1 million. Typically, commercial paper is backed up by a line of credit from a commercial bank, which reduces the risk that an issuer may not be able to pay off or roll over the maturing paper. Large finance companies such as GE Capital or Ford Motor Credit are the major issuers of commercial paper. Only firms of good credit quality can issue commercial paper because it is unsecured.

8 A negotiable CD is a bank deposit that can be traded in the secondary market before its maturity. Most negotiable CDs are sold in denominations of $1 million and carry maturities of 1 to 4 months.

9 A banker's acceptance is a time draft drawn on and accepted by a commercial bank. Most banker's acceptances arise in international trade. The U.S. secondary market consists primarily of dollar acceptance financing in which the acceptor is a U.S. bank and the draft is denominated in dollars. Banker's acceptances typically trade in lots of $100,000 and $500,000 and mature in 30, 60, or 90 days. The default risk on banker's acceptances is very low.

10 Commercial banks use the money markets extensively, continuously adjusting their liquidity positions of the short-term nature of their liabilities. The Federal Reserve System, perhaps the most important participant in the money market, controls the nation's money supply through open-market operations in which it buys and sells Treasury securities. The Treasury Department uses the money market to manage its liquidity, given that tax receipts tend to be concentrated around scheduled tax payment dates, but government expenditures are spread more evenly across the year. Government security dealers are private financial institutions that make a market for Treasury securities by standing ready to buy or sell from their inventory at quoted prices. Their activities greatly enhance the liquidity of the market for Treasury securities because of their willingness to buy or sell large amounts of securities. Corporations use the money markets when inflow of cash collected from accounts receivable doesn't keep up with necessary cash disbursements for payroll, tax obligations, and so on.

11 Money market instruments share many common characteristics and, therefore, they serve as close substitutes for one another. For this reason, the yields on money market instruments are highly correlated with one another.

KEY TERMS

Money market	Federal funds	Reverse repurchase agreement
Treasury bill	Immediately available funds	Commercial paper
Federal agency	Repurchase agreement	Banker's acceptance
Nonguaranteed agency debt	Repo	Letter of credit

QUESTIONS AND PROBLEMS

1. Calculate the bond equivalent yield for a 180-day T-bill that is purchased at a 6 percent asked yield. If the bill has a face value of $10,000, calculate its price.

2. What are the characteristics of money market instruments? Why must a financial claim possess these characteristics to function as a money market instrument?

3. How are U.S. Treasury and federal agency securities different? What difference primarily explains the yield differential between the two securities?

4. What types of firms issue commercial paper? What are the characteristics critical to being able to issue commercial paper?

5. Why is a bank line of credit necessary to back up an issue of commercial paper?

6. Describe the steps in a typical banker's acceptance transaction. Why is the banker's acceptance form of financing ideal in foreign transactions?

7. Explain how repurchase agreement transactions provide short-term loans to businesses. In what sense is a repo a collateralized loan?

8. Suppose Fargood Corporation engages in a repurchase agreement with The National Bank of Nebraska. In the agreement, Fargood sells $9,987,950 worth of Treasury securities to the bank and agrees to repurchase the securities in 30 days for $10,000,000.

   a. Is this transaction a loan, and if so, who is the borrower and who is the lender? Defend your answer.

   b. Is the loan collateralized? What is the collateral? Who holds the collateral during the term of the agreement?

   c. What interest rate (or yield) is earned by the lender?

   d. Draw T-accounts for this transaction, similar to the example earlier in the chapter. Show the assets and liabilities for each party before and after the transaction.

9. Suppose 7-day fed funds trade at 1.65 percent annually. What is the yield on fed funds on a bond-equivalent basis?

10. Why did several large well-known firms find it so difficult to raise funds in the commercial paper market in 2002?

INTERNET EXERCISE

For purposes of this assignment, you can pretend that you are an analyst reporting to the treasurer of a Fortune 500 firm. Your boss needs to understand the status of the commercial paper market, because she is considering issuing commercial paper in the near future.

1. Go to http://www.federalreserve.gov/. On the left side of the Web page select "Research and Data."
2. Next, choose "Statistics: Releases and Historical Data."
3. Under "Daily Releases," choose "Commercial Paper."
4. At the very bottom of the page, select "Historical Outstandings."
5. You will then see a table of data that shows the monthly commercial paper outstanding, seasonally adjusted.
6. Using a spreadsheet program, graph the monthly amounts outstanding for both financial and nonfinancial issuers from January 2000 to the present and answer the following questions:
   a. What happened to the amount outstanding in the commercial paper market for nonfinancial issuers during the past few years? What happened with respect to financial issuers?
   b. Why do you think that there is such a remarkable difference between financial and nonfinancial firms?
   c. Using your superb Internet research skills, can you find any articles from the *Wall Street Journal*, the *New York Times*, or *The Economist* that will help you answer the questions above? What do these articles have to say about developments in the commercial paper market?

Bond Markets

It's the morning of January 23, 2001, and you're feeling great. A few weeks ago you bought $50 million of Enron investment-grade bonds for your portfolio and the morning *New York Times* reports that Enron's fourth-quarter profits are up 34 percent. Corporate bonds are unsecured debt, and investors' biggest fear is that the issuer will default.

The earnings report confirms what you heard at a meeting you attended with hundreds of Enron executives during January. At that meeting, Ken Lay, the president of Enron, strode onto a ballroom stage at the Hyatt Regency in San Antonio, walked between two giant screens that displayed his projected image, and delivered a rousing description of the firm's achievements. As waiters with bolo ties scurried about serving drinks, the crowd was festive; the clinking of glass was occasionally drowned out by applause as Ken Lay presented his vision of Enron as the "world's greatest company."

Less than a year later—December 1, 2001, to be exact—in the small, dimly lit office of Weil Gotshal Houston, a Wall Street law firm, lawyers worked through the night struggling to pull together lists of creditors and their claims. Their voices were tired, their shoulders slumped from the strain of the grueling and relentless

work. Then, early in the morning of December 2, Steve Vacek, a paralegal aid, sat down at a computer terminal and logged on to the Internet site for the federal bankruptcy court in New York City. The necessary information was filled in.

Then at 4:28 A.M., Mr Vacek carefully moved the cursor to the box titled "submit," left clicked, and, in the blink of an eye, the largest bankruptcy in American history was filed and the "world's greatest company" laid in the ruins of broken promises.

How are bondholders and other creditors of Enron doing on getting paid the $50 billion or more that Enron owes creditors? Not so good. Reports out of the bankruptcy court indicate that the company may recover only $10 billion. And, with $10 billion in bank credit having priority status over bondholders, the prospects for any meaningful recovery for bondholders does not look promising. This is a hard lesson in the stark realities of default risk. ■

1400 Smith Street

Ken Lay, former CEO of Enron, called Enron the "world's greatest company." Today Enron is a symbol of excessive risk taking, financial fraud, and deception of investors. Enron is the largest bankruptcy in American history and exemplifies what default risk is all about—companies lying in the ruins of broken promises.

The previous chapter discussed money market instruments that have minimal credit risk. These instruments are reasonably homogeneous and are issued and held by economic units as a means to adjust liquidity. This chapter, in contrast, discusses capital market instruments whose terms, conditions, and risk vary substantially, as holders of Enron bonds are painfully aware.

Capital market instruments are defined as long-term financial instruments with an original maturity of greater than 1 year. As the name implies, the proceeds from the sale of capital market instruments are usually invested in assets of a permanent nature such as industrial plants, equipment, buildings, and inventory. The chapter begins with a discussion of the function of the major participants in capital markets. We then turn our discussion to the bond markets: the markets for long-term Treasury and agency securities, corporate bonds, state and local government tax-exempt bonds, and Eurobonds. We then discuss "junk" bonds, the securitization of debt, and the globalization of long-term debt markets. Finally, we look at institutional arrangements that increase the market efficiency of capital markets such as regulatory bodies and the bond-rating agencies. The market for mortgages will be discussed in Chapter 9 and the market for equities in Chapter 10. ∎

 ## LEARNING OBJECTIVES

The objectives of this chapter are to:

1 Explain the role and function of capital markets. How does their role differ from that of the money markets?

2 Explain what STRIPs are and how they can be helpful in immunizing a bond portfolio against interest rate risk.

3 Discuss how the municipal bond market differs from the market for corporate bonds and the instruments traded in each market.

4 Explain what "junk" bonds are and why the market developed in the late 1980s.

5 Explain what is meant by the term "securitization of debt."

6 Identify some of the reasons that bond markets are becoming global.

FUNCTIONS OF THE CAPITAL MARKETS

In the capital markets, the motive of firms issuing or buying securities is very different from in the money market. In the money markets, firms are warehousing idle funds until needed for some business activity or borrowing temporarily until cash is collected. Firms buy capital goods such as plant and equipment to produce some product to earn a profit. Most of these investments are central to the firm's core business activities. Capital goods normally have a long economic life, ranging from a few years to 10, 20, or 30 years or more. Capital assets usually are not highly marketable. As a result, firms like to finance capital goods with long-term debt or equity to lock in their borrowing cost for the life of the project and to eliminate the problems associated with periodically refinancing assets.

For example, say a firm buys a plant with an expected economic life of 15 years. Since short-term rates are typically lower than long-term rates, at first glance, short-term financing may look like a real deal. However, if interest rates rise dramatically, as they did in the early 1980s, the firm may find its borrowing cost skyrocketing as it has to refinance its short-term debt. And in the worst case, the firm may find it does not have adequate cash flows to support the debt and may be forced into bankruptcy. Similarly, if market conditions become unsettled, as they did during the 2001 recession, issuers may find themselves unable to refinance their short-term debt; if no other lenders are found, bankruptcy could again be the end result.

On the other hand, if long-term securities such as bonds are used, the cost of funds is known for the life of the asset and there should be fewer refinancing problems. It should be no surprise, then, that when issuing debt for capital expenditures, firms often try to match the expected asset life with the maturity of the debt. However, there is a price to reduce interest rate and reinvestment risk, in that long-term interest rates tend to be higher than short-term rates due to risk premiums.

CAPITAL MARKET PARTICIPANTS

Capital markets bring together borrowers and suppliers of long-term funds. The market also allows people who hold previously issued securities to trade those securities for cash in the secondary capital markets.

As Exhibit 8.1 shows, the largest purchasers of capital market securities are individuals, households, and, from time to time, foreign investors. Financial institutions are also important participants in capital markets, though their net posi-

EXHIBIT 8.1
Net Financial Positions of Major Sectors of the Economy, December 2003 ($ in billions)

Sector	Financial Assets	Financial Liabilities	Net Financial Position Surplus	Deficit
Households and nonprofits	$34,341.0	$9,756.7	$24,584.3	
Nonfinancial business	12,704.7	13,945.1		$1,240.4
State and local government	1,544.2	2,270.3		726.1
Federal government	633.6	5,016.1		4,382.5
Financial institutions	43,428.4	43,032.9	395.5	
Remainder	8,599.4	4,295.9	4,303.5	
Total	$101,251.3	$78,317.0	$29,283.3	$6,349.0

Households are the largest supplier of funds in financial markets. To no one's surprise, the federal government has a large deficit position.

Source: Board of Governors, Federal Reserve System. *Flow of Funds Accounts of the United States,* March 4, 2004.

tion (asset – liabilities) is not large because of their roles as financial intermediaries. That is, they purchase funds from individuals and others, and then issue their own securities in exchange. Hence, individuals and households may invest directly in the capital markets but, more than likely, they purchase stocks and bonds through financial institutions such as commercial banks, insurance companies, mutual funds, and pension funds.

The major issuers of capital market securities are the federal government, state and local governments, and corporations. The federal government and its agencies issue notes and bonds to finance their operations or to refinance existing debt that is about to mature. State and local governments issue debt to finance the myriad of capital projects that municipal governments engage in, such as water treatment plants, roads, airports, convention centers, schools, prisons, and, at times, professional sports facilities. The list is restrained only by taxpayers' willingness to support these projects at the ballot box and the willingness of Congress to grant tax-exempt status. Government units cannot issue stock since they are not allowed to sell ownership in themselves. Corporations can issue both bonds and stock. The decision to issue debt and what type of debt is complex and depends upon management's philosophy toward capital structure, their willingness to bear risk, and the receptivity of lenders to the securities being offered.

SIZE OF CAPITAL MARKETS

The capital markets are massive in scope, exceeding $41.9 trillion. As Exhibit 8.2 shows, the equity market (Chapter 10) is the largest single capital market, with nearly $15.5 trillion outstanding. The mortgage market (Chapter 9) is also large, amounting to nearly $9.5 trillion. Long-term government securities (Treasury and agency) are also quite large, totaling over $8.7 ($2.6 + $6.1) trillion. By far the

---

EXHIBIT 8.2
Capital Market Instruments Outstanding ($ in billions)

Instrument	1970	1980	1990	2000	2003	Annual Growth Rate (%)
Treasury debt (over 1 year)	$124	$407	$1,668	$2,320	$2,646	9.7
Federal agency debt (over 1 year)	44	277	1,446	4,345	6,096	16.1
Municipal bonds (over 1 year)	144	350	956	1,223	1,450	7.2
Corporate bonds	202	495	1,706	5,050	6,840	11.3
Corporate stock (at market value)	906	1,634	3,543	17,566	15,497	9.0
Mortgages	470	1,449	3,808	6,934	9,465	9.5
Total	$1,890	$4,612	$13,127	$37,438	$41,994	9.9

In recent years, federal agency debt has been the fastest-growing sector of the capital markets. Much of this growth can be attributed to growth by government-sponsored entities, such as Fannie Mae and Freddie Mac.

Source: Board of Governors, Federal Reserve System, *Flow of Funds Accounts of the United States,* various issues, and Bureau of the Public Debt, *Monthly Statement of the Public Debt of the United States,* various issues.

fastest-growing debt market during the last 30 years is that for federal agency debt.

U.S. TREASURY NOTES AND BONDS

Treasury notes (T-notes) and **bonds** (T-bonds) are similar to T-bills in that they are issued by the U.S. Treasury and are backed by the full faith and credit of the U.S. government. Hence, they are considered to be free of default risk. They differ from bills in that they are coupon issues (paying interest semiannually) and have maturities greater than 1 year. Notes have an original maturity of 1 to 10 years, and bonds have an original maturity of more than 10 years. The primary and secondary markets for Treasury notes and bonds are similar to those for bills: new issues are sold at auction by the Treasury Department, and existing issues can be purchased or sold in the secondary market from securities dealers.

In recent years, notes and bonds have become a less important financing vehicle because the federal government has increasingly relied on shorter maturity debt (mostly bills). In fact, on October 31, 2001, the U.S. Treasury announced that it would stop issuing 30-year Treasury bonds. As a result, the 10-year Treasury note has become the new benchmark security in the long-term Treasury market.

Many of the characteristics of U.S. Treasury securities were discussed in Chapter 7. Government debt is primarily sold in frequent well-publicized auctions and is bid upon by the approximately 30 "primary" government securities dealers who may resell the debt to the public. In addition, individuals may enter "noncompetitive bids" at each Treasury securities auction through the Treasury Direct program run by each Federal Reserve bank. Because the maximum noncompetitive bid is $5 million for any one bidder, the primary dealers, who buy in large quantities, have to bid specific "competitive" rates. Each bid is stated to two and a half decimal places, and the Treasury accepts the best bids (lowest rates) until it sells all the notes or bonds that it has offered to sell.

Exhibit 8.3 shows part of Treasury note and bond price and yield information from the *Wall Street Journal* for May 14, 2004. The right-hand portion of the exhibit shows the same information for Treasury STRIPs, which will be discussed later in the chapter. Column 1 in the exhibit, labeled Rate, lists the coupon rate for the Treasury security. Note that the coupon rates change in increments of one-eighth of a percent and coupons are paid semiannually. Column 2, labeled Maturity, is the month and year in which the security matures; an "n" after the date means the security was originally issued as a T-note and, hence, had an original maturity of less than 10 years. Column 3, labeled Bid, is the price at the close of the day in percentage terms and is the price at which dealers will buy Treasury securities from investors. Prices are quoted as a percentage of the security's face value and quotes vary by increments of 32nds. For example, using a face value of $1,000, the bid price on a 6.50 percent coupon Treasury note maturing October 2006 was $1,084.0625 ($108 + {}^{13}/_{32}$). Column 4, labeled Asked, is the price at the close of the day and is the price at which dealers will sell securities to investors. Again, coupon increments are in 32nds and the price calculation is similar to that computed for the bid. Column 5, labeled Chg, is the change in the ask price from the previous day's closing price in 32nds. For example, for our October 2006 note, the price increased $^{1}/_{32}$ from the previous day. Finally, Column 6, labeled Ask Yld,

EXHIBIT 8.3
Selected Quotations on Treasury Bonds and Notes on May 14, 2004

| | Government Bonds and Notes | | | | | U.S. Treasury Strips | | | | | |
Rate	Maturity Mo/Yr[a]	Bid[b]	Asked	Chg	Ask Yld	Maturity	Type[c]	Bid	Asked	Chg	Ask Yld
1.500	May 06n	98:06	98:07	+6	2.48	May 06	ci	94:31	94:31	+6	2.61
6.500	Oct 06n	108:13	108:14	+7	2.85	Oct 06	np	93:11	93:11	+6	2.87
3.625	Jan 08i	109:17	109:18	+3	0.96	Feb 08	ci	87:19	87:19	+10	3.57
11.750	Feb 10	107:12	107:13	−1	1.70	Aug 10	ci	76:05	76:05	+10	4.41
6.250	May 30	109:02	109:03	+27	5.58	Nov 12	np	67:01	67:01	+11	4.77

[a] n designates a note; i designates an inflation-indexed issue; and no designation following the maturity year indicates a bond.
[b] Colons in bid and asked quotes represent 32nds. For example, 100:02 means $100\frac{2}{32}$.
[c] ci designates stripped coupon interest; np designates stripped principal from a Treasury note.

Source: Wall Street Journal Online, May 17, 2004.

is the asked price converted into the bond's yield-to-maturity. The yield-to-maturity calculation is the same yield-to-maturity presented in Chapter 5 (using semi-annual coupon payments). Conceptually, the yield-to-maturity is the interest rate that makes the price of the security equal to the present value of the coupon payments and the security's face value (principal).

INFLATION-INDEXED NOTES AND BONDS

In addition to the fixed-principal notes and bonds discussed above, the Treasury also issues notes and bonds that adjust for inflation. These securities are commonly referred to as **Treasury Inflation Protection Securities (TIPS)**. TIPS were first issued in January 1997. Just like the fixed-coupon notes and bonds, the coupon rate on a TIPS issue is determined via the auction process. Unlike the fixed-principal securities, however, the principal amount upon which the coupon payments are based changes as the inflation rate changes. Specifically, the principal amount adjusts in response to changes in the Consumer Price Index for All Urban Consumers (CPI-U).

For example, consider an investor who purchases a Treasury inflation-indexed note with an original principal amount of $100,000, a 3 percent annual coupon rate (1.5 percent semiannual coupon rate), and 10 years to maturity. If the semi-annual inflation rate during the first 6 months is 1 percent, the principal amount for the first coupon payment will be adjusted upward by 1 percent or $1,000 to $101,000. Therefore, the first coupon payment will be $1,515 ($101,000 × 1.5%). This adjustment in principal amount will take place before each and every coupon payment. At maturity, the investor receives the greater of either the final principal amount or the initial par amount.

TIPS are sold three times a year and can be bought directly from the Treasury in denominations starting at $1,000. TIPS are designed to provide investors with a way to protect their investment against inflation. Since their introduction, the inflation-indexed bonds have proven popular with investors. In addition, TIPS provide government policy makers with a simple way to calculate the expected rate of inflation in the economy. The reason is that the principal and interest payments on TIPS are adjusted for changes in price levels and, hence, the interest rate on these bonds provides a direct measure of the real rate of interest. The expected rate of inflation can be obtained by subtracting the real rate of interest from the nominal interest rate of a comparable security. That is:

$$\Delta P_e = i - r,$$

which is Equation 4.3 from Chapter 4, algebraically rearranged.

For example, on July 13, 2004, the yield on a 5-year Treasury note was 3.49 percent and the yield on 5-year TIPS was 1.10 percent. Thus, the implied expected rate of inflation for the next 5 years is

$$\Delta P_e = 3.49 - 1.10 = 2.39\%.$$

Our calculation tells us that as of July 13, 2004, 2.39 percent is the market's best estimate of the inflation rate for the next 5 years. Needless to say, this is valuable information for government policy makers, investors, and other persons in the private sector. However, as we have mentioned before, as with any expectations, they may not be realized. Our calculated value of 2.39 percent is the market's best estimate at a point in time. As new information becomes available, the market participants will, more than likely, revise their estimate.

STRIPS

The **Separate Trading of Registered Interest and Principal (STRIPs)** program began in 1995. A strip is just a Treasury security that has been separated into its component parts: each interest payment and the principal payment become a separate zero-coupon security. For example, a 10-year Treasury note consists of 1 principal payment, which the holder receives at maturity, and 20 semiannual interest payments. When this note is stripped, 21 separate securities are created. Today, most fixed-principal and inflation-indexed T-notes and T-bonds are eligible for the Treasury's strip program. The only restriction on strips is that the components of a strip must be sold in multiples of $1,000 (e.g., $2,000, $3,000) with the minimum face value of $1,000.

The Treasury does not issue strips directly to investors. Instead, financial institutions or registered dealers and brokers buy Treasury securities whole at auction and then create strip components to meet the demands of customers. To do this, the firms instruct the Treasury Department to electronically recode each coupon payment and the face value payment as a separate security in the book entry system. With this done, the firm now can sell the "new" strip securities individually or collectively in the secondary market.

Creation of a Strip.   To give you a better feel for how strip securities are created and work, let's go through an example. Suppose that Chase Bank out of New York City decides to buy a T-note at the Treasury auction and convert it into a strip. The T-note has the following characteristics: maturity of 4 years,

EXHIBIT 8.4
Present Value of Strip Components

Maturity (in years)	CUSIP Number	Cash Flow at Maturity	PV of Cash Flow @5.80%
0.5	1	$300	$291.55
1.0	2	300	283.33
1.5	3	300	275.34
2.0	4	300	267.58
2.5	5	300	260.04
3.0	6	300	252.71
3.5	7	300	245.59
4.0	8	300	238.67
4.0	9	10000	7,955.67
			$10,070.49

The present value of strip components for a 4-year Treasury note with a 6 percent coupon, a 5.80 percent yield-to-maturity, and a $10,000 face value is $10,070.49, assuming semiannual compounding.

coupon rate of 6 percent (semiannual), face value of $10,000, and at its purchase price, the yield-to-maturity is 5.8 percent (see Exhibit 8.4). To convert the T-note to a strip, Chase instructs the Treasury to separate the coupon payments from the principal and give each individual cash flow a separate CUSIP number. CUSIP (Committee on Uniform Security Identification Procedures) numbers are identification numbers given to each individual security. For illustrative purposes, we have given each cash flow a CUSIP number from 1 to 9 to emphasize the point that the original T-note is now nine separate securities. The price of the original T-note to Chase was $10,070.49 and Chase expects to sell the nine strip securities for a higher price. The reason for the premium is that there are a number of investors who desire zero-coupon bonds to manage their portfolios. In particular, zero-coupon bonds are much easier to use than whole bonds (coupon payments and principal) to immunize portfolios against interest rate risk.

Using Strips to Hedge against Interest Rate Risk.   Strips are effective vehicles for immunizing portfolios against interest rate risk. Recall from Chapter 5 that we can eliminate both price risk and reinvestment risk by structuring our bond investment such that the duration of our bond portfolio matches our holding period. Also recall that this is a dynamic problem and that we must rebalance the duration of our bond portfolio periodically to make sure its duration continues to match our holding period as our holding period shortens. By using strips, however, we avoid having to rebalance our portfolio because the duration of a strip is the same as its maturity. If we have a holding period of 5 years and we buy a strip that matures in 5 years, we are assured of receiving the face amount of the strip in 5 years.

GOVERNMENT AGENCY SECURITIES

Recall from Chapter 7 that a federal agency is an independent federal department or corporation established by Congress and owned or underwritten by the U.S. government. Federal agency securities result from selected government lending programs. Initially these programs were designed to attract private capital to sectors of the economy where credit flows were considered insufficient. Housing and agriculture were traditionally the principal beneficiaries of federal credit programs. In recent years, the objectives of federal credit programs have expanded to include social and economic goals and to promote conservation and resource utilization. See Exhibit 7.7 for a list of the major government agencies authorized to issue debt.

DO YOU UNDERSTAND?

1. Why do businesses use the capital markets?
2. What is the difference between a T-bill, T-note, and T-bond?
3. What is a strip? Explain how they are created.
4. Explain how strips can be used to immunize portfolios against interest rate risk.

State and local government bonds, often called **municipal bonds**, encompass all issues of state governments and their political subdivisions, such as cities, counties, school districts, and transit authorities. The municipal bond market is one of the largest fixed-income securities markets. The market is unique among major capital markets in that the number of issuers is so large. Estimates indicate that more than 50,000 entities have debt outstanding and an additional 30,000 have legal access to the market. No other direct capital market accommodates so many borrowers. As of January 2004, there was nearly $1.7 trillion of municipal debt outstanding.

STATE AND LOCAL GOVERNMENT BONDS

THE TYPE AND USE OF MUNICIPAL BONDS

State and local government debt generally consists of either **general obligation bonds** or **revenue bonds**. General obligation bonds are backed by the "full faith and credit" (the power to tax) of the issuing political entity; there are no assets pledged in the event of default. Full faith and credit means that in the event of default, the bankruptcy court will require the city or local government to raise taxes to pay coupon or principal payments. Thus, the creditworthiness of these bonds depends upon the income levels of the households and the financial strength of businesses within the municipality's tax base. General obligation bonds are typically issued to provide basic services to communities, such as education, fire and police protection, and health-care facilities. They typically require voter approval and, as a result, in recent years the market for general obligation bonds has been the slowest-growing portion of the municipal debt market.

Revenue bonds are sold to finance a specific revenue-producing project; in event of default, only the revenue generated from the project backs these bonds. Typical revenue projects are toll roads and bridges, water and sewage treatment plants, university dormitories, parking facilities, and port facilities.

Depending on the type of project, revenue bonds may be riskier than general obligation bonds. For instance, Chesapeake Bridge and Tunnel Authority bonds went into default when a section of the bridge was destroyed. When revenue bonds default, bondholders can take control of the assets pledged and liquidate them. Revenue bonds typically do not require voter approval, which can account for their growth in recent years. The ratio of revenue bonds to general obligation bonds tends to rise during difficult economic times, when voters are less likely to approve new bond issues.

Industrial development bonds (IDBs) are a controversial use of revenue bonds. IDBs were first issued to help stimulate local businesses following the Great Depression. When issuing an IDB, the municipality merely gives its approval to the sale of the bonds and assumes no legal liability in the event of default. The recipient of the funds benefits because of the lower borrowing cost associated with tax-exempt debt. Because of IDB abuses of the tax-exempt interest privileges, federal legislation passed in 1984 limited the amount of IDBs sold in each state.

Mortgage-backed bonds are another area of abuse in the tax-exempt market. These bonds are issued by city housing authorities based on mortgage pools generated under their jurisdiction. Because interest paid on the bonds is tax-exempt, the issuer can borrow funds at low interest and then make low-interest mortgage loans. Congress intended these bonds to fund homes for low- and moderate-income people. Because of widespread abuse by some municipalities, Congress now has restricted the use of mortgage-backed municipal bonds.

THE CHARACTERISTICS OF MUNICIPAL BONDS

Municipal bond issues are typically issued in the minimum denomination of $5,000 and are sold as serial bond issues. A **serial bond issue** contains a range of maturity dates rather than all of the bonds in the issue having the same maturity date. Exhibit 8.5 shows an example of the structure of a typical serial bond issue. In the example, the issue is a serial bond issue of $1 million and has a final maturity of 8 years. The bond issue contains bonds with eight different maturity dates, ranging from 1 year to 8 years. Also, notice that each maturity has a different coupon rate. Typically, when the bond issue is sold, the coupon rates are assigned to correspond to the prevailing term structure in the municipal bond market. In the example, the yield curve is upward sloping. The principal payments correspond to the payment schedule that the municipality has decided for the debt service: $100,000 per year for 7 years with a final balloon payment of $300,000 for the final year.

THE TAX-EXEMPT FEATURE

Municipal securities can be distinguished from other types of securities by the fact that coupon interest payments are exempt from federal income tax. This feature lowers the borrowing cost of state and local governments because investors are willing to accept lower pretax yields on municipal bonds than on taxable securi-

---

EXHIBIT 8.5
Example Structure of a Serial Tax-Exempt Bond Issue

Maturity (in Years)	Coupon Rate (%)	Principal Payment (in $)
1	5.00	100,000
2	5.50	100,000
3	5.90	100,000
4	6.20	100,000
5	6.45	100,000
6	6.60	100,000
7	6.70	100,000
8	6.75	300,000

This exhibit illustrates the structure of a serial tax-exempt bond issue for an issue size of $1 million and a maturity of 8 years.

---

ties of comparable maturity and risk. To the extent that these securities are substitutes, investors will choose the security that provides the greatest after-tax return. Recall from Chapter 6 that the appropriate yield comparison is between after-tax yields on municipal securities and taxable securities:

$$i_m = i_t(1 - t), \tag{8.1}$$

where i_m and i_t are pretax yields on municipal and taxable securities of comparable maturity and risk, and t is the marginal tax rate that equates the after-tax yield on municipals and taxable securities.

Given t and i_t, the equation determines the minimum municipal yield to induce investors in tax bracket t to buy municipals rather than taxable bonds. If the investor's marginal tax rate is sufficiently high, municipal securities will generate higher yields after tax than taxable securities. If the investor's tax rate is sufficiently low, the opposite will hold—taxable securities will yield relatively more than tax-exempts. For the two markets to clear, tax-exempt and taxable security yields will adjust so that at the margin the last investor who views these securities as substitutes will be indifferent; the after-tax yields of the two alternatives are equal. Thus, it is the marginal tax rate of the last investor that determines the relative rate relationship between comparable tax-exempt and taxable securities.

INVESTORS IN MUNICIPAL BONDS

The demand for tax-exempt securities is concentrated among three groups of investors that face high marginal tax rates: commercial banks, property and casualty insurance companies, and high-income individuals who may purchase them either directly or through mutual funds. Exhibit 8.6 shows the ownership of tax-exempt securities as of December 31, 2003.

Historically, commercial banks were the major purchasers of municipal bonds. In the late 1960s and 1970s, banks typically owned more than 50 percent

EXHIBIT 8.6
Holders of Municipal Bonds (December 31, 2003)

Holder	Amount ($ in Billions)	Percentage of Total
Households	$680.6	35.8
Commercial banks	132.5	7.0
Casualty insurance companies	200.6	10.6
Money market mutual funds	297.3	15.7
Mutual funds	291.1	15.3
Other	297.3	15.7
Total	$1,899.4	100.0

Individuals are the largest purchasers of municipal bonds. They buy them directly and indirectly through the purchase of mutual funds.

Source: Board of Governors, Federal Reserve System, *Flow of Funds Accounts of the United States,* March 4, 2004.

of all outstanding tax-exempt debt. Since then, bank ownership has declined; in 2003, banks owned only 7.0 percent of outstanding tax-exempt debt. In the past, bank demand for municipal securities was strongly influenced by banks' ability to engage in a form of tax arbitrage. In the past, commercial banks were allowed to deduct from their taxable income the interest expense on debt (e.g., time deposits) used to obtain funds to finance the purchase of tax-exempt securities. As a result, banks had incentives to borrow money and purchase tax-exempt securities as long as the after-tax cost of debt was below the tax-exempt interest rate. The Tax Reform Act of 1986 put an end to deductibility of bank interest expenses for funds used to purchase tax-exempt securities after 1986 (except for small issues).

Today, bank demand for tax-exempt securities is strongly influenced by bank incentives to purchase tax-exempt securities because of state pledging or collateral requirements for public deposits. That is, many states require banks to collateralize public deposits with in-state tax-exempt securities. In these states, banks have additional incentives to purchase tax-exempt securities issued in the bank's home state.

Demand for tax-exempt securities by property and casualty insurance companies has always varied widely over time. For example, in 1969 these companies owned only 11.3 percent of outstanding tax-exempts, and in 1980 they owned 22.9 percent. Since 1980, property and casualty company demand has declined, and by 2003 they owned only 10.6 percent of outstanding tax-exempts. Demand from casualty companies is primarily determined by industry profitability and insurance companies' need to obtain tax-exempt income.

When commercial banks and insurance companies purchase tax-exempt securities, they tend to concentrate their portfolios in maturities that meet their institutional preferences. Specifically, banks tend to emphasize tax-exempts of high credit quality with short maturities for liquidity as well as those with maturities up to 10 years for investment. In contrast, property and casualty insurance companies concentrate on holding securities with longer-term maturities, higher yields,

How Orange County Got It Wrong

The treasurer of Orange County, California, Robert Citron, had developed a reputation as a highly successful investor who was able to earn higher-than-usual returns on short-term investment funds. As a result, many municipalities in Orange County and throughout California invested their temporarily excess funds in the Orange County investment pool. In late 1994, people were shocked to learn that the fund had lost nearly $2 billion on a fund whose initial size was around $7.0 billion and, supposedly, invested only in safe securities.

The question arises, though, how one person could lose so much money in "safe" investments—particularly someone who was reputed to be an investment genius. The initial explanation offered was that the fund invested in dangerous "derivative securities" that caused it to incur major losses. While some of the losses were the result of derivative security investments, the fund's basic problem was that it did not manage its interest rate risk. Let see how this financial tragedy happened.

In early 1994, Robert Citron had a profound belief that interest rates would decline, so he did not protect his fund against the possibility that rates might rise. Furthermore, he bought derivative securities and invested in such a way that he would gain only if interest rates fell. These specialized derivative securities are "inverse floaters." However, Citron's major problem was that he bought U.S. Treasury securities with maturities of several years and then financed those purchases by using the securities as collateral in the repurchase agreement (repos) market so he could borrow more money. Because the Treasury securities had a yield of 4 percent or more and the repo rate was only 3 percent until early 1994, Citron earned additional profits by financing his securities with borrowed funds. He then used the borrowed funds to buy more Treasury

securities and repeated the process. As a result, even though the original fund had a net worth of about $7.0 billion, Citron was eventually able to acquire over $20 billion in Treasury and agency securities—which had little default risk but were not immune from price changes caused by changes in market interest rates (interest rate risk).

Citron's procedure of using borrowed money to buy more securities worked well at first, since he earned more interest on the portfolio of longer-term securities than the interest paid to finance them in the overnight repo market. That is how he made greater returns than other investment funds. Thus, his reputation as an investment genius hinged on the fact that interest rates were low and falling.

Unfortunately for Citron, that idyllic interest rate environment changed on February 4, 1994, when the Federal Reserve decided to let interest rates rise in steps. And soon the repo interest rate exceeded $5^1/_2$ percent. The result was that financing costs soon exceeded the returns on the fund's portfolio of Treasury securities, while the present value (and market price) of his investment securities declined.

Believing that the interest rate rise would cease, Citron doggedly held on to the securities in the fund while interest rates continued to rise. By the time county auditors discovered the Orange County fund's problems in late 1994, the fund had lost nearly $2 billion worth of its $7 billion initial value. Unfortunately, the fund losses meant that a number of municipalities in California ran short of money to pay their bills. As a result, they raised taxes, fired people, and cut services.

The moral of this story is that "no one can consistently predict future interest movements." A second moral is "before giving your money to someone to invest, make sure that the investment 'genius' is not just a risk taker who was lucky."

and lower credit ratings. Insurance companies have been especially important buyers in the market for long-term revenue bonds.

Given the supply of tax-exempt securities and the demand from banks and insurance companies, any tax-exempt securities issued in excess of those desired by firms taxed at the full corporate rate must be purchased by individuals. The greater the excess, the higher tax-exempt yields must rise relative to taxable yields to induce individuals to purchase additional tax-exempt securities. With the decline of tax-exempt holdings by insurance companies and banks since 1980, individual holdings increased from 25 percent in 1980 to 35.8 percent of outstanding tax-exempts by 2003.

THE EFFECT OF THE TAX REFORM ACT OF 1986

The Tax Reform Act of 1986 notably altered the demand for tax-exempt securities by investors and the supply of new issues from municipalities. On the demand side, the Act substantially reduced investors' marginal tax rates. Specifically, the Act reduced the structure of individual tax rates from 14 marginal rate categories to 2, and it lowered the maximum tax rate from 50 to 28 percent. The Tax Reform Act also reduced the top corporate rate from 46 percent to 34 percent. In addition, as previously mentioned, the Act put an end to deductibility of bank interest expense for tax-exempt securities purchased after 1986. Thus, the Tax Reform Act resulted in an increase in the tax-exempt interest rate relative to taxable rates, especially for the short maturities favored by banks.

On the supply side, the Tax Reform Act significantly restricts private-purpose tax-exempt securities. Pollution-control projects of private firms, sports and convention centers, parking facilities, and industrial parks no longer have access to the tax-exempt market. Furthermore, private colleges and universities and non-profit organizations other than hospitals are limited to a maximum of $150 million per organization in outstanding tax-exempts. Finally, other private-purpose bonds such as home mortgage bonds are subject to volume restrictions. Overall, private-purpose bonds are limited by states to $50 per capita or $150 million, whichever is greater. The Tax Reform Act of 1986 reduced the volume of new issues and increased municipal interest rates relative to taxable rates. However, after the 1993 tax bill raised marginal tax rates for individuals to 39.6 percent in the highest tax brackets, the interest rate spread between municipal bonds and corporate bonds began to widen once again.

AFTER-TAX YIELD COMPARISONS

When investors buy bonds, they should always make a comparison between similar taxable and exempt securities to see which option has the highest after-tax yield to the investors. To make this yield comparison, Equation 8.1 can be restated as follows:

$$i_a = i_b (1 - t) \qquad\qquad (8.2)$$

where

i_a = after-tax yield on the taxable security
i_b = before-tax yield on a taxable security
  t = marginal tax rate for the investor (the sum of the marginal federal, state, and local tax rates)

To properly apply Equation 8.2, the comparison needs to be done between securities that are similar in all respects, except that one is taxable and the other is tax-exempt. By similar, we mean that both securities have the same default risk, marketability, and maturity.

Let's look at an example. Say your father is considering the purchase of some 5-year sewer bonds issued by San Diego County, rated triple-A, and at a yield of 8 percent. His broker recommended these bonds. You have an extra $5,000 and are wondering if it would be a good investment for you since you both live in San Diego County. Your father's total marginal tax rates for federal, state, and county tax is 35 percent. Since you are a student and work part time, your total marginal tax rate is only 14 percent. You look in the newspaper and notice that 5-year, triple-A-rated corporate bonds are yielding 10 percent. What is the correct decision for both you and your father?

For your father, the after-tax return on the corporate bond is 6.5 percent [10%(1 − 0.35)]. Thus, the tax-exempt bond yielding 8 percent provides the highest after-tax return for him. Your marginal tax rate is much lower than your father's (14 percent versus 35 percent) and, as a result, your after-tax return on the corporate bond is 8.6 percent [10%(1 − 0.14)], which makes it a better investment for you. In general, people in high-income tax brackets (the wealthy) find it advantageous to buy tax-exempt securities and the rest of us, in lower tax brackets, taxable securities.

THE MARKET FOR MUNICIPAL BONDS

Primary Market.   The **primary market** for municipal bonds has a large number of relatively small bond issues. These bonds tend to be underwritten by small regional underwriters in the immediate area of the issuing municipality. Bond issues of well-known governmental units—states, state agencies, and large cities—attract bidding syndicates of major underwriters throughout the country and are sold in a national market. The reason for the existence of local markets is the high cost of gathering information about smaller issues and the tax treatment of these bonds (most local buyers are exempt from local as well as federal taxes on their coupons). Most general obligation bonds are sold by competitive bid.

Secondary Market.   In general, the **secondary market** for municipal bonds is very thin and is primarily an over-the-counter market. Although the bonds of some large, well-known municipalities do have active secondary markets, small local issues are traded infrequently, with commercial banks and local brokerage houses making the market. Because of the inactive secondary market, dealers (including local banks) find it difficult to match buyers and sellers of such bonds; thus the bid–ask spreads on municipal bonds are usually large compared to those of corporate bonds. Because of their limited marketability, municipal bonds may have higher yields than one might otherwise expect (given their ratings and tax-exempt interest feature).

Corporate bonds are debt contracts requiring borrowers to make periodic payments of interest and to repay principal at the maturity date. Corporate bonds can be **bearer bonds**, for which coupons are attached that the holder presents for

CORPORATE BONDS

payment when they come due, or **registered bonds**, for which the owner is recorded and payment due is mailed to the owner. Corporate bonds are usually issued in denominations of $1,000, are coupon-paying bonds, paying interest semiannually, and their coupon payments are fully taxable to the investor. Corporate debt can be sold in the domestic bond market or in the Eurobond market, which is a market for the debt of U.S. companies denominated in U.S. dollars but traded overseas. Most corporate bonds are **term bonds**, which means that all of the bonds that comprise a particular issue mature on a single date. In contrast, most bonds issued by state and local governments are serial bond issues, which means that the issue contains a variety of maturity dates.

Corporate bonds have an **indenture** or bond contract. The bond indenture is the legal contract that states the rights, privileges, and obligations of the bond issuer and the bondholder. To see that the covenants in the bond indenture are carried out and to ensure the timeliness of the coupon payments, the indenture is overseen by a trustee who is appointed as the bondholder's representative. The trustee, who is usually the trust department of a large well-known bank, initiates legal actions on behalf of the bondholders if any provision of the indenture is violated.

The indenture usually specifies the security or assets to which bondholders have prior claim in the event of default. Mortgage bonds pledge land and buildings; equipment trust certificates pledge specific industrial equipment or "rolling stock," such as railroad cars, trucks, or airplanes; and collateral bonds are secured by stocks and bonds issued by other corporations or governmental units. If no assets are pledged, the bonds are secured only by the firm's potential to generate cash flows and are called **debenture bonds**. Bond contracts that pledge assets in the event of default have lower yields than similar bonds that are unsecured.

Corporate bonds can differ in ways other than security. The debentures can be **senior** debt, giving the bondholders first priority to the firm's assets (after secured claims are satisfied) in the event of default, or **subordinated** (junior) debt, in which bondholders' claims to the company's assets rank behind senior debt.

In addition, many corporate bonds have sinking fund provisions, and most have call provisions. A **sinking fund** provision requires that the bond issuer provide funds to a trustee to retire a specific dollar amount (face amount) of bonds each year. The trustee may retire the bonds either by purchasing them in the open market or by calling them, if a call provision is present. It is important to notice the distinction between a sinking fund provision and a call provision. With a sinking fund provision, the issuer *must* retire a portion of the bond as promised in the bond indenture. In contrast, a **call provision** is an option that grants the issuer the right to retire bonds before their maturity. Most security issues with sinking funds have call provisions, because that guarantees the issuer the ability to retire bonds as they come due under the sinking fund retirement schedule.

Convertible bonds are bonds that can be converted into shares of common stock at the discretion of the bondholder. This feature permits the bondholder to share in the good fortune of the firm if the stock price rises above a certain level. That is, if the market value of the stock the bondholder receives at conversion exceeds the market value of the bonds, it is to the bondholder's advantage to exchange the bonds for stock, thus making a profit. As a result, convertibility is an attractive feature to bondholders because it gives them an option for additional profits that is not available with nonconvertible bonds. Typically the conversion ratio will be set such that the stock price must rise substantially, usually 15 to 20 percent, before it is profitable to convert the bond into equity.

Because convertibility gives investors an opportunity for profits not available with nonconvertible bonds, convertible bonds usually have lower yields than similar nonconvertible bonds. In addition, convertible bonds usually include a call provision so that the bond issuer can force conversion by calling the bond rather than continue to pay coupon payments on a security that has greater value upon conversion than the face amount of the bond.

INVESTORS IN CORPORATE BONDS

Life insurance companies and pension funds (private and public) are the dominant purchasers of corporate bonds. Households and foreign investors also own large quantities of them. Corporate bonds are attractive to insurance companies and pension funds because of the stability of the cash flows they experience and the long-term nature of their liabilities. That is, by investing in long-term corporate bonds, these firms are able to lock in high market yields with maturities that closely match the maturity structure of their liabilities, thereby reducing their interest rate risk. In addition, both life insurance companies and pension funds are in low marginal tax brackets, and taxable corporate bonds provide them with higher after-tax yields than do tax-exempt bonds. Finally, both federal and state laws require these companies to be "prudent" in their investment decisions. This usually translates to purchasing investment-grade bonds—bonds rated Baa and above by Moody's and BBB and above by Standard & Poor's.

THE PRIMARY MARKET FOR CORPORATE BONDS

New corporate bond issues may be brought to market by two methods: public sale or private placement. A public sale means that the bond issue is offered publicly in the open market to all interested buyers; a private placement means that the bonds are sold privately to a limited number of investors.

Public Sales of Bonds.   Public offerings of bonds are usually made through an investment banking firm, which "underwrites" them by purchasing the bonds from the issuer at a fixed price and then reselling them to individuals and institutions. The investment banker can purchase the bonds either by competitive sales or through negotiation with the issuer. A **competitive sale** is, in effect, a public auction. The issuer advertises publicly for bids from underwriters, and the bond issue is sold to the investment banker submitting the bid that results in the lowest borrowing cost to the issuer. In contrast, a **negotiated sale** represents a contractual arrangement between the underwriter and the issuer whereby the investment banker obtains the exclusive right to originate, underwrite, and distribute the new bond issue. The major difference between the two methods of sale is that in a negotiated sale, the investment banker provides the origination and advising services to the issuer as part of the negotiated package. In a competitive sale, the issuer or an outside financial adviser performs origination services. As a rule, most public entities, such as public utility companies, are required by law to sell their bond issues by competitive sale. It is generally believed that issuers will receive the lowest possible interest cost through competitive rather than negotiated sales.

Private Placement. **Private placements** emerged as a distinct method of issuing securities because of the Securities and Exchange Act of 1934, which required publicly sold securities to be registered with the Securities and Exchange Commission (SEC). The provisions of the Act were intended to protect individual investors by forcing issuing firms to disclose a modicum of information about their securities. Unregistered securities (that is, private placements) could be sold only to large, financially sophisticated investors (in practice, usually large insurance companies or perhaps other institutional investors) as long as fewer than 35 investors were involved and as long as the securities did not change hands quickly. The rationale for exempting private placements from registration and disclosure requirements was that large institutional investors possessed both the resources and sophistication to analyze the risks of securities.

In recent years, there has been a trend toward private placements relative to public sales. However, the ratio of private placements to public offerings is sensitive to the business cycle. During periods of low interest rates or stable market conditions, many smaller companies of lower credit quality will enter the capital markets and obtain financing by a public sale. During these times, the ratio of public sales to private sales will increase; during periods of high interest rates or unstable market conditions, these same firms will sell debt privately. On the other hand, larger, better-known firms of high credit standing can shift between the two markets and select the market that provides the lowest borrowing cost, net of transactions costs.

Since the 1980s the securities markets have become driven by institutions, with individual investors having little influence on market movements. Also, the private placement market has grown rapidly. These trends led the SEC to adopt **Rule 144A** in 1990 to liberalize the regulation of the private placement market. Most significantly, Rule 144A allows secondary trading of private securities by large institutional investors. By increasing liquidity and decreasing regulatory oversight in the capital markets, the rule should lower corporations' cost of capital. Investors such as pension funds and mutual funds, which have traditionally avoided investing in private placements because of their illiquidity, now find private placements more attractive. Further, foreign corporations, which have historically shunned the highly regulated U.S. capital markets, find it more attractive to issue securities in the United States through the private placement market.

THE SECONDARY MARKET FOR CORPORATE BONDS

Most secondary trading of corporate bonds occurs through dealers, although some corporate bonds are traded on the New York Stock Exchange (NYSE). The secondary market for corporate bonds is **thin** compared to the markets for money market securities or corporate stock. The term "thin" means that secondary market trades of corporate bonds are relatively infrequent. As a result, the bid–ask spread quoted by dealers of corporate bonds is quite high compared to those of other, more marketable, securities. The higher bid–ask spread compensates the dealer for holding relatively risky and illiquid securities in inventory.

Corporate bonds are less marketable than money market instruments and corporate equities for at least two reasons. First, corporate bonds have special features such as call provisions or sinking funds that make them difficult to value. Second, corporate bonds are long term; in general, longer-term securities are riskier and less marketable. To buy or sell a corporate bond in the secondary market, one must contact a broker, who in turn contacts a dealer (or the NYSE for exchange-listed bonds) who provides bid–ask quotes.

JUNK BONDS

During the 1980s **junk bonds** became a popular form of corporate financing. Junk bonds are corporate bonds with high default risk and, hence, low bond ratings (below Moody's Baa or Standard & Poor's BBB). Junk bonds were not common in the primary market before the late 1970s and early 1980s, although they could be found in the secondary market. These secondary market junk bonds, the so-called fallen angels, were investment grade (Baa/BBB or greater) when originally issued but were subsequently downgraded by the rating agencies because of deterioration in the financial condition of issuing firms.

Why weren't many junk bonds sold in the primary market before the late 1970s? As discussed earlier in this book, higher-risk bonds tend to be less marketable. In 1977, however, Drexel Burnham Lambert innovated the marketing of junk bonds in the primary market by promising investors that they would act as a dealer for junk bonds in the secondary market. Investors, therefore, were willing to take on the extra risk of junk bonds because they knew that Drexel would buy the bonds back at quoted bid prices, thereby providing liquidity to the market. However, the junk bond market experienced difficulties in the late 1980s as prices fell, and Drexel Burnham failed in 1990, thereby causing further price declines. While prices of many bonds later recovered, this episode showed that junk bonds retain substantial risk.

The supply of junk bonds in the 1980s was part of the trend toward disintermediation, a process whereby firms raise capital in the direct financial markets rather than from financial intermediaries such as commercial banks. High-quality firms with investment-grade credit ratings, for example, issued commercial paper rather than borrowing from banks. These firms were able to borrow more cheaply in the commercial paper market because their credit quality was higher than that of most commercial banks.

Low-quality firms with speculative-grade credit ratings, on the other hand, found that they could issue marketable debt in the direct market (that is, the junk bond market) with longer maturities than the debt they could obtain from commercial banks. Before the development of the junk bond market, low-quality firms relied on short-term or floating-rate bank loans. Banks prefer making short-term or floating-rate loans because such a strategy minimizes their interest rate risk by letting loan interest rates change in step with changes in their deposit interest rates. Borrowing firms that use short-term or floating-rate instruments to finance long-term projects, however, experience increased risk because the timing of cash inflows from their projects does not match the pattern of interest payments on short-term or floating-rate debt when short-term interest rates fluctuate.

The demand for junk bonds came from financial institutions such as life insurance companies, savings and loan associations, pension funds, and mutual funds. Junk bonds were attractive investments because investors believed they consistently outperformed high-rated bonds and even Treasury securities on a risk-adjusted basis. In the growing economy of the 1980s, the performance of junk bonds can be explained by the fact that there were far fewer defaults than expected, but during the late 1980s and early 1990s the number of defaults increased substantially. Losses from these defaults reduced the capital of many financial institutions, exacerbating the thrift crisis and contributing to the failure of several major life insurance firms. Default rates for various grades of bonds are shown in Exhibit 8.7. It should be noted, however, that even though usually not all is lost when a bond defaults, the default rates for lower-quality junk-rated bonds are very high.

EXHIBIT 8.7
Cumulative Default Rates on Corporate Bonds

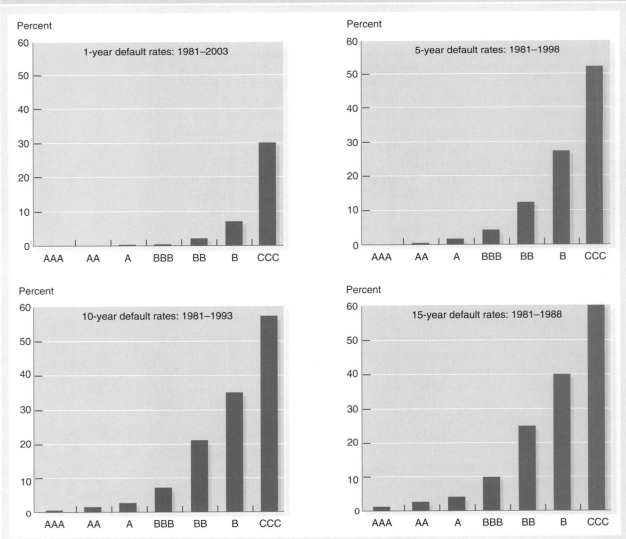

High-rated bonds rarely default in their early years of life. Over time, however, default rates increase. Junk bonds (rated BB or below) have experienced modest default rates even in their first year of existence and have very high cumulative default rates over longer horizons.

Source: Standard and Poor's *CreditWeek,* January 28, 2004, p. 12.

Because of these failures, many observers and policy makers associate junk bonds with the so-called financial excesses of the 1980s. More specifically, critics have blamed junk bonds for the merger mania of the 1980s, for the overall rise in corporate leverage encouraged by the 1986 tax reform, and for the increased volatility of the financial markets in the 1980s. These critics called for laws or regulations that would have limited the corporate use of junk bonds and limited the ability of financial institutions to invest in them.

The record suggests that the growth of the junk bond market was coincidental with the trends described above rather than causing them. Only a small portion of mergers were actually financed with junk bonds; most junk bonds were issued to finance capital investment of small, growing companies. Further, researchers have uncovered numerous other causes of the financial market volatility of the 1980s; the evidence suggests little association between junk bonds and volatility. It is true that junk bond defaults may have contributed to the failures of some financial institutions, but in many cases these institutions were in deep financial trouble before investing in junk bonds. The managers of these institutions, attempting to "hit it big" and keep their firms from going under, may not have adequately diversified their investments in junk bonds. In the end, restricting the use of junk bonds might force many small- and medium-sized companies back to the more expensive short-term intermediated credit markets, increasing their cost of capital and financial risk.

DO YOU UNDERSTAND?

1. Explain why sinking funds on corporate bond issues play the same role as the serial structure found on municipal bond issues.

2. When buying bonds, explain why investors should always make a tax-exempt and taxable comparison. What are the ground rules for making the comparison?

3. Why are commercial banks large investors in municipal bonds and property and casualty insurance companies are not?

4. How do the secondary markets differ between municipal bonds and corporate bonds?

5. Explain how and why the junk bond market had an impact on commercial bank lending.

The use of **financial guarantees** has grown dramatically in recent years. Financial guarantees cover the payment of principal and interest to investors in debt securities in the event of a default. Large, well-known insurance companies or commercial banks provide most financial guarantees. Insurance companies write insurance policies to back bond issues; commercial banks write letters of credit to back commercial paper issues or swap transactions.

FINANCIAL GUARANTEES

Convertible Bonds: The Lunch May Not Be Free

During the late 1990s when the U.S. economy was booming and interest rates were high, many large corporation turned to convertible bonds as a way to obtain cheap financing. Convertibles are hybrid securities that are a cross between a bond and a stock: they are "bonds" that pay a coupon or dividend, but can be converted into equity if a share-price target is hit – usually 15 to 20 percent increase in the stock price.

During this time, convertible bonds seemed to be the closet thing to free money for businesses. First, by issuing bonds that feature a large balloon payment of debt and accrued interest, years later companies still enjoyed huge tax breaks. What's more, convertible bonds carry borrowing costs of any where between 2 to 5 percent lower than similar nonconvertible bonds. Investors snatch them up at high prices (low interest) because they expected to convert the bonds into stock at an attractive conversion price.

As we all know expectation may not be realized. The 2001 recession proved to be much longer than expected. During the last quarter of 2002 as the country struggled to move out of the recession, the market for convertible securities went bust. The market crashed for two fundamental reasons. First, stock prices in the economy dropped sharply sending shock waves through the economy. Second, many convertible bonds issued in the late 1990s came due. As they came due, firms were forced to buy them back at their original value. For firms that weathered the recession

well, this was no problem. However, for firms whose business was in the tank, the redemptions created a cash time bomb: these issuers had trouble refinancing the issue and faced higher borrowing cost because of their financial problems. This is not what management had in mind when they issued the convertible bonds back in the 1990s.

An interesting situation that arose during 2002 was "busted" convertibles. In the parlance of Wall Street, convertible bonds were busted when they traded as straight bonds with little equity value because the underlying common stock value had declined so far. For example, during this time the stock prices of Tyco and WorldCom became virtually worthless and it was unlikely that in the future that these stocks would every recover and trade near their share price target. With little chance of conversion, these bonds were for practical purpose de facto straight bonds that now carry a very large default risk premium. Thus, many of these convertibles offered investors double-digit yields and were touted as "hot" investments by security analysts.

What is the lesson learned here? What appeared initially to many businesses as low cost money turned out to be very expensive. A firm's management must do a careful analysis of a financial alternative's risk and not be swept away by the sirens of the market place. There is no substitute for informed judgment and there is no free lunch when taking risk!

The quality of the financial guarantee depends on the reputation and financial strength of the guarantor. When an investor buys a guaranteed security, the security issuer with a lower credit standing is, in effect, "leasing" the reputation of the guarantor that has a higher credit standing. Thus, the investor in a guaranteed security is ultimately exposed to the default risk of the guarantor or insurer, not that of the issuer. Because of the reduction in default risk, guaranteed securities are typically more marketable than similar nonguaranteed securities and they pay lower yields to investors.

In recent years many loans have been "securitized" as "mortgage-backed" or "asset-backed" securities. The securities created have been sold in the nation's capital markets in competition with other capital market instruments.

The basic idea involved in securitizing a pool of loans is that separate claims on the principal and interest payments on the loans can be sold to different people. Since different people may be more interested in buying a claim on the first repayments of principal and interest than the last repayments, they may pay a higher price for a security interest in the payments that are most desirable to them. As a result, it may be possible to sell the security interests in separate payments on the pool of loans for more than the initial cost of the loans. This can be done by setting up a trust that buys a large number of loans (a loan "pool") of similar types. The trust can then sell securities of different types that "pass through" various payments of principal and interest on the loans and may even vary the payments on different securities as interest rates vary up or down. By creating attractive pieces, the creator of the trust hopes to sell the restructured pieces of the loans for more than it had to pay to buy the whole pool of loans.

For example, if 100 auto loans worth $2 million were sold to a trust, the trust could sell separate interests in the auto loans. Some interests, called "tranche A" might receive a predetermined interest rate plus all principal payments made By people repaying the amount they borrowed on their loans until the tranche was repaid in full. One thousand tranche A units might be created with a face value of $1,000 each, for a total of $1 million. People might accept a 7 percent interest payment on that tranche even though the auto loans paid 12 percent interest because they would receive their principal repayments quickly. Another $1 million tranche of security interests would also be created, called "tranche B." That tranche would consist of 1,000 securities that would be repaid only after $1 million in principal repayments had been repaid to holders of tranche A securities. The holders of tranche B might be promised 12.5 percent interest because their repayments would not be as quick or as certain as those of tranche A. Each holder of class B security would receive his or her pro rata share of all repayments of principal after the tranche A securities had been repaid in full.

Even though the tranche B securities might receive a premium interest rate, because the holders of tranche A securities were willing to accept a relatively low interest rate, the trust would pay an *average* interest rate to holders of the tranches that would be less than the amount of interest it earned on the loans. Thus, it would have money left over to pay servicing costs on the loans and tranches, as well as to absorb possible losses and leave a small profit (see Exhibit 8.8). Because the total income on the loans is likely to exceed the total payments to purchasers of the security interests in the loans, the creator of the trust and service provider (collector of payments) for the loans can often make a good profit from securitization. This is particularly true when the creator of the trust securities is able to create securities that are in strong demand, so people are willing to pay a particularly high price for those securities and accept a low rate of return on that tranche.

In recent years a wide variety of asset-backed securities have been created—particularly in the mortgage market, where federal government agencies frequently guarantee mortgage loans or securities that pass through payments of principal and interest on the mortgages (see Chapter 9). In addition, the popular-

---

EXHIBIT 8.8
Hypothetical Securitization of Auto Loans

Trust

Assets	Liabilities
100 auto loans worth $2,000,000 in face value (principal amount)	1,000 Tranche A securities with a total value of $1,000,000 at $1,000 each
	1,000 Tranche B securities with a total value of $1,000,000 at $1,000 each

Payments on a pool of loans can be divided into separate tranches. For instance, one tranche might receive only interest payments and the other only principal repayments made on loans in the pool. However, in this simple example we assume that the tranche A securities are repaid in full from the first $1,000,000 in repayments of principal for loans in the pool. Consequently, because of the quick, sure repayment, tranche A securities may need to pay only 7 percent interest to buyers. Tranche B securities will be repaid in full only after Tranche A securities are fully repaid. Since they have more risk and longer maturities, they may promise to pay 12.5 percent interest. They can pay higher interest than the 12 percent rate paid on the underlying auto loans because tranche A holders receive less. If the average rate paid on both tranches is less than the 12 percent earned, money will be left over to pay for loan-servicing costs, losses, and profits.

---

ity of privately originated asset-backed securities has greatly improved as the private sector has provided them with a variety of "credit enhancements" to reduce their default risk. The credit enhancements reduce the risk of default of various tranches and thereby allow them to obtain favorable credit ratings so they need not offer high yields (and low prices) to attract buyers.

FINANCIAL MARKET REGULATORS

The most important regulator of the U.S. capital markets is the Securities and Exchange Commission (SEC), established in 1933 after the stock market crash of 1929 helped precipitate the Great Depression of the 1930s. The SEC requires that any security sold to the general public be "registered" with it and that any potential buyer of the security be provided with a "prospectus" that fully describes the nature of the security and its issuer and all risks associated with an investment in the security. Issuers of publicly held securities must also file detailed reports with the SEC that provide complete and timely financial information and all relevant information regarding the management of the company, changes in ownership or major policies, and any other information that might materially affect the value of the company's security issues.

Because the registration process is costly and time-consuming, many firms prefer to issue private placements. Others issue securities to the public but take advantage of the SECs "shelf-registration" process that allows them to complete much of the general registration procedure early so they can quickly define the terms of the securities and complete the registration process for offering their securities to the public when market conditions are most favorable.

At the state level, state securities laws, sometimes called blue-sky laws, require that securities be registered and meet state standards so state residents can't be sold anything under the blue sky without being informed. In some states, securities registration requirements are very restrictive; in others they are lax.

In addition to state and federal regulation, individuals and firms that participate in the capital markets are subject to regulations imposed by self-regulatory bodies. These bodies are established to preserve the integrity of the market and the reputation of the industry so people will entrust their money to members of the industry. The National Association of Securities Dealers (NASD) is one of the foremost of the private regulatory authorities. It can fine people or ban them from the industry if they have violated its regulations. In addition, the various securities exchanges each have a detailed set of rules that their members must follow in their dealings with each other and the general public. Violators of the rules can be fined or expelled from membership in the exchange. The self-regulatory bodies are very important to the securities markets because it is essential that the markets retain the trust of the public. If they did not have that trust, people would be reluctant to give them money or do business with them and their business would decline. That is why extensive private regulation of the capital markets has developed to supplement public regulation of those markets.

BOND MARKETS AROUND THE WORLD ARE INCREASINGLY LINKED

With the growth of multinational corporations and the relaxation of international restrictions on capital flows, many companies and government entities have begun to obtain financing in countries other than their home country. When bonds are issued outside the home country of the issuer, they must conform to the regulations imposed by the country in which they are issued. For instance, "**Yankee bonds**" are bonds issued by foreign entities in the United States. They are denominated in U.S. dollars and must comply with the regulations imposed by the U.S. Securities and Exchange Commission. Some Yankee bonds are traded frequently and are listed as "foreign bonds" at the bottom of the New York Bond Exchange listings in the *Wall Street Journal*.

At the end of 2001 U.S. residents owned more than $700 billion in foreign debt, of which $487 billion consisted of foreign bonds. At the same time, foreigners held even more debt issued by U.S. governments, corporations, and individuals. In addition, U.S. corporations owed many billions of dollars on debt issued in other countries. U.S. countries frequently issue dollar-denominated debt in the Eurobond market, where the debt is issued and traded outside the United States. Eurodollar markets originated as a way for large well-known U.S. borrowers to obtain dollar financing from foreigners who were willing to buy the issuers' bonds and might offer better financing terms than the issuer could obtain in the United States. In the past some buyers preferred Eurobonds issued in countries that allowed unregistered bearer bonds to be issued and did not require that withholding taxes be levied on interest payments. Such rules might allow some people to avoid taxes. In addition, with relaxed regulations in some countries, it often was cheaper and easier for U.S. corporations to obtain funding abroad than in the United States.

While most large U.S. corporations have obtained financing from European markets, in recent years they also have obtained financing by issuing "**Samurai bonds**." Samurai bonds are issued by foreign companies in Japan. Since the Japanese are possibly the world's most prolific savers, interest rates in Japan tend to be low, but, of course, the Samurai bond issues are denominated in Japanese yen and must be repaid in yen, so the borrower will incur foreign exchange risk if it converts the yen to other currencies after borrowing them. Nonetheless, because yen interest rates have been so low, the Japanese Samurai bond market has expanded dramatically since 1994. By 1996, Samurai issues accounted for a quarter of the yen-denominated debt issues in Japan and exceeded the volume of yen-denominated debt issues in the Euromarkets.

Interestingly, credit ratings importantly influence the interest rates paid on Samurai debt issues by foreigners but have little effect on the rates paid by Japanese companies that issue yen-denominated debt in Japan. This shows that as the global financial markets develop, international credit ratings have become increasingly important—as foreigners who buy debt of others, even if it is issued in their own countries, must rely on international credit ratings rather than their own knowledge of a company when assessing its soundness. This is particularly true because an important determinant of international credit ratings is "country risk," as countries sometimes restrict currency flows out of their countries or otherwise cause companies to default on their debts. Thus, it is rare for any corporation to have an international credit rating higher than that of its home country.

DO YOU UNDERSTAND?

1. Why are asset-backed securities becoming increasingly important in capital markets?
2. Why are financial guarantees becoming increasingly important in financial markets both domestically and internationally?
3. What types of credit enhancement can be obtained to make asset-backed securities more desirable?
4. Why are financial markets regulated, and who is the principal U.S. regulator?

CHAPTER TAKE-AWAYS

1 The capital markets are where businesses finance assets that produce core business products for the firm; they produce these products to earn a profit. These products also normally have a long economic life; hence, capital market instruments have long maturities, typically 5 years or longer. Money markets are where firms warehouse idle funds until needed or borrow money temporarily until cash is collected

2 A strip is a Treasury note or bond that has been separated into two securities: (1) coupon interest payments and (2) principal payments. Strips are created from book-entry securities by the Treasury Department at the request of large commercial banks or Wall Street investment firms from Treasury securities purchased at the Treasury auctions. Zero-coupon bonds are excellent for immunizing against interest rate risk. This is done by purchasing zero-coupon bonds with a maturity that matches the duration of the liabilities to be immunized.

3 There are two major differences between the municipal and corporate bond market. First, municipal securities are tax-exempt and corporate securities are taxable. The issuers of corporate bonds are large businesses; in the municipal bond market, there are over 50,000 issuers, some of which are large municipalities or states, but the vast majority are small governmental units. The secondary market for municipal bonds of smaller municipalities is quite limited.

4 Junk bonds are bonds that have a credit rating below investment grade. Historically, firms with below-investment-grade ratings could not sell public debt and could only obtain longer-term financing through loans from commercial banks. In the 1980s, Drexel Burnham Lambert developed a public market for junk bonds by creating a secondary market for these securities. The attractiveness of this market for corporations was that they could finance their business borrowing at lower interest rates than bank loans of similar maturity.

5 Securitization of debt is pooling loans such as automobile loans that, by themselves, have no secondary market and creating a financial instrument that can be sold in the secondary markets. Securitization gives financial institutions the opportunity, if they desire, to sell loans that formerly were highly illiquid.

6 Some of the reasons that bond markets are becoming more global are as follows: the globalization of business, the advent of computer and telecommunication technology that can move information and financial data around the world in seconds, and the political and economic détente that has allowed the reduction of trade barriers and standardization of regulations and business practices.

KEY TERMS

Treasury notes and bonds
Treasury Inflation
 Protection Securities
 (TIPS)
Separate Trading of
 Registered Interest and
 Principal (STRIP)
Municipal bonds
General obligation bonds

Revenue bonds
Industrial development
 bonds
Mortgage-backed bonds
Serial bond issue
Primary market
Secondary market
Bearer bonds
Registered bonds

Term bonds
Indenture
Debenture bonds
Senior
Subordinated
Sinking fund
Call provision
Convertible bonds
Competitive sale

Negotiated sale
Private placement
Rule 144A
Thin
Junk bonds
Financial guarantees
Yankee bonds
Samurai bonds

QUESTIONS AND PROBLEMS

1. Calculate the gross profit that an underwriter would make if it sold $10 million worth of bonds at par (face value) and paid the firm that sold the bonds 99.25 percent of par.

2. If a bond dealer bought a $100,000 municipal bond at 90 percent of par and sold it at 93 percent of par, how much money did the dealer make on the bid–ask spread?

3. If a corporate bond paid 9 percent interest, and you are in the 28 percent income tax bracket, what rate would you have to earn on a general obligation municipal bond of equivalent risk and maturity in order to be equally well off? Given that municipal bonds are often not easily marketable, would you want to earn a higher or lower rate than the rate you just calculated?

4. If a trust is established to securitize $100 million in auto loans that paid 13 percent interest and the average rate paid on the tranches issued was 10 percent, while financial guarantees to protect against default on the loans cost 1.5 percent, how much money would the creator of the trust have available to pay for loan servicing and profits if the financial guarantee was purchased?

5. Why are private placements of securities often popular with both the buyer and seller of the securities?

6. Give a concise definition of the following types of municipal bonds: (*a*) general obligation, (*b*) revenue, (*c*) industrial development, and (*d*) mortgage-backed.

7. What features make municipal bonds attractive to certain groups of investors? Why do other groups not want to hold municipal securities?

8. Define the following terms: (*a*) private placement, (*b*) asset-backed security, (*c*) callable securities, (*d*) sinking fund provisions, and (*e*) convertible features of securities.

9. Explain how securities are brought to market under (*a*) a competitive sale and (*b*) a negotiated sale. How do the two methods of sale differ?

10. List and describe the different forms of financial guarantees seen in the bond markets.

INTERNET EXERCISE

The Bureau of Public Debt's Web page provides useful information about Treasury securities and the national debt. Go to the Web page (www.publicdebt.treas.gov/opd/opd.htm) and answer the following questions:

1. Determine to the penny the total U.S. Treasury debt. How much of the debt is held by the public? How much is in the form of intragovernmental holdings?
2. Referring to the Monthly Statement of Public Debt, what is the total amount of marketable securities outstanding? How much is in Treasury bills? Notes? Bonds? Inflation-indexed notes? Inflation-indexed bonds?
3. Click on the "Auction Information" link. Click on the "Treasury Bill Auction Results" link. Can you identify any trends in the rates for 182-day Treasury bills?

9

Mortgage Markets

CHAPTER PREVIEW

The mortgage market is the largest of the long-term debt markets. At year-end 2003, mortgages outstanding in the United States totaled $9.47 trillion while corporate bonds outstanding totaled only $6.84 trillion.

Mortgages are loans for which the borrower pledges real property as collateral to guarantee that the debt will be repaid. If the borrower does not repay the debt as promised, the collateral can be seized and sold through legal foreclosure; proceeds from the sale help repay the debt. Mortgage loans typically are repaid in monthly installments that include both interest due and repayments of a portion of the principal due on the loan. However, mortgage loan borrowers often repay the full amount due early if they move or refinance the loan.

For many years, mortgages were not traded frequently in the nation's capital markets because people found it expensive to check the creditworthiness of individual borrowers and the collateral value of homes located in many different parts of the country. Furthermore, savers often didn't want to buy securities that paid varying amounts of principal and interest from month to month.

In recent years the mortgage market has changed dramatically. Federal insurance, federal agencies, and private insurance now guarantee repayments on mortgages to reduce investors' credit risk. In addition, new types of highly marketable **mortgage-backed securities (MBSs)** have been developed. Such securities pass through all or part of the principal and interest payments on "pools" of many mortgages to buyers of the MBSs. MBSs can reduce the illiquidity risk and payment uncertainties associated with the ownership of individual mortgages. Furthermore, many new mortgages and MBSs are designed to reduce the **interest rate risk** of their purchasers. Such securities may have adjustable interest rates or, if part of a pool of mortgages, relatively certain repayment patterns. Because the credit risk, liquidity risk, and, for some (not all) MBSs, interest rate risk have been reduced by the innovations, mortgages are much more attractive investments than they were 60 years ago. ∎

Though your home may not be a castle, the mortgage markets are used by Americans to finance the homes of their dreams.

This chapter describes major mortgage market instruments and major participants in the mortgage markets. It also explains the important role played by government insurance, federal agencies, and regulations in shaping the mortgage market. In addition, it will help you learn how mortgage payments are calculated, how mortgage principal and interest payments typically vary over time, and why mortgage-backed securities have become so popular. ■

LEARNING OBJECTIVES

The objectives of this chapter are to:

1 Explain the basic structure of mortgages as debt instruments.

2 Describe the various types of mortgages that exist and discuss how the different types of mortgages allocate interest rate and inflation risks to the borrower or lender.

3 Explain how government and private-market innovations have led to a vastly expanded popularity for mortgages and mortgage-backed securities in the nation's capital markets.

4 Discuss the wide variety of mortgage-backed securities and mortgage-backed debt issues.

5 Describe the key roles that Fannie Mae, Freddie Mac, Ginnie Mae, mortgage bankers, and mortgage insurers have played in developing secondary mortgage markets.

6 Describe the role of mortgage bankers and how they earn profits.

7 Discuss how the nature of mortgage markets has evolved over time.

THE UNIQUE NATURE OF MORTGAGE MARKETS

Mortgage markets exist to help individuals, businesses, and other economic units finance the purchase of a home or other property. It is one of the few markets we discuss in this textbook that you, as an individual, are likely to participate in as an issuer. Unless you are independently wealthy or rent for the rest of your life, you will probably borrow in the mortgage market to finance the purchase of a home.

Fortunately, when you decide to buy a house (if you have not already done so), you will almost certainly find that lenders are eager to lend to you. As you will learn in this chapter, the markets for mortgages and mortgage-backed securities have developed to the point where there seems to be an almost limitless supply of funds for borrowers.

Like other capital market segments, mortgage markets bring together borrowers and suppliers of long-term funds. Most of the similarities end there, however, because mortgage markets have several unique characteristics. First, mortgage loans are always secured by the pledge of real property—land or buildings—as collateral. If a borrower defaults on the loan, the lender can "foreclose" and take ownership of the collateral.

Second, mortgage loans are made for varying amounts and maturities, depending on the borrower's needs. Because of their lack of uniform size, individual mortgages are not readily marketable in secondary markets.

Third, issuers (borrowers) of mortgage loans are typically small, relatively unknown financial entities. Thus only the mortgage lender will gain from investigating the borrower's financial condition fully. In contrast, corporate securities are often held by many thousands of people. Thus any changes in the financial condition of a major corporation are widely reported. In short, more people have an incentive to monitor the financial condition of General Motors than of John and Sue Jones.

Fourth, because uniform sizes and types of capital market debt instruments exist and information on the issuers of those instruments is generally widely available, secondary capital markets for stocks and bonds are highly developed and work very efficiently. Even though secondary trading in mortgage market instruments has increased recently, particularly for insured mortgages, it is much smaller relative to the value of securities outstanding than is the case in the capital markets.

Fifth, mortgage markets are both highly regulated and strongly supported by federal government policies. Federal participation in the operations of other capital markets is much more limited.

TYPES OF MORTGAGES

One of the most important financial decisions homebuyers face is selecting the type of mortgage that best suits their needs. The traditional 30-year, level-payment, fixed-rate mortgage may make sense for many borrowers, but it may be completely inappropriate for others. The traditional fixed-rate mortgage is well suited for those borrowers who plan to remain in the same home for many years and prefer the security of fixed monthly payments. It tends to be the mortgage type favored by borrowers with stable and reliable incomes but who want to make small down payments. Other mortgage types may make sense for homebuyers who expect to move in a few years or those who are willing to accept some of the interest rate risk associated with an adjustable-rate mortgage.

The mortgage types described in this section represent the majority of mortgages issued in the United States. If the mortgages described here don't meet a borrower's needs, however, a variety of less common mortgage types exist to meet the needs of just about any borrower.

STANDARD FIXED-RATE MORTGAGES (FRMs)

In a traditional **fixed-rate mortgage (FRM)**, the lender takes a lien on real property and the borrower agrees to make periodic repayments of the principal amount borrowed plus interest on the unpaid balance of the debt for a predetermined period of time. The mortgage is **amortized** over time to the extent that the periodic (usually monthly) payments exceed the interest due; any payment in excess of interest is credited toward repayment of the debt. When the mortgage is fully amortized (that is, repaid), the borrower obtains a clear title to the property. Until then, the lien prevents the borrower from selling the property without first repaying the debt or agreeing to repay the lender from proceeds of the sale. If the borrower fails to make payments on the property before it is fully amortized, the lender may foreclose and, through legal processes, cause the property to be sold or obtain title to the property.

Exhibit 9.1 shows amortization tables for two $200,000 mortgages, one with a 15-year maturity and one with a 30-year maturity. Both mortgages are fixed-rate mortgages that pay 6 percent interest. Thus the interest charge in the first month is $1,000 for each (which equals $200,000 × 6% divided by 12, since there are 12 months in a year). However, the 15-year mortgage shown in Frame A has a $1,687.71 monthly payment requirement while the 30-year mortgage shown in Frame B has an $1,199.10 payment requirement.

The balance due on the 15-year mortgage falls by $687.71 in the first month, by $691.15 in the second month, and by greater amounts thereafter (since the monthly interest due equals the principal balance due times 6 percent divided by 12—or 0.50 percent—each month, the interest due falls monthly as the balance due on the mortgage declines). While the balance due falls relatively slowly at first, the mortgage is fully repaid by the end of the 15th year. In the last year the mortgage balance falls sharply because, with a small balance left, interest charges are low and almost all of the $1,687.71 monthly payment can be used to repay the balance due.

Frame B of Exhibit 9.1 shows that the monthly payment on the 30-year $200,000 mortgage is substantially lower, at $1,199.10 per month, even though the interest rate and starting balance of the 30-year and 15-year mortgages are the same. The lower payment is the primary appeal of a 30-year mortgage. However, because the first month's interest is still $1,000, only $199.10 is left over to reduce the balance due on the mortgage after the first payment. Thus, the second month's interest due is $999.00, and the mortgage balance falls only by $200.10 after the second payment is made. Because of the slow repayment of principal on the 30-year mortgage, most of the mortgage balance is still due after 15 years. In the last year of the 30-year mortgage, once again, the mortgage balance is low, so interest charges are low, and most of the mortgage payment is used to repay principal.

The mortgages are fully amortized in both cases when the initial $200,000 mortgage debt has been repaid. Note, however, that total payments are $303,788.46 on the 15-year mortgage and $431,676.38 on the 30-year mortgage. Naturally, the difference in total payments is due to the much higher total interest payment on the 30-year mortgage. Thus, by making higher monthly payments for a shorter period of time, the 15-year-mortgage debtor saves more than $125,000 in total interest due. Consequently, even though the 30-year-mortgage borrower's monthly payment is lower each month, that borrower's interest bill over the life of the mortgage is much greater. (Note that these comparisons are on a pretax basis, however; for as long as the government allows mortgage interest payments to be deducted from taxable income, the federal government will absorb part of the extra interest cost.)

ADJUSTABLE-RATE MORTGAGES (ARMs)

As a general rule, fixed-rate mortgages make sense for borrowers who like the certainty of knowing the interest they will pay on their mortgages. For borrowers who are willing to accept some uncertainty, however, an **adjustable-rate mortgage (ARM)** may make sense. An ARM is a mortgage with an interest rate that

EXHIBIT 9.1
Mortgage Balances and Payments

A. 15-year, 6%, $200,000 level-payment, fixed-rate mortgage

Month	Beginning Balance	Monthly Payment	Interest Payment	Principal Payment	Ending Balance
1	$200,000.00	$1,687.71	$1,000.00	$687.71	$199,312.29
2	199,312.29	1,687.71	996.56	691.15	198,621.13
3	198,621.13	1,687.71	993.11	694.61	197,926.53
.	.	.	.	.	.
.	.	.	.	.	.
.	.	.	.	.	.
178	5,012.93	1,687.71	25.06	1,662.65	3,350.28
179	3,350.28	1,687.71	16.75	1,670.96	1,679.32
180	1,679.32	1,687.71	8.40	1,679.32	0.00
Totals:		$303,788.46	$103,788.46	$200,000.00	

B. 30-year, 6%, $200,000 level-payment, fixed-rate mortgage

Month	Beginning Balance	Monthly Payment	Interest Payment	Principal Payment	Ending Balance
1	$200,000.00	$1,199.10	$1,000.00	$199.10	$199,800.90
2	199,800.90	1,199.10	999.00	200.10	199,600.80
3	199,600.80	1,199.10	998.00	201.10	199,399.71
.	.	.	.	.	.
.	.	.	.	.	.
.	.	.	.	.	.
178	143,548.99	1,199.10	717.74	481.36	143,067.63
179	143,067.63	1,199.10	715.34	483.76	142,583.87
180	142,583.87	1,199.10	712.92	486.18	142,097.69
.	.	.	.	.	.
.	.	.	.	.	.
.	.	.	.	.	.
358	3,561.63	1,199.10	17.81	1,181.29	2,380.33
359	2,380.33	1,199.10	11.90	1,187.20	1,193.14
360	1,193.14	1,199.10	5.97	1,193.14	0.00
Totals:		$431,676.38	$231,676.38	$200,000.00	

Both mortgages are fully amortized when the $200,000 mortgage debt has been repaid. Note, however, that the total payments on the 15-year mortgage are $127,887.92 less than the total payments on the 30-year mortgage.

adjusts periodically in response to changes in market conditions. The interest rate adjustment is based on a published market index, such as the weekly average yield of 1-year U.S. Treasury securities.

ARMs are typically structured so that there is an initial interest rate that remains fixed for a period of time ranging from 1 year to 10 years. After the initial fixed-rate period has ended, the interest rate increases or decreases depending on the reference rate of interest. For example, a 3/1 ARM will have a fixed rate of interest for the first 3 years of the mortgage. Each year after that, the interest rate adjusts.

ARMs with an initial fixed rate that last 3 years or longer are often referred to as "hybrid" ARMs because they are a mix of a fixed-rate mortgage and an adjustable-rate mortgage. The initial fixed rate of interest in a hybrid ARM is lower than the rate on a fixed-rate mortgage, which makes hybrid ARMs attractive to borrowers who expect their income levels to increase during the initial fixed-rate period and those homebuyers who expect to move in a few years. Hybrid ARMs are now more popular than traditional 1/1 ARMs in which the interest rate adjusts at the end of the first year and every year thereafter.

ARMs are popular with lenders because they reduce the lender's interest rate risk. Whenever interest rates rise, borrowers' adjustable-rate mortgage payments will also rise (after the initial fixed-rate period). That, in turn, will make it easier for lenders to afford the higher interest rates they will have to pay to their depositors and other creditors at such times.

ARM Rate Adjustments.   Adjustable-rate mortgages use various measures for adjusting their rates, including Treasury security rates, current fixed-rate mortgage indexes, savings and loan cost-of-funds indexes, the prime rate, and the LIBOR rate (London Interbank Offer Rate). In addition, ARM rates can be adjusted with varying lags—such as monthly, quarterly, or every year or two. Most ARMs are adjusted annually. In no case, however, can the rate be adjusted solely at the lender's discretion, and in all cases the exact method of rate adjustment must be fully disclosed when the loan is originated. In particular, ARM regulations give flexibility to both the lender and borrower. They allow contractual rate adjustments to be implemented through changes in payment amounts, the outstanding principal loan balance, or loan maturity, provided that the method of adjustment is specified in the contract.

Rates can be adjusted according to any rate index that is readily verifiable to the borrowers and beyond the control of the lender. Furthermore, borrowers must be provided with 30- to 45-day advance notice of pending rate changes and be allowed to prepay the loan without penalties. These provisions make it possible for dissatisfied borrowers to seek alternative financing sources during the term of the loan.

ARM Caps.   Although ARMs help lenders reduce their interest rate risk, they might increase lenders' credit risk. If rates rise sufficiently, monthly payments could rise to the point that the borrower is unable to make the monthly payment. The credit risk of the loan would rise and a default could occur. Without limiting the potential increase in monthly payments, the lender incurs greater credit risk on ARMs as interest rates rise. With an interest rate "cap," however, the likelihood of default is limited. Of course, by limiting the potential increase in interest rates, the lender still bears some interest rate risk. For instance, if the initial rate is 5 percent, a mortgage with a 5 percent lifetime "cap" could never charge a rate greater than 10 percent.

At first many ARMs had no limit on the amount by which interest rates could increase. For obvious reasons, however, such loans were not very popular with potential borrowers. Borrowers preferred "capped" ARMs, which may have a payment cap, an interest rate cap, or both.

Payment caps limit the maximum amount by which the monthly payment can increase each year or over the life of the loan. If payments greater than the cap are called for at the new interest rate, the maturity of the loan is increased. If the payment limit is less than the new interest payment, "negative amortization" occurs and the amount due on the loan increases each month until interest rates fall once again. If interest rates increase without limit and never fall, the borrower may never be able to repay the debt.

Interest rate caps limit the amount that the interest rate on a loan can increase during each interest rate period or over the life of the loan. Interest rate caps typically limit maximum interest rate increases to 1 or 2 percent per year and to 5 percent over the life of the loan; thus, they help keep the monthly payment from rising to a level that the borrower cannot repay.

Because of the popularity of capped ARMs with consumers, in 1987 Congress required that all ARMs have a cap. Although capped ARMs have less default risk than uncapped ARMs, they still leave the lender with a small amount of residual interest rate risk.

Pricing Risk Transfers.   Lenders like adjustable-rate loans because they reduce their interest rate risk. Thus lenders are willing to "pay" borrowers to assume interest rate risk by offering lower rates on ARMs than contractual rates for long-term FRMs. However, borrowers incur the interest rate risk that lenders avoid with ARMs. Thus borrowers are willing to pay higher rates to have the lender assume the interest rate risk inherent in a fixed-rate, long-term mortgage. The market, then, prices risk differences in variable- and fixed-rate obligations by setting the degree of rate reduction for adjustable-rate mortgages that will satisfy both borrowers and lenders (see Exhibit 9.2).

Consumers' willingness to assume ARM obligations also varies with their expectations for future interest rate movements. If they think rates are likely to fall, they may be more willing to borrow with ARM mortgages even if ARM rates are close to FRM rates. However, if they expect interest rates to rise, they will want a larger discount from the FRM rate. At such times, the term structure of interest rates is likely to be upward sloping, so lenders may be able to accommodate their wishes. However, some lenders may go further and "sweeten" the initial ARM rate discount from FRM rates by offering especially attractive "teaser rates" for the first year of the ARM. After the first year, the ARM rate adjusts to whatever the rate-setting formula requires. Consumers must be cautious when they take on ARMs with teaser rates, since rates on such loans may increase when the initial fixed-rate period is over even if market interest rates don't change. Exhibit 9.3 illustrates the fact that ARM rates are usually well below new FRM rates.

OTHER MORTGAGES

Although FRMs and ARMs represent the majority of mortgages, other types have been developed to meet the diverse needs of borrowers and lenders or for specific

EXHIBIT 9.2
Rate Difference Needed for Borrowers to Take the Risk of an Adjustable-Rate Mortgage

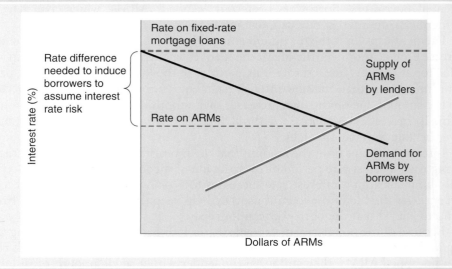

Typically, lenders will offer rates on ARMs that are marked up by a certain percentage (usually 2 to 3 percent) over a short-term index rate. One popular type of ARM charges a rate equal to the 1-year T-bill rate plus 2.754 percent. Consumer demand will determine the maximum markup lenders can obtain.

Note: When ARM rates equal rates in fixed-rate mortgage loans, it is assumed that the demand will be zero, because the borrower will receive no compensation for taking on the extra risk. As the ARM rate falls further below the fixed-rate loan rate, however, the demand for such loans will increase. At the same time, the supply of ARMs falls when lenders must give up more to reduce their risks.

circumstances. We now discuss some of the most widely used. These are also summarized in Exhibit 9.4.

Balloon Payment Mortgages.   Popular in the United States prior to the Great Depression, **balloon payment mortgages** have a relatively low fixed rate of interest for a predetermined period of time (typically 7 years). The remaining balance of the mortgage comes due at the end of that period in the form of a *balloon payment.* Alternatively, the balance can be refinanced at prevailing interest rates. This type of mortgage is popular with borrowers who plan to sell or refinance within a few years and want a low payment until that time. In the event that borrowers choose to refinance, they typically do not need to requalify as long as they have made their payments on time.

Rollover Mortgages (ROMs) and Renegotiated-Rate Mortgages (RRMs).   Like balloon payment mortgages, **rollover mortgages (ROMs)** and **renegotiated-rate mortgages (RRMs)** protect the lender from being locked into a long-term low rate of interest. In ROMs and RRMs, the interest rate is reset to prevailing interest rates at predetermined periods. For example, the interest rate may change

EXHIBIT 9.3
Fixed and Adjustable Mortgage Rates

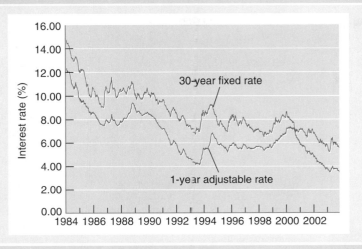

Note how fixed rates on mortgages began declining in June 2000 in anticipation of the 2001–2002 recession. Meanwhile, note that ARM mortgage rates rose in the early part of 2000, which was a period when monetary policy kept short-term interest rates high. As the Fed forced short-term interest rates lower during 2001, however, ARM mortgage rates fell. By March 2004, both fixed and adjustable rates were at near-historic lows.

Source: Federal Home Loan Mortgage Corporation.

every 5 years. Note that this is similar to an ARM except that the number of years between interest rate adjustments is longer than with the typical ARM.

Interest-Only Mortgages.   Another way for a borrower to secure financing with low payments is to borrow using an **interest-only mortgage**, whereby he or she pays only the interest for the first 10 or 15 years. After the interest-only period, the payments increase so that the loan is fully amortized by the end of 30 years.

Construction-to-Permanent Mortgages.   For those homebuyers who are planning to build their own home, a construction-to-permanent mortgage may make the most sense. In these mortgages, the purchase of the land and the construction of the home is financed in increments, with the borrower paying only the interest payments during this phase. Once construction is completed, the outstanding balance is rolled over into an FRM, ARM, or one of the other types of mortgages described above.

Reverse Annuity Mortgages (RAMs).   **Reverse annuity mortgages (RAMs)** are designed for older people who own their homes and need additional funds to meet current living expenses but do not want to sell their homes. RAMs allow people to borrow against the equity in their homes at relatively low interest rates.

RAMs are written so that instead of making regular monthly payments, the borrower receives them. At the end of the payment term, often 10 or 15 years, the

EXHIBIT 9.4
Mortgage Characteristics

Type	Minimum Down Payment	Maturity	Payments	Rate
Conventional fixed-rate (FRM)	Usually 20% or more, unless privately insured	Fixed, usually 15, 20, or 30 years	Fixed	Fixed
FHA and VA	3–10% for FHA, 0% for VA	Fixed, usually 30 years	Fixed	Fixed, cannot exceed government-set limit; insurance fee is extra
Adjustable-rate (ARM)	Same as conventional	Often 30 years, but can vary as rates change; if it does not vary, then payments will vary with rates	Can be fixed or variable; will vary if maturity does not	Variable according to predetermined rate indexes, but some may have fixed rates for the first 2 to 10 years
Balloon payment	Same as conventional	Typically 5 or 7 years, then the remaining balance must be refinanced at current rates	Fixed	Usually fixed
Rollover (ROM) and renegotiated-rate (RRM)	Same as conventional	Same as balloon, but the ability to refinance may be guaranteed	Fixed	Fixed for a period, then recontracted
Interest only	Same as conventional	Usually 30 years	Interest only for the first 15 years; amortized over the remaining 15 years	Fixed
Construction-to-Permanent Financing	Same as conventional	Same as conventional once it becomes permanent	Increase over time	Fixed
Reverse annuity (RAM)	None	Fixed, usually 20 years or less, may be for lifetime of borrower	Fixed payments are made to the borrower	Fixed

The various mortgage types have considerably different characteristics. People who deal in the mortgage market often differentiate them by their initials (FRM, ARM, etc.).

mortgage on the borrower's home equals a predetermined amount. The value of the borrower's equity in the home is also reduced by that amount—a fact that has limited the popularity of RAMs. Many have an annuity feature guaranteeing that payments will be made for the life of the borrower.

Home Equity Loans and Lines.   **Home equity loans** and **home equity lines of credit** were created so that homeowners can borrow against the equity they have accumulated in their home. If the borrower already has a mortgage on the property, the home equity loan or line would be considered a second mortgage. In the event of default and liquidation, the second-mortgage holder gets repaid only after the first-mortgage principal has been repaid.

Home equity loans are often used for debt consolidation, home improvement, education, and emergencies (e.g., medical bills). In recent years, some homebuyers have used second mortgages to borrow part of their down payment for their first mortgages.

After the 1986 tax changes, the popularity of second mortgages increased greatly, because interest on such mortgages could be deducted (within limits) from taxes, whereas interest deductions for other types of consumer credit were phased out. Subsequently, many lenders began to offer home equity credit lines that let consumers borrow on a credit line secured with a second mortgage on their homes. Many lenders let borrowers use credit cards to access those credit lines.

MORTGAGE QUALIFYING

Given the increase in real estate values over the past several years, it has become increasingly difficult for many borrowers to qualify for a mortgage. A borrower's ability to qualify depends on several factors, including income level, the amount available for a down payment, credit history, and other financial obligations.

Borrower Income.   Like any other lender, mortgage lenders focus on the sources of repayment in determining whether to accept or reject a loan application. In the typical residential mortgage loan, the primary source of repayment will be the borrower's income. Lenders use payment-to-income ratios to assess a borrower's ability to repay a loan. Although there is substantial variation in allowable maximums, some conservative rules of thumb are used: (1) a borrower's monthly mortgage payment (P&I) should be no more than 25 percent of monthly gross income; (2) the monthly P&I plus monthly property tax payments (T), homeowner's insurance premiums (HI), and any mortgage insurance premiums (MI) should be no more than 28 percent of monthly gross income; and (3) the monthly P&I, T, HI, and MI plus other debt service should be no more than 33 percent of monthly gross income.

Down Payment.   Historically, the most important determinant of whether borrowers will default on a mortgage loan is how much of their own money they put toward the purchase of the property. In addition, the equity in a home represents a secondary source of repayment in the event the borrower defaults on the loan. Therefore, the typical minimum loan-to-value ratio in a conventional mortgage is 80 percent, meaning that the borrower must provide a down payment of 20 percent of the purchase price. A borrower who is not able to provide that large a down payment may be required to purchase mortgage insurance.

Mortgage Insurance.   Mortgage contracts can be either conventional or federally insured. Mortgages whose ultimate payment is guaranteed by the Federal Housing Administration (FHA) are called **FHA mortgages**. FHA mortgages must have terms that comply with FHA requirements, and a small fee is added to cover the costs of insurance. **Veterans Administration (VA) mortgages** are similar, except that the mortgage and borrower must both meet the requirements of the Veterans Administration. VA and FHA mortgages usually have very low or zero down payment requirements, so people with such mortgages can borrow nearly all the money needed to buy a home.

Conventional mortgages are not insured by a federal government agency. Down payment requirements on conventional mortgages are usually much higher than those on federally insured mortgages. However, if conventional mortgages are privately insured, the borrower typically pays an extra charge to cover the mortgage insurance premium and, in turn, can borrow with a low down payment. The use of **private mortgage insurance (PMI)** is illustrated in Exhibit 9.5. That figure shows that, with insurance, the lender can extend more credit and not bear additional risk. The mortgage insurer accepts the additional risk in return for the insurance premium payment. The consumer pays the insurance premium in addition to the principal and interest on the loan (and thereby pays a higher effective annual percentage rate, since the monthly payments include the insurance premium). However, the insurance feature allows the consumer to buy a house with a far lower down payment than would otherwise be possible. Also, if the house rises in value such that the mortgage is less than 75 to 80 percent of its value, the borrower need no longer make private mortgage insurance payments.

Exhibit 9.5 illustrates the reallocation of credit risk that is possible with private mortgage insurance. The left side of the exhibit illustrates an uninsured con-

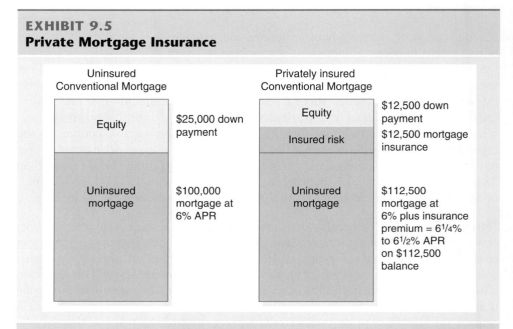

EXHIBIT 9.5
Private Mortgage Insurance

Uninsured Conventional Mortgage		Privately insured Conventional Mortgage	
Equity	$25,000 down payment	Equity	$12,500 down payment
		Insured risk	$12,500 mortgage insurance
Uninsured mortgage	$100,000 mortgage at 6% APR	Uninsured mortgage	$112,500 mortgage at 6% plus insurance premium = 6¼% to 6½% APR on $112,500 balance

With an uninsured conventional mortgage, the lender extends a $100,000 mortgage at 6 percent interest and is at risk in case of default only if the house value falls by more than $25,000. With a privately insured conventional mortgage the lender extends a $112,500 mortgage at 6 percent interest and is still at risk only if the house value falls by more than $25,000. In the second case, the private mortgage insurance company bears the risk if the house value falls by $12,500 to $25,000 and the borrower defaults. In return, the insurer receives an insurance premium equal to between 0.25 and 0.5 percent additional interest on the $112,500 debt.

ventional mortgage in which the lender extends a $100,000 mortgage on a house costing $125,000 at 6 percent interest. The consumer makes a down payment of $25,000. In this case the lender may experience default only if the house value falls by more than $25,000, which is the cushion provided by the borrower's down payment. The right side of the exhibit illustrates the effect of private mortgage insurance. In this case, the lender extends a $112,500 mortgage at 6 percent interest and is still at risk only if the house value falls by more than $25,000. In the second case, however, the private mortgage insurance company bears the risk if the house value falls by $12,500 to $25,000 and the borrower defaults. Note, however, that with the insurance the consumer needs a down payment of only $12,500, rather than $25,000, to buy a house worth $125,000. In return for bearing some default risk, the insurer receives an annual insurance premium equal to between 0.25 and 0.5 percent of the $112,500 mortgage.

DO YOU UNDERSTAND?

1. If you had a 6 percent, $100,000, 15-year mortgage, and you paid it as scheduled, how much interest would you pay in the first month of the sixth year on that mortgage? How much principal would you pay?

2. What would your principal and interest payments be if the mortgage were a 30-year mortgage at 6 percent?

3. If you had a mortgage with an initial rate of 2 percent that adjusted its rate once a year to equal the 1-year Treasury bill rate plus 2.75 percent, with a cap on rate increases of 2 percent per year and 5 percent rate increase cap over the life of the mortgage, what rate would you pay in the second year of the mortgage if the 1-year Treasury bill rate was 1.5 percent when the new rate was calculated?

4. In the mortgage described above, what is the maximum rate you could be charged if the Treasury bill rates rose to 10 percent and stayed there?

MORTGAGE-BACKED SECURITIES

In the early part of the 20th century, mortgage markets were very illiquid and inefficient. There was no secondary market for mortgages, so lenders (commercial banks, savings and loans, and mutual savings banks) were forced to hold the mortgages they originated until the loans were repaid. Therefore, mortgage rates and the availability of mortgage credit varied from one region to another and fluctuated over time depending on loan repayments and new deposits at lending institutions.

In 1934, Congress tried to strengthen the housing market by passing the National Housing Act, which created the FHA (Federal Housing Administration) to provide mortgage insurance on loans made by approved lenders. In addition, a 1938 amendment to the National Housing Act created the FNMA (Federal National Mortgage Association) for the purpose of developing a secondary market for FHA-insured mortgages. FNMA was authorized to purchase FHA-insured mortgages using the funds allocated to it by Congress.

It wasn't until 1968, however, that the secondary market for mortgages began to develop into what it is today. In that year, FNMA was split into two entities, GNMA (Government National Mortgage Association) and FNMA. Today, GNMA guarantees the timely payment of principal and interest on pools of qualifying FHA, VA, and other government-guaranteed mortgages. Lenders combine qualifying mortgages into pools, acquire a GNMA guarantee on the pool, and then sell security interests in the pool. Many of these securities are bought by investors that would not otherwise invest in mortgage markets.

Mortgage-backed securities have attributes that are lacking in individual mortgages but that are desirable for capital market instruments:

1. They are issued in standardized denominations. Thus, they are more readily tradable in both the primary and secondary capital markets.

2. They either are issued by large, well-known borrowers or are insured by a well-known institution whose credit standing can be checked and evaluated relatively easily. This increases their marketability.

3. They are usually insured and highly collateralized. Thus, they have low degrees of risk and high credit ratings. Many have their principal and interest payments guaranteed by the U.S. government or its agencies.

4. They have repayment schedules (for principal and interest) more similar to those offered on government or corporate debt issues.

Because of these considerations, secondary mortgage market instruments compete effectively for funds in the conventional capital markets and allow mortgage-lending institutions to attract funds more easily. A wide variety of mortgage-backed securities have been developed to allow mortgage lenders to obtain funds from the nation's capital markets. These are summarized in Exhibit 9.6.

PASS-THROUGH MORTGAGE SECURITIES

Pass-through mortgage securities pass through all payments of principal and interest on pools of mortgages to holders of security interests in the pool. The security interests represent a fractional share in the pool. Thus, if someone owns a security that represents a 1 percent ownership share in a pool of securities, that person is entitled to receive 1 percent of all principal and interest payments made on the underlying mortgages.

Pass-through mortgage securities are popular because, unlike the underlying mortgages, they are initially sold in standard denominations and, if the guarantor of the pool is well known, they are readily marketable.

Since GNMA began guaranteeing pass-through securities in 1968, their growth has been great. They now total more than $5 trillion.

GINNIE MAE PASS-THROUGHS

The **Government National Mortgage Association (GNMA–Ginnie Mae)** issues securities that pass through all payments of interest and principal received on a pool of federally insured mortgage loans. Ginnie Mae guarantees that all payments of principal and interest will be made on a timely basis. Because many mortgages are repaid before maturity, investors in Ginnie Mae MBS pools usually recover most of their principal investment well ahead of schedule.

Ginnie Mae mortgage pools are originated by mortgage bankers, commercial banks, or other mortgage-lending institutions. Once a pool of mortgages is assembled according to Ginnie Mae specifications, pass-through securities are issued that are collateralized by interest and principal payments from the mortgages in the pool and are guaranteed by Ginnie Mae.

Ginnie Mae I MBSs are based on a pool of mortgages of the same type, having the same interest rate, and having the same lender. Ginnie Mae II MBSs allow for the pool of mortgages to be from multiple lenders. In addition, Ginnie Mae II MBSs allow for the interest rate on the underlying mortgages to vary by as much as 0.75%. The minimum denomination of both Ginnie Mae MBSs is $25,000. For providing its guarantee and services, GNMA charges a fee, typically equal to $1/2$ of 1 percent (50 basis points). Investors are quite willing to "pay" the fee by accepting lower yields on GNMAs than on mortgages that are uninsured and less readily marketable.

FREDDIE MAC PARTICIPATION CERTIFICATES

The **Federal Home Loan Mortgage Corporation (FHLMC—Freddie Mac)** was established by Congress in 1970 as a subsidiary of the Federal Home Loan Bank system. Its initial purpose was to assist savings and loan associations and other mortgage lenders attract capital market funds.

Savings and loan associations primarily make conventional mortgages, which are not eligible for inclusion in GNMA pools. Furthermore, such loans often are not privately insured. Thus, before 1970, most savings and loans could not easily sell their mortgage holdings to obtain funds in the secondary markets.

Freddie Mac was established to provide a secondary market for conventional mortgages. Freddie Mac can purchase mortgages for its own account. It also issues pass-through securities—called participation certificates (PCs)—and other mortgage-backed securities.

Participation certificates issued by Freddie Mac are similar to GNMA pass-throughs in that they are backed by pools of mortgages and pass through all principal and interest payments made on mortgages in those pools. However, they are unlike GNMA securities in that (1) they contain conventional mortgages, (2) the mortgages are not federally insured, (3) the pools are assembled by the FHLMC rather than by private-sector mortgage originators, (4) the mortgages in the pools may be made at more than one interest rate, and (5) the underlying mortgage pools are much larger than GNMA pools, with values ranging up to several hundred million dollars. In addition, the minimum denomination for a participation certificate is $100,000.

FNMA PASS-THROUGHS

The **Federal National Mortgage Association (FNMA—Fannie Mae)** was started in the 1930s and was originally a government agency whose primary purpose was to buy government-guaranteed (FHA) mortgages in the secondary market. In 1968, however, FNMA was turned into a private corporation, although it still retains a credit line with the Treasury and some government

EXHIBIT 9.6
Mortgage-Backed Securities

Type	Issuer	Security	Payments	Insurance
Pass-Through Securities				
Ginnie Mae I, II MBSs	Government National Mortgage Association	Pools of government-insured (FHA and VA) mortgages	All principal and interest payments are passed through to security holders	FHA and VA plus GNMA guarantee
Participation certificate (PC)	Federal Home Loan Mortgage Corporation	Pools of new conventional mortgages	Same as GNMA	FHLMC guarantees ultimate payment of principal and interest
Fannie Mae MBS	Federal National Mortgage Association	Pools of government-insured or conventional mortgages	Same as GNMA	FNMA guarantees ultimate payment of principal and interest
Privately issued pass-through (PIP)	Various private institutions	Pools of conventional mortgages—can have varied rates and orginators	Same as GNMA	Privately insured
Other MBSs				
CMOs and REMICs	GNMA, FNMA, FHLMC	Same as pass-through securities	Contractual, according to class or tranche	Same as pass-through securities
IO and PO Stripped MBSs	FNMA, FHLMC	Same as pass-through securities	IO-interest payments on pool; PO-principal payments on pool.	Same as pass-through securities.

Mortgage-backed bonds

	Issuer	Collateral	Payments	Federal guarantees
FNMA or FHLMC debt issue	FNMA or FHLMC	FNMA's or FHLMC's assets (mostly mortgages) and government credit line	Regular, contractual payments	None, except FNMA and FHLMC have access to implicit federal guarantees or exilicit FHLMC guarantee federal credit lines
Privately issued mortgage-backed bonds, including CMOs (collateralized mortgage obligations) and REMICs (real estate mortgage investment conduits)	Varies with issuer	Pools of mortgages, often overcollateralized (up to 150%) or collateralized with GNMA, FNMA, or FHLMC pass-through securities	Regular, may be on contractual basis; some tranches (subdivision of mortgage pools) are scheduled to receive all principal payments first or second, etc., until fully repaid. Other CMOs may pay only interest to one class of security (IO) and only principal (PO) to another class. The "residual class" is repaid last.	None, but mortgages used as collateral often are insured or backed by government agency guarantees and pools may be backed with letters of credit
State or local mortgage revenue bond	State housing authorities or municipalities	Mortgage revenues earned on specific housing (finance) programs	Regular contractual payments	None

representatives on its board of directors. Because of its credit line, FNMA debt is considered to be government agency debt. As a privately run agency, FNMA has been able to develop a variety of pass-through securities similar to FHLMC's PCs. FNMA can issue pass-throughs for either federally insured or conventional mortgages.

PRIVATELY ISSUED PASS-THROUGHS (PIPs)

Freddie Mac's success in purchasing mortgages and issuing mortgage-backed securities sparked a number of imitators in the private sector. Some began their operations because private sellers of mortgages thought that FHLMC's insurance and administrative charges were excessively high relative to the risk of default on conventional mortgages.

Privately issued pass-throughs (PIPs) first appeared in 1977. PIPs are issued by private institutions or mortgage bankers, which pool mortgages, obtain private mortgage insurance, obtain ratings for the security issue, and sell the securities using underwriters' services to compete for funds in the bond markets. Privately issued pass-throughs are often used to securitize nonconforming mortgage loans that do not qualify for FHA insurance, often because the mortgage exceeds FNMA's or FHLMC's purchase limit ($333,700 in 2004 for single-family mortgages) or fails to meet their underwriting standards. Some institutions specialize in high-risk, over 100 percent loan-to-value ratio mortgages that FNMA and FHLMC do not make; others specialize in "jumbo" mortgages that exceed FNMA's and FHLMC's $333,700 purchase limit.

CMOs AND REMICs

Although pass-through securities have been tremendously successful in attracting capital market funds to mortgage markets, new varieties of mortgage-backed debt securities have been invented to further broaden the appeal of mortgage investing. **Collateralized mortgage obligations (CMOs)** consist of a series of related debt obligations, called **tranches**, which divide up the principal and interest payments made on a pool of mortgages and pay principal and interest to various investors according to a predetermined schedule. For instance, tranche A securities usually receive a fixed interest rate plus all principal payments until the entire tranche is repaid. Each obligation in the debt series except the "residual series" has a fixed maturity priority and interest payments similar to a corporate bond. Wall Street investment banks sell CMOs on behalf of originating thrift institutions and their subsidiaries. CMO tranches typically have a variety of maturity dates that can be tailored to lenders' needs. Some other CMOs may contain interest-only (IO) tranches, coupled with principal-only (PO) tranches; some CMOs may even have tranches that have floating rates if the tranche is backed by a pool of floating-rate mortgages or is paired with an "inverse floater" tranche. Rates on inverse floaters vary inversely with market interest rates.

The major advantage of CMOs is that, except for the interest-only or (residual) class, the size and value of their payments are more certain than payments on their underlying mortgages unless prepayments vary unexpectedly. The major problem with CMOs is that they may create tax problems for various originators, because most originators cannot pass through all interest payments tax-free when they issue multiple debt securities. To solve this problem, the 1986 Tax Reform Act authorized the creation of a new form of mortgage-backed security. The new form was called a **real estate mortgage investment conduit (REMIC)**, which was treated like a trust that could pass through all interest and principal payments to buyers of the pass-through securities before taxes were levied. REMICs are pass-through securities in the same manner as CMOs. They differ from CMOs only in their legal structure. Often pass-through securities issued by the FHLMC or FNMA are used to back issues of CMOs or REMICs.

CMOs and REMICs are popular because they create securities that have liquidity, payment, or risk characteristics that are desirable to borrowers. Because of the attractive attributes of various tranches, the tranches created by a CMO or REMIC can be sold at a higher average price (or with lower average interest rates) than the underlying pool of mortgages.

STRIPPED MORTGAGE-BACKED SECURITIES (SMBSs)

Like pass-through securities, **stripped mortgage-backed securities (SMBS)** pass through all payments of principal and interest on pools of mortgages to holders of security interests in the pool. The cash flows received by the holders of the interest only (IO) security are based solely on the interest payments being made on the underlying pool of mortgages. The interest payments are directly related to the principal amount outstanding on the pool of mortgages. Therefore, the cash flows received by the holders of the IO securities decline as the principal amount declines. The holders of the principal only (PO) securities, on the other hand, receive cash flows based on the principal payments made on the pool of underlying mortgages. Because there is a finite and fixed principal amount associated with the underlying mortgages, the cash flows received by the holders of the PO security will total a finite and fixed amount.

The values of IO and PO securities are extremely sensitive to changes in interest rates due to the effect interest rates have on prepayment rates. As interest rates decrease, the holders of a PO security expect to receive the principal amount sooner and the value of the security increases. When interest rates increase, on the other hand, the value of a PO security decreases because its cash flows will be deferred further into the future as prepayment rates extend further into the future.

The value of the IO security, on the other hand, tends to decline (increase) as interest rates decline (increase). As interest rates decrease, the principal amount outstanding on the pool of underlying mortgages also decreases due to the increased rate of prepayments. As the principal amount outstanding declines, the size of the cash flows flowing to the holder of the IO security also declines, causing a decline in the value of the security. If interest rates increase, the expected amount of principal outstanding also increases, so the expected cash flows increase and the value of the IO security increases.

MORTGAGE-BACKED BONDS

Freddie Mac, Fannie Mae, and other institutions that hold large quantities of mortgages will often fund their operations by issuing **mortgage-backed bonds**. A variety of mortgage-backed bonds are available.

FHLMC and FNMA Debt.   In addition to pooling mortgages and securitizing them, Fannie Mae and Freddie Mac issue notes and bonds backed by their mortgage holdings. Because mortgages provide excellent collateral for their note and bond issues and they both have government credit lines, the FNMA and FHLMC are able to issue securities at very favorable rates.

Private Mortgage-Backed Debt.   Mortgage-backed bonds can be issued by any holder of mortgages. They pay interest semiannually and have a fixed maturity (often 5 or 10 years) just like corporate, government, or federal agency bonds. However, they are collateralized by a specific pool of mortgages. The trust agreements associated with such bond issues often call for high collateral maintenance levels (150 percent or more of the value of the bonds). As a result, they obtain very high ratings (often AAA) and can compete effectively for funds in the capital markets.

Mortgage-backed bonds provide financial institutions with an effective way to obtain relatively low-cost funds by issuing bonds when their other sources of funds are expensive or inadequate. These bonds can be particularly helpful when a credit crunch occurs and the term structure of interest rates inverts, so short-term financing is very expensive.

In contrast with private pass-throughs (which are backed by issues of new mortgages) and new GNMA pools (which contain only mortgages written within the last year), mortgage-backed bonds allow financial institutions to borrow against the value of mortgages already in their portfolios. Such bonds greatly expand those institutions' borrowing potential and eliminate the possibility that they might have to sell (at a loss) some old, low-rate mortgages so that they can obtain more funds during financial crises. If the old bonds were sold at a loss, an institution would have to write down its profits and net worth.

State and Local Government Housing Revenue Bonds.   Mortgage-backed bonds may be issued by particular state and local government agencies, such as state housing finance agencies or municipalities. The interest paid on housing revenue–backed bonds is usually exempt from federal taxes because they are municipal obligations. Thus, they can be sold at advantageous rates, and the proceeds from their sale allow municipalities and housing authorities to provide mortgage credit at relatively low rates.

MORTGAGE PREPAYMENT RISK

Mortgages usually have interest rates that exceed rates available on Treasury bonds. Since some mortgages and mortgage-backed securities, such as GNMA securities, have a U.S. Treasury guarantee, one might wonder why the mortgage-backed securities have premium interest rates. The reason is that mortgages have a special type of interest rate risk. Unlike U.S. Treasury securities, which typically are not callable, mortgages can be prepaid (in essence, "called") at the discretion of the borrowers. When interest rates are low, many people **refinance** their old mortgages by obtaining new mortgages with lower interest rates and paying off the balance due on the old mortgages; this exposes the mortgage owner to **call** or **prepayment risk**, since the mortgage will be repaid sooner than expected. If a mortgage-backed security paid a high interest rate, a purchaser might expect to receive high interest payments for a long time and, therefore, might pay a high price (probably more than face value) for the mortgage-backed security. However, if the mortgage were prepaid early, before the owner expected, he or she would earn far less interest than expected and would probably lose a substantial amount of money if the mortgage were quickly repaid (at face value) and the high interest income ceased.

Conversely, when interest rates are high, people may be reluctant to move and buy a new house when they will have to borrow money to finance the new house at high interest rates. In addition, they will not want to refinance their old mortgage if they would have to pay higher interest rates on a new mortgage. Thus, mortgage repayments will be slower than normal when interest rates are high; this may expose mortgage owners to **extension risk**. Extension risk is the risk that the expected timing of mortgage repayment extends further into the future.

Prepayment risk and extension risk are a concern to mortgage investors because of their impact on mortgage valuations. Unlike noncallable bonds, which increase in value at an increasing rate when interest rates decline, mortgages and mortgage pass-through securities increase in value at a decreasing rate when interest rates decline due to the increased likelihood of prepayments and the shortened expected timing of mortgage repayment. When interest rates increase, on the other hand, the value of a mortgage or mortgage pass-through security will tend to decrease at an increasing rate because borrowers will be less likely to prepay their low-interest mortgages.

Repayment rate assumptions make a huge difference in the realized yield a buyer will earn on a mortgage-backed security. For instance, a pool of GNMA mortgages with a 7 percent interest rate might be priced at 107 (percent of par) and have a stated yield of 5.5 percent based on an assumed repayment rate. However, if all the mortgages were repaid at par at the end of 1 year, the realized yield would actually be about zero percent as the fall in price from 107 percent of par to par (a price of 100) would roughly equal the interest rate earned on the invested funds. Conversely, if a mortgage-backed pool of principal-only (PO) securities were purchased at a price of 80 (percent of par) and repaid at par in a year, the buyer would earn a 25 percent rate of return over that year. However, if the securities were purchased at a price of 80 and not repaid for 20 years, the investor in the POs would actually earn a compound annual rate of return of 1.1 percent, not 25 percent.

Because mortgages contain both prepayment risk and extension risk, financial institutions that provide mortgage financing often securitize the loans by issuing securities that pass through all payments of principal and interest on a pool of mortgages to buyers of the securities. The ultimate buyers of the mortgage-backed securities, then, bear the interest rate risk. The financial institution no longer owns the mortgages or earns interest on them. However, the originating institution usually earns fees for "originating" and "servicing" the mortgages, and it keeps its customers happy by providing mortgage financing when they need it.

Exhibit 9.7 shows that mortgage refinancing rates vary greatly over time, rising sharply when mortgage rates fall and falling sharply when mortgage rates rise again.

EXHIBIT 9.7
Refinancing Activity and Mortgage Rates

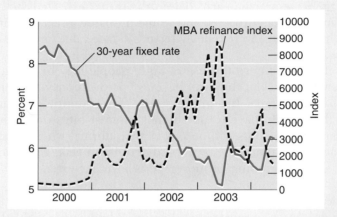

Refinancing activity varies strongly over time, rising sharply when mortgage rates fall and peaking when mortgage rates start to rise again.

Source: Mortgage Bankers Association of America.

DO YOU UNDERSTAND?

1. If you owned a $100,000 security interest in a pass-through mortgage pool that contained $200,000,000 in mortgages and received $20,000,000 in interest payments and $2,000,000 in principal payments in its first year, how much principal and interest would you receive (if there were no mortgage servicing costs) that year?

2. If your security interest in the mortgage pool described above were a PO, or principal-only, security, rather than a regular pass-through security, how much would you have received after the first year?

3. Why are securitized mortgage-backed securities often more attractive to investors than pass-through securities on the same pool of mortgages would be?

4. Why is government or private insurance important to the mortgage markets?

PARTICIPANTS IN THE MORTGAGE MARKETS

MORTGAGE HOLDERS

The major holders of mortgage instruments are shown in Exhibit 9.8. They include thrift institutions, commercial banks, life insurance companies and pension funds, government-sponsored enterprises (GSEs) such as FHLMC and

EXHIBIT 9.8
Mortgages Outstanding by Holder (1958–2003)

	1958	1968	1978	1985	1995	2003
Amount Outstanding ($ in billions)	$172.50	$412.50	$1,169.40	$2,312.30	$4,602.70	$9,465.4
Percentage Held						
Thrift institutions	39.9%	44.6%	45.1%	33.1%	13.0%	9.2%
Commercial banks	14.8	15.9	18.3	18.6	23.7	23.8
Insurance companies and pension funds	22.4	19.3	10.1	8.8	5.3	3.4
U.S. government	2.5	2.3	2.4	2.3	1.3	0.8
Government agencies (GSEs)	2.0	3.2	6.2	5.9	5.4	4.7
Mortgage pools, government agency	0.1	0.6	6.0	16.0	34.1	36.9
Mortgage pools, private	—	—	—	0.6	6.4	12.7
Households	16.6	11.8	8.7	5.4	2.5	1.2
State and local governments	0.6	0.8	1.4	3.2	2.5	1.6
REITs	0.2	0.2	0.5	0.3	0.3	0.5
Credit unions	—	0.2	0.3	0.5	1.4	1.9
Finance companies	—	—	—	1.2	1.6	2.2
Other	0.9	1.1	1.0	4.1	2.5	1.2

The rapid growth of mortgage pools has reduced thrifts' and life insurance companies' direct holdings of mortgages, as these institutions have substituted more marketable mortgage-backed securities for individual mortgages in their portfolios.

FNMA, holders of government and private pools of mortgage-backed securities, and others.

Thrifts and Banks. Participation in the mortgage markets has been dramatically altered over time. Thrift institutions expanded their presence in the mortgage markets considerably after World War II. A tax and regulatory environment favorable to those institutions, coupled with the requirement that they invest a large portion of their portfolios in mortgages, contributed to that growth. However, beginning in the 1970s, high costs of funds reduced flows of funds to thrift institutions and reduced their desire to acquire long-term, fixed-rate mortgages. Consequently, thrifts' direct participation in the mortgage markets fell sharply. The decline is overstated, however, because thrifts swapped many of their mortgage holdings for FNMA and FHLMC participation certificates starting in late 1981.

Government-sponsored agencies (FNMA and FHLMC), mortgage pools, and commercial banks picked up much of the slack as thrifts reduced their participation in the mortgage markets after the 1970s.

Insurance Companies and Pension Funds.   Life insurance companies and pension funds often acquire mortgages to guarantee long-term returns. After World War II they held 11 percent of all mortgages outstanding, and that percentage grew in the postwar years. After the mid-1960s, however, these institutions sharply decreased their participation in the direct mortgage market. Nonetheless, they did not withdraw from the mortgage markets; they mainly acquired highly marketable pass-through securities instead of less-marketable direct mortgages.

Pools.   Pass-through securities are recorded in Exhibit 9.8 as pools. Before the establishment of the Government National Mortgage Association (GNMA) in 1968, pools were unimportant. By the end of 2003, however, over $4.6 trillion (or nearly half of all mortgages outstanding) were held in pools to back pass-through securities, participation certificates, swap certificates, and so on, and they were the largest single component of the mortgage market.

Government Holdings.   Federal as well as state and local government agencies play a direct role in the mortgage markets. Federally owned or supported institutions, such as the FNMA, the FHLMC, the Federal Land Banks, or the Farmers Home Administration, may directly acquire and hold mortgage debt. In addition, state or local housing authorities may issue housing revenue bonds and use the proceeds to acquire mortgage loans.

The mortgage markets generate many billions of dollars per year in new mortgages. This vast amount of financing has been facilitated by the operations of mortgage insurers, mortgage bankers, and numerous government agencies.

MORTGAGE INSURERS

FHA Insurance.   The federal government pioneered the development of mortgage insurance during the 1930s. As real estate values plummeted and many foreclosures occurred, investors became reluctant to invest in mortgaged property without substantial down payments. Thus, the Federal Housing Administration offered FHA insurance to guarantee lenders against default on mortgage loans. FHA insurance initially had a monthly premium equal to $1/2$ of 1 percent of the outstanding balance on a loan; now the premium is paid in advance and varies with mortgage terms.

Federally insured mortgages were popular. Lenders were willing to make FHA loans to borrowers at favorable interest rates with the minimal down payments required by the FHA because of the insurance.

However, their popularity was hindered at times because the FHA refused to insure loans that (1) were above a certain maximum size, (2) carried an interest rate above what the FHA thought was politically expedient to allow, and (3) did not comply with FHA appraisal and paperwork requirements. Of these, the loan size restrictions and interest rate caps caused the most problems. When FHA-approved interest rate ceilings were below market interest rates, lenders charged discount "points" on FHA loans. Loan discounts of 10 percent or more were sometimes needed before lenders could earn a market rate of return. As a result, lenders were reluctant to make FHA loans at such times.

VA Insurance.   In 1944, the Veterans Administration (VA) was allowed to insure mortgage loans to military veterans on even more lenient terms than the FHA.

VA-insured loans can be made for larger amounts and require no down payment at all. However, they require cumbersome paperwork, and they, too, have sometimes been adversely affected by low rate ceilings.

Private Mortgage Insurance. Because of the administrative drawbacks associated with FHA- and VA-insured mortgage lending, many institutions (particularly thrifts) prefer to make conventional mortgage loans. These are usually made with down payments that are substantially higher than those for government-insured loans in order to protect the lender against loss. However, their higher down payments make them unpopular with some borrowers.

Private mortgage insurance companies (such as PMI) have helped fill the need for low down-payment conventional mortgages. These companies insure a portion of the total mortgage debt—the riskiest 10 to 20 percent—in return for a relatively high premium on the insured portion (see Exhibit 9.5). This can let a borrower buy real property with as little as 5 percent down. In addition, the overall rate (APR) on the mortgage is not substantially elevated. This is so because the insured portion is only a fraction of the total mortgage.

Effects of Mortgage Insurance. Mortgage insurance has facilitated the development of secondary mortgage markets. The buyer of an insured mortgage need know only the financial strength and credibility of the insurer instead of the financial strength and credibility of the mortgage issuer. This reduces the buyer's information costs considerably—from having to know about thousands of Jane Does' mortgages to merely knowing about the performance of the FHA, VA, PMI, or other mortgage insurers. As a result, more people are willing to buy mortgages, and mortgages are more marketable than would otherwise be the case.

MORTGAGE BANKERS

Mortgage bankers have grown in importance since mortgage insurance increased the secondary market for mortgages. **Mortgage bankers**, or mortgage companies, are private firms that originate mortgages and collect payments on them. However, they generally do not hold mortgage loans in their own portfolios for long. Instead, they sell them and obtain their income from "servicing fees" that they charge the ultimate buyers for collecting payments and keeping records on each loan. The service fees, along with loan "origination" and application fees that they receive when they make the loan, cover their costs of loan origination and collection.

Origination fees are usually expressed as "points," that is, percentages of the mortgage's principal amount. A typical origination fee is one point. Mortgage bankers typically originate mortgages that meet the "underwriting standards" (loan terms, collateral, and borrower risk requirements) imposed by major purchasers of mortgages. FNMA (Fannie Mae) and FHLMC (Freddie Mac) publish their underwriting standards and give people computer access to see if pending loans will qualify for purchase. If a mortgage is "nonconforming" under FNMA and FHLMC standards—primarily because it is for a larger amount or has a lower down payment than government guidelines allow FNMA and FHLMC to purchase—it may be sold to a private mortgage purchaser who, in turn, may securitize it—just as FNMA and FHLMC do with most of the mortgages they purchase.

Once a mortgage is sold to a final holder—such as FNMA, FHLMC, a life insurance company, or a pension fund—or to GNMA, a REMIC (real estate mortgage investment conduit), or other trust that passes through payments on securitized mortgages, a mortgage banker may continue to profit by "servicing" the mortgage in exchange for a servicing fee. A mortgage servicer collects and records mortgage payments and calculates the portion of payments that are from principal and from interest before passing the payments on to the mortgage owner. The mortgage servicer may also make insurance and tax payments due if such payments are required to be part of the borrowers' mortgage payments. The mortgage servicing fee is usually expressed as a percentage of the principal outstanding. It can range as high as 0.44 percent (44 basis points) and for many years was most often $3/8$ (37.5 basis points) percent; however, it has fallen in recent years as computer technology has reduced bookkeeping costs and competition among mortgage servicers has reduced servicing fees. Mortgage bankers must beware that they don't compete too hard, however. The typical mortgage's principal balance and the associated dollar amount of servicing fees tend to fall over time as a mortgage ages. However, a fixed-rate mortgage's payments, and the work required to process those payments, stay the same over time. Thus, servicing fee net income will fall over time on aging mortgages. As a result, initially adequate servicing fees may become inadequate when a mortgage gets old. In the past, some mortgage bankers have experienced financial difficulty because they forgot this point.

Mortgage bankers may obtain "commitments" from FNMA or FHLMC to purchase mortgages in the future on preagreed terms. They pay a "commitment fee" for that privilege but, in turn, can guarantee mortgage rates to potential borrowers before the pending sale of a property is closed and the mortgage is originated.

Mortgage bankers do not take substantial interest rate risk because they do not own mortgages for long—only until the mortgages are assembled into "pools" and sold to final purchasers. In addition, by buying interest rate put options or by obtaining advance purchase commitments for mortgages, they can insulate themselves against interest rate risk that might occur if interest rates rose after they had guaranteed a rate on a mortgage.

In recent years, mortgage banking has become increasingly efficient with the use of computers, telecommunications, and the Internet. Mortgage bankers are now able to access FNMA or FHLMC computers and determine whether a loan will qualify for purchase according to the current underwriting standards of the agency. In addition, they can access credit bureau computers and obtain an almost instantaneous credit report on mortgage loan applicants, and they can verify borrower incomes and credit histories easily. Thus, it is possible to tell a loan applicant within minutes or hours, instead of days, whether the applicant qualifies for a mortgage loan (subject to all information on the credit application being complete and true once it is further verified, and subject to the real estate appraisal and condition being confirmed upon final inspection).

One potential problem for mortgage bankers is that they constantly have to discover and implement new technologies in order to match the services that the competition offers in terms of speed, convenience, and price. New technologies (1) have simplified the speed and convenience with which the loan applications can be processed (by using computerized underwriting evaluations), (2) have allowed interest rate risks to be hedged (with interest rate futures and options and advance purchase commitments), and (3) have facilitated the collection of both current and delinquent mortgage payments (through automated clearinghouses).

The popularity of mortgage-backed securities has led to a tremendous flow of capital market funds into mortgage markets. This has opened up the possibility of homeownership for many subprime borrowers who would otherwise have difficulty in getting a mortgage loan. Subprime borrowers are those graded as A–, B, C, or D. Unfortunately, the grades are not well defined, but A– borrowers typically have FICO credit scores between 600 and 650. B and C borrowers tend to have scores between 540 and 600. D borrowers have scores below 540. Prime (A) borrowers generally have scores above 650.*

Although the subprime mortgage market has seen rapid growth and many lenders specialize in making subprime loans, the characteristics of subprime mortgages are such that subprime lenders must charge higher fees and interest rates than prime lenders. The chief reason for the high rates and fees on subprime mortgages is the high default rates on these mortgages relative to prime mortgages. The delinquency rate and foreclosure rate on subprime mortgages tend to be about five times as high as on prime mortgages. In addition to having higher risk than prime mortgages, subprime mortgages tend to be for smaller amounts, are more costly to originate, and are prepaid faster. All of these characteristics combine to force subprime lenders to charge higher rates and fees than prime lenders.

Unfortunately, the dramatic growth in the subprime mortgage market and the relatively high rates and fees have attracted some lenders that engage in abusive lending practices, collectively called **predatory lending** practices. It is important to recognize that predatory lenders represent a subset of subprime mortgage lenders and that many subprime lenders do not engage in predatory practices.

Excessively high interest rates and fees as well as abusive terms and conditions characterize predatory loans. Further, the sales practices employed by predatory lenders discourage borrowers from questioning or challenging the terms of their loan. Not surprisingly, the lenders that engage in predatory lending tend to target those members of society who are most vulnerable.

Defining predatory lending is difficult due to the complexities of determining what constitutes excessively high interest rates or fees. In addition, the loan terms that many consider abusive might, in some circumstances, be viewed as reasonable. For example, by agreeing to a prepayment penalty, some borrowers in the prime mortgage market are able to negotiate for a lower interest rate. However, some experts have argued that prepayment penalties should be prohibited in subprime mortgage markets.

Those who argue for prohibiting prepayment penalties point out that one of the legitimate and useful functions performed by the subprime lending market is to provide a source of funds for high-risk borrowers that will help those borrowers solve their short-term financial problems. Ultimately, many of these subprime borrowers will be able to improve their credit standing so that they are able to borrow in the prime market. By imposing prepayment penalties on subprime loans, however, predatory lenders prevent such borrowers from being able to refinance out of a subprime loan and into a prime loan. Further, analyzing whether the reduced interest rate is sufficient to offset the cost of agreeing to a prepayment penalty is a relatively sophisticated financial decision. In fact, only 2 percent of prime conventional mortgage borrowers choose prepayment penalties in exchange for a lower interest rate, yet Mortgage Information Corporation (MIC) statistics indicate that over 70 percent of subprime mortgage loans include a prepayment penalty.

Those who argue against prohibiting prepayment penalties counter that, due to the high cost of originating subprime mortgages, subprime lenders must be able to charge a prepayment penalty to protect themselves from losing money on mortgages that are repaid quickly. By allowing prepayment penalties, subprime lenders are promised an investment that is sufficiently long term for them to recoup their up-front costs in the form of the interest rate they earn on the loan or a prepayment penalty that compensates the lender for the up-front costs.

---

* FICO scores are the credit scores developed by Fair Isaac & Company, the leader in the development of credit scoring models. The range of possible FICO scores is 350 to 850, with higher scores representing higher credit quality. Note that the scores given here are generalizations and that there is tremendous variation within the industry.

Since new technologies require extensive investment in computers and staff training, mortgage bankers may need to process a large volume of transactions to recoup the expense of the new technology. This need may induce mortgage bankers to merge in order to spread the overhead costs of acquiring and implementing new technology. Also, in order to attract a large volume of business, mortgage bankers may tend to shave servicing fees—which could pose future problems if a mortgage banker continued to service aging mortgage portfolios once mortgage balances and servicing fees started to fall below profitable levels. In recent years, mortgage bankers have done well because many mortgage loans were refinanced before their balances were paid down. If mortgages are repaid more slowly in the future, however, some mortgage bankers may find that their servicing fee income has fallen while their costs have not.

RELATIONSHIP BETWEEN MORTGAGE MARKETS AND THE CAPITAL MARKETS

As you can see from Exhibit 9.9, interest rates on mortgage obligations move in step with those on other capital market obligations, particularly 10-year government securities. Mortgage rates on 30-year fixed-rate mortgages closely track changes in the 10-year Treasury note rate, since both have similar durations due to the accelerated repayment of mortgages. The mortgage rate is higher than the note rate, however, since mortgages have both call risk and extension risk and, if not government guaranteed, some small credit risk. Long-term fixed-rate mortgages are little affected by changes in short-term interest rates.

EXHIBIT 9.9
Mortgage Interest Rates and Other Market Rates

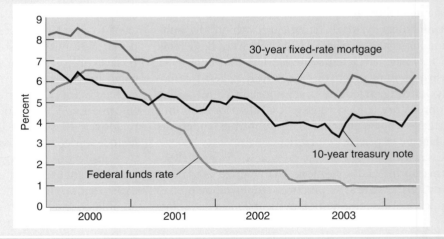

Mortgage rates on 30-year fixed-rate mortgages closely track changes in the 10-year Treasury note rate since both have similar durations due to the accelerated repayment of mortgages. The mortgage rate is higher than the note rate, however, since mortgages have both prepayment risk and extension risk and, if not government guaranteed, some small credit risk. Long-term fixed-rate mortgages are little affected by changes in short-term interest rates.

Chapter Take-aways

1 Mortgages are collateralized loans that are amortized over time. Monthly mortgage payments include interest and principal. Periodic interest payments are based on the remaining principal balance due—so, in the early years, the mortgage principal declines slowly and it may take two-thirds of the mortgage's life before even one-half of the loan is repaid.

2 A wide variety of mortgages have been developed. Fixed-rate mortgages are common but cannot adjust returns if inflation occurs and interest rates rise. ARMs, flexible ARMs, ROMs, RRMs, and balloon payment mortgages all call for periodic adjustments in interest. Home equity loans and second mortgages allow people to borrow against the accumulated equity in their homes.

3 After the development of federal mortgage insurance (FHA, VA, etc.), private mortgage insurance, GNMA, and government-sponsored agencies (FNMA, FHLMC) that guarantee mortgage loans, a national secondary market in mortgages developed. Insurance and other financial guarantees reduce credit risk in the market.

4 A wide variety of mortgage-backed securities (MBSs) were developed that increased the appeal of MBSs relative to the original mortgages by reducing call (prepayment) risk, extension risk, or payment uncertainties for some types or tranches of MBSs. The development of MBSs increased the ability of mortgage lenders to obtain financing from the nation's capital markets and led to rapid growth in mortgages outstanding and more uniform mortgage rates across the country. These innovations also improved liquidity in the mortgage markets.

5 Most mortgages are now sold in the secondary mortgage markets. Mortgage bankers and government agencies (such as FNMA and FHLMC) facilitate secondary mortgage market operations. These government agencies set underwriting (credit) standards, purchase mortgages, and often securitize pools of mortgages by providing "pass-through" or other mortgage-backed securities that can be sold or used to back other securities issued in the mortgage markets.

6 Mortgage bankers originate and service mortgage loans. They bear little interest rate risk because they hold on to mortgages only long enough to sell them in the secondary market. Mortgage bankers earn income from two sources. First, on origination of the loan, they receive an origination fee, which is a fixed percentage of the original loan amount. Second, they receive servicing fees that are a fixed percentage of the outstanding loan balance.

7 The nature of the mortgage markets has changed over time. Regional mortgage markets dominated by local lending institutions, such as savings banks or savings and loans, have given way to national mortgage markets dominated by key government agencies, mortgage bankers, and commercial and investment banks (the investment banks help create and sell many of the mortgage-backed securities). Insurance companies and pension funds provide substantial amounts of funding for mortgage loans, but now they are more likely to buy mortgage-backed securities than individual mortgages.

KEY TERMS

Mortgage
Mortgage-backed security (MBS)
Interest rate risk
Fixed-rate mortgage (FRM)
Amortization
Adjustable-rate mortgage (ARM)
Balloon payment mortgage
Rollover mortgage (ROM)
Renegotiated-rate mortgage (RRM)
Interest-Only Mortgage
Reverse annuity mortgage (RAM)
Home equity loan
Home equity line of credit
FHA mortgage

Veterans Administration (VA)
  mortgage
Private mortgage insurance (PMI)
Government National Mortgage
  Association (GNMA—Ginnie
  Mae)
Federal Home Loan Mortgage
  Corporation (FHLMC—Freddie
  Mac)
Federal National Mortgage
  Association (FNMA—Fannie
  Mae)
Privately Issued Pass-Throughs
  (PIPs)

Collateralized mortgage obligation
  (CMO)
Tranches
Real estate mortgage investment
  conduit (REMIC)
Stripped mortgage-backed securities
  (SMBS)
Mortgage-backed bonds
Refinance
Call Risk
Prepayment Risk
Extension Risk
Mortgage banker
Predatory lending

QUESTIONS AND PROBLEMS

1. If you had a 7 percent, $100,000 30-year fixed-rate mortgage, how long would it take before you had repaid half the loan balance due? If you paid an extra $100 per month to reduce the principal due on the mortgage, how long would it take to repay half the principal due? In the case where you paid an extra $100 per month, how long would it take to repay the entire loan? (Hint: It probably would help to use a computer spreadsheet program to make these calculations; set it up in the same way that Exhibit 9.1 is set up.)

2. If your bank held 1 percent of the units issued by a unit trust and the mortgages in the trust repaid $10,500,000 in interest and $1,500,000 in principal in its first year, how much principal and interest would your bank receive that year?

3. If your mortgage balance was $60,000 and you had a floating-rate mortgage that called for you to pay interest at an annual rate of 2.75 percent over the 1-year T-bill rate and the T-bill rate has been averaging 2.05 percent, how much interest would you owe on your mortgage next month?

4. Describe the factors that affect a borrower's ability to qualify for a mortgage.

5. Suppose your gross monthly income is $5,000. Assume that property taxes, homeowner's insurance, and mortgage insurance payments total $200 a month. In addition, assume you have automobile and student loan payments that total $400 a month. If 30-year fixed-rate mortgages have a current annual percentage rate of 6 percent, how much will you qualify to borrow based on the payment-to-income ratios described in the chapter?

6. Assume you set up a REMIC that guaranteed that the class B tranche would bear all the credit risk and the class A tranche would lose only if the class B tranche holders were not repaid. What is the maximum interest rate you could offer the class B tranche holders and still make a profit from securitizing the loans if the class A tranche buyers were willing to accept a 7 percent return on their 90 percent interest in a pool of mortgages that generated an 8 percent interest return? (The class B holders would hold the other 10 percent interest in the pool.)

7. Why was the development of mortgage insurance necessary before secondary mortgage markets could develop?

8. How has the development of secondary mortgage markets allowed mortgage issuers to attract additional funds from the capital markets?

9. Explain how mortgage-related securities have become more similar to capital market instruments over time.

10. Why have mortgage market interest rates become more uniform across the country in recent years?

11. How has the government encouraged the development of secondary mortgage markets?

12. What is the difference between conventional mortgages and FHA and VA mortgages?

13. If you expect prices and incomes to rise, what type of mortgage would you rather have on your house: FRM or ARM? What if you expected prices to fall? Explain your answer. Also explain how your answer would differ if you were a mortgage lender.

14. Why have CMOs and REMICs made it easier for the mortgage markets to compete for funds with corporate bonds? What problems do their "residuals" pose?

15. If mortgage bankers originate more mortgages than other types of financial institutions, why don't they also hold more mortgages in their asset accounts?

INTERNET EXERCISE

A majority of the mortgages originated in the United States are sold or securitized at some time. Mortgage bankers are among the most important originators and sellers of mortgages. The GSEs—government-sponsored enterprises such as Ginnie Mae, Freddie Mac, and Fannie Mae—are the most important buyers of mortgages and issuers of mortgage-backed securities. The Web site for the Mortgage Bankers Association of America, http:www.mbaa.org, provides useful news releases on mortgage legislation, mortgage delinquency rates, and mortgage interest rates. The Web sites of all the GSEs (www.freddiemac.com, www.fanniemae.com, and www.ginniemae.gov) contain useful descriptions of the various types of mortgage-backed securities one is most likely to encounter in the financial markets.

1. Go to the Fannie Mae Web site. Click on "Mortgage-Backed Securities." Then click on "Basics of Fannie Mae MBSs" and "Basics of REMICs." Finally, click on "Classes." (a) What are three types of tranches that are adversely affected by extension risk. (b) What type of tranche is least likely to be adversely affected by extension risk? (c) What type is most likely to be adversely affected by prepayment (call) risk?
2. Beginning at Fannie Mae's home page, click on the "Homepath" link and then the "Adjustable-Rate Mortgages" link. Use the links to different types of ARMs to identify the advantages and disadvantages of 1-year ARMs versus fixed-period ARMs.
3. The Web site of the Mortgage Bankers Association of America, http://www.mbaa.org, contains useful information on the current state of the mortgage market. Use that site to find the following
   a. How delinquency rates on mortgages have changed over the last year
   b. How much the ARM rate differs from the 30-year mortgage rate.

10

Equity Markets

Equity securities are certificates of ownership of a corporation. Equities are the most visible securities on the U.S. financial landscape. At the end of 2003 over $15 trillion worth of equity securities were outstanding. Every day in newspapers and on tele- vision, reporters eagerly and with rapt interest describe the ups and downs of the stock market because many in society view the perform- ance of the stock market as an impor- tant indicator of the economy's health. The term **equity** implies an ownership claim, and holders of equity securities have a right to share in a corporation's profits. People dream of reaping riches from invest- ing in the stock market and, in fact, whether we realize it or not, most of us own equity securities indirectly through pension or investment funds. ∎

Equity securities, which represent ownership of cor- porations, are traded on exchanges such as the New York Stock Exchange. The trading activity on a stock exchange is fast, furious, and frenzied, and every day has the potential to be a bad hair day.

The purpose of this chapter is to answer the following questions about equity securities: Who owns them? How are they bought and sold? How are stock markets regulated? What determines the prices of equity securities? How do we measure the risk of equities? What is the meaning of various stock indexes such as the Dow Jones Industrial Average or the S&P 500? Do movements in the stock market predict changes in economic activity?

The chapter begins with a description of the types of equity securities: common stock, preferred stock, and convertible securities. We then discuss how equity securities are traded in primary and secondary markets before describing the major venues for trading equities in the United States. Next we briefly describe government regulation of the equity markets. The focus then turns to valuing equity securities and measuring their risks. We then describe the major stock indexes and, finally, address whether the stock market is a good predictor of economic activity. ■

LEARNING OBJECTIVES

The objectives of this chapter are to:

1 Describe the three types of equity securities.

2 Explain how equity securities are sold in the primary market and discuss the determinants of underwriter spreads.

3 Explain how equity securities are traded in the secondary markets and discuss the determinants of a security's bid–ask spread.

4 Describe the basics of equity valuation.

5 Explain the risks associated with equity securities and discuss how to measure these risks.

6 Describe the major stock-market indexes and how they are constructed.

7 Discuss whether the stock market is a good predictor of economic activity.

WHAT ARE EQUITY SECURITIES?

Equity securities take several forms. As the name implies, **common stock** is the most prevalent type of equity security. The term "common stock" usually means equity securities that have no special dividend rights and have the lowest priority claim in the event of bankruptcy. Owners of **preferred stock**, in contrast, usually receive preferential treatment over common stockholders when it comes to receiving dividends or cash payoffs in bankruptcy. Most convertible securities are preferred stock or corporate bonds that are convertible into the firm's common stock. We now discuss the characteristics of these three types of equity securities.

COMMON STOCK

Common stock represents the basic ownership claim in a corporation. The most distinguishing feature of common stock is that it is the **residual claim** against the firm's cash flows or assets. In the event of a firm's liquidation, common stock-holders cannot be paid until claims of employees, the government, short-term creditors, bondholders, and preferred stockholders are first satisfied. After these prior claims are paid, the stockholders are entitled to what is left over, the resid-ual. Common stockholders, therefore, directly share in the firm's profits. The residual nature of common stock, however, means that it is more risky than a firm's bonds or preferred stock.

Legally, common stockholders enjoy **limited liability**, meaning that their losses are limited to the original amount of their investment. Limited liability also implies that the personal assets of a shareholder cannot be obtained to satisfy the obligations of the corporation. In contrast, a sole proprietor is *personally* liable for the firm's obligations. Given limited liability, it is not surprising that most large firms in the United States are organized as corporations.

Dividends.   Corporate payments to stockholders are called **dividends**. Common stock dividends are not guaranteed, and a corporation does not default if it does not pay them. Dividends are paid out of the firm's after-tax cash flows. Because dividend income is taxable for most investors, corporate profits are doubly taxed—once when the corporation pays the corporate income tax, and once more when the investors pay their personal income taxes. To avoid double taxation, some investors hold stocks in "growth companies" that reinvest their accumulated earnings instead of paying larger dividends. Reinvestment of earnings allows the company to accumulate capital and grow faster than it otherwise might. As a firm's earnings grow, its stock price usually rises. Stockholders, therefore, can sell their stock and pay capital-gains taxes on their profits.

The Tax Reduction Act of 1997 set a lower tax rate on capital gains than on dividends. The maximum tax rate on assets held for more than 18 months was lowered to 20 percent from 28 percent. Note, also, that taxes on capital gains are paid only upon realization of the gain. Thus, investors can reduce their tax bills in present value terms by deferring the sale of securities to postpone realization of capital gains. Because investors have different portfolio preferences and corpora-tions have different growth opportunities, corporate strategies toward growth versus current dividend payments vary widely.

Voting Rights.   While stockholders own the corporation, they do not exercise control over the firm's day-to-day activities. Control of the firm is in the hands of corporate managers who are supposed to act in the interests of shareholders. Shareholders exercise control over the firm's activities through the election of a board of directors. It is the task of the board of directors to monitor the managers' activities on behalf of the shareholders. Shareholders elect directors by casting votes at an annual meeting. As a practical matter, most shareholders do not actu-ally attend the meeting, voting instead by **proxy**, a process in which shareholders vote by absentee ballot.

In general, one vote is attached to each share of stock, although there are exceptions, called **dual-class firms**. During the 1980s many firms recapitalized with two classes of stock having different voting rights. By issuing stock with limited voting rights compared to existing shares, the managers of a firm can raise equity capital while maintaining voting control of the firm. Needless to say, dual-class firms are controversial. Many view the dual-class recapitalizations as attempts by managers to entrench themselves. Opponents of dual-class recapitalizations argue that managers of dual-class firms are insulated from the disciplining effects of the proxy or takeover processes, through which ineffective managers can be replaced. Proponents say that managers of dual-class firms are free to pursue riskier, longer-term strategies that ultimately benefit shareholders without fear of reprisal if the short-term performance of the firm suffers.

There are two procedures for electing directors: cumulative voting and straight voting. In **cumulative voting**, all directors are elected at the same time and shareholders are granted a number of votes equal to the number of directors being elected times the number of shares owned. In most cumulative voting schemes, shareholders are permitted to distribute their votes across directors as they wish. They may even decide to cast all of their votes for one director. The effect of cumulative voting is to give minority shareholders, those owning small proportions of the stock, a voice in the firm's decisions. With cumulative voting, minority shareholders are guaranteed of being able to elect the largest percentage of the directors that is less than the percentage of shares the minority shareholders control. For example, if five directors are being elected and the minority shareholders control 42 percent of the shares, they are assured of being able to elect two directors because each director requires 20 percent of the total votes cast to be elected. However, if only three directors are being elected, then the minority shareholders would be able to elect only one director because each director requires 33.3 percent of the total votes. In **straight voting**, directors are elected one-by-one. Thus, the maximum number of votes for each director equals the number of shares owned. Under this scheme, it is difficult for minority shareholders to obtain representation on the board of directors because any shareholder who owns even slightly over 50 percent of the shares can elect the entire board of directors.

PREFERRED STOCK

Like common stock, preferred stock represents ownership interest in the corporation, but as the name implies, it receives preferential treatment over common stock with respect to dividend payments and the claim against the firm's assets in the event of bankruptcy or liquidation. In liquidation, preferred stockholders are entitled to the issue price of the preferred stock plus accumulated dividends after other creditors have been paid and before common stockholders are paid.

Dividends.   Preferred stock is usually designated by the dollar amount of its dividend, which is a fixed obligation of the firm, similar to the interest payments on corporate bonds. Most preferred stock is **nonparticipating** and **cumulative**. Preferred stock is nonparticipating in that the preferred dividend remains constant regardless of any increase in the firm's earnings. Firms can decide not to pay the dividends on preferred stock without going into default. The cumulative feature of preferred stock means, however, that the firm cannot pay a dividend on its common stock until it has paid the preferred shareholders the dividends in arrears. Some preferred stock is issued with adjustable rates. **Adjustable-rate preferred stock** became popular in the early 1980s when interest rates were rapidly changing. The dividends of adjustable-rate preferred stock are adjusted periodically in response to changing market interest rates.

Voting.   Generally, preferred stockholders do not vote for the board of directors. Exceptions to this general rule can occur when the corporation is in arrears on its dividend payments.

CONVERTIBLE SECURITIES

Convertible preferred stock can be converted into common stock at a predetermined ratio (such as two shares of common for each share of preferred stock). By buying such stock, an investor can obtain a good dividend return plus the possibility that, should the common stock rise in price, the investment would rise in value.

Convertible bonds are bonds that can be exchanged for shares of common stock. However, until conversion they are corporate debt; thus their interest and principal payments are contractual obligations of the firm and must be made lest the corporation default. Most convertible bonds are subordinated debentures. Hence, their holders have lower-ranking claims than most other debt holders, although their claims rank ahead of stockholders.

Because convertible bonds both increase in value with rising stock prices and provide the fixed income and security of bonds, they are popular with investors, who are usually willing to pay more to acquire convertible debt than conventional debt issued by the same corporation. From the corporation's perspective, convertible bonds provide a means by which the corporation can issue debt and later convert it to equity at a price per share that exceeds the stock's present market value. This feature is attractive because it allows the corporation to "sell" stock at a higher future price.

EQUITY MARKETS

Exhibit 10.1 shows the distribution of ownership for equity securities in the United States at the end of 2003. Households dominate the holding of equity securities, owning over 36 percent of outstanding corporate equities. Pension funds (private and public) are the largest institutional holders of equity, followed by mutual funds and foreign investors. These investors come to own equity securities through either primary market or secondary market transactions. In this section, we discuss the primary and secondary markets for equity securities and the costs of buying or selling securities in these markets.

PRIMARY MARKETS

New issues of securities are called **primary offerings** because they are sold in the primary market. The company can use the funds raised by the sale of equity securities to expand production, enter new markets, further research, and the like. If the company has never before offered a particular type of security to the public, meaning the security is not currently trading in the secondary market, the primary offering is called an unseasoned offering or an **initial public offering (IPO)**. Otherwise, if the firm already has similar securities trading in the secondary market, the primary issue is known as a **seasoned offering**. All securities undergo a single primary offering in which the issuer receives the proceeds of the offering

EXHIBIT 10.1
Holders of Corporate Equity Securities (December 31, 2003)

Holder	Amount (Billions)	% of Total
Households	$5,709	36.8
Pension funds	3,272	21.1
Mutual funds	3,062	19.8
Foreign investors	1,613	10.4
Insurance companies	1,143	7.4
Bank personal trusts	213	1.4
Other	480	3.1
Total	$15,498	100.0

Although households are the category with the single largest holdings of equity securities, institutional investors, as a group, hold more.

Source: Board of Governors, Federal Reserve System.

and the investors receive the securities. Thereafter, whenever the securities are bought or sold, the transaction occurs in the secondary market.

New issues of equity securities may be sold directly to investors by the issuing corporation, but they are usually distributed by an investment banker in an underwritten offering, a private placement, or a shelf registration. The most common distribution method is an **underwritten offering** in which the investment banker purchases the securities from the company for a guaranteed amount known as the net proceeds and then resells the securities to investors for a greater amount, called the gross proceeds. The difference between the gross proceeds and the net proceeds is the **underwriter's spread**, which compensates the investment banker for the expenses and risks involved in the offering.

Also, some equity securities are distributed through **private placements** in which the investment banker acts only as the company's agent and receives a commission for placing the securities with investors. In addition, occasionally a company will place equity securities directly with its existing stockholders through a **rights offering**. In a rights offering, a company's stockholders are given the right to purchase additional shares at a slightly below-market price in proportion to their current ownership in the company. Stockholders can exercise their rights or sell them.

Shelf registration is an important method of selling both equity and debt securities. Shelf registration permits a corporation to register a quantity of securities with the SEC and sell them over time rather than all at once. Thus, the issuer is able to save time and money through a single registration. In addition, with shelf registrations, securities can be brought to market with little notice, thereby providing the issuer with maximum flexibility in timing an issue to take advantage of favorable market conditions. Chapter 19 discusses in more detail the process by which investment bankers assist companies in conducting primary offerings of their securities.

FACTORS AFFECTING UNDERWRITER SPREADS

In an underwritten offering, the difference between the gross proceeds and the net proceeds is the underwriter's spread, which compensates the investment banker for the expenses and risks involved in the offering. Several factors affect the size of the spread.

First, the underwriter's spread is inversely related to the size of the offering. In other words, the larger the offering, the smaller the spread tends to be as a percentage of the amount of funds being raised by the company. Second, the more uncertain the investment bankers are concerning the market price of the equity securities being offered, the larger the underwriter's spread tends to be. The reason is that in an underwritten offering, especially an unseasoned offering, the investment bankers bear all of the price risk. Third, shelf registrations tend to have lower spreads than ordinary offerings. This is due, in part, to the fact that larger, more well-known companies employ shelf registrations.

SECONDARY MARKETS

Any trade of a security after its primary offering is said to be a secondary market transaction. When an investor buys 100 shares of IBM on the New York Stock Exchange (NYSE), the proceeds of the sale do not go to IBM but rather to the investor who sold the shares. In the United States, most secondary market equity trading is done either on organized exchanges, such as the New York Stock Exchange, or in the over-the-counter market.

Exhibit 10.2 shows a portion of the stock exchange quotations from the *Wall Street Journal* and also shows the explanatory notes that accompany the listings. From the exhibit you can see that Anheuser-Busch's stock price has fluctuated between a low price of $48.51 and a high price of $54.10 over the previous 52 weeks. Anheuser-Busch pays dividends of 88 cents per share, which equates to a dividend yield (Yld%) of 1.7 percent. Note that the P/E ratio for Anheuser-Busch is 20. This means that Anheuser-Busch's current price per share is 20 times its earnings per share. You might be asking why on earth anyone would pay *20 times* a company's earnings for a share of its stock. The answer is that the market expects substantial growth in the company's earnings. You can also see from the exhibit that trading volume in Anheuser-Busch stock was 1,824,600 shares (Vol 100s) and that its closing price, under the column labeled "Close," was $51.81 per share, up 6¢ over the previous day's closing price.

From an investor's perspective, the function of secondary markets is to provide liquidity at fair prices. Liquidity is achieved if investors can trade large amounts of securities without affecting the prices. Prices are fair if they reflect the underlying value of the security correctly.

There are several liquidity-related characteristics of a secondary market that investors find desirable. First, a secondary market is said to have **depth** if there exist orders both above and below the price at which a security is currently trading. When a security trades in a deep market, temporary imbalances of purchase or sales orders that would otherwise create substantial price changes encounter offsetting, and hence stabilizing, sale or purchase orders. Second, a secondary market is said to have **breadth** if the orders that give the market depth exist in significant volume. The broader the market, the greater the potential for stabilization of temporary price changes that may arise from order imbalances. Third, a market is **resilient** if new orders pour in promptly in response to price changes

EXHIBIT 10.2
Stock Exchange Quotations from the *Wall Street Journal* (May 20, 2004)

52 Weeks		Stock (Sym)	Div	Yld %	P/E[a]	Vol 100s	Close	Net Chg
Hi	**Lo**							
61.15	31.16	Amazon.com (AMZN)	—	—	cc	72,982	41.69	−0.30
54.10	48.51	Anheuser-Busch (BUD)	0.88	1.7	20	18,246	51.81	+0.06
20.00	12.93	Callaway Golf (ELY)	0.28	1.8	25	6,379	15.85	+0.23
52.88	38.09	Citigroup (C)	1.60	3.6	12	161,741	45.00	−0.15
37.18	29.23	Dell Computer (DELL)	—	—	32	171,030	34.05	−0.31
19.43	12.70	Avista Utilities (AVA)	0.50	3.2	19	2,067	15.81	−0.19
23.47	16.32	Gap, Inc. (GPS)	0.09	0.4	21	54,576	22.40	+0.20
34.60	18.51	Intel (INTC)	0.16	0.6	28	757,501	27.11	−0.04
30.00	23.60	Microsoft (MSFT)	0.16	0.6	38	584,520	25.62	−0.21
29.18	13.00	Yahoo! (YHOO)	—	—	cc	253,771	27.95	+0.18

Column YTD % Chg: −20.8, −1.7, −5.9, −7.3, +0.2, −12.7, −3.5, −15.4, −6.4, +24.1

The *Wall Street Journal* provides daily listings of prices, trading volume, and other information for stocks traded on the NYSE, AMEX, and NASDAQ.
[a] Explanatory notes: cc: P/E ratio is 100 or more. dd: Loss in the most recent four quarters.

Source: Wall Street Journal, May 20, 2004.

that result from temporary order imbalances. For a market to be resilient, investors must be able to quickly learn of such price changes.

However, what investors are most concerned with is having complete information concerning a security's current price and where that price can be obtained. There are four types of secondary markets: direct search, brokered, dealer, and auction. Each of these types of secondary markets differs according to the amount of information investors have concerning prices.

Direct Search.   Perhaps the secondary markets furthest from the ideal of complete price information are those in which buyers and sellers must search each other out directly. Since the full cost of locating and bargaining with a compatible trading partner is borne by an individual investor, there is only a small incentive to conduct a thorough search among all possible partners for the best possible price. Failure to conduct a search implies a high probability that, at the time a trade is agreed upon by the two participants, at least one of the participants could have gotten a better price were he or she in contact with some undiscovered participant. Securities that trade in **direct search markets** are usually bought and sold so infrequently that no third party, such as a broker or a dealer, has an incentive to provide any kind of service to facilitate trading. The common stock of small companies, especially small banks, trades in direct search markets. Buyers and sellers of those issues must rely on word-of-mouth communication of their trading interests to attract compatible trading partners.

Brokered.   When trading in an issue becomes sufficiently heavy, brokers begin to offer specialized search services to market participants. For a fee, called a commission, brokers undertake to find compatible trading partners and to negotiate acceptable transaction prices for their clients.

Since brokers are frequently in contact with many market participants on a continuing basis, they are likely to know what constitutes a "fair" price for a transaction. Brokers will usually know whether the offering price of a seller can easily be bettered by looking elsewhere or whether it is close to the lowest offer price likely to be uncovered. Their extensive contacts provide them with a pool of price information that individual investors could not economically duplicate. By charging a commission less than the cost of direct search, they give investors an incentive to make use of that information.

Dealer.   Whatever its advantages over direct search, a **brokered market** has the disadvantage that it cannot guarantee that investor orders will be executed promptly. This uncertainty about the speed of execution creates price risk. During the time a broker is searching out a compatible trading partner for a client, securities prices may change and the client may suffer a loss. However, if trading in an issue is sufficiently active, some market participants may begin to buy and sell their own inventory at their quoted prices. **Dealer markets** eliminate the need for time-consuming searches for trading partners, because investors know they can buy or sell immediately at the quotes given by a dealer.

Dealers earn their revenue, in part, by selling securities at an offer price greater than the bid price they pay for the securities. Their **bid–ask spread** compensates them for providing to occasional market participants the liquidity of an immediately available market, and also for the risk dealers incur when they position an issue in their inventory.

In most cases dealers do not quote identical prices for an issue because they disagree as to its value or because they have different inventory objectives. Even in a dealer market it is therefore incumbent upon investors to search out the best prices for their trades. The expense of contacting several dealers to obtain comparative quotations is borne by investors. However, since dealers have an incentive to advertise their willingness to buy and sell, their identity will be well known and such contacts can usually be completed quite readily. The ease of searching among dealers guarantees that those dealers quoting the best price will be most likely to do business with investors.

Auction. **Auction markets** provide centralized procedures for the exposure of purchase and sale orders to all market participants simultaneously. By doing so they virtually eliminate the expense of locating compatible partners and bargaining for a favorable price. The communication of price information in an auction market may be oral if all participants are physically located in the same place, or the information can be transmitted electronically.

FACTORS AFFECTING BID–ASK SPREADS

Spreads between dealers' bid and ask prices are not the same for all equity securities. They range from as low as $1/_{32}$ of a dollar on frequently traded issues to several dollars on securities that seldom trade. The wide range of spread sizes reflects differences in the costs of trading various securities, and it is a function of issue characteristics and the trading patterns. In particular, the factors affecting the size of the bid–ask spread for equity securities include the price of the issue, the size of the transaction, the frequency of transactions, and the presence in the market of investors trading on inside information.

Other things being equal, the bid–ask spread for a security should be proportional to its price. That is, higher-priced securities tend to have larger absolute spreads. However, due to fixed transaction costs, higher-priced stocks tend to have lower bid–ask spreads in percentage terms.

Extremely small transactions and extremely large transactions tend to have larger bid–ask spreads in percentage terms. Due to the inconvenience of trading in less than round lots of 100 shares, transactions of less than a round lot generate larger spreads. For larger transactions, the spread between bid and ask prices is larger because the dealer is providing more of a liquidity service than would be the case for a normal-sized trade.

The frequency of trades for a particular security also impacts the bid–ask spread. Since the dealer is providing a liquidity service, the more frequent the trades, the less costly it is for the dealer to provide investors with the desired liquidity. This is because the dealer can hold a smaller inventory of securities when trading is more frequent, and thus the dealer's inventory costs are smaller.

The presence of traders with inside information about the value of a stock will cause dealers to widen the bid–ask spread for such stocks. Dealers may lose in transactions with better-informed traders. Traders with inside information are presumed to sell when they believe the current price of the security is too high or buy when they believe the current price is too low. Dealers who transact with such traders end up paying a price that is too high when the inside information is unfavorable and selling at a price that is too low when the inside information is favorable. Unfortunately, dealers find it difficult to separate traders acting on inside information from those without such information. When there is potential for trading against investors with superior information, dealers increase the spread to compensate for the potential losses they incur.

EQUITY TRADING

Several thousand stocks are listed and traded on organized stock exchanges, while there exist perhaps 30,000 other stock issues that are not restricted from public trading but that are not listed on any exchange. These "unlisted" stocks trade in the **over-the-counter**, or **"OTC,"** market.

OVER-THE-COUNTER AND NASDAQ

Securities not sold on one of the organized exchanges are traded over the counter (OTC). A stock may not be listed on an exchange for several reasons, including lack of widespread investor interest, small issue size, or insufficient order flow.

The OTC stock market is primarily a dealer market. Since different OTC issues are not usually close substitutes for each other, a dealer with limited capital can make a successful market even in a relatively narrow range of stocks. As a result, there are a large number of relatively small OTC dealers. OTC dealers, however, often concentrate their trading in particular industry groups or geographical areas. It is estimated that about 30,000 various types of equity securities are traded in the OTC market. However, only about 15,000 of these securities are actively traded.

When a customer places an order to buy or sell a security in the OTC market, the broker or dealer contacts other dealers who have that particular security for sale. Public orders for purchase or sale are often executed by brokers acting as agents for their customers. When handling a public order a broker will contact several dealers to search out the most favorable price. When a broker is satisfied with a dealer's quoted price, he or she will complete the transaction with that dealer and charge his or her customer the same price plus a commission for brokerage services. Investors use brokers to locate the most favorable dealer because they are usually unfamiliar with the identities of the dealers making markets in specific issues and because brokers can contact dealers at lower cost. More generally, brokers can capitalize on economies of scale in search.

When handling a customer's order, a broker has two questions to answer. First, which dealers are market makers? Second, which of those dealers is quoting the most favorable price for his customer? Before 1971 the first question was easily resolved by looking at the "pink sheets" of the National Quotation Bureau (NQB). These sheets, printed on pink paper, were distributed daily to subscribing dealers and listed bid and/or ask prices submitted by dealers to NQB the previous afternoon.

Because of the delay of nearly a day between submission of a quote to NQB and the dissemination of the pink sheets to market participants, pink sheet quotes were always "stale" by the time a broker saw them. More generally, a dealer could not be expected to sell a stock on Thursday morning at the offer price quoted Wednesday afternoon. The pink sheets' real value was to identify which dealers were active in a given issue.

After a broker has determined which firms are dealing in a security, he or she next must locate the best price for his or her customer. Until 1971 this search process was conducted exclusively by telephone and teletype. A broker handling an order typically called several dealers, incurring telephone charges and the opportunity cost of his or her time. These costs reduced the incentive of the broker to make a complete search of the OTC dealer market and often resulted in executions away from better (but undiscovered) prices.

A major development in the OTC market occurred in 1971 when the National Association of Securities Dealers (NASD) introduced an automatic computer-based quotation system (**NASDAQ**). The system provides continuous bid-and-ask prices for the most actively traded OTC stocks. NASDAQ is basically an electronic pink sheet, and as such was compatible with the existing structure of the OTC market. NASDAQ so accelerated the disclosure of price information, however, that it fundamentally altered the structure of the OTC market.

NASDAQ's most important contribution to enhancing the OTC market was accelerating the disclosure of dealer quotations to brokers. NASDAQ did little to increase the identifiability of dealers beyond what was possible with the pink sheets, but it did greatly increase the efficiency of a broker's search for the best bid-and-ask prices. Thus NASDAQ greatly reduced the occurrence of trading away from the best available prices.

STOCK EXCHANGES

The New York Stock Exchange, the preeminent securities exchange in the United States, is an example of an auction market. Other stock exchanges in the United States include the American Stock Exchange located in New York, the Pacific Stock Exchange in both San Francisco and Los Angeles, the Chicago Stock Exchange (formerly the Midwest Stock Exchange), the Philadelphia Stock Exchange, the Boston Stock Exchange, and the Cincinnati Stock Exchange. Exhibit 10.3 shows the trading volume on the New York exchange, the American exchange, and NASDAQ. The NASDAQ and the NYSE account for most trading. The American Stock Exchange and the regional exchanges account for a much smaller proportion of trading.

All transactions in a stock listed on the NYSE and completed within the structure of that exchange's market occur at a unique place on the floor of the exchange, at a so-called post. There are three major sources of active bids and offerings in an issue available at a post: (1) floor brokers executing customer orders, (2) limit price orders left with the specialist for execution, and (3) the specialist in the issue buying and selling for his own account. Since trading is physically localized, the best available bid-and-offer quotes are readily available. Competition and ease of communication among market participants gathered at a post enforce price priority of execution and guarantee the absence of bids above the lowest offer or offerings below the highest bid.

Orders from the public are telephoned or telexed from brokerage house to brokers located on the floor of the NYSE, who bring the orders to the appropriate posts for execution. Most of these orders are either market orders or limit orders.

A **market order** is an order to buy or sell at the best price available at the time the order reaches the post. The broker bringing a market order to a post might execute the order immediately upon his arrival, or he might hold back all or part of the order for a short time to see if he can attract a better price than is currently available. He may also choose to quote a price on his transaction that is inside the

EXHIBIT 10.3
Stock Exchange Trading Volume on May 20, 2004

Exchange	Trading Volume (millions of shares)
New York Stock Exchange	1,534.80
NASDAQ	1,780.20
American Stock Exchange	11.20

Most equity trading in the United States takes place in the New York Stock Exchange, NASDAQ, and the American Stock Exchange.

Source: Wall Street Journal, May 20, 2004.

current bid-and-ask price, thereby getting in front of other orders at the post and reducing the amount of time he anticipates he will have to wait until completing the trade.

A **limit order** is an order to buy or sell at a designated price (the limit price stated on the order) or at any better price. Thus, a limit order is actually a bid for, or offering of, securities. A floor broker handling a limit order to buy at or below a stated price, or to sell at or above a stated price, will usually stand by the post with the order if the limit price on the order is near the current bid-and-ask prices.

When a limit order carries a price that is not close to current market prices, the broker handling the order knows it is unlikely the order will be executed anytime soon. For example, a bid or purchase order at $50 on a stock currently trading at $55 may not be satisfied for days—and may never be satisfied. The broker presenting the order wants to ensure the order is executed as soon as possible but does not want to stand around tendering the order for hours or days. As an alternative to maintaining a physical presence at the post, the broker can enter the limit order on the order book maintained by the specialist. Orders on the book are treated equally with other orders in terms of price priority. No trades can take place at a particular price unless all bids above and all offerings below that price have been cleared from the book. Entering a limit order on a specialist's book provides an economical alternative for a floor broker who would otherwise have to maintain a physical presence at a post to keep a limited-price bid or offer active.

Specialists provide the third source of bids and offerings in listed securities. At least on the NYSE, specialists are members of the exchange who combine the attributes of both dealers and order clerks. Specialists have an affirmative obligation to maintain both bid-and-offer quotations at all times, good for at least one round lot (usually 100 shares) of the issues in which they specialize. In this respect specialists act as dealers, trading for their own account and at their own risk. NYSE specialists also maintain the book of limit orders left by floor brokers, and in this respect they act as order clerks.

Trading on the floor of the NYSE in a few dozen issues is sufficiently heavy that there are always active bids and offerings available from either floor brokers or the limit order book. For these issues the dealer function of the specialist as a source of the liquidity service of immediate execution is relatively unimportant. In

In what seems to be just one more in a series of problems plaguing the NASDAQ stock market lately, damaging evidence has emerged alleging that through the avoidance of odd-eighth quotes such as $3/8$ or $5/8$, market makers have been able to maintain unusually wide spreads even in the market's most active stocks. If true, market makers have been protecting huge profit margins at the expense of customers who wish to invest capital in some of the nation's fastest-growing companies, including Intel and Microsoft.

The problem surfaced in a well-known study conducted by William Christie, a finance professor at Vanderbilt University, and Paul Schultz, a finance professor at Ohio State University. In their research Christie and Schultz presented trading statistics that suggested that something other than market forces was influencing the spreads of NASDAQ stocks in a manner contrary to the behavior of spreads of the stocks on the New York Stock Exchange and the American Stock Exchange.

A portion of the study's conclusions read as follows: "The almost complete absence of odd-eighth quotes for 71 percent of the Nasdaq sample, including such heavily traded stocks as Apple Computer and Lotus Development, imposes obvious and real costs on investors. . . . One possible explanation for our results is that we are observing the quote-setting behavior that emerges when individual market makers implicitly agree to maintain spreads of at least $0.25 by not posting quotes on odd-eighths. This inference is strengthened by the persistence of this result through time and across stocks."

The implications of the study reinforced a growing feeling among some NASDAQ customers that the market fails to serve their best interests. As a result, the U.S. Justice Department launched an antitrust investigation of the NASDAQ stock market, followed by a Securities and Exchange Commission inquiry. In addition, Christie and Schultz's study has prompted numerous lawsuits against NASDAQ charging the major NASDAQ dealers with, among other things, collusion and price fixing.

Soon after the release of the Christie and Schultz paper, the NASD convened a closed-door meeting of the major NASDAQ market makers on May 24, 1994. At the meeting, they were told that their spreads on many stocks were too wide and they were urged to narrow the spreads before a regulatory crackdown occurred.

In a second study, Christie and Schultz, and a new coauthor, Jeffrey Harris, detailed trading activity on the days following May 24. The study found that following the NASD's meeting with market makers, the spreads on many of the most active stocks decreased dramatically while the number of odd-eighth quotes increased. Spreads on some issues fell nearly 50 percent according to the study.

As a result of this controversy, the NASD's regulatory functions were separated from its control of NASDAQ. Furthermore, in early 1998, settlement of the lawsuit was announced. More than 36 NASDAQ dealers agreed to pay more than $1 billion to investors who traded any of 1,659 stocks between May 1, 1989, and July 17, 1996.

Now the entire issue is moot. Since 2001 all U.S. stocks have been priced and traded in dollars and cents, rather than in fractions of a dollar such as $1/16$, $1/8$, and $1/4$. The tradition of trading stocks in fractions of a dollar dates back to the 1700s and the birth of U.S. financial markets. Now stock prices can move 1¢ at a time. According to preliminary analysis by the Securities and Exchange Commission conducted during the first half of 2001, bid–ask spreads on NASDAQ stocks dropped by 50 percent after decimalization, while average spreads on the New York Stock Exchange declined by 28 percent.

Sources: William G. Christie and Paul H. Schultz, "Why Do NASDAQ Market Makers Avoid Odd-Eighth Quotes?" *Journal of Finance* 49, No. 5 (December 1994), p. 1813; William G. Christie, Jeffrey H. Harris, and Paul H. Schultz, "Why Did NASDAQ Market Makers Stop Avoiding Odd-Eighth Quotes?" *Journal of Finance* 49, No. 5 (December 1994), p. 1841.

many issues, however, public trading interest is more sporadic and infrequent. In these cases the obligation of the specialist to provide the liquidity service of immediate execution can be quite important. Indeed, if the prices of the best purchase and sales orders on the specialist's book have a wide spread (which is common for infrequently traded stocks), the specialist may be the sole source of an economical market for immediate transaction.

THE AMERICAN STOCK EXCHANGE AND NASDAQ MERGE

The National Association of Securities Dealers (NASD) and the American Stock Exchange announced the completion of their merger on October 30, 1998, after receiving all necessary approvals. This combination creates the world's first financial market that brings together central auction specialists (AMEX) and multiple market makers (NASDAQ).

The principal objective of The NASDAQ-AMEX Market Group is to provide more efficient markets for both investors and issuers. They continue to invest in new technology to provide investors with more efficient pricing, faster trade execution, and reduced transaction costs, and issuers with better liquidity, cost efficiency, and increased market visibility. One recent investment was to enhance AMEX's equity market technology with a new electronic limit order book, which will allow investors and market professionals to enter and electronically execute orders from on and off the trading floor. The new limit order book provides greater transparency by enabling investors to view orders in the book beyond those at the inside bid-and-ask prices.

The new organization's financial-information-based Web site, www.NASDAQ-AMEX.com, averages 12 million hits a day and has been redesigned to increase listed company visibility among shareholders and investors. Information is available for NASDAQ and AMEX companies, including analyst and stock reports, SEC filings, Web site links, and company logos.

GLOBAL STOCK MARKETS

The secondary markets for equity securities are becoming increasingly competitive. Improved communications and computer technology have reduced transaction costs, making it easier for other financial intermediaries to compete with securities firms and promoting competition among national exchanges, regional exchanges, over-the-counter markets, and foreign exchanges. Several trends are related to the forces of technology and competition: the emergence of a so-called national market system, the move toward 24-hour trading of equity securities, and the globalization of equity markets.

The Securities Act Amendment of 1975 mandated that the Securities and Exchange Commission, the primary regulator of U.S. financial markets, move toward implementing a national market system. In its ideal form, a national market system would include a computer system that records and reports transactions regardless of where they take place, a system that allows investors to obtain price information from any exchange instantaneously, and a means to buy or sell securities at the best price, regardless of location. Although some progress has been made toward electronically linking the national exchanges, regional exchanges, and over-the-counter markets, we are still many years away from a truly nationwide system.

There is competitive pressure to link international equity markets as well. Many U.S. firms are issuing stocks overseas to take advantage of differences in tax laws, to increase their visibility and reputation worldwide, and to avoid driving down their stock prices by flooding local markets. In 1986, the London Stock Exchange created a computer network similar to the U.S. NASDAQ system and permitted U.S. and Japanese investment firms to enter trades on the system. This development was important because it created virtual 24-hour global trading, given the time zone differences among New York, London, and Tokyo. Many U.S. companies are listed on exchanges in all three locations.

Stock exchanges in the United States are fearful of losing business to the overseas markets. As a step toward increasing the global competitiveness of the U.S. financial markets, the SEC has permitted after-hours trading on the NYSE. Before, trading on the NYSE took place between 9:30 A.M. and 4:00 P.M. The NYSE now has several after-hours trading sessions during which shares trade electronically at the day's closing price. The biggest beneficiaries of the NYSE's move toward globalization will be U.S. companies that expect to broaden the market for their securities. The flow of capital across international boundaries will make it easier for firms to raise money and should ultimately lower the cost of capital in the United States.

Another aspect of the globalization of stock markets is that many foreign companies, such as Sony and Nestlé, have discovered the benefits of trading their stock in the United States. Unfamiliar market practices, confusing tax legislation, incomplete shareholder communications, and the lack of effective avenues for legal recourse tend to discourage U.S. investors from buying equity securities in foreign markets. In addition, the disclosure and reporting requirements mandated by the U.S. Securities and Exchange Commission historically have discouraged all but the largest foreign firms from directly listing their shares on the New York Stock Exchange, the American Stock Exchange, or NASDAQ.

Many foreign companies overcome these obstacles and tap the U.S. equity market by means of **American Depositary Receipts (ADRs)**. ADRs are dollar-denominated claims issued by U.S. banks representing ownership of shares of a foreign company's stock held on deposit by the U.S. bank in the issuing firm's home country. Because ADRs are issued in dollars by a U.S. bank to U.S. investors, they are subject to U.S. securities laws.

With over 1,600 ADRs from 63 countries trading in the United States, they have proven to be very popular with U.S. investors, at least partly because they allow investors to diversify internationally. However, they are still holding a claim that is covered by American securities laws and that pays dividends in dollars (dividends on the underlying shares are converted from local currency into dollars and then paid to U.S. investors). Each ADR can represent a fraction or a multiple of a share of the foreign company, so that the price of the ADR is within the range of share prices for comparable companies traded in the United States. Because an ADR can be converted into ownership of the underlying shares, arbitrage ensures rational dollar valuation of this claim against foreign-currency-denominated stock.

Trading in securities markets in the United States is regulated by several laws. The two major laws are the Securities Act of 1933 and the Securities Exchange Act of 1934. The 1933 act requires full disclosure of relevant information relating to the

REGULATION OF EQUITY MARKETS

issue of new securities in the primary market. This is the act that requires registration of new securities and the issuance of a prospectus that details the recent financial history of the company. SEC acceptance of a prospectus or financial report does not mean that it views the security as a good investment. The SEC is concerned only that the relevant facts are disclosed to investors. Investors must make their own evaluations of the security's value. The 1934 act established the Securities and Exchange Commission to administer the provisions of the 1933 act. It also extended the disclosure of the 1933 act by requiring firms with outstanding securities on secondary exchanges to periodically disclose relevant financial information.

The 1934 act also allowed the SEC to register and regulate securities exchanges, OTC trading, brokers, and dealers. The 1934 act thus established the SEC as the administrative agency responsible for broad oversight of secondary securities markets.

In addition to federal regulations, security trading is subject to state laws. The laws providing for state regulation of securities activities are generally known as blue-sky laws because they attempt to prevent the false promotion and sale of securities representing nothing more than blue sky.

DO YOU UNDERSTAND?

1. What characteristics of an asset determine the type of secondary market in which it is most likely to trade?
2. What are the four types of secondary markets?
3. Explain the differences among the OTC market, NASDAQ, and a stock exchange.
4. What are the functions of market makers and specialists? How do they differ?

EQUITY VALUATION BASICS

Similar to bond valuation, which we discussed in Chapter 5, equity valuation requires us to apply the mathematics of present value. For any security, including common stock or preferred stock, the valuation process involves three steps. First, identify the timing and the size of the cash flows. Second, decide upon the appropriate discount rate. The discount rate, which is the interest rate used in the present value calculation, should reflect the opportunity cost of investing in the security. The opportunity cost is the rate of return offered by a security with similar characteristics, including risk, that is trading in the market. Third, apply the discount rate to the cash flows in each period to obtain present values and sum the present values to obtain the price of the security.

PREFERRED STOCK VALUATION

Preferred stock is relatively simple to value because most preferred shares entitle the holders to regular, fixed dividend payments. Since preferred stock usually has no maturity, the payments are assumed to continue forever. Suppose that a preferred stock promises to pay dividends of D per share, forever. Further, assume that the appropriate discount rate is r. Using the present value formula of Chapter 5, the value is

$$P_0 = \frac{D}{(1+r)} + \frac{D}{(1+r)^2} + \cdots$$
$$= \sum_{t=1}^{\infty} \frac{D}{(1+r)^t}. \tag{10.1}$$

This formula is difficult to implement because the payments are assumed to continue forever. Luckily, mathematicians have figured out a simple shortcut. The series of cash flows in Equation 10.1 is a special kind of cash-flow stream called a **perpetuity**. A perpetuity pays equal cash flows at the end of each period forever. Equation 10.2 is the perpetuity formula applied to preferred stock:

$$P_0 = \frac{D}{r}. \tag{10.2}$$

Suppose a firm pays dividends on its preferred stock of $10 at the end of each year and that the required return for the stock is 7.5 percent. The value of the preferred stock from Equation 10.2 is

$$P_0 = \frac{\$10}{0.75} = \$133.33.$$

If you know the current market price of the preferred stock and the annual amount of its dividend, you can calculate the required rate of return by solving Equation 10.2 for r:

$$r = \frac{D}{P_0}. \tag{10.3}$$

Suppose the current price per share of preferred stock is $75 and that the firm pays an annual dividend of $6 per share. Applying Equation 10.3, the market's required return on this preferred stock is

$$r = \frac{D}{P_0} = \frac{\$6}{\$75} = .08,$$

or 8 percent.

COMMON STOCK VALUATION

The same general valuation principles apply to calculating the price of a common stock. Simply calculate the present value of the stream of expected cash flows with the appropriate discount rate. Let P_0 be the current stock price and P_1 be the expected stock price 1 year from now. Assume the firm pays a dividend of D_1 at the end of the first year. Using the present value formula we can write

$$P_0 = \frac{D_1}{(1+r)} + \frac{P_1}{(1+r)}. \tag{10.4}$$

Equation 10.4 assumes that we purchase the stock today, hold it for 1 year, and then sell it after collecting the dividend. One problem with implementing Equation 10.4 is that it requires an estimate of P_1. We can estimate the price 1 year from now in the same way we calculated P_0:

$$P_1 = \frac{D_2}{(1+r)} + \frac{P_2}{(1+r)}. \tag{10.5}$$

Substituting Equation 10.5 for P_1 in Equation 10.4 and simplifying, we obtain Equation 10.6:

$$P_0 = \frac{D_1}{(1+r)} + \frac{D_2}{(1+r)^2} + \frac{P_2}{(1+r)^2}. \tag{10.6}$$

Continuing this process, we obtain Equation 10.7, which says that the price of a stock is equal to the present value of the stream of dividends:

$$P_0 = \frac{D_1}{(1+r)^1} + \frac{D_2}{(1+r)^2} + \cdots = \sum_{t=1}^{\infty} \frac{D_t}{(1+r)^t}. \tag{10.7}$$

Equation 10.7 works because the present value of the stock price approaches zero, the further we push it to the future. Of course, Equation 10.7 is difficult to implement because it requires estimates of dividend payments that begin 1 year from now and continue forever. Fortunately, we can make some assumptions about the nature of future dividends that will simplify our calculations.

No Growth in Dividends.   A common stock whose dividends are not expected to grow can be valued in the same way as preferred stock because all dividends are equal; that is, $D_1 = D_2 = \cdots = D$, which is a constant. The price, therefore, is $P_0 = D/r$, where r is the required return on the stock. Suppose a firm has a policy of paying dividends of $15 per share every year. If the firm intends to maintain this dividend forever and the required return on the stock is 12 percent, what is the value of the stock? This stock is basically a perpetuity, so its value is $P_0 = \$15/0.12 = \$125$ per share.

Constant Dividend Growth Rate.   Many firms increase their dividends over time. Say we know that a firm has just paid a dividend of $2 per share and that this firm's dividends grow at 5 percent per year. The dividend 1 year from today is $D_1 = \$2 \times (1.05) = \$2.10$. Two years from today the dividend will be $D_2 = \$2 \times (1.05)^2 = \$2.20$. In general, if we know that the dividends of a company grow at some rate, g, we can calculate any future dividend as follows:

$$D_t = D_0 \times (1 + g)^t, \tag{10.8}$$

where D_0 is the dividend just paid.

If the dividend grows at the same rate forever, the stream of dividends meets the definition of a growing perpetuity. As long as the growth rate, g, is less than the discount rate, r, the present value of the dividends can be written as:

$$P_0 = \frac{D_0 \times (1+g)}{r-g} = \frac{D_1}{r-g}. \tag{10.9}$$

Letting $r = 0.12$ and completing the example, we obtain

$$P_0 = \frac{\$2 \times (1.05)}{.12 - .05} = \frac{\$2.10}{.07} = \$30.$$

The constant dividend growth model gives us a convenient way to summarize the total return on common stock. If we solve Equation 10.9 for r, we obtain

$$r = D_1/P_0 + g. \tag{10.10}$$

The first term of the expression is called the **dividend yield**, which is the expected dividend expressed as a proportion of the price of the stock. The second term, g, can be interpreted as the **capital-gains yield**, which is the rate at which the value of the firm is expected to grow.

To illustrate, suppose that we have a stock selling for $78 per share that just paid a dividend of $3 per share. The dividend is expected to grow at 6 percent per year forever. What is the required return on this stock? By substituting the information into Equation 10.10 we obtain

$$r = (\$3.18/\$78) + 0.06 \cong 0.04 + 0.06 \cong 0.10,$$

or approximately 10 percent.

Variable Dividend Growth Rate. It may be unreasonable to assume that a firm will grow at the same rate forever. A typical course of events is for growth to proceed rapidly for a period of time after which the growth rate settles to a more "normal" level. The present value formulas we have used so far can be easily adapted to deal with situations in which firms grow at different rates over different time periods. If the dividend grows at a constant rate *after t* periods, the price of the stock is

$$P_0 = \frac{D_1}{(1+r)^1} + \frac{D_2}{(1+r)^2} + \cdots + \frac{D_t}{(1+r)^t} + \frac{P_t}{(1+r)^t}, \tag{10.11}$$

where $P_t = [D_t \times (1 + g)] / (r - g)$. The use of Equation 10.11 is best explained through an example.

Suppose the current dividend is $1.50 per share and that it is expected to grow at a 15 percent rate for the next 3 years. After the 3-year period, dividends are expected to grow at the more "normal" rate of 8 percent per year indefinitely. If the required return on the stock is 12 percent, what price would you be willing to pay for a share of the stock?

Finding the price involves several steps. First, calculate the dividends in the "above-normal" period of growth and in the first period of "normal" growth. In this example, we must calculate the dividends for the first 4 years:

$$D_1 = \$1.50 \times (1.15)^1 = \$1.72$$
$$D_2 = \$1.50 \times (1.15)^2 = \$1.98$$
$$D_3 = \$1.50 \times (1.15)^3 = \$2.28$$
$$D_4 = \$2.28 \times (1.08) = \$2.46.$$

Second, calculate the price at the end of the "above-normal" growth period. In our example, we must calculate the price of the stock at the end of year 3. Because after year 3 the dividends grow at a rate of 8 percent forever, we can use a variation of the growing perpetuity formula, Equation 10.8: $P_3 = D_4/(r - g) = \$2.46 / (0.12 - 0.08) = \$61.60$.

Finally, substitute the values for $D_1, D_2, D_3,$ and P_3 into Equation 10.11:

$$P_0 = \frac{1.72}{(1.21)^1} + \frac{1.98}{(1.12)^2} + \frac{2.28}{(1.12)^3} + \frac{61.60}{(1.12)^3} = \$48.58.$$

Thus, the current price of the stock is $48.58.

EQUITY RISK

Risk-averse investors require higher returns, the greater the risk of the security. In this section we discuss the types of risk faced in equity markets and how risk is reflected in the required returns of stocks.

SYSTEMATIC AND UNSYSTEMATIC RISK

The total risk of a security can be thought of as the sum of two types of risk: systematic risk and unsystematic risk. To understand the distinction between these two types of risk, we must briefly discuss the benefits of **diversification**, which is just a fancy term for not putting all of your eggs in one basket.

Investors measure the total risk of a security or a portfolio with the variance or standard deviation of returns. Variance or standard deviation measures the "width" of a probability distribution of returns. The larger either of these measures of return dispersion, the greater the total risk and the greater the probability of changes in the value of your position. The good news is that we can reduce the total risk of our investment in equities by diversifying across many securities. Exhibit 10.4 illustrates the effects on a portfolio's total risk of increasing the number of securities in the portfolio. As can be seen from the exhibit, the total risk of a portfolio decreases with the number of securities.

Diversification works because **unsystematic risks** (unique or security-specific risks) of different securities tend to partially offset one another in a portfolio. This could occur, for example, because when the price of one stock in the portfolio goes down, the price of another tends to go up, at least partially off-

EXHIBIT 10.4
The Effect of Diversification on Portfolio Risk

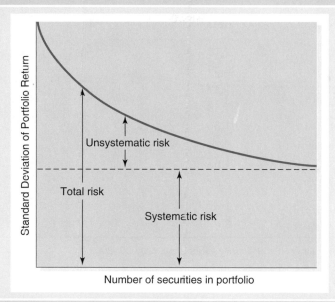

As the number of securities increases, the diversification effect reduces the standard deviation of portfolio return, a measure of the portfolio's total risk. Total portfolio risk can be reduced, however, only to the level of systematic risk, which cannot be diversified away because it is caused by general market movements that tend to affect all stocks similarly.

setting the loss. The diversification effect can help even if, when one stock tends to go down, the other stock does not tend to go down by as much, on average. As long as the returns of two securities are *not* perfectly, positively correlated (perfect positive correlation means that changes in one stock are matched exactly by changes in the other), one can reduce total risk by combining the securities in a portfolio. By adding enough securities to a portfolio, it is possible to eliminate unsystematic risk. For that reason, unsystematic risk is also called diversifiable risk. Examples of unsystematic risks that could reduce a stock's price include unanticipated strikes, lawsuits, changes in government regulation affecting a particular industry, environmental disasters, or changes in production technology.

Note, however, that no matter how many securities we add, the total risk of the portfolio can only be reduced to the level of **systematic risk**. Systematic risk is also called market risk or nondiversifiable risk. No matter how many securities we add to a portfolio, we cannot reduce systematic risk because it is the risk that tends to affect the entire market in a similar fashion.

MEASURING SYSTEMATIC RISK: BETA

If most investors hold reasonably well-diversified portfolios, the relevant measure of risk is systematic risk, because the unsystematic risk is diversified away to the

EXHIBIT 10.5
Betas of Selected Firms (May 20, 2004)

Firm	Beta
Amazon.com	2.18
Anheuser-Busch	−0.09
Callaway Golf	1.39
Citigroup	1.38
Dell Computer	1.66
Avista Utilities	0.24
Gap, Inc.	1.66
Intel	2.07
Microsoft	1.62
Yahoo!	3.20

Source: Yahoo! Finance, http://finance.yahoo.com, May 20, 2004.

extent possible. Most investors, therefore, are primarily concerned with systematic risk, which is usually measured by how closely a security's returns are correlated with the returns of the entire market.

The extent to which a stock's returns are related to general market swings is measured with **beta** (β). Understanding beta is easy. Let's assign a beta of 1.0 to the market as a whole. As a practical matter, we might represent the market with a broadly based stock index such as the NYSE Composite Index or the S&P 500. (We discuss stock indexes in the next section.) Suppose a stock has a beta of 2 relative to the NYSE Composite Index. This means that the stock is expected to be twice as volatile as the NYSE index. Stocks with betas greater than 1.0 are referred to as **aggressive stocks** because they carry greater systematic risk than the market and tend to magnify the effects of market movements on the returns of a portfolio. If another stock has a beta of 0.5, it means that this stock will only be half as volatile as the market. Stocks with betas less than 1 are called **defensive stocks** because they carry less systematic risk than the market and tend to subdue the effects of market movements on the returns of a portfolio. The stocks of most U.S. corporations have betas between 0.5 and 1.5. Exhibit 10.5 gives the betas of some well-known U.S. firms.

THE SECURITY MARKET LINE

The required (or expected) return on a stock depends on the amount of its systematic risk. To see how the beta of a stock affects its expected return, consider the following definition of a **risk premium**.[1]

---

[1] Remember that in Chapter 6, we defined the default risk premium on a bond as the bond's return (or yield) minus the return on a risk-free security.

Risk premium = Required (or expected) return on a risky security minus the return on a risk-free security

= Total reward for bearing systematic risk

= Amount of systematic risk × Average reward in the market per unit of systematic risk.

Given the definition, we can write an expression for the risk premium on any stock, j.

First let's define some terms:

$E(R_j)$ = Expected return on stock j.

$E(R_M)$ = Expected return on the market portfolio, which consists of all assets in the market.[2]

R_F = Rate of return on a risk-free asset, such as a T-bill.

β_j = The beta of stock j.

β_M = The beta of the market portfolio.

In this case the risk premium is $E(R_j) - R_F = \beta_j \times ([E(R_M) - R_F] / \beta_M)$. The left-hand side of the expression is the total reward for bearing the risk in security j. On the right-hand side, the term β_j is the amount of risk. $[E(RM) - R_F] / \beta_M$ represents the average reward per unit of risk in the market. The numerator is the risk premium of the market portfolio, also called the **market risk premium**. The denominator is the amount of risk in the market. The expression for the risk premium of stock j simplifies because we know that the beta of any portfolio with respect to itself equals 1. Therefore, the risk premium of security j is

$$E(R_j) - R_F = \beta_j \times [E(R_M) - R_F], \qquad (10.12)$$

which is the equation for the **security market line (SML)**. Equation 10.12 is also referred to as the capital asset pricing model (CAPM). The SML is more typically written as

$$E(R_j) = R_F + \beta_j [E(R_M) - R_F]. \qquad (10.12a)$$

Equation 10.12a shows that the required return on a security equals the return on a risk-free asset plus a premium for bearing systematic risk in the amount β_j. The graph of the SML in Exhibit 10.6 shows that the relationship between risk and return is linear. The slope of the SML is the average reward per unit of risk in the market, $[E(RM) - R_F]$. This means that an increase in beta increases the required return on a stock. If, for example, stock A has a beta of 1.0 and stock B has a beta of 1.2, the expected return of stock B will exceed that of stock A by an amount $(0.2) [E(R_M) - R_F]$.

Let's illustrate the use of the SML with an example. Suppose the risk-free rate is 3.5 percent and that the market risk premium, $[E(R_M) - R_F]$, is 8.6 percent. A stock with a beta of 1.25 would have a required return of $E(R_j) = R_F + \beta_j [E(R_M) - R_F]$ = 3.5 percent + 1.25(8.6 percent) = 14.25 percent. Using a similar calculation, the required return on a stock with a beta of 1.5 would be 16.4 percent. More systematic risk implies a higher required return.

[2] Consider the market portfolio as the "ultimate" in diversified portfolios.

EXHIBIT 10.6
The Security Market Line

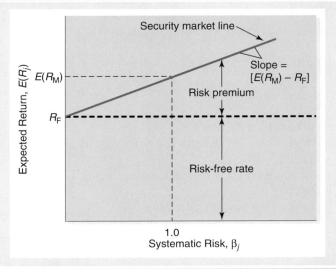

The security market line is the relationship between risk and return. Investors are concerned only with systematic risk, measured by beta, because in a well-diversified portfolio, unsystematic risk is eliminated. As a beta increases, the security's risk premium increases, thereby increasing the expected rate or required return of the security.

DO YOU UNDERSTAND?

1. Describe the general approach to valuing a share of stock.
2. What cash flows are relevant to the value of stock?
3. Describe what happens to the total risk of a portfolio as the number of securities is increased.
4. Suppose a firm's stock has a beta of 1.2. What will probably happen to the value of the stock if the market decreases by 20 percent?

STOCK MARKET INDEXES

Stock market indexes provide a useful tool to summarize the vast array of information generated by the continuous buying and selling of stocks. At the same time, the use of market indexes presents two problems. First, many different indexes compete for our attention. Second, indexes differ in their composition and construction, and they can often give contradictory information regarding stock market movements.

When constructing a market index, the first decision is what will be the base index value and what will be the starting date. That is, at what value and on what date will the index begin? The choice is completely arbitrary, since absolute index

During December 2002, United Airlines, once the world's largest airline, declared bankruptcy and, on the same day, its executives rushed to pledge "even better service" to their customers. You may wonder, "How could a firm that is bankrupt still be in business?" United, of course, was operating under the protection of Chapter 11 of the federal bankruptcy code.

The rationale for Chapter 11 is that it provides companies that are insolvent but may still be viable entities a second chance, rather than shutting their doors and liquidating their assets. However, a growing number of critics say that Chapter 11 has lost it effectiveness and prolongs companies' lives beyond sensible limits. In Britain and continental Europe, for example, firms that enter into bankruptcy are typically liquidated rather than restructured.

Chapter 11 provides an orderly and, at times, a routine process for corporate bankruptcy. Firms in financial trouble go to the court and apply for a 120-day breathing space from creditors. For large firms with complex legal structures, judges routinely extend the deadline. During this time, the firm's existing management prepares and submits to the bankruptcy court a plan to reorganize the firm into a going concern. The business plan is then submitted to creditors, who decide whether the plan has merit or come up with their own reorganization plan. Though the court makes the final decision, creditors have a significant say in whether the firm keeps operating or is liquidated. The key question in the analysis is whether the present value of the restructured firm's future cash flows exceeds the expected cash flows if the firm is liquidated. If the value of the restructured firm exceeds its liquidation value, the bankruptcy judge will typically allow the firm to continue operating. In these cases, creditors usually end up with much of the firm's equity and gain outright control of the firm. At this time, creditors almost always elect to bring in a new management team to lead the restructured firm out of bankruptcy.

Critics of Chapter 11 are concerned that court-ordered restructurings may give these firms an unfair advantage in the marketplace. A particular concern in industries such as telecommunications and airlines is that bankrupt firms will return with manageable cost and debt structures and, thus, be better able to compete, with the result that they force hitherto healthier rivals into bankruptcy. As a result, Chapter 11 may create zombie companies that live on only to drag innovative and better-managed companies into the grave. There is no shortage of zombie firms. Of the ten biggest bankruptcies since 1978, seven are still in the courts, dragging behind them nearly $300 billion of assets.

Chapter 11's tolerance for bad credit decisions is also underscored by the number of so-called Chapter 22s and Chapter 33s, which are firms that have used Chapter 11 two and three times, respectively. Currently, more than sixty firms have appeared in federal bankruptcy court two times and three firms have appeared three times. Much to our surprise, there is one firm that has had four trips into federal bankruptcy court.*

Those favoring Chapter 11 note that a firm can emerge from Chapter 11 only if creditors agree that the firm is worth more alive than dead. They also note that not all large firms get a second chance: Enron, for example, is self-liquidating itself. Thus, a few zombie companies may be the price that the U.S. economy pays for second chances.

Regardless of the arguments advanced, a congressional backlash to modify the federal bankruptcy codes may be coming. In truth, it is hard to point to a successful big bankruptcy in which a firm emerged from Chapter 11 revitalized and strong enough to be an industry leader. Competitive market theory says that the economy is best served if weak firms are allowed to fail and their assets liquidated. These assets—labor and capital—are reinvested by firms that are more competitive, better managed, and able to earn a higher rate of return on their investments.

---

* The firm is Harvard Industries, whose major skill appears to be its notable ability for repeated failure: performing poorly in the marketplace, declaring bankruptcy, then getting up off the canvas and hatching a restructuring plan plausible enough that a bankruptcy judge and a group of creditors bought into it. Harvard's final demise came during the summer of 2004, when the bankruptcy court made the decision to liquidate the firm.

values are meaningless. Only the *relative* changes in index values convey useful information. For example, knowing only that a particular stock market index finished the year at a level of 354.7 is of no value. However, if we also know that the same index finished the previous year at a level of 331.5, then we can calculate that the stock market, as measured by this particular index, rose by approximately 7 percent over the past year.

The next decision is, which stocks should be included in the index? There are three methods for deciding stock market index composition: (1) the index can represent a stock exchange and include all the stocks traded on the exchange, (2) the organization producing the index can subjectively select the stocks to be included, or (3) the stocks to be included can be selected based on some objective measure such as market value, which is simply the number of shares outstanding times the price per share. Often the stocks in an index are divided into groups so that indexes represent the performance of various industry segments such as industrial, transportation, or utility companies. Regardless of the method chosen for selecting the stocks, the composition of an index can change whenever included companies merge or are delisted from an exchange.

Once the stocks to be included in an index are selected, the stocks must be combined in certain proportions to construct the index. Each stock, therefore, must be assigned some relative weight. One of two approaches typically is used to assign relative weights when calculating stock market indexes: (1) weighting by the price of the company's stock or (2) weighting by the market value of the company. After next explaining the calculation of stock indexes, we describe the major stock indexes in the United States. Exhibit 10.7 provides recent statistics on the major stock indexes.

PRICE-WEIGHTED INDEXES

A **price-weighted index** is first computed by summing the prices of the individual stocks composing the index. Then the sum of the prices is divided by a "divisor" to yield the chosen base index value. Thereafter, as the stock prices change, the divisor remains constant unless there is a stock split, a stock dividend, or the composition of the index changes. If such a situation arises, then the divisor is adjusted so that the index value is not affected by the event in question.

For example, if the prices per share of the three stocks A, B, and C in a price-weighted index were $20, $10, and $50, respectively, then the prices would sum to $80. If the base index value is to be 100, then the initial divisor would be 0.8 (100 = 80/0.8). Then on the next trading day, if the prices per share were, respectively, $25, $10, and $40, the sum would now be $75 and the price-weighted index value would be 93.75 ($75/0.8), or 6.25 percent lower.

Now, assume that stock C undergoes a two-for-one stock split after the market closes on the second day such that its price per share declines to $20 ($40/2). The sum of the three prices is now only $55, but the index should remain the same. Thus, the divisor must be adjusted so that the index value continues to be 93.75. The new divisor would be approximately 0.5867 ($55/0.5867 = 93.75) and it would remain constant until it again had to be adjusted.

MARKET VALUE–WEIGHTED INDEXES

A **market value–weighted index** is computed by calculating the total market value of the firms in the index and the total market value of those firms on the

EXHIBIT 10.7
Statistics on Major Stock Indexes from the *Wall Street Journal*'s "Markets Lineup" (May 20, 2004)

| Index | Daily | | | | | 52-Week | | | YTD |
	High	Low	Close	Net Chg	% Chg	High	Low	% Chg	% Chg
Dow Jones 30 Industrials	10,093.21	9,933.11	9,937.71	–30.80	–0.31	10,737.70	8,516.43	+16.69	–4.94
Standard & Poor's 500	1,105.93	1,088.49	1,088.68	–2.81	–0.26	1,157.76	923.42	+17.90	–2.09
Standard & Poor's 600 SmallCap	272.88	267.61	268.00	–0.54	–0.20	293.64	201.77	+32.82	–0.89
NASDAQ Composite	1,963.04	1,898.16	1,898.17	+0.35	+0.02	2,153.83	1,489.87	+27.41	–5.25
NYSE Composite	6,369.66	6,276.51	6,287.16	+10.63	+0.17	6,780.03	5,223.22	+20.37	–2.38

Stock indexes measure general stock market movements, but they are also used to track movements in specific industry or firm-size groups. Some indexes are price-weighted, such as the Dow Jones Industrial Average, and others are value weighted, for example, the New York Stock Exchange Composite Index.

Source: Wall Street Journal, May 20, 2004.

previous trading day. The percentage change in the total market value from one day to the next represents the change in the index. Market value–weighted indexes do not require adjustments for stock splits and stock dividends because they do not affect the market capitalization. However, market value–weighted indexes do require adjustment when the composition of the index changes.

For example, if stocks A, B, and C described above had outstanding shares of 100 million, 200 million, and 10 million, then the total market value for the three stocks on the first day would be $4.5 billion. The total market value on the second day would be $4.9 billion, for an increase of 8.8 percent. If the market value–weighted index began with a base index value of 10 on the first day, then its value on the second day would be 10.88, or 8.8 percent higher.

If we again assume that stock C undergoes a two-for-one stock split after the market closes on the second day such that its price per share declines to $20, we can see that there is no impact on the market value–weighted index. This is because the number of shares outstanding will double to 20 million and company C's market value will remain at $400 million. Thus, the total market value of the three stocks in the market value–weighted index continues to be $4.9 billion on the second day and the index will remain at 10.88.

Notice the different conclusions concerning the stock market performance given by the price-weighted and market value–weighted indexes in the above examples. Both indexes used the same stocks and the same price changes. However, the price-weighted index decreased by 6.25 percent while the market value–weighted index increased by 8.8 percent. This example clearly shows that both the composition of an index and its weighting scheme can have a significant impact on its results.

Both market value–weighted and price-weighted indexes reflect the returns to buy-and-hold investment strategies. If one were to buy each share in an index in proportion to its outstanding market value, the market value–weighted index would perfectly track capital gains on the underlying index although the return from dividends would not be included. Similarly, a price-weighted index tracks the returns on a portfolio composed of equal shares of each company.

DOW JONES AVERAGES

The most widely cited stock market index is the Dow Jones Industrial Average (DJIA), which was first published in 1896. The DJIA is a price-weighted index that originally consisted of 20 stocks with a divisor of 20; thus, the value of the index was simply the average of the price of the 20 stocks. In 1928 the DJIA was enlarged to encompass 30 of the largest U.S. industrial stocks. Dow Jones also publishes a price-weighted index of 20 transportation companies, a price-weighted index of 15 utility companies, and a composite index that includes the 65 companies making up the industrial, transportation, and utility indexes. None of the Dow Jones indexes are adjusted for stock dividends of less than 10 percent.

NEW YORK STOCK EXCHANGE INDEX

The New York Stock Exchange Composite Index, published since 1966, includes all the common and preferred stocks listed on the NYSE. In addition to the composite index, the NYSE stocks are divided into four subindexes that track the performance of industrial, utility, finance, and transportation issues. All the NYSE indexes are market value weighted, and the base index value for all five indexes was 50 on December 31, 1965.

STANDARD & POOR'S INDEXES

The Standard & Poor's (S&P) 500 Index is a market value–weighted index that consists of 500 of the largest U.S. stocks drawn from various industries. The stocks included in the S&P 500 account for over 80 percent of the market capitalization of all the stocks listed on the NYSE, although a few NASDAQ issues also are included. The base index value for the S&P 500 Index was 10 in 1943. The index is computed on a continuous basis during the trading day and reported to the public. The S&P 500 is divided into two subindexes that follow the performance of industrial and utilities companies.

The S&P 400 MidCap Index also is published by Standard and Poor's. It is market value weighted and consists of 400 stocks with market values less than those of the stocks in the S&P 500. The S&P 400 MidCap Index is useful for following the performance of medium-sized companies.

In addition, Standard & Poor's publishes a market value–weighted SmallCap Index that tracks 600 companies with market values less than those of the companies in its MidCap Index. The S&P 1500 Index includes the companies in the S&P 500, the MidCap 400, and the SmallCap 600.

NASDAQ

The NASDAQ Composite, with a base year of 1970, has been compiled since 1971. The composite consists of three categories of companies: industrial, banks, and insurance. It consists of all of the stocks traded through NASDAQ, including those traded in the National Market System and those that are not. In 1984 the NASDAQ National Market System introduced two new indexes, the NASDAQ/NMS Composite Index and the NASDAQ/NMS Industrial Index. Both are weighted by market capitalization and have a base of 100.

OTHER STOCK INDEXES

The American Stock Exchange Composite Index includes all the common stocks listed on the AMEX. It is a market value–weighted index.

The Russell 3000 encompasses the largest companies ranked by market capitalization, while the Russell 1000 includes the largest 1,000 market capitalization companies. The Russell 2000 includes the bottom 2,000 companies in the Russell 3000, so it represents a small-capitalization market index.

The Value Line Composite Index measures the values of about 1,700 common stocks, most of which are on the NYSE. Its components make up more than 96 percent of all dollar trading volume in U.S. markets. The equally weighted geometric average of stock prices is expressed in index form with June 30, 1961, set at 100. The composite consists of about 1,500 industrial issues, 180 utilities, and 20 railroads.

The Wilshire 5000, published since 1971, includes more than 7,000 companies, more common stocks than any other index. It consists of all the stocks on the NYSE and AMEX as well as most of the actively traded NASDAQ issues. It is a market value–weighted index.

THE STOCK MARKET AS A PREDICTOR OF ECONOMIC ACTIVITY

In the wake of the October 1987 stock market crash, there was concern as to whether a recession (or depression!) would follow. Such fears were based on memories of the 1929 stock market crash and the subsequent Great Depression. Why do some economists and many laypeople believe that the stock market can predict economic recessions? First, even if stock prices have no direct effect on the economy, changes in stock prices may precede a recession. If the market consensus is that a recession is imminent, investors may forecast lower corporate profits. Given that stock prices are the discounted sums of future corporate profits, stock prices would then decline. Second, stock price declines reduce the wealth of consumers and, therefore, may lead to reduced consumption spending and a reduction in national income (GDP, gross domestic product). Third, if consumer confidence is adversely affected by stock price declines, consumption spending may decrease. Finally, lower stock prices may increase the cost of raising capital and result in a reduction in business investment.

Empirical evidence suggests the stock market is not very successful in predicting economic activity. A study by the Federal Reserve Bank of Kansas City showed that only 11 of the 27 recessions between 1900 and 1987 were successfully predicted by stock market declines.[3] Exhibit 10.8 shows the movement of the

EXHIBIT 10.8
The Relationship Between Recessions and the Stock Market

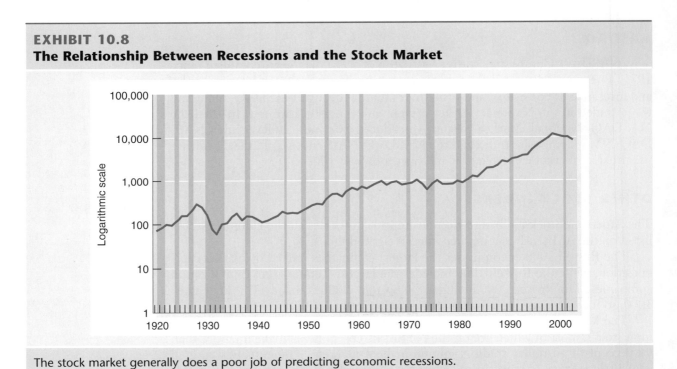

The stock market generally does a poor job of predicting economic recessions.

Source: Dow Jones & Company, Inc.; National Bureau of Economic Research.

[3] See Bryon Higgins, "Is a Recession Inevitable This Year?" *Economic Review*, Federal Reserve Bank of Kansas City, January 1988, pp. 3–16.

Dow Jones Industrial Average of 30 stocks since the early 1900s. As can be seen, there seems to be little correlation between stock market declines and recessions. Note, however, that the 2001–2002 recession was predicted by the stock market. The crash of 1987, on the other hand, was followed by 3 more years of economic expansion.

CHAPTER TAKE-AWAYS

1 There are three general forms of equity securities: common stock, preferred stock, and securities that are convertible into common stock. Common stock is the basic form of corporate ownership. Common stockholders typically vote on the corporation's board of directors, may receive periodic cash payments called dividends, and are last in priority of payment in the event of bankruptcy. Preferred stockholders typically do not vote, but they receive preference in receiving dividend payments over common shareholders. Preferred stockholders are just ahead of common stockholders in priority of payment in bankruptcy. Convertible securities are either corporate bonds or preferred stock that convert to common stock at the investor's option.

2 New issues of equity securities may be sold directly to investors by the issuing corporation, but they are usually distributed by an investment banker in an underwritten offering, a private placement, or a shelf registration. The most common distribution method is an underwritten offering in which the investment banker purchases the securities from the company for a guaranteed amount known as the net proceeds and then resells the securities to investors for a greater amount, called the gross proceeds. The difference between the gross proceeds and the net proceeds is the underwriter's spread, which compensates the investment banker for the expenses and risks involved in the offering. The smaller the offering amount and the more uncertain investment bankers are about the price of the offering, the larger the underwriter spreads. Shelf-registered offerings tend to have lower underwriter spreads than those sold by traditional methods.

3 Any trade of a security after its primary offering takes place in the secondary market. Secondary markets take four possible forms: direct search, brokered, dealer, and auction markets. Bid–ask spreads vary with the price of the security, the size of the trade, the frequency of trading in a security, and the incidence of informed versus uninformed trading in a security. Stocks trade over the counter, on the NASDAQ system, and on organized exchanges such as the New York Stock Exchange. Stocks of major U.S. firms also trade globally on the stock exchanges of other countries.

4 Equity securities are valued similarly to bonds but are more complicated because they are assumed to exist forever and because corporations can change the amount of the dividend at any time. Valuing an equity security requires estimating the future stream of dividend payments and coming up with an assumed sale price at the end of a holding period. Once the timing and the magnitude of the cash flows (i.e., dividends and a future sale price) are determined, one must determine the discount rate that reflects the risk of holding the stock. This discount rate is then used to calculate the present value of the future cash flows. There are some convenient formulas, such as the perpetuity and growing perpetuity formulas, which can be easily adapted to value most types of common and preferred stock.

5 The total risk of an equity security (or portfolio) is the sum of unsystematic and systematic risk. Total risk is usually measured with the standard deviation of the returns on a stock or portfolio of stocks. Unsystematic risk can be reduced by diversification; systematic risk cannot. Investors measure systematic risk with beta (β), which is

an indicator of how closely a security's returns are correlated with the returns of the entire stock market.

6 Stock market indexes track movements of prices in the stock market or in some portion of the stock market, such as a firm size or industry segment. Stock market indexes are constructed by selecting a sample of stocks and calculating the weighted average of stock prices in the sample. The indexes can be price-weighted or market value weighted. The most visible stock indexes are the Dow Jones Industrial Average, the New York Stock Exchange Composite Index, and the S&P 500 Index.

7 Market observers believe that changes in the stock market can predict changes in overall economic activity for a number of reasons. First, stock prices should reflect the market's expectation of a firm's future profits. Second, when stock markets go up or down, the wealth of individuals is affected and may, in turn, affect their willingness to spend. Third, the stock market may reflect or impact changes in consumer confidence about the economy. Finally, as the stock market goes up or down, the cost of capital of corporations may be affected, which could influence corporate investment spending. While some economic recessions have been preceded by declines in the stock market, the empirical evidence suggests that the stock market is generally a poor predictor of economic activity.

KEY TERMS

Equity	Convertible preferred stock	Brokered market	Unsystematic risk
Common stock	Convertible bonds	Dealer market	Systematic risk
Preferred stock	Primary offerings	Bid–ask spread	Beta
Residual claim	Initial public offering (IPO)	Auction market	Aggressive stocks
Limited liability	Seasoned offering	Over-the-counter (OTC) market	Defensive stocks
Dividends	Underwritten offering	NASDAQ	Risk premium
Proxy	Underwriter's spread	Market order	Market risk premium
Dual-class firms	Private placement	Limit order	Security market line (SML)
Cumulative voting	Rights offering	Specialist	Price-weighted index
Straight voting	Shelf registration	American Depositary Receipt (ADR)	Market value–weighted index
Nonparticipating preferred stock	Market depth	Perpetuity	
Cumulative preferred stock	Market breadth	Dividend yield	
Adjustable-rate preferred stock	Market resilient	Capital-gains yield	
	Direct search market	Diversification	

QUESTIONS AND PROBLEMS

1. Describe the major differences between common stock and preferred stock.

2. Why are convertible securities more attractive to investors than simply holding a firm's preferred stock or corporate bonds?

3. Rowell Inc. has 100 million shares of common stock outstanding and the company is electing seven directors by means of cumulative voting. If a group of minority shareholders controls 31 million shares, how many directors is the group certain of electing? If straight voting were used, how many directors would the group be certain of electing?

4. Weber Corporation has 10 million shares of a preferred stock issue outstanding that pays a cumulative $6

annual dividend on a quarterly basis. However, due to poor profitability the company has not paid the preferred stock dividend for the last five quarters. The company also has 20 million shares of common stock outstanding. Weber Corporation's profitability has improved recently and the board of directors believes that the company can pay $100 million in dividends next quarter. How much of a dividend can the company pay on its common stock?

5. Arbuckle Corporation is selling 2 million shares of common stock in its initial public offering (IPO). The company's investment banker, Jones Securities, will offer the stock to the public at $15 per share and charge Arbuckle Corporation an underwriting spread of 7 percent. What will be the gross proceeds from the IPO? What will be Arbuckle Corporation's net proceeds from the offering? How much will Jones Securities earn for conducting the offering?

6. List and explain the factors affecting underwriter spreads.

7. Define the following terms as they relate to secondary markets: depth, breadth, and resiliency.

8. List and explain the factors affecting bid–ask spreads.

9. How did the introduction of NASDAQ in 1971 affect price discovery in secondary markets? Explain.

10. Briefly describe the role of the NYSE specialist. How does this role differ from that of a dealer?

11. Explain the difference between a market order and a limit order.

12. Lance Garrison and Jennifer Stock both have decided to buy 100 shares of WWW.COM, a hot Internet stock. The market price is $240 per share when Lance places a market order and Jennifer places a limit order at $230 per share. One week later, the price of WWW.COM is $305 per share after having increased steadily since Lance and Jennifer placed their orders. How much profit has Lance made? How much profit has Jennifer made?

13. Winters Hi-Hook Inc., a golf club manufacturer, is currently paying dividends of $0.50 per share. These dividends are expected to grow at a 20 percent rate for the next 2 years and at a 3 percent rate thereafter (forever!). What is the value of the stock if the appropriate discount rate is 14 percent?

14. Kaes Power Company promises to maintain dividends of $5 per share on its preferred stock, indefinitely. The stock currently sells at $37.50 per share. What is the required return on the stock?

15. Chastain's Gardening Supplies, Inc. is a young start-up company. It plans to pay no dividends over the next 5 years because it needs to reinvest all earnings in the firm to finance planned growth. The firm then plans to begin paying dividends of $3 per share, which are anticipated to grow at 10 percent per year for 3 years and 6 percent per year in perpetuity beyond that. If the required return on Chastain stock is 15 percent, what should be today's stock price?

16. You purchase 100 shares of Adams Trading Company stock today for $22.50 per share. At the end of 1 year, you collect a dividend of $2.75 and then sell the stock at $24.50 per share. What is your total return on the stock? What is the dividend yield? What is the capital-gains yield?

17. Farrell Motors stock has a beta of 1.3. If the market risk premium is 8.5 percent and the risk-free rate is 4 percent, what is the expected return of the stock according to the security market line?

18. The market's required return on Gitche Gumee Oil Company stock is currently 13.8 percent. If the expected return on the market portfolio is 12.6 percent and the risk-free rate is 3.5 percent, what is the beta of Gitche Gumee stock?

19. Explain the difference between systematic and unsystematic risk. Explain how beta captures systematic risk.

20. You have decided to create stock market indexes using three representative stocks. At the end of day 1, stock X has a price of $20 per share and 20 million shares outstanding, stock Y has a price of $25 per share and 50 million shares outstanding, and stock Z has a price of $35 per share and 40 million shares outstanding. You are going to calculate a price-weighted index and a market capitalization–weighted index. You have decided that the beginning value of each index at the end of day 1 will be 100. What is the value of each index at the end of day 2 if stock X's price is $23 per share, stock Y's price is $22 per share, and stock Z's price is $36 per share?

INTERNET EXERCISE

In this exercise you will learn how to access the Dow Jones Industrial Average on the Internet and get some practice doing some simple analysis of the DJIA.

1. Go to the Dow Jones Indexes home page at www.djindexes.com.
2. Select "Averages" under the "Blue Chip Indexes" column on the left.
3. Notice the column on the left headed with "Dow Data." Under "Dow Data," click on "2000–2009" and print the chart. What impact did historical events have on the DJIA in the early part of the 2000s? Describe what has happened to the DJIA since January 2000?
4. After viewing and printing the historical chart, go back to the "Dow Jones Averages" page and select "Index Data" from the menu bar. You will see boxes highlighting three steps. Under Step 1, select "Historical Values," which appears under a heading labeled "Performance." Under Step 2, select "Industrial (DJI)." Enter your birth date in the "from date" space and click "Get Report." What was the Dow Jones Industrial Average on the day you were born? (If you were born before May 26, 1896, skip this exercise. You have better things to do with the little time you have remaining.) What was the DJIA on your last birthday? What has the compound annual return for the DJIA been during your lifetime?

11

Derivatives Markets

What are interest rates going to do? What about exchange rates? What about the stock market? Should I bet that interest rates will fall and stocks rise, or should I bet that the exchange rate will fall and stocks fall? How much risk can I take? Should I gamble to try to earn a higher return? Will I lose my job if my portfolio or transactions lose money? Most financial institutions hate risk and will fire people who take too much risk. How can I protect myself and my transactions and portfolio against loss? Many bond traders, market makers, exporters and importers, and managers of financial institutions and investment funds must ask themselves questions like these daily.

Because many people are concerned with interest rate, exchange rate, or stock market risk, the financial futures markets have grown explosively in recent years. "Financial engineers" have developed a wide variety of financial instruments so that individuals and institutions can alter both their risk exposure and return possibilities. The new "financial derivative" securities derive their value from changes in the value of other assets (such as stocks or bonds), values (such as interest rates), or events (such as credit defaults, catastrophes, or even temperature changes in certain localities). Derivative securities also generate substantial fee income for the financial institutions that invent and market them. ∎

He's no rock star. The guy in the backwards baseball cap is Nick Leeson, who piled up $1.4 billion in losses trading derivative securities at Barings Bank's Singapore office. The result was that the 232-year old bank had to declare bankruptcy. Leeson was fired, convicted of security trading violations, and jailed in Singapore--a bad hair month by any standard.

This chapter describes the nature of the most important markets for financial derivatives. It starts with forward and futures markets, then discusses the swaps and options markets. It discusses how markets work, what financial instruments are traded in each, who the major participants are, and how the markets are regulated. It also describes how the financial futures markets can be used to reduce risk—particularly the interest rate risk of financial intermediaries—and how new types of risk, such as basis risk and counterparty risk, may be relevant to claims traded in the financial derivative markets. ∎

LEARNING OBJECTIVES

The objectives of this chapter are to:

1 Explain the characteristics of forwards, futures, options, and swaps.

2 Explain how market participants use derivative securities.

3 Describe the advantages and disadvantages of each derivative security.

4 Discuss the risks involved in using futures contracts to hedge an underlying risk exposure.

5 Discuss why some people prefer options to forward or futures contracts, and why options protect against risk only if someone pays a price—the option "premium."

6 Explain how swaps work and how they can be used to reduce interest rate risk.

THE NATURE OF DERIVATIVE SECURITIES

The securities discussed in previous chapters have diverse payoff characteristics, and most financial institutions and other investors pursue their investment objectives by picking and choosing among those securities. At any given point in time, however, these investors may be exposed to more or less risk than they desire in one or more securities or markets. This is where derivative securities come in.

A derivative security is a financial instrument whose value depends on, or is derived from, some underlying security. For example, the value of a futures contract to buy Treasury bills at some future point in time is derived from the value of Treasury bills. The most common types of derivative contracts are forwards, futures, options, and swaps. In fact, virtually all derivative securities are some combination of these four basic contracts.

Derivatives are an integral part of a successful risk management program because they offer an inexpensive means of changing a firm's risk profile. A firm's risk profile describes how the firm's value or cash flows will change in response to changes in some risk factor. Common risk factors are interest rates, commodity prices, stock market indexes, and foreign exchange rates. By taking a position in a derivative security that offsets the firm's risk profile, the firm can limit the extent to which firm value is affected by changes in the risk factor. Similarly, investors can use derivative securities to speculate on these risk factors.

Given the effectiveness of derivative securities in managing a firm's risk exposures, it is not surprising that the markets for derivative securities have seen tremendous growth in the past 20 years. In fact, according to a recent survey by the International Swaps and Derivatives Association (ISDA), 92 percent of the world's largest companies use derivatives to manage their risks. The total notional principal amount of interest rate derivatives outstanding was over $140 trillion at the end of 2003, according to ISDA statistics. We now turn to a discussion of the four basic derivative securities: forwards, futures, options, and swaps.

FORWARD MARKETS

Frequently people enter into contracts that call for future delivery of domestic or foreign currency, a security, or a commodity. A **forward contract**, for example, involves two parties agreeing today on a price, called the **forward price**, at which the purchaser will buy a specified amount of an asset from the seller at a fixed date sometime in the future. This is in contrast to a cash market transaction in which the buyer and seller conduct their transaction today at the **spot price**. The buyer of a forward contract is said to have a **long position** and is obligated to pay the forward price for the asset. The seller of a forward contract is said to have a **short position** and is obligated to sell the asset to the buyer in exchange for the forward price. The future date on which the buyer pays the seller (and the seller delivers the asset to the buyer) is referred to as the **settlement date**.

Forward markets let people arrange exchanges "forward" in time. In a forward market one party enters into a contract with a **counterparty** to purchase (or sell) a specified amount of an asset at the forward price on the settlement date. Ordinarily, both parties to the contract are bound by the contract and will not be released from that obligation early unless they renegotiate the contract prior to its fulfillment. Individual parties to forward contracts are exposed to potential loss should their counterparty default rather than honor his or her obligation on the settlement date.

The forward price for an asset is that price which makes the forward contract have zero net present value. Consider, for example, an asset that does not cost anything to store (a financial asset) and doesn't pay any income (a discount bond). Whether we purchase this asset forward, say six months forward, or borrow the current price of the asset, buy it today, and pay back the loan in six months, we end up owning the asset in six months. Therefore, we can say the forward price must be equal to the current price plus what it would cost us to borrow for six months. For example, consider Hilary, a portfolio manager who plans to buy 1-month Treasury bills in two months. The total face amount of securities she plans to buy is $5 million. The current price for 3-month Treasury bills is $992,537 per $1 million face amount. If the current effective annual risk-free rate over the two months is 3 percent, the fair forward price would be

$$F = \$992,537[1 + (0.03/12)]^2 = \$997,506.$$

So, the total forward price Hilary should pay is $4,987,530 ($997,506 × 5). If the asset had any storage costs or paid any income, the forward price would be adjusted upward (to incorporate the storage costs) or downward (to incorporate the income).

The forward markets for foreign exchange (money) are the most active forward markets. Markets in foreign currencies let people guarantee a currency exchange rate at some specific forward point such as 30, 60, or 90 days or more hence. When an exporter wishes to guarantee a forward exchange rate, he or she can go to any one of a number of banks or foreign exchange dealers and enter into a forward contract. The contract guarantees delivery of a certain amount of foreign currency (say, 2 million British pounds) for exchange into a specific amount of dollars ($3.7 million, if the exchange rate is $1.85 = £1) on a specific day (90 days hence).

If a corn exporter sold 1 million bushels of corn at £2 per bushel with payment due in 90 days, the exporter could guarantee the dollar price of the corn by entering into a forward exchange contract with a major bank. The exporter would agree to sell the £2 million it will receive to the bank for $1.85 per pound, or a total of $3.7 million.

A risk of counterparty default exists if, for instance, the exporter does not receive prompt payment of the £2 million and is unable to keep its end of the contract, or if the bank fails (and is not bailed out) before maturity of the contract. Losses due to a default are relatively low as long as the pound–dollar exchange rate is close to $1.85 per pound on the designated delivery day because the unfilled end of the contract can be offset in the spot exchange market at a price close to the prearranged rate of exchange. The **spot market** calls for immediate delivery of foreign exchange.

Because the future spot rate is uncertain, exporters do not want to risk their profits by gambling that they can predict it. Furthermore, since the risk of counterparty default on forward exchange contracts is very small, they would rather take that risk and pay their bank a fee for arranging the forward exchange than receive a currency whose future value is uncertain. Forward exchange contracts let importers and exporters offset the price risk inherent in future dealings by guaranteeing future exchange rates and prices.

The individual banks and foreign exchange dealers that make up the forward market balance the supply of and demand for funds by exporters, importers, investors, and speculators in various countries and alter the forward exchange rate as necessary so that the demand for and supply of funds will be equal.

Forward exchange dealers make their money on the spread between their buying and asking prices for foreign exchange. For instance, an exchange dealer might exchange dollars supplied by Japanese exporters for yen at ¥109 per dollar and exchange yen supplied by U.S. exporters for dollars at ¥110 per dollar. The dealer profits by buying low and selling high.

FUTURES MARKETS

Like forward contracts, **futures contracts** involve two parties agreeing today on a price at which the purchaser will buy a given amount of a commodity or financial instrument from the seller at a fixed date sometime in the future. In fact, futures and forwards serve many of the same economic functions. The markets for the two types of instruments are sufficiently different, however, that the two contracts warrant being called by different names.

DIFFERENCES BETWEEN FUTURES AND FORWARD MARKETS

Futures contracts differ from forward contracts in several ways. Many of the differences can be attributed to the fact that futures contracts are traded on an organized exchange, such as the Chicago Board of Trade or the Chicago Mercantile Exchange, while forward contracts are traded in the informal over-the-counter market.

One of the most important differences between futures and forwards is that futures contracts are standardized in quantities, delivery periods, and grades of deliverable items, whereas forward market contracts are not. Most futures contracts call for the delivery of specific commodities, securities, or currencies either on specific future dates or over limited periods of time. For example, 10-year U.S. Treasury note futures call for a contract size of one U.S. Treasury note having a face value of $100,000. Available delivery months are limited to the nearest March, June, September, and December. This standardization results in a relatively large volume of transactions for a given contract. This makes trading in the contract easy and inexpensive.

In addition, although there must be a buyer and seller when any new contract is initiated, both parties in a futures market transaction hold formal contracts with the **futures exchange**, not with each other. Every major futures exchange operates a clearinghouse that acts as the counterparty to all buyers and all sellers. While individual traders interact with each other face-to-face in a futures "pit" (trading area), the actual contract drawn up to formalize this trade will break this direct link between buyer and seller and will instead insert the clearinghouse as the opposite party. This means that traders need not worry about the creditworthiness of the party they trade with (as forward market traders must), but only about the creditworthiness of the exchange itself. This reduces the risk of default on futures contracts. Forward contracts are riskier because one party may default if prices change dramatically before the delivery date.

The futures exchange is protected from default risk by requiring daily cash settlement of all contracts, called **marking-to-market**. By its very nature, a futures contract is a zero-sum game in that whenever the market price of a commodity changes, the underlying value of a long (purchase) or short (sale) position also changes—and one party's gain is the other party's loss. By requiring each contract's loser to pay the winner the net amount of this change each day, futures exchanges eliminate the possibility that large unrealized losses will build up over time. Market participants post **margin** money (if necessary) to take account of gains or losses accruing from daily price fluctuations. In a forward contract, on the other hand, there are no cash flows between origination and termination of the contract.

Because the futures exchange acts as the counterparty in all futures contracts and all contracts are marked to market daily, either party in a futures contract can liquidate its future obligation to buy (or deliver) goods by offsetting it with a sale (or purchase) of an identical futures contract prior to the scheduled delivery date. In the forward exchange markets, contracts are ordinarily satisfied by actual delivery of specified items on the specified date. In the futures market, almost all contracts are offset prior to delivery,

EXAMPLE OF A FUTURES MARKET TRANSACTION

The futures markets typically call for delivery of specific items during specific months of the year. For instance, as indicated above, a 10-year U.S. Treasury note contract calls for the delivery of $100,000 face amount of 10-year Treasury notes during the months of March, June, September, or December. A person may purchase (or sell) a futures contract for receipt (or delivery) of $100,000 worth of 10-year Treasury notes for any of those months for the next year. Treasury note futures prices are quoted in points and one-half of $1/32$ of a point. For example, a quote of 110'12.5 indicates a futures price of $110,391 (110 12.5/32 percent of $100,000).

10-year U.S. Treasury notes are limited in number, so the Chicago Board of Trade allows any U.S. Treasury note maturing in at least 6.5 years, but in no more than 10 years, to be delivered in the event delivery actually takes place. In addition, because there are differences in values between 6.5-year Treasury notes and 10-year Treasury notes, the exchange uses conversion factors to adjust the futures settlement price for these differences. The conversion factors are based on prices that yield 6 percent.

Agreeing to Trade.   Suppose that in December 2004, Paige decides to buy a Treasury note futures contract for delivery in June 2005 at a price of 110'12.5. At the same time, Jake decides to sell a Treasury note futures contract if he can get a price of 110'12.5 or higher. Both place their orders with their brokers, who take them to the trading floor (in practice, the order would probably be executed electronically) at the Chicago Board of Trade. Paige's broker offers to buy one contract and Jake's broker offers to sell one contract. Once they agree on the price, the brokers signal their agreement to buy and sell a June 2004 contract to each other at a price of 110'12.5 and record their orders with the exchange. The exchange, in turn, agrees to sell one Treasury note contract to Paige at 110'12.5 and to buy one contract from Jake at 110'12.5. Because there are both a new buyer and a new seller, the **open interest**, or total number of contracts to deliver a Treasury note in June 2005 through the exchange, increases by one. This process is illustrated in Exhibit 11.1. Note that even though the agreement to buy and sell

---

EXHIBIT 11.1
Buyers and Sellers Agree on a Price through the Futures Exchange

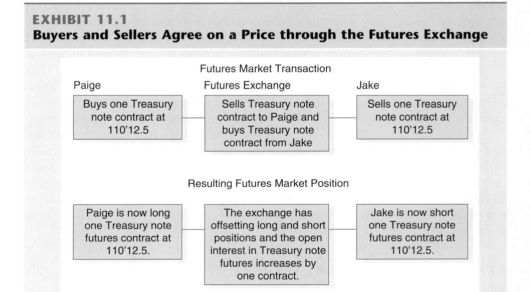

When a person buys or sells a futures contract, the futures exchange is legally the other party to the contract. However, the exchange has a neutral net position, because it always simultaneously buys and sells contracts to the public. The total number of long (or short) contracts outstanding in a futures contract is called the *open interest*.

was between individuals, the exchange wrote separate contracts with each. This, combined with marking-to-market, allows each participant to liquidate his or her position at will.

The payoff diagrams for the long and short positions are shown in Exhibit 11.2. If the price of Treasury notes increases, Paige benefits from the contract because she is guaranteed a price of 110′12.5, or $110,391, and Jake is worse off because he is obligated to sell Treasury notes for 110′12.5, or $110,391, which is less than what he could sell them for in the spot market. If, on the other hand, Treasury note prices decrease, Paige is worse off because she must pay $110,391 for Treasury notes that are not worth that much. Jake's futures position would provide him with a benefit if Treasury note prices decrease, however, because the

---

EXHIBIT 11.2
Payoff Diagrams for Treasury Note Futures Contracts

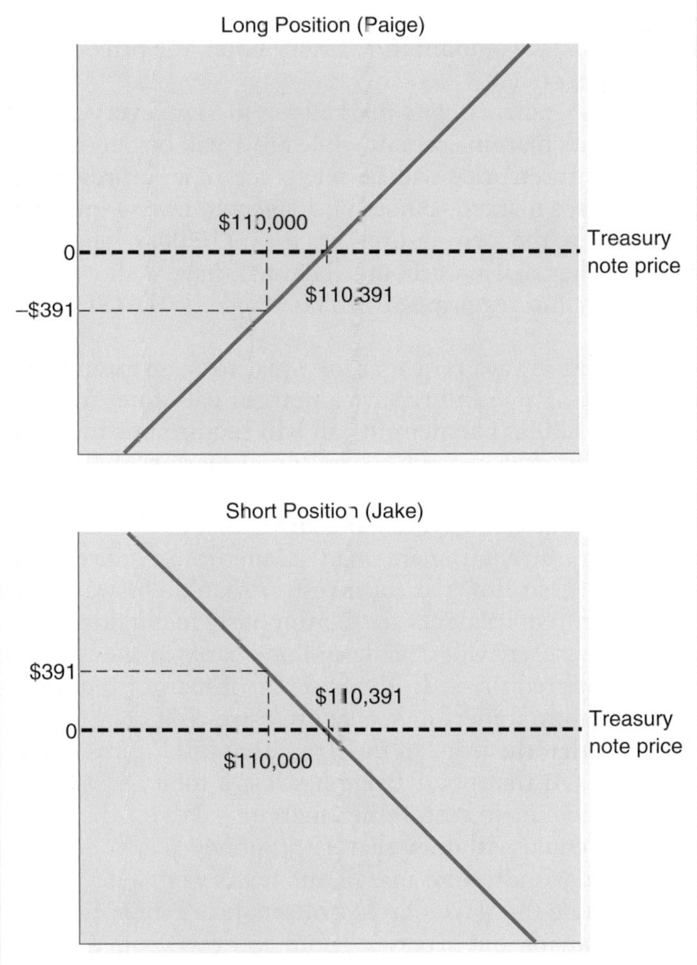

Long positions benefit from price increases. Short positions benefit from price decreases.

futures contract enables him to sell Treasury notes for a price that is greater than their market value.

Margin Requirements.   When Paige and Jake initiate their futures positions (as in forward contracts, an agreement to buy is called a long position and an agreement to sell is called a short position), they each must deposit money with the exchange to guarantee that they will keep their part of the bargain. This deposit is called the **initial margin** requirement. The initial margin for Treasury note futures is $1,620. If the market price of new contracts on the exchange moves adversely, Paige or Jake may have to deposit more money in order to meet the **maintenance margin** requirement imposed on investors by the exchange. Maintenance margin requirements are imposed to ensure that people do not default on their contracts if prices move adversely for them. The Treasury note maintenance margin is $1,200.

Assume that Paige and Jake each posted an initial margin requirement of $1,620 with the exchange, so the exchange holds a total of $3,240 in margin deposits. Now suppose that the price of the Treasury note futures contract fell to 110′00.0. At that point, Paige's long contract has lost $391 in value and Jake has gained an equal amount. Jake's contract has gained value because it gives him the right to sell $100,000 face amount in Treasury notes at a price that is $391 higher than the new futures price.

Because futures contracts are marked to market every day, $391 will be deducted from Paige's margin account while $391 will be deposited in Jake's margin account. The futures price will be set to the new futures price of 110′00.0. After the contracts are marked to market, Paige will have a long futures contract with the exchange at the new futures price of 110′00.0. She will have $1,229 ($1,620 − $391) in her margin account. Jake will have a short position with the exchange at the new futures price of 110′00.0 and $2,011 ($1,620 + $391) in his margin account.

Because she must always post margin equal to or greater than maintenance margin requirements, Paige will receive a **margin call** if her margin account balance drops below $1,200. The margin call will require her to add money to her margin account to bring it back up to the initial margin of $1,620. Margin calls are necessary to ensure that futures traders will always keep a positive balance in their accounts and will not have an incentive to default on their obligations. Because futures margin requirements may at any time require interim cash outlays, they pose more cash-flow risk for investors than do forward contracts. However, because margin requirements are continuously maintained, they also reduce the risk that a counterparty will default and one party to the transaction will suffer a loss because of credit risk. In the absence of margin requirements, as with over-the-counter trades, traders may take excessive risks.

Let us suppose that the price of the Treasury note futures contract continues to fall—to 109′12.5. At that point Paige has lost a total of $1,000 and must add that much to her account to restore her margin. Jake, on the other hand, has a gain of $1,000. He could withdraw that extra money at will or decide to sell out and take his gain and withdraw his margin money as well. This is shown in Exhibit 11.3, where we assume that Jake's broker offsets Jake's short position by going to the exchange and buying one Treasury note contract from Carl's broker. Since Carl's broker sold a contract to deliver one Treasury note on Carl's behalf, Carl is now short one Treasury note contract instead of Jake.

EXHIBIT 11.3
Transfer of Futures Contracts

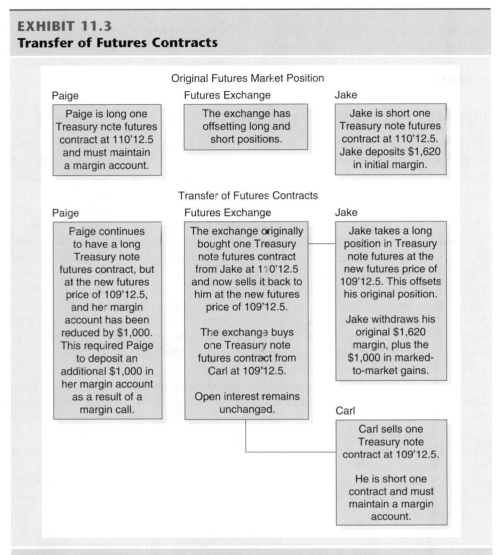

Original Futures Market Position

Paige

Futures Exchange

Jake

| Paige is long one Treasury note futures contract at 110'12.5 and must maintain a margin account. | The exchange has offsetting long and short positions. | Jake is short one Treasury note futures contract at 110'12.5. Jake deposits $1,620 in initial margin. |

Transfer of Futures Contracts

Paige

Futures Exchange

Jake

| Paige continues to have a long Treasury note futures contract, but at the new futures price of 109'12.5, and her margin account has been reduced by $1,000. This required Paige to deposit an additional $1,000 in her margin account as a result of a margin call. | The exchange originally bought one Treasury note futures contract from Jake at 110'12.5 and now sells it back to him at the new futures price of 109'12.5.

The exchange buys one Treasury note futures contract from Carl at 109'12.5.

Open interest remains unchanged. | Jake takes a long position in Treasury note futures at the new futures price of 109'12.5. This offsets his original position.

Jake withdraws his original $1,620 margin, plus the $1,000 in marked-to-market gains. |

Carl

| Carl sells one Treasury note contract at 109'12.5.

He is short one contract and must maintain a margin account. |

When a person closes out a futures position, a payment is made to settle the change in value that has occurred since the initial purchase, and the contract with the exchange is canceled. This procedure provides liquidity, as it allows one party to the initial trade (Jake) to liquidate his position without requiring the consent of the party who initially took the other side of the contract (Paige). This is one advantage of futures over forward contracts.

Delivery on Futures Contracts. Although the vast majority of all futures contracts are offset before delivery, a few are completed by delivery from the seller to the buyer. For instance, in Exhibit 11.3, if Carl continues to hold his contract in June 2005, he may fulfill his contract to sell by delivering $100,000 in Treasury notes on any business day of his choosing during the month. The holder of the "long" (buy side) futures position is invoiced to pay for the Treasury notes at the current settlement price, net of gains or losses, that he or she has accrued on the futures contract. Both the long and the short contracts, then, are canceled by delivery. Note that Paige will not necessarily be the buyer. In fact, if she has offset her position, then she will certainly not be the buyer. The exchange selects the long position with the oldest outstanding contract to be the buyer of any Treasury notes being delivered.

FUTURES MARKET INSTRUMENTS

Futures markets can be started for any type of security, foreign currency, or commodity for which a sufficient number of people want to exchange future price risk. An interesting aspect of futures contracts is that "the fittest survive." Initially, several exchanges may issue similar contracts, or one exchange may issue several closely related contracts. However, over time one contract will tend to gain popularity at the expense of other closely related contracts, and trading will tend to be concentrated in that single contract. This happens because the contract with the highest volume generally provides the greatest liquidity and lowest bid–ask spreads. Eventually, trading in the other contracts will be discontinued. For instance, the New York Futures Exchange (NYFE) T-bill contracts were unable to compete with the Chicago Mercantile Exchange's International Monetary Market (IMM) contracts for the same instruments because the IMM had larger volumes of trading. Because of the survival-of-the-fittest tendency of futures contracts, usually only one contract is traded for each type of asset. Exhibit 11.4 lists a few examples of exchange-traded futures contracts.

There are several futures exchanges, as indicated in Exhibit 11.4, and a great deal of competition exists among them. The U.S. futures markets, particularly the Chicago Board of Trade (CBOT) and the Chicago Mercantile Exchange (CME), used to dominate futures trading, while the Chicago Board Options Exchange (CBOE) was the largest options exchange in the world. In recent years, however, all three have been exposed to competitive pressure from foreign exchanges, particularly as the European exchanges have consolidated following Europe's introduction of a common currency. In addition, the European exchanges have been quicker to develop all-electronic trading facilities, while the U.S. exchanges have retained a greater interest in floor trading facilities. Floor trading facilities may provide greater liquidity but are more expensive to operate than all-electronic systems.

Each futures exchange determines the specifications for contracts traded on that exchange. The specifications show delivery dates for each contract, the value of items to be delivered when each contract is exercised, the types of items that can be delivered, and the method of delivery. The exchange also dictates the minimum price change that can occur in the contract and (to prevent panics) the maximum price change that can occur in 1 day. Initial and maintenance margins, trading rules and hours, and trading methods (electronic or pit-traded) for each type of contract are also specified by the exchange. Finally, each exchange enforces trading rules, contract agreements, and margin requirements applicable to that exchange.

FUTURES MARKET PARTICIPANTS

There are two major types of participants in futures and forward markets: **hedgers** and **speculators**. Hedgers try to reduce price risk inherent in their balance sheets

EXHIBIT 11.4
Examples of Exchange Traded Futures Contracts

Contract	Exchange	Contract Size
Grains and oilseeds		
Corn	Chicago Board Of Trade	5,000 bushels
Oats	Chicago Board Of Trade	5,000 bushels
Wheat	Chicago Board Of Trade	5,000 bushels
Livestock and meat		
Cattle—feeder	Chicago Mercantile Exchange	50,000 lbs.
Cattle—live	Chicago Mercantile Exchange	40,000 lbs.
Pork bellies	Chicago Mercantile Exchange	40,000 lbs.
Food and fiber		
Cocoa	Coffee, Sugar & Cocoa Exchange, New York	10 metric tons
Coffee	Coffee, Sugar & Cocoa Exchange, New York	37,500 lbs.
Sugar—world	Coffee, Sugar & Cocoa Exchange, New York	112,000 lbs.
Sugar—domestic	Coffee, Sugar & Cocoa Exchange, New York	112,000 lbs.
Cotton	New York Cotton Exchange	50,000 lbs.
Orange juice	New York Cotton Exchange	15,000 lbs.
Metals and petroleum		
Copper	Comex, New York Mercantile Exchange	25,000 lbs.
Gold	Comex, New York Mercantile Exchange	100 troy oz.
Platinum	New York Mercantile Exchange	50 troy oz.
Silver	Comex, New York Mercantile Exchange	5,000 troy oz.
Crude oil	New York Mercantile Exchange	1,000 bbls.
Natural gas	New York Mercantile Exchange	10,000 MMBtu
Interest Rate		
Treasury bonds	Chicago Board Of Trade	$100,000
10-year Treasury notes	Chicago Board Of Trade	$100,000
30-day federal funds	Chicago Board Of Trade	$5 million
LIBOR	Chicago Mercantile Exchange	$3 million
Eurodollars	Chicago Mercantile Exchange	$1 million
Euro bund	Eurex	€100,000
Index		
Dow Jones Industrial Average	Chicago Board Of Trade	$10 × avg.
Mini-sized Dow	Chicago Board Of Trade	$5 × avg.
S&P 500	Chicago Mercantile Exchange	$250 × avg.
Mini-sized S&P 500	Chicago Mercantile Exchange	$50 × avg.
NIKKEI 225	Chicago Mercantile Exchange	$5 × avg.
Currency		
Japanese Yen (¥)	Chicago Mercantile Exchange	¥12.5 million
Euro (€)	Chicago Mercantile Exchange	€125,000
British pound (£)	Chicago Mercantile Exchange	£62,500

PEOPLE & EVENTS

Rogue Traders Can Sink Large Institutions

One of the advantages of futures and options markets is that they let people control large amounts of assets with relatively small amounts of equity required to back their positions. Thus, people who make correct decisions can earn very large percentage returns. Conversely, people who make wrong decisions can quickly incur huge losses. Thus, it is imperative for all financial institutions to monitor the operations of their traders closely to ensure that they don't cause the institution to take horrendous losses. Unfortunately, institutions have often been remiss in their internal monitoring, thereby causing them to take great losses or even fail in response to trades made by rogue traders in their employ.

In the late 1990s, the venerable Barings Bank in England failed because of the actions of a rogue trader in its Singapore branch. Nick Leeson didn't start out as a rogue trader; the year before he had made $25 million for Barings Bank. Thus, Barings Bank didn't watch what he was doing very closely. However, Leeson guessed wrong on the future direction of Japan's Nikkei stock index, whose futures are traded both in Japan and on the Singapore exchange. As his losses grew, he doubled and tripled his positions, thinking that he surely would be right eventually, and his eventual gain would more than compensate for his past losses. Because Barings wasn't watching closely, he was able to cover up his bad trades and post more margin money to support his futures positions. Finally, Barings' home office per-

sonnel noted the large cash outflows from the bank and went to Singapore to investigate. By the time they got there, Leeson had lost over $1 billion of the bank's capital, and the venerable bank failed.

One would think that other banks would learn from Barings' mistake, and, indeed, many did. Banks employ risk managers that analyze each trader's and the bank's trading position risk every single day with the idea that constant monitoring will prevent any given trader from exposing the bank to too much risk. However, not all banks have been so careful. In 2002, John Rusnak, a foreign currency trader at All-first, a U.S. subsidiary of Allied Irish Banks, Ireland's largest bank, caused the bank to lose more than $750 million. Once again, a trader had gotten into trouble by taking too much risk in highly leveraged markets and doubling up to try to erase his earlier losses. In this case, Rusnak disguised his losses as they grew by creating artificial offsetting trades in over-the-counter foreign currency options that had (mythical) gains that exceeded his losses. Because over-the-counter transactions are not cleared through an exchange clearinghouse, where marking-to-market is required and the counterparty to the transaction is clearly identified and assigned an offsetting position, no one in the marketplace alerted the bank to the fictitious trades. Consequently, since the bank did not monitor Rusnak closely enough, by the time it found out, his losses had seriously undermined the bank's financial stability.

or future business dealings by guaranteeing buying or selling prices for closely related futures contracts. In our earlier example, Jake may have been holding a portfolio of Treasury securities. If so, his transaction to sell Treasury note futures contracts reduced his price risk; thus he was a hedger. Other hedgers might try to guarantee their costs of feed (by buying corn futures contracts) or the value of their livestock at market time (by selling cattle or hog futures contracts). By so doing, they can guarantee their costs of raising cattle or hogs and ensure that they will make a profit. Similarly, banks can guarantee their cost of funds over the period they make a loan by selling interest rate futures short. Insurance companies can guarantee a return on planned annuity policies by buying Treasury bond futures before they actually sell the policies.

In short, there are many ways that people can use futures contracts to hedge their financial and business transactions. In the process, some will be buyers and some will be sellers. Their major objective, however, is to guarantee a future price that will reduce their risk.

Speculators take risks in the futures markets. They are willing to enter a futures transaction in hopes that the market price will move in a favorable direction. If they are right, like Jake in our example, they can make a great deal of money in a hurry. If prices move unfavorably, however, they can also lose a great deal of money. Speculators may either speculate on a rise in prices by buying futures contracts (going long) or speculate on a fall in prices by selling futures contracts (going short). They also may enter into **spreads** or **straddles**, in which they buy one futures contract and sell a closely related contract (such as a contract for the same commodity that is due in a different month, or a contract for a closely related commodity) in the hope that the price of one contract will move more favorably than the other.

Traders are a special class of speculators that speculate on very short-term changes in prices. Most operate on the floor of the exchange and try to "scalp" short-term changes in market prices by buying and selling quickly when prices seem to be changing. Traders provide a valuable function because their activity adds liquidity to markets and reduces the disparity between bid and ask prices on the exchanges. Consequently, exchanges encourage trading activity in order to broaden the market appeal of their futures contracts.

DO YOU UNDERSTAND?

1. Explain the major differences between futures contracts and forward contracts.
2. What is the economic role of the margin account on a futures exchange?
3. What determines the size of the margin requirement for a particular futures contract?
4. What is the difference between hedging and speculating?

USES OF THE FINANCIAL FUTURES MARKETS

Financial futures markets have grown rapidly because they provide a way for financial market participants to insulate themselves against changes in interest rates and asset prices. Financial futures can be used to reduce the systematic risk of stock portfolios or to guarantee future returns or costs. In general, financial futures prices move inversely with interest rates and directly with financial asset prices, so the sale of futures can offset asset price risk.

REDUCING SYSTEMATIC RISK IN STOCK PORTFOLIOS

In 1982, **stock-index futures contracts** became available. They derived their value from averaging the prices of a "basket" of underlying stocks that were included in the stock index. The New York Stock Exchange Composite Index includes all stocks listed on the New York Stock Exchange while the S&P 500 Index obtains its value from the 500 stocks included in the Standard & Poor's 500 stock index. The use of stock-index futures has grown rapidly, and they now are among the most actively traded contracts in the U.S. futures markets. There are also stock-index futures (usually traded in foreign markets) that derive their value from foreign stocks. In 2002, futures on individual stocks started to trade in the United States. The primary advantage of stock-index futures contracts is that they let an investor alter the market risk (or systematic risk) intrinsic to his or her portfolio. They can also be tailored to the type of portfolio one holds. People who wish to hedge price movements in stock values in general or in only large stocks may want to use the S&P 500 futures or, possibly, the Dow Jones Index futures, while people who wish to hedge price movements in smaller stocks may wish to use the Russell 2000 index futures.

Systematic risk measures a stock portfolio's tendency to vary relative to the market as a whole. It is measured by calculating a stock's average covariance with the market, or its beta. If the value of a stock or stock portfolio typically moves up or down 1.2 times as much as the general stock market, it is said to have a beta of 1.2. Systematic risk is important because, unlike unsystematic risk (which measures the tendency of a stock's price to change because of factors particular to that specific stock), systematic risk cannot be diversified away. Thus, before the development of stock-index futures, it was difficult for investors to eliminate systematic risk from their portfolios.

Stock-index futures can be used to control the systematic risk in an investor's portfolio. For instance, assume that someone has a portfolio worth $30 million with a beta of 1. On average, therefore, the value of the portfolio will move up and down in step with the stock market as a whole. Further assume that the S&P 500 futures contract is selling at 1,200. Since one S&P 500 futures contract is worth $250 per point, it is worth $300,000 in stocks ($250 × 1,200) when it is priced at 1,200. Thus if the investor sold 100 contracts of the S&P 500 futures short, it would have the same effect as selling $30 million worth of stocks with an average beta of 1 (the beta of the S&P 500 is usually assumed to be 1, because that index is often used as a measure of market price movements). By selling the 100 futures contracts short, the investor would fully offset the systematic risk in his or her portfolio. He or she would be long $30 million worth of stocks with a beta of 1 and short $30 million worth of futures contracts (also with a beta of 1), so the net portfolio beta would be zero.

If the investor's portfolio had a beta of 1.2, he or she could still offset its systematic risk. In that case, however, the investor would sell 120 S&P 500 futures contracts short. The investor would have to sell 20 percent more contracts short because the systematic risk of his or her portfolio would be 20 percent higher than the systematic risk of the futures contract (which means that its value moves up or down by 20 percent more than the market as a whole).

By selling futures contracts short, the investor need no longer fear that the value of his or her stock portfolio would change substantially if stock market prices generally rose or fell. However, one might wonder why the investor would want to sell stock-index futures short, since those short sales would cause losses that would offset part of the gain on the investor's stock portfolio if stock prices rose. For one thing, the investor might believe that the market was likely to fall and thus would want to buy portfolio insurance to protect against a possible market decline. Such insurance has a cost because it reduces investors' potential gains as well as their potential losses.

Stock investors may also desire to eliminate the systematic risk from their portfolios for several reasons unrelated to portfolio insurance. For instance, stock dealers profit by bidding to buy stocks at a lower price than they offer to sell them. However, after buying stocks at their bid price, dealers take the risk that the price of the stocks they own may decline before they can resell them. Thus, dealers may want to reduce the systematic risk of their portfolio by hedging in the futures markets. In addition, investors who believe that they are superior stock pickers may want to profit by finding undervalued stocks while still protecting themselves from general stock market declines. They too might use stock futures to reduce the systematic risk of their portfolio while still allowing them to capture the excess returns (if any) available to people with superior stock-picking abilities. Finally, stock-index futures can be used by people who wish to earn either riskless returns greater than the Treasury bill rate or returns greater than the popular stock indexes.

STOCK-INDEX PROGRAM TRADING

Program trading often has substantial short-term effects on stock market price movements. However, many people who engage in program trading do not want to own stocks per se, but just want to obtain an investment that will generate a higher risk-free rate of return than T-bills. Program traders enter the market when the price of stock-index futures is too far out of line with the prices of the stocks that make up the stock index. For instance, if S&P 500 futures are selling at 1,230 and expire in 3 months, whereas the underlying stocks in the S&P 500 stock index are selling for an equivalent price of 1,200 right now, a person could buy those stocks now, sell futures short, and know that he or she would gain a "riskless" 2.5 percent (1,230/1,200 represents a 2.5 percent gain) in 3 months. The return is guaranteed because the value of the futures must equal the value of the underlying stocks in the stock index when it expires in 3 months. In addition, by owning the stocks for 3 months, the investor might accrue dividends worth an additional 0.5 percent of the stocks' value. Thus, the investor who undertook this arbitrage would earn a "riskless" return of 3.00 percent (2.5 percent in capital gains plus 0.50 percent in dividends) per quarter, or 12 percent per year. If that return exceeded the T-bill rate, the index arbitrage would be a superior "risk-free" investment. As a result, when stock-index futures prices rise too far above stock prices, program traders sell the futures index and quickly buy great amounts of stock that replicate the price movement of the underlying stock index (it takes at least 50 stocks to replicate price movements in the S&P 500). This sudden buying of stocks can drive the stock market up sharply. However, the stock market rises not because the stock buyers want to own stocks, but only because they want to earn a riskless return higher than the T-bill rate.

On the downside, if an investor in stocks wants to earn a return equal to a specific stock index (as many fund managers do), that investor may be able to earn a greater return through index arbitrage. In the previous example, if both stocks and the equivalent stock-index future sold at 1,200, a portfolio manager could buy the futures and sell his or her stocks. The proceeds from the stock sale could be invested in T-bills to earn possibly $1\frac{1}{4}$ percent a quarter. At the end of the quarter, the stock fund would have 101.25 percent of 1,200, or 1.215 dollars for every 1,200 dollars in stocks sold, but because the investor owned a futures contract purchased at a price of 1,200, he or she would be able to reinvest in the same stocks for a net price of 1,200 when the future expired. Even after allowing for a loss of dividends (of $\frac{1}{2}$ percent), the investor would have earned $\frac{3}{4}$ percent more in the

3-month period than would have been possible without entering the index arbitrage. If this could be done every quarter, the fund would outperform the index by 3 percent over the course of a year. Consequently, the fund manager would likely earn a nice bonus for outperforming the stock indexes during the year.

Index arbitrageurs try to profit either by earning a riskless return that is a little greater than the T-bill rate or by selling stocks and investing in T-bills to beat the stock market. To do so, they buy and sell huge quantities of stocks whenever the value of a stock-index futures contract is not equal to the value of its underlying stocks (adjusted for dividend yields and T-bill rate considerations). Through their actions, they provide the socially valuable function of keeping stock-index futures prices in line with the value of underlying stocks. However, when they buy or sell in quantity, they can also cause stock prices to rise or fall sharply in a few minutes.

GUARANTEEING COSTS OF FUNDS

When a corporation plans a major investment, it typically commits itself to major cash outlays for several years in the future. Although a project can be forecast to yield a good return, it might not be profitable if interest rates unexpectedly rise and the corporation has to pay substantially more to borrow needed funds. The corporation can avoid such a risk by borrowing all funds at the time the investment is planned and investing excess funds in short-term securities until they are needed. However, because short-term rates are often lower than long-term rates, it could be costly to borrow long term and invest the temporarily excess money at a lower rate. Thus the corporation may wish to use the futures market to guarantee its future financing costs.

If the corporation usually pays a 2 percent premium over the T-bond rate to borrow, it can use the T-bond market to hedge its cost of funds. Suppose it needs to borrow $10 million now and $10 million in another year. It could sell $10 million in long-term bonds now and simultaneously sell T-bond futures with a market value of $10 million for a delivery 1 year hence. If it continues to pay 2 percent more interest than T-bonds in 1 year, its hedge will allow it to obtain a known interest cost on its future sale of corporate bonds. It would figure its expected interest cost by adding 2 percent (the usual premium it pays over the corporate bond rate) to the yield implied by the T-bond future, which is sold short.

If interest rates rise during the next year, the corporation will have to pay more to borrow. However, if interest rates rise, futures prices will fall. Thus the corporation will have a capital gain on its futures contracts. The capital gain (assuming it is not taxed) can be used to reduce borrowing requirements. By so doing, the corporation's total interest costs can be held to the level previously anticipated. If the corporation had not hedged, the annual interest costs on its debt would have increased in line with the change in market interest rates. However, it should be noted that, by hedging, the corporation will also lose the ability to obtain funding at a lower rate if rates fall because, even though it might sell bonds at a lower rate 1 year hence, it would lose on its sale of the futures contracts—which will rise in price as market interest rates fall.

FUNDING FIXED-RATE LOANS

Bank customers often prefer to borrow on a fixed-rate basis so that they will know their interest costs in advance. The futures market can be used to accommodate such customers. For instance, if a bank customer wants a 1-year loan at a fixed rate, a bank could sell additional certificates of deposit to finance the loan for the first 6 months and, following that, sell Eurodollar futures. Exhibit 11.5 illustrates such a case.

In the exhibit, a bank that traditionally pays 25 basis points more than the Eurodollar rate, which is the interest rate banks pay on dollars outside the United States, uses the Eurodollar futures market to lock in its future cost of funds. It first sells a 6-month CD and then sells consecutive 3-month Eurodollar futures. By

---

EXHIBIT 11.5
Financing a Fixed-Rate Loan of $1 million

I. Bank Funding Plan

- Sell a 6-month $1 million CD at 3.25% for funding January through June.
- Sell a 3-month $1 million Eurodollar future in June at 96.6 (Eurodollar futures are quoted at 100 minus the Eurodollar interest rate, indicating a Eurodollar rate of 3.40%), guaranteeing funding costs of 3.65% (3.40% plus 25 basis points that the bank usually pays on its CDs relative to the Eurodollar rate).
- Sell a 3-month $1 million Eurodollar future in September at 96.4 (a 3.60% rate) to guarantee funding costs of 3.85%.

This gives an average cost of funds per quarter of

$$\frac{3.25\% + 3.25\% + 3.65\% + 3.85\%}{4} = 3.50$$

Adding a 2.75% spread, the bank offers to make a fixed-rate 1-year loan for $1 million at 6.25%.

II. Bank Funding Costs (after the fact)

- First 6 months, 3.25% CD.
- Next 3 months, 3.75% CD (10 basis points more than expected).
- Last 3 months, 4.05% CD (20 basis points more than expected).

Interest costs in the third quarter, then, were $250 ($1,000,000 × 0.10% × $\frac{1}{4}$ year) more than expected. Interest costs in the fourth quarter were $500 ($1,000,000 × 0.20% × $\frac{1}{4}$ year) more than expected. Thus, the total interest expenses were $750 more than expected.

- In June, the bank offsets the short Eurodollar futures position at 96.5, for a gain of 10 basis points, or $250.
- In September, the bank offsets the short Eurodollar futures position at 96.2, for a gain of 20 basis points, or $500.

Total gains on futures transactions, then, were $750, minus commission of less than $100.

III. Net Result

The gain on the futures transactions approximately offset the increased interest costs. Thus, the bank realized its expected spread on the loan even though interest rates rose.

adding its 25-basis-point premium to the rate on the Eurodollar futures, it calculates its average cost of funds for the next year as 3.50 percent. It then adds a suitable spread and makes a 1-year fixed-rate loan at 6.25 percent.

However, interest rates unexpectedly rise, and the bank must pay more interest on its CDs. In fact, its total interest costs rise by roughly $750. This leaves it with an average cost of funds of 3.575 percent, which is higher than expected when the bank made the loan at 6.25 percent. Nonetheless, the bank gains approximately $750 on its short sales of Eurodollar futures contracts. As a result, it can offset its increased interest cost and earn the spread it desired on the fixed-rate loan transaction.

Banks use futures to provide fixed-rate loans to borrowers who are reluctant to pay variable rates on loans. They also can show such customers how they can lock in their costs of funds by borrowing on a variable-rate basis and selling Eurodollar or Treasury bill futures in the forward markets. The latter approach has gained considerable popularity with banks. Consequently, many large banks have established futures-trading subsidiaries, called futures commission merchants (FCMs). FCMs provide brokerage services to customers who wish to guarantee their costs of funds or use futures for other purposes.

HEDGING A BALANCE SHEET

Financial futures can be used to protect a financial institution against interest rate risk. For instance, assume that a thrift institution has $300 million in liabilities, all with maturities of 1 year or less, and $15 million in capital. At the same time, assume that it holds $300 million in fixed-rate mortgages and only $15 million in assets with maturities under 1 year. It will have a negative 1-year GAP (see Chapter 14 for GAP definitions) of $285 million (since its 1-year rate-sensitive assets, $15 million, less its 1-year rate-sensitive liabilities, $300 million, equals –$285 million). Thus it will be highly exposed to loss should interest rates increase. If interest rates do rise, the thrift's revenues on its mortgage portfolio will change very little and, with a higher discount rate, the value of those mortgages will fall. At the same time, its liabilities will mature, and it will find that it will either have to pay more interest to its liability holders or lose its deposits. Thus, its interest costs will rise more than interest revenues (and its asset values fall). Consequently, the thrift will suffer large losses.

However, the thrift can insulate its balance sheet against interest rate risk by using interest rate futures to neutralize its long position in mortgages. In the simplest case, in which all securities are priced at par, the thrift could sell $300 million in U.S. Treasury 10-year note futures to offset the interest rate risk of the $300 million in mortgages held in its portfolio. Then, if interest rates rose and prices changed in a similar manner on both its mortgages and its Treasury securities, it would receive a capital gain on the futures sufficient to offset the loss that it would take because the present value of its fixed-rate mortgages fell as interest rates rose. Its returns on capital then would vary only with the returns on its $15 million in short-term assets. If it wanted its returns on capital to vary with long-term assets, it would hedge only the GAP of $285 million.

PRICE SENSITIVITY RULE OF HEDGING

To hedge properly, an institution must create a futures position that has the same sensitivity to interest rate changes as the asset or portfolio whose value the institution desires to hedge. This requires that the institution create a hedge that follows the *price sensitivity rule:*

$$\Delta P_A/\Delta r_M = N \times \Delta P_F/\Delta r_M, \qquad (11.1)$$

where $\Delta P_A/\Delta r_M$ equals the change in the price of the asset that will occur for a 1 percent change in market interest rates, $\Delta P_F/\Delta r_M$ equals the change in the price of the futures contract that will occur for a 1 percent change in market interest rates, and N equals the number of futures contracts purchased to create the hedge. If the price sensitivity rule is followed, the change in the price of the asset that occurs when market interest rates change will be exactly offset by an (inverse) change in the value of the futures position, thereby leaving the hedging institution's total portfolio value unchanged.

Complicating matters is the fact that slope of the term structure of interest rates can change as well as the level of interest rates. Usually, for example, when interest rates rise, short-term interest rates tend to increase more than long-term rates. Thus, the hedging firm might want to try to match the durations of the hedged asset and the futures contract fairly closely. That is why the thrift that wished to hedge a fixed-rate mortgage portfolio would probably use long-term futures contracts, such as 10-year Treasury note futures, to hedge. However, an institution that wanted to hedge short-term costs of funds would be likely to use Treasury bill or Eurodollar futures contracts.

INCOME VERSUS NET WORTH HEDGING

Entire balance sheets can be hedged by following a basic "duration rule." The duration rule notes that an institution can calculate a duration gap (D_G) by comparing the market value and interest rate sensitivity of its assets to the market value and interest rate sensitivity of its liabilities. Assuming that interest rates applicable to liabilities and assets change equally when market interest rates change, the duration gap, D_G, can be expressed as follows:

$$D_G = MV_A \times D_A - MV_L \times D_L + MV_F \times D_F, \qquad (11.2)$$

where
  MV_A = the market value of an institution's assets
  MV_L = the market value of its liabilities
  MV_F = the market value of futures contracts purchased (this value will be negative if futures are sold)
  D_A = the duration of its assets
  D_L = the duration of its liabilities
  D_F = the average duration (rate sensitivity) of futures contracts purchased (or sold)

An institution can calculate its duration gap on the assumption that it buys or sells no futures (that is, $MV_F = 0$). After calculating its portfolio duration on the assumption that no futures are owned (or $MV_F = 0$), the institution then can buy or sell futures contracts with appropriate durations to immunize its portfolio against interest rate changes. In general, an institution that has a positive futures-free duration GAP (because the market value–weighted duration of its assets is greater than the market value–weighted duration of its liabilities) will want to sell futures market instruments to immunize its balance sheet. An institution that has a negative futures-free duration GAP (because it has assets with a much lower duration than its liabilities) will want to buy futures market instruments in order to immunize. In general, the institution will be fully immunized when its duration GAP equals zero.

Before planning its immunization strategy, however, an institution must decide whether it wishes to immunize its earnings or the market value of its net worth against rate risk because it cannot immunize both at once. For instance, assume an institution immunizes its earnings so that they remain unchanged as interest rates vary. If interest rates rise, the discounted present value of the (constant) future earnings stream will fall. Thus, the net worth of the institution will also fall. Consequently, a financial institution with immunized earnings will find that the present value of its earnings will vary inversely with interest rates.

To immunize its net worth against changes in interest rates, an institution's earnings would have to rise or fall in step with interest rates. Typically, since most institutions have more assets than liabilities, this can be done if the institution is somewhat "asset sensitive," with more short-maturity assets than liabilities. Then, if all interest rates rise, its earnings will also rise. If the institution is properly immunized, the discounted value of its new (increased) earnings flow will be the same before and after interest rates rise; if so, its net worth will be immunized against changes in rates.

RISKS IN THE FUTURES MARKETS

The previous illustrations have all been constructed so that investment in futures will prove to be profitable. However, there are substantial risks in the futures markets, some of which we shall now discuss.

BASIS RISK

Basis risk exists because the value of an item being hedged may not always keep the same price relationship to contracts purchased or sold in the futures markets. For instance, in the corporate financing example, the corporation might find that its cost of borrowing was 250 basis points above the Treasury bond rate after 1 year. As a result, a futures hedge would only partially offset its increase in interest costs. The same would be true in the bank cost-of-funds example (Exhibit 11.5) if the bank had to pay 50 basis points more, rather than 25 basis points more than the Eurodollar rate in the futures markets when it issued its CDs.

Frequently, basis risk is the result of **cross-hedging**. Cross-hedging is hedging with a traded futures contract whose characteristics do not exactly match those of the hedger's risk exposure. For instance, an S&L that wishes to hedge its assets for more than 1 year may wish to hedge in the Treasury note rather than the mortgage-backed security futures market, because trading in distant futures contracts is more active in the former. However, mortgage rates and Treasury note rates, although closely related, do not always move together. As the spread between the rates changes, so does the basis risk. In general, cross-hedges have more basis risk than hedges involving a precise match between the futures contract and the underlying risk exposure.

RELATED-CONTRACT RISK

Hedges can also fail because of a defect in the contract being hedged. In the bank cost-of-funds example, interest rates conceivably could fall (thereby causing a loss on the short sale of the Eurodollar contracts) and the borrower could prepay the loan. Although commercial loan contracts ordinarily do not allow for prepayments, consumer borrowers frequently prepay their debts. Thus, the bank would lose on the futures contract and would not be receiving compensatory loan revenues.

MANIPULATION RISK

The commodity markets are federally regulated because there have been instances of manipulation in the past. Most manipulations involve **short squeezes**, whereby an individual or group tries to make it difficult or impossible for short sellers in the futures markets to liquidate their contracts through delivery of acceptable commodities. Then the "shorts" will have to buy their contracts back at inflated prices.

Manipulations can take many forms and are hard to predict. In the early 1970s, a strike at grain elevators in Chicago made it impossible to deliver corn to the elevators as called for by the Chicago Board of Trade's corn contract. As a result, futures prices shot upward even though there was a bumper harvest and cash corn prices were low. In another instance, federal regulation of the pork belly market was initiated after a consortium of buyers executed a short squeeze that caused many public losses. In 1977, the activities of the Hunt family of Texas, who, because of their immense wealth, held contracts for more deliverable bushels of soybeans than were readily available in Chicago, caused a short squeeze in soybeans. Then, in 1980 and 1981, the Hunts attempted to squeeze the silver market. Their activities created a short panic that sent the silver price over $50 per ounce before it collapsed following changes in exchange rules.

Because manipulations cannot be foreseen and because they cause large price movements, they add an element of risk to trading in some futures contracts. However, futures that use cash settlement procedures, such as Eurodollar or stock-index futures that allow cash instead of an underlying asset to be delivered at expiration, are safe from short squeezes. With cash settlement, futures prices at expiration are simply marked to market to reflect the value of the underlying assets at the designated settlement time. Thus, such contracts are safe from potential short squeezes because holders of short futures positions do not need to obtain physical commodities (which may be hard to obtain) to deliver to satisfy their open futures contracts' requirements on delivery day.

MARGIN RISK

An individual with illiquid assets can also encounter difficulty by hedging in the futures markets if the futures price moves adversely and the individual must constantly post more maintenance margin funds. This could cause a cash shortage that might force him to liquidate his futures contracts at a loss before the illiquid asset matured.

The fact that maintenance margin requirements rise when futures prices move adversely should be taken into account lest they cause an unexpected cash squeeze. Forward contracts are sometimes preferred to futures contracts because they do not cause maintenance margin problems.

DO YOU UNDERSTAND?

1. Suppose you own a portfolio of stocks currently worth $100,000. The portfolio has a beta of 1.2. Describe in detail the futures transaction you would undertake to hedge the value of your portfolio. Which futures contract would you use? How many contracts would you buy or sell?

2. Suppose your desired holding period is 5 years, but you find yourself with a bond portfolio having a duration of 7 years. Describe the futures transaction you would undertake to hedge the value of your portfolio at the end of 5 years. What futures contract would you use? Would you buy or sell these futures contracts to shorten the duration of your bond portfolio?

3. Why does cross-hedging lead to basis risk?

OPTIONS MARKETS

One drawback of hedging with futures is that the hedging process can totally insulate a firm against price changes. Not only will it reduce the firm's losses if prices move adversely, but it also will eliminate potential gains if prices move favorably. Because hedging with futures eliminates gains as well as losses, some people prefer to use options rather than futures contracts to ensure themselves against various risks. Options have been available on stocks for many years, and they have been traded on organized exchanges since 1973. Options have been available in the United States on financial futures contracts only since October 1982.

THE NATURE OF OPTIONS

Options allow people to enter into contracts to buy or sell stocks, commodities, or other securities at a predetermined price, called the **strike** or **exercise price**, until some future time. Unlike futures contracts in which both the long and the short position have obligations, an option buyer has a right but not an obligation, while the option seller has an obligation if the long position exercises the option. Obviously, the option seller will not agree to such an arrangement unless he or she is compensated. We call the price that an option buyer pays the option seller an **option premium**. In addition, an option is only good for a limited time. With an **American option**, the option can be exercised at any time prior to and including the expiration date. With an **European option**, the option can be exercised only on the expiration date.

An option provides the buyer with a one-sided choice. If price movements are advantageous, the buyer exercises the option and realizes a gain. If price movements are harmful, the buyer can limit potential losses by letting the option expire unexercised. Because of this feature, options can provide their buyers with insurance against adverse price moves. If the price move is adverse, the buyer loses only the premium paid to buy the option. If the price move is favorable, however, the buyer can exercise the option and realize a gain. The option premium is the price of this insurance.

Calls and Puts. There are two types of options—calls and puts. **Call options** give the buyer the right to buy a security or futures contract at the strike price. **Put options** give the option buyer the right to sell a security or futures contract at the strike price. The writer of a call agrees to sell the security (or futures contract) at the strike price if the buyer exercises the option; the writer of a put agrees to buy the security (or futures contract) for the strike price if the buyer exercises the option.

Exhibit 11.6 shows a few of the listed quotations for options on individual stocks. Individual options trade up to 9 months in advance of expiration; leap options trade up to several years in advance. Under each option name, the first column below the stock's name is the strike price of the option. The second col-

---

EXHIBIT 11.6
Sample Listed Stock Option Quotations (July 16, 2004)

Listed Stock Options

Option/Strike	Exp.	Call Vol.	Last	Put Vol.	Last
Gen El				Underlying Stock Price: $33.09	
30	Sep	392	3.30	44	0.20
32.50	Sep	1705	1.30	1319	C.70
32.50	Dec	57	2.05	202	1.40
35	Sep	1648	0.40	33	2.00
35	Dec	1528	0.85	81	2.75
HewlettPk				Underlying Stock Price: $19.64	
17.50	Nov	5	2.85	21	0.50
20	Aug	308	0.55	1070	0.85
20	Feb	2	1.65	21	1.85
22.50	Aug	35	0.10	473	2.85
25	Aug	8	0.05	4	5.11
Microsft				Underlying Stock Price: $27.48	
20	Jan	5	8.10	734	0.20
22.50	Oct	330	5.50	24	0.15
25	Aug	1418	2.70	3250	0.20
25	Jan	142	3.40	368	0.85
32.50	Oct	1055	0.15	37	5.20
32.50	Jan	816	0.40	391	5.40

(table continues)

EXHIBIT 11.6
Sample Listed Stock Option Quotations (July 16, 2004) *(continued)*

LEAPS

Option/Strike	Exp.	Vol.	Call Last	Put Vol.	Last
BankAm				Underlying Stock Price: $84.47	
60	Jan 06	...	...	130	1.75
90	Jan 06	55	4.6	...	...
Calpine				Underlying Stock Price: $4.34	
2.50	Jan 06	...	...	85	0.60
5	Jan 06	50	1.05	1511	2.00
7.50	Jan 07	45	0.85	...	...
Cendant				Underlying Stock Price: $23.84	
25	Jan 06	92	2.90	16	3.30
Cisco				Underlying Stock Price: $21.53	
20	Jan 06	111	4.80	3	2.15
40	Jan 06	246	0.25	...	...
eBayInc				Underlying Stock Price: $80.36	
65	Jan 06	18	24.80	265	6.70
80	Jan 06	29	15.80	32	13.00
100	Jan 06	20	8.30	9	24.90
Yahoo				Underlying Stock Price: $29.19	
20	Jan 06	36	11.80	510	1.80
25	Jan 07	724	10.90	21	4.40

Quotes are for the close of trading July 16, 2004. Dots occur for options that did not trade on the indicated day.

Source: Wall Street Journal Online, July 19, 2004.

umn shows the expiration month (the third Friday of the expiration month will be the last trading day). Call trading volumes are listed next, followed by the closing price of the call with the indicated strike price and expiration month. The last two columns then show the trading volume and closing price for puts with the same strike price and expiration month. For example, Exhibit 11.6 shows us that on July 16, 2004, an investor could have purchased on August 2004 call option on Hewlett Packard stock with a strike price of $20 for a premium of $55 ($0.55 per share) for a 100-share option when Hewlett Packard was trading at $19.64.

Option Exercise.   Since the Hewlett Packard option is an American option, the buyer can exercise the call at any time up to, and including, the third Friday in August and buy 100 shares of Hewlett Packard stock for a price of $2,000 ($20 per share). Clearly the option would be highly valuable if Hewlett Packard's price rose to $25 per share before the third Friday in August because the option could be exercised and the stock could quickly be sold for a profit.

Stock options like the Hewlett Packard option are exchanged for stock, for which the exercise price is paid, when they are exercised. However, there are options that trade on a wide variety of financial instruments and indexes, including stocks, stock indexes, stock-index futures, interest rate futures, currencies, and commodity futures. Options on indexes are usually cash settled, meaning that the value of the contract, rather than an asset, is exchanged between the buyer and the seller when the option is exercised. For example, options on the NASDAQ 100 index, which are traded on the Chicago Board of Trade, are cash settled at $100 times the difference between the exercise price and the value of the index at expiration. If an investor owns a call option on the NASDAQ 100 index with a strike price of $1,410 when the index is 1,420, the option would cash settle for $1,000 (10 × $100).

Futures options exercise into a futures position. For example, when a call option is exercised on the S&P 500 future, the owner surrenders the option and obtains a long position in the futures contract at the strike price. For instance, if the futures contract is trading at 1,250 when the owner of a 1,200 call exercises his or her option, in exchange for the option, he or she will receive a futures contract with a cost basis of 1,200. Since S&P 500 futures are based on $250 per index point, his or her account will immediately be credited with a mark-to-market gain of $12,500 (50 times $250 per point gained). The gain might be nearly enough to meet his or her margin requirement and can be withdrawn immediately if the futures position is offset (sold) at a price of 1,250. If a put option is exercised on a futures contract, the option owner surrenders the option and obtains a short position in the futures contract at the strike price. Thus, if the futures price is at 1,180 and a put is exercised with a strike price of 1,200, the owner will have a potential gain of $5,000 (20 times $250 per point) if the futures contract is bought back at 1,180.

Gains and Losses. Potential gains and losses are quite different for buyers and writers of puts and calls. They also differ for options and futures contracts. Exhibit 11.7 illustrates this. Frame A shows how gains and losses vary as the underlying security price changes for the buyer and the writer of a call option on a security with a strike price of $40 and a premium of $5 if the option is exercised on expiration day. The call buyer's potential gain is unlimited and the writer's potential loss is unlimited if the security price rises. Meanwhile, if the security price falls, the buyer's maximum loss is limited to the premium paid for the option, whereas the call option writer's maximum gain is limited to the premium paid for the option. Put options are similar, as shown in Frame B, except that the put buyer gains when the security price declines and the put buyer loses the amount of the premium if the security price rises. In contrast with options, buyers and sellers of futures gain and lose symmetrically and without limits as futures prices vary. This is illustrated in Frame C.

Covered and Naked Options. Because the option writer's maximum loss is virtually unlimited, many option writers write **covered options** wherein they already own the security that they have agreed to sell or have already sold short the security that they have agreed to buy. Option writers may also write **naked**

EXHIBIT 11.7
Gains and Losses on Options and Futures Contracts, if Options Are Exercised at Expiration

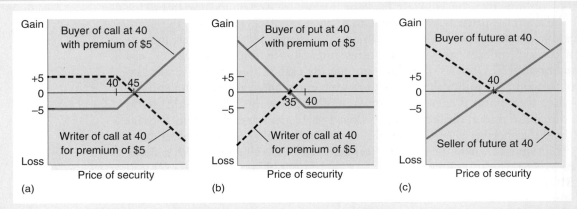

(a)   (b)   (c)

In all of these examples, the gain to the buyer of an option or future equals a loss to the seller (or writer) of the contract, and vice versa. Note that in Frame A, the buyer of a call exercisable at 40 breaks even on the call but loses the $5 premium if the underlying stock is at 40 when the call expires. If the stock is at 45, the $5 gain on the call exactly offsets the $5 premium; thus the net gain is zero. Above 45, the buyer of the call gains, and the writer of the call loses more than the premium and ends up with a loss. In Frame B, puts pay off at expiration in a way that is opposite to calls. Futures, however, have no premium and provide symmetric gains and losses, as shown in Frame C.

(that is, uncovered) **options.** In this case, they need not own an offsetting security position. However, writers of naked options typically must deposit margin requirements with the exchange to guarantee that they will honor their commitments. If the underlying security price moves adversely, writers of naked options have to deposit additional money to maintain their margin requirements.

The Value of Options.   The option premium varies positively with (1) the price variance of the underlying commodity or security, (2) the time to the option's expiration, and (3) the level of interest rates. Its value also varies with changes in the price of the underlying asset relative to the option's exercise price and, for options based on stocks, with the dividends of the underlying stocks. The more price variability a stock has, the greater the chance that the buyer can exercise the option for a larger profit. However, the buyer will never exercise the option and take a loss. Thus, options with greater price variance tend to have higher premiums. Similarly, given a longer period of time, bigger cumulative price changes can be expected. Thus, options have greater value when they have a longer time to expiration.

Because the purchase of an option allows the buyer to conserve capital until the option is actually exercised and the underlying stock or commodity is purchased, call options on stocks have a higher value when interest rates are high. If a buyer purchases a call option instead of a stock and then invests the money saved, the buyer still shares in the price appreciation of the stock but earns more on the invested funds when interest rates are high. Thus, buyers are willing to pay more for options when interest rates are high, particularly if the option has a long time to maturity. In addition, as can be seen by analyzing Exhibit 11.7, a call on a stock will be more valuable when its strike price is lower relative to the stock's value. Conversely, a put option will be more valuable when its exercise price is higher relative to the stock's value. Finally, since stock options are not protected against dividend payouts, call options will lose value (and put options will gain value) when a company distributes some of its assets as dividends to shareholders and thereby reduces its stock's price.

The value of an option changes over time in a systematic manner, as shown in Exhibit 11.8, which applies to a call option with a stock price of 100. As shown in line A, just before expiration, the value of a call is equal to its **intrinsic value**, or the value that could be realized by exercising the option immediately. A call option's intrinsic value is equal either to the value of the underlying asset minus the exercise price or to zero (whichever is greater). However, before expiration an option will have an additional time value as shown in line B. The time value of an option usually is positive prior to expiration. Even if the option has an intrinsic value of zero (as it does in Exhibit 11.8 when the stock price is 90 and the exercise price is 90 or 100), as long as the underlying asset is sufficiently volatile and there is enough time left until expiration, the option will have a chance of becoming valuable before it expires. The time value of an option reflects this chance. Because the chances that an option will become valuable before expiration are

EXHIBIT 11.8
Value of a Call Option

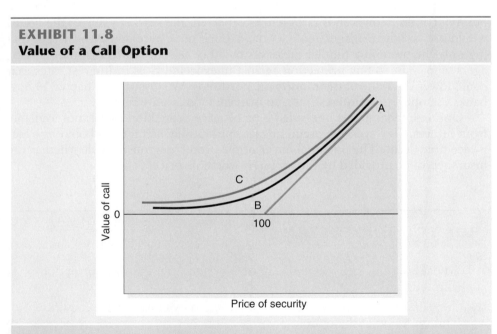

Options have a time premium that exceeds their intrinsic value by a greater amount as the volatility of the underlying security or the time to expiration increases. As an option approaches expiration, its value will experience time decay until it is worth only its intrinsic value.

A – value at expiration (intrinsic value)

B – value shortly before expiration

C – value substantially before expiration

greater the longer the time to expiration, the option value will be higher if there is a longer time to expiration or the stock is more volatile (see line C). Conversely, because there is less chance that the option can still become valuable as expiration approaches, the option value will experience "time decay" and lose value as expiration approaches, shifting from line C to line B. Finally, when the option is due to expire, it will retain only its intrinsic value, as shown by line A.

OPTIONS VERSUS FUTURES

The gains and losses to buyers and sellers of futures contracts are quite different from those for buyers and sellers of option contracts (see Exhibit 11.7). For futures, both gains and losses can vary virtually without limit. Therefore some buyers (or sellers) prefer options to futures contracts. For instance, suppose a portfolio manager thinks that interest rates will decline but is not sure. To take advantage of the rate decline, the manager might want to buy many long-term bonds that would increase in value as rates fell. However, if rates rose, the bond would lose value and the manager might lose his or her job. If the manager hedged in the futures market by selling T-bond futures, he or she would be safe if rates rose, because the loss on the bonds in the portfolio would be offset by the gain on the short sale of the T-bond futures. However, if rates fell, the loss on the T-bond futures would eliminate the gain in value of the bonds in the portfolio. Consequently, the portfolio manager might prefer to buy a T-bond put option. If T-bond prices fell, the put option would rise in value and offset the loss on the bond portfolio. However, if rates fell, as expected, the market value of the bonds would rise and the manager could let the T-bond put expire unused—thereby losing only the premium. Similar measures could be used by thrift institution managers who want to buy protection against unexpected rises in interest rates that could lower the value of their mortgage portfolios. We discuss in Chapter 14 how banks use options on interest rates to manage interest rate risk.

Options, then, give a one-sided type of price protection that is not available from futures. However, the premiums on options may be high, and options experience time decay. The potential buyer of the protection must decide whether the insurance value provided by the option is worth its price.

DO YOU UNDERSTAND?

1. What are some considerations in the decision to use futures or options for hedging?
2. Explain the relationship between the time to expiration for a call option and the value of the option.
3. Explain the relationship between the price variance of an asset and the value of an option written on that asset.
4. If you hold some shares of stock and would like to protect yourself from a price decline, without giving up a lot of upside potential, should you purchase call options or put options? Explain.

THE CFTC

REGULATION
OF THE
FUTURES
AND
OPTIONS
MARKETS

The primary regulator of the futures markets is the Commodity Futures Trading Commission (CFTC), a five-member federal commission whose members are appointed to staggered 5-year terms by the president with the consent of the Senate. The CFTC was formed in 1974 to centralize government regulation of the futures markets. Although the federal government had regulated some futures markets as far back as the 1920s, not all futures markets were subject to consistent scrutiny.

The CFTC monitors futures trading to detect actual or potential manipulation, congestion, and price distortion. It reviews proposed contracts to see if they have an economic purpose and analyzes the terms of proposed trading contracts to ensure that they meet commercial needs and serve the public interest. It also monitors enforcement of exchange rules, registers industry professionals, and audits brokerage houses and clearing associations. Finally, it investigates alleged violations of CFTC regulations and the Commodity Exchange Act and refers apparent violations of federal laws to the Justice Department for prosecution.

The extensive enforcement responsibilities of the CFTC suggest that a major purpose of the commission is to prevent abuse of the public through misrepresentation or market manipulation. In the past, such abuses occurred with some frequency. Because of the low margin requirements relative to the value of futures contracts, it is possible for large amounts of money to be made (or lost) with only small price movements. In addition, the zero-sum nature of the commodity markets means that, unlike the stock market, if one person gains, another loses. Thus wild trading activities sometimes occur in the futures markets, and it is the CFTC's job to ensure that the public will not be harmed by violations of exchange rules or federal laws.

THE SEC

The Securities and Exchange Commission (SEC) regulates options markets that have equity securities as underlying assets. Thus, the SEC regulates all individual stock options traded on the Chicago Board Options Exchange as well as all **stock-index options**, which are based on the value of an underlying index of stocks. The CFTC, however, regulates all options that are settled with the delivery of a futures contract, even if that contract will eventually be settled based on the value of an index of stocks. For instance, the CFTC regulates the S&P 500 options contracts traded on the Chicago Mercantile Exchange (CME) because those options involve the purchase or sale of futures contracts for the S&P 500 stock index. In contrast, the SEC regulates the S&P 500 index options contracts traded on the Chicago Board Options Exchange (CBOE) because those options involve immediate payments based on the current value of the underlying stocks in the S&P 500 index. However, the SEC and CFTC jointly regulate individual stock futures and narrowly based stock-index futures.

The confusing state of regulation for stock-index products has caused turf wars between the SEC and CFTC, particularly after the October 1987 stock market crash, when the SEC maintained that it should be the sole regulator of stocks and all contracts that derived their value from stock price movements. Congress did not go along with the SEC proposal, however, and the CFTC remains the sole regulator of broad-based stock-index futures contracts.

EXCHANGE REGULATION

The commodity exchanges also impose many rules on their members. The rules are designed to ensure that members keep proper accounts, maintain sufficient funds on deposit with the exchange clearinghouse, and do not engage in practices that could affect the ability of the exchange to honor its contracts or otherwise endanger the financial solvency of the exchange. In addition, exchange rules determine trading procedures, contract terms, maximum daily price movements for commodities, margin requirements, and position limits. Position limits impose maximum contract holdings for any one speculator and are designed to prevent manipulation of the futures markets.

Because the commodity exchanges have numerous rules designed to regulate trading behavior, they argue that federal regulation of futures market activities is unnecessary. The counterargument is that the exchanges are organized to serve the purposes of their members, not the public. If push comes to shove, the public may lose.

The exchanges' laxity in enforcing rules was illustrated in early 1989, when an FBI sting operation found that many exchange rules had been violated over a long period of time. As a result, many exchange members and traders were subpoenaed and numerous changes in futures market regulation and monitoring systems were proposed. Subsequently, the exchanges adapted their computer systems to be able to determine more quickly and effectively when all transactions occur and to prevent prearranged trades from taking place.

SWAP MARKETS

In the last 25 years a new form of financial transaction has developed called a **swap**. In a swap contract two parties agree to exchange payment obligations on two underlying financial liabilities that are equal in principal amount but differ in payment patterns. A swap works much like a forward contract in that it guarantees the exchange of two items of value between counterparties at some time (or at several times) in the future. However, unlike the forward market, a swap for only a *net* transfer of funds is usually arranged. For instance, if the first party to a swap owes the second party 9 percent interest on a **notional principal** of $1 million and the other party owes the first party 8 percent interest on the same notional principal, they need only exchange the difference, or $10,000 per year, to settle the annual interest difference due on the $1 million swap. The principal amount is notional (or fictional) in that the $1 million is never actually transferred between counterparties; it serves only as the basis for calculating the swapped interest payments. Also, unlike a forward contract, the exact terms of trade are usually not prespecified, but rather they typically vary with interest rates, exchange rates, or some other future price. For instance, one party may pay a 9 percent fixed-interest rate on the notional principal while the other may pay 2 percent over the T-bill rate, which would be 8 percent if the T-bill rate were 6 percent, but could vary over time.

Swaps are frequently used to offset interest rate risk by exchanging fixed-interest-rate payments for variable-interest-rate payments. Such swaps may also be used to take advantage of credit risk premium differences for different maturities of securities (i.e., the differences in yield between the debt of an Aaa firm and that of a Baa firm are likely to be much greater for long-term bonds than for commercial paper issues—but rate differences may reflect the fact that the Baa firm may have financial troubles in the future, so such credit-risk-differential swaps can be risky). In addition, swaps may also be used to offset the risk of future foreign currency flows (such as the income that a firm expects to receive from a foreign subsidiary or foreign investment) or the risk that foreign interest rates may move differently from domestic interest rates.

There is some theoretical debate as to why swap opportunities exist. It may be that some institutions have information-cost, transaction-cost, or location advantages in raising or lending funds in certain sectors of the credit markets; however, the sectors that each serves may not be well matched internally. For instance, saving associations typically have a branch structure and deposit production process that allows them to attract relatively short-term deposits at relatively low interest rates. Many savings associations specialize as mortgage lenders because they know both their depositors and their local mortgage markets well. However, if an S&L makes fixed-rate mortgages, its revenues will be stable even if interest rates rise. Also, if interest rates rise, the S&L has to pay more to obtain and retain its short-term deposits; thus, its profits will suffer and it will be exposed to interest rate risk when it strictly pursues its usual lines of business. As a result, a savings association frequently can benefit from swap transactions, particularly if it can find a counterparty with opposite interest-rate-risk problems.

For example, assume that a commercial bank was able to sell $50 million more in long-term (10 years) IRA (individual retirement account) certificates of deposit paying 8 percent interest than it could profitably lend out to long-term borrowers since most bank assets (such as commercial loans and T-bills) are short term. Unless the bank could invest $50 million more in long-term assets, it would probably acquire $50 million more in short-term assets. However, this would increase the GAP between its short-term assets and short-term liabilities by $50 million. As a result, it would be exposed to interest rate risk. Consequently, if market rates fell, it would earn lower rates on its short-term assets and might not be able to afford the fixed rate of interest it had agreed to pay to its IRA depositors for the next 10 years.

The bank can offset its potential interest rate risk, however, by entering into a swap with an institution that has too many long-term assets, such as our mortgage-oriented savings association. Thus, let us assume that the bank enters into a swap agreement in which it arranges to make short-term interest payments at a rate equal to LIBOR (the London Interbank Offering Rate) minus $1/8$ percent in exchange for a fixed-interest return of $8^3/_4$ percent for 10 years on a notional principal of $50 million. The savings bank, in turn, offers to pay a fixed rate of $8^3/_4$ percent for 10 years in return for a variable rate of return equal to LIBOR minus $1/8$ percent on $50 million. The swap is diagrammed in Exhibit 11.9.

The swap can be advantageous to both parties. For instance, a bank with good credit can usually borrow funds at the LIBOR rate, so it will earn a $1/8$ percent profit on its short-term funding of the $50 million (because it pays the S&L 44 $1/8$ percent less than LIBOR). In addition, it will earn a $3/_4$ percent spread (an 8 $3/_4$ percent fixed return less the 8 percent interest cost) on its long-term IRA deposits. The savings association, in turn, is likely to have a portfolio of mortgages on which it earns 9 $3/_4$ percent, so it can make a sure profit by agreeing to make 8 $3/_4$ percent interest payments for 10 years. Furthermore, because savings banks can usually pay as much as 1 percent less than LIBOR to their retail depositors, the savings bank can be assured that it will generally be able to add to its profits by issuing short-term retail deposits to fund its LIBOR minus $1/8$ percent interest

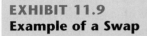

EXHIBIT 11.9
Example of a Swap

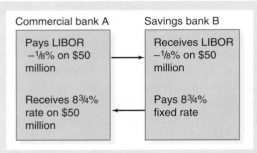

The savings bank is obligated to pay $8^3/_4$% of $50 million, or $4.375 million per year in interest less the amount of interest owed it by the bank. If LIBOR – $^1/_8$% equals $8^3/_4$%, no net interest payment is required. However, if LIBOR averages $9^7/_8$%, the commercial bank must pay the savings bank 1% of $50 million, or $0.50 million. Conversely, if LIBOR rates average $6^7/_8$% throughout the year, the savings bank must pay the net difference of $(8^3/_4\% - 6^7/_8\% + ^1/_8\%) \times$ $50 million, or $1 million to the commercial bank in that year.

rate obligation. The key to making the swap work is that the savings bank has a relative cost advantage in issuing short-term deposits and making long-term mortgage loans, while the commercial bank has a cost advantage in making short-term commercial loans and, temporarily, in issuing long-term IRA deposits.

The risks involved in a swap are not great. Since only the net difference in interest payments is exchanged, if one party defaults, the potential loss is just a small rate difference, not the entire notional principal. However, credit risk does exist, and defaults are more likely when the rate movement is disadvantageous to the defaulting party.

Because credit evaluation of potential counterparties is required to reduce the risks of swaps, and also because it is difficult for individual parties to agree on the exact amount, timing, and rate-determination characteristics of swaps, an extensive dealer market has developed in swaps. Commercial banks are among the most active participants in the swaps market, accompanied by investment banks and, to some degree, foreign exchange dealers. By the start of 2004, the swaps market exceeded $140 trillion in notional principal.

SWAP DEALERS

Because it takes specialized skill to assess credit risk and because individual institutions' needs in a swap transaction are usually not perfectly matched with respect to desired maturities, rate indexes on which floating rates are based, or payment timing, swap dealers who serve as counterparties to both sides of swap transactions have emerged. Commercial banks play a major role as swap dealers because of their easy access to money markets and foreign currency markets and their ability to assess credit risks. Investment banks also have the requisite skills and market access to serve as swap dealers.

Each dealer in the swaps market runs a "book" of swaps for which it serves as a counterparty. The dealer tries to keep its "book" as closely matched as possible with respect to short-term or long-term interest rate exposures, foreign currency exposures, or floating-rate-index exposures. If its book is temporarily mismatched, the dealer will usually try to hedge any residual exposure in the financial futures or options markets.

Swap dealers take some risk running their book because they may not be able to match it perfectly or because they may experience the unexpected default of a counterparty at a time when it is expensive to replicate that counterparty's position at low cost. Because of their risks and the fact that they provide a service by matching counterparties' needs, swap dealers usually charge a fee equal to 5 to 10 basis points (0.05 percent to 0.10 percent) of the notional principal of a swap.

SWAP MARKETS REGULATION

Swap markets, in general, are subject to very little regulation. There is no central clearinghouse for swaps and no central regulatory agency. Nonetheless, while default risks on a swap are low because only one side has an incentive for default at one time, and the risk of loss is limited to the price that must be paid to rehedge the swap at current market interest rates, bank regulators are concerned with the risks banks take when acting as counterparties to a swap. Commercial banks, therefore, must apply risk-based capital requirements to swap-risk exposures. Because most swaps are short term and deal in low-risk assets, the risk-based capital requirements are typically low. Nonetheless, since investment banks and insurance companies, which also deal in the swap market, are not subject to bank risk-based capital requirements, commercial banks often claim that their risk-based capital requirements put them at a disadvantage in pricing swaps. Still, in spite of their capital requirements, because of their easy access to money and foreign currency markets and their expertise in evaluating credit risk, commercial banks still retain a dominant role in the swap dealer markets.

Regulators are probably correct to require that institutions provide capital to hedge against potential swap defaults. If defaults do occur, they are likely to occur in a crisis, when many defaults occur on one side of the dealer's book. However, in ordinary circumstances, defaults are not likely to be frequent. Consequently, it is difficult to ascertain just what level of capital must be maintained to protect against possible losses on swaps.

CHAPTER TAKE-AWAYS

1 Forward contracts and futures contracts are agreements between two parties to exchange a specified amount of an asset for a predetermined price at a predetermined point in time in the future. An option contract grants the option buyer the right to buy (call) or sell (put) a specified amount of an asset for a specified price for a specified period of time. A swap contract involves two parties exchanging periodic payments for a predetermined length of time.

2 Derivatives markets allow people to guarantee the price of future transactions with greater certainty. They can be used either by hedgers, to reduce risk, or by speculators, who assume risk in hopes of earning a return.

3 Regulated futures and options markets differ from forward and swaps markets in that they involve the trading of standardized contracts on organized exchanges by people who typically don't know who has taken the opposite side of their transactions and look only to the exchange to guarantee their contracts.

4 Basis risk, related-contract risk, and manipulation risk may all affect the returns to hedging with standardized exchange-listed contracts. Counterparty default risk must be guarded against in over-the-counter forward, swaps, and options markets.

5 Options markets provide an opportunity for one-sided returns in exchange for the payment of a "premium" to the seller of the option. The premium is much like an insurance premium. Call option premiums increase with uncertainty, interest rates, and the time to maturity of each option. Option prices also increase as an option becomes more in-the-money, which means that the intrinsic value is greater than zero.

6 Swaps markets involve two parties agreeing to exchange payment obligations. Swap terms may vary with future foreign or domestic interest rates or foreign exchange rates. Because of their great flexibility in transferring interest rate or currency risk, swaps markets have grown explosively since 1982.

KEY TERMS

Forward contract	Marking-to-market	Stock-index futures contracts	Call option
Forward price	Margin	Basis risk	Put option
Spot price	Open interest	Cross-hedging	Covered option
Long position	Initial margin	Short squeeze	Naked option
Short position	Maintenance margin	Option	Intrinsic value
Settlement date	Margin call	Strike (or exercise) price	Stock-index options
Counterparty	Hedgers	Option premium	Swap
Spot market	Speculators	American option	Notional principal
Futures contract	Spread (or straddle)	European option	
Futures exchange	Traders		

QUESTIONS AND PROBLEMS

1. What are the differences between futures and forward markets? What are the pros and cons associated with using each one?

2. What role does the exchange play in futures market transactions?

3. How can a thrift institution guarantee its costs of funds for a period of time by using the futures markets?

4. Why do you think some futures contracts are more widely traded than others?

5. What agency is the chief regulator of futures markets? Why is federal regulation necessary?

6. Explain the difference between a put and a call. Draw a diagram showing the payoffs of puts and calls at expiration. Draw it from the perspective of both the option buyer and seller.

7. Why do you think exchanges are more concerned with writers of naked options than with writers of covered options?

8. Explain the difference in the gain and loss potential of a call option and a long futures position. Under what circumstances do you think someone would prefer the option to the future or vice versa?

9. Futures contracts on stock indexes are very popular. Why do you think that is so? How do you think they might be used?

10. Which do you think has more default risk, a futures contract or a swap contract? Why?

11. Assume that in March a farmer and a baker enter into a forward contract on 1,000 bushels of wheat at a price of $3.00 per bushel for delivery in September. In

September the spot price of wheat is $2.50 per bushel. Who has profited from entering into the forward contract and who has lost? How much is the gain and how much is the loss?

12. Assume the initial margin on a Eurodollar futures contract is $750 and the maintenance margin is $500. If the contract price declines by 25 basis points, by how much do the long and short positions' margin balances change? Which position, if any, gets a margin call?

13. Referring to Exhibit 11.6, what is the time value and what is the intrinsic value of a call option on Hewlett Packard with a strike price of $20 and February expiration? What is the time value and what is the intrinsic value of a put option on Hewlett Packard with a strike price of $20 and February expiration?

14. A bank wants to have a duration gap of zero. The market value of its assets is $700 million and the assets have an average duration of 5 years. The market value of the bank's liabilities is $640 million and the liabilities have an average duration of 3 years. A futures contract on $100,000 of Treasury bonds with a duration of 10 years is available. Should the bank take a long or short position in the Treasury bond futures contract? How many contracts should comprise the bank's position?

15. A bank has entered into an interest rate swap. The swap has a notional principal amount of $100 million and calls for the bank to make annual fixed-interest-rate payments of 8 percent and to receive an annual floating-interest-rate payment of LIBOR plus 2 percent. If LIBOR is 5 percent, what payment will the bank make or receive?

16. Assume the S&P 500 index settles at 1242.15 on expiration day in December 2006,

    a. What would be the value of regular SPX index calls expiring in that month with a strike price of 1220? (Hint: S&P 500 index options are cash settled with a multiplier of $100.)

    b. What would be the value of an SPX 1250 call expiring at the same time?

    c. What would be the value of an S&P 500 futures put option with a strike price of 1250 that expired at the same time? (Hint: S&P 500 futures are cash settled with a multiplier of $250.)

INTERNET EXERCISE

The major U.S. exchanges have excellent Web sites where people can obtain educational information, contract information, delayed quotes, and market volume and open-interest data for the futures and options products traded on each exchange. The Web sites can be found at www.cboe.com, www.cbot.com, and www.cme.com. Go to each site and find the following: (a) at the CBOE, find what time of the month the SPX (S&P 500) and the OEX (S&P 100) options, respectively, obtain their settlement prices; (b) at the CME, find current performance bond (margin) requirements for the S&P 500 and the NASDAQ-100 futures contracts; and (c) at the CBOT, note that there is a free online tutorial, then go to the site map and find the most recent daily volume and open-interest for the Dow Jones Industrials stock-index future.

CHAPTER PREVIEW

English is the international language for airlines. If there were not a single language, imagine the difficulty pilots would have, with nearly 250 languages spoken in the world. Similarly, for U.S. citizens and businesses, it would be nice if the whole world used the U.S. dollar to conduct business transactions. Then U.S. citizens would never have to worry about the dollar value of revenues denominated in foreign currencies, the dollar value of assets they own abroad, or the dollar cost of materials they obtain from foreign sources. This would make accounting and planning much easier for all people who invest or do business internationally.

Unfortunately, people around the world are not willing to use a foreign currency to conduct their domestic transactions. Consequently, the world's citizens and businesses use many different currencies. The fact that U.S. business firms conduct business in foreign countries with different currencies introduces two additional risks for domestic businesses: (1) currency risk and (2) country risk. **Currency risk** is derived from the fact that the values of currencies fluctuate relative to each other. **Country risk** is derived from the fact that financial claims and other business contracts can be repudiated or become unenforceable because of a change in government policy or a change in government. ∎

Hong Kong is one of the leading international business centers, best known for its unbridled, free-market, capitalist economy. It is also one of the world's most important foreign exchange markets. Foreign exchange trading is in the trillions of dollars worldwide and transactions take place 24 hours a day, every day of the year.

This chapter examines the major economic and political forces that influence foreign exchange markets. In order to reduce currency risk, foreign exchange markets developed so people can convert their cash to different currencies as they conduct business or personal affairs. Furthermore, because payments across borders can be difficult to enforce and creditworthiness can be hard to assess, elaborate "credit procedures" have developed to facilitate international loans and financing. As we will see, commercial banks play a major role in financing and arranging foreign exchange transactions because of their expertise in financing business, checking credit, and transferring money. In addition, investment banks and foreign exchange dealers play important roles in the foreign currency markets. Finally, a number of organizations have developed to help reduce some of the risks of international trade. ■

LEARNING OBJECTIVES

The objectives of this chapter are to:

1 Explain the types of risks that U.S. firms face when engaging in international trade.

2 Explain how a country can run a deficit in its balance of trade and still have a strong currency given the conventional wisdom suggesting that a trade deficit should lead to a decline in a currency's value.

3 Explain how the foreign exchange markets facilitate international trade.

4 Explain why the Eurodollar deposit and Eurobond markets have become so important in recent years.

5 Explain why Europe introduced the euro as its currency

THE DIFFICULTIES OF INTER-NATIONAL TRADE

When U.S. manufacturers need to buy raw materials, they want to get the best possible deal. Hence they investigate several potential suppliers to determine the availability and quality of materials from each, how long it takes to receive an order, and the total delivered price. When all potential suppliers are located in the United States, comparison of the alternatives is relatively easy. Both suppliers and customers keep their books, price their goods and services, and pay their employees in the same currency—the U.S. dollar. Furthermore, since the federal government regulates interstate commerce, it is unlikely that there will be any problems in shipping between states. If a dispute arises, the buyer and the seller are governed by the same legal traditions and have access to the federal court system.

When potential suppliers are not located in the United States, comparisons are more difficult because the evaluation process is complicated by at least three factors. The first problem is that the American buyer prefers to pay for the purchase with dollars, but the foreign supplier must pay employees and other local expenses with its domestic currency. Hence one of the two parties to the transaction will be forced to deal in a foreign currency. The second difficulty is that no single country has total authority over all aspects of the transactions. Nations may erect barriers to control international product and capital flows, such as high tariffs and controls on foreign exchange. Also, countries may have distinctly different legal traditions—such as the English common law used in the United States or the French civil law, which is encountered in many other nations. Finally, banks and other lending agencies often find it difficult to obtain reliable information on which to base credit decisions in many countries.

EXCHANGE RATES

The first complicating factor mentioned above—comparing suppliers who price their goods in currency units other than the U.S. dollar—is the easiest to overcome. To make such comparisons, the American buyer can check the appropriate exchange rate quotation in the foreign exchange market. An **exchange rate** is simply the price of one monetary unit, such as the British pound, stated in terms of another currency unit, such as the U.S. dollar.

As an example of how exchange rates facilitate comparisons, assume that the American manufacturer has to pay $190 per ton for steel purchased in the United States and £116 per ton for steel bought from a British supplier. Furthermore, a Japanese steel company is willing to sell steel for ¥20,000 per ton. Which supplier should the American firm chose?

If the exchange rate between dollars and pounds is $1.65/£, British steel will cost (£116) × ($1.65/£) = $191.40. At this dollar price, the American firm will prefer to buy steel from the American supplier. If the exchange rate between the yen and the dollar is ¥110/$, the Japanese steel will cost (¥20,000)/(¥110/$) = $181.82 per ton. Assuming that the price quotation of ¥20,000 includes all transportation costs and tariffs, or that the sum of those costs is less than $8.18, the American manufacturer will find it cheaper to purchase steel from the Japanese supplier. Hence the contract will be awarded to the Japanese steel company, and dollars will be exchanged for yen in the foreign exchange market to make the purchase.

However, exchange rates are not constant. Today most exchange rates are free to move up and down in response to changes in the underlying economic environment. If for some reason the exchange rate between the dollar and the pound falls from $1.65/£ to $1.50/£, British steel could be bought for (£116) × ($1.50/£) = $174.00. Now the British firm becomes the low-cost supplier even though it has done nothing itself to lower its price. See Exhibit 12.1 for a summary of the steel purchase analysis.

Notice that now it takes fewer dollars to buy one British pound, or conversely, more pounds are needed to purchase one U.S. dollar. It is correct to say that the value of the pound has fallen against the dollar or that the value of the dollar has risen against the pound. These two statements are equivalent. Both statements indicate that goods and services priced in pounds are now cheaper to someone holding dollars or that purchases priced in dollars are now more expensive to someone holding pounds. In our example, initially £1 was worth $1.65. As the value of the pound fell relative the dollar, £1 was now worth only $1.50.

Note that if the price of the British steel remains unchanged, the demand for a country's products (British steel) will be higher when the country's exchange rate declines relative to other currencies. The reduction in the exchange rate for the pound from $1.65/£ to $1.50/£ led to a reversal of the purchase decisions; at $1.65/£ British steel was the most expensive, but when the exchange rate fell to $1.50/£ it was the cheapest.

EXHIBIT 12.1
Foreign Exchange Rates and the Price of Steel in International Markets

Supplier	Price in Local Currency	Foreign Exchange Rate	Conversion to Price in U.S. $	Price of Steel in U.S. $
American	$190	–	–	$190.00
English	£116	$1.65/£	£116 × $1.65/£ =	$191.40
Japanese	¥20,000	¥110/$	¥20,000/¥110/$ =	$181.82
English	£116	$1.50/£	£116 × $1.50/£ =	$174.00

THE EQUILIBRIUM EXCHANGE RATE

Note that when the foreign demand for a country's goods and services increases, the demand for its currency will also increase as more people seek to obtain currency to pay for their purchases. This is illustrated by the downward-sloping demand curve shown in Exhibit 12.2. For our British steel example, this demand curve illustrates that the lower the dollar price of pounds, the lower the dollar price of British goods. The lower the price of British goods in terms of dollars, the higher will be the demand for British goods by foreigners. Thus, as the demand for pounds increases, the price of the pound in U.S. dollars also increases.

From the point of view of a British importer, though, the lower the price of pounds, the more pounds must be given up in order to obtain dollars (or other foreign currencies) to buy foreign goods. Thus, the lower the price of the pound in terms of dollars, the more likely British residents are to switch from imported to domestic products. When purchases are diverted in this way to domestic goods, the demand by British residents for foreign currencies to buy imported products is reduced. This also means that they will supply fewer pounds to the foreign exchange markets because they no longer want to buy as many imports. This is shown by the upward-sloping supply curve in Exhibit 12.2.

As illustrated by the point of intersection of the supply and demand curves in Exhibit 12.2, the equilibrium exchange rate occurs at the price at which the quantity of the currency demanded exactly equals the quantity supplied. At that rate of exchange (price), participants in the foreign exchange market will neither be accumulating nor divesting a currency they do not wish to hold.

The key, therefore, to understanding movements in exchange rates (prices) will be to identify the factors that cause shifts in the supply and demand curves for foreign currency. In general, whatever causes U.S. residents to buy more or less foreign goods shifts the demand curve and whatever causes foreigners to buy more or less U.S. goods shifts the supply curve of foreign currency.

CURRENCY QUOTATIONS

Exhibit 12.3 shows the foreign exchange rate quotations for all major currencies as shown in the *Wall Street Journal* on June 30, 2004. Column 2, labeled U.S. $ Equivalent, shows how much U.S. currency exchanges for one British pound or Brazilian real; in other words, it show how much U.S. currency it takes to buy one unit of foreign currency. For example, it takes $1.80 to buy one British pound (for

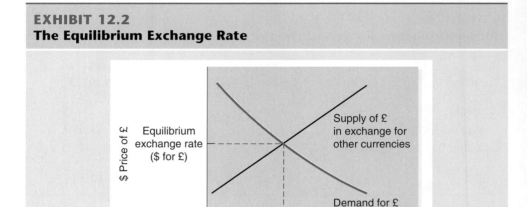

EXHIBIT 12.2
The Equilibrium Exchange Rate

The equilibrium exchange rate for a currency is the point of intersection of the supply and demand curves for the country's currency.

now, ignore the forward rates), 32¢ to buy one Brazilian real, and about 3¢ to buy a Taiwan dollar.

Column 3, labeled Currency per U.S. $, shows how much foreign currency exchanges for one U.S. dollar; that is, how much foreign money it takes to buy one American dollar. For example, $1 would get you about 55 British pence, 3.11 Brazilian reals, and 34 Taiwan dollars.

For the major world currencies such as the U.S. dollar, the British pound, and the Japanese yen, the *Wall Street Journal* lists both the spot price (current price) and the forward rates for 1-month, 3-months, and 6-months. The spot price is what you pay to buy currency today—it's today's price for the currency. Forward prices, as the name implies, are what you pay for money if you sign a contract today to buy the money on a date in the future, such as 1 month or 3 months from now. In making foreign business transactions, many businesses buy currencies forward because they anticipate they will need foreign currencies in the future. By contracting now to buy or sell foreign currencies at some date in the future, the business locks in the cost of foreign exchange at the beginning of the transaction and does not have to worry about the risk of an unfavorable movement in the exchange rate in the future.

The last entry in Exhibit 12.3 is for the **euro**, which is the new common currency for countries that are members of the European Union (EU). When the currency was introduced in January 1999, you could write checks or get loans in euros but could not make cash transactions. Cash transactions were made in a country's national currency until January 1, 2002. Now the euro circulates as the EU's single currency, and most national currencies have been phased out.

The original 11 member counties of the EU were Austria, Belgium, Finland, France, Germany, Ireland, Italy, Luxembourg, The Netherlands, Portugal, and Spain. Today, 25 European countries are EU members, but not all EU members

EXHIBIT 12.3
Selected Foreign Exchange Quotations (June 28, 2004)

Country (Currency)	U.S. $ Equivalent	Currency per U.S. $
Argentina (Peso)	.3373	2.9647
Australia (Dollar)	.6901	1.4491
Brazil (Real)	.3220	3.1056
Canada (Dollar)	.7437	1.3446
Chile (Peso)	.001570	636.94
China (Renminbi)	.1208	8.2781
Hong Kong (Dollar)	.1282	7.8003
Hungary (Forint)	.004776	209.38
India (Rupee)	.02175	45.977
Japan (Yen)	.009228	108.37
1-month forward	.009240	108.23
3-months forward	.009266	107.92
6-months forward	.009320	107.30
Mexico (Peso)	.0869	11.5075
Poland (Zloty)	.2669	3.7467
Russia (Ruble)	.03444	29.036
Singapore (Dollar)	.5826	1.7164
South Korea (Won)	.008677	1152.47
Switzerland (Franc)	.7900	1.2658
1-month forward	.7906	1.2649
3-months forward	.7922	1.2623
6-months forward	.7946	1.2585
Taiwan (Dollar)	.02972	33.647
United Kingdom (Pound)	1.8073	.5533
1-month forward	1.8022	.5549
3-months forward	1.7928	.5578
6-months forward	1.7795	.5620
SDR	1.4675	.6814
Euro	1.2083	.8276

SDR (special drawing rights) are based on the U.S., U.K., and Japanese exchange rates.

Source: Wall Street Journal, June 30, 2004.

have adopted the euro as their national currency: Denmark, Great Britain, and Sweden have not.[1] Perhaps the most notable is Britain, which continues to regard itself as more or less separate from Europe. Nonetheless, British prime minister

[1] Nations that are members of the EU can elect to join the European Monetary System, which operates the EU's central bank, called the European Central Bank (ECB).

Tony Blair has announced plans to consider adopting the euro sometime between 2002 and 2005. In all three nations there is strong public anxiety that dropping their national currencies would involve giving up too much independence.

The EU motivation for adopting a common currency is to make member countries more competitive in global markets by better integrating their national economies and reducing the economic inefficiency cause by large fluctuations in foreign exchange rates. In addition, a European Central Bank (ECB) was established to set a single monetary policy and interest rates for the adopting nations. Finally, the establishment of the EU is widely regarded as a major step toward European political unification.

For the major world currencies, such as the dollar or Japanese yen, holdings of one currency can be converted into any other monetary unit. To keep prices consistent among the various currencies, arbitrageurs continually operate in the market to take advantage of any price disparities between currencies or between two trading centers. Thus, if a profit can be made by converting pounds into yen and then yen into dollars in New York City, then selling the dollars for pounds in London, an arbitrageur will do so and gain the profit. The action of foreign exchange arbitrageurs tends to keep exchange rates among different currencies consistent with each other within narrow limits.

BALANCE OF PAYMENTS

At the heart of the movement of foreign exchange rates is the change in a county's balance of payments. The balance of payments is a convenient way to summarize a country's international balance of trade (imports – exports) and the payment to and the receipts from foreigners. Though they look complicated, it is similar to the way a family would keep records of all of its expenditures and receipts. For example, a deficit in the family budget means that family members spent more money than was collected. A deficit in the U.S. balance of payments means that, collectively, we are paying out more money abroad for imports than we are collecting from foreigners who buy our exports.

Of course for the U.S. balance of payments, all of the transactions are between residents of two countries and the transactions are formally recorded in a set of accounts known as the **balance of payments**. These accounts are kept in accordance with the rules of double-entry bookkeeping; thus debit entries must be offset by corresponding credit entries. This implies that, overall, total debits must equal total credits and that the account must always be in balance. If not, an errors and omissions account is required to balance international flows. Because of smuggling, tax evasion, poor data, and unrecorded transfers, sometimes the international errors and omissions account is quite large.

THE CURRENT ACCOUNT

The **current account** in the balance of payments summarizes foreign trade in goods and services plus investment income and gifts or grants made to other countries. As shown in Exhibit 12.4 in line 1, the United States has a substantial merchandise trade deficit (negative sign) because its imports of foreign goods exceeded its exports of goods to foreigners. U.S. consumers may prefer foreign goods for a variety of reasons, such as image or higher quality in the choice of German cars or lower prices in the choice of Chinese textiles or Southeast Asian electronics products.

EXHIBIT 12.4
U.S. Balance of Payments, 2003 (in millions of $)

Current Accounts

1	Merchandise trade, net		$–547,552
2	• Merchandise exports	$713,122	
3	• Merchandise imports	–1,260,674	
4	Services, net		51,044
5	• Services exports	307,381	
6	• Services imports	–256,337	
7	Investment & other income		33,279
8	• U.S. income from abroad	294,385	
9	• U.S. income payments to foreigners	–261,106	
10	Foreign unilateral transfers		–67,439
11	Total balance of accounts		$–530,668

Capital Accounts

12	U.S. assets abroad, net		$–283,414
13	• U.S. official reserve assets	$1,523	
14	• Other U.S. government assets	537	
15	• U.S. private assets	–285,474	
16	Foreign assets in the U.S.		829,173
17	• Foreign official assets	248,573	
18	• Other foreign assets	580,600	
19	Statistical discrepency		–12,012
20	Other capital account transactions		–3,079
21	Total capital accounts		$530,668

Current accounts reflect balances on merchandise trade and services as well as net investment income and the effect of unilateral transfers. Capital accounts reflect changes in U.S. citizens' asset holdings abroad and foreign holdings of U.S. assets. Because of major reporting problems, often a large statistical discrepancy account is needed to balance the current and capital accounts.

Source: U.S. Department of Commerce, Bureau of Economic Analysis.

While the U.S. merchandise trade balance is strongly negative, the United States often runs a surplus on the "services" component of the balance-of-payments current accounts, as is shown on Line 4 of Exhibit 12.4. The services component includes royalty income, licensing fees, foreign travel and transportation, and some military expenditures and transfers. Because the U.S. services sector generates substantial fee income from transportation, insurance, and other financial services, and various royalties and licensing fees, the services component usually creates a positive entry in the U.S. balance-of-payments current account.

The net investment income of U.S. citizens usually contributed positively to the U.S. balance of payments because of large U.S. investments abroad since World War II. However, in the late 1980s the United States changed from a net creditor nation to a net debtor nation as it sold many of its assets, including many U.S. government bonds, to foreigners to finance its large government deficits and its chronic deficit on its merchandise trade account. Consequently, U.S. net investment income surpluses have narrowed and may be negative. For 2003, however, the investment account was positive, as shown in line 7 of Exhibit 12.4.

Finally, the balance of payments on current account shows that foreign unilateral transfers (line 10) such as foreign aid, for which no compensating payment is received, have consistently been negative. This adds to the net amount of U.S. dollars transferred to foreigners and makes the total balance of payments on current account more negative than it otherwise would be.

As Exhibit 12.5 shows, in recent years, the U.S. deficit on current account has been very large and increasing. Line 11 in Exhibit 12.4 only confirms this trend. As the exhibit shows, for 2003 the total U.S. deficit for the current account is $531 billion. As in our family analogy, the U.S. balance-of-trade deficit means that collectively, we are paying out more money abroad to buy imports than we are taking in selling exports.

EXHIBIT 12.5
U.S. Current Account Trade Deficit

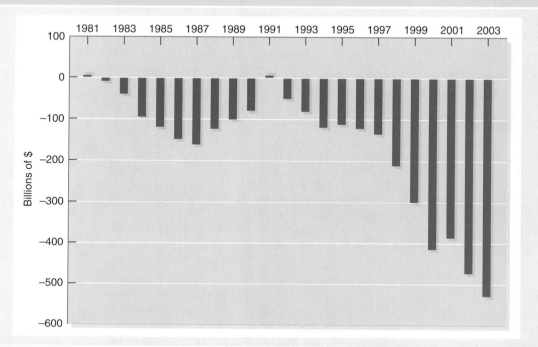

Because of rising imports and falling or stagnant exports, the U.S. deficit on current account has fallen sharply since 1997.

Source: U.S. Department of Commerce, Bureau of Economic Analysis.

CAPITAL ACCOUNTS

The balance-of-payments **capital accounts** measure capital flows into or out of the country. Capital flows can be used to finance private long-term investments of more than 1 year, or they may be short-term flows invested in bank deposits or short-term securities. Long-term capital flows often involve investments in land, plant and equipment, real estate, or stocks or bonds in other countries. Such investments occur when long-term potential seems to be substantially greater in one country than another. They may be driven, in part, by breakdowns in purchasing power parity that make it cheaper to buy assets in one country than another.

Government-motivated financial flows often play an important role in the flow-of-funds accounts. If a country is trying to support the value of its currency, its government can sell various reserve assets such as gold or special drawing rights (SDRs), also known as "paper gold."

The capital accounts therefore keep track of the investment capital flows into and out of a country. A positive balance in these accounts indicates that foreign investors purchased more U.S. assets than U.S. investors purchased foreign assets, creating a capital flow into the United States. A negative balance in these accounts indicates that U.S. investors purchased more foreign assets than foreign investors purchased U.S. assets, creating a capital outflow out of the United States.

Turning to Exhibit 12.4, line 12 shows that net U.S. assets purchased abroad, such as U.S. investors buying stock in a Japanese company, totaled $283.4 billion. The major component of this amount was the $285.5 billion in private assets purchased by U.S. citizens, as shown in line 15. Other factors affecting this account are changes in foreign currency reserves (line 13) and government asset purchases such as special drawing rights (line 14).

Line 16 in Exhibit 12.4 shows that net foreign purchases of assets in the United States, such as the Japanese investors purchasing Treasury securities, total $829.2 billion. This account is comprised of foreign government assets in the United States (line 17) and other foreign assets in the United States (line 18), which is by far the largest component of this account. The capital account flows (line 21) total $530.7 billion.

Since all current account flows (line 11) must be offset by capital account flows (line 21), these two values should be equal. If they are not equal, the difference is called a "statistical discrepancy" (line 19), which is defined to make the balance-of-payments accounts balance exactly. Unfortunately, because many international transactions are not reported, such as smuggling proceeds, illegal activity transactions, and tax evasion, the statistical discrepancy is often quite large and can be positive or negative. As a result, substantial imprecision exists in the balance-of-payments accounts.

Admittedly, the balance-of-payment accounts are difficult to understand, but it may help our understanding to explain them in terms of a family. If a family spends more money on goods and services than it earns, the family runs a current account deficit balance. To deal with this problem, the family has two choices: (1) it can borrow money to finance the deficit or (2) it can sell off some of the family's financial assets such as stock or bonds. The United States has the same problem when it runs a deficit. Running a deficit in the current accounts means that U.S. citizens have bought more foreign goods than foreigners have bought from us; hence, imports exceed exports. In this situation the United States has two choices: (1) it can borrow abroad or (2) it can sell financial assets such as domestic equities or real estate to foreigners. Thus, the country needs to have sufficient net capital inflows to finance the current account deficit. Throughout the 1990s and early 2000s, the United States has run a deficit and has financed this trade gap by both borrowing abroad and selling assets such as Treasury securities, stocks, and real estate.

The exchange rate is determined by the interaction of market forces that give rise to the supply of and demand for currency. Supply of and demand for currency, though, depend on both the underlying demand for and supply of goods and services and net capital in or out of the country. Thus, both trade and capital flows matter. We will now examine in the next three sections, in turn, how exchange rates are influenced by (1) international trade flows of goods and services, (2) capital flows, and (3) government intervention in foreign exchange markets.

INTERNATIONAL TRADE AND EXCHANGE RATES

According to the classical theory of international trade, nations produce the goods and services for which they enjoy a comparative advantage, and then they trade with foreigners to obtain other goods and services. Anything that affects the demand for a country's exports or imports has the potential to cause shifts in the supply and demand curves for foreign currency and, hence, alter the price of its currency in the foreign exchange market. We discuss five factors that influence long-run supply and demand conditions.

Relative Prices.   The relative costs of the factors of production can give one country an advantage over another. Wage rates in many Asian nations such as China and Korea are less than the value added to production by labor. Thus, the cost of goods imported from those nations may be less than that for comparable goods produced in the United States. Hence, the production of labor-intensive goods is shifting to these countries, and imports are starting to displace domestic products that require substantial amounts of unskilled labor. Thus, for example, as people buy more Nike shoes made in China, the RMB (China's currency) tends to appreciate and the value of the dollar declines.

Barriers to Trade.   Barriers to trade, such as tariffs, quotas, and other trade restrictions and taxes affect the supply of and demand for traded goods and services that underlie the supply of and demand for foreign currencies. For example, the U.S. government decides to impose a tariff or quota on the importation of Japanese steel. The trade barriers will increase the domestic demand for U.S. steel and decrease the demand for Japanese steel. As a result, the dollar should appreciate against the Japanese yen because of the decrease in demand for yen to buy Japanese steel.

Resource Endowment.   Another factor that determines the supply and demand for traded goods and services is the relative resource endowment among nations. The Asian nations tend to have abundant supply of inexpensive labor, South Africa has large concentrations of diamonds, Middle Eastern countries have an abundance of petroleum, and Western nations have large amounts of capital. Thus, for example, Middle Eastern countries can produce oil more cheaply than Western countries, while capital-intensive production enjoys an advantage in the United States. Thus, depending on the relative balance of trade between oil and capital goods, the dollar will appreciate or depreciate against the Saudi riyal.

Tastes. The relative tastes for U.S. goods versus foreign goods also affects the supply and demand for traded goods. Before the OPEC oil embargo caused oil prices to rise in the 1970s, consumers in the United States had a preference for large, powerful automobiles. Poor gas mileage was simply not an important issue to most drivers because gasoline was abundant and cheap. Therefore, small fuel-efficient cars represented a market niche that U.S. companies were content to leave to imports. After the oil embargo, however, the small-car niche became the dominant segment of the market, and Detroit was unable to respond in the short run. This created a tremendous demand for imported cars (and the foreign currency to pay for them) that was caused by a fundamental shift in consumer tastes. Because of the increase in Japanese imports, the yen appreciated in value against the dollar or the dollar declined in value against the yen.

Productivity. Another factor influencing a nation's exports and imports is a country's productivity relative to other countries. Suppose U.S. computer companies discover a way to make computer chips at a much lower cost than foreign competitors. The result will be an increase in U.S. exports of computer chips and a decrease in the import of foreign chips. The net effect will be an appreciation of the dollar relative to the currencies of Asian countries that manufacture chips. In general, countries that have high productivity experience rapid economic growth and, as such, will experience an increase in demand for their goods and services, including imports, whereas countries that are less productive will not grow as rapidly and will not experience a change in demand for imports.

PURCHASING POWER PARITY

A theory that explains international trade flows is **purchasing power parity**. Purchasing power parity means that exchange rates will tend to move to levels at which the cost of goods in any country is the same in the same currency. For instance, if a Big Mac hamburger costs $3 in the United States and ¥330 in Japan, purchasing power parity would exist when the ¥/$ exchange rate was ¥110 for $1, as then the Big Mac would cost the same in the same currency in both countries.

If purchasing power parity holds for exchange rates, all goods cost the same in the same currency in all countries, so there would be no net cost saving from buying goods in one place rather than another. However, if one currency is undervalued, goods produced in that country will tend to cost less than similar goods produced elsewhere. As a result, that country's exports will grow and its imports will diminish unless trade barriers, transportation costs, or the perishability of products make it infeasible for people to buy the same products in various places. For instance, computer parts are easy and cheap to ship, and we would expect there to be purchasing price parity among countries. On the other hand, steel prices may not be equal depending on the source because of high transportation costs, and McDonald's hamburgers would spoil (or, at least, cool off) in transit. Thus steel and hamburger prices might be less closely equated across various currencies than computer prices.

Because of transportation costs and trade restrictions, purchasing power parity is only an abstract concept. Factors such as relative prices, productivity, and tastes are at the heart of what affects the flow of goods and services between countries and has an affect on exchange rates. While exchange rates tend to adjust so similar products cost the same amount in the same currency in different countries, the adjustment may not be complete for all products and may take

PEOPLE & EVENTS

Burgernomics Tests the Purchasing Power Parity Theory

One of the most prominent theories of how exchange rates are determined is the theory of purchasing power parity (PPP). It states that in the long run, the exchange rate between countries that produce identical products will adjust over time to a level at which the costs of similar goods in any country are the same. Simply put, a dollar should buy the same things anywhere in the world. As a lighthearted test of whether exchange rates for currencies are at their "correct" level, in 1986 *The Economist* began publishing the Big Mac Index. Big Macs are a relatively homogeneous product in that the recipe is roughly the same in the 118 countries in which McDonald's operates. Comparing a country's PPP rate with the market-determined exchange rate is a test of whether a country's currency is overvalued or undervalued.

The table shows the price of Big Macs in dollars for select countries from *The Economist*. If purchasing power parity holds, the Burgernomics test should show that that the cost of a Big Mac is the same worldwide. Column 2 of the table shows the current price of a Big Mac in a country's local currency. Column 3 converts the price into dollars at the prevailing market foreign exchange rate. The average price of a Big Mac in major American cities during April 2003 was $2.71. The most expensive burger was in Switzerland, priced at $4.52. The cheapest burger was China, at $1.20. As can be seen, the prices of Big Macs are hardly the same throughout the world.

The Hamburger Standard

	Big Mac Prices		Implied PPP* of the Dollar	Actual Dollar Exchange Rate April 22	Under (–)/over (+) Valuation against the Dollar, %
	In Local Currency	In Dollars			
United States	$2.71	2.71			
Argentina	Peso 4.10	1.40	1.51	2.88	–47
Brazil	Real 4.55	1.44	1.68	3.07	–45
Britain	£1.99	3.08	1.36‡	1.58	+16
Canada	C$3.20	2.17	1.18	1.45	–18
China	Yuan 9.90	1.20	3.65	8.28	–56
Denmark	DKr27.75	3.99	10.2	6.78	+51
Euro area	€2.71	2.89	1.00	1.10	+10
Hong Kong	HK$11.50	1.47	4.24	7.80	–46
Japan	¥262	2.18	96.7	120	–19
Mexico	Peso 23.00	2.14	8.49	10.53	–19
New Zealand	NZ$3.95	2.15	1.46	1.78	–18
Poland	Zloty 6.30	1.56	2.32	3.89	–40
Russia	Ruble 41.00	1.31	15.1	31.1	–51
Singapore	S$3.30	1.85	1.22	1.78	–31
Sweden	SKr30.00	3.50	11.1	8.34	+33
Switzerland	SFr6.30	4.52	2.32	1.37	+69

Source: The Economist, April 26, 2003.

(continues)

To determine how much a currency is over- or undervalued, column 4 calculates a country's PPP rate. For example, dividing the local Chinese Big Mac price by the American price gives a dollar PPP of 3.65 yuan (9.90/2.71). Column 5 shows the prevailing market exchange rate, which is 8.28 yuan. The fact that the market exchange rate is much higher than the PPP exchange rate suggests that the yuan is undervalued by −55.9 percent [(8.28 − 3.65)/8.28]. This comes as no surprise, since China's government has pegged the yuan at a very low rate to stimulate export sales of its goods. On the other hand, the Swiss franc is overvalued by 69.3 percent [(1.37 − 2.32/2.32)]. Anyone who has traveled to Switzerland knows that, at least for Americans, it is a very expensive place to visit.

Why doesn't burgernomics validate the theory of purchasing power? First, regardless of the Big Mac Index outcome, economists are comfortable with the theory of purchasing power parity as the major behavioral force that drives the exchange rate to PPP equilibrium. Second, it is no surprise that the Big Mac prices are not in PPP equilibrium. The theory assumes that products can be easily traded across boarders; in the case of perishable Big Macs, this does not seem likely. Furthermore, prices between countries in the real world are distorted by taxes, tariffs, differences in profit margins, and differences in the cost of nontradable items like rent. Finally, in the long run there are a number of other factors that influence exchange rates, such as relative price levels, preferences for foreign versus domestic goods, and a country's productivity.

---

years to happen. Thus, we must look for some additional factors that drive the volatility of foreign exchange rates.

CAPITAL FLOWS AND EXCHANGE RATES

As Exhibit 12.5 illustrates, the United States has run a deficit in its current account for a number of years. The current account deficit means that foreign citizens will be increasing their holdings of dollars and other claims on U.S. assets. If foreigners sell their extra dollars to obtain their domestic currency, the value of the dollar will fall. Thus, many people think that when the United States runs a deficit on its balance-of-payments current account, the dollar should fall in value relative to other currencies.

However, the dollar does not always fall when the United States runs a current account deficit. As Exhibit 12.6 shows, in recent years the deficit has grown until the 2001 recession, and the value of the dollar has increased. The reason is that foreigners can buy U.S. capital assets as well as U.S. manufactured goods and services. If interest rates in the United States are high and U.S. inflation is expected to be low, foreigners can expect to earn high real returns if they invest in the United States. Thus, net foreign demand for both short-term and long-term investments may be great enough to support a high price for the dollar even if the United States runs a current account balance-of-payments deficit.

In fact, if the net foreign demand for investments in the United States is high enough, as foreigners buy dollars to finance investments, they may bid up the value of the dollar and make the U.S. current account merchandise trade deficit even larger. The large trade deficit transfers more dollars to foreigners' hands so they can afford their desired investments in the United States. As shown in Exhibit 12.7, this happened in the late 1990s and early 2000s as foreigners acquired more U.S. stocks, bonds, and investments than U.S. citizens acquired abroad. Thus, it is overly simplistic to say that a large U.S. trade deficit will make the dollar fall in value. The change in the dollar value cannot be predicted unless desired intracountry investment (capital) flows are also taken into account.

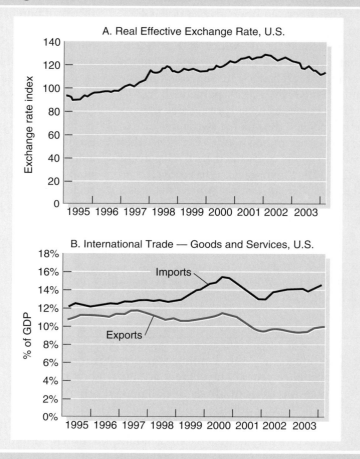

EXHIBIT 12.6
U.S. Exchange Rates and International Trade

Between 1995 and 2001, the U.S. exchange rate trended upward in terms of the dollar's purchasing power versus the currencies of the major trade partners. Consequently, U.S. imports rose sharply until the 2001 recession and exports rose slowly if at all.

Source: Federal Reserve Bank of St. Louis.

There are at least two types of international capital flows that can affect a currency's exchange rate and explain the volatility of exchange rates. They are investment capital flows and political capital flows.

INVESTMENT CAPITAL FLOWS

Investment capital flows are either short-term money market flows motivated by differences in interest rates or long-term capital investments in a nation's real or financial assets. Changes in long-term investment flows can result either from a change in the perceived attractiveness of investment in a country or from an increase in international holdings of that country's currency. For example, foreign direct investment in the United States increased dramatically during the 1980s because of favorable taxes, a strong currency, and high expected real rates of

EXHIBIT 12.7
Inflows and Outflows of Capital for Securities

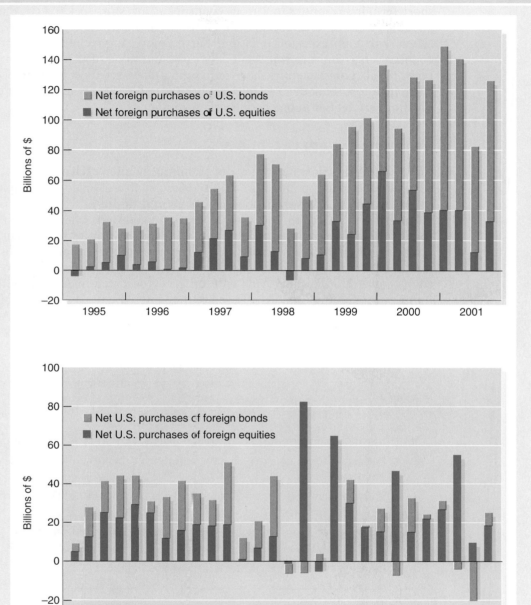

The United States was able to sustain large current account deficits in the late 1990s and early 2000s, in part because foreigners' net purchases of U.S. stocks and bonds far exceeded U.S. purchases of foreign stocks and bonds.

Source: U.S. Department of Commerce, Bureau of Economic Analysis.

return on investment. Foreign investors perceived the United States as both a safe and profitable place to invest.

Changes in short-term investment flows usually respond to differences in short-term interest rates in various countries as investors seek to earn the highest possible return on their excess cash. However, high interest rates are usually associated with high expected inflation. Furthermore, higher inflation rates in one country versus another will eventually cause the value of the first country's currency to fall. Consequently, short-term capital flows are most likely to occur only when investors think that *real interest rates* (i.e., interest rates adjusted for expected inflation) are higher in one country than another.

POLITICAL CAPITAL FLOWS

Political capital flows at times can significantly alter exchange rates. When a country experiences political instability because of war or domestic upheaval, it will often experience the phenomenon of **capital flight**, in which owners of capital transfer their wealth out of the country. In addition, when a country adopts socialist economic policies that reduce the value of private investment, private capital flight often occurs. In addition, when people fear war or social disruption, they transfer their investment funds to safer countries. Thus, when an aborted coup against USSR leader Mikhail Gorbachev occurred in August 1991, European investment funds quickly flowed to the United States; as a result, the dollar's value shot upward temporarily. Large capital outflows also occurred in Argentina in the early 2000s as people feared the value of their Argentine pesos would fall when Argentina abolished its currency board.

DO YOU UNDERSTAND?

1. Why should purchasing power parity exist? Why might it not hold?
2. What can cause a country to have a deficit in its current account balance of payments?
3. Is it always true that when a country has a deficit in its trade balance, the value of its currency will decline? Explain.
4. What types of capital flows exist between countries and what can motivate each type of flow?
5. Why must the balance of payments always balance?

GOVERNMENT INTERVENTION IN FOREIGN EXCHANGE MARKETS

By buying or selling assets, a government can influence the extent to which private transactions affect the exchange rate of its domestic currency. If a government sells assets to foreigners, it acquires foreign currencies. The government can then use these currencies to support the prices of its own domestic currency by buying its currency in the foreign exchange markets. Alternatively, foreigners can be required to pay for their asset purchases with the domestic currency. In this case, foreigners who wish to buy assets will first have to trade their currencies in the foreign exchange markets for the government's domestic currency. As more people try to buy a country's currency, its price will rise.

Governments can also seek to depress currency prices. A government that believes its currency is becoming overvalued may fear that currency appreciation will hinder its producers' abilities to export goods and will encourage imports. In this case, a government may buy assets from abroad. As the government trades its money for foreign assets, foreigners will hold more of its money, and if they sell that money in the foreign exchange markets, its value will fall.

Governments may also sell securities abroad or borrow from foreign governments to obtain claims on foreign funds. Those funds, in turn, can be used by the government to purchase its country's currency in foreign exchange markets, thereby supporting the exchange rate. If these asset flows are reversed, domestic funds leave the country, and the price of the domestic currency will fall in the foreign exchange markets. Exhibit 12.8 illustrates that when the net effect of government action is to increase the total demand for a currency, the currency's exchange rate will rise. If the net effect of government action is to increase the supply of domestic currency, its exchange rate will fall. Demand and supply decreases have opposite effects.

FIXED EXCHANGE RATES

Before 1971, the world adhered to a system of **fixed exchange rates** known as the **Bretton Woods** System. Under that system, a government was obligated to intervene in the foreign exchange markets in the manner depicted in Exhibit 12.8 to keep the value of its currency within a narrow range. If the government did not have the reserve assets to sell to support the currency's floor value, either the fixed parity relationship with other currencies had to change or the government had to

EXHIBIT 12.8
Government Intervention in the Foreign Exchange Markets

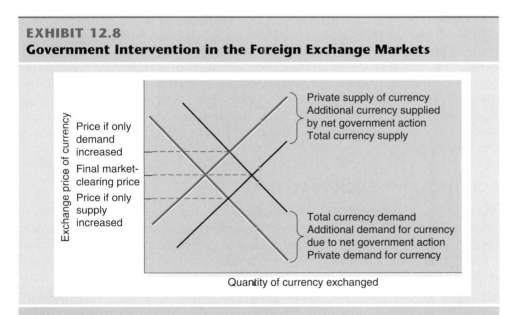

By intervening in the market for their country's currency, governments can influence its price relative to other currencies in the short run.

undertake new economic policies that would change the fundamental forces within the domestic economy that underlie the supply of and demand for goods and services. Because of this imperative, reserve asset balances such as gold or foreign currency holdings were key indicators of a government's ability to keep its exchange rate stable.

Since the collapse of the Bretton Woods System in 1971, governments in general are no longer required to impose discipline on the domestic economy to maintain a stable exchange rate. Rather, any pressures can be relieved by letting the value of the currency fluctuate in the foreign exchange market to determine a new equilibrium. For most countries, this is what has happened since the early 1970s.

Nonetheless, if currency fluctuations become too severe and disruptive to the economy, countries may borrow funds from the International Monetary Fund (IMF) to stabilize their currency. Often, the IMF requires that countries reduce their budget deficits and the growth rate of their money supplies as a condition for lending them money. Because such actions not only reduce inflation but also can cause recession, many countries prefer to borrow from the IMF only in emergencies.

INFLATION AND EXCHANGE RATES

One of the most important effects governments have on foreign currency values is through their monetary policies, insofar as those policies affect domestic inflation. A country with high inflation will tend to have higher nominal interest rates, often coupled with lower real interest rates and a deteriorating balance of merchandise trade. Because interest rates and trade flows are tied closely to exchange rates, it should not be surprising that exchange rates are materially affected by changes in a country's rate of inflation.

As inflation causes prices to rise in the United States relative to other countries, American buyers are likely to switch from domestic goods to imported foreign goods. Similarly, foreigners are likely to switch from American products to those of other countries. Thus, the demand for American goods will tend to fall at the same time that Americans supply more dollars in exchange for foreign currencies so that they can buy foreign goods. Thus, these inflation-generated supply and demand shifts will cause the dollar's exchange rate to fall relative to other currencies. Conversely, as the U.S. inflation rate falls relative to another country, the exchange value of the dollar should rise relative to that country's currency, and vice versa.

POLITICS AND EXCHANGE RATES

At times one hears that the U.S. dollar is overvalued and that its value needs to fall substantially. In a competitive market such as the foreign exchange market, though, the value is always "fair" in the sense that it represents the equilibrium point of supply and demand. Thus, what is really meant by the term "overvalued" is that the equilibrium exchange rate established in a competitive currency market results in aberrations in the domestic economy that are politically unacceptable. Today, the huge deficit in the current account is thought to result in the "exporting of jobs." At a lower value for the dollar, U.S. products would be more price-competitive internationally, and both Americans and foreigners would shift from foreign products to those produced in the United States. This, it is thought, would increase American employment and stimulate the U.S. economy. Consequently, weak-dollar policies are often supported by businesses, labor unions, and farmers who think a weak dollar would increase the demand for domestically produced goods in foreign markets.

On the other hand, a strong U.S. dollar also encourages foreigners to invest in the United States by buying capital and financial assets. Foreigners will continue to invest as long as the U.S. dollar remains strong relative to their domestic currencies. Thus, strong-dollar policies are favored by Wall Street firms who help place foreign investments. In addition, a strong dollar reduces the cost of imported goods, pressures local producers to lower their prices to meet import competition, and as a result lowers the domestic cost of living and inflation. Thus, a strong-dollar policy benefits domestic consumers and borrowers even though domestic producers often don't like it.

FOREIGN EXCHANGE MARKETS

Many references have been made in this chapter to markets for foreign exchange. In these markets, individuals, corporations, banks, and governments interact with each other to convert one currency into another. It was also mentioned that these markets are quite efficient and competitive. In fact, foreign exchange transactions total over $1.5 trillion per day and hundreds of trillions of dollars per year.

The primary explanation of why foreign exchange markets exist is that they provide a mechanism for transferring purchasing power from individuals who normally deal in one currency to people who generally transact business using a different monetary unit. Importing and exporting goods and services are facilitated by this conversion service because the parties to the transactions can deal in terms of media of exchange instead of having to rely on bartering. The currencies of some countries, such as those of centrally planned socialist countries, are not convertible into other currencies. If a corporation chartered in another country wants to do business with a country whose currency is nonconvertible, the corporation may be required to accept locally produced merchandise in lieu of money as payment for goods and services. This practice is known as **countertrade**.

A second reason that efficient foreign exchange markets have developed is that they provide a means for passing the risk associated with changes in exchange rates to professional risk takers. This "hedging" function is particularly important to corporations in the present era of floating exchange rates.

The third important reason for the continuing prosperity of foreign exchange markets is the provision of credit. The time span between shipment of goods by the exporter and their receipt by the importer can be considerable. While the goods are in transit, they must be financed. Foreign exchange markets are one device by which financing and related currency conversions can be accomplished efficiently and at low cost.

MARKET STRUCTURE

There is no single formal foreign exchange market such as the one that exists for the sale of stocks and bonds on the New York Stock Exchange. In fact, the foreign exchange market is an over-the-counter market that is similar to the one for money market instruments. More specifically, the foreign exchange market is composed of a group of informal markets closely interlocked through international branch banking and correspondent bank relationships. The participants are linked electronically. The market has no fixed trading hours, and, since 1982 when a forward market opened in Singapore, foreign exchange trading can take place at any time every day of the year. There are also no written rules governing operation of the foreign exchange markets; however, transactions are conducted according to principles and a code of ethics that have evolved over time. The extent to which a country's currency is traded in the worldwide market depends, in some measure, on local regulations that vary from country to country. Virtually every country has some type of active foreign exchange market.

MAJOR PARTICIPANTS

The major participants in the foreign exchange markets are the large multinational commercial banks, although many investment banking houses have established foreign exchange trading operations in recent years. In the United States, the market is dominated by large money-center banks, with about half of them located in New York City and the remainder in major financial centers such as San Francisco, Chicago, and Atlanta. These banks operate in the foreign exchange market at two levels. First, at the retail level, banks deal with individuals and corporations. Second, at the wholesale level, banks operate in the interbank market. Major banks usually transact directly with the foreign institution involved. However, many transactions are mediated by foreign exchange brokers. These brokers preserve the anonymity of the parties until the transaction is concluded.

The other major participants in the foreign exchange markets are the central banks of various countries. Central banks typically intervene in foreign exchange markets to smooth out fluctuations in currency exchange rates. Additional participants in the foreign exchange markets are nonfinancial businesses and individuals who enter the market through banks for various commercial reasons.

TRADING FOREIGN EXCHANGE

In commercial banks, the trading in foreign exchange is usually done by only a few persons. As in the money markets, the pace of transactions is rapid, and traders must be able to make on-the-spot judgments about whether to buy or sell a particular currency. They have a dual responsibility in that, on the one hand, they must maintain the bank's position (inventory) to meet customer needs but, on the other hand, they must not take large losses if the value of a currency falls. The task is difficult because currency values tend to fluctuate rapidly and often widely, especially since currencies are always subject to possible devaluations by their governments. Banks are not permitted to engage in foreign exchange transactions for speculative purposes. However, if a currency is expected to fall in value, banks may want to sell it to reduce their foreign exchange losses.

TRANSFER PROCESS

The international funds-transfer process is facilitated by interbank clearing systems. The large multinational banks of each country are linked through international correspondent relationships as well as through their worldwide branching systems. Within each country, regional banks are linked to international banks'

Parmalat Global Scandal isn't Milk Money

In a majestic courtroom with towering gothic windows, eyes cast downward, the former CEO of a major multinational firm admits to magistrates that he cooked the books and skimmed off $640 million from his publicly trade company. Given the recent financial scandals at Enron, Tyco International, and WorldCom, the scene was most likely another American CEO headed for incarceration. Wrong! Much to the surprise of European business executives, who have long insisted that no such fraud could occur in Europe, the executive is Calisto Tanzi, the founder and former CEO of Parmalat, the jewel of Italian capitalism.

Parmalat is one of Europe's largest and most global companies. The firm has 36,000 employees in more than 30 countries and does $3.3 billion of business in North America, under its own name and other brand names such as Black Diamond Cheese, Archway Cookies, and Sunnydale Farms.

The financial crisis was triggered when Parmalat defaulted on a $185 million bond payment in mid-November of 2003, which prompted auditors and banks to scrutinize the company's financial accounts. Much to their surprise, $4.9 billion of assets supposedly in a Bank of America account in the Cayman Islands did not exist. In ensuing investigations, Italian prosecutors discovered that Parmalat management simply invented assets to offset as much as $16.2 billion in liabilities and falsified accounts over a 15-year period, which ultimately forced the $9.3 billion company into bankruptcy on December 27, 2003. Parmalat went bankrupt because of its inability to pay its debt obligations.

Parmalat is a story of globalization gone bad. Evidence indicates that investment bankers in Italy, Germany, and London harbored serious reservations for years about Parmalat's accounting numbers and the firm's superheated growth. Many wonder whether Parmalat's multinational banks were complicit in the fraud or were duped in a colossal financial hoax shrouded by assets spread around the world. The global clout of top banks was the underpinning that allowed Parmalat to sell its falsified debt from London to Alaska, with more than $1.5 billion sold to U.S. investors. Top executives at Citibank, Bank of America, and Deutsche Bank all deny any wrongdoing.

Others question whether Parmalat's auditors, Grant Thornton International and Deloitte Touche Tohmatsu, were asleep at the wheel, guilty of sloppy audit work, or complicit. There is mounting evidence of shredded documents and a Cayman Island special-purpose entity with many irregularities. For example, it was recently discovered that the audit confirmation of the $4.9 billion Cayman Island bank account was a forgery concocted by someone in Parmalat's home office on Bank of America stationery. The very size of the account should have been a red flag to the auditor—it is a standard auditing procedure to cross-verify accounts as small as $1 million.

Although the allegation against Parmalat's two auditors appear to be serious, it is unlikely they will face the legal assault that destroyed Arthur Andersen. First, both firms are willingly cooperating with authorities, whereas Andersen executives arrogantly tried to stonewall much of the investigation. Second, even if the auditors are found liable, there is unlikely to be a legal attack to destroy the firm. Europe is much less litigious than the United States, and authorities rarely file criminal action against companies.

Much of the Parmalat story has been told before: billons in missing assets, discovery of assets on the books that never existed, fake invoices, millions in bogus sales, a bewildering constellation of offshore subsidiaries, and, most importantly, involvement and complicity at the highest levels within the firm. Overall, the Parmalat collapse seems to be déjà vu all over again, but with a distinctly European flare.

main offices, either through nationwide branching systems or through domestic correspondent networks. In the United States, practically every bank has a correspondent relationship with a bank in New York City or with a large bank in a regional financial center. As a result, virtually every bank, large or small, is able to provide its customers with international payment services.

<table>
<tr><td>

SPOT AND FORWARD TRANS- ACTIONS

</td><td>

There are two types of foreign exchange quotations—spot and forward. The **spot market** is the market in which foreign exchange is sold or purchased "on the spot." The rate at which a currency is exchanged in this market is called the **spot rate**. Delivery of the currency in the spot market must be made within 2 business days, but it is usually done immediately upon agreeing to terms. Retail foreign exchange markets are mainly spot markets.

</td></tr>
</table>

FORWARD MARKET

In the **forward market**, the parties agree to exchange a fixed amount of one currency for a fixed amount of a second currency, but actual delivery and exchange of the two currencies occurs at some time in the future, or "forward." Typically, forward contracts are written for delivery of currency 30, 60, 90, or 180 days and sometimes even longer into the future. However, it is possible to tailor the maturity of the contract, as well as the amount of currency exchanged, to meet the special needs of the parties involved. The exchange rate for these transactions is called the **forward rate**. Note that the forward rate is established on the date on which the agreement is made, but it defines the exchange rate to be used on the date of the transaction. Parties to a forward contract eliminate all uncertainty about the amounts of currency to be delivered or received in the future. Note in Exhibit 12.1 that forward rates are quoted along with spot rates for major currencies.

EXAMPLE OF A FORWARD TRANSACTION

As an example of the way in which foreign exchange markets are used by businesses, suppose that an American exporter sells farm equipment to a British firm for £100,000 to be paid in 90 days. If at the time of the transaction the spot rate is £1 = $1.60, the delivery of the farm equipment is worth $160,000. However, the actual number of dollars to be received for the machinery, which is the relevant price to the American firm, is not really certain. That is, if the American firm waits 90 days to collect the £100,000 and then sells it in the spot market for dollars, there is a risk that the dollar price of the pound sterling may have declined more than the market expected. For instance, if sterling is worth only $1.50, the American exporter will receive only $150,000 and would realize a loss of $10,000 because of the change in the exchange rate. To ensure a certain future exchange rate, the American company can hedge by selling the £100,000 forward 90 days. If the forward rate at the time of sale is £1 = $1.58, the American exporter will deliver the £100,000 to the banks in 90 days and receive $158,000 in return. In this case, since the spot rate on the day the exchange is made is £1 = $1.50, the "savings" from hedging is $8,000 (a $10,000 "loss" without hedging minus a $2,000 "loss" with hedging).

What about the $2,000 loss incurred even with hedging? Can this be prevented? The answer is that forward contracts cannot protect against *expected* changes in exchange rates, only against *unexpected* changes. At the time of sale, the 90-day forward rate was £1 = $1.58 and is the best estimate of what the rate will be in 90 days. Of course, in 90 days the spot rate for dollars may be £1 = $1.58, but more than likely it will be more or less. Thus, in this example, a true loss of $8,000 is realized if the transaction is not hedged, and no unexpected loss occurs if it is hedged.

What would happen if the spot rate in 90 days rose to $1.80? The unhedged transaction would yield $22,000 over the expected return of $158,000. However, the forward contract would again provide exactly the number of dollars anticipated. Although there may be regrets after the fact because the forward contract prevented the company from receiving the benefits of the strengthening pound, most businesses would call leaving the account receivable exposed (that is, unhedged) "speculation." It is generally believed that foreign exchange speculation is not a logical or legitimate function of businesses that import or export goods or services. However, there is a way to avoid large losses while not precluding the possible receipts of large gains without having to engage in speculation. This involves the use of foreign currency options.

OPTION TRANSACTION

Another alternative for managing foreign exchange risk is a currency option. If the American exporter were to buy a put option on the £100,000 maturing in 90 days at a strike price of $1.60, the firm would be protected against deterioration of the pound below that price. If the spot rate in 90 days is $1.50, the exporter can exercise the put and receive $160,000. On the other hand, if the rate goes up to $1.90, the American company can let the put expire and sell the sterling at the spot rate. The cost of this asymmetrical protection is the price of the option. The exporter's commercial banker will usually sell the exporter an option that suits the exporter's needs. Commercial banks earn fee income by selling options as well as by arranging forward currency transactions.

One of the most important services provided by international banks is the financing of imports and exports among countries. International transactions are far more complicated than equivalent domestic financing because of the additional sources of risk that are involved. Three problems must be overcome before trade deals can be executed. First, exporters often lack accurate information about the importer's current and past business practices and, hence, the likelihood of payment. Importers are similarly concerned about the ability or inclination of the exporter to fulfill all contractual obligations once payment has been made. Second, before the transaction can be hedged with a forward contract (or an option contract) to reduce foreign exchange risk, the exact amounts and dates of payments must be known. Finally, before a bank is willing to finance an international transaction, a means has to be found to insulate the bank from nonfinancial aspects of the transaction that could lead to disputes and to protracted legal proceedings, which delay recovery of its money. A number of specialized financial instruments have been developed to overcome these three problems, thereby

FINANCING INTERNATIONAL TRADE

minimizing the risk of engaging in international transactions. These instruments are letters of credit, drafts, and bills of lading.

LETTERS OF CREDIT

A letter of credit or **LC** is a financial instrument issued by an importer's bank that obligates the bank to pay the exporter a specified amount of money once certain conditions are fulfilled. Legally, the bank substitutes its credit standing for that of the importer in that the bank guarantees payment if the correct documents are submitted.

From the perspective of the exporter, letters of credit have several advantages over sales on open account. First, because an exporter's knowledge about a foreign importer is frequently vague, the company is hesitant to ship merchandise without advance payment. With a letter of credit, however, the creditworthiness of the bank is substituted for that of the importer, and exporters see little risk of nonpayment when the bank is the guarantor. Second, as soon as the exporter documents that he or she has met the terms and conditions specified in the LC, payment is assured. This is particularly important, because it eliminates the possibility that payment might be held up because of disputes arising from some alleged deficiency in the actual goods. As long as the paper documents are in order, the bank is obligated to pay, even if the importer no longer wants the merchandise. The final advantage of letters of credit is that they eliminate a major risk facing exporters: the possibility that governments may impose restrictions on payment. There are few cases on record in which governments have prevented banks from honoring letters of credit that have already been issued.

From the perspective of the importer, there are two definite advantages to using letters of credit. Since the LC specifies the actions that must be taken before the exporter can be paid, the chance of noncompliance by the seller is reduced. This is most useful when the importer has little knowledge of the business practices of the exporter. The second advantage to the importer is that funds do not have to be paid out until the terms set out in the LC have been met and the documentation is in order.

DRAFTS

A second important document that serves to facilitate international trade is a **draft**. A draft is simply a request for payment that is drawn up by the exporter and sent to the bank that drew up the letter of credit for the importer. If the draft conforms to several legal requirements, it becomes a negotiable instrument that is particularly useful for financing international trade flows.

Drafts can be of two types: **sight drafts** or **time drafts**. Sight drafts, as the name implies, require the bank to pay on demand, assuming that all documentation is in proper order and that all conditions have been met. Time drafts, however, are payable at a particular time in the future, as specified in the letter of credit. When a time draft is presented to the importer's bank for payment, it is checked to make certain that all terms and conditions set forth in the letter of credit have been met, and then it is stamped "accepted" and dated on the face of the draft. The importer's bank then returns the "accepted" draft to the exporter or the exporter's bank. Alternatively, the importer's bank may elect to pay the exporter or the exporter's bank a price that reflects the discounted present value of the draft, after which it may hold the acceptance for its own account or sell it in the banker's acceptance market. In either situation, when the time draft matures, the importer must pay the amount due unless other arrangements have been made in advance. The "accepting" importer's bank must make payment if the importer does not.

BILLS OF LADING

A third document of particular importance for international trade is the **bill of lading**. The bill of lading is a receipt issued to the exporter by a common carrier that acknowledges possession of the goods described on the face of the bill. The bill of lading serves as a contract between the exporter and the shipping company. In this role it specifies the services to be performed, the charges for those services, and the disposition of the goods if they cannot be delivered as instructed.

If it is properly prepared, a bill of lading is also a document of title that follows the merchandise throughout the transport process. As a document of title, it can be used by the exporter either as collateral for loans prior to payment or as a means of obtaining payment (or acceptance of a time draft) before the goods are released to the importer.

EXAMPLE OF AN IMPORT TRANSACTION

To better understand how these three documents are used in international trade, let us examine a hypothetical transaction between an American importer and a British exporter. The steps involved in this transaction are shown in Exhibit 12.9. In step 1, the American importer applies for a letter of credit from its American bank. In step 2, if the bank is willing to guarantee payment for the goods upon presentation of the required documentation, it prepares a letter of credit and sends it to the exporter in England. The letter specifies the documentation and other conditions that were agreed on to receive payment.

In step 3, the British exporter ships the goods to the American importer and collects the necessary documentation. In step 4, the British exporter prepares a draft in accordance with the terms set out in the letter of credit, and it takes the letter of credit, the draft, and all other required documentation to its London bank. The documentation required may include bills of lading, commercial invoices, certificates of quantity, and certificates of quality or grade, among others. In step 5, the British bank examines the documents carefully for full compliance. If it is satisfied that everything is in proper order, it normally *confirms* the credit (adds its own promise to pay) and pays the exporter. Usually this payment is made in the exporter's own currency (in this case pounds sterling). Note that the British bank's inspection is limited to an examination of the documents; the bank's employees do not physically examine or even see the shipping containers or merchandise. A letter-of-credit transaction does not protect an importer from a dishonest exporter shipping crates of sawdust. However, the documentation may require certifications necessary to prevent such fraud.

EXHIBIT 12.9
Steps in a Letter-of-Credit Transaction

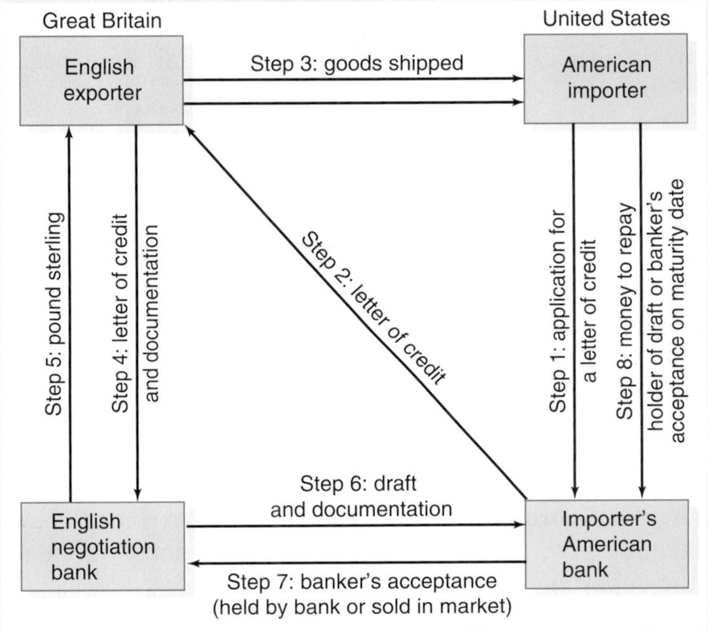

Great Britain — United States

English exporter — Step 3: goods shipped → American importer

Step 2: letter of credit

Step 5: pound sterling

Step 4: letter of credit and documentation

Step 1: application for a letter of credit

Step 8: money to repay holder of draft or banker's acceptance on maturity date

English negotiation bank

Step 6: draft and documentation

Importer's American bank

Step 7: banker's acceptance (held by bank or sold in market)

The bank that provides the letter of credit legally substitutes its credit promise for that of the importer and guarantees payment if the correct documents are submitted to prove the right goods were shipped appropriately.

In step 6, the British bank sends the draft and documentation to the importer's bank. The American bank examines the draft and accompanying documentation. If the draft is a sight draft, the American bank pays on demand and collects from the importer. If it is a time draft, the banks stamps it "accepted," signs it, and then either returns it to the exporter's bank or pays the exporter's bank a discounted price. If the American bank pays the exporter's bank for a time draft, the draft becomes a **banker's acceptance**. The bank can hold the acceptance and be repaid by the importer when the time draft matures. In this case, the draft acts much like a loan from the bank to the importer. Alternatively, the bank can sell the banker's acceptance in the money markets (step 7)—in which case the time draft is similar to "commercial paper" issued by the importer and guaranteed by its bank. Because the importer's bank has "accepted" the time draft, the accepting bank must pay and is at risk if the importer does not pay the obligation at maturity (step 8). Consequently, the banker's acceptance has no more credit risk than other bank obligations, and it might have less (if the importer has a superior credit rating). By selling the banker's acceptance, however, the bank can receive immediate cash to finance the transaction.

DO YOU UNDERSTAND?

1. What could a government do to support the value of its currency in the foreign exchange market?

2. How can a firm reduce its risk by engaging in forward currency transactions? Why are losses on such transactions often more apparent than real?

3. When a country has high inflation, why is it risky for a foreigner to invest in that country?

4. Why might consumer groups support government policies that maintain a "strong" U.S. dollar?

5. If the United States has a high rate of inflation, what will likely happen to the value of the dollar? Why?

INTERNATIONAL MONEY AND CAPITAL MARKETS

Many business contracts all over the world call for payments in U.S. dollars because the U.S. economy is very large, politically stable, and subject to less regulation than other economies. Consequently, businesses, governments, and individuals choose to hold dollars. Dollar-denominated deposits provide a high degree of liquidity that can be deployed to conduct international trade or exchanged for other currencies.

Prior to World War II the vast majority of these deposits were in large money-center banks in New York City. However, with the start of the Cold War in the 1950s, the Soviet Union feared that the U.S. government might expropriate deposits held on U.S. soil to repay defaulted czarist bonds that the Soviet government had repudiated. Some large London banks responded to this business opportunity by offering to hold dollar-denominated deposits in British banks. The transaction creating Eurodollars is illustrated in Exhibit 12.10. As shown, the Soviets withdrew their deposits from American banks and deposited them with European banks. The European banks then issued dollar-denominated deposit liabilities (Eurodollars) to the Soviets, which were backed by the deposit claims on American banks that the Soviets had transferred. By holding the dollar-denominated claims in Europe, the Soviets were able to avert the threat that the United States might freeze or expropriate their American bank deposits. These deposits were soon dubbed **Eurodollars**.

Today, the Euromarkets are vast, largely unregulated money and capital markets with centers in Europe, the Middle East, and Asia. The short-term Euromarkets are called **Eurocurrency markets**. A Eurocurrency is any currency held in a time deposit account outside its country of origin. Thus, for example, a Eurodollar is a dollar-denominated time deposit held in a bank outside the United States. The long-term market is called the **Eurobond market,** and a Eurobond is any bond issued and sold outside of its country of origin. Thus, a Eurodollar bond is a bond issue denominated in U.S. dollars and sold in Europe.

EXHIBIT 12.10
Transfer of Funds to the Eurocurrency Market

Initial Situation

U.S. Bank		European Bank	
Assets	**Liabilities**	**Assets**	**Liabilities**
	USSR deposits ($)		

Transfer of Deposits to Europe

U.S. Bank		European Bank	
Assets	**Liabilities**	**Assets**	**Liabilities**
	European bank deposits ($)	Deposits in U.S. banks ($)	USSR dollar-denominated deposits ($)

The Eurodollar market allows individuals or firms to hold dollars in banks outside the United States. By holding dollar-denominated deposits outside the United States, the deposit holders may be able to avoid restrictions on capital flows or other sanctions imposed by the U.S. government while still owning dollar-denominated deposits.

EUROCURRENCY MARKET

Eurocurrency markets serve three vital functions in international finance. First, they are a particularly attractive source of working capital for multinational corporations. They are attractive because the rates on Eurocurrency loans may be lower than for equivalent loans in the domestic economy. For Eurodollars, the rates are lower in the Euromarkets because (1) there are no reserve requirements or insurance costs associated with the deposits, and thus the overhead costs are lower; and (2) the Euromarkets are wholesale, mainly interbank markets, meaning that all participants are particularly creditworthy, the minimum transaction size is $500,000, and credit-checking and other processing costs are minimal. Because of these factors, lending rates can be lower than in the domestic U.S. market and deposit rates can be higher without sacrificing profitability.

The second function of the Eurocurrency markets is serving as storehouses for excess liquidity. Corporations, international banks, and central banks find it convenient to hold their idle funds in these markets and earn highly competitive rates of return. There is less regulation in the Eurocurrency markets. This makes them attractive to investors who wish to hold securities in bearer form to preserve their anonymity. The absence of tax withholding on interest earned in some of the Eurocurrency markets also makes them attractive to foreigners.

Finally, the Eurocurrency markets facilitate international trade. Even when trade is financed by letters of credit, banks find it attractive to use Eurocurrency loans to make payments. Corporations sometimes borrow directly in the Eurocurrency markets and pay cash in return for discounts on goods and services. Without this source of capital at very competitive rates, the volume of international trade would be lower because of the higher cost of less flexible financing arrangements.

The outstanding amount of this "stateless money," as it has been called, is extremely difficult to measure, but the gross size of the Eurocurrency market is many trillions of dollars. Because about half of Eurocurrency deposits are inter-bank transfers, the net, or retail, size of the market is somewhat smaller but still consists of many trillions of dollars. In practice, Eurocurrency deposits are highly liquid because many have maturities ranging from less than a day to a few months. Nearly one-third have a maturity of 8 days or less, and nearly 90 percent have maturities of under 6 months. Relatively few deposits have maturities longer than 1 year.

LIBOR

The Eurodollar markets began as wholesale markets for interbank transactions. The markets are now used by banks around the world as a source of overnight borrowing. The interest rate on this borrowing is known as **LIBOR**, the *London Interbank Offering Rate*. The funds in wholesale Eurodollar markets are a very close substitute for the U.S. federal funds. Loans in both markets are typically 1-day, unsecured loans denominated in U.S. dollars. As a result, the fed funds and LIBOR rates tend to be very closely related and move together, as can be seen in Exhibit 12.11. On the wholesale commercial lending side, LIBOR and the U.S. prime rate are the base rates used to determine the borrower's interest cost in nearly all international lending.

While the fed funds and LIBOR markets are close substitutes, the fed funds rate tends to be slightly lower because of the relative strength of the U.S. banking system and the fact that U.S. bank deposits are covered by deposit insurance. Moreover, there is a perception based on historical action by U.S. bank regulators that U.S. money-center banks are "too big to fail" and that, in effect, the federal government will not allow one of these large banks to fail. Foreign banks have no such guarantees. Historically, the spread between the two rates has been in the neighborhood of 10 to 12 basis points.

EUROBOND MARKETS

Eurobonds are long-term bonds issued and sold outside of the country of origin. Eurobonds were first sold in 1963 as a way for issuers to avoid taxes and government regulations. At the time, U.S. government currency policy was aimed at keeping domestic dollars invested at home. As a result, U.S. businesses were limited in the amount of funds they could borrow to invest overseas, while the bond issues of foreign firms sold in the United States were subject to a 30 percent tax on their coupon interest. The first Eurobonds were denominated in dollars and other currencies, and were not subject to U.S. regulations. Even though the U.S. currency regulations were later abandoned, the Eurobond market remained and has grown in popularity. U.S. firms found that, at times, they could sell Eurodollar bonds for domestic investment at substantially lower borrowing costs than similar domestic issues. The savings could be as large as 50 to 100 basis points compared to similar domestic bond issues. Thus, Eurobonds became an alternative source of long-term domestic financing for U.S. multinational firms.

Eurobonds are underwritten by an international syndicate of large commercial banks and securities underwriters. Large selling syndicates then take the

EXHIBIT 12.11
The Fed Funds and LIBOR Interest Rates

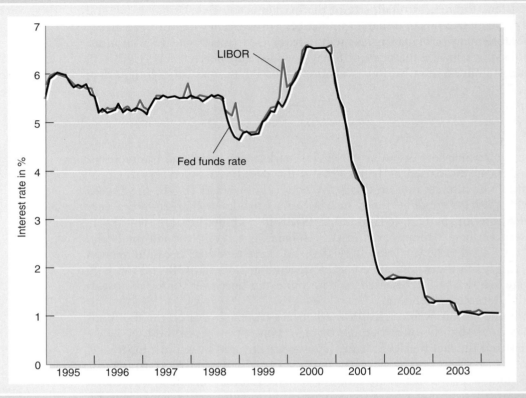

The fed funds and LIBOR interest rates are both short-term unsecured loans denominated in dollars and are close substitutes for one another. The fed funds rate is typically 10 to 20 basis points lower than the LIBOR rate.

bonds to market. Eurobonds tend to be issued in bearer form, pay interest once a year using a 360-day year, are issued in denominations of $5,000 and $10,000, and are traded in the over-the-counter market, mainly in London and Luxembourg. In contrast, bond issues sold in the United States are typically registered bonds and pay coupon interest semiannually. The fact that most Eurobonds are bearer bonds increases their marketability because the identity of the owner is not a matter of public record. In the early years of the market, many of the investors in Eurobonds were wealthy individuals and small investors with an eye toward tax avoidance. During this time, the secondary market for Eurobonds was weak and most of the issues did not have bond ratings. However, in recent years more issues are rated as individual investors are overshadowed in importance by large institutional investors such as mutual funds and pension funds. The fact that most countries regulate securities denominated in foreign currencies only loosely, if at all, means that disclosure requirements and registration costs for Eurobond issues are much lower than those for comparable domestic issues. Hence, Eurobond issues are widely perceived as a cost-effective means of raising long-term debt capital.

During the past 30 years, we have witnessed the globalization of business and the exponential growth of international financial markets. Financial instruments and even entire markets that did not exist in the early 1970s have developed and grown to maturity. A complex interaction of historical, political, and economic factors drive the globalization of financial markets. Historical and political factors include the demise of the Bretton Woods System of fixed exchange rates, the economic disruption caused by widely fluctuating oil prices, the large trade deficits experienced by the United States, Japan's rise to financial preeminence during the 1980s and its weakness in the 1990s and early 2000s, the global economic expansion that began in late 1982, the Asian economic crisis in the late 1990s, the fall of the USSR, and the adoption of the euro in 1999. Long-term economic and technological factors that have promoted the internationalization of financial markets include the global trend toward financial deregulation, the standardization of business practices and processes, the ongoing integration of international product and service markets, and breakthroughs in telecommunications and computer technology. We now discuss factors that have led to the globalization of financial markets.

THE INTER-NATIONAL-IZATION OF FINANCIAL MARKETS

EMERGENCE OF FLOATING EXCHANGE RATES

Under the Bretton Woods fixed exchange rate system, which lasted from 1944 to 1971, corporations had little need for protection against exchange rate movements. The floating exchange rate regime that came about in the 1970s, however, was characterized by rapid and extreme changes in currency values in response to changes in the supply and demand for currencies. This induced an increased demand for foreign exchange and hedging services. International banks quickly developed large, expert, and profitable foreign exchange trading staffs to meet the needs of their corporate clients.

AMERICA AS A DEBTOR NATION

Much has been written about the economic and political consequences of the transformation of the United States from the world's largest creditor in 1980 to the world's largest debtor by 1988. Relatively little, however, has been written about the purely financial impact of this phenomenon. There have been two major effects. First, since corporate capital spending actually rose as the budget and trade deficits mushroomed in the 1980s, the United States had to borrow money from foreigners on a scale never before imagined. This caused the world's most sophisticated financial system to become even larger, more efficient, and more innovative. Second, as the national debt zoomed upward, the U.S. Treasury security market emerged as a truly global bond market of immense size and liquidity.

RISE OF MULTINATIONAL COMPANIES

As the economies of the world have become increasingly interdependent in recent years, large multinational companies have grown ever more powerful. For these companies, capital is almost completely mobile, and their approach to financial management is global in scope and sophisticated in technique. Most large multinational firms have integrated sales and production operations in 100 or more countries, which also require state-of-the-art systems for currency trading, cash management, capital budgeting, and risk management. The financial needs of these companies have been met by the major international banks that have followed their customers as they expanded around the world.

TECHNOLOGY

Breakthroughs in telecommunications and computer technology have transformed international finance at least as much as they have transformed our own lives and careers. Daily international capital movements larger than the gross national products of most countries have now become routine as a result of the speed, reliability, and pervasiveness of information-processing technology. Computers now direct multibillion-dollar program trading systems in equity, futures, and options markets around the world, and a telecommunications "global village" has become a reality for currency traders operating 24 hours a day, 365 days per year from outposts on every continent. The future will certainly bring even more rapid innovation.

THE DOLLAR AS THE "NEW GOLD STANDARD"

One of the problems that currencies encounter is that governments develop reputations for the way they conduct monetary policy. For example, say a country conducts monetary policy in an irresponsible manner by issuing too much currency, which leads to high rates of domestic inflation and possible devaluation of the currency. People soon become reluctant to hold the currency. Because of the devaluation risk, people who lend money in that currency demand higher interest rates as compensation for risk bearing.

Because people wish to trade with stable currencies that are widely accepted, the U.S. dollar has benefited. For instance, it is estimated that roughly two-thirds of all U.S. currency outstanding is held outside the United States. The reason, in part, is because the U.S. dollar is highly valued for trade and as a store of value since the United States has low inflation relative to most countries. This works out as a good deal for the United States. That is, by printing pieces of paper that are used as currency in many countries around the world, the United States and its citizens are able to obtain valuable goods in exchange. Thus, the United States profits from **seigniorage** whenever it prints money at low cost and trades its currency for valuable foreign goods. Seigniorage is the difference between the cost of the printed currency and the exchange value of the currency.

Some countries have adopted the U.S. currency as a medium of exchange. Panama, for example, accepts the U.S. dollar in trade. Such countries are said to have "dollarized" their economies. Through **dollarization**, countries can obtain a stable currency widely used in world trade, which makes their accounting and international transactions easier. In addition, their borrowers no longer have to pay an interest rate risk premium to international lenders who fear the currency will be devalued before their loans are paid back.

CHAPTER TAKE-AWAYS

1 The major risks for a U.S. firm importing goods are currency risk, country risk due to the fact that the exporter is not a citizen and may be from a country with a different legal system, and, finally, the difficulty of getting reliable credit information.

2 International capital flows by themselves can cause the value of a currency to rise or fall even though the country has a trade deficit. Exchange rates are affected by both trade flows and capital flows, and capital flows can offset trade deficits. For example, in the late 1990s and early 2000s, the U.S. dollar rose in value due to large capital inflows that more than offset its large balance-of-payments deficits on current account.

3 Foreign exchange markets facilitate international trade by allowing firms to compare the cost of foreign goods in the home currency. Without foreign exchange markets, firms would have to engage in barter, which is an inefficient means of conducting international trade.

4 The Eurodollar deposit and Eurobond markets have become important in recent years because the markets provide a large pool of U.S. dollars available for U.S. and foreign firms to borrow or lend. Because of the strength and size of the U.S. economy, the dollar has become an important medium of exchange throughout the world.

5 The euro was introduced to eliminate exchange rate uncertainties so trade and financial planning would become easier among European countries.

KEY TERMS

Currency risk	Investment capital flows	Forward market	Eurodollar
Country risk	Political capital flows	Forward rate	Eurocurrency market
Exchange rate	Capital flight	Letter of credit (LC)	Eurobond market
Euro	Fixed exchange rates	Draft	LIBOR
Balance of payments	Bretton Woods	Sight draft	Eurobond
Current account	Countertrade	Time draft	Seigniorage
Capital account	Spot market	Bill of lading	Dollarization
Purchasing power parity	Spot rate	Banker's acceptance	

QUESTIONS AND PROBLEMS

1. If a bushel of corn costs $3.00, and a British pound is worth $1.50, how many pounds would a person receive for 100,000 bushels of corn sold in Britain in the spot market? If the delivery were to occur in 3 months and the U.S. interest rate exceeded the British rate by 2 percent per year, what would be received in the forward exchange market for a conversion arranged now if the current spot rate is $1.50 per British pound? Explain.

2. If a dollar can buy 98 Japanese yen and a British pound costs $1.50, how many yen would it take to buy £1? If a pound of copper £1 in Britain, ¥1,600 per pound in Tokyo, and $1.45 per pound in the United States, where is a pound of copper most expensive and where is it least expensive?

3. Assume that the spot and 1-year forward rates for the British pound are $1.60 and $1.55, and in Germany are $0.90 and $0.92 per euro. If interest rates are 4 percent in the United States, 6 percent in Britain, and 3 percent in Germany, where can you get the best return on a covered 1-year investment?

4. If the United States runs a balance-of-payments deficit on current account of $100 billion and receives a net inflow of $60 billion on long-term investments in a year, by how much will its short-term capital flows have to change in order to accommodate all these flows?

5. Why are international banks able to earn large fees by providing letters of credit and forward currency transactions?

6. If purchasing power parity applied to Big Macs, and a Big Mac cost $2.50 in the United States while the British pound cost $1.50 and €0.90 could be obtained for $1.00, how much would the Big Mac cost in Britain and Germany, respectively? Why might it actually have a different price?

7. If the Japanese yen were to change from 100 per dollar to 90 per dollar, would the U.S. balance of payments improve (become more positive) or not? Consider what effect this exchange rate change would have on both U.S. exports to and imports from Japan, as well as on purchase decisions made by manufacturers or importers located in other countries.

8. Assume that the United States and Canada are both initially in an economic recession and that the United States begins to recover before Canada. What would you expect to happen to the U.S. dollar–Canadian dollar exchange rate? Why?

9. The newly industrializing countries (NICs) of the Far East, such as Korea, Taiwan, and Hong Kong, dramatically increased their merchandise exports during the

1980s. Based on what you know about the determinants of international trade flows, explain why this export success occurred and what effect it should have on the exchange value of the NICs' currencies.

10. Explain the role that letters of credit and banker's acceptances play in international transactions. Is a banker's acceptance a sight draft? Why or why not?

11. Why do domestic governments often try to limit domestic flows of funds abroad for investment in foreign countries? How did such limitations in the United States contribute to the development of the Eurodollar markets?

12. Will the domestic balance of payments be helped or hurt if foreign investment inflows into the country increase?

13. How can government intervention affect the exchange value of a currency? Will the currency generally rise or fall if a government sells assets to foreigners?

14. How can an arbitrageur make a profit if interest rates are higher in a foreign country than at home? Describe circumstances under which one could make a profit if interest rates were *lower* abroad than at home.

15. How does inflation affect a country's spot and forward exchange rates? Why? Is it absolute inflation or inflation relative to other countries that is important?

16. Describe the factors that promoted the internationalization of financial markets during the last 15 years. Are any of these factors reversible?

INTERNET EXERCISE

The United States conducts its monetary policy and foreign exchange operations through the Federal Reserve Bank of New York. For this reason, the president of the New York Fed always has a vote on the Federal Open Market Committee. Because it is intimately connected with the U.S. and foreign financial markets, the New York Fed compiles useful data both on U.S. financial markets and on international currency exchange rates. The New York Fed Web page can be reached at http://www.ny.frb.org/, and its daily foreign currency quotes can be obtained from its 12:00 noon foreign exchange (forex) rate site, which can be found easily on its site map. Another useful site is the IMF's site, http://www.imf.org, which contains analyses of the world economy and country conditions, as well as exchange rate data and financial data related to IMF loans.

1. At the New York Fed site, some currencies are stated in terms of the amount of U.S. dollars needed to buy them, and others are priced according to the number of foreign currency units one gets per dollar. List all the currencies priced according to the number of units received per dollar. How do their values seem to differ from those priced the other way?

2. The New York Fed also publishes data on expected currency volatility based on option prices for major currencies. Find that location on the Fed's site map and answer the following:

   a. Over the next 6 months which currency is expected to be most volatile relative to the U.S. dollar?

   b. Which country do you think has the highest-priced 6-month at-the-money options for its currency quoted in U.S. dollars?

3. Go to the IMF site and find its site map. Use that map to look up countries and find out the last time Argentina was given authority to borrow from the IMF.

COMMERCIAL BANKING

13

Commercial Bank
Operations

CHAPTER PREVIEW

Like other businesses, banks are profit-maximizing firms—a fact you are probably reminded of whenever you get charged a fee or service charge. If you are at all like other depositors, you probably do not like paying fees for letting your bank use your money. Banks and other finan- cial intermediaries are unique because their creditors are also their customers. Whenever you deposit money in your bank account, you are effectively lending money to your bank, so it is understandable that you would grumble over paying fees and service charges associated with your checking account. The purpose of this chapter is to explain bank opera- tions. Hopefully, by the time you fin- ish reading this chapter and Chapter 14, you will understand why your bank charges those fees and service charges. You probably still won't like the fees, but at least you will under- stand why the bank charges them. ■

The fundamental business of banking is to accept deposits as a source of funds and then to make loans to consumers and businesses. In the past, most transactions were face-to-face, with people dropping in on a weekly basis to see the banker and get free coffee and donuts. Today, customers rarely visit their bank, instead conducting most transactions over the phone, by wire, over the Internet, or at an ATM machine.

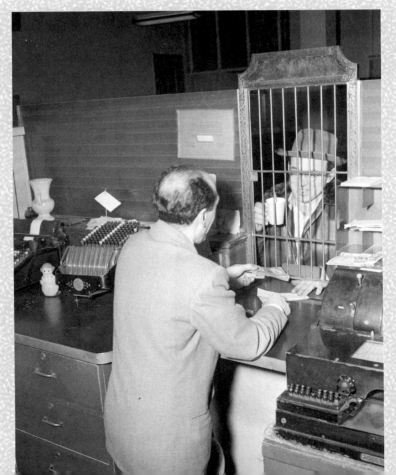

This is the first chapter on how commercial banks operate, and it is intended to lay the foundation for the three chapters that follow. We begin the chapter by providing an overview of the banking industry. We continue by examining the principal business activities of banks as summarized on their balance sheets. Then we discuss in detail how banks set interest rates and make loans. We also examine the fee-based activities of banks: wealth management and advisory services, correspondent banking, and the off-balance-sheet transactions of loan commitments, letters of credit, loan sales, and derivative securities. Finally, we discuss the role of bank holding companies and financial holding companies. ■

 LEARNING OBJECTIVES

The objectives of this chapter are to:

1 Describe the size and structure of the U.S. banking industry.

2 Discuss banks' sources of funds as reflected in their liabilities and equity capital.

3 Describe banks' uses of funds as reflected in their assets.

4 Explain how banks make lending decisions and how they price their loans.

5 Discuss how banks set interest rates on deposits.

6 Describe the various fee-based activities of banks.

7 Explain the various off-balance-sheet activities of banks and describe how these activities generate revenue for banks, and the conditions under which they will become on-balance-sheet activities.

8 Discuss the development and structure of bank holding companies and the newly formed financial holding companies.

AN OVERVIEW OF THE BANKING INDUSTRY

There are currently about 7,800 banks in the United States. Although this number may seem large, Exhibit 13.1 shows that more than three times as many banks were operating in the 1920s. Frequent bank panics and the collapse of the nation's financial system during the Great Depression (1930–1933) reduced the number of banks from more than 30,000 at the beginning of the 1920s to about 15,000 by 1933. After the Great Depression, the number of banks continued to decline gradually until the 1960s, primarily because of bank mergers rather than bank failures. After 1960, the number of banks increased slightly, stabilizing at around 15,000 until the late 1980s. Then, in the late 1980s and the 1990s the number of banks declined as a result of failures and mergers. Since the early 1980s, however, the number of total banking offices (branches plus main offices) has been increasing despite the downward trend in the number of banks. The reason is the increase in the number of branches. Even though the number of banks has decreased, geographic restrictions on banking have relaxed in the past 20 years, resulting in more branches per bank.

BRANCHING AND CONSOLIDATION

Although the number of banks has declined in recent years, the number of banking offices has grown dramatically because of a sharp increase in the number of branches. In 1941, there were only 3,564 branch offices in this country. By 2003, there were almost 75,000 banking offices, and about 67,000 of these were branch offices. This rapid growth was a result of banks following their cus-

EXHIBIT 13.1
Number of Banks and Branches of Commercial Banks (1920–2003)

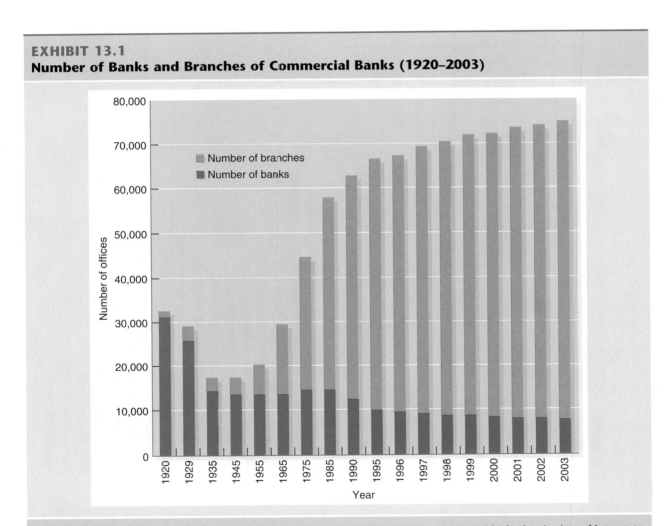

After the 1950s, the number of banks and branches increased until the late 1980s. With the beginning of interstate banking and the emergence of electronic banking, the number of banks began declining. The number of branches per bank, however, continues to increase.

Source: FDIC, *Statistics on Banking.*

tomers as they moved from the cities to the suburbs and of the easing of state branching restrictions.

The decline in the number of banks can be attributed to the rapid pace of consolidation taking place in the industry during the past 20 years. The growth in bank mergers is illustrated in Exhibit 13.2. While many of the mergers that took place during the late 1980s were the result of failed banks being acquired by healthy banks, the majority of mergers in the past two decades have been the result of deregulation and the reduction in branching restrictions.

In recent years, the pace of consolidation was slowed at the same time the economy was slowed, and many banks began to focus more on their internal operations. In addition, there are fewer potential acquisitions to choose from, and many banks are still trying to digest some of their earlier acquisitions. In fact,

EXHIBIT 13.2
Mergers in the Banking Industry (1970–2003)

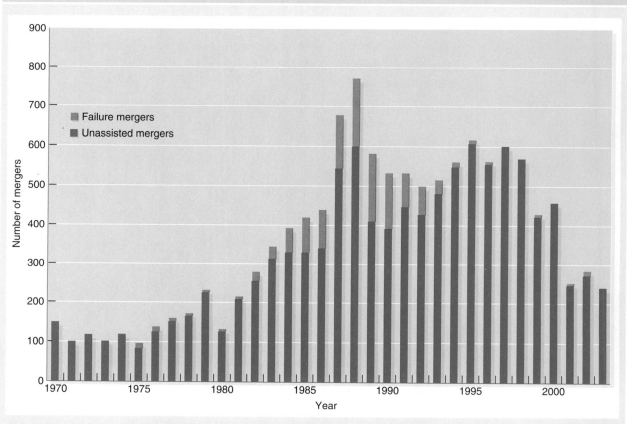

Beginning in the 1980s, the number of mergers in the banking industry grew steadily until the peak in the mid-1990s. The vast majority of these mergers have been voluntary mergers with the exception of several mergers of failed banks in the late 1980s and early 1990s.

Source: FDIC, *Statistics on Banking.*

PEOPLE & EVENTS

Crutchfield and McColl

It is not the Hatfields and the McCoys, but Edward Crutchfield and Hugh McColl were intense rivals and competitors throughout the 1990s. Edward Crutchfield was chief executive officer of First Union Corp. until retiring in 2000. Hugh McColl was head of NationsBank and then Bank of America until retiring in 2001. Under McColl's direction, NationsBank acquired Bank of America and changed the name of the merged bank into Bank of America. At the time of their retirements, both Bank of America and First Union were ranked among the top 10 banks in total assets and both banks were based in Charlotte, North Carolina.

The rivalry between the two men became legendary as the two banks competed for customers and acquisitions. When First Union built an office tower in Charlotte that was taller than McColl's office tower, for example, McColl got permission from the Federal Aviation Administration to build an even taller building. By all accounts, however, the rivalry was not personal even though the competition was fierce.

Both men had a significant impact on the banking industry, and their institutions are a barometer of sorts for the rest of the banking industry. Both men took a relatively small bank and grew it into a megabank through aggressive acquisitions. Not surprisingly, such aggressive growth can create problems and challenges. As the two men approached retirement, their institutions were still trying to digest many of the companies they had acquired and both banks were experiencing larger than expected loan losses. The challenges faced by these two companies mirror some of the same challenges faced by the banking industry as a whole.

So, just as the Hatfields and the McCoys are the names most often associated with family feuds, Edward Crutchfield and Hugh McColl, as much as anybody else, represent the period of rapid consolidation of the banking industry in the 1990s.

Source: "McColl Shuts Books on an Era," *Washington Post,* January 23, 2001, p. E1.

---

many banks are in the process of selling off some of the branches they previously acquired in order to streamline their operations and reduce redundancies.

It seems unlikely, however, that the decline in mergers and acquisitions will continue for very long. Most industry observers view the slowdown as being temporary. As the economy continues to recover from the recession of the early part of this decade and more small banks grow into attractive acquisition targets, the pace of consolidation is likely to accelerate again.

SIZE DISTRIBUTION OF BANKS

We can further increase our understanding of the structure of commercial banking by examining the size distribution of banks. As shown in Exhibit 13.3, the overwhelming majority of U.S. banks are very small. Currently, the smallest 6,369 banks (or about 82 percent of all banks) in this country hold only 8 percent of the total assets of the banking industry. Most of these small banks are located in small one- or two-bank towns. In contrast, the largest 83 banks (about 1 percent of all banks) control 73 percent of the total assets of the industry.

Exhibit 13.4 shows the largest bank holding companies (BHC) in the United States ranked by total assets. Bank holding companies are simply companies that

EXHIBIT 13.3

Size Distribution of All Insured Commercial Banks (December 31, 2003)

Asset Size	Number of Banks	Total Assets (in Millions)	Number of Banks		Total Assets	
			%	Cumulative %	Percent	Cumulative %
Less than $25 million	701	$11,860	9	9	0	0
$25 to 50 million	1,253	46,833	16	25	1	1
$50 to 100 million	1,957	141,996	25	50	2	3
$100 to 300 million	2,458	420,563	32	82	6	8
$300 to 500 million	597	228,794	8	90	3	11
$500 to 1 billion	379	260,658	5	95	3	15
$1 to 3 billion	246	405,677	3	98	5	20
$3 to 10 billion	95	541,610	1	99	7	27
$10 billion or more	83	5,544,499	1	100	73	100
Total	7,769	$7,602,489	100		100	

Although there are about 7,800 banks in the United States, the largest 1 percent of the banks control over 70 percent of all banking assets.

Source: FDIC, *Statistics on Banking,* December 31, 2003.

EXHIBIT 13.4

The 10 Largest Bank Holding Companies in the United States (March 31, 2004)

Rank	Bank Holding Company	State	Total Assets (Billions)
1	Citigroup, Inc.	New York	1,317.6
2	Bank of America Corporation	North Carolina	819.8
3	J.P. Morgan Chase & Co.	New York	801.1
4	Wachovia Corporation	North Carolina	411.0
5	Wells Fargo & Company	California	397.4
6	Taunus Corporation	New York	336.8
7	Bank One Corporation	Illinois	319.6
8	Fleetboston Financial Corporation	Massachusetts	199.8
9	U.S. Bancorp	Minnesota	192.1
10	ABN AMRO North America Holding Company	Illinois	136.1

Citigroup, Inc. is the largest holding company in the United States. It is almost 10 times larger than the nation's tenth largest bank holding company. Because of consolidation in the industry, 7 of the top 10 bank holding companies are headquartered in cities other than New York, the nation's traditional financial center.

Source: Federal Financial Institutions Examination Council, *Top 50 Bank Holding Companies,* March 31, 2004.

have an ownership interest in at least one bank. Most banks are owned by bank holding companies. At the end of 2003, there were 5,152 bank holding companies that controlled 6,298 commercial banks with about 96 percent of all commercial bank assets. Citigroup, Inc. is the largest BHC, with total assets over $1.3 trillion. Citigroup owns Citibank as well as many other bank and nonbank subsidiaries. Interestingly, while 3 of the top 10 are located in New York City, the country's financial center, recent consolidation in the industry has led to more of the top 10 BHCs being located elsewhere.

BALANCE SHEET FOR A COMMERCIAL BANK

We now turn our attention to examining the operations of a commercial bank. A good place to start is a commercial bank's balance sheet. The balance sheet lists what the business owns (assets), what the firm owes to others (liabilities), and what the owners have invested (capital) as of a given time. The basic balance sheet equation for any organization expresses the relationship between these accounts as:

$$\text{Assets} = \text{Liabilities} + \text{Capital}.$$

The capital account (or net worth) is a residual that can be calculated by subtracting liabilities owed to creditors from the total assets owned by the organization. The right-hand side of the equation can be viewed as the sources of funds for a bank. Funds are supplied by either creditors (liabilities) or the owners (capital). The left-hand side of the equation shows the uses of funds (assets) that the bank has obtained from the creditors and owners.

THE SOURCE OF BANK FUNDS

In Exhibit 13.5, the major liability and capital items in dollars and percentages are shown for all insured commercial banks and for small, medium, and large banks. The principal source of funds for most banks is deposit accounts—demand, savings, and time deposits. Economically, deposit accounts are similar to other sources of funds borrowed by the bank. Legally, however, deposits take precedence over other sources of funds in case of a bank failure. Furthermore, the Federal Deposit Insurance Corporation (FDIC) insures the holders of such accounts against any loss up to a maximum of $100,000 per individual depositor.

TRANSACTION ACCOUNTS

Banks offer a number of transaction accounts, which are commonly called checking accounts. They serve as the basic medium of exchange in the economy, accounting for about half of the total money supply (M1). Transaction accounts account for about 17 percent of all deposits.

Demand Deposits. A **demand deposit** is a checking account in which the owner is entitled to receive his or her funds on demand and to write checks on the account, which transfers legal ownership of funds to others. Individuals, government entities, and business organizations can own demand deposits.

The demand deposits of individual corporations and state and local governments are held primarily for transaction purposes. The U.S. Treasury Depart-

EXHIBIT 13.5
Liabilities and Capital Accounts of Commercial Banks (December 31, 2003)

Liabilities and Capital Accounts	All Insured Commercial Banks[a]		Small Banks[b]	Medium-Sized Banks[c]	Large Banks[d]
	Billions	%[e]	%[e]	%[e]	%[e]
Liabilities					
Deposits, total	$5,029	66	84	81	64
Noninterest-bearing	$957	13	14	13	12
Interest-bearing	$4,072	54	71	68	51
Borrowed funds, total	$1,540	20	4	8	22
Federal funds purchased and securities sold under repurchase agreements	$528	7	1	3	8
Trading liabilities	$274	4	0	0	4
Other borrowed money	$739	10	3	6	11
Subordinated notes and debentures	$101	1	0	0	2
All other liabilities	$239	3	1	1	4
Total liabilities	**$6,909**	**91**	**89**	**90**	**91**
Capital Accounts					
Common and preferred stock	$387	5	6	5	5
Undivided profits	$305	4	5	5	4
Total equity capital	**$692**	**9**	**11**	**10**	**9**
Total liabilities and equity capital	**$7,601**	**100**	**100**	**100**	**100**

Deposits are the largest source of funds for most banks, but they are a much more important source for small and medium-sized banks. Borrowed funds are a more important source of funds for large banks. Banks in general are thinly capitalized, but small banks tend to be better capitalized than large ones.

[a] This group consists of 7,770 insured commercial banks.
[b] This group consists of the country's 3,912 smallest banks. These banks have assets of less than $100 million.
[c] This group consists of the country's 3,434 medium-sized banks. These banks have assets between $100 million and $1 billion.
[d] This group consists of the country's 424 largest banks. These banks have assets of $1 billion or more.
[e] Columns may not add to 100 percent because of rounding.
Source: FDIC, Statistics on Banking, December 31, 2003.

ment also holds deposits in commercial banks. The Treasury accounts are maintained to help banks avoid the large fluctuations in reserves that would occur if the Treasury deposited consumers' and businesses' tax and loan payments directly at the Fed. Treasury deposits are called tax and loan accounts and are held by many commercial banks. Small banks also hold substantial demand deposit balances in large urban banks; these are called **correspondent balances**.

NOW Accounts. Until 1980, most banks could not pay explicit interest on checking accounts. Because these deposits provided banks with funds to lend and invest, banks competed for these "costless" funds by providing individual customers with "free" services or services sold for less than their cost. Such services include check writing, safekeeping, accounting, and the sale of traveler's checks. These constituted implicit interest payments to the holders of these deposits.

In 1972 Congress experimented by allowing financial institutions in Massachusetts and New Hampshire to pay interest on a special class of transaction accounts called **NOW accounts** (negotiable order of withdrawal). NOW accounts are just demand deposits that pay interest. They were subject to a $5^1/_4$ percent interest rate ceiling (Regulation Q). In 1976 Congress expanded the authority to offer NOW accounts to financial institutions in all of the New England states, and in 1980 the Depository Institutions Deregulation and Monetary Control Act (DIDMCA) removed the $5^1/_4$ percent interest rate ceiling and allowed all depository financial institutions in the nation to offer NOW accounts.

NOW accounts are currently available only to individuals, government entities, and nonprofit organizations. Recent trends in banking legislation suggest that it is only a matter time, however, before banks are allowed to pay interest on all demand deposits, including business accounts.

SAVINGS DEPOSITS

Savings accounts are the traditional form of savings held by most individuals and nonprofit organizations. They are a more important source of funds for small banks than for large banks. Since the beginning of the deregulation of the financial system in 1980, these accounts are becoming a less important source of funds for all banks as consumers switch to higher-yielding and more convenient checkable accounts. Historically, savings deposits had low handling costs because of their low activity level. The basic types of savings accounts are passbook and money market deposit accounts.

Savings Accounts. A blue or green passbook was the standard symbol of savings for generations of Americans. When funds were deposited or withdrawn from a savings account, the passbook had to be presented and the transaction recorded in it. Today most consumers do not receive passbooks. Instead, they receive quarterly statements from the bank and do most of their savings transactions electronically. Savings accounts comprise about 15 percent of all deposits and are most often held by individuals and nonprofit organizations. Since 1975 they may also be held by private businesses.

Money Market Deposit Accounts. To allow banks to be more competitive with money market mutual funds (MMMFs), the Garn–St. Germain Act of 1982 authorized banks to issue accounts "directly equivalent" to MMMF accounts. In the past, MMMF accounts had grown rapidly whenever market rates of interest rose above the legal limit banks could pay on deposits (Regulation Q). MMMF accounts allowed the public to earn the market rate of interest and offered limited checking features. The regulatory response, in December 1982, was the **money market deposit account (MMDA)**.

MMDAs are federally insured and pay an interest rate that is set at the discretion of the issuing bank. The exact features, such as minimum balance requirements, vary from bank to bank. However, by law depositors are limited to six third-party transfers each month. The account is available to all bank customers, including for-profit corporations. MMDAs quickly proved to be popular with consumers and helped banks attract funds from MMMFs. They account for about 39 percent of bank deposits.

TIME DEPOSITS

Time deposits have increased rapidly since 1960 and have become the largest source of funds for commercial banks, accounting for about 29 percent of bank deposits. Time deposits are unlike demand deposits in that they are usually legally due as of a maturity date and funds cannot be transferred to another party by a written check. Technically, a time deposit cannot be withdrawn for 7 days, and if withdrawn after that an interest rate penalty must be invoked. Both consumers and corporations can own them, and their characteristics vary widely with respect to maturity, minimum amount, early withdrawal penalties, negotiability, and renewability. Since April 1, 1986, there is no interest rate ceiling on time deposit accounts. The principal types of bank time deposits are certificates of deposit and negotiable (or jumbo) certificates of deposit.

Certificates of Deposit.   Primarily consumers or other small depositors hold **certificates of deposit**, which have grown in popularity during the last 20 years. They are an important source of funds for small, consumer-oriented banks. Certificates of deposit are bank liabilities issued in a designated amount, specifying a fixed rate of interest and maturity date. The interest rate is generally higher than on savings accounts.

Negotiable Certificates of Deposit.   Negotiable certificates of deposit, commonly referred to as jumbo CDs, are very large, unsecured liabilities of commercial banks issued in denominations of $100,000 or more to business firms and individuals. They have a fixed maturity date, pay an explicit rate of interest, and are negotiable if they meet certain legal specifications. Negotiable CDs are issued by large, well-known commercial banks of the highest credit standing and are traded actively in a well-organized secondary market.

Negotiable CDs are attractive both to holders of large funds and to commercial banks. They can be redeemed at any time in the secondary market without loss of deposit funds to the bank. CDs have allowed large commercial banks to attract temporary funds that had previously been invested in other money market instruments. Smaller banks can issue large CDs, but their CDs do not have active secondary markets and thus lose much of their appeal to large investors. The interest rate on CDs is competitive with the rates on comparable money market instruments. Since 1973 there has been no interest rate ceiling on CDs in denominations of $100,000 or more.

BORROWED FUNDS

Borrowed funds are typically short-term borrowings by commercial banks from the wholesale money markets or a Federal Reserve bank. They are economically similar to deposits but are not insured by the FDIC. Although they account for only 20 percent of all bank funds, borrowed funds have grown in importance as high levels of loan demand have increasingly provided banks with the incentive to

EXHIBIT 13.6
Liabilities and Capital Accounts of Commercial Banks (1935–2003)

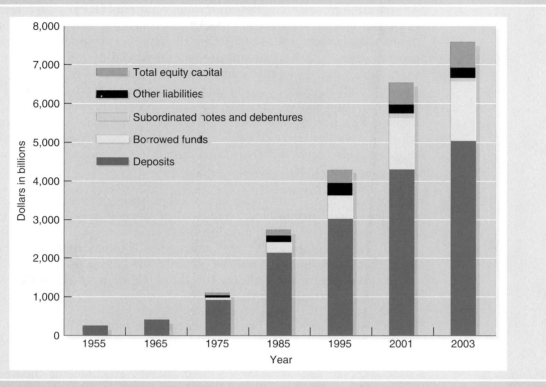

Increased demand for loans at banks has outpaced the growth in deposits at banks in recent years. As a result, banks have had to rely more heavily on borrowed funds to finance their operations. Banks made little use of money market sources of funds until the mid-1980s. In recent years, however, banks have made greater use of borrowed funds. They currently account for about 20 percent of all funds raised by banks.

Source: FDIC, *Statistics on Banking.*

develop other sources of funds. As loan demand has outpaced deposit growth, banks have increasingly turned to borrowed funds to fill the funding gap. Exhibit 13.6 illustrates this growth.

Federal Funds. For liquidity reasons, banks may hold reserves in excess of those required by law. A bank with more excess reserves than it desires may lend reserves to another bank that does not have its required level of reserves or that desires additional reserves to make more loans. The buying (borrowing) and selling (lending) of reserves on deposit at the Federal Reserve banks is called trading in **federal funds** (or **fed funds**).

The maturity of federal funds is usually 1 day, but the loans may be continuously renewed with the same or other banks in the federal funds market. Trading units tend to be very large, generally $1 million or more. About 150 large banks participate in the federal funds market regularly, and a number of other large banks participate intermittently. Recently, small banks that typically hold excess reserves have become more actively engaged in the federal funds market as suppliers (sellers) of fed funds to their larger correspondent banks in amounts as small as $50,000.

Repurchase Agreements.   **Repurchase agreements (RPs)** are a form of loan in which the bank sells securities (usually government securities) to the lender but simultaneously contracts to repurchase the same securities either on call or on a specified date at a price that will produce an agreed-upon yield. For example, a corporation with idle cash balances agrees to buy a 90-day Treasury bill from a bank at a price to yield 2 percent with a contract to sell the bills back 1 day later. The RP transaction is attractive to the corporation because, unlike demand deposits, RPs pay explicit interest. Most RP transactions are for $1 million or more and have a maturity of 1 day; however, the RP can be renewed continuously on a day-to-day basis. There are also term RP transactions that are written for maturities up to 30 days.

Eurodollars.   Short-term deposits at foreign banks or foreign branches of U.S. banks are called **Eurodollars**. They are denominated in U.S. dollars. U.S. banks may also borrow funds from individuals or other banks in the Eurodollar market for short periods of time. The interbank market is similar to the fed funds market except that interbank loans may be obtained for as long as 6 months. The base rate in this market is the **London Interbank Offer Rate (LIBOR)**. Only large banks actively participate in the Eurodollar market.

Banker's Acceptances.   A **banker's acceptance** is a draft drawn on a bank by a corporation to pay for merchandise. The draft promises payment of a certain sum of money to its holder at some future date. What makes such drafts unique is that a bank accepts them by prearrangement, thereby guaranteeing their payment at the stated time. In effect, the bank has substituted its credit standing for that of the issuer. Banker's acceptances can be held by the bank or sold in the secondary market as a source of funds. Most banker's acceptances arise in foreign trade transactions. Export and import firms find it less risky to deal in drafts guaranteed by well-known banks than those drawn against the bank accounts of firms with whom they are less familiar. Banker's acceptances are primarily a source of funds for large banks.

Federal Reserve Bank Loans.   Banks can borrow funds from their district Federal Reserve bank for short periods of time. The purpose of this type of borrowing is to cover short-term deficiencies of reserves. The traditional term of a discount loan is 15 days, although loans may be renewed with the approval of the Federal Reserve bank. Borrowing from the discount window requires that the bank apply to the Federal Reserve bank for the loan and receive its approval. Federal Reserve banks exercise close administrative control over this type of borrowing, and the amount of borrowing at the discount window is quite small, representing less than 1 percent of funds for all banks.

CAPITAL NOTES AND BONDS

Issuing bonds to raise funds is a common practice for most industrial firms. It is only in recent years that a few large commercial banks began raising funds by selling short-term capital notes or longer-term bonds. In the early 1960s, the Comptroller of the Currency ruled that debentures subordinate to the claims of depositors could be used to raise funds and that a limited amount of this debt could be counted as part of a bank's capital for regulatory purposes. Subordinated notes and debentures account for only a small percentage of the liabilities of commercial banks.

CAPITAL ACCOUNTS

Bank capital represents the equity or ownership funds of a bank, and it is the account against which bank loan and security losses are charged. The greater the proportion of capital to total funds, the greater the protection to depositors. Banks maintain much lower capital levels than other businesses, and currently bank capital accounts for 9 percent of total bank funds. Notice that capital is a more important source of funds for small banks than for large banks.

There are three principal types of capital accounts for a commercial bank: capital stock, undivided profits, and special reserve accounts. Capital stock represents the direct investments into the bank in the form of common or preferred stock; retained earnings comprise that accumulated portion of the bank's profit that has not been paid out to shareholders as dividends; special reserve accounts are set up to cover anticipated losses on loans and investments. Reserve accounts involve no transfers of funds or setting aside of cash. They are merely a form of retained earnings designed to reduce tax liabilities and stockholders' claims on current revenues.

DO YOU UNDERSTAND?

1. Approximately how many banks operate in the United States? Discuss trends in the number of banks versus the number of banking offices. What do these trends tell us about the future structure of the banking industry?

2. The interest rate on borrowed funds is usually higher than the interest rate on small time deposits. Given that, why do large banks continue to rely more heavily on borrowed funds as a source of funds?

3. What are the major sources of bank funds? How do these differ between large and small banks?

4. How does the proportion of capital for a typical bank compare with that of a typical industrial firm? Do you believe banks have adequate capital? Why or why not?

5. Why do you think that small banks are financed by a higher proportion of capital than large banks?

BANK USES OF FUNDS: BANK INVESTMENTS AND CASH ASSETS

The earning assets of a bank are typically classified as either loans or investments, and there are important differences between these two classes. Loans are the primary business of a bank and usually represent an ongoing relationship between the bank and its borrowers. A loan is a highly personalized contract between the borrower and the bank and is tailor-made to the particular needs of the customer. Investments, on the other hand, are standardized contracts issued by large, well-known borrowers, and their purchase by the bank represents an impersonal or open-market transaction; consequently, they can be resold by the bank in secondary markets. Unlike loans, investments represent pure financing, because the bank provides no service to the ultimate borrower other than the financing. Exhibit 13.7 shows the major asset accounts for all insured commercial banks in the United States and for samples of large and small banks. In this section, we discuss bank investments and other assets. We will save our discussion of bank loans for the next section.

CASH ASSETS

Cash items account for 5 percent of the total assets of the commercial banking system. They consist of vault cash, reserves with the Federal Reserve banks, balances held at other banks, and cash items in the process of collection. Cash assets are non-interest-bearing funds; banks try to minimize their holdings of these idle balances within their liquidity constraints. Because large banks must hold larger amounts of legal reserves and have more checks drawn against them than small banks, cash item accounts are typically a greater percentage of total assets for larger than for smaller banks.

Vault Cash.   Vault cash consists of coin and currency held in the bank's own vault. Banks typically maintain only minimum amounts of vault cash because of the high cost of security, storage, and transfer. Vault cash does, however, perform two important functions for banks. First, it provides banks with funds to meet the cash needs of the public. Second, banks can count vault cash as part of their legal reserve requirements.

Reserves at Federal Reserve Banks.   Deposits held by banks at their district Federal Reserve bank represent the major portion of the banks' legal reserve requirements and serve as check-clearing and collection balances. Rather than physically transferring funds between banks, check clearing and collection can be done by simply debiting or crediting a bank's account at the Federal Reserve bank. Banks may also transfer funds to other banks for reasons other than check clearing. For example, transactions in the federal funds market are performed as bookkeeping entries between banks and are accounted for on the books of the Federal Reserve banks.

Balances at Other Banks.   Banks hold demand deposit balances at other banks for a number of reasons. In most states, small banks that are not members of the Federal Reserve System can usually meet state reserve requirements by holding balances at approved large banks. Also, many small banks use their deposits at other banks to secure correspondent services from large city banks.

Cash Items in the Process of Collection.   This account, often written as **CIPC**, is the value of checks drawn on other banks but not yet collected. After a check written on another bank is deposited into a customer's account, the receiving bank attempts to collect the funds through the check-clearing mechanism. This is done by presenting the check to the bank on which the check is drawn. Before collection, the funds are not available to the bank and show up in the CIPC account. At the time the funds become available to the bank, the CIPC account is decreased (reversing the original entry), and the bank's reserves are increased by the same amount. The CIPC account is analogous to the accounts receivable on the balance sheet of a nonfinancial corporation.

EXHIBIT 13.7
Assets of Commercial Banks (December 31, 2003)

Asset Accounts	All Insured Commercial Banks[a] $ Billions	All Insured Commercial Banks[a] %[e]	Small Banks[b] %[e]	Medium-Sized Banks[c] %[e]	Large Banks[d] %[e]
Cash and due from depository institutions	387	5	6	4	5
Securities, total	1,456	19	25	24	18
U.S. Treasury	74	1	1	1	1
U.S. government agency	932	12	18	17	11
State and local government	110	1	5	4	1
Other	340	4	1	2	5
Federal funds sold and securities purchased under repurchase agreements	332	4	5	3	5
Loans and lease financing, Total	4,429	58	61	65	57
Commercial and industrial	871	11	10	11	12
Depository institutions	143	2	0	0	2
Real estate	2,272	30	38	46	27
Residential	1,358	18	17	18	18
Commercial	602	8	12	19	6
Other real estate	312	4	9	8	3
Agriculture	46	1	6	2	0
Consumer	770	10	6	6	11
Credit cards	354	5	0	1	5
Other consumer	417	5	6	5	6
Lease financing receivables	149	2	0	0	2
Other	177	2	1	1	3
Less loan loss allowance	(77)	(1.01)	(0.90)	(0.94)	(1.03)
Trading account assets	448	6	0	0	7
Bank premises and fixed assets	83	1	2	2	1
Intangible assets	158	2	0	1	2
Other assets	384	5	2	3	5
Total Assets	7,601	100	100	100	100

Loans are the most important earning assets held by banks. They have high yields, but they are typically not very liquid. Securities are much more important for small and medium-sized banks than for large ones. Large banks concentrate in commercial and industrial loans while small and medium-sized banks focus on real estate loans.

[a] This group consists of 7,770 insured commercial banks.

[b] This group consists of the country's 3,912 smallest banks. These banks have assets of less than $100 million.

[c] This group consists of the country's 3,434 medium-sized banks. These banks have assets between $100 million and $1 billion.

[d] This group consists of the country's 424 largest banks. These banks have assets of $1 billion or more.

[e] Columns may not add to 100 percent because of rounding.

Source: FDIC, *Statistics on Banking,* December 31, 2003.

FEDERAL FUNDS SOLD AND REVERSE REPURCHASE AGREEMENTS

Federal funds sold correspond to the lending of excess bank reserves in the federal funds market discussed earlier. Banks that sell (lend) excess reserves in the federal funds market acquire assets (federal funds sold) and lose a corresponding amount of reserves on the balance sheet. Banks that borrow federal funds gain reserves but acquire a liability (federal funds purchased). These transactions are reversed when the borrowing bank returns the reserves to the selling bank.

Reverse repurchase agreements are counterparty positions to the repurchase agreements discussed earlier. They are a form of lending in which the bank buys securities (usually government securities) from the borrower and simultaneously contracts to resell the same securities on a specified future date at a price that will produce an agreed yield.

INVESTMENTS

The investment portfolios of commercial banks are a major use of funds by the banking system, accounting for 19 percent of total assets. Bank investments consist primarily of U.S. government bonds, municipal securities, and bonds issued by agencies of the U.S. government. Bank investment portfolios serve several important functions. First, they contain short-term, highly marketable securities that provide liquidity to the bank. These short-term securities are held in lieu of non-interest-bearing reserves to the maximum extent possible. Second, the investment portfolio contains long-term securities that are purchased for their income potential. Finally, they provide the bank with tax benefits and diversification beyond that possible with only a loan portfolio.

Investment securities are more important to the portfolios of smaller banks than to those of larger banks. Larger banks have access to many more sources of liquid funds than do smaller banks, and therefore they do not need to rely as heavily on investment securities for liquidity.

Treasury Securities.   Commercial banks hold U.S. Treasury securities for various reasons. First, they are highly marketable. A bank in need of cash can find purchasers for its government securities nearly instantly. Second, funds held for liquidity must be safe from default, and Treasury securities are virtually default free. Third, although yields on Treasury securities are not as high as on other securities of similar maturity, they do provide banks with earned interest income on their liquid asset holdings.

Government Agency Securities.   These are securities issued by federal agencies that administer selected lending programs of the government, such as the Federal Home Loan Mortgage Corporation. The default risk of agency securities is slightly higher than that of Treasury securities because most agency securities are not direct obligations of the federal government. Some have active secondary markets whereas others do not, although none have secondary markets as broad or as active as those for U.S. Treasury securities. Because agency securities have somewhat greater default risk and lower marketability, they sell at yields above comparable Treasury obligations.

Municipal Securities.   These are securities sold by city, state, and local governments to finance education, water, electricity, recreation, and other community services. The default risk varies widely from issuer to issuer. Municipal securities, except those of very short term, are not considered liquid investments.

The principal attraction of municipal securities for commercial banks is their tax-exempt status. All coupon interest payments are exempt from federal income taxes. Depending on the marginal income tax bracket of an investor, the after-tax yield on municipal bonds may be higher than that on comparable taxable securities.

BANK USES OF FUNDS: LOANS AND LEASES

Bank loans and leases are the primary business activity of a commercial bank, accounting for about 58 percent of all bank assets. They generate the bulk of a bank's profits and help attract valuable deposits. Although loans are very profitable to banks, they take time to arrange, are subject to greater default risk, and have less liquidity than most bank investments. Also, they do not have the special tax advantage of municipal bonds.

Most bank loans consist of promissory notes. A **promissory note** is an unconditional promise made in writing by the borrower to pay the lender a specific amount of money, usually at some specified future date. Repayment can be made (1) periodically, in installments; (2) in total on a single date; or (3) in some cases, on demand. If the loan is due on demand, either the borrower or lender can end the contract at any time.

Bank loans may be **secured** or **unsecured**. Most are secured. The security, or **collateral**, may consist of merchandise, inventory, accounts receivable, plant and equipment, and, in some instances, even stocks or bonds. The purpose of collateral is to reduce the financial injury to the lender if the borrower defaults. An asset's value as collateral depends on its expected resale value. If a borrower fails to meet the terms and conditions of his or her promissory note, the bank may sell the collateralized assets to recover the loan loss.

Banks make either **fixed-rate** or **floating-rate loans**. The interest rate on a fixed-rate loan does not change over the loan's term. The interest rate on a floating-rate loan, on the other hand, is periodically adjusted to changes in a designated short-term interest rate, usually a Treasury rate or LIBOR. In periods of stable interest rates and upward-sloping yield curves, banks are eager to make long-term loans at fixed rates above the rates they pay on their short-term liabilities. As long as rates do not rise too quickly, banks can roll over their deposits at relatively low rates, maintaining a positive spread. When interest rates rise quickly or become more volatile, on the other hand, banks have a preference for making short-term or floating-rate loans.

Most bank loans carry fixed rates. While many commercial loans have floating rates, consumers are generally less willing to bear the interest rate risk of a floating-rate loan. With a fixed-rate loan, the bank assumes all of the interest rate risk. Borrowers will shift to floating-rate loans, however, if they are offered sufficient inducement in the form of a lower initial interest rate on the floating-rate loan.

COMMERCIAL AND INDUSTRIAL LOANS

As shown in Exhibit 13.7, loans to commercial and industrial firms constitute 11 percent of total assets. Most are short-term loans with maturities of less than 1 year. The type of loans made by a bank will reflect the composition of the bank's customers. Consequently, business lending is typically more important to large banks than to small retail banks.

There are three basic types of business loans, depending on the borrower's need for funds and source of repayment. A **bridge loan** supplies cash for a specific transaction with repayment coming from an identifiable cash flow. Usually, the purpose of the loan and the source of repayment are related; hence the term bridge loan. For example, an advertising company enters into a contract to produce a TV commercial for the Ford Motor Company. The total contract will be for $850,000; however, the advertising company needs approximately $400,000 in financing to produce the commercial. The loan is a bridge loan because it supports a specific transaction (making the commercial) and the source of repayment is identifiable (completing the commercial).

A **seasonal loan** provides term financing to take care of temporary discrepancies between business revenues and expenses that are due to the manufacturing or sales cycle of a business. For example, a retail business may borrow money to build inventory in anticipation of heavy Christmas sales and may expect to repay it after the new year begins. The uncertainty in this type of loan is whether the inventory can be sold for a price that will cover the loan.

Long-term asset loans are loans that finance the acquisition of an asset or assets. An example would be a manufacturing company purchasing new production equipment with a 7-year expected life. The new equipment should increase the firm's cash flow in future years. The loan would then be repaid over 7 years from the firm's yearly cash flow. Banks' long-term asset loans typically have maturities ranging between 1 and 10 years.

LOANS TO DEPOSITORY INSTITUTIONS

Banks make loans to other depository institutions, such as their respondent banks, savings and loan associations, and foreign banks. These loans differ from federal funds sold and reverse repurchase agreements. While federal funds sold and reverse repurchase agreements tend to be overnight loans, the loans in this category have a variety of maturities and can be for a variety of purposes. These loans are usually made by large banks and account for only 2 percent of bank assets.

REAL ESTATE

Real estate loans account for 30 percent of banks' total assets. These mortgage loans finance the purchase, construction, and remodeling of both residential housing and commercial facilities. About two-thirds of all mortgage loans are for residential housing, and the remainder are for commercial property and land development.

Mortgage loans are secured by the real estate they finance. They are long-term loans with an average maturity of about 25 years, but maturities may vary between 10 and 30 years. Historically, mortgages had a fixed interest rate, with borrowers paying the loans back in fixed monthly installments. In recent years, more mortgage loans have been variable-rate mortgages (VRMs), in which the interest rate and monthly payments vary with a market index, usually within a prescribed range. The amount of down payment affects the interest rate charged on a mortgage loan. Higher down payments reduce the risk of loss to the mortgage holder in the event that the home must be repossessed for the owner's failure to make mortgage payments or for some other breach of the contract. Down payments typically range from 10 to 30 percent of the purchase price.

AGRICULTURAL LOANS

Agricultural loans are both short-term and long-term loans to farmers to finance farming activities. Although agricultural loans make up only 1 percent of all bank assets, they represent an important form of lending at many small rural banks. Small banks (<$100 million in assets) devote about 6 percent of their assets to agricultural lending. Short-term agricultural loans are generally seasonal and are made primarily to provide farmers with funds to purchase seed, fertilizer, and livestock. In making these loans, specialized knowledge of farming is required, and the lending officer usually inspects the applicant's farming operation once a year.

CONSUMER LOANS

Bank loans to individuals are known as consumer loans. Their maturities and conditions vary widely with the type of purchase. Maturities can be as short as 1 month or as long as 5 years for automobile loans. Long-term loans, which are typically paid on an installment basis, are generally secured by the item purchased, as in the case of automobile loans. Short-term loans are usually single-payment loans.

Consumer loans account for about 10 percent of total bank assets. Commercial banks furnish approximately one-half of total consumer installment credit outstanding. Their emergence as a major supplier of consumer credit is a relatively new phenomenon. Prior to the 1930s, commercial banks were primarily engaged in business loans. It was in part the failure of banks to satisfy the growing demand for consumer credit that led to the emergence and rapid growth of consumer-oriented financial institutions such as finance companies, credit unions, and savings and loan associations.

Bank Credit Cards. The first bank credit card plan was started in 1951 by Franklin National Bank of New York. Early bank credit card plans were local or regional in nature, were run by individual banks, did not provide revolving credit, and did not charge a membership fee. In 1958, revolving credit became a feature of bank credit card plans. In 1966, the first nationwide card plan was started by Bank of America, using the name BankAmericard.

Before 1966, high start-up costs and the acceptance of credit cards only by merchants in the issuing bank's immediate area were obstacles to the growth and widespread use of credit cards. The advent of the nationwide clearing of bank-card slips as well as nationwide licensing of banks to issue credit cards was a turning point in the credit cards' development. These factors transformed local credit cards into national credit cards and made bank cards acceptable to a large number of merchants and consumers. Today, Visa (formerly BankAmericard) and MasterCard are the most widely known plans. Worldwide, more than 14 million merchants accept MasterCard, Visa, or both, and about 20,000 financial institutions issue the cards. The merchant who accepts a credit card pays a service charge ranging from 2 to 5 percent, depending on the average sale price and volume generated.

For the consumer, the holder of a credit card is guaranteed a credit limit at the time the card is issued. The dollar amount of the credit lines varies with the cardholder's income and employment record. The cardholder is entitled to purchase items up to the credit limit without prior approval of the bank. If the purchases are paid for in full within 25 days after the monthly billing by the bank, generally no interest is charged. However, the cardholder does not have to pay the full amount within the billing period and may elect to pay the balance off in installments. The bank sets a minimum monthly payment that must be paid. The interest charged for credit card installments usually varies between 1 and 2 percent per month (12 and 24 percent per annum) on the unpaid balance. The cardholder may receive the card free or may pay an annual membership fee of between $15 and $500, depending on the services the card offers to the cardholder. It is estimated that the annual maintenance cost to the bank for a credit card account ranges between $35 and $55. These costs escalate quickly with the number of delinquent accounts or fraudulent credit card transactions.

LEASE FINANCING

In recent years, leasing has been a fast-growing area of business for commercial banks, particularly large banks. The impetus for bank entry into leasing was provided by a 1963 decision by then Comptroller of the Currency James Saxon to allow national banks to purchase property upon a customer's request and lease it to a customer. Since then, almost every state allows state-chartered banks to enter into lease-financing arrangements.

The main economic justification for leasing is taxation. When the lessee (e.g., consumer) is in a lower tax bracket than the lessor (e.g., bank), leasing an asset becomes a viable alternative to borrowing and purchasing the asset. This is because with a leasing arrangement, the bank may get a larger tax deduction than the lessee and may pass part of it along to the lessee as a discount on lease payments. Banks enter into leasing because the rate of return on leasing activities is comparable (after risk adjustment) to that earned on bank lending. Leasing is viewed by most bankers as an extension of their commercial lending activities.

The market for lease equipment is quite large, and it is estimated that leasing and equipment financing account for about 25 percent of the total annual expenditures on equipment. In the United States, banks and their leasing affiliates are making major inroads into these markets. Bank leasing activities for large banks involve big-ticket items, such as commercial aircraft, oceangoing tankers, computers, and nuclear generators for utilities. Other items leased by both large and small banks include office equipment, automobiles, trucks, and machinery. The majority of bank leasing activities are with business firms, although the leasing of automobiles to individuals is gaining in popularity. Many bank holding companies have started or purchased equipment-leasing companies, and the majority of the nation's 100 largest banks are engaged in equipment leasing. Furthermore, large correspondent banks have been increasingly involving their respondent banks in leasing activities. As these smaller banks gain knowledge of the methodology and techniques of leasing, it is likely that many will enter the leasing markets in the near future. This is because there appear to be no notable economies of scale in the leasing industry. Thus, the only significant barrier to entry is knowledge and expertise in the field.

OTHER ASSETS

Trading account assets represent the inventory of securities held by banks for resale to investors as part of their securities dealer activities. The types of securities included in the trading account are the same as those included in the investment portfolio. They are listed separately, however, because they are expected to be held for only a short time. Given that trading account assets are held for dealer activities, it is not surprising that trading account assets are concentrated in large banks.

Fixed assets include such real assets as furniture, banking equipment, and the bank's real estate holdings. Other items are intangible assets (e.g., goodwill), prepaid expenses, income earned but not collected, foreign currency holdings, and any direct lease financing. Small banks have a higher proportion of fixed assets than do large banks. Small banks, with a greater consumer/retail emphasis, require more "bricks and mortar" than do large banks.

LOAN PRICING

Because most of a bank's assets are loans, loan pricing is one of the most critical decisions made by a bank manager. There are three important facets of loan pricing. First, the bank must earn a high enough interest rate on the loan to cover the costs of funding the loan, whether the funds are from deposits, money market securities, or capital accounts. Second, the rate on the loan must be sufficient to cover the administrative costs of originating and monitoring the loan. Finally, the loan's interest rate must provide adequate compensation for the credit (or default) risk, liquidity risk, and interest rate risk generated by the loan. Of course, the primary concern in loan pricing is the borrower's credit risk.

THE PRIME RATE

Historically, the **prime rate** served as a benchmark, or base rate, on short-term business and agricultural loans and was the lowest loan rate posted by commercial banks. At that time, the prime rate was the rate banks charged their most creditworthy customers, and all other borrowers were typically quoted rates as some spread above prime, depending on their risk.

Recently, the role of the prime rate has changed. Over the last 20 years, fewer loans have been priced using the prime rate as a benchmark. While the prime is still used as a benchmark for certain types of consumer loans, its use in business and agricultural lending has declined. Now, lenders choose from among several other benchmark rates when pricing loans. A common alternative benchmark for pricing loans to large corporate borrowers is the LIBOR, which is the price of short-term Eurodollar deposits. Other popular alternatives include Treasury rates or the federal funds rate. Despite the declining role of the prime rate as a benchmark for loan pricing, the popular media continue to use it as a barometer of conditions in the nation's money markets because banks are the major suppliers of commercial credit in the economy.

In the past it was commonly believed that the prime rate was a bank's lowest lending rate. In recent years, however, the competitive factor has led to the widespread bank practice of below-prime lending. Beginning in the 1970s and 1980s, banks made loans at below the prime rate for firms that had the opportunity to obtain cheaper funds elsewhere. Below-prime customers are usually large, financially sophisticated customers who have access to the commercial paper market or the Eurocurrency market. These borrowers do not seek customer relationships, so a loan to them is more like pure financing. The conventional borrower, on the other hand, needs the advice and counsel of a bank and has fewer borrowing alternatives. The majority of below-prime loans are made by large money-center banks because many of their customers borrow money in wholesale amounts ($1 million or more) and have access to other sources of funding.

BASE-RATE LOAN PRICING

Most banks have adopted a loan-pricing procedure of setting a base interest rate for their most creditworthy customers and then using this rate as the markup base for loan rates to all other customers. The base rate may be the prime rate, the federal funds rate, LIBOR, or a Treasury rate. It is expected to cover the bank's administrative costs and provide a fair return to the bank's shareholders. The markups include three adjustments. The first is an adjustment for increased default risk above the risk class associated with the base rate. The bank's credit department determines the risk assignment. The second is an adjustment for term-to-maturity. Most bank business loans are variable rate with the rate varying with the underlying base rate. Thus, as the base rate increases or decreases, the customer's loan rate is adjusted accordingly. If the customer wants a fixed-rate loan for a certain maturity period, say, 1 year, the bank will adjust the variable-rate loan rate (short-term base rate) by an amount consistent with the current market yield curve (e.g., the Treasury yield curve). Finally, an adjustment is made that takes into account the competitive factor—a customer's ability to borrow from alternative sources. If, for example, a loan officer believes the customer has an alternative source of cheaper funding such as the commercial paper market, the bank may lower the rate to keep the customer's business. The greater the competition, the lower the loan rate. Expressed mathematically, the loan rate to a particular bank customer is:

$$r_L = BR + DR + TM + CF, \qquad (13.1)$$

where:

r_L = individual customer loan rate
BR = the base rate
DR = adjustment for default risk above base-rate customers
TM = adjustment for term-to-maturity
CF = competitive factor

For example, a bank's base rate is 7 percent and two customers—a small firm and a large firm—want loans. The large firm is well known nationally, has sold commercial paper on occasion, and wants a floating-rate loan. The smaller firm wants a 1-year fixed-rate loan. The bank's money market manager reports that 1-year Treasury securities sell for 75 basis points above a 3-month Treasury bill. Given this information, the bank's loan-pricing scheme may be as follows:

Pricing Factor	Small Firm	Large Firm
Prime rate (the base rate)	7.00%	7.00%
Default risk adjustment	3.00	2.00
Term-to-maturity adjustment	0.75	0.00
Competitive factor adjustment	1.00	0.00
Loan rate	11.75%	9.00%

The small firm's less favorable borrowing rate is due to greater default risk, a premium for a fixed rate, and the competitive factor—the intensity of competition from other banks or alternative, nonbank borrowing sources such as commercial paper. Exhibit 13.8 shows that the interest rate on small loans is commonly about 200 basis points (2 percent) higher than the rate charged for larger loans.

NONPRICE ADJUSTMENTS

Banks can also make nonprice loan adjustments to alter the effective loan rate. The most common of these are changes in compensating balances. **Compensating balances** are minimum average deposit balances that bank customers must maintain at the bank, usually in the form of non-interest-bearing demand deposits. Compensating balances—usually about 10 percent of the amount of outstanding loans—also encourage borrowers to use other services of the bank and raise effective loan rates. As an example, assume that a firm has a $100,000 line of

EXHIBIT 13.8

Interest Rate Spread of Commercial and Industrial Loans over the Federal Funds Rate (1986–Second Quarter 2004)

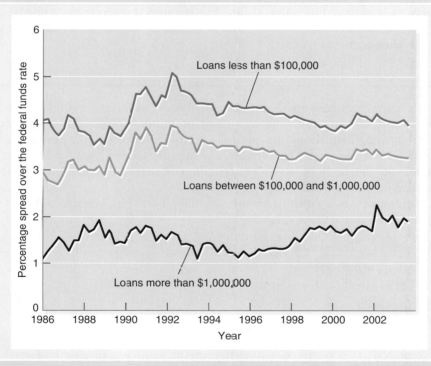

The largest loans tend to be made to the lowest-risk borrowers. Therefore, it is not surprising that the interest rates on these loans are the lowest. During recessions, the yield spread over the federal funds rate remains relatively constant on the largest loans. On smaller, higher-risk loans, however, the yield spread over the federal funds rate tends to get larger, as it did in the early 1990s.

Source: Board of Governors, Federal Reserve System, *E2 Statistical Release.*

credit at an 8 percent rate of interest that requires a 10 percent compensating balance. If the firm borrowed the maximum amount ($100,000) for 1 year, it would have to maintain $10,000 in a deposit account with the bank; since the firm has only $90,000 ($100,000 – $10,000) available to use during the year, the annual effective rate of interest is 8.9 percent ($8,000/$90,000), rather than the stated nominal rate of 8 percent ($8,000/$100,000).

Other methods of adjusting the effective loan rate without altering the nominal rate include reclassifying borrowers from lower to higher credit risk classes (carrying higher loan rates), increasing the amount of collateral (lowering the default risk), and changing the maturity of the loan (moving along the yield curve). Finally, the ability of banks to adjust the effective loan rate and other aspects of the customer relationship explains why the prime rate tends to be more inflexible, or "sticky," than other short-term interest rates.

MATCHED-FUNDING LOAN PRICING

One way that banks can control the interest rate risk of fixed-rate loans is through matched funding of loans. **Matched funding** means that fixed-rate loans are funded with deposits or borrowed funds of the same maturity. If, for example, a bank makes a 1-year fixed-rate loan, it might fund the loan with a 1-year CD. Assuming that the cash inflows from the loan match the cash outflows on the CD, the bank is able to reduce interest rate risk because if interest rates change, the rate on the loan and the CD change by approximately the same amount since they have the same maturity.

ANALYSIS OF LOAN CREDIT RISK

One of a lending officer's major tasks is to analyze a customer's creditworthiness—that is, to determine a customer's default risk premium. Credit analysis determines whether or not a loan should be granted and to which credit risk category a customer should be assigned. Of course, in making loans, it is illegal for banks to discriminate on the basis of sex, race, religion, or marital status; only economic factors can be considered.

In attempting to quantify a customer's default risk characteristics, banks typically analyze the five Cs of credit:

1. Character (willingness to pay)
2. Capacity (cash flow)
3. Capital (wealth)
4. Collateral (security)
5. Conditions (economic conditions)

Character reflects a borrower's integrity, credit history, and past business relationship with the bank. Basically, banks want to lend to persons who want to repay their debts. Capacity analyzes a borrower's projected income statements or cash flow generated from a job. Capital looks at a borrower's balance sheet or residual wealth (e.g., stock or land ownership). Collateral refers to assets that can be taken by the bank and liquidated if a loan is not repaid. Finally, conditions refers to economic conditions at the time of the loan and a borrower's vulnerability to an economic downturn or credit crunch.

MANAGING RISK: CREDIT SCORING

Credit scoring is an efficient, inexpensive, and objective method for analyzing a potential borrower's character. Credit scoring involves assigning a potential borrower a score based on the information in the borrower's credit report. The factors and weights that determine the score are based on a statistical analysis of the historical relationships between loan default rates and specific borrower characteristics. A higher credit score indicates a lower risk of default. Generally, credit-scoring models focus on these five factors: (1) the borrower's payment history, (2) the amount owed, (3) the length of the borrower's credit history, (4) the extent of new debt by the borrower, and (5) the type of credit in use. According to Fair, Isaac, and Company (FICO), the following factors are ignored in their credit scoring model: race, color, religion, national origin, sex, marital status, age, salary, occupation, title, employment history, and any other information not found in a person's credit report.

Most banks and other financial institutions use credit scoring to analyze the character of borrowers in almost all consumer, residential real estate, and small business loan applications. One advantage of credit scoring is that it allows lenders to make very fast loan decisions. While a conventional analysis and verification of a borrower's character could take days, credit scoring takes only seconds. Thus, lenders are able to provide instant credit for many loan products. A second advantage is that a person's credit score is based on objective criteria, which minimizes the potential for discriminatory lending practices. The disadvantage of credit scoring is that it is impersonal and does not allow for special circumstances. In addition, critics of credit scoring argue that the secretiveness behind credit-scoring models makes it difficult for potential borrowers to improve their score. For example, consumers who try to improve their rating by consolidating their debt onto one or two cards may actually hurt their rating because credit-scoring models may interpret the behavior as an effort to manipulate their credit rating.

DEFAULT RISK PREMIUMS

Once the five Cs are analyzed, a customer is assigned to a credit-rating category. The default risk premium for each category is determined from an analysis of the bank's credit losses over several business cycles.

For example, a bank with five credit categories may develop the following loan-pricing scheme:

Credit Category	Default Risk Premium
1	Prime-rate customers
2	10 to 50 basis points
3	50 to 100 basis points
4	100 to 200 basis points
5	Reject credit

At some point, however, potential borrowers become too risky, and the bank will refuse to grant them credit as indicated by credit category 5.

Determining the appropriate default risk premium for a given credit category is a delicate process. Lending officers who set their default risk premiums too high will tend to drive away the most creditworthy borrowers in a given category because those borrowers will be able to borrow cheaper elsewhere. Lending officers who set their default risk premiums too low will eventually lose their jobs as the bank's loan losses exceed the expected loan loss rate, particularly during periods of severe economic downturns.

DO YOU UNDERSTAND?

1. Why do you think small banks have a higher proportion of assets in investments than do large banks?
2. Describe a typical fed funds transaction. Why do you think small banks sell more fed funds as a proportion of total assets than large banks?
3. How does loan portfolio composition differ between large and small banks? Can you provide an explanation?
4. What factors go into setting the loan interest rate? Explain how each factor affects the rate.
5. What customer characteristics do banks typically consider in evaluating consumer loan applications? How do each of these factors influence the decision of the bank to grant credit?

PRICING BANK DEPOSITS

Because most of a bank's funds come from deposits, another critical decision of bank managers is determining the interest rates offered to depositors. Before the 1980s, the pricing of deposits was neither a challenging nor imaginative management problem. Banks were not even permitted to pay interest on demand deposits until 1980 and the advent of NOW accounts. Further, Regulation Q set ceilings on the interest rates banks could pay on savings deposits until it was phased out in 1986. Because interest rates in the money markets exceeded the regulatory ceiling, banks had to offer rates equal to the ceiling to slow the process of disintermediation.

Since the deregulation of the 1980s, however, the pricing of deposits has been a much more interesting and difficult function of bank managers. The pricing of deposits is a complex process, but here are two factors to consider. First, the bank must offer a high enough interest rate to attract and retain deposits. If, however, it offers a rate so high that it squeezes the spread between the average return on assets and the average cost of liabilities, then the bank's profitability suffers. Second, in banking markets with intense competition, this problem is compounded. To meet competition, banks may not only have to lower rates charged on loans, but also have to increase rates paid on deposits. Thus, under extremely competitive conditions, bank managers should recognize that they ultimately have little control of deposit rates (or loan rates, for that matter) over the long run.

Why is the competition for deposits so intense? From the perspective of a depositor with less than $100,000, all deposit accounts look pretty much the same because they are insured by the FDIC; that is, the deposits are risk free. Accordingly, depositors will put their money where it will earn the highest return, all other things, such as service charges on accounts or loan relationships, held constant. Also, banks have to offer rates that are competitive with money market mutual funds. For deposits greater than $100,000, banks must compete not only with other banks, but also with other money market instruments. The money market will price large, negotiable certificates of deposit in line with the riskiness of the bank's loan and investment portfolios, given that these large CDs are uninsured. Essentially, all CDs that represent a given level of risk are close substitutes for one another in the money market and therefore must offer similar rates.

There are times when banks may price deposits above or below competitive market rates. If, for example, a bank is aggressively growing, it may offer higher-than-market rates to penetrate a new market. Such banks will attempt to make loans or sell fee-based services to new depositors to cover the higher cost of funds. On the other hand, a bank with few profitable loan or investment opportunities may reduce deposit rates below market to reduce liability costs.

FEE-BASED SERVICES

Our examination of the balance sheet of a commercial bank has given us a great deal of insight into its business activities. However, some activities in which commercial banks engage are not easily classified, and they do not readily show up in balance-sheet summary accounts. Some of these services are performed directly by banks and other by subsidiaries of bank holding companies. The income from these activities comes in the form of fees rather than interest payments. In the 1980s and 1990s, banks shifted away from the traditional services of deposit taking and lending toward providing more fee-based services. These fee-based services are subject to less risk and provide more stable income to banks during uncertain conditions in the economy and the financial markets.

CORRESPONDENT BANKING

Correspondent banking involves the sale of bank services to other banks and to nonbank financial institutions. Correspondent banks typically act as agents for respondent banks in check clearing and collection, purchases of securities, the purchase and sale of foreign exchange, and participation in large loans. Traditionally, correspondent services are sold in packages of services, with payment being made by the respondent bank holding compensating balances with the correspondent bank. For example, investing a $100,000 compensating balance from a respondent bank at 12 percent would generate $12,000 gross income for the correspondent bank. If the bundle of services the respondent receives has a fair market value of $12,000, then both parties should be satisfied. In recent years, a trend has developed to unbundle correspondent services and to pay a direct fee for each service. This trend is particularly true in the area of computer and book-keeping services.

Correspondent banking is not a recent development; it was a common practice in this country by the 1800s. It is unique to the United States, however, and derives its origin from the structure of our financial system. In the United States there are about 7,800 banks, most of them relatively small and operating only one office. These banks find it either impossible or inefficient to provide certain types of services needed by their customers.

Though informal in nature, the structure of correspondent banking is highly complex. Small rural banks often maintain correspondent relationships with five or more larger banks in regional financial centers. Regional financial center banks maintain correspondent balances with 30 or more banks in national financial centers as well as with banks in other regional financial centers. The center of American correspondent banking is New York City. This is because New York is the nation's financial center, with its short-term money markets, foreign exchange markets, and long-term capital markets. Almost every important bank in the world maintains an operating office in New York, and almost every large bank in the United States maintains a correspondent relationship with at least one large bank in that city.

The most important service that correspondent banks provide today is still check clearing and collection. Most banks, particularly nonmember banks, prefer clearing their checks through local or regional correspondent banks rather than through the Federal Reserve network of clearinghouses. One reason for this is that the correspondent banks often give immediate credit for cash items in the process of collection, whereas the Federal Reserve may withhold credit for up to 2 days, depending on the respondent bank's location. In addition to check clearing, correspondent banks often participate in loans arranged by respondents. The respondent bank may want outside help with some loans because demand outstrips regional supplies of funds or because the loan exceeds the bank's legal lending limit. Loan participations also help respondents diversify their loan portfolios and reduce overall risk on their loans. Correspondent banks also provide electronic data processing for deposit accounts, installment loans, and payrolls. They provide investment and trust department advice, prepare reports on economic and financial market conditions, and allow respondent banks to participate in their group insurance and retirement programs. Correspondent banks buy and sell government securities, foreign exchange, federal funds, and other financial securities for respondent banks. They may also serve as clearinghouse for job applicants, assist in forming holding companies or opening new branches, or help respondents find sources of equity capital or other long-term funds.

TRUST OPERATIONS

Banks have been involved in trust operations since the early 1900s. The trend in recent years, however, is to call a bank's trust operations something more contemporary, such as "wealth management and advisory services" or "private banking." Currently, about one-fourth of all banks offer trust services to their customers even if they call them something else. Trust operations involve a bank acting in a fiduciary capacity for an individual or a legal entity, such as a corporation or the estate of a deceased person. This typically involves holding and managing trust assets for the benefit of a third party. Equity investments constitute about two-thirds of the total assets of bank trust departments. Banks administer these securities rather than own them. By law, banks are not allowed to own equity securities for their own accounts.

Currently, bank trust departments manage or maintain more than 24 million trust accounts holding almost $13 trillion in assets. Nearly one-half of all trust assets are managed for individual accounts. This frequently involves the settlement of estates, which is the activity most people associate with bank trust departments, but trust departments also provide other wealth management services. As part of the estate settlement function, the trust assures that the terms and conditions of the will are fulfilled, sees that claims against the estate are settled, and manages the assets of the estate during the interim period. Banks also administer personal trusts for those not wishing or unable to undertake this responsibility for themselves. Examples of this situation would be children unable to care for an estate or a beneficiary considered to be a "spendthrift" by the originator. Banks usually follow conservative investment practices in managing personal trusts. As part of the wealth management function, trust departments may provide investment management services, estate planning, and wealth-transfer services.

The second largest group of trust assets managed by banks are for pension funds. Bank pension fund holdings account for nearly four-fifths of all pension fund assets. Bank trust departments also perform functions other than managing or investing assets. They frequently act as transfer agents, registrars, dividend disbursement agents, and coupon and bond payment agents for corporations. They also serve as bond trustees, seeing that the conditions of the bond contract are carried out by the issuer.

IN PRACTICE

Banks Learn from Wal-Mart and Other Retailers

In a quest for market share and profits, many banks are turning to the examples set by Wal-Mart, Nordstrom, Starbucks, and other retailers. While some banks are still pursuing a strategy of cost cutting and efficiency, others are pursuing a customer-oriented strategy that is allowing them to grow faster than the rest of the industry. Commerce Bancorp and Washington Mutual (a Seattle-based thrift) are examples of financial institutions that have adopted a customer-friendly approach to banking.

Commerce and Washington Mutual have been successful in attracting deposits due, in large part, to their unorthodox approach to branch banking. Customers who walk into a Washington Mutual (WaMu) branch, for example, may not recognize it as a bank. At first, customers might be disoriented by the concierge whose job it is to greet customers as they walk in the door. Bank employees are dressed in khaki pants and blue shirts rather than suits. In addition, there are no glass barriers to separate the tellers from the customers. Instead, tellers assist customers at 'towers," while the customers' kids play in the WaMu Kids Corner.

Of course, WaMu is not doing all this just to be nice. The goal is to get more retail customers in the door. By offering free checking accounts and free ATM transactions, as well as making the banking experience less intimidating and more customer-friendly, WaMu tends to attract relatively young and lower-income customers. The idea is that by attracting them now, WaMu will be able to keep them when they grow older and more affluent. As a result of these efforts and an aggressive acquisition strategy, WaMu has grown from $21 billion in total assets in 1990 to $275 billion in 2003.

Not surprisingly, many other banks are following the lead of WaMu and Commerce. For example, Bank of America is experimenting with unique and innovative branches.

The ultimate success of these innovative approaches to branch banking remains to be seen, however. When depositors expect both great service and a competitive interest rate, it will be interesting to see whether WaMu and other customer-friendly retail banks continue to enjoy the same success.

INVESTMENT SERVICES, INSURANCE, AND OTHER FINANCIAL PRODUCTS

In the 1980s and 1990s, deposit growth slowed as more people invested in equity shares and **mutual funds**. Rather than allowing depositors to withdraw their funds and invest them elsewhere, however, many banks (through the nonbank affiliates of their bank holding companies) began aggressively marketing mutual funds and offering **brokerage services**. In this way, banks were able to generate noninterest fee income to help offset some of the increased interest costs of relying on borrowed funds to finance their growth.

In addition, beginning in 1987, the Federal Reserve allowed banks to form so-called Section 20 affiliates that allowed them to offer **investment banking** services as long as the revenue these subsidiaries generated made up only a small percent of the company's total revenue. Section 20 of the Banking Act of 1933 (the Glass-Steagall Act) separated commercial banking from investment banking. The Federal Reserve's interpretation of Section 20 allowed many bank holding companies, such as Citicorp, to acquire investment banking firms.

At the same time that banks have been offering more products and services that have traditionally been the domain of investment companies and investment banks, they have been expanding their offerings of products and services that are traditionally associated with insurance companies. However, the limitations on the allowable activities of banks limited the extent of banks entry into insurance.

Finally, on November 12, 1999, President Clinton signed the **Financial Services Modernization Act** (or the **Gramm-Leach-Bliley Act**). Gramm-Leach-Bliley (GLB) formally removed the Glass-Steagall restrictions and limitations on these activities. After GLB, banks, insurance companies, and securities firms can form financial holding companies and offer "one-stop shopping" for financial services.

OFF-BALANCE-SHEET BANKING

During the past 20 years, there has been a substantial increase in what is called off-balance-sheet banking at large U.S. commercial banks. Like other fee-based activities, off-balance-sheet activities generate fee income for banks. Unlike other fee-based activities, however, off-balance-sheet activities have the feature of representing either contingent assets or contingent liabilities. Contingent assets are those off-balance-sheet activities that may ultimately become on-balance-sheet assets. Examples of off-balance-sheet assets are loan commitments and unrealized gains on derivative securities contracts. Contingent liabilities are those off-balance-sheet activities that may ultimately become obligations of the bank. Examples of contingent liabilities are letters of credit and unrealized losses on derivative securities contracts. The off-balance-sheet activities of banks are summarized in Exhibit 13.9.

LOAN COMMITMENTS

Most bank loans begin as loan commitments. A loan commitment is a formal promise by a bank to lend money according to the terms outlined in the commitment. The type of loan commitment that most consumers are familiar with is the available credit on their credit cards. At the end of 2001, consumers had drawn on less than 20 percent of the available credit on their credit cards, leaving almost $3 trillion in

EXHIBIT 13.9
Off-Balance-Sheet Activities of Commercial Banks (December 31, 2003)

Off-Balance-Sheet Items	All Insured Commercial Banks[a] Billions	All Insured Commercial Banks[a] Percent of Assets[e]	Small Banks[b] (Percent of Assets[e])	Medium-Sized Banks[c] (Percent of Assets[e])	Large Banks[d] (Percent of Assets[e])
Unused Commitments, Total	5,395	71	49	30	77
Credit Card Lines	3,386	45	40	16	49
Other Unused Commitments	2,009	26	9	14	29
Letters of Credit, Total	373	5	0	1	6
Commercial	24	0	0	0	0
Financial Standby	295	4	0	0	4
Performance Standby	54	1	0	0	1
Derivative Contracts	71,356	939	0	1	1,099
Credit Derivatives	1,001	13	0	0	15
Bank is the guarantor	471	6	0	0	7
Bank is the beneficiary	529	7	0	0	8
Interest Rate Contracts	61,858	814	0	1	953
Notional Value of Swaps	42,107	554	0	0	649
Futures and Forward Contracts	7,210	95	0	0	111
Written Option Contracts	6,184	81	0	0	95
Purchased Option Contracts	6,357	84	0	0	98
Foreign Exchange Contracts	7,455	98	0	0	115
Notional Value of Swaps	1,805	24	0	0	28
Futures and Forward Contracts	4,351	57	0	0	67
Written Option Contracts	554	9	0	0	10
Purchased Option Contracts	644	8	0	0	10
Other Commodity Contracts	1,043	14	0	0	16

Off-balance-sheet banking has become an important part of many bank's activities. Many large banks act as dealers in the markets for derivative securities. It is not surprising, therefore, that the derivative holdings of these banks dwarf their on-balance-sheet assets.

[a] This group consists of 7,770 insured commercial banks.

[b] This group consists of the country's 3,912 smallest banks. These banks have assets of less than $100 million.

[c] This group consists of the country's 3,434 medium-sized banks. These banks have assets between $100 million and $1 billion.

[d] This group consists of the country's 424 largest banks. These banks have assets of $1 billion or more.

[e] Columns may not add to 100 percent because of rounding.

Source: FDIC, Statistics on Banking, December 31, 2003.

available credit. There are three types of loan commitments that may be agreed upon by business borrowers and commercial banks: line of credit, term loan, and revolving credit. Consumers usually do not enter into these types of arrangements. The purpose of the loan commitment is to (1) provide some assurance to the borrower that funds will be available if and when they are needed and (2) provide the lender with a basic format for structuring the customer's loan request properly.

A **line of credit** is an agreement under which a bank customer can borrow up to a predetermined limit on a short-term basis (less than 1 year). The line of credit is a moral obligation, not a legal commitment on the part of a bank. Thus, if a company's circumstances change, a bank may cancel or change the amount of the limit at any time. With a line of credit, it is also customary for a bank to require an annual cleanup period, usually 1 month. This ensures the bank that funds are not being used as permanent capital by the firm. A firm does not have to use a line of credit and incurs a liability only for the amount borrowed.

A **term loan** is a formal legal agreement under which a bank will lend a customer a certain dollar amount for a period exceeding 1 year. The loan may be amortized over the life of the loan or paid in a lump sum at maturity. **Revolving credit** is a formal legal agreement under which a bank agrees to lend up to a certain limit for a period exceeding 1 year. A company has the flexibility to borrow, repay, or reborrow as it sees fit during the revolving credit period. At the end of the period, all outstanding loan balances are payable, or, if stipulated, they may be converted into a term loan. In a sense, revolving credit is a long-term, legally binding line of credit.

LETTERS OF CREDIT

A letter of credit is a contractual agreement issued by a bank that involves three parties: the bank, the bank's customer, and a beneficiary. In a **commercial letter of credit**, the bank guarantees payment for goods in a commercial transaction. The buyer of the goods arranges for the bank to pay the seller of the goods once the terms of the purchase agreement are satisfied. As shown in Exhibit 13.9, commercial letters of credit represent only a small part of banks's off-balance-sheet activities.

In a **standby letter of credit (SLC)**, the bank promises to pay a third party in the event the bank's customer fails to perform according to a contract the customer has with the third party. In this way, the bank substitutes its creditworthiness for that of its customer. Thus, if the bank's customer fails to meet the terms and conditions of its contract with the third party, the bank guarantees the performance of the contract as stipulated by the terms of the SLC. The bank's obligation under an SLC is a contingent liability, because no funds are advanced unless the contract is breached by the bank's customer and the bank has to make good on its guarantee.

Traditionally, most SLCs are used as backup lines of credit to support commercial paper offerings, municipal bond offerings, and direct loans such as construction lending. These are referred to as financial SLCs. Newer applications for financial SLCs, such as for mergers and acquisitions, are emerging. Another type of SLC involves the bank guaranteeing performance of a nonfinancial contract, such as the timely delivery of merchandise or completion of a construction project. These SLCs are called performance SLCs.

LOAN BROKERAGE

Banks have always sold commercial loan participations to other banks and have entered into syndicated loan agreements when a loan was too large for any single bank. Recently, however, large commercial banks have, to an increasing extent, originated loans with a view to selling them or offering participations. When acting as a loan broker, banks typically negotiate large loans through their credit departments and then sell participations to various investors, including thrifts, life insurance companies, pension funds, and other banks. Although most loan sales are business loans, some banks, with the aid of investment bankers, have structured sales of automobile loans, credit card receivables, and home mortgage loans.

There are several reasons, besides earning fee income, that a bank may want to broker loans. First, loan sales permit banks to invest in and diversify across a different set of loans than they originate and service. Second, a bank may sell loans because it has a competitive advantage in booking certain types of loans and, therefore, can use the funds from loan sales to fund additional similar loans. Finally, banks may sell loans to avoid burdensome regulatory taxes. Specifically, the argument is that banks have a comparative advantage in originating loans, but they are at a disadvantage in keeping loans on their books because of bank regulations. This disadvantage stems from the regulatory tax that banks must pay in the form of federal deposit premiums, forgone interest from holding required reserves, and mandatory capital requirements that exceed those that would be maintained in the absence of regulations. Thus, firms not subject to stringent banking regulations have a comparative advantage in holding loans on their balance sheet.

SECURITIZATION

Banks became increasingly involved in the securitization of loans in the 1980s and 1990s. The **securitization** process begins with banks segregating loans into relatively homogeneous pools with regard to the maturity and type of loan. These pools of loans are then transferred to a trust, which then, with the help of an underwriter, sells securities (usually called certificates) backed by the loans to ultimate investors. The originating bank usually provides some form of credit enhancement, which pays promised cash flows to the ultimate investors in the event of default. Also, securitized issues are typically rated for default risk by one of the major rating agencies. Exhibit 13.10 illustrates the typical securitization process.

Securitization offers several benefits to banks. First, by selling rather than holding loans, banks reduce the amount of assets and liabilities, thereby reducing reserve requirements, capital requirements, and deposit insurance premiums. Note that securitized assets are not listed in Exhibit 13.9 because they are not contingent assets or contingent liabilities. Second, securitization provides a source of funding loans that is less expensive than other sources. Finally, banks generate fees from the securitization process. Banks collect origination fees and loan-servicing fees, and recently banks have been permitted to underwrite securitized issues. Thus banks can also collect underwriting fees in the securitization process.

DERIVATIVE SECURITIES

Banks participate in the markets for interest rate and currency forwards, futures, options, and swaps. Banks participate in these markets for several reasons. First, banks use derivatives to hedge the risks they are exposed to as a result of the asset transformation functions they perform. We will discuss some of these uses in the next chapter. Second, banks may use derivatives to speculate on the direction of changes in interest rates or currency exchange rates. Bank regulators frown upon this type of activity, but it is difficult for outsiders to determine when a bank is using derivatives to hedge and when they are using derivatives to speculate. And finally, some banks act as dealers by serving as the counterparty in derivative con-

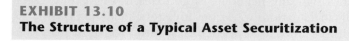

EXHIBIT 13.10
The Structure of a Typical Asset Securitization

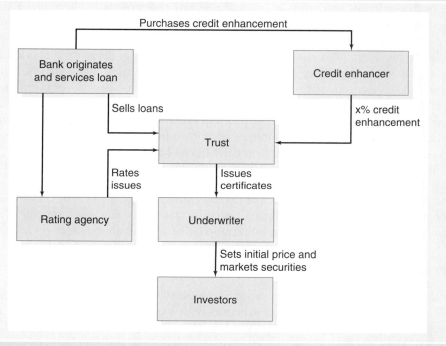

In a securitization, banks sell loans to a trust that issues securities backed by the loans. Not only does securitization improve a bank's capital and liquidity positions, but it also allows banks to generate fee income.

tracts for their clients. Derivative securities are both contingent assets and contingent liabilities because they offer potential gains as well as potential losses. In addition, banks that act as derivatives dealers earn fee income by matching up parties that wish to take a long position in a derivative contract and parties that wish to take short positions.

Exhibit 13.9 shows that the notional values of banks' derivative contract positions dwarf the value of banks' assets. Recall from Chapter 11, however, that these notional values are fictional in nature and are used only for calculating the swapped payments. Further, the notional values of the swap contracts shown in Exhibit 13.9 do not represent net positions, but the sum of the notional value of all the contracts of a given type. Therefore, some banks may have a net position of zero but show a large notional principal amount on their financial statements.

Derivative securities were discussed at length in Chapter 11, so we will not go into detail here about the different types. Needless to say, however, is that many banks, especially large banks, are relying heavily on derivative securities for the purposes mentioned above. The active use of derivatives by banks has caused bank regulators and other policy makers to be more concerned about whether derivative securities are increasing or decreasing the overall risk exposure of the banking industry. Fortunately, the use of derivatives by banks has not yet caused any large-scale losses in the industry.

The **bank holding company** is the most common form of organization for banks in the United States. The prominence of the holding company structure is attributable to three important desires on the part of bank management. First is the desire to achieve some form of interstate banking/branching in the face of restrictive laws, almost all of which have been eliminated in recent years. Second is the desire by some banks to diversify into nonbanking activities. Finally, bank holding companies can reduce their tax burden relative to the taxes they would pay if they operated as a bank.

DE FACTO BRANCHING

One of the motivations for adopting the holding company structure was to circumvent geographic restrictions on bank branching and acquisitions. By forming multibank holding companies, banks were able to expand beyond regulated geographic boundaries. This organizational form allowed banks to operate in larger units and thereby achieve economies of scale, and it also allowed greater geographic diversification within states for greater safety.

In 1994, Congress passed the Riegle-Neal Interstate Banking and Branching Efficiency Act. This Act allowed banks to acquire banks in other states. Previously, out-of-state bank acquisitions were regulated by individual states. Many states had established reciprocal arrangements with other states that allowed for acquisitions across state lines for banks located in the participating states. Beginning June 1, 1997, these reciprocal arrangements were made moot by the passage of the Riegle-Neal Act. In addition, banks can now branch across state lines if allowed by individual states. Consequently, banks no longer need to form a holding company to expand geographically.

NONBANKING ACTIVITIES

The reason many large banks formed bank holding companies was the opportunity to engage in a wide range of business activities. The scope of activities permitted is broader than those activities granted individual banks under the Banking Act of 1933. The Board of Governors of the Federal Reserve System has the authority to define what activities are closely related to banking activities. The Federal Reserve gradually expanded the list of allowable activities for the affiliated nonbank subsidiaries of bank holding companies over the last 20 years until, finally, the Financial Services Modernization Act of 1999 (the Gramm-Leach-Bliley Act) expanded the list of allowable activities for financial holding companies to include virtually all financially related businesses.

Under GLB, any well-managed, well-capitalized banking firm that has a satisfactory Community Reinvestment Act rating can convert to a **financial holding company**. subject to approval by the Federal Reserve.[1] Financial holding companies are allowed to own subsidiaries that engage in virtually any financial business. Therefore, many bank holding companies have become certified as financial holding companies and acquired insurance and investment banking affiliates. Likewise, some insurance and investment banking firms have

---

[1] The Community Reinvestment Act (CRA) and CRA ratings are discussed in Chapter 16.

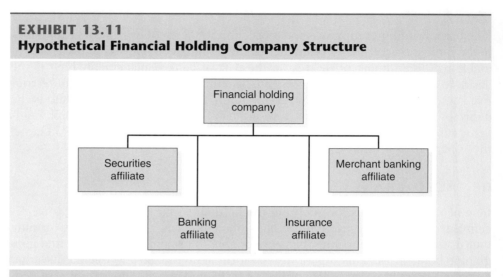

EXHIBIT 13.11
Hypothetical Financial Holding Company Structure

Banks are now allowed to affiliate with securities firms, insurance companies, and merchant banking firms as part of a financial holding company structure.

acquired bank holding companies and become certified as financial holding companies. A hypothetical structure of a financial holding company is shown in Exhibit 13.11.

TAX AVOIDANCE

One of the most important reasons for smaller banks to form a bank holding company is the tax consideration. For example, approximately 90 percent of bank holding companies are one-bank holding companies, and of these, about half are single-subsidiary companies. Product or geographic market motivation cannot account for the existence of these single-subsidiary holding companies. The principal tax benefit of a holding company organization is that interest paid on debt is a tax-deductible expense and most dividends received from subsidiaries provide tax-exempt revenues for the parent firm. In addition, nonbanking subsidiaries can be structured to avoid local taxes.

DO YOU UNDERSTAND?

1. What are the main factors a bank must consider when setting the interest rate to offer on deposits?
2. List and describe the major fee-based services offered by commercial banks.
3. Discuss the uses of standby letters of credit (SLCs). What benefits do SLCs offer to a bank's commercial customers?
4. What are the major reasons that banks sell loans?
5. What are the major benefits to banks of securitization?

CHAPTER TAKE-AWAYS

1 The elimination of branching restrictions and mergers has reduced the number of commercial banks from about 15,000 in 1985 to about 7,800 today. In addition, the industry is dominated by a small number of very large institutions.

2 For most banks, the principal source of funds is deposit accounts. These funds are payable on demand or have very short maturities, and the owners of such accounts are insured by the FDIC against any loss up to $100,000.

3 Over half of the funds obtained by banks are utilized in making a wide variety of loans. In addition, banks hold large portfolios of investment securities. Short-term investments, such as Treasury securities, afford banks a source of income while also providing liquidity. Long-term securities, such as municipal bonds, are held for their higher after-tax returns. Because cash assets earn no interest, banks keep their cash holdings to a minimum.

4 Banks' lending decisions and how they price their loans are based largely on the credit risk of borrowers. Credit risk is measured using the five Cs of lending: character, capacity, capital, collateral, and conditions.

5 Banks must set deposit interest rates high enough to attract and retain depositors, but not so high that they are no longer profitable. The problem is further compounded in competitive markets where loan interest rates are relatively low.

6 Fee-based services provide stable income during uncertain economic conditions, while allowing banks to avoid the usual risks of financial intermediation. These services include correspondent banking, trust services, mutual fund sales, and securities brokerage.

7 Banks' major off-balance-sheet activities include loan commitments, standby letters of credit, loan brokerage, securitization, and derivative securities. These also generate income for banks in the form of fees or gains in the value of the contracts.

8 Banks organize into bank holding companies to achieve geographic expansion, to conduct limited nonbanking activities, and to reduce their taxes. Many bank holding companies have sought financial holding company status in order to offer additional nonbanking activities through affiliated companies.

KEY TERMS

Demand deposit
Correspondent balances
NOW account (negotiable order of withdrawal)
Money market deposit account (MMDA)
Certificates of deposit
Borrowed funds
Federal funds (fed funds)
Repurchase agreements (RPs)
Eurodollars

London Interbank Offer Rate (LIBOR)
Banker's acceptance
Cash items in the process of collection (CIPC)
Promissory note
Secured/unsecured loan
Collateral
Fixed-rate/floating-rate loan
Bridge loan
Seasonal loan
Long-term asset loan

Prime rate
Compensating balances
Matched funding
Credit scoring
Correspondent banking
Mutual fund
Brokerage services
Investment banking
Financial Services Modernization Act (Gramm-Leach-Bliley Act)
Line of credit

Term loan
Revolving credit
Commercial letter of credit
Standby letter of credit (SLC)
Securitization
Bank holding company
Financial holding company

QUESTIONS AND PROBLEMS

1. What is the primary goal of a commercial bank? Why may this goal be translated into maximizing the firm's stock share price?

2. Why are demand deposits a more important source of funds for small banks than for large banks? Why are demand deposits considered to be a more stable source of funds for small banks than for large banks?

3. What are borrowed funds? Give some specific examples. Have borrowed funds become more or less important as a source of funds for banks?

4. Why are negotiable CDs and federal funds primarily sources of funds for very large banks?

5. Define "bank capital." What is the economic importance of capital to a firm?

6. What are the major uses of funds for a bank? What are the differences between large and small banks? Explain the difference.

7. What are the important differences between investments and loans in a bank portfolio of assets?

8. What are the advantages and disadvantages of using credit scoring to evaluate a loan application?

9. Distinguish between a line of credit and a letter of credit.

10. Give the reasons banks hold Treasury securities and municipal bonds in their investment portfolios.

11. Explain why banks buy and sell federal funds. Also explain the role of the Federal Reserve System in the federal funds market. Show the T-accounts for a federal funds transaction.

12. Define "correspondent banking." Why do banks enter into correspondent relationships?

13. What is the prime rate? Why do some banks make loans below the prime rate?

14. What do we mean by "off-balance-sheet" activities? If these things are not on the balance sheet, are they important? What are some off-balance-sheet activities?

15. What are the major benefits of getting assets "off the balance sheet" through either loan sales or securitization?

16. Give the reasons that banks select the bank holding company form of organization. Why would a bank holding company seek to convert to a financial holding company?

17. With the passage of the Riegle-Neal Banking and Branching Efficiency Act, what do you expect to happen to the number of banks in the United States?

18. What is a contingent asset? What is a contingent liability? Provide an example of each.

INTERNET EXERCISE

There are several useful Internet sites for gathering information about commercial banks and bank holding companies. In this chapter, we discussed the various sources and uses of funds by commercial banks, the growth in off-balance-sheet activities of banks, and the typical structure of banking organizations. In this Internet exercise, your task is to examine the sources and uses of funds for a specific bank in your local community. Data on the balance sheet, income statement, and structure of individual banks and bank holding companies can be found at the Federal Financial Institutions Examination Council's National Information Center (NIC) Web site, http://www.ffiec.gov/nic/. Search the NIC Web site for the name of your local bank. Once you have found the bank in the database, you can generate reports on the balance sheet, income statement, performance ratios, deposits, and loan portfolio. In addition, you can determine the organizational hierarchy of the bank. Up-to-date data on the banking industry as a whole can be found at the FDIC's Web site, http://www.fdic.gov.

1. Once you have found your bank on the NIC database, determine which bank regulatory agency is responsible for regulating your bank.
2. Determine whether the bank is part of a holding company structure. If so, determine whether there are other commercial banks owned by the same parent company. Are there any nonbank subsidiaries of the parent company?
3. Print out or download data on the balance sheet of your bank. Import the data into a spreadsheet and determine how your bank stacks up against industry norms. Do this by calculating the percentages that were calculated in Exhibits 13.5 and 13.7. How do the averages for your bank differ from the averages for other banks of similar size?

14

Bank Management and Profitability

CHAPTER PREVIEW

Thirty or forty years ago, bankers managed by the so-called 3-6-3 rule. According to this rule, a smart banker would borrow at 3 percent from his depositors (there were few female bankers at the time), lend at 6 percent to his borrowers, and be on the golf course by 3 o'clock. Banking was a much simpler business at the time.

For better or worse, banking has evolved into a much more challenging business. Certainly for the better,

there are more female bankers. Possibly for worse, depending on your perspective, bankers have to work much harder and the business has become much more challenging.

Just as it was 30 or 40 years ago, bank managers are in a constant quest for profits. However, profits must be earned without sacrificing bank safety; that is, bank managers must maintain adequate liquidity and capital. Further, banks must manage the risks they face in order to protect

their liquidity and capital positions. Failure to manage these risks effectively can lead to, at a minimum, greater regulatory scrutiny and limits on the bank's activities. At worst, a failure to maintain adequate capital and liquidity can lead to the bank being taken over by bank regulators, shareholders losing their investment, and bank managers being the target of legal action. A bank that takes very little risk, on the other hand, will not generate enough profits to satisfy the demands of shareholders.

Among the differences between today and 30 or 40 years ago are that the competition for profitable lending opportunities is much greater, interest rates are more volatile, attracting and keeping depositors are more difficult, and shareholders are more demanding. Consequently, the challenges of managing a profitable bank are more difficult. Fortunately, the tools that managers use in their quest to maximize profits and minimize risk have also evolved. ■

In the relaxed regulatory environment of the 1980s, Hugh McColl (on the right), then CEO of North Carolina National Bank, began building an interstate banking empire that resulted in the creation of NationsBank. McColl's drive to create a truly nationwide bank culminated in the merger of NationsBank with Bank of America in 1998, a $62.5 billion transaction. The photograph shows McColl and David Coulter, then CEO of Bank of America, talking to reporters about the merger.

The previous chapter discussed what banks do to generate profits. This chapter examines some of the issues that arise in the pursuit of those profits and discusses how bank managers address those issues. The chapter begins with a description of bank income statements and a discussion of some of the trends in the income and expense items on banks' income statements. Next, we discuss measures of bank performance. Then we discuss the dilemma of bank profitability versus bank safety and how managers minimize the risk of failure while they attempt to maximize shareholder wealth. Specifically, the major risk management topics covered in this chapter are asset and liability management strategies for minimizing the risk of failing due to liquidity risk, and interest rate risk management and credit risk management strategies for minimizing the risk of failure due to solvency risk. ∎

LEARNING OBJECTIVES

The objectives of this chapter are to:

1 Describe the primary sources of income and expenses for banks.

2 Discuss the recent trends concerning bank earnings and performance.

3 Explain the profitability-versus-safety trade-off faced by banks.

4 Discuss how banks manage their liquidity risk.

5 Describe the capital requirements faced by banks.

6 Explain the methods employed by banks to manage credit risk.

7 Describe how banks measure interest rate risk.

8 Discuss how banks can minimize their interest rate risk.

BANK EARNINGS

Before we discuss the management problems banks face, let us examine the performance of commercial banks by examining the bank income statement. The major items on the income statement for all federally insured commercial banks and for small, medium, and large banks are shown in Exhibit 14.1. For comparison purposes, we scaled the income and expense items by total assets.

The major source of income for commercial banks is interest on loans, accounting for $335 billion, or 4.42 percent when measured as a percent of assets. Small banks' interest and fee income on loans is greater than that of large banks (small banks, 5.22 percent; and large banks, 4.29 percent). These differences can be attributed to differences in the lending practices of large and small banks. Recall from Chapter 13 that small banks tend to make more real estate and agricultural loans, while large banks tend to make more commercial and industrial loans.

The interest earned on investment securities provides another 0.71 percent. This source of revenue is more important for small banks (0.88 percent of assets)

EXHIBIT 14.1
Income Statement for Commercial Banks (December 31, 2003)

	All Insured Commercial Banks[a]		Small Banks[b]	Medium-Sized Banks[c]	Large Banks[d]
	Millions[e]	% of Assets[f]	% of Assets[f]	% of Assets[f]	% of Assets[f]
Total interest income	**335,764**	**4.42**	**5.22**	**5.18**	**4.29**
Loans	254,410	3.35	4.20	4.23	3.20
Lease financing receivables	8,872	0.12	0.02	0.03	0.13
Balances due from dep. institutions	2,723	0.04	0.04	0.02	0.04
Investment securities	54,150	0.71	0.88	0.84	0.69
Assets held in trading accounts	7,881	0.10	0.00	0.00	0.12
Federal funds sold and securities purchased under agreements to resell	5,100	0.07	0.06	0.04	0.07
Other Interest income	2,627	0.03	0.02	0.03	0.04
Total interest expense	**95,768**	**1.26**	**1.54**	**1.50**	**1.22**
Deposits	63,089	0.83	1.41	1.28	0.75
Federal funds purchased and securities sold under agreements to repurchase	8,076	0.11	0.01	0.03	0.12
Other borrowed money	20,371	0.27	0.12	0.20	0.28
Subordinated notes and debentures	4,231	0.06	0.00	0.00	0.06
Net interest income	**239,996**	**3.16**	**3.68**	**3.67**	**3.07**
Provisions for loan and lease losses	**34,777**	**0.46**	**0.26**	**0.31**	**0.48**
Total noninterest income	**186,474**	**2.45**	**1.14**	**1.58**	**2.62**
Fiduciary activities	21,039	0.28	0.07	0.23	0.29
Service charges on deposit accounts	31,733	0.42	0.42	0.41	0.42
Trading account gains and fees	11,474	0.15	0.00	0.00	0.18
All other noninterest income	122,228	1.61	0.66	0.93	1.73
Total noninterest expense	**245,948**	**3.24**	**3.41**	**3.36**	**3.21**
Salaries and employee benefits	107,798	1.42	1.76	1.64	1.38
Premises and equipment	31,324	0.41	0.44	0.41	0.41
All other noninterest expense	106,826	1.41	1.22	1.31	1.42
Pretax net operating income	**145,744**	**1.92**	**1.14**	**1.58**	**1.99**
Gains (losses) on securities	5,600	0.07	0.04	0.04	0.08
Applicable income taxes	49,227	0.65	0.27	0.44	0.69
Income before extraordinary items	102,117	1.34	0.90	1.19	1.38
Extraordinary items, net	429	0.01	0.00	0.03	0.00
Net income	**102,546**	**1.35**	**0.90**	**1.22**	**1.38**

The interest income earned on loans continues to be the most important source of income for banks, especially small banks. Large banks supplement their relatively low net interest income by generating substantial revenue in the form of noninterest income.

[a] This group consists of 7,770 insured commercial banks.
[b] This group consists of the country's 3,912 smallest banks. These banks have assets of less than $100 million.
[c] This group consists of the country's 3,434 medium-sized banks. These banks have assets between $100 million and $1 billion.
[d] This group consists of the country's 424 largest banks. These banks have assets of $1 billion or more.
[e] Columns may not add to 100 percent because of rounding.
[f] Measured as a percent of total assets.
Source: FDIC, *Statistics on Banking*, December 31, 2003.

than for large banks (0.69 percent of assets) because small banks hold proportionally more investment securities (see Exhibit 13.7 in the previous chapter).

The interest paid on deposits is one of the largest expense items for banks, accounting for $63 billion, or 0.83 percent when measured as a percent of assets. Small banks pay more interest on their deposits (1.41 percent of assets) than large banks (0.75 percent) because of their greater reliance on deposits as a source of funds (see Exhibit 13.5 in the previous chapter). Large banks, on the other hand, pay more than small banks for federal funds purchased and securities sold under repurchase agreements as well as other borrowed money. The bottom line is that all banks pay gross interest expenses equal to about 1.26 percent of assets, on average.

The net interest income (or **net interest margin**) of $240 billion represents the difference between **gross interest income** and **gross interest expense**. Small banks tend to earn a greater net interest income as a percent of assets than large banks (small banks, 3.68 percent; large banks, 3.07 percent) because small banks generate more interest income than large banks.

Illustrations of the historical trends in interest income and interest expense are shown in Exhibit 14.2. The difference between the two lines in the exhibit represents net interest income. Gross interest income and gross interest expense

EXHIBIT 14.2
Interest Income and Expense (1935–2003)

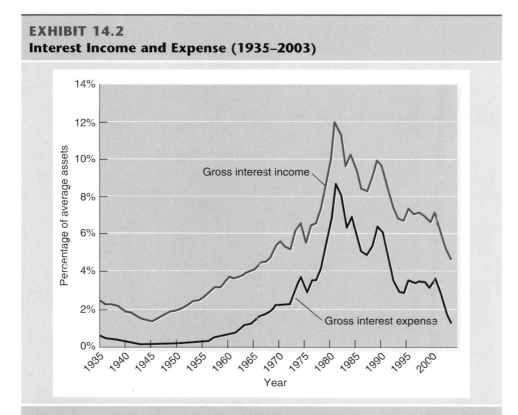

The difference between gross interest income and gross interest expense is net interest income. Net interest income is the traditional source of income for banks.

Source: FDIC, *Statistics on Banking.*

have been relatively volatile in the last 30 years and tend to follow market rates of interest. Note that both are at lows that have not been seen since the 1960s. However, net interest income has remained relatively stable. In fact, net interest income has increased in the last 20 years as banks have shifted from holding government securities to holding higher-yielding assets such as mortgages, mortgage-backed securities, and consumer loans.

The **provision for loan losses** is an expense item that adds to a bank's loan loss reserve. The loan loss reserve is a contra-asset account that is deducted from gross loans to determine the net loan amount shown on the bank's balance sheet. Banks add to their loan loss reserve in anticipation of credit quality problems in their loan portfolio. Exhibit 14.1 shows that large banks added more to their loan loss reserve than small banks. The provision for loan and lease losses was 0.48 percent for large banks when measured as a percent of assets. It was only 0.26 percent for small banks. Much of the difference can be attributed to the high delinquency rates on credit card debt holdings of some large banks.

Exhibit 14.3 gives a historical perspective on the loan loss provisions of commercial banks since 1935. The increase in loan loss provisions in the mid-1980s was due to many of the loans to less developed countries (LDCs) that ultimately went bad. The LDC debt crisis in the mid-1980s forced many of the country's largest banks to write off billions of dollars in loans. In the late 1980s and early 1990s, some banks continued to suffer losses in their LDC loans. In addition, many banks experienced losses in their real estate loan portfolio. The recent increase in the provision for loan losses is largely due to delinquencies in credit card portfo-

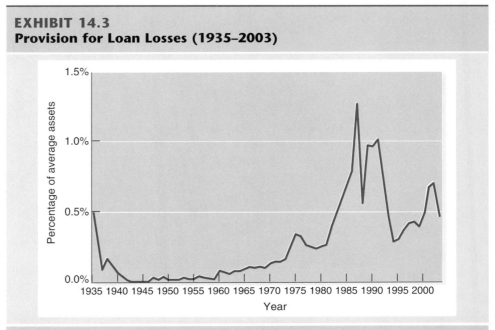

EXHIBIT 14.3
Provision for Loan Losses (1935–2003)

Provision for loan losses is an expense item that adds to the reserve for loan losses. It increases in anticipation of loan losses.

Source: FDIC *Statistics on Banking.*

EXHIBIT 14.4
Noninterest Income and Expense (1935–2003)

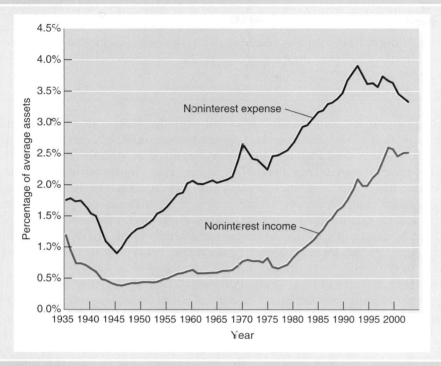

Noninterest income includes fees and service charges earned by the bank. They are the fastest growing source of income for banks, especially large banks. Noninterest expense has been growing in response to increased information-processing costs and merger restructuring fees.

Source: FDIC *Statistics on Banking.*

lios and commercial loan portfolios. Fortunately, as the economy showed modest improvements in 2003, banks were able to reduce their provisions for loan losses.

A source of revenue of growing importance in the last 20 years, especially for large banks, is **noninterest income**, which consists mainly of fees and service charges. Noninterest income was 2.45 percent of assets for all banks in 2003, up from 1.6 percent in 1990. Some of the fastest-growing noninterest income items are those in the "all other noninterest income" category, including ATM surcharges, credit card fees, and fees from the sale of mutual funds and annuities. Exhibit 14.4 shows the increase in noninterest income in recent years.

While noninterest income has been growing in recent years, **noninterest expense** peaked in the early 1990s and has even shown signs of declining in recent years. It is about 3.24 percent of assets for all banks. Most of small banks' noninterest expenses are in the form of salaries and employee benefits, while large banks' noninterest expenses are more balanced between the "salaries and employee benefits category" and the "other noninterest expense category," which includes, among other things, merger restructuring charges, marketing expenses, fees for information-processing services, and fees for loan servicing performed by others. Small banks are less automated and have a greater retail emphasis than large banks; therefore, small banks have more employees per dollar of assets than large banks. For the industry as a whole, however, salaries and employee benefits have remained a relatively stable 1.42 percent of assets in recent years. Much of the recent decline in noninterest expenses can be attributed to the economies of scale and improved efficiencies resulting from the consolidation the industry went through in the 1980s and 1990s.

BANK PERFORMANCE

Although net income for banks has varied over the years, the general trend in bank profitability has been upward. Low profit margins but high volume characterize bank operations. Profitability can be measured in several ways. The rate of return on average assets (net income/average total assets) allows for the comparison of one bank with another. The **return on average assets (ROAA)** is the key ratio in evaluating the quality of bank management, because it tells how much profit bank management can generate with a given amount of assets. Bank management is responsible for the utilization and selection of a bank's assets, and in recent years, ROAA for commercial banks varied between 0.48 percent and 1.40 percent in the 1990s and early 2000s.

Another measure of bank profitability is the rate of return on average equity capital (net income/average equity capital). **Return on average equity (ROAE)** tells the bank owners how management has performed on their behalf—the amount of profits in relation to their capital contribution to the firm. Because banks are very highly leveraged (low capital-to-assets ratios), their ROAEs are quite respectable even though their ROAAs are very low. During the 1990s and early 2000s, banks' ROAEs have ranged between 7.55 and 15.31 percent. Exhibit 14.5 shows the return on average assets and return on average equity capital from 1935 to 2003. The left axis indicates the return on average assets, while the right axis indicates the return on average equity. Changes in the difference between ROAA and ROAE, as illustrated in the exhibit, are due to changes in banks' capital-to-assets ratios. ROAE will be high relative to ROAA during periods when banks have relatively low capital-to-assets ratios. For example, banks' capital-to-assets ratios declined during the 1970s and 1980s. In the past 10 years, however, banks' capital-to-assets ratios increased. Consequently, ROAAs have increased faster than ROAEs.

A BANKING DILEMMA: PROFITABILITY VERSUS SAFETY

As profit-maximizing firms, commercial banks can increase expected profits by taking on more credit risk, interest rate risk, or liquidity risk, all of which jeopardize bank safety. Bank safety concerns a bank's ability to survive as a going concern—staying in business. For a bank to survive, it has to balance the demands of three constituencies: shareholders, depositors, and bank regulators. If bank managers do not generate adequate profits, shareholders may become dissatisfied with management and sell their stock, driving the bank's stock price lower. If bank managers take on too much risk, bank depositors (especially uninsured ones) may become concerned about the safety of their deposits and they remove them, creating a liquidity crisis for the bank. If bank regulators believe that the actions of managers are imprudent, they may intervene in the management of the bank or,

EXHIBIT 14.5
Return on Average Assets and Average Equity (1935–2003)

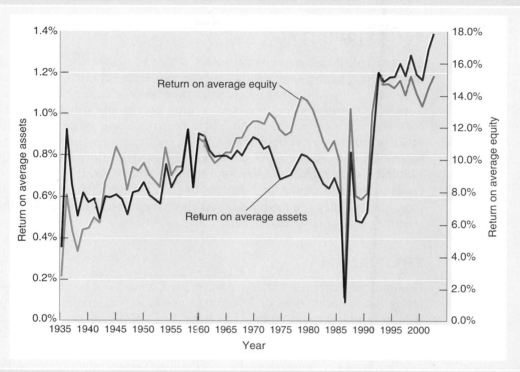

ROAA and ROAE tend to move together over time. When ROAA and ROAE do not move together, it is due to changes in capital-to-assets ratios. ROAE increases relative to ROAA when capital-to-assets ratios decrease, as they did in the late 1960s and early 1970s. ROAA increases relative to ROAE when capital-to-asset ratios increase, as they did in recent years.

Source: FDIC *Statistics on Banking.*

at the extreme, revoke the bank's charter. Bank managers can avoid the problems of taking too many risks by taking very little risk, but then the bank would not be very profitable. In this section we discuss the trade-offs faced by bank managers in balancing profitability against liquidity and solvency.

BANK SOLVENCY

As discussed in the previous chapter, the capital-to-total-assets ratio for a commercial bank is about 9 percent, which is low compared to other industries. What are the managerial implications of commercial banks having such low capital-to-assets ratios? First, it means that the owners provide only 9 percent of the money to purchase the bank's total assets. The remaining 91 percent of the funds are furnished by the bank's creditors. Second, and more important, a relatively small depreciation in the value of the bank's assets could make it insolvent. A firm is **insolvent** when the value of its liabilities exceeds the value of its assets; the firm is legally bankrupt. For example, if a commercial bank invests all of its funds in

Treasury bonds that fall in price by 9 percent, the bank becomes bankrupt. Thus, given commercial banks' extremely low capital position, they are vulnerable to failure if they accept excessive credit risk or interest rate risk.

BANK LIQUIDITY

Another risk facing commercial banks is that of inadequate liquidity. **Bank liquidity** refers to the bank's ability to accommodate deposit withdrawals and loan requests, and pay off other liabilities as they become due. Normally, some depositors will be withdrawing funds or writing checks and others will be adding to their deposit accounts. Similarly, some borrowers will be paying off loans while other borrowers are taking down lines of credit or other loan commitments. On some occasions, however, a large number of depositors withdraw their funds simultaneously, such as occurred in the 1920s and 1930s. If a bank has insufficient funds to meet its depositors' demands, it must close its doors. Banks fail, therefore, because they are unable to meet their legal obligations to depositors, other creditors, and borrowers.

THE DILEMMA

Commercial banks can fail in two ways. First, a bank can become insolvent by suffering losses on its loans or investment portfolio (i.e., credit risk or interest rate risk), resulting in a depletion of its capital. Second, a bank can be a profitable business operation but fail because it cannot meet the liquidity demands of its depositors or borrowers (i.e., liquidity risk).

Exhibit 14.6 summarizes the profitability-versus-safety dilemma facing bank management. The central problem for bank management is reconciling the conflicting goals of solvency and liquidity on the one hand and profitability on the other. Unfortunately, it is a set of conflicts not easily resolved. For example, liquidity could be achieved by holding only Treasury securities. In this strategy, bank management would sleep well but eat poorly because profits would be low.

EXHIBIT 14.6
Profitability Goal versus Liquidity and Solvency

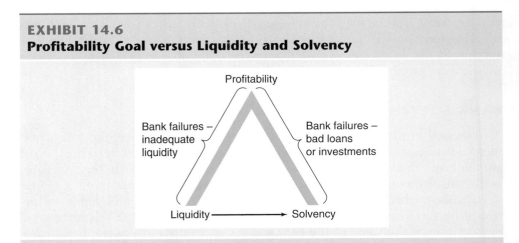

The goal of bank management is to maximize the value of the firm. However, higher profits must not be achieved at the expense of bank safety

At the other extreme, the bank could shift its asset portfolio into high-yielding, high-risk loans at the expense of better-quality loans or liquid investments. Bank management would eat well temporarily because of increased profits but would sleep poorly because of the possibility of a bank failure later on caused by large loan losses or inadequate liquidity. Finally, bank liquidity is ultimately related to bank solvency. That is, most bank runs are triggered by depositors' and other creditors' expectations of extraordinary losses in the bank's loan or investment portfolios.

We now turn our attention to how banks attempt to solve the problem of maximizing profits while maintaining adequate liquidity and capital. We begin with how banks manage their liquidity.

LIQUIDITY MANAGEMENT

We now examine current bank strategies for maintaining sufficient liquidity and solvency while maximizing overall bank profits. Several important developments in bank liquidity practices have taken place since the 1960s. The first is asset management, which is a codification of previous theories. The second is liability management—acquiring liquidity from the liability side of the balance sheet. In practice, of course, banks obtain liquidity from both sides of the balance sheet.

ASSET MANAGEMENT

A commercial bank requires liquidity to accommodate deposit withdrawals, pay other liabilities as they become due, and accommodate loan requests. Sources of liquidity are new deposits, increases in other liabilities, loan repayments, and the sale of assets. Cash accounts are available to the bank for payment of immediate withdrawals at no cost to the bank. All other assets must be converted into cash assets before they can be used for liquidity purposes. The conversion process involves the time and expense to sell the assets as well as the risk that they may be sold below their purchase price (price risk).

We can draw the following general conclusions when examining the assets held by commercial banks: (1) investment securities are more liquid than bank loans because of their superior marketability, and (2) short-term investments are more liquid than long-term investments because of the smaller price risk. Let us see how bank management uses these conclusions in asset management. **Asset management** classifies bank assets into four basic groups: primary reserves, secondary reserves, bank loans, and investments for income and tax shields.

Primary Reserves. **Primary reserves** are the cash assets on a bank's balance sheet. They consist of vault cash, deposits at correspondent banks, and deposits held at the Federal Reserve banks. Primary reserves are immediately available at no cost to the bank to accommodate liquidity demands. However, because they yield no interest, banks try to minimize their holdings of primary reserves.

Secondary Reserves. **Secondary reserves** are short-term assets that can be converted quickly into cash at a price near their purchase price. Their main purpose is to provide the bank with additional liquidity while safely earning some interest income. Treasury bills and short-term government agency securities make up the majority of the bank's secondary reserves. Because the securities that compose secondary reserves are highly marketable and have low default risk, they typically have yields below the yields of loans and other investment securities held by the bank.

Bank Loans.   After the bank has satisfied its potential liquidity needs, bank management can concentrate on its primary business—making loans to business firms and individuals. Business loans are generally less liquid and riskier than other bank assets and, as a result, typically carry the highest yield of all bank assets and offer the greatest potential for profit.

Investments.   After the bank has satisfied its loan demand, the remaining funds are then available for open-market investments. The primary function of the investment portfolio is to provide income and tax advantages to the bank rather than liquidity. Open-market investments are typically longer-term securities that are less marketable and have higher default risk than secondary reserves. These investments therefore offer greater income potential to the bank. Investments for income include long-term Treasury securities, municipal bonds, and government agency securities. Banks usually prefer to hold municipal instead of corporate bonds because they offer a higher after-tax yield.

The Asset Mix.   The proportion of liquid assets a bank should hold brings us back to the dilemma between bank profitability and liquidity. The greater the proportion of primary and secondary reserves the bank holds, the greater the liquidity of its portfolio. Unfortunately, highly liquid assets that are low in default risk typically have low interest returns. Overall bank strategy, then, is to hold the minimum amounts of primary and secondary reserves consistent with bank safety. Exhibit 14.7 shows assets commonly held in bank asset management strategy and the liquidity–yield trade-off that bank management must make. The exhibit provides a useful review of the concepts involved in asset management.

At a minimum, banks are required to hold enough primary reserves to satisfy reserve requirements. In addition, banks usually hold additional primary and secondary reserves. The total amount of primary and secondary reserves that a bank holds is related to reserve requirements, deposit variability, other sources of liquidity, loan commitments outstanding, bank regulations, and the risk posture of the bank's management. Deposit variability is often determined by examining past deposit behavior, particularly in regard to deposit inflows and outflows. Deposit variability also depends on the type of account and bank customer. For example, demand deposits are more variable than time deposits.

LIABILITY MANAGEMENT

Prior to the 1960s, it was believed that liquidity came almost entirely from the asset side of the balance sheet. **Liability management** argues that banks can use the liability side of their balance sheets for liquidity. Historically, banks had always treated their liability structure as a fixed pool of funds, at least in the short run. Bank asset holdings were tailored to the deposit variability characteristics of their liabilities. Under liability management, however, banks take asset growth as given and then adjust their liabilities as needed. Thus, when a bank needs additional funds for liquidity or any other purpose, it merely buys the funds in the money markets.

EXHIBIT 14.7
Summary of Asset Management Strategy

Category and Type of Asset	Purpose	Liquidity	Yield
Primary reserves Vault cash Deposits at the Fed Deposits at other banks	Immediately available funds	Highest	None
Secondary reserves Treasury bills Federal funds sold Short-term agency securities	Easily marketable funds	High	Low
Bank loans Business loans Consumer loans Real estate loans Agriculture loans	Income	Lowest	Highest
Investments Treasury securities Agency securities Municipal bonds	Income when safe loans are unavailable and tax advantages	Medium	Medium

To maintain adequate liquidity, banks hold both primary and secondary reserves. Secondary reserves allow banks to earn some interest income while still meeting their liquidity needs.

Liability Management Theory.   Liability management is based on the assumption that certain types of bank liabilities are very sensitive to interest rate changes. Thus, by raising the interest rate paid on these liabilities above the market rate, a bank can immediately attract additional funds. On the other hand, by lowering the rate paid on these liabilities, a bank may allow funds to run off as the liabilities mature.

Some of the bank liabilities employed in liability management are negotiable certificates of deposit (CDs), federal funds, repurchase agreements, commercial paper, and Eurodollar borrowings. These securities are sensitive to interest rates and have markets large enough to accommodate the activities of the commercial banking system. Other bank liabilities, such as savings accounts or demand deposits, are not as sensitive to interest rates, and changes in the posted offering rate will not result in notable immediate inflows or outflows of funds. Long-term debt and bank capital are not appropriate for use in liability management because of the time it takes to bring these securities to market.

Using Liability Management.   The liquidity gained by liability management is useful to a bank in several ways. First, it can be used to counteract deposit inflows and outflows and reduce their variability. Sudden or unexpected deposit outflows can be offset immediately by the purchase of new funds. Second, funds attracted by liability management may be used to meet increases in loan demand by the bank's customers. Customers need not be denied loans because of a lack of funds. As long as the expected marginal return of the new loans exceeds the expected marginal cost of funds, the bank can increase its income by acquiring the additional funds through liability management. Third, the ability to immediately attract additional funds allows banks to engage in more off-balance-sheet activities. As discussed in Chapter 13, off-balance-sheet activities generate fees for banks but also represent contingent commitments of the bank. Those banks that use liability management have the funding flexibility that allows them to safely participate in contingent commitments.

Summary.   Liability management supplements asset management but does not replace it as a source of bank liquidity. Asset management still remains the primary source of liquidity for banks, particularly smaller banks. If used properly, liability management allows banks to reduce their secondary reserve holdings and invest these funds in higher-yield assets, such as loans or long-term municipal bonds. Liability management is not well suited to smaller banks, because they do not have direct access to the wholesale money markets where liability management is practiced.

Liability management is not a panacea for bank liquidity problems. There may be times when banks are unable to attract or retain funds through liability management because of tight credit periods or because of uncertainty about the soundness of a particular bank.

DO YOU UNDERSTAND?

1. Explain how liquidity risk can lead to a bank's failure.
2. What defines a bank's insolvency? What characteristic of a bank's balance sheet makes it vulnerable to insolvency?
3. Explain some simple strategies banks can follow to avoid insolvency or illiquidity. Why don't more banks adopt these strategies?
4. Why do banks try to minimize their holdings of primary reserves in the practice of asset management?
5. What asset accounts comprise secondary reserves? What role do these accounts serve in an asset management strategy?

BANK CAPITAL MANAGEMENT

Both bank management and regulators are concerned about banks maintaining adequate amounts of capital. Bank capital performs several important roles. First, it provides a financial cushion that enables banks to continue to operate even if they suffer temporary operating losses. Second, adequate capital helps maintain public confidence in the soundness and safety of individual banks and the banking system. This role protects the U.S. economy against the destabilizing consequences of massive bank failures. Third, adequate capital provides some protection to depositors whose bank accounts are not fully insured. Finally, capital is a source of funds for the bank's growth and the addition of new products, services, or facilities.

TRENDS IN BANK CAPITAL

In the early 1970s, bank regulators and public officials became concerned about erosion of key capital ratios (see Exhibit 14.8). Their concern was heightened by the failure of several large banks in 1973 and 1974 and again during the early 1980s following two back-to-back recessions. The debate over capital adequacy focuses on how much bank capital is necessary to provide a stable and safe banking system. Although opinions differ as to the amount of capital that provides reasonable protection, there is agreement that the capital ratios of the banking system declined appreciably in the 1960s and 1970s. Exhibit 14.8 shows that equity capital declined from about 8 percent of total assets in 1960 to less than 6 percent by 1974. The decline in bank capital is partly attributable to the unparalleled economic prosperity of the 1960s and early 1970s, which caused banks' assets to grow rapidly while their capital grew more slowly.

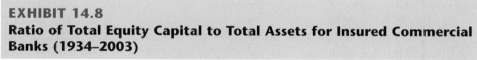

EXHIBIT 14.8
Ratio of Total Equity Capital to Total Assets for Insured Commercial Banks (1934–2003)

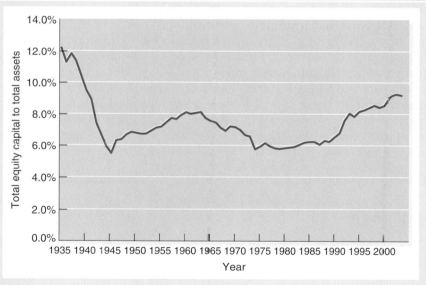

Capital levels declined in the late 1960s and early 1970s. The decline in capital levels was due to asset growth exceeding capital growth. In recent years, capital levels have improved in response to more stringent capital adequacy standards.

Source: FDIC *Statistics on Banking.*

Beginning in the 1980s, capital adequacy once more became an issue with bank regulators. Though the number of bank failures was less than 10 per year in 1979, the number of failures reached record numbers in the 1980s, with 118 banks failing in 1985 and more than 200 in 1987. Given this environment, bank regulators started increasing bank capital requirements in a series of steps beginning in December 1981. By 1985, the minimum ratio of equity capital to total assets increased to 5.5 percent of total assets.

CAPITAL ADEQUACY REGULATION

Basel I.   In July 1988, the central banks of the major industrial countries adopted a sweeping proposal assessing the capital adequacy of international banks.[1] The central banks reached this agreement as part of an effort to coordinate bank supervisory policies, with the goal of strengthening the international banking system and alleviating competitive inequities. The new guidelines define capital uniformly across all nations, apply risk weights to all assets and off-balance-sheet exposures, and set minimum levels of capital for international banks.

In the United States, the effort to develop a risk-based capital measure began in 1985. Of concern was the rapidly growing risk exposure of large money-center banks stemming from their off-balance-sheet activities. For example, standby letters of credit issued by the 10 largest bank holding companies had increased from 7.6 percent of total assets in 1981 to more than 12 percent by 1985. Likewise, interest rate swaps, first introduced in 1981, had increased to more than 14 percent of total assets by 1985. Neither of these or other off-balance-sheet activities were factored into existing U.S. capital guidelines, which focus on balance sheet assets.

Current capital adequacy requirements in the United States define two forms of capital. **Tier 1 capital** includes the sum of common stock, paid-in-surplus, retained earnings, noncumulative perpetual preferred stock, and minority interest in consolidated subsidiaries minus goodwill and other intangible assets. Tier 1 capital is commonly referred to as core capital. **Tier 2 capital** includes cumulative perpetual preferred stock, loan loss reserves, subordinated debt instruments, mandatory convertible debt instruments, and other debt instruments that combine both debt and equity features. Tier 2 capital is commonly referred to as supplemental capital. These capital measures are measured against **risk-weighted assets**. Risk-weighted assets are a measure of total assets that weights high-risk assets more heavily than low-risk assets. The minimum capital requirements require the following:

1. The ratio of Tier 1 capital to risk-weighted assets must be at least 4 percent.
2. The ratio of total capital (Tier 1 capital plus Tier 2 capital) to risk-weighted assets must be at least 8 percent.

Notice that the regulatory definition of Tier 2 capital includes debt. In the economic sense, debt is not capital; operating losses cannot be written off against debt. However, the debt included in Tier 2 capital is not insured by the Federal Deposit Insurance Corporation (FDIC) and represents a residual claim against the assets of the bank. The holders of the debt securities included in Tier 2 capi-

---

[1] The agreement, called the Basel Accord, included central banks from the following countries: Belgium, Canada, France, West Germany, Italy, Japan, the Netherlands, Sweden, the United Kingdom, the United States, Switzerland, and Luxembourg.

tal are ahead of common stockholders in terms of their claim against the assets of the bank, but they are behind the claims of the FDIC, uninsured depositors, secured creditors, and other debt holders. Banks are allowed to include these debt sources of funds as Tier 2 capital because they represent a buffer between losses by the bank and losses by the FDIC Bank Insurance Fund.

The basic purpose of the new capital guidelines is to relate a bank's capital to its risk profile so that high-risk activities require relatively more bank capital. The risk weightings applied to bank assets for capital adequacy calculations are shown in Exhibit 14.9. The risk weightings applied to off-balance-sheet activities are

---

EXHIBIT 14.9
Risk Weights for Assets

Category 1—Zero Percent Weight

Cash

Balances due from Federal Reserve banks and claims on central banks in other OECD countries[a]

U.S. Treasury and government agency securities and claims on or unconditionally guaranteed by OECD central governments

Federal Reserve stock

Claims collateralized by cash on deposit or by securities issued or guaranteed by OECD central governments or U.S. government agencies

Category 2—20 Percent Weight

Cash items in the process of collection

All claims on or guaranteed by U.S. depository institutions and banks in OECD countries

General obligation bonds of state and local governments

Portions of claims secured by U.S. government agency securities or OECD central government obligations that do not qualify for a zero percent weight

Loans or other claims conditionally guaranteed by the U.S. government

Securities and other claims on U.S. government-sponsored agencies

Category 3—50 Percent Weight

Loans secured by first liens on 1- to 4-family residential property and certain multifamily residential properties

Certain privately issued mortgage-backed securities

Revenue bonds of state and local governments

Category 4—100 Percent Weight

All loans and other claims on private obligors not placed in a lower risk category

Bank premises, fixed assets, and other real estate owned

Industrial development revenue bonds

Intangible assets and investment in unconsolidated subsidiaries, provided they are not deducted from capital

---

[a] The group of countries associated with the Organization for Economic Cooperation and Development (OECD) includes the United States and 24 other major industrial countries.

Category 1 is the least risky asset category; category 4, the riskiest. The weights reflect that regulators require banks to have more capital set aside to cover riskier activities.

Source: Commercial Bank Examination Manual, Board of Governors, Federal Reserve System, May 2004.

slightly more complicated because the off-balance-sheet amounts must be adjusted to reflect their potential on-balance-sheet exposure. In other words, off-balance-sheet amounts must be converted to on-balance-sheet amounts using a conversion factor. The conversion factor is a percentage that reflects the percentage of the off-balance-sheet exposure that will potentially end up on the balance sheet. The current risk weights and conversion factors for sample off-balance-sheet activities are shown in Exhibit 14.10.

The degree of regulatory scrutiny faced by a bank depends on the bank's level of capital. As capital declines, regulators clamp down harder on bank activities. The new capital requirements are based not only on the risk-based capital ratios described above, but also on the so-called leverage ratio. The leverage ratio is defined as Tier 1 capital divided by total assets.

The regulatory implications of declining capital are severe. Critically under-capitalized banks are subject to being seized by the FDIC, the worst possible penalty. All banks in the undercapitalized categories must submit improvement plans to the FDIC within 45 days of falling below the minimum. The FDIC will also restrict the asset growth of undercapitalized banks. Banks in the significantly undercapitalized category could face caps on deposit rates, forced sale of subsidiaries, or the firing of bank executives. These banks could also be forced to fire the board of directors and elect new members. Needless to say, the new guidelines provide a strong incentive to bank managers to maintain adequate capital. Financial economists have stated that the new capital standards hampered the ability of banks to make new loans, contributing to the early 1990s credit crunch and slowing the pace of recovery from the early 1990s economic recession.

EXHIBIT 14.10
Risk Weights and Conversion Ratios for Selected Off-Balance-Sheet Activities

Weight (%)	Conversion Factor	Off-Balance-Sheet Item
0	0	Short-term loan commitments
50	0[a]	Short-term interest rate derivatives
50	0.005[a]	Long-term interest rate derivatives
50	0.01[a]	Short-term foreign exchange derivatives
50	0.05[a]	Long-term foreign exchange derivatives
100	0.2	Commercial letters of credit
100	0.5	Long-term loan commitments
100	1	Standby letters of credit

Long-term off-balance-sheet activities require more capital than short-term activities. This is reflected in the weights associated with long-term activities.

[a] In addition to holding capital against potential on-balance-sheet exposures as measured by conversion factors, banks must also hold capital against the current value (replacement cost) of derivative securities.

Source: Commercial Bank Examination Manual, Board of Governors, Federal Reserve System, May 2004.

Although interest rate, credit, and liquidity risks are the primary risks that bankers worry about, there are plenty other risks that get their attention. For example, operational risk is the risk that has been drawing much of the banking industry's attention in recent years. This is due, in part, to the endorsement of the Basel II Accord on June 26, 2004. The Basel Committee defines operational risk as "the risk of direct or indirect loss resulting from inadequate or failed internal processes, people, and systems, or from external events." This catchall risk category includes losses from fraud, theft, terrorism, litigation, and even reputation problems. According to the Basel II Accord, large international banks will be required to hold capital against their operational risk.

These risks have been around for a long time but have taken on new importance in recent years. Some of the increased focus on these risks can be blamed on the tragedy of September 11, 2001, and recent corporate scandals. In addition to these reasons, however, banks are increasingly concerned about these risks due to increased reliance on technology, increased complexity in organizational structures, and the ever-increasing pace of change in the industry.

The biggest worries faced by banks concern the infrastructure costs associated with developing an operational risk management system, a lack of operational risk data with which to measure the risk, and lack of sufficient regulatory guidance on implementation issues. Fortunately, most bankers feel that improving their operational risk management systems will help them be competitive and improve their profitability.

Basel II. On June 26, 2004, the Basel Committee endorsed Basel II, a 251-page document outlining how capital standards will be implemented over the next several years. Having been in the works for several years, Basel II is an attempt to more effectively incorporate credit, market, and operational risks into capital standards. It is now up to individual countries to implement these standards. In the United States, the Federal Reserve is expected to implement regulations based on its interpretation of Basel II on a test basis beginning in 2007. Under Basel II, large international banks will be expected to use sophisticated models to measure credit, market, and operational risks and then use those models to determine their regulatory capital requirement.

MANAGING CREDIT RISK

Historically, the primary risk bank management dealt with was the risk of loan defaults. In fact, as recently as the late 1980s and early 1990s many banks failed because of credit risk losses. In response to these failures, bank managers and regulators have made substantial efforts in recent years to more effectively monitor and manage banks' credit risk exposure.

The credit risk associated with an individual loan concerns the losses the bank can experience in the event that the borrower does not repay the loan. The credit risk associated with a bank's loan portfolio concerns the aggregate credit risk of all the loans in the bank's portfolio. Obviously, bank shareholders and bank regulators will be most concerned about a bank's overall risk exposure, but bank managers must also focus on managing the credit risk of individual loans if they are to be successful. It is important that bank managers effectively manage both dimensions of a bank's credit risk.

In recent years, the market for **credit derivatives** has grown substantially, especially after the collapse of Enron and loan defaults by Argentina. Credit derivatives are relatively new and come in many forms but can be thought of as being similar to the types of derivatives discussed in Chapter 11. Rather than having a payoff that is tied to the value of some underlying asset such as shares of stock, bonds, or some other traded financial instrument, credit derivatives have a payoff that is tied to credit-related events such as default or bankruptcy. In effect, these instruments provide lenders with insurance against the risk of default.

This section describes strategies for how banks can manage the credit risk associated with individual loans as well as strategies for managing the credit risk associated with loan portfolios. In addition, the section provides a brief discussion of how credit derivatives can be used to supplement these strategies.

MANAGING THE CREDIT RISK OF INDIVIDUAL LOANS

Managing credit risk begins with the lending decision as discussed in Chapter 13. Once a loan is on the books, bank managers are responsible for ensuring that the performance of individual loans is being closely monitored, that problem loans are identified as quickly as possible, and that the bank recovers as much as possible from problem loans.

Identifying Problem Loans.   Bank managers rely on several indicators to identify problem loans. Obviously, the first of these is failing to make promised payments on the loan. In addition, other events can cause bank managers to become concerned about a borrower's risk of default. Some of these additional indicators of potential problem loans are (1) adverse changes in the customer's credit rating, (2) adverse changes in deposit balances, (3) adverse changes in sales or earnings, and (4) delays in supplying financial statements or other documents.

Loan Workouts.   Once a problem loan is identified, the goal of the bank manager is to recover as much as possible from the borrower. In many cases, it is possible for the bank to recover all or most of the loan amount by restructuring the loan such that the borrower has a greater chance of successfully making the payments on the new loan. Some of the issues the bank manager is concerned about in the loan recovery process are (1) other creditors and other claims against the borrower's assets, (2) the ability of the borrower to service the debt if it is restructured, and (3) the losses to the bank if the loan is not restructured.

MANAGING THE CREDIT RISK OF LOAN PORTFOLIOS

Traditionally, monitoring the performance of each individual borrower was sufficient for successful credit risk management in most financial institutions. In recent years, however, a number of developments in the banking industry have forced bank managers to become more sophisticated in how they manage credit risk. For example, banks are larger, are more geographically dispersed, and offer a wider range of loan products than ever before. These developments have led to increased complexity in banks' loan portfolios and increased challenges for bank managers.

"Bank of Presidents" Loses More Than a Sock in the Laundry

A dramatic example of the potential for losses due to operational risk is offered by Riggs Bank. Riggs Bank was once known as the "Bank of Presidents" because of its Washington, D.C., location and history of catering to the Beltway elite. Several presidents, including Abraham Lincoln, banked at Riggs. Most recently, however, Riggs was in the news because of a money-laundering scandal. According to Carl Levin, who led a U.S. Senate subcommittee inquiry into Riggs, the institution was involved in money laundering as evidenced by "million-dollar cash deposits, offshore shell accounts, suspicious wire transfers, and alterations of account names." The money laundering that Riggs is accused of involved several alleged activities, including questionable payments made to government officials of Equatorial Guinea on behalf of U. S. oil companies and millions of dollars of suspicious transactions by Saudi Arabian diplomats.

The scandal at Riggs amplifies concerns that bank regulators have not done an adequate job of enforcing anti-money-laundering laws. According to the Senate subcommittee looking into the scandal, the Office of the Comptroller of the Currency (OCC), which is the primary regulator of national banks, knew of suspicious activities at Riggs as long ago as 1997. The failure of the OCC and other bank regulators may lead to enhanced authority for the Financial Crimes Enforcement Network, an agency of the Treasury Department.

Unfortunately for the employees of Riggs, the damage to Riggs's reputation is already done. Coincidentally, on the same day that Martha Stewart was sentenced to jail for insider trading, it was announced the Riggs was being acquired by PNC Financial Services Group.

Internal Credit Risk Ratings.   Increasingly, bank managers are relying on **internal credit risk ratings** to measure and manage the credit risk of loan portfolios. Much like the credit rating assigned to bonds by Moody's and Standard & Poor's, many banks assign internal credit risk ratings to the loans in their portfolio. Some banks have as few as three grades, while others have as many as eight or ten. The rating systems with only a few grades typically base their ratings on whether the loan is delinquent or not and how long it has been delinquent. More sophisticated credit risk rating systems will also consider some of the variables discussed in the "Identifying Problem Loans" section above. For example, if a borrower's external credit rating changes, the internal credit risk rating assigned by the bank to that borrower's loan may also change. These internal credit risk ratings are used for a range of purposes, including:

1. **Identifying problem loans**. The credit risk rating of individual loans is based on the probability of default on the loan and may also consider the dollar amount likely to be recovered in the event of default. By having several gradations in potential credit risk ratings, bank managers can identify the quantity and volume of loans that are most likely and least likely to become problem loans. If the bank has only a few credit risk rating grades, managers are limited as to how the rating system is used. For general monitoring and management reporting, having only a few gradations is fine. For more sophisticated use of the rating system, however, the more gradations, the better.

2. **Determining the adequacy of loan loss reserves**. Credit risk ratings can also be used to assess whether a bank's loan loss reserves are sufficient for the level of substandard or doubtful loans in their portfolio. In addition, if the credit risk ratings have several gradations, bank managers may use the ratings to forecast future loan losses.

3. **Loan pricing and profitability analysis**. Many banks use their internal credit risk ratings to analyze the profitability of loan types. The ratings can be used to identify the expected losses and expenses associated with individual loans. The expected losses and expenses can be subtracted from the yield on the loan or loan type to determine the net yield. This type of analysis is especially useful to bank managers who are responsible for deciding the types of loans a bank should pursue and the types the bank should avoid. For example, the bank may change its marketing strategy to attract more loans that tend to generate a high net yield. This type of profitability analysis can also be a useful input into loan officers' compensation packages. Finally, bank managers can use the results of this profitability analysis to price future loans of a given type. For example, if a certain type of loan consistently generates a low net yield, bank managers may want to raise the interest rate they charge on loans of that type.

Loan Portfolio Analysis.   Increasingly, banks and other lenders recognize the need to consider the performance of the loan portfolio as a whole in addition to the performance of individual loans. Modern portfolio theory teaches us that there are benefits to holding a well-diversified portfolio of assets. We can apply the same principles to bank loan portfolios as long as the default rates on individual bank loans are less than perfectly correlated. Banks can minimize portfolio credit risk by minimizing the degree of correlation among default rates on the loans in their portfolios.

The most common way of monitoring and managing bank loan portfolios is by using **concentration ratios**. Concentration ratios measure the percentage of loans or loan commitments allocated to a given geographic location, loan type, or business type. Higher concentration ratios imply higher correlation among default rates for banks' loan portfolios. For example, a bank that makes all of its loans to businesses and individuals in a small town will have a higher geographic concentration ratio, and higher portfolio credit risk, than a bank that makes loans to similar businesses and individuals throughout the state. If a business in that small town goes bankrupt and closes, not only are the individuals employed by that company more likely to default on their loans from the bank, but other businesses in the town will also be more likely to default because of a decline in revenue they can expect to experience.

Similarly, banks that concentrate on making certain types of loans are exposed to more portfolio credit risk than banks that make a variety of loans. For example, in recent years there has been a sharp increase in the default rate on credit card debt. Consequently, those banks that specialize in issuing credit cards have much more portfolio credit risk than other banks that are better diversified in terms of the variety of loan products in their portfolio. A classic example of losses due to loan portfolio credit risk is the experience of the savings and loan industry in the 1980s. Savings and loans tend to concentrate on making mortgage loans. During the mid-1980s, however, real estate values in the oil-producing states of the

Southwest declined sharply when the price of oil dropped during that period. As a result, loan default rates increased drastically for savings and loans. Banks in those regions did not suffer as much because their loan portfolios were not overly concentrated in real estate lending.

Finally, banks also avoid concentrating on making too many business loans to any single industry. Banks use either Standard Industrial Classification (SIC) codes or North American Industry Classification System (NAICS) codes to monitor their business lending concentration ratios. Banks that concentrate on lending to a specific industry will have relatively high loan portfolio credit risk due to the high correlation among default rates within specific industries. Some banks have gone so far as to employ sophisticated modeling of macroeconomic variables to arrive at default rate probabilities for specific industries that can be applied to their business loan portfolio. The bank can develop comprehensive estimates of overall loan portfolio credit risk using these macroeconomic forecasts, the correlation among historical or projected default rates within industries, and the bank's business lending concentration ratios.

CREDIT DERIVATIVES

Even if they are trying to minimize credit risk by effectively monitoring individual loans and minimizing loan concentration ratios, many banks still feel that they have too much credit risk exposure. Alternatively, many banks tend to specialize in making certain types of loans and, therefore, have relatively high concentration ratios. Increasingly, both types of banks are turning to the market for derivative securities for help in reducing their credit risk.

The market for credit derivatives offers a variety of instruments, which lenders can use to minimize their credit risk exposure. These instruments are called credit derivatives because, just like the derivative securities discussed in Chapter 11, credit derivatives have cash flows tied to some underlying asset. In the case of credit derivatives, the underlying asset is a loan or portfolio of loans. In a **credit swap**, for example, the holder of a loan makes periodic payments to the seller of the swap in exchange for a promise to pay the holder of the loan the face amount of the loan in the event the borrower defaults. **Credit insurance** offers the same kind of protection that a credit swap offers, but in the form of an insurance contract. This form of credit protection is useful for those lenders that are either unwilling or unable to trade in "derivatives" due to regulatory or tax reasons.

The market for credit derivatives has grown rapidly in recent years. Exhibit 13.9 shows that the banking industry has over $1 trillion in credit derivatives outstanding, with banks acting as the guarantor about half the time and the beneficiary about half the time. In addition to credit swaps and credit insurance, there are many other types of credit derivatives, including credit-linked notes, credit options, and synthetic securitizations. As demand for these instruments increases, we can expect to see an even greater variety of instruments become available.

There are several advantages of using a credit swap, credit insurance, or other credit derivative to reduce or eliminate the credit risk associated with a lending relationship. First, and most important, is the reduction in credit risk. Second, in addition to reducing the credit risk of a loan, the lender can do so while maintaining the relationship with the borrower. Unlike a loan sale, which typically requires borrower notification, the borrower does not need to be notified when a credit swap is used to insure against the risk of default by a borrower.

MANAGING INTEREST RATE RISK

Exhibit 14.2 showed that both gross interest income and gross interest expense have become more volatile in the last 30 years. In response to the increased volatility of interest rates, interest rate risk has become a concern to both bank management and regulators. The risk of unexpected interest rate changes affects both sides of a bank's balance sheet and arises because of differences in the sensitivity of bank assets and liabilities to changes in market rates of interest.

To make a profit, banks must earn higher rates of return on their loans and investments (assets) than they pay out to attract deposits and other funds (liabilities). The essence of managing interest rate risk is to ensure that the bank will always be able to profit from the spread between its borrowing (and deposit) rates and its rates of return on investment, even if market interest rates change. The focus of interest rate risk management is first on measuring interest rate risk and next on innovating ways to control it. Before discussing these two issues, however, we first show how unexpected changes in interest rates affect the earnings of a commercial bank.

EFFECTS OF CHANGING INTEREST RATES ON COMMERCIAL BANKS

Recall from our examination of the typical bank balance sheet in Chapter 13 that most banks operate by using shorter-term deposits to fund longer-term (or fixed-rate) loans. This strategy takes advantage of the fact that long-term interest rates usually exceed short-term interest rates (that is, the term structure is usually upward sloping) and earns the bank a positive spread, or net interest income. But the strategy exposes the bank to decreasing earnings when interest rates rise because the liabilities reprice before the assets, on average.

To illustrate the effects of changing interest rates (interest rate risk), let us examine what happens to the cash flows of a commercial bank that borrows short and lends long if interest rates increase. We use a simple example, which is given in Exhibit 14.11. Suppose that a bank makes a 1-year, single-payment loan at the beginning of the year. This loan has a face value of $1,000 and pays 9 percent interest; thus, at the end of 1 year the borrower pays the bank $1,090 ($1,000

EXHIBIT 14.11
Net Cash Flow Example Assuming No Change in Interest Rates

Action	Elapsed Time (Months)				
	0	3	6	9	12
Cash Inflows					
Issue 3-month CD	$500	$506	$513	$519	
(percent)	(5)	(5)	(5)	(5)	
Issue 6-month CD	500		515		
(percent)	(6)		(6)		
1-year loan					$1,090
Total cash inflow	$1,000	$506	$1,028	$519	$1,090
Cash Outflows					
1-year loan	1,000				
(percent)	(9)				
Payoff		506	513	519	525
3-month CD					
Payoff			515		530
6-month CD					
Total cash outflow	$1,000	$506	$1,028	$519	$1,055
Net cash flow =	$0	$0	$0	$0	$35
Total cash inflow –					
Total cash outflow					

Net cash flow from funding a $1,000 loan with a 3-month CD and a 6-month CD (assuming no change in interest rates).

principal plus $90 interest). The bank funds this loan by issuing a $500 denomination, 3-month certificate of deposit (CD) with the idea of renewing the CD every 3 months over the life of the 1-year loan. The bank funds the other $500 of the loan with a $500-denomination, 6-month CD with the idea of renewing the CD every 6 months over the life of the loan. Initially the 3-month CD pays 5 percent interest and the 6-month CD pays 5 percent.

After 3, 6, and 9 months the bank must "roll over" the 3-month CD. The 6-month CD rolls over after 6 and 12 months. Thus, every 3 months the bank issues a new CD in an amount sufficient to pay off the principal and interest on the old CD. At the end of the first 3 months of the year, for example, the bank would issue one 3-month CD of $506 [$500 $(1.05)^{0.25}$] to pay off the first 3-month CD (see Exhibit 14.11). At the end of 6 months, the bank would issue another 3-month CD to retire the second 3-month CD and a 6-month CD of $515 [$500 $(1.06)^{0.5}$] to retire the first 6-month CD. Assuming that interest rates do not change over the year, Exhibit 14.11 shows that the anticipated net cash flow (that is, the loan repayment plus interest minus the amount required to pay off the last two CDs) from funding the 1-year loan with a portfolio of 3-month and 6-month CDs is $35, or a net yield of 3.5 percent on an investment of $1,000 over the year. Notice that the 3.5 percent figure is the difference between the average yield on assets of 9 percent and the average cost of liabilities of 5.5 percent [(5% + 6%)/2].

What happens to the bank's net cash flow if, immediately after making the loan and issuing the first batch of CDs, all interest rates in the market rise by 100 basis points, or 1 percent? The bank's cash inflows from the loan will not be affected because the loan is fixed-rate; assuming no default risk, the loan will pay $1,090 after 1 year. Unfortunately, the rates on 3-month and 6-month CDs will rise by 1 percent so that when they are rolled over, the bank's cost of funds increases. Exhibit 14.12 shows that the bank's anticipated net cash flow at the end of 1 year falls to $28 if interest rates rise by 100 basis points. It is easy to show that the bank's cash flows would have increased had interest rates declined.

EXHIBIT 14.12
Net Cash Flow Example Assuming a 1 Percent Change in Interest Rates

	Elapsed Time (Months)				
Action	0	3	6	9	12
Cash Inflows					
Issue 3-month CD	$500	$506	$514	$521	
(percent)	(5)	(6)	(6)	(6)	
Issue 6-month CD	500		515		
(percent)	(6)		(7)		
1-year loan					$1,090
Total cash inflow	$1,000	$506	$1,029	$521	$1,090
Cash Outflows					
1-year loan	1,000				
(percent)	(9)				
Payoff		506	514	521	529
3-month CD					
Payoff			515		533
6-month CD					
Total cash outflow	$1,000	$506	$1,029	$521	$1,062
Net cash flow =	$0	$0	$0	$0	$28
Total cash inflow −					
Total cash outflow					

Net cash flow from funding a $1,000 loan with a 3-month CD and a 6-month CD (assuming a 1 percent increase in interest rates).

MEASURING INTEREST RATE RISK

In the preceding example, why did the bank's net cash flow decline when interest rates increased? Because the liabilities were shorter term than the assets (4.5 months on average versus 1 year), the liabilities repriced before the assets. Thus the cost of liabilities increased faster than the yields on assets with the interest rate increase; the liabilities were more rate sensitive than the assets. The rate sensitivity of bank earnings can be measured by the gap between the maturity or duration of assets and liabilities (hereafter referred to as *GAP*).

Maturity Gap Analysis.   In a typical GAP management process, bank management divides all assets and liabilities on the balance sheet according to their interest rate sensitivity. An asset or a liability with an interest rate subject to change within a year is considered rate sensitive. One whose interest rate cannot change for more than a year is considered fixed. The GAP between **rate-sensitive assets (RSA)** and **rate-sensitive liabilities (RSL)** is defined as:

$$GAP = RSA - RSL. \tag{14.1}$$

The GAP can be expressed either as dollars or as a percentage of total earning assets. If RSA is greater than RSL, the GAP is positive; if RSA is less than RSL, the GAP is negative; and if RSA equals RSL, the GAP is zero. Exhibit 14.13 shows the rate-sensitive GAP for a bank balance sheet and identifies the most important rate-sensitive and fixed-rate financial instruments. For the balance sheet shown, the GAP = 50% − 20% = 30%.

Controlling the size of the GAP is an important decision that depends both on the degree of risk that a bank's management is willing to accept and on its forecast of future interest rate movements. For example, assume that we are at the bottom of a business cycle and that interest rates are low and expected to rise. Under such circumstances, bank management would want a large positive GAP. The reason is that, given expected higher interest rates in the future, the bank wants to hold rate-sensitive assets in order to take advantage of future higher interest rates and to hold fixed-rate liabilities in order to lock in the current low interest rates—thus a positive GAP. On the other hand, at the top of the business cycle, when interest rates are high and expected to decline, a negative GAP is desirable. In this case the desired balance-sheet portfolio consists of fixed-rate assets and rate-sensitive liabilities. Finally, if the bank's management wishes to minimize interest rate risk, a zero GAP is the desired portfolio strategy. In sum, the greater the GAP—either positive or negative—the greater the bank's exposure to interest rate risk.

The size of the GAP has a major influence on the volatility of bank earnings. If, for example, all variable interest rates changed by 1 percent, a 30 percent GAP would have a $9 million effect on the pretax earnings of a bank with $3 billion in assets. The size of a bank's GAP, then, varies with the bank management's expectations of future interest rates and the risk it is willing to take.

The tendency is for banks that are expecting higher interest rates to accept large positive GAPs and to plan to decrease the GAPs as interest rates turn down. However, because the demand for short-term (or variable-rate) loans is usually heaviest when interest rates are high, most banks cannot close the GAP when they want to. To overcome this problem, bank fund managers are increasingly turning to the use of financial futures contracts to hedge exposed asset and liability risk positions.

EXHIBIT 14.13
Rate-Sensitive GAP for a Bank Balance Sheet

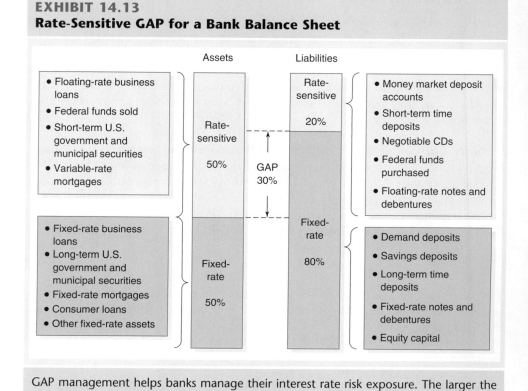

GAP management helps banks manage their interest rate risk exposure. The larger the GAP, the greater the risk exposure.

The technique just discussed is **maturity GAP** analysis. It is probably the most widely used technique for assessing interest rate risk. It compares the value of assets that will either mature or be repriced within a given time interval to the value of liabilities that will either mature or be repriced during the same time period. It is possible to calculate cumulative GAPs for assets and liabilities due to be repriced during any period desired, such as 1 day, 1 week, 1 month, 1 quarter, 6 months, or 1 year. Large banks compute GAPs on a daily basis, whereas smaller banks often compute monthly GAPs.

In addition to cumulative GAPs, a financial institution may wish to compute incremental GAPs. Incremental GAPs show how much the cumulative GAP will change during a future interval. For instance, bank A may have a cumulative GAP of +$40 million over 1 year, with incremental GAPs of +$30 million in the first quarter, +$15 million in the second quarter, –$10 million in the third quarter, and +$5 million in the final quarter. Incremental GAPs can be useful for determining how and when a bank should offset interest rate risk. Thus, bank A's risk-offset strategy would likely be quite different from the strategy undertaken by bank B, which also had a cumulative GAP of +$40 million over 1 year but had incremental GAPs of +$10 million per quarter.

Maturity GAP analysis is widely used by banks because it is relatively easy to compute and it makes good intuitive sense. By ensuring that its assets have maturities similar to its liabilities, a financial institution can ensure that its assets will mature or be repriced at the same time that an approximately equal amount of liabilities is repriced.

Duration GAP Analysis. Maturity GAP provides only an approximate rule for analyzing interest rate risk. Consider, for instance, a bank that issues a $10,000 zero-coupon deposit that promises to double the depositor's money in 7 years (i.e., pays interest at an annual compound rate of 10.4 percent) and uses the proceeds to buy a $10,000 7-year bond paying annual interest at a 12 percent rate. Provided that the bank reinvests all interest coupons paid on the bond each year-end at a 12 percent rate, it would have $22,107 at the end of 7 years—more than enough to pay back the depositor and to book a gross profit of over $2,000 before costs. However, if interest rates fell to the extent that the coupon interest could be reinvested only at a 5.5 percent rate (recall reinvestment risk from Chapter 5), at the end of 7 years the institution would have accumulated only $19,920—not enough to repay the $20,000 obligation to the depositor, even before costs. Clearly, then, matching the maturities of liabilities and assets is not sufficient to guarantee that an institution will not bear interest rate risk.

To reduce the reinvestment risk, banks try to match the durations of their assets and liabilities, not their maturities.[2] As discussed in Chapter 5, duration is a measure of the average time it takes for a security (or portfolio) to return its present value to the owner, and it can also be viewed as the effective time until an asset reprices. Although duration is a complicated concept, it is quite useful for immunizing an institution's balance sheet against interest rate risk. If an institution's assets and liabilities have equal values and the same durations, their values will change similarly as interest rates change. Thus, by matching the duration of its assets to the duration of its liabilities, an institution can immunize its balance sheet against changes in value caused by interest rate changes.

If an institution wants to use duration GAP analysis to immunize the value of its equity against interest rate changes, it will compute and set at zero its duration GAP, D_G. Its duration GAP accounts for differences in the respective market values of a firm's assets and liabilities, MV_A and MV_L. The formula for **duration GAP** is

$$D_G = D_A - (MV_L/MV_A) \times D_L. \qquad (14.2)$$

When a bank adjusts its asset and liability durations such that $D_G = 0$, interest rate changes will affect the value of the firm's assets and its liabilities similarly, leaving the market value of its equity unchanged.

Duration GAPs are opposite in sign from maturity GAPs for the same risk exposure. For instance, if an institution is asset sensitive—in other words, subject to income declines if interest rates fall—its assets will have shorter duration than its liabilities. Thus, it will have a negative duration GAP. At the same time, it will ordinarily have more rate-sensitive (short-maturity) assets than rate-sensitive liabilities, so it will have a positive maturity GAP.

Duration matching to immunize against interest rate risk is complicated, however, because asset and liability durations change every day. Except for zero-coupon securities, asset and liability durations change whenever interest rates

---

[2] See Chapter 5 for a detailed discussion of duration and its use as a measure of interest rate risk.

change, just as bond present values change whenever interest rates change. Furthermore, it is difficult to assess the duration of loans on which customers have the option to prepay or the duration of deposits that customers can withdraw at any time. These customer options pose problems for computing both duration and maturity GAPs.

Because it requires a great deal of computation on a continuing basis, only the largest institutions use duration GAP analysis. Most smaller institutions prefer to use maturity GAP analysis to reduce interest rate risk because of its greater simplicity. These banks should recognize, however, that their management of interest rate risk will be less precise by using maturity GAP instead of duration GAP because maturity GAP ignores the reinvestment risk associated with intermediate cash flows.

To illustrate how duration GAP works, let's return to the example presented earlier, Exhibits 14.11 and 14.12. Recall in our example that the bank funded a $1,000 fixed-rate, single-payment, 1-year loan with a 3-month and 6-month CD having face values of $500.

The duration GAP calculation is simple in this case because the assets and liabilities have no intermediate cash flows (that is, they are zero-coupon instruments); thus, their durations equal their maturities (0.25 years for the 3-month CD and 0.5 years for the 6-month CD). The duration GAP is calculated below:

$$D_G = D_A - (MV_L/MV_A) \times D_L$$
$$= 1 - (1 \times 0.375)$$
$$= 0.625$$

Note that D_L is the weighted average of the durations of the two CDs:

$$D_L = [(\$500/\$1,000) \times 0.25] + [(\$500/\$1,000) \times 0.5]$$
$$= 0.375 \text{ years.}$$

The duration of assets exceeds the duration of liabilities in this case, suggesting that the liabilities reprice before the assets. The "average" dollar of liabilities reprices after 0.375 years (4.5 months) whereas the assets do not reprice until the end of the year. Thus, an interest rate increase will result in declining earnings for this bank.

On the other hand, had the bank issued a 6-month CD and an 18-month (1.5 years) CD, the duration of the liabilities would have equaled 1 year.

$$D_L = [(\$500/\$1,000) \times 0.5] + [(\$500/\$1,000) \times 1.5]$$
$$= 1 \text{ year.}$$

Thus, the duration of the assets equals the duration of the liabilities, the duration GAP is zero, and the bank's cash flows are immunized from interest rate changes.

MANAGING RISK: VALUE AT RISK

The interest rate risk measures discussed in this chapter focus on the risk that arises as a result of banks' deposit taking, lending, and investment activities. **Value at risk (VAR)** is a common approach to assessing risk in financial firms' trading accounts and is gaining popularity in evaluating overall riskiness for banks. VAR measures the loss potential up to a certain probability within a given time period.

Using recent historical data, we can estimate the mean and standard deviation of changes in the underlying risk factors (e.g., interest rates) that affect the value of the assets in our trading account. After estimating the mean and standard deviation of the risk factor, we can use the asset's duration to estimate the change in asset values for the maximum probable change in the risk factor. The VAR is calculated as follows:

$$VAR = \frac{\Delta V}{\Delta r} \times \Delta r^*$$

where:

$\Delta V / \Delta r$ = the sensitivity of changes in asset values to changes in the risk factor.[3]

Δr^* = the potential adverse change in the risk factor within the relevant time period for a given confidence level. For example, a 95 percent confidence level implies that $\Delta r^* = 1.65\ \sigma$, where σ is the standard deviation of changes in the risk factor.[4]

For example, consider Bank of Pullman, which holds a portfolio of Treasury bills in its trading account. The trading desk manager of Bank of Pullman has estimated that the mean change in the Treasury bill yield over the next month is 0 basis points with a standard deviation of 50 basis points. Based on a 95 percent confidence level, this implies that the potential change in the Treasury bill yield is 82.5 basis points, or 0.00825 (1.65×0.005). The duration for the Treasury bills is 0.50 years. The bank holds $10,000,000 in Treasury bills and the expected Treasury bill yield in 1 month is 7 percent per year. Based on this information, the VAR is calculated as follows:

$$VAR = -\frac{0.5}{(1+0.35)} \times \$10,000,000 \times 0.00825 = -\$39,855$$

Put another way, we can say with 95 percent confidence that the worst loss Bank of Pullman can expect to experience in the next month as a result of changes in the Treasury bill yield is $39,855.

The advantage of VAR as a method for assessing the extent of a firm's risk exposure is that it summarizes the potential for bad outcomes in a single number. However, there are several limitations to VAR. First, VAR relies on a normal

---

[3] Note that we can use duration in calculating the VAR for a portfolio of fixed-income securities to arrive at the following:

$$\frac{\Delta V}{\Delta r} = -\frac{D}{(1+r)} \times P$$

[4] Recall from the principles of statistics that 95 percent of the area under a normal probability distribution is below +1.65 standard deviations from the mean.

distribution. Changes in risk factors may not be normally distributed, and the standard deviation we estimate for the risk factor is subject to estimation error. Second, VAR is sensitive to the time horizon we choose. A VAR that is accurate over a 1-month period may not be accurate when it is extended over a year.

HEDGING INTEREST RATE RISK

Hedging means taking actions to reduce or eliminate risk. The simplest form of hedging is matched funding of loans, which we discussed in Chapter 13. With matched funding, the bank funds a loan with a CD (or other liability) that has exactly the same maturity (or duration, if the instruments involved have intermediate cash flows). Matched funding means that the interest rate sensitivity of the loan and the CD are identical, or that they have the same effective time to repricing. Thus, changes in cash flows of the asset due to interest rate changes are matched exactly by changes in the cost of financing the asset. One should remember, however, that by hedging the bank not only eliminates downside risk, but it also eliminates upside potential.

Matched funding is a form of **microhedging**, which is hedging a specific transaction. **Macrohedging**, on the other hand, involves using instruments of risk management, such as financial futures, options on financial futures, and interest rate swaps (see Chapter 11) to reduce the interest rate risk of the firm's entire balance sheet. We will now discuss how financial futures, options on financial futures, and interest rate swaps can be used in managing interest rate risk.

FINANCIAL FUTURES

The interest rate risk of a bank with a negative maturity GAP or positive duration GAP (in either case, recall that the assets are more rate sensitive than the liabilities) can be reduced through the use of financial futures. In Chapter 11 we showed that the prices of financial futures behave similarly to those of bonds when interest rates change; thus, there is an inverse relationship between the price of a financial futures contract and interest rates.

A short-funded bank will experience a decline in earnings with a rise in interest rates, as shown in our earlier example. To offset this risk, the bank should sell (or short) financial futures. Recall from Chapter 11 that if interest rates rise, a short position in financial futures increases in value. A short position in the futures market, therefore, offsets the decline in the bank's earnings should interest rates rise.

Exhibit 14.14 illustrates the effects of macrohedging on a typical bank with financial futures. The graph shows that as interest rates increase, the bank's net cash flow declines. At the same time, the value of the short futures position increases. The logic here is simple. Recall that when a bank sells futures contracts, it does so at a given price for the underlying security. As interest rates rise, the price of the underlying security declines, as does the value of the futures contract. To get out of the short position, the bank does not have to deliver the underlying security; it simply purchases an identical futures contract in the secondary market. With an interest rate increase (that is, a price decrease), therefore, the bank has "sold high and bought low" in the futures market, making a profit that offsets the decline in bank cash flows. Notice from Exhibit 14.14 that after hedging with futures, the bank's cash flows do not fluctuate with changes in interest rates.

EXHIBIT 14.14
Using Financial Futures to Reduce the Interest Rate Risk of a Commercial Bank

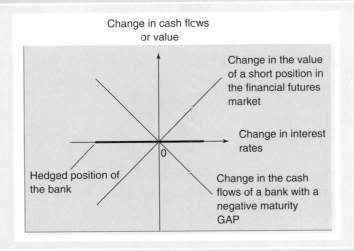

Banks can reduce interest rate risk by selling short financial futures. Notice, however, that by hedging, the bank eliminates the upside potential that comes from a decline in interest rates.

Chapter 11 provided a detailed example of how financial futures can be used to microhedge a fixed-rate loan.

OPTIONS ON FINANCIAL FUTURES

Banks can develop more sophisticated hedges against interest rate risk by using options on financial futures. Recall from Chapter 11 that options on financial assets can reduce downside risk without eliminating all of the upside potential. A common use of options on financial futures is to create so-called **caps**, **floors**, and **collars** on interest rates. A cap on interest rates is created by purchasing a put option (that is, an option to sell) on a financial futures contract. Banks can use caps to limit increases in the cost of their liabilities without sacrificing the possibility of benefiting from interest rate declines. On the other hand, a floor on interest rates is created by selling a call option (i.e., an option to buy) on a financial futures contract. The floor sets a lower limit for liability costs.

By simultaneously buying a cap and selling a floor, the bank creates a collar. Collars limit the movement of a bank's liability costs within a specified range. If, for example, a bank purchases a cap at 9 percent and a sells a floor at 5 percent, the bank's liability costs will fluctuate between 5 and 9 percent. Exhibit 14.15 shows the cash flows of caps, floors, and collars. As shown in Frame A of Exhibit 14.15, if interest rates rise above the cap rate, the bank purchasing the cap receives a cash flow from the writer (seller) of the cap (or the value of the put option on the futures contract increases). Frame B shows that if the bank has written (sold)

EXHIBIT 14.15
Using Options on Financial Futures to Create Caps, Floors, and Collars

Panel A: Cash flows from buying an interest rate cap

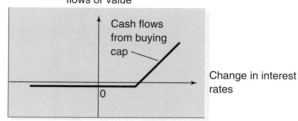

Panel B: Cash flows from selling an interest rate floor

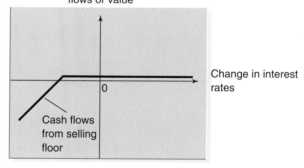

Panel C: Cash flows from simultaneously buying an interest rate cap and selling an interest rate floor (interest rate collar)

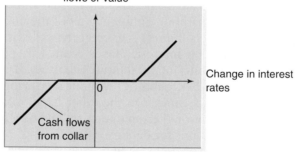

By simultaneously buying a put option on financial futures (a cap) and selling a call option on financial futures (a floor), a bank creates a collar, which limits the movements of a bank's liability costs within a specified range.

a floor, it must pay the purchaser of the floor a cash flow if rates decrease below the floor rate. Frame C shows the cash flows from the collar.

Exhibit 14.16 shows the cash flows of a bank with a negative maturity GAP (or positive duration GAP) after creating a collar. Notice that if rates increase beyond the cap rate or decrease below the floor rate, the bank's cash flows are unchanged. The caps and floors illustrated here eliminate only the effects of extreme movements in interest rates, allowing the bank's cash flows to fluctuate within a specified range.

Exhibits 14.15 and 14.16 naturally raise the question of why a bank would want to limit reductions in its liability costs by selling a floor. To understand the answer to this question, one must understand that purchasing a cap is equivalent to buying an insurance policy against increasing interest rates and that selling a floor is equivalent to selling an insurance policy to someone who fears a decline in interest rates. As everyone knows, insurance is not free. We all must pay premiums for insurance protection. By simultaneously selling insurance (in the form of a floor) to a third party, a bank generates "premium" income that offsets the cost of obtaining the cap. Thus, banks are willing to give up some of their upside potential from decreasing interest rates as a way of reducing the cost of downside protection.

While caps, floors, and collars can be created by buying and selling options on financial futures, this strategy is difficult because exchange-traded options with sufficiently long maturities do not exist. Most caps, floors, and collars, therefore, are privately negotiated agreements (that is, over the counter) between buyers and sellers of interest rate "insurance." These privately negotiated agreements are called interest rate options.

INTEREST RATE SWAPS

Banks also use interest rate swaps (see Chapter 11) to manage interest rate risk. Recall from Chapter 11 that in an interest rate swap, two counterparties literally swap cash flows based on relative movements of two interest rates that are agreed on in the swap agreement. In the simplest and most common form, parties to a swap will periodically exchange cash flows (monthly, quarterly, or semiannually) based on the difference between an agreed-on fixed interest rate and a variable interest rate.

To illustrate, we shall consider the case of a short-funded bank, one whose liabilities are more rate sensitive than its assets. Such a bank has a problem with rising interest rates because liability costs are "variable" compared to the relatively "fixed" asset returns. Thus liability costs increase faster than yields on assets. The bank, therefore, pays out variable cash flows and receives relatively fixed cash flows with respect to interest rate changes. This logic leads to the same cash flow profile of a bank shown previously in Exhibit 14.14. What a short-funded bank needs to offset the risk position, therefore, is to receive a variable cash flow and pay a fixed cash flow.

To hedge interest rate risk, the bank should enter into an interest rate swap in which the bank receives cash flows based on a floating interest rate and pays cash flows based on a fixed interest rate. In an interest rate swap, the cash flows are based on what is called a notional amount of principal. The principal is notional in that it never actually changes hands. The counterparties to the swap simply pay

EXHIBIT 14.16
Using Collars to Manage Interest Rate Risk

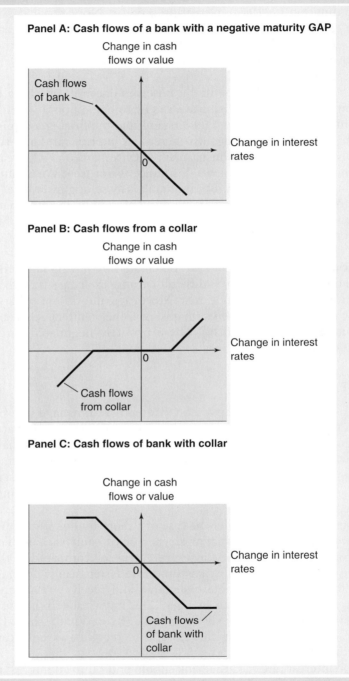

Panel A: Cash flows of a bank with a negative maturity GAP

Change in cash
flows or value

Cash flows
of bank

Change in interest
rates

0

Panel B: Cash flows from a collar

Change in cash
flows or value

Change in interest
rates

0

Cash flows
from collar

Panel C: Cash flows of bank with collar

Change in cash
flows or value

Change in interest
rates

0

Cash flows
of bank with
collar

A collar eliminates the effects of extreme movements in interest rates, allowing the bank's cash flows to fluctuate within a specified range.

each other difference checks based on the interest rate changes as applied to the notional amount of principal.

Suppose a bank enters into a swap and agrees to pay a fixed rate and receive a cash flow based on a variable rate. If interest rates rise in the first settlement period, the bank would receive a difference check because the variable interest rate increased relative to the fixed interest rate. If, for example, the variable rate is 100 basis points higher than the fixed rate on the settlement date, the bank would receive a difference check from the counterparty of $1 million on a notional principal of $100 million. If the variable interest rate declines, the bank would have to pay a difference check to the counterparty. This type of interest rate swap results in a net cash inflow to the bank if interest rates rise, offsetting the decrease in net interest income that occurs when liability costs increase faster than asset yields. Of course, the swap also eliminates the upside potential from an interest rate decline because even though a bank with a negative maturity GAP would ordinarily benefit from the decline, it must pay a difference check that offsets that benefit.

If we were to draw the cash-flow profile of the type of interest rate swap just described, it would be identical to the change in value of a short position in the financial futures market shown in Exhibit 14.14. If financial futures and interest rate swaps can accomplish essentially the same objective, why do they both exist? Recall from Chapter 11 that financial futures are standardized agreements, trading on organized exchanges. Financial futures are cash-settled (or marked to market) daily. Unfortunately, there is not a corresponding financial futures contract for every financial instrument. Interest rate swaps, on the other hand, are privately negotiated agreements that can be tailor-made to fit the circumstances of particular counterparties. Swaps can be made for more varied maturities than is possible with futures, tailored to particular interest rates, and the settlement dates can be designed to fit the cash-flow patterns of the counterparties. The trade-off for the increased flexibility of designing swaps is that swaps are less marketable and carry more default risk than financial futures.

DO YOU UNDERSTAND?

1. What is meant by repricing? What happens to the cash flows of a bank whose liabilities reprice before assets as interest rates increase?

2. If a bank's liability costs increase faster than yields on assets as interest rates rise, does the bank have a positive or negative maturity GAP? What kind of duration GAP would such a bank tend to have—positive or negative? Explain.

3. Should banks use maturity GAP or duration GAP to manage interest rate risk? What are the important considerations in this decision?

4. Explain how financial futures can be used by banks to reduce interest rate risk.

5. What trade-offs should banks consider when choosing between a cap or a collar to manage interest rate risk?

CHAPTER TAKE-AWAYS

1 Commercial banks are profit-maximizing business firms whose primary source of income is interest earned on loans and investment securities. The primary expenses for banks are interest paid on deposits and borrowed funds along with salaries and employee benefits.

2 The fastest-growing source of income for banks is the noninterest income earned from fees and service charges.

3 Like all business firms, banks strive for higher profits consistent with safety. The trade-off between profitability and safety is more acute for banks than for most other businesses because banks have low capital-to-assets ratios and because most bank liabilities are short term. Banks can fail because of inadequate liquidity and inadequate capital.

4 Banks have two basic tools for maintaining sufficient liquidity: (1) asset management and (2) liability management. Under asset management, banks use liquidity stored on the asset side of the balance sheet in the form of primary reserves and marketable securities. Under liability management, banks obtain liquidity by increasing liabilities such as fed funds purchased or by issuing certificates of deposit.

5 Banks must meet capital requirements that are based on risk-weighted assets. Failure to satisfy the requirement can result in regulatory intervention in the bank's activities.

6 Banks manage the credit risk associated with individual loans by closely monitoring loan performance, identifying problem loans quickly, and recovering as much as possible in the event of default. Banks manage the credit risk of loan portfolios by diversifying across geographic regions, loan type, and borrower type. Banks supplement these efforts by using credit derivatives.

7 Banks manage interest rate risk by controlling the maturity or duration GAP between the bank's rate-sensitive assets and liabilities. The greater the size of the GAP, the greater the bank's interest rate exposure.

8 When interest rates are expected to rise, the proper strategy is to have a positive maturity GAP; if interest rates are expected to decline, there should be a negative maturity GAP; and if bank management wishes to minimize interest rate risk, it should strive for a zero GAP. Banks use futures, options on futures, and interest rate swaps to manage interest rate risk.

KEY TERMS

Net interest margin
Gross interest income
Gross interest expense
Provision for loan losses
Noninterest income
Noninterest expense
Return on average assets (ROAA)
Return on average equity (ROAE)

Insolvent
Bank liquidity
Asset management
Primary reserves
Secondary reserves
Liability management
Tier 1 capital
Tier 2 capital
Risk-weighted assets
Credit derivatives

Internal credit risk ratings
Concentration ratios
Credit swaps
Credit insurance
Rate-sensitive assets (RSA)
Rate-sensitive liabilities (RSL)
Maturity GAP
Duration GAP

Value at risk (VAR)
Microhedging
Macrohedging
Cap
Floor
Collar

QUESTIONS AND PROBLEMS

1. What are the major differences between large banks and small banks on the income statement? Why are there differences between the two groups of banks? For example, why is the net interest income higher for small banks?

2. Describe some of the recent trends affecting bank income statements? For example, has net interest income increased or decreased in recent years? What about other components of the income statement?

3. Explain the profitability versus solvency and liquidity dilemma facing bank management.

4. What are the two ways a bank can fail? Explain how these two conditions cause failure. Give examples of times when we have had the two different types of failures.

5. Liquidity management can be practiced on either side of the balance sheet. How are asset and liability management similar and how do they differ? Why do smaller banks have limited access to liability management?

6. Discuss the debt instruments used in liability management. What are the common characteristics of these debt instruments and what type of bank is most likely to issue them?

7. How do banks decide on the proper amount of primary and secondary reserves to hold?

8. What are risk-based capital standards? What are they designed to do?

9. Assume you are the manager of a bank with the balance sheet as shown below. Determine the maturity GAP and duration GAP for the bank. What will happen to the value or net income for the bank if interest rates go up or down?

Assets		Liabilities and Equity Capital	
Cash assets	$15M	Demand deposits	$10M
Short-term investments ($D = 0.35$ years)	$30M	Interest-bearing deposits maturing in less than 1 year ($D = 0.40$ years)	$10M
Long-term investments ($D = 5.00$ years)	$5M	Interest-bearing deposits maturing in more than 1 year ($D = 2.5$ years)	$45M
Loans maturing in less than 1 year ($D = 0.5$ years)	$25M	Borrowed funds ($D = 0.25$ years)	$5M
		Equity capital	$10M
Loans maturing in more than 1 year ($D = 10.0$ years)	$5M		
Total assets	$80M	Total liabilities and equity capital	$80M

10. Describe how internal credit risk ratings can be used to allocate funds to different types of loans.

11. What are the major sources of revenue and expenses for commercial banks? What has been the trend in these accounts in recent years?

12. Explain what happens to the cash flows or market value of a typical bank when interest rates decline. What happens if interest rates increase?

13. Explain how financial futures are used to reduce bank interest rate risk. How does the value of a futures contract change when interest rates change?

14. Explain how one can use options on financial futures to manage interest rate risk.

15. A bank economist projects that interest rates in the future are expected to decline. What is the bank's proper funds management strategy? Why?

16. Why is capital adequacy more of a problem for commercial banks than for most other businesses?

17. Explain why bank regulators are so concerned about capital adequacy for the banking system.

INTERNET EXERCISE

In the previous chapter, you were asked to use the Federal Financial Institutions Examination Council's National Information Center (NIC) Web site to look up balance-sheet information about a bank in your local community. In this Internet Exercise, your task is to expand on the analysis you did in Chapter 13's Internet Exercise. (Note: It is not necessary for you to have completed Chapter 13's Internet Exercise for you to do this exercise.) In this chapter, we discussed the income statement, performance measures, and the various risks that bankers must manage. Data on the income statement of individual banks and bank holding companies can be found at the NIC Web site, http://www.ffiec.gov/nic/. Search the NIC Web site for the name of your local bank. Once you have found the bank in the database, you can generate reports on the balance sheet, income statement, performance ratios, deposits, and loan portfolio. In addition, you can determine the organizational hierarchy of the bank. Up-to-date data on the banking industry as a whole can be found at the FDIC's Web site, http://www.fdic.gov.

1. Once you have found your bank or bank holding company on the NIC database, print out or download data on the income statement of your bank. You will also need the balance sheet to calculate the common-size ratios similar to those shown in Exhibit 14.1. Import the data into a spreadsheet and determine how your bank stacks up against industry norms. Do this by calculating the percentages that were calculated in Exhibit 14.1. How do the averages for your bank differ from the averages for other banks that are of similar size as your bank?

2. The performance ratios that you can download from the NIC Web site are very useful for analyzing the performance and level of risk faced by your bank relative to its peers. Download or print out the summary performance ratios for your institution.

3. Compare the performance and riskiness of your bank to its peer institutions by examining whether your bank has performed better than its peers in recent periods. Also, look at some of the risk measures to determine whether your bank takes more risk than its peers. Based on the relative performance and relative riskiness of your bank, comment on whether the bank is earning an appropriate return for its shareholders given its risk level.

International Banking

Imagine depositing $225,000 in a branch of Citibank and then being forced to stand by helplessly while the value of your deposits declines to $75,000. That is exactly what happened to Maria Carmen de los Santos during a 4-month period beginning in December 2001. How is this possible? Unfortunately for Dr. de los Santos, her Citibank account was in Argentina, not in the United States. When the Argentinean government froze bank accounts at all banks, including foreign banks, and ordered that any deposits denominated in dollars be converted to pesos, many depositors lost large sums.

The experience of Dr. de los Santos illustrates one of the risks involved in overseas banking. Although Citibank is not responsible for the order to freeze deposits by the Argentinean government, its depositors have lost millions and its reputation has been significantly harmed. Many Argentinean depositors blame Citibank for their losses because they

say that Citibank led them to believe that their deposits were safer at Citibank. Many of these depositors claim that, because their deposits were being held by a U.S.-based bank, they thought their deposits were just as safe as they would be if they were deposited in the United States. Unfortunately for these depositors, an American bank operating overseas is not the same as an

American bank operating in the United States.

This chapter focuses on the development of international banking, the structure of American overseas banking, international lending, and foreign bank activities in the United States. In addition, it discusses some of the risks involved in international banking. ■

Tokyo, New York, and London are the most important international banking centers and foreign exchange markets. In Asia, most currency conversions are the U.S. dollar to the Japanese yen, the dollar to Euro, Euro to yen, and the U.S. dollar to the Australian dollar. On most days, exchange rate fluctuations in Tokyo are insignificant, but there are days when the fluctuations are breathtaking.

This chapter examines international banking—the banking practices, regulations, and market conditions by which American banks compete in the global marketplace and foreign banks operate in the United States. ■

LEARNING OBJECTIVES

The objectives of this chapter are to:

1 Describe the evolution of U.S. overseas banking activities.

2 Explain the reasons for growth in U.S. banking operations overseas.

3 Discuss the regulation of foreign banking activities.

4 Describe the organizational forms that banks can use to conduct overseas operations.

5 Explain the risks involved in foreign lending.

6 Describe the nature of foreign bank activities in the United States.

DEVELOPMENT OF INTERNATIONAL BANKING

The establishment of an international presence by American banks is a relatively recent development. European financial institutions, though, have conducted overseas activities for centuries. From the twelfth to the mid-sixteenth century, Italian banks dominated international finance. With the establishment of colonial empires, British, Dutch, and Belgian banks became conspicuous by their worldwide presence. Many of them were established in colonial territories, whereas others were in countries having close trading ties to the bank's home country. During this period, Great Britain emerged as the center of international finance, a position it maintained until after World War II.

Until 1960, few American banks had international operations. In fact, national banks were not permitted to establish branches or accept bills of exchange outside the United States until the passage of the Federal Reserve Act of 1913. In an effort to stimulate penetration of American banks into international finance, Congress enacted the Edge Act in 1919. The Edge Act, proposed by Senator Walter E. Edge of New Jersey, provided for federally chartered corporations to be organized that could engage in international banking and financial operations. These activities could be entered into directly by the Edge Act corporation or through subsidiaries that owned or controlled local institutions in foreign countries. Edge Act corporations could make equity investments overseas, an activity denied domestic banks. This and other expanded powers allowed American banks to compete more effectively against stronger and better-established European banking houses.

Although these provisions were important, American banks did not rush into the international banking arena. It was not until after World War II that American banks established any significant foreign presence. This occurred as American corporations began to establish overseas offices and affiliates. These businesses required financial services and expertise that could best be provided by banks located in the host countries, but there was also a need to maintain a strong relationship with the companies' main U.S. banks. This trend toward substantial direct foreign investments forced some large American banks to consider establishing a network of foreign branches or affiliates to serve the expanding needs of their large corporate customers more fully. Although the demand was growing for international banking services, by 1960 only eight American banks had established overseas branches.

THE DECADE OF EXPANSION

Beginning in 1960, a profound change took place in the international banking activities of American banks. At that time eight large banks, with overseas assets totaling $3.5 billion, dominated U.S. foreign banking. By 1965, there were 13 large banks with 211 branches and foreign assets totaling $9.1 billion. Then the rush to establish foreign branches began in earnest. By 1970, there were 79 banks with foreign branches. By 1980, when the rush slowed, 159 U.S. banks were operating 787 branches overseas, with total assets of $343.5 billion.

Exhibit 15.1 shows that, since that time, the overseas operations of U.S. banks seem to have declined. In truth, the recent decline in the number of banks

EXHIBIT 15.1
Foreign Branches of U.S. Commercial Banks

Year	Number of Banks with Foreign Branches	Number of Foreign Branches
1955	7	115
1960	8	131
1965	13	211
1970	79	532
1975	126	762
1980	159	787
1985	162	916
1990	122	833
1995	102	788
2000	91	998
2003	47	773

The number of banks with foreign branches increased substantially between 1960 and 1980 but has declined in recent years.

Source: Board of Governors, Federal Reserve System.

and branches is the natural consequence of mergers between banks with overseas operations. By the end of 2003, the number of banks with overseas operations had declined to 47 while the number of branches had declined to 773 after peaking at 998.

THE REASONS FOR GROWTH

There are a number of reasons for this dramatic growth in American banking overseas, among them being the overall expansion of U.S. world trade, the growth of multinational corporations, the effects of government regulations on domestic profit opportunities, and the impetus for financing trade deficits that changes in petroleum prices generated in some foreign countries. First, the 1960s were a decade marked by rapid growth of international trade, full convertibility of most of the world's major currencies, and rapid expansion by major U.S. corporations abroad. As American firms expanded overseas, American banks found it advantageous to follow them. Corporations prefer to deal with familiar banks that understand their operations and can provide a full range of services. U.S. banks financed this expansion through letters of credit, banker's acceptances, and other credit instruments.

Interest in foreign banking operations has also been encouraged by the regulatory environment in the United States. Specifically, a set of government programs designed to restrain the outflow of funds from the United States in 1964–1965 and help the country's balance-of-payments problems exerted a strong influence on the international activities of U.S. banks. The federal government's capital control program consisted of the Foreign Direct Investment Program (FDIP), the Interest Equalization Tax (IET), and the Voluntary Foreign Credit Restraint (VFCR) program. Under these various programs, U.S. banks and other corporations were limited in the amount of funds they could transfer overseas. As a result of these restrictions, U.S. corporations had to rely on sources outside the United States to finance their growing investments abroad. Thus, to accommodate their overseas corporate customers, many U.S. banks established networks of foreign branches to tap international sources of funds.

Other domestic regulations also accelerated the growth of American banks abroad. Regulation Q, which limited the rate that domestic banks were allowed to pay on deposits, was one such regulation. In 1966 and again in 1969, when market interest rates increased, U.S. banks were unable to pay rates that were competitive with alternative financial instruments. As a result, banks experienced large runoffs in deposits at domestic offices. To offset these lost funds, U.S. banks turned to foreign branches, which were not subject to the Regulation Q interest rate ceilings. Foreign branches could attract funds because they were free to pay the market rate of interest. Deposits at overseas branches were transferred back to the United States for use by domestic offices. In 1980, the Depository Institutions Deregulation and Monetary Control Act phased out Regulation Q.

As a reaction to restrictive domestic regulations and the internationalization of American business operations, the growth in overseas activities by U.S. banks was dramatic. Interestingly, the growth was not limited to banks located in major financial centers, such as New York and San Francisco, which are traditional international trade centers. Banks headquartered in such cities as Chicago, Pittsburgh, Atlanta, Dallas, Seattle, Detroit, and other regional money centers also found it profitable to enter the foreign markets aggressively. Banks without foreign branches soon found themselves at a considerable competitive disadvantage in international as well as domestic business.

RECENT ACTIVITY

Currently, a small number of American banks have a large network of international banking affiliates throughout the world. A larger number of American banks maintain a small number of overseas offices. In addition, the number of U.S. banks having correspondent relationships with foreign banks is in the hundreds.

As many of the largest U.S. banks merged over the last two decades, the number of banks having overseas operations shrank. We see this in Exhibit 15.1. The relative importance of these institutions increased, however, as the size of the merged institutions increased. Exhibit 15.2 shows the 10 largest banks in the world ranked in terms of total assets at two points in time: December 31, 2002 and December 31, 1990. In 1990, not a single U.S. bank was in the top 10 in the world in terms of its asset holdings. By 2002, however, two of the top 10 were based in the United States.

In 1990, most of the 10 largest banks in the world were headquartered in Japan. In recent years, however, concerns about problem loans at Japanese banks have forced the managers of some banks to sell off some of their foreign subsidiaries. In addition, many of the largest banks in Japan have merged with other large banks. By the end of 2002, only two Japanese banks were in the top 10, but they are numbers one and three in terms of their asset holdings.

As we know, banking in the United States has traditionally been a highly regulated industry. The broad objectives of federal bank regulations have been (1) to promote bank safety, which fosters economic stability by minimizing economic disturbances originating in the banking sector; (2) to promote competition within the banking system; and (3) to maintain a separation of banking from other business activities in order to promote soundness in banking and to prevent concentration of economic power. For the most part, this overall regulatory framework has been extended to the overseas operations of American banks.

This philosophy is in contrast with that of many other countries, where banks are allowed to engage in a wider range of business activities than are American banks. Japan adopted most of the U.S. financial regulatory system during the postwar American occupation, but most Western nations grant their banks either limited or full merchant banking powers. Furthermore, most bank regulatory authorities, including those in the United States, have historically focused on the domestic operations of banks, often ignoring activities conducted by the banks outside their own national borders.

This stance has changed over the last 30 years as foreign regulatory authorities begin to understand the global nature of financial markets. In particular, the 10-nation agreement on bank capital adequacy standards worked out under the auspices of the Bank for International Settlements (BIS) in July 1988 is tangible evidence that bank regulators are concerned with, and are addressing, international issues. This agreement mandated at least an 8 percent capital-to-assets ratio for all international banks and also defines precisely what will be counted as pri-

REGULATION OF OVERSEAS BANKING ACTIVITIES

EXHIBIT 15.2
World's 10 Largest Banks (December 31, 2002, and December 31, 1990)

December 31, 2002

Rank	Company Name	City	Total Assets (in billions)
1	Mizuho Holdings	Tokyo	$1,135.6
2	Citigroup	New York	1,097.2
3	Sumitomo Mitsui Financial Group	Tokyo	873.0
4	UBS AG	Zurich	852.2
5	Allianz AG	Munich	850.4
6	Deutsche Bank	Frankfurt	791.7
7	J.P. Morgan Chase & Co.	New York	758.8
8	HSBC Holdings PLC	London	757.4
9	ING Group NV	Amsterdam	751.7
10	BNP Paribas	Paris	744.6

December 31, 1990

Rank	Company Name	City	Total Assets (in billions)
1	Dai-Ichi Kangyo Bank	Tokyo	$428.2
2	Sumitomo Bank Ltd.	Osaka	409.2
3	Mitsui Taiyo Kobe Bank	Tokyo	408.8
4	Sanwa Bank	Osaka	402.7
5	Fuji Bank	Tokyo	400.0
6	Mitsubishi Bank	Tokyo	391.5
7	Credit Agricole Mutuel	Paris	305.2
8	Banque Nationale de Paris	Paris	291.9
9	Industrial Bank of Japan	Tokyo	290.1
10	Credit Lyonnais	Paris	287.3

In 1990, Japanese banks dominated other banks in terms of asset holdings. In the last 20 years, however, problems in the Japanese banking industry combined with consolidation in the U.S. and European banking industry has resulted in U.S. and European bank dominance of the top 10.

Source: "The World's Top Banking Companies by Total Assets," *American Banker,* September 17, 2003, and "The World's Largest Banks," *American Banker,* July 26, 1991.

mary (Tier 1) and secondary (Tier 2) capital. At least 4 percent of the 8 percent total must be Tier 1 capital.

THE REGULATORY FRAMEWORK

The regulatory framework for the international operations of U.S. banks can be summarized briefly:

1. The Federal Reserve Act of 1913 allowed federally chartered banks to establish branches outside the United States.

2. The 1916 amendment to the Federal Reserve Act permitted national banks to form agreement corporations.

3. The 1919 Edge Act allowed the formation of federally chartered corporations to engage in foreign banking and such financial operations as owning stock in foreign financial institutions.

4. In 1966, national banks were allowed to invest directly in the stock of foreign banks.

5. In 1970, amendments to the Bank Holding Company Act provided a regulatory framework for international activities of U.S. bank holding companies.

6. In 1978, the International Banking Act extended federal regulation to foreign banks operating in the United States.

7. In 1980, the Depository Institutions Deregulation and Monetary Control Act broadened the scope of the Federal Reserve Board's authority to impose reserve requirements on foreign banks international and permitted U.S. banks to establish international banking facilities (IBFs).

8. The International Lending Supervision Act, passed by Congress in late 1983, mandated the reporting of country-specific loan exposure information by commercial banks and established standardized procedures for dealing with problem loans.

9. The Foreign Bank Supervision Enhancement Act (FBSEA) of 1991 provided the Federal Reserve with greater authority over foreign banks and limited the service offerings of foreign banks to those that U.S. banks are allowed to offer.

The Federal Reserve System and the Office of the Comptroller of the Currency (OCC) have primary responsibility for supervising the activities of U.S. banks' foreign operations: the OCC examines national banks that make up the majority of banks operating overseas, and the Federal Reserve System examines state-chartered member banks, approves national banks' foreign branches, and supervises the operation of Edge Act corporations and IBFs Also, foreign acquisitions by domestic bank holding companies come under the jurisdiction of the Federal Reserve. The Federal Deposit Insurance Corporation (FDIC) has only a limited role in international banking because few purely international banks are members. However, since enactment of the International Banking Act of 1978, foreign banks operating in the United States have been allowed to establish federally chartered foreign branches, and their deposits up to $100,000 must be insured by the FDIC. Other foreign banking institutions may, at their option, obtain FDIC insurance.

In the past, U.S. bank regulators relied primarily on home office records in conducting examinations of the overseas operations of U.S. banks. This procedure was acceptable as long as the number of banks with overseas operations was small and foreign activities of a bank did not pose a substantial risk to the bank's domestic operations. This is not always true today. On-site examinations are becoming both more necessary and more frequent. The OCC now maintains a permanent staff in London, and both the Federal Reserve Board and the FDIC are increasing the frequency of their overseas on-site examinations. These are used primarily to check the accuracy of head office records and the adequacy of internal controls. The cost of regular examinations of the quality of all foreign offices' assets would be prohibitive.

ALLOWABLE BANKING ACTIVITIES

In general, U.S. banks have been permitted to engage in a wider range of business activities in foreign countries than at home. Even after the passage of the Financial Services Modernization Act of 1999 (Gramm-Leach-Bliley), which allowed banks operating in the United States the ability to engage in a broader range of activities, U.S. banks abroad can engage in activities that are still not available to domestic banks. For example, U.S. banks abroad may make limited equity investments in nonfinancial companies in connection with their financing activities. The major reason for the wider latitude in overseas markets has been to enhance the competitive effectiveness of U.S. banks in foreign markets. Most banks in foreign countries have broader powers than those possessed by American banks. Thus, to promote the participation of U.S. banks in overseas markets, Federal Reserve policy has been to broaden powers as long as they did not impinge on domestic policy considerations. Furthermore, because many domestic constraints on banks are concerned with the competitive environment and the concentration of financial resources in the United States, the Federal Reserve has accordingly refrained from restricting the international activities of domestic banks.

However, certain overseas activities have been restrained. Foreign subsidiaries are not allowed to own controlling interests in nonfinancial companies. This restriction stems from the long-standing U.S. concept of separating banking and commerce. Regulatory changes announced in August 1987 weakened these restrictions somewhat by allowing banks to purchase a controlling interest in a foreign nonfinancial corporation, but only if the firm was being sold as part of a privatization program by the foreign government. Affiliates in which U.S. banks have been allowed to own a substantial minority interest have been confined to companies of a predominantly financial nature. Also, investment in foreign companies has been severely limited. It is feared that such investments could indirectly undermine domestic policy objectives, such as the separation of finance-related businesses from other lines of business. Even though Congress effectively repealed the Glass-Steagall Act (which separated commercial and investment banking) by passing the Gramm-Leach-Bliley Act, the activities of U.S. banks, bank holding companies, and financial holding companies are still constrained when compared to banks in some other countries.

DELIVERY OF OVERSEAS BANKING SERVICES

Banks may use a number of organizational forms to deliver international banking services to their customers. The primary forms are (1) representative offices, (2) shell branches, (3) correspondent banks, (4) foreign branches, (5) Edge Act corporations, (6) foreign subsidiaries and affiliates, and (7) international banking facilities. Exhibit 15.3 shows a possible organizational structure for the foreign

EXHIBIT 15.3
Possible Organizational Structure for a U.S. Bank's International Operations

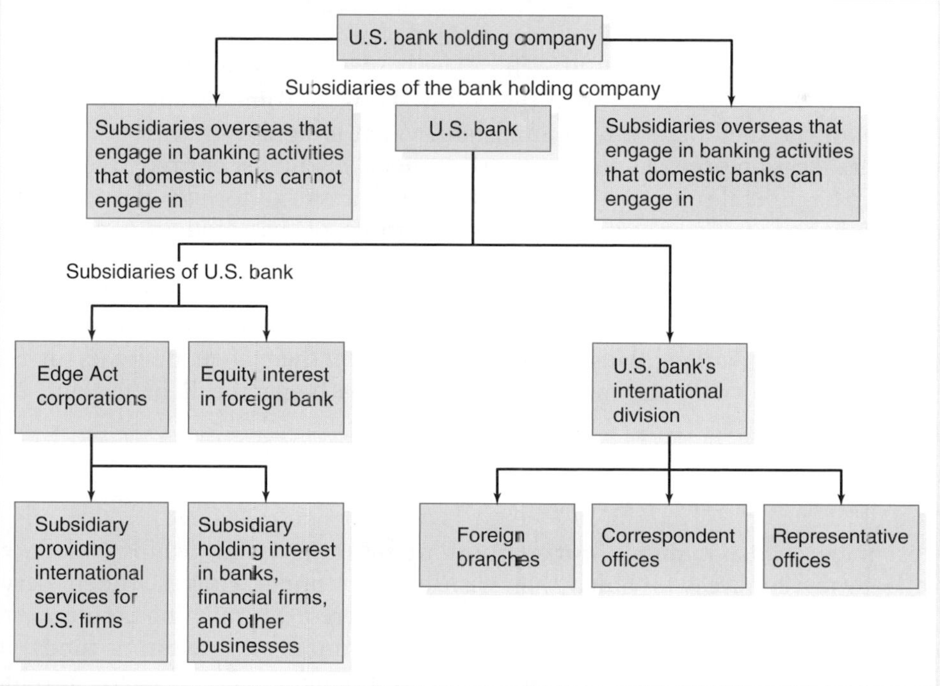

Because of regulatory changes over the years, the structure of U.S. banks' international operations varies from bank to bank. This exhibit shows one possible structure for a U.S. bank.

operations of U.S. banks. Though possible, all these forms need not exist for any individual bank. We shall now discuss each organizational form, focusing on its advantages and disadvantages for the parent bank.

REPRESENTATIVE OFFICES

Representative nonbanking offices are established in a foreign country primarily to assist the parent bank's customers in that country. Representative offices cannot accept deposits, make loans, transfer funds, accept drafts, transact in the international money market, or commit the parent bank to loans. In fact, they cannot cash a traveler's check drawn on the parent bank. What they may do, however, is provide information and assist the parent bank's clients in their banking and business contacts in the foreign country. For example, a representative office may introduce businesspeople to local bankers, or it may act as an intermediary between U.S. firms and firms located in the country of the representative office. A representative office is a primary vehicle by which an initial presence is established in a country before setting up formal banking operations.

SHELL BRANCHES

The easiest and cheapest way to enter international banking is to establish a **shell branch**. This is a booking office for bank transactions located abroad that has no contact with the public. Activities of shell branches are primarily limited to inter-bank money market transactions (mostly in the Eurodollar market), foreign currency transactions, and the purchase of small shares of syndicate loans. In most cases, transactions at the shell branch reflect banking decisions made at the U.S. head office or at branches around the world. Thus, to some extent, the physical location of the shell branch is unimportant. What is significant, however, is that the shell's location provides an environment that (1) is almost entirely free of local taxes, (2) has liberal rules for the conversion and transfer of foreign currencies, (3) has simple and unencumbered banking regulations, (4) has modern communication facilities linked to other financial centers around the world, and (5) has a relatively stable political environment. The establishment of shell branches is not limited to small banks. All large banks operate shell branches to escape taxes and government regulations. Most U.S. banks operate their shell branches in the Caribbean Basin, with the most popular locations being the Bahamas and the Cayman Islands.

CORRESPONDENT BANKS

Most major banks maintain **correspondent banking** relationships with local banks in market areas in which they wish to do business. Correspondent services include accepting drafts, honoring letters of credit, furnishing credit information, collecting and disbursing international funds, and investing funds, in international money markets. Typically, correspondent services center around paying or collecting international funds, because most transactions involve the importing or exporting of goods. In addition, the correspondent bank will provide introductions to local businesspeople. Under a correspondent relationship, the U.S. bank usually will not maintain any permanent personnel in the foreign country.

FOREIGN BRANCHES

Branch offices of U.S. banks are widely distributed throughout the world and represent the most important means by which U.S. banks conduct overseas business. A **foreign branch** is a legal and operational part of the parent bank. Creditors of the branch have full legal claims on the bank's assets as a whole, and, in turn, creditors of the parent bank have claims on its branches' assets. Deposits of both foreign branches and domestic branches are considered to be total deposits of the bank, and reserve requirements are tied to these total deposits.

Foreign branches are subject to two sets of banking regulations. First, as part of the parent bank, they are subject to all legal limitations that exist for U.S. banks. Second, they are subject to the regulation of the host country. Domestically, the OCC is the overseas regulator and examiner of national banks, whereas state banking authorities and the Federal Reserve Board share the authority for state-chartered member banks. Granting power to open a branch overseas resides with the Board of Governors of the Federal Reserve System. As a practical matter, the Federal Reserve System and the OCC dominate the regulation of foreign branches.

The attitudes of host countries toward establishing and regulating branches of U.S. banks vary widely. Typically, countries that need capital and expertise in lending and investment welcome the establishment of U.S. bank branches and allow them to operate freely within their borders. Other countries allow the establishment of U.S. bank branches but limit their activities relative to domestic banks because of competitive factors. Some foreign governments may fear that branches of large U.S. banks might hamper the growth of their country's domestic banking industry. As a result, growing nationalism and a desire for locally controlled credit have slowed the expansion of American banks abroad in recent years.

The major advantage of foreign branches is a worldwide name identification with the parent bank. Customers of the foreign branch have access to the full range of the parent bank's services, and the value of these services is based on the worldwide value of the client relationship rather than just the local office relationship. Furthermore, deposits are more secure, having their ultimate claim against the much larger parent bank, not just the local office. Similarly, legal loan limits are a function of the size of the parent bank, not of the branch. The major disadvantages of foreign branches are the cost of establishing them and the legal limits placed on the activities in which they may engage.

EDGE ACT CORPORATIONS

Edge Act corporations are subsidiaries of U.S. banks that were formed to permit U.S. banks to engage in international banking and financing activities and to engage in activities that they could not conduct within the United States. Edge Act corporations operate under federal charter and are not subject to the banking laws of the various states. There also exists a number of **agreement corporations** that operate similarly to Edge Act corporations but remain under state charter. At year-end 2003, there were 78 Edge Act and agreement corporations. The principal difference between these two types of organizations is that agreement corporations must engage primarily in banking activities, whereas Edge Act corporations may undertake banking as well as some nonbanking activities. The most important nonbanking activity in which Edge Act and agreement corporations may engage is investing in equities of foreign corporations. Ordinarily, U.S. banks cannot participate in investment activities. Hence, this power has been the main advantage of the Edge Act and agreement corporations' form of organization; it has helped U.S. banks achieve an improved competitive position relative to foreign banks, which are typically allowed to make equity investments. The largest class of these have been investments in foreign banking institutions. Purchases have been made as an alternative to establishing a branch network or to strengthening foreign correspondent relationships. Edge Act and agreement corporations have in recent years also taken equity positions in finance and investment companies.

FOREIGN SUBSIDIARIES AND AFFILIATES

A **foreign subsidiary** bank is a separately incorporated bank owned entirely or in part by a U.S. bank, a U.S. bank holding company, or an Edge Act corporation. A foreign subsidiary provides local identity and visibility of a local bank in the eyes of potential customers in the host country, which often enhances its ability to

Coming Soon: The Bank of Europe

The creation of a common European currency and the economic consolidation of Europe into the European Union present several interesting benefits, challenges, and opportunities for all banks that compete internationally. One of the benefits for banks that operate in Europe is the reduced foreign exchange risk of dealing in a single currency. In the past, those banks that lent funds across borders within Europe were subject to foreign exchange risk due to fluctuations in individual currency values. Additional benefits include the increased freedom of capital flows and the increased ability of banks to diversify geographically. With fewer barriers to capital flows, it will be easier for banks based in one country to lend to borrowers in other countries. This will allow for lower transaction costs and increased allocational efficiency in European financial markets. At the same time, banks will become more geographically diversified as they lend to borrowers in more countries.

Increased freedom of capital flows also leads to increased competition in financial markets. The challenge to European banks is to respond to these opportunities more effectively than their competitors do. To be successful in this environment, European banks will have to do many of the same things that U.S. banks have been doing in recent years: taking advantage of improvements in information technology, trimming excess personnel, eliminating duplicate functions, and merging with other banks when there are opportunities for cost savings.

When interstate branching restrictions were lifted in the United States, it didn't take long for Bank of America to spread nationwide. Now that doing business across national boundaries within the European Union is relatively easy, it seems like only a matter of time before there is a European version of Bank of America. Surprisingly, there have been relatively few cross-border mergers in Europe. It is not as though there is little room for consolidation. The European banking industry has been consolidating much like the U.S. banking industry, but the vast majority of mergers have been within-country mergers. For example, one of the biggest recent deals involved Credit-Agricole and Credit-Lyonnais, two French banks.

Although the creation of the European Union (EU) makes it easier to do business across national borders, a cross-border merger in the EU is still much more challenging than an interstate merger in the United States. Legal, regulatory, and tax differences still exist within the EU. In addition, there is political and cultural resistance to foreign takeovers.

Some have suggested that cross-border mergers in the EU are more likely to be initiated by an American bank than a European bank. In fact, there are rumors that Bank of America had merger talks with Barclays Bank of London and that Citibank had talks with Deutschbank. What's next? Bank of the World?

attract additional local deposits. Furthermore, management is typically composed of local nationals, giving the subsidiary bank better access to the local business community. Thus, foreign-owned subsidiaries are generally in a stronger position to provide domestic and international banking services to residents of the host country.

Closely related to foreign subsidiaries are foreign affiliate banks, which are locally incorporated banks owned in part, but not controlled, by an outside parent. The majority of the ownership and control may be local, or it may be other foreign banks.

INTERNATIONAL BANKING FACILITIES

Effective in December 1981, the Federal Reserve Board permitted the establishment of **international banking facilities (IBFs)**. These facilities may be established by a U.S.-chartered depository institution, a U.S. branch or agency of a foreign bank, or the U.S. office of an Edge Act or agreement bank. IBFs are not institutions in the organizational sense. They are actually a set of asset and liability accounts segregated on the books of the establishing institutions.

IBFs are allowed to conduct international banking operations that, for the most part, are exempt from U.S. regulation. Deposits, which can be accepted only from non-U.S. residents or other IBFs and must be at least $100,000, are exempt from reserve requirements. The deposits obtained cannot be used domestically; they must be used for making foreign loans. In fact, to ensure that U.S.-based firms and individuals comply with this requirement, borrowers must sign a statement agreeing to this stipulation when taking out the loan.

DO YOU UNDERSTAND?

1. What are the reasons for growth in American banking overseas in recent decades?
2. What are the organizational forms banks use to deliver international banking services to their overseas customers?
3. Compare the U.S. philosophy of bank regulation to that of other countries.

INTERNATIONAL LENDING

As is the case with domestic operations, the greatest amount of income from international operations is derived from lending. The bulk of the lending is accomplished through foreign branches, subsidiaries, or affiliate banks in foreign countries. The total amount of international lending by U.S. banks is not known precisely, because published data are not available on loans made by affiliates of U.S. banks or banks owned jointly by U.S. banks and other foreign banks. However, as of year-end 2003, the Federal Reserve Board reported that foreign lending by U.S. banks totaled more than $592 billion. As Exhibit 15.4 shows, foreign branches are located throughout the world. In amounts of assets, branches in Latin America, Europe, and Japan account for over 80 percent of all the assets of U.S. branches abroad. However, despite the impressive record of American banks overseas, the market remains dominated by a few giant multinational banks. Currently about 10 banks dominate the market, and many of the 82 banks operating outside the United States have only single *shell branches* in offshore money markets, such as Nassau or the Cayman Islands. Increasingly, however, regional and superregional banks are increasing their loans and investment activities overseas.

EXHIBIT 15.4
Amount Owed U.S. Banks by Foreign Borrowers (March 2004)

Area	$ in Billions	%
European countries, except those below	$192.9	32.5
Germany	120.9	20.4
United Kingdom	60.6	10.2
France	47.2	8.0
Japan	38.2	6.4
Latin America and Caribbean (except Mexico)	37.6	6.3
Asia, excluding Japan	35.8	6.0
Canada	19.4	3.3
Mexico	18.3	3.1
Australia and New Zealand	13.3	2.2
Africa	1.1	0.2
Other	7.6	1.3
Total	$592.9	100

Although the lending activities of U.S. banks extend worldwide, most U.S. banks' claims are on companies or individuals in Latin America, Europe, or Japan.

Source: Federal Reserve System, *Country Exposure Lending Survey,* March 31, 2004.

CHARACTERISTICS OF INTERNATIONAL LOANS

In many ways, the loans that banks make to international customers are similar to domestic business loans. Most loans are intermediate-term, floating-rate credits made to moderate- to high-quality borrowers. There are, however, important differences relating to one or more of the following factors: (1) funding, (2) syndication, (3) pricing, and (4) collateral. A further difference is that international loans can be denominated in almost any major currency, although dollars are the overwhelming favorite. International loans tend to be larger in size than typical domestic loans, and borrowers are generally sovereign governments or large multinational companies, so the perceived credit risk tends to be lower.

Most large international loans are negotiated and funded in the Eurocurrency market. International banks operating in this market accept time deposits from nonbank investors and then make short- or intermediate-term loans. Funds can be lent directly to nonbank borrowers, or they can be lent in the interbank market to other international banks if the original bank does not have sufficient loan demand. The interest rate paid to depositors and charged to borrowers will be related to the home-country interest rate for the currency in question, but for a variety of reasons, the spread between borrowing and lending rates tends to be smaller in the Eurocurrency market. Most Eurocurrency loans are priced with respect to the **London Interbank Offer Rate (LIBOR)**, which is the rate at which international banks lend to each other in London, historically the center of the Eurocurrency market.

A loan to a nonbank borrower will typically be priced at some premium above LIBOR, with the premium being related to the credit risk of the borrower. For example, a loan made to a highly rated multinational company or to a European government might be priced at 0.10 percent above LIBOR, whereas a credit made to a less well-known company or to a developing country might have a premium as high as 1.5 percent or more above LIBOR.

If the loan extends for more than one credit period (such as a month), the interest rate charged on the loan for the coming period will be determined by the level of LIBOR at the beginning of the period. These floating-rate loans allow banks to fund the credits in the Eurocurrency market at the beginning of the period and lock in a lending spread for the coming period. At the end of this period, the loan will again "roll over" and be repriced for the subsequent period. This **rollover pricing** mechanism, which was first used in the Eurocurrency market in 1969, allows banks to make intermediate-term loans without exposing themselves to the interest rate risk inherent in fixed-rate loans. The sheer volume of credit available, the low cost of funds, and the sophistication of the banking service provided have also made the Eurocurrency market a favorite source of funds for nonbank borrowers.

Most large (greater than about $50 million) international bank loans are **syndicated**. This means that several banks participate in funding the loan, which is packaged by one or more lead banks. This allows banks to spread their risks among a large number of loans, and it allows borrowers to obtain larger amounts of capital than would be available through other means. This is especially true for sovereign borrowers (national governments). Indeed, the intermediate-term, floating-rate, general obligation (unsecured and backed by the taxing power of the government), syndicated bank loan was the principal instrument through which financial capital was channeled to developing countries during the 1970s and early 1980s. The total level of such debt grew from essentially nothing in 1971 to over $300 billion in August 1982, when the Mexican debt moratorium effectively ended voluntary bank lending to **less developed countries (LDCs)** at that time.

Finally, most international bank loans are unsecured (made without specific collateral). Business loans are generally made only to large, creditworthy, multinationals and, with public-sector loans, are generally backed by the "full faith and credit" of the borrowing nation. Ironically, during the period when the OPEC surplus was being recycled to developing countries, bankers comforted themselves with the statement that "nations don't go bankrupt." Although true in a legal sense, this idea was shown to be tragically misguided when LDCs began experiencing severe financial difficulties during the mid-1980s, and the market value of the creditor banks was knocked down to reflect the underlying value of these sovereign loans.

RISK IN INTERNATIONAL LENDING

In many respects, the principles applicable to foreign lending are the same as those applicable to domestic lending—that is, to define and evaluate the credit risk that the borrower will default. In international lending, bankers are exposed to two additional risks: *country risk* and *currency risk*. In this section, we discuss each of these three risks in turn and then suggest ways in which bankers can reduce them.

Credit Risk.   Credit risk involves assessing the probability that part of the interest or principal of the loan will not be repaid. The greater the default risk, the higher the loan rate that the bank must charge the borrower. As noted previously, this is the same type of risk that bankers face on the domestic scene. However, it may be more difficult to obtain or assess credit information abroad. U.S. banks are less familiar with local economic conditions and business practices than are domestic banks. It takes time and practice to develop appropriate sources of information and to correctly evaluate such information. As a result, many U.S. banks tend to restrict their foreign lending to major international corporations or financial institutions. This policy reflects the cost of gathering reliable information. A foreign government will sometimes offer assurances against default or rescheduling of loans by private borrowers, making such loans more attractive to international lenders.

Country Risk.   **Country (sovereign) risk** is closely tied to political developments in a country, particularly the government's attitude toward foreign loans or investments. Some governments attempt to encourage the inflow of foreign funds whether the funds come from private or public sources. Others, however, make it difficult to maintain profitable lending operations. Minor obstacles, such as wage–price controls, profit controls, additional taxation, and other legal restrictions can inhibit the ability of borrowers to repay loans.

At the extreme, foreign governments may expropriate the assets of foreigners or prohibit foreign loan repayments, either of which could drastically alter risk exposure. Worldwide, there are only a few cases in which countries have refused to repay or have refused permission for their citizens to repay foreign loans. The reason for this is that the borrowing country does not want to preclude the possibility of obtaining foreign credit in the future. Any nationalization or government refusals to repay international loans may virtually halt the inflow of foreign funds into the country involved. However, rebellions, civil commotions, wars, and unexpected changes in government do occur from time to time, and, as a result, risk is real and must be considered in granting international loans. Somewhat soothing to international lenders is the fact that, with the exception of Chile and Cuba, there have been few large-scale nationalizations by foreign governments in recent years. However, U.S. banks have been forced out of Iran, and some South American countries have taken the properties of some U.S. citizens.

A major problem for banks in the 1980s was the rescheduling of sovereign loans. Rescheduling refers to rolling over a loan, often capitalizing interest arrears or extending the loan's maturity. Because of repayment problems, multiyear rescheduling agreements were introduced in 1984. These typically involve (1) a consolidation of several individual public and private loans into a smaller number of standardized debt issues; (2) the extension of government guarantees to private-sector debts; (3) the granting of a grace period of 1 to several years, during which the loans do not need to be serviced; and (4) an extension of the loan maturity date to as long as 15 years.

Although little attention has been paid to LDC debt in recent years, some analysts are raising concerns about the possibility of a crisis similar to that experienced in the 1980s. According to the Federal Reserve, exposure to developing country risk has increased steadily in recent years. As of December 2001, exposure to developing country risk is more than $100 billion.

Currency Risk. **Currency risk** is concerned with currency value changes and exchange controls. More specifically, some loans are denominated in foreign currency rather than dollars, and if the currency in which the loan is made loses value against the dollar during the course of the loan, the repayment will be worth fewer dollars. Of course, if the foreign currency has a well-developed market and the maturity is relatively short, the loan may be hedged. However, many world currencies, particularly those in developing nations, do not have well-established foreign currency markets; consequently, these international loans cannot always be hedged to reduce this kind of currency risk.

Another aspect of currency risk concerns exchange controls. Exchange controls, which are not uncommon in developing countries, may limit the movement of funds across national borders or restrict a currency's convertibility into dollars for repayment. Thus, exchange risk may occur because of difficulties in the convertibility of a currency or in its exchange rate. Typically, if a country has an active market for its currency and its international payments and receipts are in approximate balance (or it has adequate reserves to pay deficits), currency risk is minimal. However, if a country persistently runs a deficit on its balance of payments, it may establish some form of exchange control. One such example is Mexico, which devalued its currency severely in 1982 and literally suspended exchange operations for a period of time. This was the result of its large balance-of-payments deficit and its inability to make current payments on its sizable international loans.

RISK EVALUATION

When lending abroad, bankers must take into account the same economic factors that they consider domestically—government monetary and fiscal policy, bank regulations, foreign exchange controls, and national and regional economic conditions. Depending on the cost, lenders employ different means of evaluating risks in foreign lending. The most direct are in-depth studies prepared by the bank's foreign lending. and economic departments. These are based on statistics and other information about a country's economic and financial condition. Information is gathered from government sources and, if available, from the bank's representatives overseas. The analyses often contain careful evaluations of expected inflation, fiscal and monetary policy, the country's trade policies, capital flows, and political stability, as well as an estimate of the credit standing of the individual borrower. Some circumstances affecting sovereign risk cannot be captured in statistical analysis, and, in such cases, practical judgment and experience play a heavy role. Here, information from government officials in this country and abroad, from branch and representative offices, and from other sources is carefully sorted out and subjectively analyzed.

When international lenders find in-depth analysis too expensive, they may turn to on-site reports, checklists, and statistical indicators to help them assess the risk of lending. However, such methods tend not to be as reliable and may signal false alarms or a false sense of security. Part of the problem with indicators is that they often are not current, and even if current, there is no assurance that they predict the future. Thus, lenders may find it expensive and difficult to gather reliable information about foreign borrowers. Lenders must decide how much information they need to negotiate a loan with a prospective borrower. The higher the cost of gathering information—or the greater the risk of lending either because of lack of information or credit quality—the higher the loan rate. If the risk of making a loan is too great, the loan applicant may be turned down.

METHODS OF REDUCING RISK

Bankers have at their disposal several ways of reducing risk in international lending. The basic avenues open to them are to seek third-party support in the form of insurance or loan guarantees, to share risk exposure by participating in loans with other lenders or, most important, to diversify their loans among different borrowers and countries.

Third-Party Help.   One way banks may reduce foreign lending risk is to get a third party to agree to pay back the principal and interest in the event that the borrower defaults. Typically, this is done by either foreign governments or central banks. Of course, these guarantees are only as good as the backer's ability and intent to repay. Such a promise from a politically unstable and underdeveloped country may not mean much. Furthermore, if the same government guarantees a number of loans, its ability to repay may be strained if several of these loans are to default simultaneously.

An alternative to foreign government guarantees is an external guarantee from an outside institution. In addition to the credit derivatives discussed in Chapter 14, banks can reduce foreign lending risk by lending to exporters who insure their trade credit with the Foreign Credit Insurance Association (FCIA). The FCIA is an organization of approximately 50 insurance companies throughout the United States. FCIA insurance covers individual transactions up to a certain percentage against nonpayment arising from credit loss and political hazards. Political risks are reinsured by the FCIA through the U.S. Export-Import Bank (Eximbank). The FCIA makes thorough credit investigations of individual borrowers as well as of the sovereign risk. Typically, the insurance covers up to 90–95 percent of the credit risk and up to 100 percent of the risk associated with political hazards. The insurance premium paid by the exporter depends on the credit rating of the borrower and the rating established for each country. It typically averages about $1/2$ of 1 percent, but it may be higher for less creditworthy firms and less stable governments.

The Overseas Private Investment Corporation (OPIC) offers programs to insure bank loans against the risk of war, expropriation, and currency inconvertibility. The OPIC also finances some loans directly. Similarly, the Eximbank guarantees medium-term loans made by commercial banks against both political and credit risks. The Eximbank deals with risk beyond the scope that private capital markets or private lenders are willing to assume. The bank's role in financing the high-risk loans may take the form of making a direct loan, participating in a loan with other lenders, or guaranteeing a loan. The Eximbank loan guarantee program is similar to the insurance provided by FCIA described earlier. As a policy matter, the Eximbank directs its international lending involvement toward the financing of capital equipment, such as hydroelectric installations, rather than consumer goods.

Pooling Risk.   Banks can also reduce international lending risk for any one institution by making **participation loans**. Under this kind of arrangement, banks join together to provide the funds for a loan and thereby directly reduce the risk exposure for individual banks. Large banks that participate in such arrangements will generally make their own assessment of the political and credit risks. Smaller lenders may rely primarily on the reports prepared by large banks. This may lead smaller banks to enter into international loans without fully appreciating or understanding the risk involved. Realistically, though, this is the only means by which smaller banks can enter the international lending arena, but one hopes that they base their decisions on intelligent analysis of the economic returns and risks involved, not on the glamour and prestige of having an international banking department. The decline in international banking activity of some small banks suggests that they have realized they do not have the expertise necessary to compete in international lending.

Diversification.   Banks may reduce foreign lending risk through portfolio diversification. That is, in the event that a borrower defaults, earnings from other investments will minimize the effect of the loan loss on the bank's total earnings. Of course, the extent that diversification reduces risk for a given portfolio of loans depends on how the returns are correlated with one another. The more highly correlated the returns, the less the portfolio risk will be reduced. Thus, in a choice between two loans having the same rate of return and riskiness, the loan that is less correlated with the bank's existing portfolio would be the more attractive loan.

Banks have pursued portfolio diversification in several ways, with geographic diversification being the most obvious means to reduce risk exposure. Geographic diversification reduces political risk, but such diversification for diversification's sake is not all good. Specifically, a bank develops expertise in certain countries and cultivates sources of primary information that may not be available to other banks. This type of information, plus long-standing experience with a particular borrower, may allow the bank to formulate better estimates of the risk involved in a particular loan. The danger is that if a bank develops expertise in an area in which the economies of all of the countries in that area depend on the same factors, specializing in the region can prove to be disastrous. This is what happened to many banks that were heavily exposed in Latin America. Although there may have been good diversification among the various countries, the whole region's fortunes were tied to a continuation of economic growth in the industrialized countries and to high prices for their export commodities. When these factors started to deteriorate, the entire region suffered, and banks were left with problem loans in many of the countries.

MANAGING RISK: HOW BANKS REDUCE COUNTRY RISK

After suffering huge losses on loans to less developed countries, U.S. banks have been reluctant to make new loans in countries like Mexico and Brazil. These countries and others in Latin America, Eastern Europe, and Asia are perceived as being risky places in which to make loans. Bankers are reluctant to lend in these countries because of potential political developments. For example, at the extreme, the government of one of these countries could restrict payment of foreign debt obligations.

This country (sovereign) risk is responsible for keeping U.S. banks from making loans in these countries. This is beginning to change, however, because of innovations that are allowing banks to lend in these countries without bearing

Swiss Banking: Neutrality and Confidentiality after the Holocaust Banking Scandals

Nestled in the heart of Europe, Switzerland has historically remained neutral through more than a century of European political instability and, more recently, neutral between the tensions of Eastern Communism and Western countries. As a result, Swiss banking has always enjoyed a unique position in the international banking community as a haven for those seeking political stability and banking confidentiality. The Swiss banking formula has been extremely successful. Swiss banks hold deposits disproportionately large relative to the size of the small Swiss economy.

The most mysterious and least understood of all Swiss bank activities is the handling of numbered deposit accounts. Banks in Switzerland, as well as in several other countries, allow bank or security safe-keeping accounts to be identified only by a number and not listed by the name of the depositor. Not commonly known, however, is that Swiss banking law requires Swiss banks to identify the owner of the funds by name in order to know who is entitled to transact with the funds. Thus, every numbered account has a name attached to it, just as every named account has a number. Furthermore, in May 1991 the Swiss government abolished "Form B" accounts, which had allowed depositors to hide their true identities by registering the accounts in the names of lawyers or other agents. The primary purpose of a numbered account is to restrict the knowledge of the customer's identity to a small number of high-ranking bank officials. Numbered accounts merely provide protection from possible indiscretions on the part of the bank staff.

The moral justification for such practices has always been that it protects innocent victims from tyrannical governments and others that might wish to confiscate the wealth of these victims. Faith in this argument was forever eroded, however, after it was learned that Swiss banks failed to turn over to family members the secret deposits of thousands of Jews who were killed during the Holocaust. Further, there is evidence suggesting that some Swiss banks assisted in the laundering of gold stolen from Holocaust victims. In an effort to put the wrongdoings of the past behind them, Swiss banks agreed to a $1.25 billion settlement with Holocaust survivors.

At the same time as they were settling with Holocaust survivors, Swiss banks were showing signs of becoming less secretive and more willing to assist authorities with information about potential criminals and to turn over funds held in secret accounts by such persons. For example, in October 1998, Swiss banking officials froze $114.4 million in accounts that were linked to Raul Salinas de Gortari, brother of Carlos Salinas, Mexico's former president. Raul is accused of controlling the Mexican drug-smuggling industry while Carlos was president. Swiss bank officials also participated in the seizure of $180 million in Swiss accounts held by Julio Cesar Nasser David. Nasser is accused of controlling one of the Colombian drug cartels.

substantial country risk. For example, the International Finance Corporation (IFC), a unit of the World Bank, is creating loan syndications to private borrowers in developing countries that make it possible for U.S. banks to make loans in these countries without bearing the country risk normally associated with such loans. These IFC loans are typically for amounts between $5 million and $100 million, with the IFC holding 25 percent of the debt and selling the rest of it to participating banks.

U.S. banks are attracted to these loan participations because they offer attractive yields, typically 2 to 3.5 percent above the LIBOR, and have minimal country risk. Country risk is small for two reasons. First, because the IFC is a unit of the World Bank, it is protected against the risk that a particular country will restrict the payment of debt obligations to foreign banks. And second, because the loans are syndicated, the risk exposure for individual banks is reduced. Note that although country risk is minimized, these loans still have credit risk associated with them. If the borrower fails, the participants will lose, but it will not be because of political developments in the country; it will be because of economics.

DO YOU UNDERSTAND?

1. In what ways may an international loan differ from a domestic loan?
2. What is the difference between currency risk and country risk?
3. Compare the strategies of pooling risk and diversification as methods of reducing the risks of international lending.

Foreign banks have operated in the United States for more than a hundred years. Beginning in the mid-1970s, however, they began to attract attention by their rapid expansion into major U.S. financial centers. Their rapid growth alarmed many U.S. bankers and regulators because, until the passage of the International Banking Act, foreign banks were able to escape federal control almost entirely. Exhibit 15.5 shows the number of foreign banks that have established offices in the United States in recent years. The number of foreign bank offices grew rapidly during the 1980s. Most of the growth in foreign bank offices was due to the overseas expansion of Japanese banks that was occurring during that period. When the Japanese financial system began experiencing difficulties in the early 1990s, however, many Japanese banks began to consolidate their overseas activities.

FOREIGN BANKS IN THE UNITED STATES

GROWTH OF FOREIGN BANKS

Before World War II, the primary motive for foreign banks to establish banking offices in the United States was to facilitate trade and the flow of long-term investments between the United States and their home countries. Following the war, the American dollar emerged as the major world currency, primarily because of the dominance of the U.S. economy relative to the rest of the world. With the importance of U.S. money and capital markets, additional foreign banks began to locate here. By 1965, there were 41 foreign banks conducting business in the United States, with assets totaling $7 billion. Most of these foreign banks were located in New York City, the major attraction being the direct access to the city's money and capital markets. Most of the other foreign banks were concentrated in California.

The rapid expansion of foreign banking activities in the United States began in the early 1960s. This spurt can be characterized as a worldwide response by the banking industry to the multinationalization of major manufacturing corpora-

EXHIBIT 15.5
Number of Foreign Banks in the United States (1982–2003)

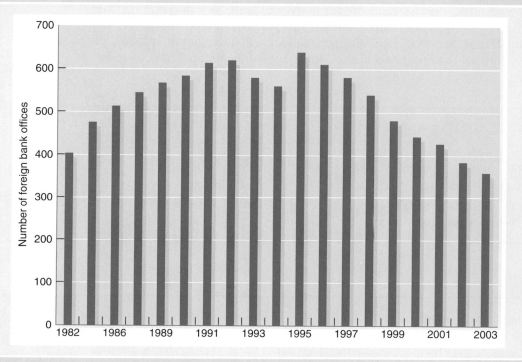

The number of foreign bank offices grew rapidly during the 1980s. In the 1990s and early 2000s, however, difficulties in their home countries and the pace of consolidation in the U.S. banking industry have caused a decline in the number of foreign bank offices in the United States.

Source: American Banker, various issues, 1983–1995, and Federal Reserve System, *Structure Data for U.S. Offices of Foreign Banks,* 1996–2003.

tions, as previously discussed. For foreign corporations, the United States represented a major market, and many of these firms made sizable direct investments in the United States. In short, foreign banks followed their corporate customers. The financial services provided were merely a continuation of long-established relationships. Similarly, U.S. corporations also provided some of the impetus for foreign banks to locate in the United States. As American corporations expanded abroad, they established relationships with major local foreign banks, which found it to be good business to extend the banking relationships to the corporate headquarters of U.S. firms by establishing offices in the United States. The banking services that were provided centered on financing the shipment of parts and semi-finished products between the corporate headquarters in the United States and the affiliated suppliers of foreign countries.

However, demand was not the only factor that caused this growth. It was also fostered by both the lack of a federal regulatory framework and the ability of foreign banks to establish an interstate banking network in a form denied U.S. banks. During this period, the entry of foreign banks into the United States was controlled by the individual states. No federal legislation governed their entry. A foreign bank's activities were regulated by federal law only if the bank joined the Federal Reserve System or if it controlled a subsidiary bank, in which case the foreign bank would be subject to the provisions of the Bank Holding Company Act. Thus, as long as the foreign bank operated branches or agencies, it was not subject to federal banking laws. Foreign banks could engage in some nonbanking activities denied to U.S. banks, and they were not required to hold reserves with the Federal Reserve System, a situation that tended to complicate monetary management. For all of the reasons previously discussed, the number of foreign bank offices in the United States increased from 85 to over 600 between 1965 and 1992. The growth of foreign bank assets in the United States relative to U.S. domestic bank assets is shown in Exhibit 15.6. Although the number of banks operating in the United States has increased dramatically, the 50 largest foreign banks tend to dominate foreign banking activities in the United States. According to a recent study by Thomson's International Bank Regulator, the 50 largest banks booked over 80 percent of the loans by all foreign banks. Exhibit 15.7 shows the foreign banks with the largest U.S. asset holdings. Clearly, a handful of foreign banks dominate the holdings of all foreign banks.

EXHIBIT 15.6
Growth in Foreign Bank Assets in the United States (1982–2003)

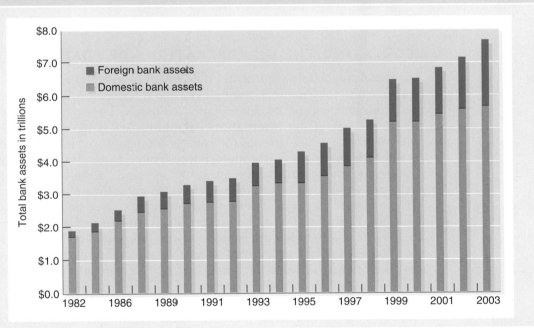

Foreign banks now control about 20 percent of all banking assets in the United States. Foreign bank assets grew rapidly in the 1980s, especially the assets held by branches of Japanese banks. In the 1990s, however, the holdings of U.S. assets by Japanese banks declined. The recent growth in foreign bank assets is due to increased holdings by Canadian and European banks.

Source: Board of Governors, Federal Reserve System.

EXHIBIT 15.7
Top Foreign Banks in U.S. Assets (December 31, 2003)

Rank	Bank	Headquarters Location	Total Assets in U.S. Offices ($ In billions)
1	Abn Amro Holdings	The Netherlands	$192.0
2	Deutsche Bank Ag	Germany	98.2
3	BNP Paribas	France	84.7
4	HSBC Holdings Plc	United Kingdom	83.6
5	Societe Generale	France	49.6
6	Mitsubishi Tokyo Fin. Group	Japan	49.2
7	Bank of Montreal	Canada	48.8
8	Landesbank Nordrhein Westfalen	Germany	46.9
9	Royal Bank of Canada	Canada	35.5
10	Rabobank	The Netherlands	33.5

Most of the U.S. assets held by foreign banks are in European banks. Japanese and Canadian banks also hold substantial U.S. assets.

Source: Board of Governors, Federal Reserve System, *Structure Data for U.S. Offices of Foreign Banks,* December 2003.

REGULATING THE U.S. OPERATIONS OF FOREIGN BANKS

The lack of regulatory control and the growth of foreign banks in the 1970s led to a recognition by the U.S. government that domestic banks were at a competitive disadvantage against foreign-controlled banks. The result of this realization was the passage of the **International Banking Act (IBA) of 1978**. The broad policy objective of the IBA was to promote competitive equality between domestic and foreign banking institutions in the United States. The policy of national treatment attempted to give foreign banks operating in the United States similar power and to subject them to the same obligations as their domestic counterparts.

There were six major statutory changes implemented under the International Bank Act. First, the IBA allowed federal chartering of foreign banking facilities. Second, the ability of foreign banks to accept interstate domestic deposits is limited. Foreign banks were allowed to establish branches in more than one state; however, branches outside the home state of a foreign bank could cannot accept deposits and could only maintain customer balances as permitted for Edge Act corporations. Such multistate banking activities were not allowed for domestic banks or bank holding companies at the time, and foreign banks' ability to engage in such activities was viewed as a competitive advantage over domestic banks. Third, the Federal Reserve Board was authorized to impose reserve requirements on foreign banks operating in the United States if they had worldwide assets in excess of $1 billion. This was done to help ensure the integrity of monetary policy actions as well as for competitive equality. Fourth, federal deposit insurance was required for foreign bank operations that engage in retail deposit taking.

Fifth, foreign banks were allowed to establish Edge Act corporations to conduct international banking and finance activities. Sixth, foreign banks that operate in the United States became subject to the nonbanking prohibitions of the Bank Holding Company Act.

With the passage of the Foreign Bank Supervision Enhancement Act (FBSEA) in 1991, the approval of the Federal Reserve was required before a foreign bank can establish offices in the United States. In addition, the Federal Reserve was required to examine each U.S. office of a foreign bank at least once a year and was given the power to close the office if it was engaging in inappropriate activities. FBSEA was passed shortly after the scandal involving the Bank of Commerce and Credit International (BCCI). Because of the complex organizational structure of BCCI, the bank was operating with very little regulatory oversight. The passage of FBSEA was an attempt to ensure that the Federal Reserve has the authority to oversee the activities of all foreign institutions operating in the United States.

After the Financial Services Modernization Act [or the Gramm-Leach-Bliley Act (GLB)] of 1999 was passed, any well-managed, well-capitalized, banking firm with a satisfactory Community Reinvestment Act rating could convert to a financial holding company, subject to approval by the Federal Reserve.[1] Financial holding companies are allowed to own subsidiaries that engage in virtually any financial business. The provisions of GLB apply to foreign and domestic banks, so it is not surprising that many foreign banks have formed financial holding companies. As of December 31, 2003, 32 of the 644 financial holding companies were foreign owned.

The foreseeable future is almost certain to be a time of dramatic change in international banking. The industry faces several challenges and opportunities:

- The recent consolidation of the European economy into a single market offers both opportunities and challenges for international banks. (See the In Practice box in this chapter.)

- The capital needs of developing nations (China, India, Russia, etc.) are likely to put pressure on world credit markets into the next decade.

- The Asian financial crisis and other shocks to the financial system in the late 1990s and early 2000s have increased financial institutions' awareness of operational risks.

- The trend toward the securitization of bank credits seems certain to continue and perhaps even accelerate as banks everywhere scramble to build up their capital bases and derive greater fee income.

- Increased competition from securities markets for the business of meeting the borrowing needs of large corporate clients is forcing banks to pursue other sources of revenue or develop new ways of competing.

- Finally, the growing interdependence among international economies and financial markets is certain to continue.

FUTURE DIRECTIONS OF INTERNATIONAL BANKING

---

[1] The Community Reinvestment Act (CRA) and CRA ratings are discussed in Chapter 15.

These trends have led the major international financial institutions, such as the International Monetary Fund (IMF) and the Bank for International Settlements, as well as the leading central banks to assume tighter regulatory and supervisory roles regarding the world's banking systems. The results have been a greater awareness of declining capital levels in some countries, some explicit regulations concerning capital adequacy and loan limits, and more supervision in such areas as international lending and foreign exchange trading. Recently the World Bank has been investigating the possibility of working with private corporations to tap larger pools of capital with which to assist countries with severe debt problems. Under one proposed arrangement, the World Bank would guarantee loans made to corporations for financing the construction of infrastructure projects in developing countries. The IMF is also looking for more ways to reduce the interest burden on developing countries while stimulating their economies to higher levels of output.

CHAPTER TAKE-AWAYS

1 U.S. banks engaged in very few international banking activities before 1914. It was not until the early 1960s that the rapid expansion of U.S. overseas banking took place.

2 The major reasons for this dramatic growth were (1) the overall expansion of U.S. world trade, (2) the growth of multinational corporations, and (3) the effect of government regulations.

3 The Federal Reserve Board and the OCC have primary responsibility for supervising the activities of U.S. banks overseas.

4 Banks can use a number of organizational forms to deliver banking services to their international customers. The most important are correspondent relationships, branch offices, Edge Act corporations, and international banking facilities.

5 The basic risk involved in foreign lending is the same as in domestic banking—the customer's default risk. However, there are two additional risks in lending abroad: sovereign risk and currency risk.

6 Although the number of foreign banks with U.S. operations is in the hundreds, a small number of large institutions tend to dominate the U.S. asset holdings of foreign banks.

KEY TERMS

Representative
  nonbanking offices
Shell branches
Correspondent banking
Foreign branches

Edge Act corporations
Agreement corporations
Foreign subsidiaries
International banking
  facilities (IBFs)

London Interbank Offer
  Rate (LIBOR)
Rollover pricing
Syndicated
Less developed countries

Country (sovereign) risk
Currency risk
Participation loans
International Banking Act
  of 1978

QUESTIONS AND PROBLEMS

1. Why were U.S. banks slow in expanding overseas? What changed to encourage oversees expansion?

2. How were the overseas expansions of U.S. nonfinancial corporations and banks related?

3. Why has the number of U.S. banks operating overseas shrunk in recent years?

4. What are Edge Act corporations? What advantages do they afford American banks that wish to engage in international banking?

5. What is a shell branch? What functions do banking shell branches perform in U.S. overseas banking? Why are so many located in Caribbean nations?

6. What is an international banking facility? In what types of business activities can such entities engage? Why did the Federal Reserve Board create these new banking entities?

7. What are the basic objectives of federal bank regulations as they apply to domestic banking? How are these basic regulatory objectives interpreted differently with respect to overseas banking? How will the BIS capital standards affect internationally active U.S. banks?

8. Explain the motivations behind the International Banking Act of 1978?

9. What were the provisions of the International Banking Act? Are some of the provisions no longer relevant? If so, which ones? Explain.

10. What is a syndicated loan? In what ways do large international loans differ from typical domestic loans? Define the term "LIBOR."

11. What risks must be evaluated in making international loans? Which of these are unique to international lending? How might these risks be reduced?

12. Do you believe that the presence of foreign banks in the United States serves the public's interest? In formulating your answer, consider the issues of bank safety and competition in banking markets.

13. In international lending, what is meant by the phrase "rescheduling of sovereign loans"? Why has rescheduling of loans become a problem to international lenders? What countries are involved?

INTERNET EXERCISE

In the previous two chapters, you were asked to use the Federal Financial Institutions Examination Council's National Information Center (NIC) Web site to look up balance-sheet and performance information about a bank in your local community. In this Internet Exercise, your task is to expand on the analysis you did in Chapters 13 and 14. (Note: It is not necessary for you to have completed the Internet Exercises in Chapter 13 or 14 for you to do this exercise.) Data on the foreign branches of U.S. banks and U.S. branches of foreign banks can be found at the NIC Web site, http://www.ffiec.gov/nic/.

1. Search the NIC Web site to determine whether your bank has any foreign branches. If so, identify the countries in which your bank has branches.
2. Search the NIC Web site to determine whether there are any foreign banks operating in your community. If so, identify the institution that is most similar to the domestic institutions identified in (1) above in terms of asset size.
3. Download or print out the summary performance ratios for the domestic institution and the foreign bank.
4. Compare the activities, performance, and riskiness of your bank to its foreign competitor. Comment on any significant differences between the two institutions.

16

Regulation of Financial Institutions

CHAPTER PREVIEW

When was the last time you performed a careful analysis of your bank to make sure it was a safe place to deposit your money? If you are like most people, you have not given much thought to the safety and soundness of your bank. If you had been a student in the early 1900s, however, you would have been keenly aware of your bank's financial strength. At that time, banks had little regulation and bank liabilities (paper money or bank accounts) were unsecured. Thus, if your bank failed, you probably lost your money. Given those consequences, it's easy to understand why "runs" on banks were a common occurrence. What's a run on a bank? Back in the good old days, when banks had little regulation and some banks engaged in unscrupulous activities that included cheating or lying, when you heard a rumor that a bank might fail, you literally "ran" to the bank to get your money back—either as hard currency (gold or silver coins) or bank notes of a sound bank. The motto of the day about banking was "better the safe than sorry." Today, people take for granted that banks are a safe place to keep their money. The reason is, of course, the extensive regulatory system developed over many years of experience and the fact that bank deposits are protected by federal deposit insurance. This chapter discusses the regulation of financial institutions, the reasons for the regulation, and the issues involved. ■

A crash in the stock market can be devastating. When markets crash, there are only sellers—no buyers—and the prices of both securities and real assets can decline in the wake of a crash. The good news is that you may be able to pick up a great used car for a hundred bucks.

This chapter focuses on the major regulations that affect financial institutions, especially commercial banks. Regulations have a major impact on how financial institutions are managed, how they deal with consumers, the types of products they offer, the structure of the industry, and the types of risks they take. In fact, the interplay between financial institutions and their regulators is so intertwined that one cannot define an institution or understand what it does without understanding the regulations that constrain its behavior.

The chapter begins with a discussion of bank failures and their impact on individual communities and the nation's economy as a whole. Drawing on the lessons from the past, we then discuss the reasons for regulating commercial banks and other financial institutions. Historically, the overriding concern of regulation has been the safety and soundness of the financial system, which includes commercial banks and other financial institutions. The primary tools to achieve safety and soundness are (1) liquidity to the banking system provided by the Federal Reserve banks; (2) federal deposit insurance, which reduces the threat of runs on banks and other depository institutions; and (3) the examination process, which monitors compliance with regulations and evaluates the quality of management. In addition, the chapter also discusses other regulations that affect the financial system, such as those affecting competition between institutions, industry structure, and the protection of consumers. The chapter concludes by discussing the powers of various regulators that oversee commercial banks. Subsequent chapters discuss other financial institutions and describe their regulators and the principal regulations that define and limit their business activities. Those chapters are Chapter 17 (Thrift Institutions and Finance Companies), Chapter 18 (Insurance Companies and Pension Funds), Chapter 19 (Investment Banking), and Chapter 20 (Investment Companies). ■

LEARNING OBJECTIVES

The objectives of this chapter are to:

1 Discuss the reasons why banks are regulated.

2 Describe the history of bank failures in the United States, the steps policy makers have taken to reduce the incidence of failure, and the lessons learned from previous bank failures.

3 Explain FDIC insurance and how the FDIC goes about paying off depositors and disposing of the assets of a failed bank.

4 Discuss the issues and concerns created by FDIC insurance.

5 Describe the bank examination process.

6 Explain the limitations on bank activities and discuss recent changes to those limitations.

7 Discuss the various consumer protection regulations that banks must comply with.

8 Describe the responsibilities of the various bank regulatory agencies.

REASONS FOR REGULATION

Financial institutions are regulated because they provide goods and services that the economy needs in order to function well. In addition, they function in an environment where asymmetric information is more the rule than the exception. Most consumers and businesses will disclose their financial affairs to a financial institution if it is a necessary condition to obtain services. However, consumers and businesses want their financial affairs to be confidential. As a result, financial institutions are honor bound to keep the information private, but in doing so it is difficult for depositors to have enough information to assess the institution's soundness. Depositors, for example, do not know whether their financial institution has made good loans and entered into sound financial contracts. Unfortunately, because of the veil of uncertainty that exists when information is limited, banks and other depository institutions in the past have been subjected to runs and the financial system as a whole has encountered "panics" when people rush to withdraw funds because they fear their bank or the banking system is unsound.

Individual bank failures can hurt a community by shrinking the money supply, disrupting borrowing relationships, and drying up sources of credit, at least temporarily. Thus, commerce in the community suffers if other institutions cannot or do not move quickly to fill the void of money and credit left by a bank failure. If a banking panic occurs, the economy will slow down because bank reserves and the money supply will shrink abruptly unless the central bank quickly takes action to provide liquidity and restore confidence in the financial system.

Because the social costs of bank failures and the resulting economic upheaval may exceed the private costs to bank shareholders, banks are heavily regulated. In addition, because national regulation often allows financial institutions to earn significant profits by creating money or borrowing at low cost due to explicit or implicit government guarantees, politicians often try to induce financial institutions to surrender some of those profits to further the politicians' social goals. Thus, financial institutions are often coerced into (1) investing in government securities, (2) making loans to classes of customers that otherwise might not qualify, or (3) making certain loans at interest rates lower than the rates that the financial institutions customarily charge on loans of that type and associated risk.

Banks and other depository institutions are willing to accept the regulation as long as they know that the net effect of regulation benefits them by increasing public confidence in their stability and public willingness to accept their liabilities, even if those liabilities pay low interest rates. However, regulated financial institutions also have an incentive to try to avoid regulation if by so doing they can increase their profits even more. Thus, over time a so-called **regulatory dialectic** or regulatory struggle has developed in which regulators impose a regulation—such as limits on activities imposed by the 1933 Glass-Steagall Act—and banks find a way to avoid the regulation, for example, by establishing separate subsidiaries to engage in the prohibited activities. As financial institutions innovate around regulation, the regulators impose new regulations and the regulatory dialectic continues. Overall, however, financial institutions comply with a heavy dose of regulation because the value of the charter to operate as a bank or other financial institution is greater than the cost associated with complying with regulation. The major bank legislative actions and their regulatory provisions since 1900 are summarized in Exhibit 16.1. As you can see from the exhibit, regulation of financial institutions is broad in scope and quite detailed. The extensive regulation makes it challenging to manage a financial institution profitably.

EXHIBIT 16.1
Major Bank Legislation and Regulatory Provisions Since 1900

Federal Reserve Act (1913)

- Establishes the Federal Reserve System

Banking Acts of 1933 Glass-Steagall) and 1935

- Prohibits payment of interest on demand deposits
- Establishes the FDIC
- Separates banking from investment banking
- Establishes interest rate ceilings on savings and time deposits

Bank Holding Company Act (1956)

- Regulates formation of bank holding companies (BHC)
- Allows nonbank subsidiaries to operate across state lines

Bank Merger Act (1966)

- Establishes merger guidelines and denotes competition as a criterion

Amendment to Bank Holding Company Act (1970)

- Regulates one-bank holding companies

Depository Institutions Deregulation and Monetary Control Act (1980)

- Establishes uniform reserve requirements for all depository institutions
- Phases out deposit rate ceilings by April 1, 1986
- Allows NOW accounts at all depository institutions
- Allows thrifts to make consumer loans and issue credit cards

Depository Institutions Act of 1982 (Garn–St. Germain)

- Allows possibility of interstate and interinstitutional mergers
- Gives thrifts authority to make some commercial loans

Competitive Equality in Banking Act (CEBA) of 1987

- Limits growth of nonbank banks
- Changes definition of bank to include FDIC-insured institutions

Financial Institutions Reform, Recovery, and Enforcement Act of 1989

- Changes structure of thrift institution regulation
- Changes federal deposit insurance structure and financing

Federal Deposit Insurance Corporation Improvement Act of 1991

- Provides for additional funding for federal deposit insurance
- Tightens regulations applicable to insured institutions
- Provides for greater capital regulation, early closure, and risk-based insurance

Interstate Banking and Branching Efficiency Act of 1994

- Allowed banks to acquire and merge with out-of-state banks by 1997 (if the host state did not disallow interstate branching)
- Requires banks to make loans to all elements of the community—including the inner city and other poor areas

Financial Services Modernization Act of 1999 (Gramm-Leach-Bliley)

- Created financial holding companies that can own commercial banking, securities, and insurance affiliates.

BANK FAILURES AND REGULATION

As indicated above, one of the main reasons that banks are regulated is that policy makers believe the public will lose more than the individual bank will lose if the bank fails and disrupts the economy or its financial system. For this reason, much of the bank legislation passed during the 1980s and early 1990s was an attempt to reduce the number of bank failures or deal with some of the problems caused by bank failures. This section discusses the reasons why banks fail, the bank legislation passed during the 1980s and 1990s, and some of the lessons learned from past bank failures.

Recall from Chapter 14 that bank failures occur for two primary reasons. First, banks fail because of illiquidity. Banks hold fractional reserves and invest in many illiquid assets, such as loans, which in many cases can be resold quickly only at a loss. If many depositors withdraw funds from the bank simultaneously, it forces the bank to liquidate assets at a loss to generate cash to pay depositors. Failures caused by illiquidity can be prevented, however, if a bank can borrow easily in such situations from another institution or, better yet, have a **lender of last resort**. Second, a bank or other financial institution can fail because the bank acquires assets that are too risky relative to the bank's capital base—in other words, inadequate capital. If the investments decline in value or if loans default, the bank's capital can erode to the extent that the bank becomes insolvent—that is, its liabilities are greater than its assets. Because banks are highly leveraged, this can easily happen when the value of assets falls by only a small amount.

Unfortunately, the failure of a single bank, whether due to inadequate capital or inadequate liquidity, can create uncertainty about the soundness of other banks. Prior to the creation of federal deposit insurance, this uncertainty would often cause **bank panics**. Thus, one bank's failure often caused the failure of many banks. Consequently, the number of bank failures per year in the United States has fluctuated widely. They have occurred both as isolated local events and in great national waves. For instance, during the business panic of 1893, nearly 500 banks out of 9,500 suspended operations. In contrast, during the business recession of 1870, only one bank closed.

Exhibit 16.2 shows the number and percentage of all banks failing in the 1921–2003 period. Prior to the 1920s, the number of bank failures averaged about 100 per year, something less than 2 percent of all banks. Beginning in the 1920s, the number of bank failures increased dramatically. The greatest number of failures occurred during the early years of the Depression, 1930–1933. All told, over 14,000 banks failed during the 1921–1933 period.

THE ROLE OF THE FED IN PREVENTING BANK FAILURES

The most important mechanism for preventing bank failures that are due to inadequate liquidity is the Federal Reserve's discount window. By acting as a "lender of last resort," the Federal Reserve reduces the incentive for depositors to panic during a financial crisis and banks do not have to liquidate assets at substantial losses in order to satisfy depositors' withdrawal requests. In fact, the Federal Reserve often turns to discount window lending to prevent a financial panic. For example, in the days that followed September 11, 2001, discount window borrowing far exceeded normal levels in part because the Fed encouraged banks to borrow at the discount window in order to ensure that financial markets were sufficiently liquid. Also recall that the Fed never has a liquidity problem because of its power to create money.

EXHIBIT 16.2
Number and Percentage of All Banks Failing (1921–2003)

Years	Number of Failures	Annual % of Active Banks	Average Number of Failures per Year
1921–1933	14807	5.07%	1139.0
1934–1940	328	0.34%	46.9
1941–1950	52	0.04%	5.2
1951–1960	20	0.02%	2.0
1961–1970	49	0.04%	4.9
1971–1980	77	0.05%	7.7
1981–1990	1178	0.88%	117.8
1991–2000	306	0.27%	32.2
2001–2003	16	0.07%	5.3

FDIC insurance became effective on January 1, 1934, and initially provided depositors with $2,500 in coverage. Its impact on public confidence in the banking system was immediate. The number of bank failures declined dramatically and stayed relatively low until the rise in banks' deposit interest costs in the early 1980s combined with the regional recessions of the 1980s and early 1990s led to a significant number of bank failures.

Source: FDIC, *Annual Report,* various issues, and *Historical Statistics on Banking.*

Through its policy tools of open-market operations and adjusting reserve requirements, the Fed can "print" all the money needed in a financial crisis. Refer back to Chapters 2 and 3 for a discussion of the Fed's powers to create money.

THE ROLE OF DEPOSIT INSURANCE IN PREVENTING BANK FAILURES

Following the large number of failures in the 1921 to 1933 period, Congress enacted legislation intended to prevent such wholesale bank failures from occurring again. The **Banking Act of 1933** (which is commonly referred to as the **Glass-Steagall Act** in recognition of the senators who sponsored the legislation) restored confidence in the commercial banking system by establishing the **Federal Deposit Insurance Corporation (FDIC)**. By guaranteeing the safety of depositors' funds, federal **deposit insurance** put an end to banking panics. Thus a potential insolvency at one bank no longer threatened deposits at other banks in the same economic region, thereby putting a stop to the domino effect that had long plagued American banking.

In addition to establishing the FDIC, the Banking Act of 1933 barred banks from paying interest on demand deposits, separated commercial banking from investment banking, and restricted the types of assets that banks could own (e.g., banks can only own investment-grade securities) on the grounds that these and other banking practices were excessively risky. Although the wisdom and effectiveness of some of these restrictions have been questioned and many have since been repealed, the effectiveness of the 1933 Banking Act in reducing bank panics and failures is undisputed.

The effectiveness of federal deposit insurance in reducing bank failures can be seen in Exhibit 16.2. Between 1934 and 1942, bank failures dropped to an average of 54 per year, and many of the banks that failed did not have deposit insurance. Following World War II, the number of bank closings slowed to a trickle, averaging less than 10 per year until the 1980s.

THE 1980s AND 1990s

At first, deposit insurance and the other regulatory initiatives in the 1930s banking acts protected financial institutions against failure. However, during the 1980s increasing interest rates, coupled with increasing competition from nonbank institutions and excessive interest rate risk on the part of thrift (savings and loans and savings banks) institutions, led to a sharp increase in depository institution failures. As a result, a number of laws were passed in the 1980s and 1990s in an attempt to strengthen financial institutions and their insurance funds. The laws also broke down traditional barriers between financial institutions by giving them more powers to issue financial liabilities and diversify their assets, in hopes that this would let institutions become more profitable. We now turn to a discussion of these new regulations.

The first major law passed was the **Depository Institutions Deregulation and Monetary Control Act of 1980 (DIDMCA)**. Basically, DIDMCA tried to "level the playing field" for all depository institutions by giving all of them the right to issue interest-bearing transactions deposits, requiring that all back their transactions deposits with reserves, and requiring that the Fed charge them all equally for the use of check-clearing services (instead of giving such services free to Fed member banks) and give them all equal access to the discount window. Furthermore, the Act phased out rate ceilings on deposits and also on certain types of loans (unless the ceilings were reimposed by individual states), and it generally tried to simplify the regulatory environment. It was hoped that the new powers and relaxed loan rate ceilings given thrift institutions and credit unions by the act would enhance their profitability and reduce their interest rate risk.

However, the DIDMCA did not do enough to help the thrift institutions. Thus, Congress passed the **Depository Institutions Act of 1982 (DIA) (Garn–St. Germain)**. That Act immediately deregulated interest rate ceilings by allowing depository institutions to issue checkable money market deposit accounts that could pay any interest rate and had no reserve requirements as long as the depositor wrote only three checks per month. It also gave thrift institutions the power to issue limited demand deposits and the ability to make commercial loans. This let thrift institutions become more competitive with banks and also made them more attractive as merger candidates for banks. However, the decline in oil prices in the mid-1980s combined with thrifts' already depleted capital led to many thrift failures and an insolvent **Federal Savings and Loan Insurance Corporation (FSLIC)** fund.

After the Garn–St. Germain Act, few regulatory acts were passed until the **Competitive Equality in Banking Act of 1987 (CEBA)**. The main provisions of that act were (1) to regulate the activities of "nonbank banks" (which were "banks" used by holding companies to evade regulatory restrictions, since they technically were not banks because they either did not have demand deposits or make consumer loans) and (2) to provide funding to bail out the failing FSLIC.

However, the aid for the FSLIC was too little and too late. Thus, in 1989 Congress passed the **Financial Institutions Reform, Recovery, and Enforcement Act (FIRREA)**. The FIRREA made major changes in the financing of deposit insurance and the structure of financial institution regulation. It also provided for the "bailout" of insolvent thrift institutions. The Act recognized that easy accommodation of thrift industry legislative interests, coupled with lax capital, accounting, and regulatory standards, had all contributed to the high rate of failure of thrift institutions and the insolvency of the FSLIC (the thrift institutions' deposit insurance fund until 1989).

The FIRREA created a new federal insurance institution (the Savings Association Insurance Fund—FDIC-SAIF) that assumed responsibilities for insuring thrifts' deposits. The new thrift deposit insurance fund was made a subsidiary of the Federal Deposit Insurance Corporation, which continued to supervise the Federal Deposit Insurance Fund for banks (now called the Bank Insurance Fund) as well as the new (separate) Savings Association Insurance Fund.

The FIRRE Act also implemented the risk-based capital standards discussed in Chapter 14 and mandated an increase in deposit insurance premiums. The deposit rate premium increases embodied in FIRREA were not sufficient to keep the bank deposit insurance fund solvent, however. Thus, in 1991 Congress passed the **Federal Deposit Insurance Corporation Improvement Act (FDICIA)**. The major purpose of the act was to provide additional funding provisions for the FDIC. However, the act also mandated that major changes be made in financial regulation and compliance procedures in order to reduce the probability of failure and any ensuing cost to the taxpayers.

Key provisions of the FDICIA included the following: (1) The Act increased the line of credit available to the FDIC from the U.S. Treasury and allowed the FDIC to borrow additional funds as needed to resolve bank failures. (2) The Act mandated that the FDIC increase deposit insurance premiums as necessary to ensure that it could repay all principal and interest on any debts it incurred. (3) The Act mandated that the FDIC start to charge risk-based deposit insurance premiums so riskier banks (that is, those less well capitalized or those with high interest rate or credit risk) would have an incentive to reduce their risk and would better compensate the insurance fund for their increased risk of loss. (6) "Undercapitalized banks" were required to develop capital restoration plans that would explain how they would restore their capital adequacy to satisfactory levels by selling stock, cutting dividends, divesting risky assets, and so forth. The FDIC was then required to monitor the implementation of the restoration plans to ensure that undercapitalized banks were, in fact, returning to "adequately capitalized" status. (7) Critically undercapitalized banks were given only a short period of time to correct their problems or they would be closed. (8) The FDICIA also required that any institution with capital below 2 percent of assets would be declared "critically undercapitalized" and would be subject to the act's "early closure" requirements. By closing weak institutions early, it was hoped that losses to the insurance fund would not accumulate as the institution continued to struggle along in a weakened status.

After the FDICIA was passed, bank failures stayed high for a year or two as the weakest institutions that could not restore their capital were liquidated; then bank failures fell to minuscule levels, falling as low as one failure per year in 1997. A strong economy helped reduce failures but so did the new emphasis on increased examinations and **prompt corrective actions** taken while banks still retained some capital.

LESSONS FROM PAST BANK FAILURES

One of the lessons learned from past bank failures is that by guaranteeing depositors' funds, the FDIC has effectively prevented runs on the banks that it insures. Depositors no longer need to operate under the rule of "better first in line than sorry." If their bank fails, depositors know the FDIC will pay them in an orderly manner. When bank runs have occurred in recent years, they have been limited to a single bank and have not spread to other insured banks.

Another lesson learned from past bank failures is that regional or industry-wide depressions are a major cause of bank failures. From 1921 through 1931, most bank failures involved unit banks that were closely tied to local economies. Only seven suspensions involved banks with more than 10 branches. California, the country's principal statewide branching state, experienced few bank failures during this period. The reason for unit banks' poor record with respect to bank failures is their lack of geographic diversification. Branch banking over wide geographic areas provides diversification for a bank's loan and deposit portfolio, resulting in reduced business risk as compared to a similar unit bank. Recent evidence suggests that regional or industry-wide depressions still cause bank failures in states whose economies are poorly diversified. This was shown by numerous bank failures in the oil-dependent Southwest and agriculturally dependent Midwest during the 1980s. However, even in an area with weak economies, it is only the most poorly managed banks (i.e., the least diversified, most illiquid holders of the poorest-quality loans) that fail.

Finally, another lesson learned from past bank failures is that fraud, embezzlement, and poor management are the most notable causes of bank failures. This has been particularly true since the 1940s. For example, of the 54 insured banks that failed between 1959 and 1970, 35 (65 percent) were classified by the FDIC as failing as a consequence of fraud or other irregularities. That percentage fell sharply in the 1980s, however, as bank failures ascribable to weak local economies increased. Nonetheless, among major bank failures, the FDIC blamed the failures of the United States National Bank of San Diego and Franklin National Bank of New York City on "irregular" banking practices, and the failures of Penn Square Bank of Oklahoma and United American Bank of Knoxville resulted from "unusual" loan losses.

United American Bank, a large bank that failed in Tennessee in 1983, had made many "floater loans," which floated down to lower-ranking loan officers from top management with the request that the loans be approved. Many of the loans were to friends or political cronies of the president of the bank, and often the loans were not repaid.

SAFETY AND SOUNDNESS REGULATION: DEPOSIT INSURANCE

When deposit insurance was first enacted in 1933, it covered only deposits up to $2,500. Its purpose was to protect people with small deposits. People with large deposits were assumed to be sophisticated enough to look after themselves. It was believed, however, that small depositors (those with small amounts of money, not those weighing less than 100 pounds) were more likely to be unable or unwilling to assess a bank's true financial status. Thus, they were thought to be both more vulnerable to bank failures and more likely to panic and cause a run on a bank to get their deposits back quickly if they heard rumors that a bank might fail.

Over time, federal deposit insurance has been increased from $2,500 per account offered by the FDIC on deposits at insured commercial banks and savings banks in 1934 to more institutions and to $100,000 per depositor. In 1934, the Federal Savings and Loan Insurance Corporation (FSLIC) extended deposit insurance of $5,000 per account to savings and loan depositors. The FSLIC was established by the National Housing Act of 1934 and continued until 1989, when it was eliminated as a separate entity and the responsibility for thrift institutions was transferred to the FDIC. The thrift insurance branch of the FDIC, the Savings Association Insurance Fund (FDIC-SAIF), now insures deposits at savings and loans and at some federally chartered savings banks. Federal insurance is also extended to credit unions' depositors' "shares" through the **National Credit Union Share Insurance Fund (NCUSIF)**, which was established in 1970. The NCUSIF provides insurance for participating credit union members' share deposits for amounts up to $100,000—the same level of insurance the FDIC provides.

All federally chartered commercial banks, savings banks, savings and loans, and credit unions must obtain deposit insurance from one of the federal insurance funds. State-chartered institutions can also obtain federal deposit insurance provided that they meet the standards imposed by the appropriate fund. Some institutions, such as savings and loans or savings banks, have sometimes changed their charters so that they could obtain insurance from the most desirable fund. In the late 1970s and early 1980s, many savings and loans and savings banks preferred FSLIC insurance in order to obtain looser regulations. After many savings and loans failed, however, the FSLIC raised its insurance premium in the mid-1980s. Subsequently, many savings institutions tried to transfer to FDIC insurance (by obtaining savings bank or commercial bank charters) so that they could pay lower rates on their deposit insurance. Such transfers were subsequently limited, however, by the fact that institutions that transferred from the FDIC-SAIF (Savings Association Insurance Fund) to the FDIC-BIF (Bank Insurance Fund) were assessed extra fees. Thus, by 2001, most savings institutions were still insured by the FDIC-SAIF fund.

HOW REGULATORS HANDLE BANK FAILURES

When a bank fails, the FDIC may have a choice of several policies to use when resolving the assets and liabilities of a failed bank. In the past it had some discretion as to which policy to use, but the FDICI Act mandates that it use the least-cost method. The most straightforward approach to resolving a failed institution is to *pay off* the insured deposits, take over the failed institution, and *liquidate* the institution's assets. Exhibit 16.3 illustrates the FDIC's payoff policy. Under a **pay-off and liquidate policy**, if sufficient funds were not realized from the liquidation of the failed institution, the insured depositors would be paid in full only up to $100,000 per depositor. After that, the depositors would obtain only a partial settlement, or no settlement at all, when the assets of the bank were liquidated. A partial settlement would often be necessary because an insolvent bank has total assets worth less than the total value of its liabilities (see Exhibit 16.3). In such a case, the FDIC would pay insured depositors in full, but the uninsured depositors might receive only 50¢ on the dollar for uninsured deposits.

EXHIBIT 16.3
FDIC Payoff Policy

Assets	Liabilities and Net Worth
Value realized from sale of assets = $75 million	Deposits under $100,000 = $50 million
	Uninsured liabilities and deposits over $100,000 = $100 million
	Net worth = –$75 million

In a deposit payoff, the FDIC pays off the $50 million in insured deposits and, in turn, is owed $50 million by the bank. The FDIC then takes possession of the failed bank's assets and liquidates them. It uses the proceeds to pay off the $150 million of deposits and other liabilities (including the $50 million that it is owed in return for paying off the insured deposits). After recovering $75 million from the asset liquidation, the FDIC can pay itself and uninsured liability and deposit holders $0.50 in payoff for each $1 ($75 million/$150 million) of the bank's liabilities that they own. The owners of the bank receive zero dollars back, because the bank is insolvent and has no positive net worth.

Exhibit 16.3 involves the simplest possible liquidation scenario. In fact, there may be different levels of financial claims outstanding when a bank is liquidated. Formerly laws differed regarding payoff priorities. However, in the Omnibus Budget Reconciliation Act of 1993, payoff priorities were established for different claimants of the failed bank's assets. Depending on the availability of funds, payoffs would be made in the following order: (1) the administrative expenses of the receiver; (2) the claims of all depositors, including the FDIC in place of the insured depositors whom it had paid off; (3) general creditors; (4) subordinated creditor claims; and, if there are any assets left, (5) the claims of shareholders. Note that subordinated debt holders are not paid off until all claims except shareholder claims have been satisfied.

Because a bank may have more value as a going concern, with valuable customer relations, locations, staff knowledge, and expertise, it may be more valuable if at least part of its operations is maintained than if it is totally liquidated. This has generated a number of alternative methods for resolving bank failures. Most commonly, various forms of "purchase and assumption" transactions are employed.

Instead of liquidating a failed bank, the insurance fund can allow another bank to enter into a **purchase and assumption agreement**, in which it would purchase the failed bank and assume all of its liabilities. In that case, the FDIC might provide financial assistance to the acquirer and relieve the bank of some or all of the bad assets in order to induce the new buyer to assume the failed bank's liabilities. Because the failed bank might have more value as an ongoing concern than as a failed bank, it could be less costly for the FDIC to provide financial assistance than to liquidate the failed bank. Furthermore, when all the liabilities were assumed, no depositor would lose a dime, regardless of how large or small the depositor's account was. Thus, the use of the purchase and assumption technique would provide de facto 100 percent deposit insurance.

Exhibit 16.4 illustrates a purchase and assumption in which the acquiring institution injects $5 million in new capital and pays a purchase premium of $5 million to cover past losses. In addition, the FDIC provides $20 million in financial assistance in this example to cover other losses.

The FDIC may use either a "whole bank" purchase and assumption or a "clean bank" purchase and assumption policy. In the latter case the FDIC retains some of the failed bank's assets and provides the acquirer with an FDIC promissory note to cover the value of the retained assets. Alternatively, the acquirer may acquire all the failed bank's assets but retain an option to "put" some of the assets back to the FDIC in exchange for an FDIC promissory note at some later point in time. It may exercise the put after it has a chance to better evaluate the failed bank's loan portfolio. In such a case, the FDIC is likely to receive all the failed bank's defaulted and doubtful loans when the put is exercised.

Finally, the FDIC may retain the failed bank's assets and transfer the insured deposits of that bank to another financial institution. Because an acquiring institution may find it cheaper to obtain additional deposit liabilities by "buying them" from the FDIC, rather than by advertising, it may be willing to pay the FDIC a small premium for being allowed to assume the failed bank's insured deposit obligations.

EXHIBIT 16.4

FDIC-Assisted Purchase and Assumption Transaction: Failed Bank Subsidiary of New Bank

Assets	Liabilities and Net Worth
$75 million, value of old bank's good assets acquired by new bank	$100 million in deposits and other liabilities of old bank assumed by new bank
$20 million in financial assistance provided by FDIC in exchange for some bad assets	
$5 million purchase premium paid by new bank's owners in the form of assumed liabilities	
$5 million in new cash injected by new bank's owners to buy capital	$5 million in new capital in new bank

In a purchase and assumption, the owners of the new bank acquire selected assets of the failed bank and assume all of its liabilities, including its uninsured as well as insured deposits. The new bank's owners may request financial assistance from the FDIC and, in turn, give the FDIC claims on some of the old bank's bad assets (defaulted or doubtful loans). Before they are allowed to acquire and operate the new bank, the owners also may have to (1) inject new money in the form of a purchase premium to make up for asset deficiencies (charged-off loans of the old bank) and (2) inject new capital into the bank. If the old bank has hidden assets, such as a valuable banking franchise, the new bank's owners may be willing to pay a substantial amount to acquire it.

DEPOSIT INSURANCE IN THE 21ST CENTURY

One of the lessons learned during the 1980s and 1990s concerns the cyclical nature of the deposit insurance system. When the economy performs well, banks perform well and there are few bank failures. During such times, deposit insurance funds build up a surplus, often leading to a reduction in deposit insurance premiums. When the economy performs poorly, however, banks perform poorly, and many banks fail. When a large number of banks fail, the deposit insurance fund is whittled away, often to the point that the FDIC must raise deposit insurance premiums.

Several policy makers argue that the deposit insurance system needs reform to address the cyclical nature of the current system. In addition, there is concern among bankers that new entrants into the banking business, such as investment banks and insurance companies, may weaken the deposit insurance fund and lead to an increase in premiums. Many bankers feel they are subsidizing these new entrants, which tend to be some of the fastest-growing and riskiest banks. Still others argue that deposit insurance coverage needs to be increased and indexed to inflation, especially for individual retirement accounts.

There have been several attempts to pass a deposit insurance reform bill in recent years. At the time of this writing, the future of deposit insurance reform is unknown. It seems likely, however, that the current deposit insurance system is likely to face significant change in the near future.

DO YOU UNDERSTAND?

1. Why are bank failures considered to be so undesirable that the government should try to prevent them?
2. What has the U.S. trend in bank failures been since 1920?
3. What is the difference between a purchase and assumption and a payoff method for liquidating a failed bank?
4. Why might it be unfair to small banks if all large bank liquidations were accomplished via purchase and assumption rather than payoff transaction?

DEPOSIT INSURANCE ISSUES

Although deposit insurance has reduced the numbers of bank failures and panics, it is not without its own issues. In fact, because of these issues, some policy makers have argued in favor of more limited coverage of deposits. This section describes the issues created by deposit insurance and discusses how policy makers attempt to deal with those issues.

MORAL HAZARD PROBLEMS

A major problem resulting from the provision of deposit insurance is that it reduces the incentive of depositors to monitor the health of institutions in which they place their money. This is a **moral hazard** in that the insured individual is less careful, and thus is more likely to incur a loss, than would be the case if he or she were not insured. Thus, since 1983, the FDIC has tried to ensure that *uninsured* depositors police more carefully the banks in which they deposit their funds. It has done so by arranging insured-deposit transfers in cases of bank failure. In such cases, only the insured deposits are transferred to another institution. The uninsured deposits are returned to the old bank, which is liquidated. Consequently, because uninsured depositors may lose some or all of their funds, they have a greater incentive to monitor the safety of the bank than they would if they expected a purchase and assumption to occur in the event of failure.

Deposit insurance can also create a moral hazard for the managers of depository institutions. In particular, even if a depository institution is risky, if it is insured, it can usually continue to issue deposits to obtain funds at much the same rate as less risky institutions. It can do so because most deposit holders do not share the risks of loss (which are primarily borne by the FDIC). Thus, unlike corporation managers, managers of insured depository institutions can usually take greater risk without greatly increasing the price they must pay to obtain (deposit) liabilities. If they do not bear the full cost of their risk taking, they may be encouraged to take more risk than they would if they could only issue uninsured liabilities.

For example, an institution with many bad loans may fear that it will have to write them off and become insolvent. If that were done, it would be liquidated, thereby costing the management team its jobs, salaries, and perquisites. However, if the institution issues more insured deposits paying its usual insured-deposit rate, makes more loans at higher rates, and charges high loan origination or application fees, it may be able to report enough profits on its newly expanded loan portfolio that it will be able to absorb the losses on past loans and still appear to be profitable. This strategy can work only if losses appear on the new loans with a lag while the income from extra fees and higher rates on loans immediately increases reported profits. Such a "profitable" institution can continue to operate. If the new loans are, in fact, sound, the management may have true profits and survive its crisis. However, if the new borrowers were willing to pay high loan rates and large up-front fees only because the borrowers' loan requests were risky, loan losses will ultimately occur as the new loans go bad. Thus, the weak institutions will have to grow still faster so that reported earnings from new loans will grow faster than reported loan losses on old loans.

This process occurred with many savings and loan associations in the 1980s, before regulators required that "loan origination fees" be amortized over the life of the loan rather than recorded as current income. Nonetheless, risky borrowers still promise to pay higher rates to obtain a loan and may be willing to purchase other services to try to gain favor with the lender. (Although the purchase of other services, with few exceptions, such as compensating balance requirements, usually cannot be explicitly required as a condition to obtain the loan, many borrowers may purchase such services if they believe it will enhance the relationship by providing more profits for the lender.) Thus, moral hazard still exists for lenders who believe they can make greater profits for their institutions if they make more risky loans.

This moral hazard problem means that managers of troubled institutions will have an incentive to gamble. If the gamble fails, they can gamble again in hopes that the gambling process will obscure their losses, buy them more time as managers, and give the institution a chance to grow out of its difficulties. Deposit insurance makes this gambling possible, as it allows remotely generated deposits to be funneled to the gamblers by deposit brokers, even if local depositors become wary of an institution that is taking too many risks.

The issue of moral hazard is not moot. A scenario like the one just described led to massive failures of Texas depository institutions in the late 1980s. The problems actually started in the early to mid-1980s as oil prices fell and the real estate market softened. Despite the market trends, Texas lenders, especially the thrift institutions, continued to lend. Many took advantage of the new powers given to them by the DIDMCA of 1980 and the Depository Institutions Act of 1982 to make commercial real estate construction and development loans. These loans were risky, but they paid high interest rates and large up-front fees. Also, they often provided the promise of an "equity kicker" so that the lending institutions' profits would be higher if the project financed with the borrowed money did well. By financing their lending by issuing insured deposits, the lending institutions were able to make risky loans without paying more to borrow. This was a moral hazard, but it made it easy to borrow, so many of the riskiest thrifts grew very rapidly. Often the risky thrifts lent new money to previous borrowers so the borrowers could pay the interest due on old loans, and the old loans would not default. They even counted loan origination fees on the new loans in their profits; regulatory accounting rules, since changed, let them do so at that time.

Ultimately, however, the risky Texas thrifts could not outgrow their portfolio of risky loans and the softening real estate and oil markets. As a result, many institutions failed after suffering great losses. Yet many survived 5 years longer through their lending strategies than they would have survived if their early losses had been promptly recognized. Consequently, even though their managers received 5 more years of income, the losses to the deposit insurance fund were gigantic by the time they ultimately were realized.

THE "TOO-BIG-TO-FAIL" PROBLEM

Purchase and assumption policies provide 100 percent coverage for all depositors whose deposits are assumed. A second policy adopted by federal regulators that provided 100 percent deposit insurance was its **too-big-to-fail (TBTF)** policy. For many years it appeared that the FDIC was reluctant to liquidate large banks. Instead, it generally arranged purchase and assumption transactions if a large bank failed. Then in 1984, when Continental Illinois National Bank essentially failed, the Comptroller of the Currency (the regulatory agency responsible for supervising national banks) announced that Continental, as well as the 11 other of the largest banks in the country, were "too big to fail." Their depositors would be paid off in full regardless of how large the deposit was or how poorly the bank performed. This policy was implemented not only in resolving the Continental Illinois failure but also in conjunction with the 1988 failures of First City Bank Corporation and First Republic Bank Corporation in Texas and with the failure of the Bank of New England in 1991. In each case, federal regulators guaranteed that 100 percent of deposits would be paid off, regardless of the deposits' size.

In response to these cases and concerns that the failure of one large institution might have a domino effect throughout the financial system, Congress enacted a "systemic risk" provision as part of the FDICI Act of 1991. This provision allows for the Treasury Secretary to rescue a bank if it is determined that the bank's failure could cause significant damage to the economy. However, the

TBTF policy has not escaped criticism. First, it has created a two-tiered banking system. All depositors at very large institutions have de facto 100 percent deposit insurance. Depositors at small banks, however, have deposit insurance only up to $100,000 per account. This creates an obvious unfair advantage for larger institutions when it comes to attracting depositors.

A second criticism is that if the federal government stands behind all big-bank liabilities, bank management may be tempted to make riskier loans in an effort to increase profits. This is because uninsured depositors, who are at risk, help monitor the bank's performance, and their willingness (or unwillingness) to purchase the bank's liabilities disciplines the bank to take prudent risks. In recent years the FDIC has hoped to strengthen market discipline in banking; however, with the Continental experience behind them, large banks' uninsured depositors may now be indifferent to the risks that these banks take because of the willingness of the FDIC or some other government agency to intervene and prevent the banks from suffering any loss. This has created a major moral hazard problem. To compensate, regulators must ensure that the top managers of all failed or reorganized banks lose their jobs.

In recent years, regulators have been reluctant to admit that a too-big-to-fail policy exists. Further, it is unlikely that regulators will ever identify those institutions that it considers too big to fail unless one of those institutions is on the brink of failure. The reason for the regulators' reluctance to admit to the policy or identify the affected institutions is that it is important for bank managers, shareholders, depositors, and other uninsured creditors to believe that the government will not save them. If these parties have this belief, then they are more likely to behave prudently.

INSURANCE AGENCIES AS "POLICE"

In the 1940s through the 1960s, deposit insurance seemed to solve the problem of bank failures. However, during the 1980s, more than one-third of all savings institutions disappeared, and bank failures rose consistently to exceed 200 per year before the end of the decade. Clearly, not all problems had been solved.

One factor that changed after deposit insurance became available was that depositors with deposits under $100,000 at small banks or deposits of any size at too-big-to-fail banks no longer had to fear bank failures. As a result, depositors no longer caused runs on banks based on unsubstantiated rumors. At the same time, most depositors no longer had an incentive to make sure that a depository institution was sound before they put their money in it; all they wanted to know was whether it had federal deposit insurance. As long as depositors know that a depository institution is federally insured for an amount greater than their individual deposits (or know that the bank is too big to fail), the depositors have no incentive to withdraw funds from a financial institution even if that institution is taking many risks. As a result, the deposit insurance funds must have a "police" mentality—as they try to protect members of the public who (by relying on deposit insurance for protection) no longer protect themselves by withdrawing funds from risky institutions.

The FDIC and other bank regulators, therefore, have enacted various policies designed to ensure that insured depository institutions are operated safely. They hire large forces of examiners and examine insured institutions regularly. If an insured institution is found to be violating any of a number of detailed regulations, its board of directors will be held responsible and asked to change policies. Such policy changes may include such things as hiring more guards; keeping less money in the vault; providing marked money so that bank robbers can be traced; using surveillance cameras; double-checking all transfers of funds; monitoring all loans made to employees or directors; complying fully with the disclosure and procedural requirements associated with accepting loan applications, granting loans, and documenting all aspects of all loan transactions; and so on.

If a bank is found to score poorly on the examiners' rating system, it will be scheduled for more frequent examinations than other banks. If the problems are serious, the institution may be subjected to "cease and desist" orders that force it to change its operations, to change directors or principal officers, to obtain more capital contributions from stockholders, or to cease operations.

STOCKHOLDERS AND DEBT HOLDERS AS "POLICE"

If a bank has inadequate net worth because of operating losses or loan charge-offs, examiners may force it to obtain more capital by selling more common stock or closely related securities, such as preferred stock or mandatory convertible debt. In this case, the bank must sell securities in the nation's capital markets, which entails a risk of loss for the buyers. Thus, if the bank is very risky, the buyers of those securities will buy them only if they are promised a very high rate of return. In that way, the capital market imposes a risk premium for risky banks that attempt to sell additional stock or subordinated debt to comply with the insurers' capital requirements.

While bank examinations are costly and infrequent, the use of uninsured subordinated debt to provide funds for the institution will ensure that a group of interested people (the owners of that debt) will find it profitable to monitor bank actions and risk-taking on an ongoing basis lest their investment in the bank debt lose value. In that way, the owners of the subordinated debt will help police the bank to ensure that it will not take excess risk. Furthermore, if the debt holders believe the institution is taking excess risk, they will often sell their debt holdings in the open market, thereby depressing the price of the debt and quickly and inexpensively alerting regulators to the fact that something may be wrong.

ARE DEPOSIT INSURANCE PREMIUMS APPROPRIATE?

One of the problems associated with deposit insurance in the past was that one rate was applied to all institutions insured by the same insurance fund. This aggravated moral hazard problems because riskier institutions did not have to pay more. Unlike auto insurance, where a person's insurance rate is likely to go up after a series of tickets or accidents, riskier institutions could obtain insurance at the same rate as the safest institutions, and this took away the riskier institutions' incentive to "drive safely" in a risky world. To solve this problem, the FDICI Act of 1991 required that the FDIC charge higher deposit insurance premiums for riskier institutions. Consequently, the FDIC has adopted a grid system to assess different deposit insurance premiums based on the insured institution's examiner ratings and capitalization status. Well-capitalized institutions with good examiner ratings may have a zero deposit insurance premium in years when their insurance fund is adequately funded, while poorly capitalized institutions with low examiner ratings may have to pay substantial premiums to obtain deposit insurance—

thereby putting them at a competitive disadvantage in obtaining deposits (since they can't pay as high a rate to depositors if they also have to pay a high insurance premium) and providing them with incentives to increase their capital and reduce their riskiness. In 2004, both the FDIC-BIF and the FDIC-SAIF levied deposit insurance premiums of $0.27 per $100 in deposits on the riskiest institutions they insured and no deposit insurance premium on well-capitalized and highly rated banks and thrifts. Institutions with a moderate level of risk paid premiums between $0.03 and $0.24 per $100 in deposits.

Historically, regulatory examinations did not become widespread until the National Bank Act of 1863. The then newly created **Office of the Comptroller of the Currency (OCC)** annually examined all banks chartered under the federal statute. By the early 1900s, every state had instituted some sort of bank examination procedure. Today all commercial banks in the United States are examined by a bank regulatory agency (federal or state). Examinations are more frequent if a bank is believed to be particularly risky.

Regulatory examinations are not equivalent to an audit by an accounting firm. A public accounting firm audit verifies the bank's financial statements and ensures that generally accepted accounting principles are followed consistently from one period to the next. Regulators' examinations are intended to promote and maintain safe and sound bank-operating practices and to ensure that all applicable regulations are followed.

THE BANK EXAMINATION PROCESS

The principal purpose of bank examinations is the prevention of bank failures resulting from poor management or dishonesty. There are two principal ways in which information is gathered for bank examinations. First, **call reports** (detailed statements of the operating and financial condition of the bank) are prepared by bank management four times a year. The examination staffs of the various bank regulators conduct second, **on-site bank examinations**. Those visits are unannounced and the examiners remain at the bank or its branches until the examination is completed. Generally, the examiners first control the records of the bank and such assets as cash and marketable securities by securing or taking physical possession of them. At this point in the examination procedure, the examiners are concerned with the possible detection of embezzlement or fraud. Next, the securities portfolio is examined to see if the securities claimed are on hand and if control procedures comply with regulations. Finally, the market value of bonds is determined, with particular attention given to bonds considered to be speculative or in default.

The most important part of the examination, and the one to which most time is devoted, is the evaluation of the creditworthiness of the bank's loan portfolio. Loans are examined for compliance with or violation of laws or regulations—such as limits on the maximum size loan that may be made to any one borrower or loans to bank officers. Next, loans are examined on a sampling basis as to their quality and are classified in one of four categories: satisfactory, substandard, doubtful, or loss. Loans classified as "loss" are thought to be uncollectible, and the bank is required to write them off (but not to stop trying to collect them). "Doubtful" loans are expected to result in some loan losses, though the exact amount is not precisely determinable. Loans classified as "substandard" have some element of risk and, if not watched closely, may result in losses to the bank. "Satisfactory" loans are those that meet the standards of prudent banking practice and appear to be in no danger of defaulting.

Another important part of the bank examination procedure is the evaluation of the quality of the bank's organizational structure. The supervision by top management and the board of directors, internal controls over bank operations, and, most important, the abilities of management are all appraised.

Based on the call reports and on-site examinations, examiners assess the overall quality of a bank's condition using the **CAMELS** rating system. Exhibit 16.5 summarizes the CAMELS rating system. The S in CAMELS is relatively new and it is intended to reflect how the impact of changes in interest rates, exchange rates, commodity prices, and equity prices can adversely affect a financial institution's earnings or capital.

Finally, a summary of the bank examination report is presented and discussed with the bank's management. If the bank's operations are in violation of the law, if poor operating procedures are detected, or if the bank's capital is below capital requirements, management is requested to bring the violation into compliance over a period of time. The bank's progress in correcting the difficulties is closely monitored. If a bank has a problem that could seriously jeopardize its safety, regulatory agencies can serve *cease and desist* orders on it. These require immediate or speedy compliance under penalty of law.

OTHER BANK EXAMINATIONS

In addition to the safety and soundness examinations discussed above, banks are subject to other examinations that are intended to determine the success or failure of a bank in satisfying other regulatory requirements. For example, banks are examined periodically with respect to their success in achieving the requirements of the Community Reinvestment Act (CRA). If a bank does not receive a satisfactory rating on its CRA examination, then it will have difficulty getting approval from regulators for acquisitions, expansions, and other actions requiring regulatory approval. In addition to CRA-related examinations, banks are also subject to other inquiries concerning their compliance with other consumer protection regulations. The CRA and other consumer protection regulations are discussed later in the chapter. Finally, bank trust departments are also subject to examination so that regulators can ensure that the bank is not violating its fiduciary responsibilities.

DO YOU UNDERSTAND?

1. What is *moral hazard* and how does deposit insurance contribute to it on the part of both depositors and bank management?
2. How can bank capital and subordinated debt help protect deposit insurance funds against losses?
3. What are the arguments for and against regulators using a too-big-to-fail policy?

EXHIBIT 16.5
The CAMELS Rating System

Rating Category	Primary Rating Criteria
Capital adequacy	• The level and quality of capital and the overall financial condition of the institution • The ability of management to address emerging needs of additional capital • Balance-sheet composition
Asset quality	• The adequacy of underwriting standards • The level, severity, and trend of problem loans • The adequacy of the allowance for loan losses • The diversification and quality of the loan and investment portfolio • The adequacy of loan and investment policies, procedures, and practices • The adequacy of internal controls
Management	• The capability of the board of directors and management to identify, measure, monitor, and control the risks of an institution's activities • The level and quality of oversight and support of all institution activities by the board of directors and management • The accuracy and timeliness of management information and risk-monitoring systems • Management depth and succession • Reasonableness of compensation policies and avoidance of self-dealing
Earnings	• The level, trend, and stability of earnings • The quality and sources of earnings
Liquidity	• The adequacy of liquidity sources compared to present and future needs • The availability of assets that can be converted to cash without undue loss • The trend and stability of deposits • Access to money markets and other sources of liquidity
Sensitivity to market risk	• The sensitivity of earnings or economic value to adverse changes in interest rates, foreign exchange rates, commodity prices, or equity prices • The ability of management to identify, measure, monitor, and control exposure to market risk given the institution's size and complexity

Banks are rated on a scale from 1 (best) to 5 (worst) for each rating category. In addition, a composite rating is formed based on the six component ratings.

Source: Department of Supervision, FDIC, *Manual of Exam Policies.*

STRUCTURE AND COMPETITION REGULATIONS

Other types of regulation faced by banks include limitations on the activities that banks are allowed to engage in, the geographic boundaries on those activities, and the organizational structures within which the activities can occur. These types of regulation have been the most controversial and the most dynamic over the past 20 years. In fact, the banking industry has seen these regulations change dramatically in just the past 10 years. This section provides some history on the initial motivation for these regulations, the arguments for and against the regulations, and the changes in the regulations over time.

BRANCHING LIMITATIONS

Until the McFadden-Pepper Act of 1927, the question of whether federally chartered banks could establish branches was unanswered. The 1927 act answered the question by subjecting national banks to the state branching regulations in their home state. Further, interstate banking was not allowed unless explicitly approved by state governments. These restrictions contributed to the development of bank holding companies as a way to avoid intrastate and interstate branching restrictions. As a result, the Bank Holding Company Act of 1956 and subsequent amendments regulated multibank holding companies and limited the ability of bank holding companies to circumvent branching restrictions.

These restrictions tended to reduce entry of new competition into local banking markets, thereby reducing competition for existing banks and enhancing their profits. However, several states allowed reciprocal operations by bank subsidiaries of bank holding companies under provisions in the Douglas Amendment to the Bank Holding Company Act. Thus, interstate banking through holding company banks developed until, in 1994, the **Interstate Banking and Branching Efficiency Act (IB&BEA)** allowed banks to merge and branch across state lines unless a potential host state "opted out" of interstate branching. As it stands now, all banks are allowed to freely branch across state lines as long as it is done through acquisition of another bank or bank branch. In addition, if allowed by state law, a bank can create a new branch (**"de novo" branching**) across state lines.

DEPOSIT RATE CEILINGS

Additional regulations incorporated in the 1933 Banking Act were also designed to restrict risk taking by banks, reduce competition among banks, and enhance bank profitability. The Glass-Steagall Banking Act of 1933, for example, prohibited the payment of interest on demand deposits (checking accounts) and mandated that the Fed regulate maximum interest rates that could be paid on bank time and savings deposits through its **Regulation Q**. Deposit rate regulation was extended to thrift institutions in 1966.

However, these rate-ceiling restrictions subsequently had very disruptive effects in financial markets as they caused financial disintermediation (as people withdrew funds from financial intermediaries) whenever market interest rates exceeded the "Reg Q" ceiling. Consequently, banks and thrifts had to drastically reduce credit availability whenever market interest rates rose. Furthermore, during the high-interest-rate period in the 1970s, disintermediated funds fled to unregulated **money market mutual funds (MMMFs)**. The MMMFs began to offer checking account withdrawals and, as a result, attracted even more funds from banks and thrift institutions. As a result, the DIDMCA Act of 1980 provided a phaseout of deposit rate ceilings and allowed banks, thrifts, and credit unions nationwide to offer checkable interest-bearing (NOW and share draft) accounts. Because the phaseout was not fast enough and banks and thrifts had to maintain reserves to back their NOW accounts, the MMMFs still had a competitive advantage. Thus the 1982 Depository Institutions (Garn–St. Germain) Act accelerated the phaseout of rate ceilings and allowed banks and thrifts to offer checkable **money market deposit accounts (MMDAs)** that had no rate ceiling and no reserve requirement if check transactions were limited.

Deposit rate ceilings are now gone, but they led to substantial financial innovation as people sought ways to avoid them. Consequently, their legacy still exists in the form of MMMFs, MMDAs, and NOW accounts, which would not have come into existence if rate ceilings had not existed.

SEPARATION OF COMMERCIAL AND INVESTMENT BANKING

The Banking Act of 1933 also tried to reduce bank risk taking by separating commercial banking from investment banking. That way commercial banks would not be exposed to price-risk fluctuations in the value of securities that they had underwritten but had not yet sold.

The Glass-Steagall prohibitions against investment banking also prevented banks from acquiring equity securities for their own accounts and from acting as equity securities dealers. The prohibition against owning equity securities not only prevents banks from carrying certain potentially risky assets on their balance sheet, which could increase their risk of failure, but also lessens potential conflicts that can arise when the ownership and creditor functions of banks are combined. Thus the prohibition reflects, in part, a long-standing American fear that unscrupulous manipulation and exercise of creditor powers could ultimately lead to ownership. In contrast, in countries such as Germany, "universal banking" is allowed in which commercial banks can also serve as investment banks and even appoint directors for businesses in which they own stock.

The U.S. Glass-Steagall restrictions were gradually relaxed during the 1980s and 1990s until the Financial Services Modernization Act of 1999 repealed most of the restrictions. This legislation allows U.S. commercial banks to engage in investment banking, insurance, and other financial activities through affiliated subsidiaries.

FINANCIAL SERVICES MODERNIZATION ACT OF 1999

The major provisions of the **Financial Services Modernization Act of 1999** (often referred to as the **Gramm-Leach-Bliley Act** in recognition of the senators who sponsored the legislation) are: (1) banks are allowed to create securities and insurance subsidiaries; (2) a new organizational form, called financial holding companies (FHCs), can establish commercial banking, insurance, security, and merchant banking affiliates, invest in and develop real estate, and engage in other finance-related activities (see Exhibit 13.11 in Chapter 13); (3) insurance companies and securities firms can acquire commercial banks and form FHCs with Federal Reserve approval; (4) financial service providers must comply with a new set of privacy rules concerning how information about customers is shared within an organization and with others; and (5) the Federal Reserve is the "umbrella" supervisor over FHCs while the bank and nonbank subsidiaries of the FHC fall under the supervision of other regulators. This approach is referred to as **functional regulation**.

The 1999 act was passed after many years of weakening restrictions on bank activities. Throughout the 1980s and 1990s, bank regulators loosened the restrictions on bank activities. For example, in 1986 the Federal Reserve allowed certain bank holding companies to own subsidiaries that engage in investment banking activities as long as those activities did not generate more than a small percent of the company's total revenue. Therefore, in many respects, the 1999 act merely formalized well-established regulatory interpretations and positions on already-existing laws. For example, even though the act explicitly allowed affiliation among commercial banks and investment banks, the restrictions on these activities had eroded so much already that there were few real barriers to such affiliation.

In contrast to the securities activities of bank holding companies, the ability to affiliate with insurance companies is new. Except for limited abilities to sell insurance products, banking firms were not allowed to engage in insurance activities, especially insurance underwriting. Following the 1999 act, however, bank and insurance companies can be separate subsidiaries within the same financial holding company. The long-term impact of Gramm-Leach-Bliley remains to be seen, but it seems likely that affiliation among banks, securities firms, and insurance companies is likely to become more common.

BALANCE-SHEET RESTRICTIONS

In addition to restrictions against equity ownership, commercial banks' balance sheets are restricted in other ways. For example, banks can loan no more than 15 percent of their capital to any one borrower. This restriction is intended to prevent the default of any one customer from imperiling the bank and also forces the bank to diversify its assets. Also, most banks are not allowed to invest in subinvestment grade securities (that is, securities rated lower than BBB or Baa by the securities (that is, securities rated lower than BBB or Baa by the major rating agencies). Furthermore, banks are required to hold adequate liquid assets by the Federal Reserve and adequate capital to comply with the restrictions imposed by regulators. Thus banks' balance sheets and operations are frequently constrained by various regulations.

CONSUMER PROTECTION REGULATIONS	The final class of regulations to be discussed is those designed to protect consumers in their transactions with commercial banks and other credit-granting institutions. Since 1968 there has been a trend toward legislation designed to protect consumers in the credit market, precipitated by an active and growing consumer movement. The regulatory philosophy behind many of the consumer regulations is twofold: (1) consumers generally have unequal market power relative to creditors and other market participants, and (2) consumer markets, when left to their own devices, may not allocate credit in the most socially desirable manner. It often is not clear, however, that the regulations have their intended effects.

LOAN RATE CEILINGS

Loan rate ceilings vary widely from state to state and historically have usually applied to consumer and mortgage credit. The DIDMCA of 1980 suspended state rate ceilings on all real estate loans and on business and agricultural loans exceeding $25,000. However, states had until April 1, 1983, to adopt new rate ceilings. In most instances they did not elect to do so.

Rate ceilings pose no problem for banks or consumers as long as the ceiling exceeds the rate of interest that would be charged in a competitive market. When rate ceilings become binding, they may cause serious problems. For instance, it is well documented that mortgage rate ceilings seriously impede the flow of mortgage credit and reduce housing starts when market interest rates rise above the maximum ceiling rate. In the consumer credit markets, because prices of goods sold on credit can be raised, credit is not usually cut off entirely as a result of rising market rates of interest, but it may become unprofitable for banks to make direct loans that are subject to the rate ceilings.

TRUTH-IN-LENDING

In 1969 Congress passed the **Consumer Credit Protection Act** (popularly known as the **Truth-in-Lending Act**) with the intent of assuring that every borrower obtained meaningful information about the cost of credit. The act applies not only to banks but also to all lenders who extend credit to consumers for personal or agricultural use up to a limit of $25,000. For commercial banks, truth-in-lending is administered by the Board of Governors of the Federal Reserve System under Federal Reserve **Regulation Z**.

The two most important disclosures required by Regulation Z are (1) the annual percentage rate and (2) the total finance charges on a loan. The purpose of the Truth-in-Lending Act is to increase consumers' awareness of true loan rates and charges. The desired result is that consumers shop more wisely for credit and obtain credit from the lowest-rate source. This has helped banks, as they often have the lowest rates on consumer loans.

FAIR CREDIT BILLING ACT

The **Fair Credit Billing Act (FCBA)** of 1974 requires that creditors provide detailed information to consumers on the method of assessing finance charges and also that billing complaints be processed promptly. The purpose of the Fair Credit Billing Act is to deal with some of the problems created by the increasing automation of credit and the proliferation of credit card transactions. The Act requires that banks and other suppliers of consumer credit send their customers a detailed description of their rights and of the procedures they must follow in making complaints about billing errors. The Act is administered by the Federal Reserve System under Regulation Z.

The FCBA raises costs to creditors by increasing legal complexities and mandating quick formal responses to complaints. However, by formalizing procedures for filing and handling complaints, it has also simplified operations and reduced some costs. In addition, because there is no longer a threat of litigation as long as the Act is complied with, lenders report that they are now less charitable in awarding disputed claims and can do so in a less costly (more routine) manner than before.

PEOPLE & EVENTS

Dual or Dueling Banking Systems?

In the U.S., banks are part of a **dual banking system**, where both state and federal authorities have significant regulatory authority. The primary federal banking authority is the Office of the Comptroller of the Currency (OCC). The OCC charters, regulates, and examines national banks. Individual states have their own bank regulatory offices. State banking authorities share regulatory authority over state-chartered banks with either the FDIC or the Federal Reserve, depending on whether the bank is a member of the Federal Reserve System.

Recent preemption actions by the OCC, under Comptroller Jerry Hawke, and the reaction by state banking authorities suggest that the dual banking system might be more appropriately called a "dueling banking system." In February 2004, the OCC issued regulations preempting state regulations concerning national banks' powers and activities. Essentially the OCC said that any state law that applies to all businesses (property laws, environmental laws, and contract law) also applies to national banks but that states may not attempt to regulate the deposit-taking and

lending activities of national banks. As you might expect, state banking authorities were not too happy with the OCC.

The current preemption battle stems largely from predatory lending and consumer protection laws passed at the state level. The OCC challenged the applicability of these laws to national banks. Because the National Banking Act of 1863 exempts national banks from state laws and oversight by state officials, the OCC has won most of the court cases concerning preemption.

State banking officials argue that the OCC is pandering to the institutions it regulates and is trying to eliminate the dual banking system. Their concern is that some state banks will drop their state charter in favor of a national charter because, according to some state authorities, the OCC favors banks' interests over consumer interests. The OCC counters that the OCC is interested in consumer issues. For example, it forced national banks to stop providing funds to payday lenders.

EQUAL CREDIT OPPORTUNITY ACT

In 1974 Congress passed the **Equal Credit Opportunity Act (ECOA)**, which requires that credit be made available to individuals without regard to sex or marital status. In 1976 Congress broadened the scope of that act to forbid discrimination by creditors based on race, age, national origin, or whether credit applicants received part of their income from public assistance benefits. It also requires women's incomes to be treated equally with men's in evaluating credit. The act is implemented through **Regulation B** of the Federal Reserve Board.

THE COMMUNITY REINVESTMENT ACT (CRA)

The **Community Reinvestment Act (CRA)** was created in 1977 to prevent "redlining," where a lender draws a hypothetical red line on a map around one part of the community and refuses to make loans in that area. While some bankers argue that "redlining" never existed, Congress passed the CRA to make sure that banks make credit available to all people in their market area regardless of where they live. Thus, under the CRA, banks must be able to show that they attempt to serve the credit needs of all people in their area and they must be able to document their efforts and make the documentation available to regulators and the general public. The upside of the Act is that it does ensure that credit will be generally available to all people who qualify. The downside of the Act is that the documentation requirements of CRA are very expensive to perform, especially after the requirements were increased by the FDIC Improvement Act of 1991 and by the Interstate Banking and Branching Efficiency Act of 1994. Some of the new requirements were intended to ensure that banks would channel credit to the neediest people and neediest areas in their communities as well as to politically favored community groups. Because banks that cannot show that they have complied faithfully with the CRA requirements may be prohibited from merging, branching, or taking other actions that require regulatory approval, many banks have made unsound loans to favored groups just to ensure that they would not encounter problems with CRA compliance and the regulators in the future.

IN PRACTICE

Recent Legislation, Regulatory Burden, and the Future of Small Banks

The cost of doing business as a bank or other financial institution just keeps going up, and many smaller institutions may not be able to survive. Recent legislation and regulation have saddled all institutions with increased compliance costs. For example, the **USA Patriot Act** of 1991 requires banks and other financial service providers to establish the identity of new customers and any customers making changes to existing accounts. The Patriot Act was passed in an effort to catch money-laundering and terrorist financing activities; while its provisions may not seem terribly costly, it is just one of many rules and regulations that financial institutions must comply with.

Another example of recent legislation that has increased the regulatory burden for financial institutions is the **Sarbanes-Oxley Act** of 2002, which put in place tougher accounting and auditing standards. Although many of the provisions in Sarbanes-Oxley represent good practice, they are difficult for some small banks to implement. For example, a small pub-

licly traded bank may find it difficult to form a competent audit committee comprised entirely of independent directors.

Another recent piece of legislation encourages greater spending in an area where small banks are weak: technology. The **Check Clearing for the 21st Century (Check 21) Act** of 2003 requires banks to accept electronic images of checks for the purpose of interbank check clearing and settling. The intent of this legislation is to reduce the costs associated with transporting paper checks, reduce labor costs for back-office processing, and facilitate faster check clearing. The challenge for small banks will be meeting this new requirement in a cost-efficient way.

For small financial institutions, the combined effect of these new rules may be that they are forced out of business. In fact, a recent FDIC study predicts that 43 percent of smaller banks will be merged out of existence by 2013, largely as a result of the costs of complying with regulation.

FAIR AND ACCURATE CREDIT TRANSACTIONS ACT

In 1970, the **Fair Credit Reporting Act (FCRA)** was passed. It was intended to promote the accuracy, fairness, and privacy of personal information assembled by credit-reporting agencies. The three major credit-reporting agencies are Equifax (www.equifax.com), Experian (www.experian.com), and Trans Union (www.transunion.com). In the 1990s and early 2000s, banks and other financial institutions began relying more and more on credit reports and credit scores to evaluate credit applications. Concerns about potential errors in credit reports and increased worries over identity theft led to the passage of the **Fair and Accurate Credit Transactions (FACT) Act** in 2003.

The FACT Act reauthorized some of the provisions of the FCRA that were expiring. In addition, it preempted individual states from enacting legislation that would impose even greater requirements on credit-granting institutions and credit-reporting agencies. In exchange for the preemptions, however, credit-granting institutions and credit-reporting agencies face increased responsibility for protecting consumers. For example, consumers are entitled to receive a free copy of their credit report once a year. In addition, banks and other lenders are required to tell customers if they report negative information about them to credit bureaus and must notify them when they are granted credit at terms less favorable than most other consumers receive.

BANK REGULATORS

Because the U.S. banking system has developed over time, and because the United States has a wide variety of other depository institutions that have evolved to serve specialized needs over time, the U.S. financial regulatory structure is quite complex. State regulators regulate state-chartered financial institutions. However, federal regulators regulate nationally chartered or insured institutions as well. Several regulators could conceivably all be responsible for the same institution (e.g., a nationally chartered bank that belongs to the Federal Reserve System and has federal deposit insurance could be examined by the Fed, the OCC, or the FDIC). Thus, the federal agencies cooperate so only one of the federal regulators will take on the responsibility for examining the bank to make sure that it complies with all applicable laws. In addition, the FDIC retains the authority to initiate an independent examination of any problem institution that presents a risk to the bank or thrift insurance fund. Furthermore, each of the various regulators remains responsible for regulating branching, mergers, entry, and exit by institutions under its jurisdiction.

Federal supervision of banks is divided between the FDIC, the Federal Reserve, and the Comptroller of the Currency. Exhibit 16.6 summarizes the regulatory responsibilities of each. In addition, state banking commissioners are responsible for the regulation and examination of banks chartered in their states. State banking commissioners also must ensure that branches of out-of-state banks chartered or located in their state comply with all applicable state laws.

Each state has its own agency that is responsible for regulating and supervising commercial banks chartered by the state. These agencies can also regulate other financial institutions in the state, such as savings and loan associations, mutual savings banks, credit unions, finance companies, and out-of-state bank branches that are located in their state. The agency directors may be called commissioner or superintendent of banking, but, in general, the scope of their duties with respect to state-chartered banks is analogous to that of the Comptroller of the Currency for national banks. Although their functions vary from one state to another, state banking authorities normally have the following responsibilities. First, they approve the charters for new state banks, the opening and closing of branch offices, and the scope of bank holding company operations within the state. Second, they examine financial institutions chartered by the state. Third, state bank agencies have powers to protect the public interest. These powers take the form of regulating the activities of finance companies and enforcing various consumer regulations, such as credit disclosure and usury laws.

It is difficult to make any broad generalizations about the quality of state banking supervision. Perhaps all that can be fairly said is that the quality varies. Some state agencies are comparable to federal agencies in the quality of their bank examinations. Others, unfortunately, are weak. Administrators may be selected by patronage; examiners may be poorly paid, undertrained, and influenced by the institutions that they are supposed to regulate. Generally, state banking agencies are more permissive in the types of banking practices they allow. As a result, we find a large number of both large and small banks preferring state charters. For example, most large New York City banks whose operations are global in scope are state-chartered banks. However, the Federal Reserve regulates bank and financial holding companies.

One of the issues addressed by the Financial Services Modernization Act concerns the allocation of regulatory authority within a financial holding company. According to the 1999 act, the Fed has "umbrella" authority over financial holding companies but functional regulation is the responsibility of the individual regulators. For example, a financial holding company that owns both a state-chartered commercial bank that is not a member of the Federal Reserve System and an investment bank will be subject to regulatory authority from the Federal Reserve, state banking authorities, the FDIC, and the Securities and Exchange Commission (SEC). Because the Federal Reserve has regulatory authority over financial holding companies, it will be responsible for reviewing the activities of the holding company. Because the commercial bank is state chartered, it will be subject to regulatory oversight by its state banking authorities. Because the commercial bank is state chartered and not a member of the Federal Reserve System, it is subject to regulation and examination by the FDIC. The investment banking affiliate will be subject to oversight by the SEC. In addition, depending on their activities, some of the financial holding company's affiliates may fall under the authority of other regulatory agencies, such as the Commodity Futures Trading Commission.

Given the complexity of the U.S. regulatory system, it is no surprise that there is an ongoing debate over regulatory reform. For example, many argue that the regulatory process would be simplified if the FDIC-SAIF and FDIC-BIF merged and the OTS (Office of Thrift Supervision) and OCC merged. Other mergers of regulators (such as a merger of the Commodity Futures Trading Commission into the SEC) are proposed from time to time, but each interest group seems to prefer to deal with its own set of regulators—possibly because they hope to "capture" the regulators so their regulators will help

EXHIBIT 16.6
Primary Supervisory Responsibilities for Commercial Bank Regulators

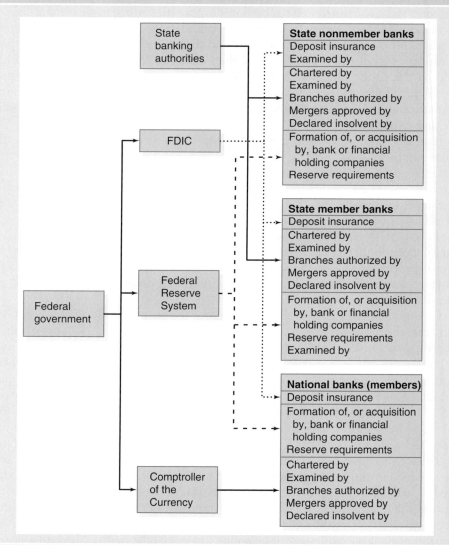

Because there are so many different bank regulators, it is often difficult to determine which regulator is responsible for which different banking activities.

advance the interests of the regulated. Otherwise, the regulated institutions could be forced out of existence and the regulators lose their reason for keeping their jobs. Thus, regulatory profusion still exists—and regulatory "capture" is still a potential problem.

DO YOU UNDERSTAND?

1. In what way did the Financial Services Modernization Act of 1999 merely formalize the regulatory interpretations of existing laws?
2. What was the justification for separating commercial banking from investment banking?
3. Why do bankers probably have more favorable attitudes toward the Truth-in-Lending Act than the Community Reinvestment Act?
4. What does it mean to say that the Federal Reserve is an "umbrella" regulator?

CHAPTER TAKE-AWAYS

1 Financial institutions are heavily regulated because politicians fear that their failures could badly damage local or national economies.

2 The greatest number of bank failures occurred during the 1930–1933 period. In recent years the number of bank failures has been minuscule. The creation of deposit insurance has done more to limit bank panics and failures than any other development. Deposit insurance helps prevent failures by ensuring that the public has confidence in insured institutions.

3 Deposit insurance was first created in 1933. In the event an insured institution fails, the FDIC attempts to resolve the institution using the least costly approach. Purchase and assumption transactions make the most sense when an institution has value as a going concern. Otherwise, the FDIC will pay off depositors and liquidate the assets.

4 Deposit insurance creates a moral hazard in that depositors do not fully monitor the riskiness of insured institutions. As a result, the institutions' managers can take more risk without having to pay higher interest rates to attract deposits.

5 Banks are examined periodically to ensure that bank managers are behaving in a safe and sound manner. These examinations monitor compliance with regulations and can provide regulators with warning signals of potential failures, providing time for corrective action to prevent failures and associated losses to deposit insurance funds.

6 New regulations have liberalized the restrictive banking laws of the 1930s by removing rate ceilings on deposits, restrictions on interstate branching, and (for well-capitalized banks) prohibitions against investment banking by commercial banks. The Financial Services Modernization Act of 1999 allows a financial holding company to own affiliates that engage in commercial banking, investment banking, and insurance activities.

7 Banks are subject to significant regulations that are intended to protect consumers from bankers that have significant influence over the consumers' quality of life. These regulations help to ensure that consumers are not exploited, but they also create an additional regulatory burden for banks and other lenders.

8 Many regulators exist at the federal level both to examine and to provide deposit insurance to various institutions. Important regulators include the Fed, FDIC, OCC, OTS, NCUSIF, and state banking commissioners.

KEY TERMS

Regulatory dialectic
Lender of last resort
Bank panic
Banking Act of 1933 (Glass-Steagall Act)
Federal Deposit Insurance Corporation (FDIC)
Deposit insurance
Depository Institutions Deregulation and Monetary Control Act (DIDMCA) 1980
Depository Institutions Act (DIA) 1982 (Garn–St. Germain)
Federal Savings and Loan Insurance Corporation (FSLIC)
Competitive Equality in Banking Act (CEBA) 1987
Financial Institutions Reform, Recovery, and Enforcement Act (FIRREA), 1989
Federal Deposit Insurance Corporation Improvement Act (FDICIA) 1991

Prompt corrective action
National Credit Union Share Insurance Fund (NCUSIF) 1970
Payoff and liquidate policy
Purchase and assumption agreement
Moral hazard
Too big to fail (TBTF)
Office of the Comptroller of the Currency (OCC)
Call reports
On-site bank examination
CAMELS
Interstate Banking and Branching Efficiency Act (IB&BEA) 1994
De novo branching
Regulation Q—deposit rate ceilings
Money market mutual fund (MMMF)
Money market deposit account (MMDA)
Financial Services Modernization Act of 1999 (Gramm-Leach-Bliley Act)

Functional regulation
Consumer Credit Protection Act (Truth-in-Lending Act) 1969
Regulation Z—truth-in-lending
Fair Credit Billing Act (FCBA) 1974
Dual banking system
Equal Credit Opportunity Act (ECOA)
Regulation B—equal credit opportunity
Community Reinvestment Act (CRA) 1977
USA Patriot Act
Sarbanes-Oxley Act
Check Clearing for the 21st Century (Check 21) Act
Fair Credit Reporting Act (FCRA)
Fair and Accurate Credit Transactions (FACT) Act

QUESTIONS AND PROBLEMS

1. Why are bank failures considered to have a greater effect on the economy than other types of business failures? Do you agree with this conclusion?

2. What are the major lessons that have been learned from past bank failures? Do you think that history can or will repeat itself?

3. Although the FDIC does not grant charters for banks to operate, it is said to have an enormous influence on the charter process. Explain.

4. Which of the bank safety regulations enacted in the 1930s do you believe are most important in actually achieving bank safety? Which of the safety regulations would you classify as being anticompetitive?

5. How would you assess the success of consumer regulation? In what areas has it failed its stated objectives?

6. Bank regulation is considered to be in the public interest. Thus the more regulation, the better. Explain why you agree or disagree with this statement.

7. What is the purpose of bank examinations? How do they differ from CPA audits?

8. How do failing bank resolution policies differ between large and small banks? Why the difference?

9. Why has Congress had to pass more and more regulatory acts for financial institutions in recent years? Cite major acts passed since 1980 and the major provisions of each.

10. What is moral hazard, and how is it created by deposit insurance?

11. Why did bank failures increase, with a lag, after deposit insurance became available to banks? What else contributed to the increase in bank failures in the 1980s?

12. How can an effective lender of last resort prevent financial panics from developing? Why was the Fed unable to prevent the Great Depression of the 1930s?

13. Why do banks and other financial institutions willingly comply with financial regulation, even though they may complain about it?

14. How might possibilities for regulatory capture contribute to the large number of financial regulators and deposit insurance funds?

INTERNET EXERCISE

All financial institution regulators have Internet sites where people can obtain extensive information on the institutions they regulate and can learn about current and pending regulations. The Internet Exercises for Chapters 13 and 14 asked you to look up information on the Federal Financial Institutions Examination Council (FFIEC) Web site. The FFIEC Web site is useful because it has links to all the other bank and thrift regulatory agencies. It also acts as a sort of clearinghouse for information about individual institutions. One of the topics of discussion in this chapter concerns the Community Reinvestment Act. Recall that institutions are examined with respect to how well they satisfy the provisions of the act. Using a bank that is in your local community, do the following:

1. Go the FDIC Web page, http://www.fdic.gov/, and click on the CRA link. This will take you to the FDIC's CRA Web page. From here, click on "CRA Ratings and Performance Evaluations." From here you can search for the CRA ratings your institution has received. What is your institution's rating?
2. Open the institution's CRA evaluation and read the summary of the institution's CRA performance. What criteria were used in evaluating the institution? Under which criteria did the institution do well? Under which criteria did the institution do poorly?
3. Can you identify any reasons why you think your institution did well or did not do well on its CRA evaluation?

FINANCIAL INSTITUTIONS

17

Thrift Institutions and Finance Companies

CHAPTER PREVIEW

If you have ever seen the movie *It's a Wonderful Life,* starring Jimmy Stewart, then you already have an understanding of why early thrift institutions were created. In the movie, Jimmy Stewart played George Bailey, the president of the Bailey Building and Loan during the late 1930s and early 1940s. **Building societies**, such as the Bailey Building and Loan, were formed by groups of people who pooled their savings so that each could eventually acquire a home. They might draw lots to see who would be first to obtain a home and, as the mortgages were repaid and more funds were deposited, the building societies could finance more home construction for their members.

Prior to World War II, commercial banks primarily served business customers, hence the name "commercial" banks. The consumer-focused institutions that emerged during this period were savings and loan associations, mutual savings banks, and credit unions. These institutions are often called thrift institutions, a term which is frequently shortened to just "thrifts." Thrifts historically accommodated the needs of working-class people who typically have small amounts to save and want to make sure that their "thriftiness" is rewarded by earning a respectable rate of interest on their deposits while taking minimal risk of loss. ■

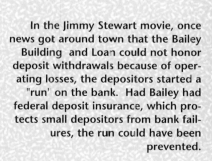

In the Jimmy Stewart movie, once news got around town that the Bailey Building and Loan could not honor deposit withdrawals because of operating losses, the depositors started a "run" on the bank. Had Bailey had federal deposit insurance, which protects small depositors from bank failures, the run could have been prevented.

This chapter is about **thrift institutions**, which are consumer-orientated financial institutions that accept deposits from and make loans to consumers. Thrift institutions are comprised of savings institutions and credit unions. There are two types of savings institutions, which focus on residential mortgage lending: (1) savings associations and (2) savings banks. The chapter also is about **finance companies**, which provide specialized financial services to consumers and businesses. Exhibit 17.1 shows in a diagram the economic roles of each type of institution that we will discuss in this chapter. As you read the chapter, you may find it convenient to refer back to Exhibit 17.1 given the complexity of the historical development and regulation of these institutions.

EXHIBIT 17.1
Types of Thrift Institutions and Finance Companies

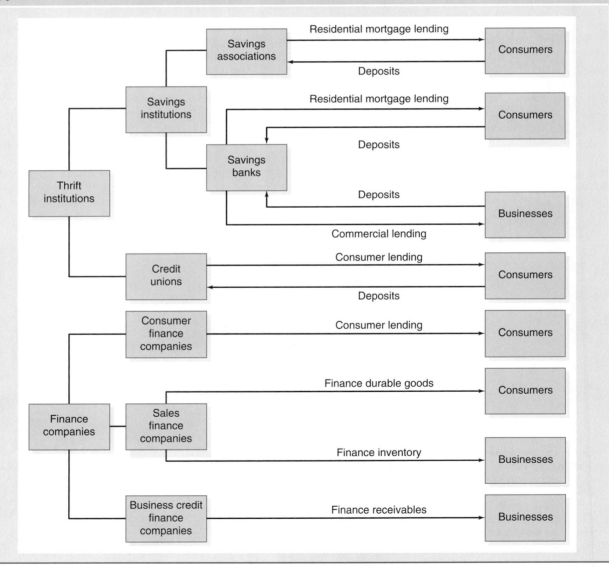

The chapter begins with a discussion of the history of mortgage-oriented thrifts, now called saving institutions. Historically, savings associations have specialized in making consumer mortgage loans, while savings banks have operated as more diversified institutions with a large concentration of residential mortgages but also holding some commercial loans, corporate bonds, and stocks as well. Because savings institutions, regardless of type, focus on long-term residential mortgages and fund them with short-term consumer savings deposits, they are exposed to considerable interest rate risk, which creates significant management challenges.

We will also discuss another class of thrifts, credit unions, which specialize in short-term consumer loans. They are unique because (1) they are nonprofit organizations, (2) they are owned by the depositors (or members), and (3) they have rules that limit their membership.

Finally, we discuss finance companies, which make loans to both consumers and businesses. They differ from thrifts in that they do not accept deposits from the public to obtain funds; instead they rely on short-term and long-term funding from the sale of commercial paper, notes, bonds, or stock. For each institution, we will discuss their regulators, their size and structure, and their operations. ■

LEARNING OBJECTIVES

The objectives of this chapter are to:

1 Discuss the historical development of savings institutions.

2 Describe the balance-sheet composition of savings institutions.

3 Explain the problems faced by savings institutions in the 1980s, how Congress addressed the problems, and the impact of the problems and regulations on the industry today.

4 Describe the operations and organizational structure of credit unions.

5 Explain the various types of finance companies and the roles they play in providing credit.

In this section we discuss the economic and political forces that have influenced the development of the two types of savings institutions: savings banks and savings associations. These institutions focus on mortgage lending to consumers.

HISTORICAL DEVELOPMENT OF SAVINGS INSTITUTIONS

SAVINGS BANKS

Savings banks were first started in the United States in 1816. They were formed as depository institutions that would allow people with small deposit balances to save and earn a respectable rate of interest on their deposits while taking prudent risk of loss. The original savings banks in the United States were **mutual institutions** that were technically owned by their depositors and were managed by a public-spirited board of trustees that sought to invest depositors' funds to earn a safe and secure rate of interest. Initially, the savings banks' trustees could invest in stocks, bonds, consumer or mortgage loans, or any other asset they deemed to be a safe investment that would earn interest for their depositors. In the 1900s, however, savings banks began to invest increasingly in mortgage loans because of the desire of their depositors to own their homes. In addition, until 1996 and because of the political importance of home ownership, the federal government gave large tax breaks to mortgage-oriented lenders who invested at least 60 percent of their assets in home-mortgage-related lending.

SAVINGS ASSOCIATIONS

The first savings associations[1] in the United States were chartered as "building societies." The first was the Oxford-Provident Building Society, chartered in 1831 in Philadelphia. Building societies were formed by groups of people who pooled their savings so that each could eventually acquire a home, in some instances drawing lots to see who would be first. As mortgages were repaid and more funds were deposited, the building societies could finance more home construction for their members. In some cases, once all the original members obtained a home, the early building societies would dissolve. In other cases, however, the society would continue to make mortgage loans and would continue to pay interest to its depositors.

Many of these early savings associations were formed as mutual institutions, which technically means that the depositors own the institution. Mutual savings associations were managed by officers who were elected by their depositors on a "one-dollar, one-vote" basis. When depositors started an account, they would typically sign over a proxy statement to the current management that let the management vote on their behalf. Thus, managements of mutual institutions often became self-perpetuating.

An alternative form of savings association was a stockholder-owned and -directed **stock association**. Stock associations issue common stock to shareholders and are operated by managers appointed by a board of directors elected by profit-seeking shareholders—just like a commercial bank or any other corporation. Until the 1980s, stock ownership of savings associations usually was not encouraged by regulators, who also discouraged conversions of mutual to stockholder-owned savings associations.

THE 1980s THRIFT CRISIS

When interest rates began to increase sharply in the late 1970s and spiked in the early 1980s, as can be seen in Exhibit 17.2, many savings associations and savings banks encountered severe financial problems. The problem was that mortgage-oriented thrifts funded themselves by selling short-term deposits to consumers and making long-term fixed-rate home mortgage loans. Thus, when interest rates rose sharply, their cost of funds rose quickly above the interest rate earned on mortgages, which remained relatively constant, causing operating losses. Because many of these institutions took too much interest rate risk, and some, too much credit risk, many mortgage-oriented thrifts failed during the 1980s. As a result, deposit insurance funds for these institutions were virtually depleted and Con-

---

[1] Historically, savings associations were known as **savings and loan associations (SLAs)** or, in brief form, "savings and loans" or "S&Ls." With the changes in the regulatory structure of the financial services industry, these institutions are now called "savings associations."

EXHIBIT 17.2
3-Month Treasury Bill Rates (June 1960–June 2004)

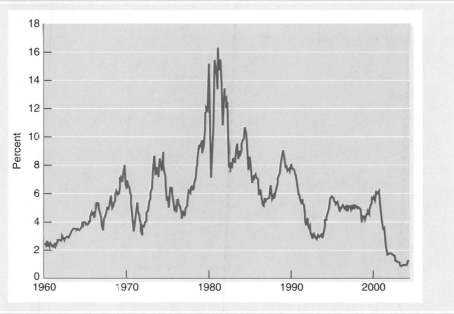

When interest rates spiked in the late 1970s, most mortgage-oriented savings institutions suffered large losses because they were forced to pay higher rates to retain deposits but did not earn additional interest on their loan portfolio.

Source: Federal Reserve Board of Governors, H15 Statistical Release.

gress established new regulatory agencies to handle the ensuing crisis. Also during this period, it became clear that mortgage-oriented thrifts needed to attract more capital investment from outside shareholders to survive and prosper.

During this thrift crisis, Congress enacted the 1980 Depository Institutions Deregulation and Monetary Control Act (DIDMCA), which permitted savings banks to obtain federal charters rather than state charters and to convert to stockholder ownership. This allowed mortgage-oriented thrifts to attract more capital investment and increased their ability to bear the losses caused by too much interest rate risk. Consequently, many of the largest and healthiest savings institutions are now stockholder-owned and are managed and directed much like commercial banks, rather than as mutual institutions, as they were originally chartered. Exhibit 17.3 shows that, while the overall number of mortgage-oriented savings institutions declined sharply in the 1990s, the relative number of stock institutions and their assets has increased.

SAVINGS BANK REGULATORS

Initially, all savings banks were chartered and regulated by state banking commissioners in the 20 states where they are allowed, which was mostly in the eastern

**REGULATION
OF SAVINGS
INSTITUTIONS**

EXHIBIT 17.3
Number and Assets of Mutual and Stock Savings Institutions (1989–2003)

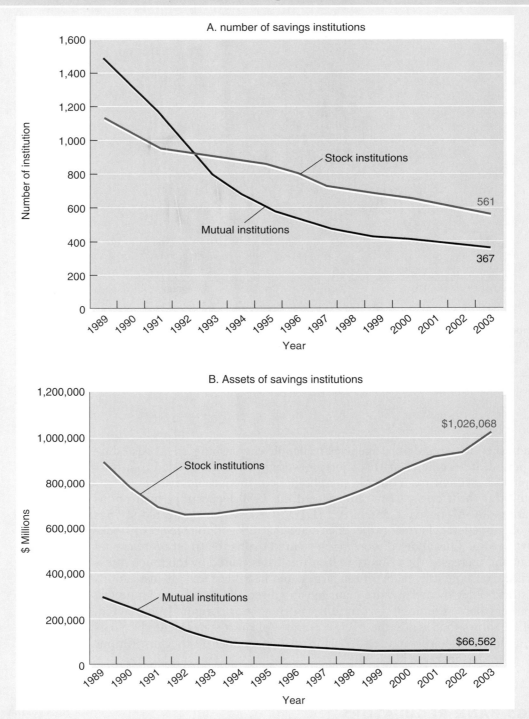

A. number of savings institutions

Stock institutions

Mutual institutions

561

367

B. Assets of savings institutions

Stock institutions

Mutual institutions

$1,026,068

$66,562

In recent years, the number of mutual and stock savings institutions has fallen sharply.

Source: Office of Thrift Supervision, *2003 Fact Book,* May 2004.

part of the United States. When federal deposit insurance became available in 1934, qualifying mutual savings banks were allowed to obtain insurance from the Federal Deposit Insurance Corporation (FDIC). Prior to that time, savings banks had obtained deposit insurance from state deposit insurance programs, a practice that continued into the 1980s when many of these state programs failed.

Because of rising interest rates in the 1960s and 1970s, as seen in Exhibit 17.2, some savings banks experienced difficulties, so their mix of products and regulatory structure began to change. First, savings banks in New England were allowed by regulators to issue checkable NOW accounts so they could pay interest on checkable deposits and better compete with commercial banks. Second, some savings banks sought to change their organizational form from mutual to stock ownership or to savings associations, so they could obtain additional capital. Finally in 1980, the DIDMCA allowed savings banks to obtain federal rather than state charters, to issue NOW accounts nationwide, and to shift to regulators at the federal level. Some savings banks shifted to federal charters and the jurisdiction of the **Federal Home Loan Bank Board (FHLBB)**, which regulated savings and loan associations; others switched from FDIC insurance to more lenient Federal Savings and Loan Insurance Corporation (FSLIC) insurance, which provided deposit insurance to savings and loan associations. Further, savings banks were also given many banking powers, in the hopes that they would become financially stronger and could operate better under the supervision of regulators that were primarily experienced in regulating mortgage-oriented institutions.

When the problems of the mortgage-oriented thrift industry worsened with continued rising interest rates in the 1980s, Congress blamed lax regulation as the source of the problem and abolished the FHLBB and the FSLIC. Congress replaced those two institutions with two new regulatory institutions: (1) the **Office of Thrift Supervision (OTS)**, which now charters and regulates savings institutions at the federal level, and (2) the FDIC Savings Association Insurance Fund (**FDIC-SAIF**), which is a deposit insurance fund run by the FDIC to provide deposit insurance to member savings associations and savings banks. Consequently, savings banks are now regulated at the federal level by the OTS and at the state level by state banking commissioners; most obtain their deposit insurance either from the FDIC-SAIF or from the FDIC Bank Insurance Fund (**FDIC-BIF**), which is the original bank insurance fund operated by the FDIC that mutual savings banks have long been allowed to join.

SAVINGS ASSOCIATION REGULATORS

Savings associations were chartered at the state level in most states until the 1930s. In 1932, because of liquidity problems experienced by mortgage lenders in the Great Depression, the **Federal Home Loan Bank** system was established. That system consisted of 12 regional Federal Home Loan Banks that were empowered to borrow in the national capital markets and make loans, called **advances**, to savings associations in their regions that were members of the Federal Home Loan Bank. Advances were much like discount window loans made by the Federal Reserve banks, with the difference that advances could be made with maturities of many years rather than a few days at rates that were usually only modestly above the Federal Home Loan Banks' borrowing rates. Because the home loan banks are government agencies with minimal credit risk, their borrowing rates are relatively low and they can make advances at attractive rates.

Because Federal Home Loan Banks' lending policies have made them politically popular, they were not eliminated in the 1980s and, indeed, have expanded their functions by allowing qualifying commercial banks (banks that make a sufficiently large number of mortgage loans) and a few credit unions to join the Federal Home Loan Bank system.

The primary regulator of savings associations at the federal level was the Federal Home Loan Bank Board, which chartered federal savings associations and supervised the Federal Home Loan Banks after it was established by the Federal Home Loan Bank Act of 1932. However, because the FHLBB curried favor with its member savings associations by being lax in accounting and regulatory rules, it was abolished in 1989 by the Financial Institutions Reform, Recovery, and Enforcement Act (FIRREA). The FHLBB was replaced by the Office of Thrift Supervision (OTS), which was subject to Treasury Department oversight and control. The OTS is now the chief federal-level regulator of savings associations in that it charters associations at the federal level and establishes federal rules with which savings associations must comply.

Savings associations could obtain federal deposit insurance after the **Federal Savings and Loan Insurance Corporation (FSLIC)** was established in 1934. Initially, the FSLIC, which was regulated by the FHLBB, issued deposit insurance on much the same terms as the FDIC. After World War II, however, because there were very few bank failures, the FDIC began to rebate part of the 0.083 percent deposit insurance premium paid by member institutions.

As the problems of savings associations grew in the late 1970s and 1980s, the FSLIC found it could not afford to give an insurance premium rebate and even raised its rate. As a result, some of the soundest institutions tried to convert to savings bank or commercial bank charters so they could obtain FDIC insurance and lower insurance premiums. To retain institutions, the FSLIC competed by allowing member institutions to meet more lenient capital requirements and accounting rules. These so-called regulatory accounting principles (RAPs) let savings associations hide their growing losses and report inflated incomes and net worth in the 1980s, while their problems grew.

When Congress finally recognized the problems and moved to solve them by passing the FIRREA of 1989, it blamed the FSLIC and the FHLBB for letting the problems become so bad. Thus, Congress abolished both the FHLBB and the FSLIC. The FSLIC was replaced with a new insurance fund (the FDIC-SAIF) managed by the FDIC, which insured the better savings associations that had previously been insured by the FSLIC. The weak or failed savings associations were placed under the jurisdiction of a new federal agency, the **Resolution Trust Corporation (RTC)**, for liquidation or sale. The RTC disposed of the weak or failed associations. The taxpayers, FDIC-SAIF, and Federal Home Loan Banks bore the associated losses, until the RTC completed its job and went out of business at the end of 1995. However, the taxpayers, Federal Home Loan Banks, FDIC-SAIF and, thus, the savings associations that receive insurance from the FDIC-SAIF are still making principal and interest payments on the debt incurred when the RTC (and, before that, the FSLIC) liquidated the failing institutions.

At present, most savings associations are regulated by the OTS and the FDIC-SAIF at the federal level. However, some former savings associations have converted to savings banks or commercial banks and may be regulated by the FDIC-BIF and the appropriate regulators for such institutions. In addition, some former savings associations have obtained FDIC-BIF deposit insurance rather than FDIC-SAIF deposit insurance. Furthermore, it is becoming increasingly likely that bank and savings association insurance funds and regulators will merge at some future time. Then students won't have to learn such a large alphabet soup of regulatory initials.

The balance sheets of savings banks and savings and loan associations are quite similar. After World War II, until 1996, they were given substantial federal income tax relief (a **bad-debt deduction**) if at least 60 percent of their assets were related to home mortgage lending. The tax breaks encouraged the mortgage-oriented thrifts to finance the great expansion in home ownership that occurred after World War II.

Because of the tax incentive to conduct residential mortgage lending, these institutions exposed themselves to substantial interest rate risk because they held too many long-term fixed-rate mortgages when interest rates rose sharply in the late 1970s and early 1980s. As we previously discussed, by the 1980s, many savings institutions were in severe financial trouble and failed because of the excessive interest rate risk. Exhibit 17.4 shows the major reasons that mortgage-oriented thrifts exited the industry. In the late 1980s and early 1990s, there were a large number of failures and charter conversions. In recent years, merger and acquisition activity is the leading reason for the decrease in the number of institutions.

OPERATIONS OF SAVINGS INSTITUTIONS

EXHIBIT 17.4

Contraction of OTS-Regulated Private-Sector Savings Institutions Due to Failures, Mergers, and Conversion to Bank Charters

	1989	1990	1991	1992	1993	1994	1995	1996 to 2000	2001 to 2003
Exits									
Failures	320	213	147	61	8	2	2	3	2
Voluntary dissolutions	0	0	6	8	10	3	5	15	44
Charter conversions	2	16	43	108	116	66	29	135	46
Mergers and acquisitions	46	48	57	71	79	78	93	374	91
Total exits	368	277	253	248	213	149	129	527	183
Entrants	15	24	6	6	15	11	23	156	43
Net change (exits)	353	253	247	242	198	138	106	371	140

In the late 1980s and early 1990s, the major reasons for savings association exit were failures, mergers, and conversions to savings bank or commercial bank charters. In recent years, mergers and charter conversions have been the primary reasons for contraction.

Source: Office of Thrift Supervision, *2003 Fact Book,* May 2004.

Because their traditional methods of operation had caused savings institutions to experience problems, the 1980 DIDMCA gave them many additional powers traditionally reserved for commercial banks, such as issuing transactions deposits (i.e., checking accounts) in addition to savings deposits and making shorter-term loans, such as consumer and credit card loans. The reasoning was that banks had broader powers and had experienced fewer problems than mortgage-oriented thrifts in the late 1970s and early 1980s. By giving savings associations additional powers, regulators hoped that savings institutions could diversify more and reduce their dependence on the long-term mortgage lending that had exposed them to such great interest rate risk. Savings institutions received additional powers with the passage of the 1982 Depository Institutions Act. The act permitted savings associations to make a limited number of commercial loans and gave them additional powers. Consequently, mortgage-oriented thrifts now own a wider variety of assets than they did in the 1970s and their operations are more complicated.

ASSETS

Exhibit 17.5 shows that the largest single type of asset held by savings institutions is 1–4-family residential mortgage loans. In addition to 1–4-family residential mortgages, savings institutions hold loans on many other types of real estate, including mortgage loans for multifamily apartments, commercial properties, construction, and land acquisition. Most savings institutions also hold substantial amounts of mortgage-backed securities. Because mortgage-backed securities are more marketable and have more desirable cash-flow characteristics than the underlying mortgages, they have grown in importance in savings institutions' total assets in recent years.

Savings institutions continue to hold many mortgages despite their interest rate risk because they obtain a number of advantages from doing so. First, savings institutions that hold a sufficiently large amount of mortgages and qualifying assets (over 60 percent) are designated as qualified lenders and are therefore eligible for more favorable regulatory treatment than banks if they are part of a single-depository-institution holding company. This treatment means that they can have commercial affiliates and are not subject to intense holding company regulation. Further, savings associations that hold sufficient mortgages can borrow on relatively advantageous terms by joining the Federal Home Loan Bank system and obtaining "advances" from their regional Federal Home Loan Bank.

Savings institutions can also hold nonmortgage loans such as loans to individual consumers, including credit card loans. However, most savings associations do not hold large amounts of such loans, which average only about 5 percent of savings institutions' total assets.

Savings institutions hold cash, deposits with other financial institutions, and investment securities to meet reserve requirements imposed on their transactions deposit holdings, to meet additional needs for liquidity, to obtain clearing and correspondent services from other financial institutions, and to earn additional income. Because of their focus on mortgage lending, their other investments are small relative to their total assets.

Savings institutions' other asset holdings include buildings, computers, other fixed assets, as well as **other real estate owned (OREO)**. OREO, unlike the famous cookie, is not very desirable because it usually consists of problem assets,

EXHIBIT 17.5
Assets of Thrift Institutions (December 31, 2003)

Asset Accounts	All Insured Thrift Institutions[a]		Small Savings Institutions[b]	Medium-Sized Savings Institutions[c]	Large Savings Institutions[d]
	Millions	%[e]	%[e]	%[e]	%[e]
Cash and due from depository institutions	$41,560	3	9	5	2
Securities, total	331,561	21	22	26	20
Federal funds sold and securities purchased under repurchase agreements	31,225	2	2	1	2
Loans and leases, total	1,059,319	68	62	64	69
Loans secured by real estate, total	927,548	59	56	57	60
Construction and land development	42,473	3	4	5	2
1–4 family residential	727,515	47	43	38	48
Multifamily residential	75,325	5	2	4	5
Commercial	81,908	5	6	10	4
Commercial and industrial loans	45,089	3	3	3	3
Loans to individuals	81,515	5	4	3	6
Other loans	5,168	0	0	0	0
Less allowance for loan losses	8,326	1	1	1	1
Bank premises and fixed assets	14,148	1	2	2	1
Other real estate owned	1,516	0	0	0	0
Goodwill and other intangible assets	30,946	2	0	0	2
Other assets	57,435	4	3	3	4
Total Assets	**$1,559,384**	**100**	**100**	**100**	**100**

Real estate lending, especially for residential properties, dominates savings institutions' asset portfolios.

[a] This group consists of 1,404 insured savings institutions.

[b] This group consists of the country's 469 smallest savings institutions. These institutions have assets of less than $100 million.

[c] This group consists of the country's 776 medium-sized savings institutions. These institutions have assets between $100 million and $1 billion.

[d] This group consists of the country's 159 largest savings institutions. These institutions have assets of $1 billion or more.

[e] Columns may not add to 100 percent because of rounding.

Source: FDIC, *Statistics on Banking,* December 31, 2003.

such as properties repossessed from defaulting mortgage borrowers. Thus, the fact that savings institutions' holdings of OREO are relatively small is a good sign. Finally, another indicator of financial health, **contra-assets,** has also been falling. Contra-assets consist of reserves to compensate for the overvaluation of other assets on the savings institutions' balance sheets. The major component of this category is the savings institutions' allowance for loan losses. Because the allowance for loan losses is a reserve account used to recognize that not all loans will be repaid in full, it is subtracted from the asset accounts to reflect possible future losses.

LIABILITIES

Deposits.   Exhibit 17.6 shows that the primary source of funds for savings institutions is from deposits—particularly relatively "small" deposits of $100,000 or

---

EXHIBIT 17.6
Liabilities and Capital Accounts of Saving Institutions (December 31, 2003)

Liabilities and Capital Accounts	All Insured Thrift Institutions[a] Millions	%[e]	Small Savings Institutions[b] %[e]	Medium-Sized Savings Institutions[c] %[e]	Large Savings Institutions[d] %[e]
Liabilities					
Deposits	$946,888	61	79	76	57
Borrowed funds, total	407,533	26	6	12	29
Federal funds purchased and securities sold under repurchase agreements	88,375	6	0	1	7
Other borrowed money	319,158	20	6	12	22
Subordinated notes and debentures	6,918	0	0	0	1
All other liabilities	27,334	2	1	1	2
Total liabilities	$1,388,673	89	86	89	89
Capital accounts					
Common and preferred stock	101,689	7	5	3	7
Undivided profits	69,022	4	9	7	4
Total equity capital	170,711	11	14	11	11
Total liabilities and equity capital	$1,559,384	100	100	100	100

Deposits are the largest source of funds for most savings institutions, but they are a much more important source for small- and medium-sized institutions. Borrowed funds are a more important source of funds for large banks. Other borrowed money consists largely of FHLB advances.

[a] This group consists of 1,404 insured savings institutions.

[b] This group consists of the country's 469 smallest savings institutions. These institutions have assets of less than $100 million.

[c] This group consists of the country's 776 medium-sized savings institutions. These institutions have assets between $100 million and $1 billion.

[d] This group consists of the country's 159 largest savings institutions. These institutions have assets of $1 billion or more.

[e] Columns may not add to 100 percent because of rounding.

Source: FDIC, *Statistics on Banking,* December 31, 2003.

less. Initially, passbook savings deposits were the primary sources of funds for savings institutions, but now they issue a wide variety of deposits. Specifically, because of the 1980 and 1982 Depository Institutions Acts, they can issue checkable deposits such as NOW accounts and transaction-limited money market deposit accounts (MMDA). In addition, they can issue demand deposits to commercial customers with whom they do business, and some savings banks have issued non-interest-bearing checkable accounts. Thus, savings associations can offer a variety of transactions deposits, and they must back those deposits by meeting the same reserve requirements applicable to commercial banks.

Savings institutions typically issue a variety of savings certificates and negotiable certificates of deposit as well as regular savings accounts. The certificates are usually tailored to meet the needs of retail customers and can be issued to customers' retirement accounts.

Borrowed Funds.   Savings institutions supplement their deposits by borrowing from other sources. The most important source of borrowed funds consists of FHLBB advances, which are included in the "other borrowed money" category. FHL Bank advances are available to FHLB member institutions. Advances are available with relatively long maturities, up to 20 years, at rates that are only a little higher than the FHL Banks' government agency borrowing rate. Thus, advances are an attractive source of funding for savings associations with long-term assets. Savings institutions also have expanded their borrowing by obtaining collateralized loans (**reverse repos**) from the repurchase agreement market. Borrowings from Federal Home Loan Banks have expanded greatly while other sources of borrowings have declined in relative importance since the restructuring of the savings institution industry in 1989.

CAPITAL

The most startling change since the regulatory structure was reformed and weak savings institutions were assigned to the RTC for liquidation in 1989 is that saving institutions now hold substantially more net worth (capital) relative to their assets. Savings institutions' net worth may be either in the form of reserves and surplus, for mutual institutions, or in the form of "stockholders' equity," for stockholder-owned institutions. While most savings institutions initially were mutual institutions, by the end of 2003 the FDIC reported that mutual institutions held under 7 percent of all savings institutions' assets but comprised 40 percent of all savings institutions. Mutual institutions are smaller because they cannot issue stock to acquire more capital for growth purposes. Thus, they can grow only slowly as their reserves and surplus accumulate (like retained earnings) over time.

Because of infusions of new capital from stockholders and the retention of earnings, OTS-regulated savings institution capital accounts grew substantially from 1989 to 1992, while their total assets contracted. Their assets contracted as institutions failed, converted to commercial or savings bank charters, or were acquired by commercial banks. With more capital and fewer assets, the capital adequacy of savings associations improved greatly in the early 1990s. Capital adequacy ratios (Exhibit 17.7) show that savings institutions' Tier 1 leverage ratios and risk-based capital ratios approximately doubled from 1989 to 1997. It has remained high since then.

EXHIBIT 17.7
Trends in Capital Adequacy, Problem Assets, and Savings Institution Earnings

Year-End	1989	1991	1996	1997	2000	2003
Capital Adequacy Ratios for OTS-Supervised Savings Institutions						
Average Tier I leverage ratio	3.83%	5.27%	7.38%	7.59%	7.39%	7.82%
Average (total) risk-based capital ratio	7.19	10.16	14.53	14.59	13.32	14.23
Problem Assets of OTS-Regulated Savings Institutions						
Total troubled assets as a % of assets	NA	3.80%	1.13%	1.00%	0.60%	0.67%
Noncurrent loans as a % of assets	NA	1.87	0.85	0.77	0.50	0.58
Noncurrent 1–4 family loans[a]	NA	1.85	1.21	1.11	0.67	0.84
Noncurrent multifamily loans[a]	NA	—	1.45	0.79	0.15	0.13
Noncurrent commercial loans[a]	NA	5.98	1.38	1.10	1.52	1.21
Noncurrent consumer loans[a]	NA	1.32	0.89	0.97	0.81	0.87
Return on Assets (ROA) for OTS-Regulated Savings Institutions						
Average ROA for savings institutions	–0.41%	0.13%	0.89%	0.84%	0.90%	1.29%
Average ROE for savings institutions	0.97	1.88	11.15	10.44	11.61	14.30

After weak savings institutions were liquidated by the RTC in the early 1990s, savings institutions' assets fell, but capital ratios, earnings, and troubled asset ratios improved. Commercial loans and multifamily loans showed the greatest improvement.

NA = not available.
[a] As a % of the loan type.
Source: Office of Thrift Supervision, *2003 Fact Book,* May 2004.

One reason for the increase in savings institution capital ratios was that savings institutions' problem assets declined substantially in the 1990s (see Exhibit 17.7). This was particularly true of the highest-risk loan categories (multifamily and commercial loans). In addition, because of a favorable interest rate environment and reduced charge-offs for problem assets, savings associations were able to increase their earnings substantially from 1989 to 2003. By the end of that period, the average return on assets (ROA) for savings institutions was almost 1.30 percent and their return on equity (ROE) exceeded 14 percent.

INCOME AND EXPENSES OF SAVINGS ASSOCIATIONS

Exhibit 17.8 shows the trend in savings institutions' net interest margin. Recall that a financial institution's net interest margin is the difference between gross interest income and gross interest expense. The exhibit shows that savings associations' net interest spread declined substantially in the early 1980s. The reason was that savings associations' cost of funds rose sharply while the interest revenue from their mortgage portfolio lagged behind. As a result, savings associations in

EXHIBIT 17.8
Net Interest Margin of Savings Institutions (1970–2003)

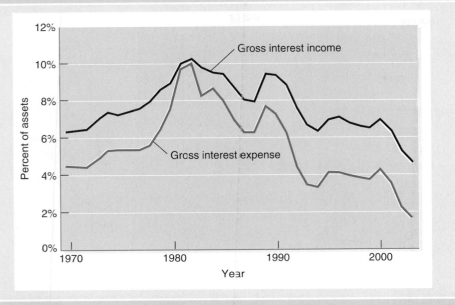

In the late 1970s and early 1980s, savings institutions' net interest margins shrank to almost nothing. In the 1990s, on the other hand, savings institutions' net interest margins grew as interest rates declined.

Source: FDIC, *Statistics on Banking,* December 31, 2003.

general suffered large losses in 1981 and 1982 due to interest rate risk. Since 1989, savings institutions have become more profitable and financially healthier. While their interest income declined, their costs of funds fell even faster. As a result, their net interest spread increased from a little under 2 percent to almost 3 percent by 2003.

Exhibit 17.9 shows the trend in savings institutions' provision for loan losses over the 1984 to 2003 period. The dramatic increase in the provision in the late 1980s can be attributed to increased risk taking by many institutions following the deregulation of the industry in the early 1980s. Many savings institutions grew rapidly in the mid-1980s by making risky loans. Recall from Chapter 16 that poorly capitalized depository institutions face a moral hazard. That was certainly the case in the savings institution industry in the early 1980s. Unfortunately, many of these risky loans ended up in default, especially those that were made in the oil-producing states of Texas, Oklahoma, Louisiana, and elsewhere.

After the FIRREA was passed in 1989 and regulators cleaned up the problem savings institutions and other savings institutions disposed of their bad assets and took care to avoid new problems, savings institutions' provisions for loan losses declined greatly in the 1990s. Consequently, because of widening interest mar-

---

EXHIBIT 17.9
Provision for Loan Losses for Savings institutions (1984–2003)

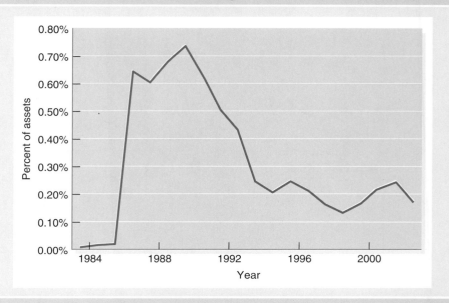

The provision for loan losses at thrift institutions increased substantially in the late 1980s as many savings institutions struggled to absorb losses on their lending portfolio, especially those loans made in oil-producing states such as Texas, Oklahoma, and Louisiana.

Source: FDIC, *Statistics on Banking,* December 31, 2003.

---

gins, greater fee income, and declining loan losses, savings associations' profits recovered sharply in the 1990s. This is shown in Exhibit 17.10.

A major reason for the savings associations' profit recovery in the 1990s is that savings institutions were able to maintain their net interest margins as interest rates declined. This occurred because of several factors. First, as interest rates fell, deposit rates fell faster than mortgage rates. Even though high-rate mortgages were refinanced, they weren't refinanced immediately. Second, after initial low "teaser" rates on adjustable-rate (ARM) mortgages expired, ARM rates adjusted upward by nearly as much or even more than the amount that market interest rates had declined. Third, savings institutions made more relatively high-rate consumer and commercial loans, such as credit card loans, on which interest rates exceed mortgage loan rates. Nonetheless, since savings institutions still used many relatively short-term deposits to fund longer-term mortgage loans, they still take considerable interest rate risk that could cause them to incur losses if interest rates began to rise at a rapid rate at some time in the future.

Fortunately, savings institutions take less interest rate risk than they did previously. They match-fund many of their long-term mortgages with long-term borrowings (advances) from the Federal Home Loan Banks. They also originate and hold relatively more adjustable-rate mortgage loans than in the past. In addi-

EXHIBIT 17.10
Net Income for Savings Institutions (1970–2003)

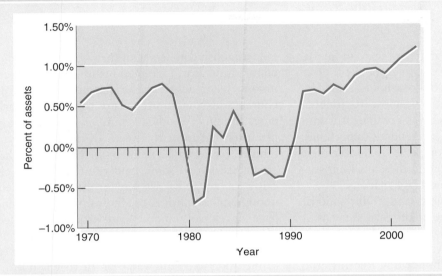

The high interest rates of the late 1970s and early 1980s caused substantial losses at savings institutions. After the deregulation of the industry in 1980 and 1982, many savings institutions grew rapidly and the industry began to show a profit again, at least on a book-value basis. When oil prices dropped in the mid 1980s, however, loan defaults mounted quickly in the oil-producing states of Texas, Oklahoma, Louisiana, and elsewhere.

Source: FDIC, *Statistics on Banking,* December 31, 2003.

tion, they hold more mortgage-backed derivative securities with floating rates and/or short maturities. Furthermore, they have acquired more business loans and consumer loans with relatively short maturities and flexible rates. Thus, changes in interest revenues and changes in interest costs are more closely correlated at most savings institutions.

DO YOU UNDERSTAND?

1. When and why were the various types of thrift institutions started in the United States?
2. Name the present federal regulators of savings institutions. Also, explain which ones no longer exist and why.
3. What are savings institutions' most important assets and liabilities?
4. What trends have recently occurred in savings associations' capital adequacy, earnings, and numbers, and why?

IN PRACTICE

Demographic Change Brings Opportunity

Between 1980 and 2000, the minority share of households increased from 17 percent to 26 percent. Over the same period, the number of households headed by unmarried women increased by almost 10 million. Both of these trends are expected to continue well into the future. This represents a tremendous opportunity for those thrifts and finance companies that make their products and services appealing to these growing segments of the consumer and mortgage markets.

Thrifts (savings institutions and credit unions) have a tradition of serving the credit-related needs of consumers, so it is natural to expect thrifts to capitalize on this opportunity. However, commercial banks are also interested in serving minorities. Recently, the Credit Union National Association (CUNA) published the *Hispanic National Resource Guide* to help credit unions develop strategies to meet the needs of Hispanics. The American Bankers Association (ABA) has published its *Best Practices in Immigrant Lending*. Not surprisingly, the two documents have much in common.

According to the CUNA and ABA, financial institutions should develop an outreach strategy to help establish contacts with members of the minority community. For example, many banks and credit unions have developed a partnership with local churches or community groups to offer financial literacy training. Another key to success is developing products that meet the needs of the minority community. For example, many immigrants do not have a credit history, so some lenders offer secured credit cards that are a low-risk way for the lender to help an immigrant establish a credit history. Other lenders have developed unique loan products targeted at Muslims. Islamic law prohibits the payment of interest, so the loan product must be carefully structured to incorporate an allowable profit that is not in the form of interest.

Although these practices make sense, a financial institution's success will also depend on who is implementing the practices. Many minorities are distrustful of the financial system because of language barriers and a lack of familiarity with how the system works. The best way to overcome these barriers is for financial institutions to hire employees who are representative of the groups they are trying to serve.

CREDIT UNIONS

Originating in Germany in the mid-1800s, the first credit union in the United States, St. Mary's Cooperative Credit Association, was organized in New Hampshire in 1909. Like savings institutions, credit unions were started both to provide an outlet for savers to deposit small amounts of funds and as organizations that would provide loans on relatively lenient terms to their members. Unlike savings institutions, however, credit unions were not instituted for the purpose of providing mortgage financing for their members. Instead, credit unions tend to focus on consumer lending.

Credit unions are strictly mutual institutions. They are organized like clubs whose members pool their savings and loan them to one another. Each member has one vote to elect members of the board of directors. Every member of a credit union must have one or more savings "shares" in the credit union in order to use its facilities, borrow funds from it, or vote for its board of directors. Often a minimum share (deposit) of $25 is required of each member who joins a credit union, but the minimum amount varies at different credit unions. The board of directors establishes major credit union policies, chooses the management of the credit union, and can change the management if necessary. To be a member of a credit union, a person must qualify under the credit union's **common bond requirements**. Most common bonds (over 80 percent) are "occupational" (e.g., members work for the same employers or in the same industry); some (around 10 percent) are "associational" (e.g., members belong to the same religion, trade association, or trade union). The rest are "residential" (e.g., members live in a qualifying sparsely populated rural county or in specified low-income areas).

The common bond requirement gives credit unions several advantages that are not available to other depository institutions. First, like other clubs, their income is not subject to federal income tax before it is paid out as "dividends." Savers who own shares (which are equivalent to other institutions' deposits) in the credit union receive "dividends" instead of interest as a return on their savings shares (deposits). Second, because their common bond requirement prevents credit unions from competing for the same customers (members), they are not subject to antitrust laws that otherwise might keep them from engaging in cooperative ventures. Consequently, they have developed strong trade associations that provide them with many jointly provided services and help them coordinate their activities. Their trade associations, cooperative ventures, and tax exemption give them advantages that are not available to other depository institutions. Thus, while the mortgage-oriented thrifts are becoming more like commercial banks, credit unions are likely to remain a distinctive form of financial institution.

CREDIT UNION REGULATORS

At first credit unions were chartered and regulated only by individual states. It was not until 1934 that the Federal Credit Union Act was approved by Congress. That act allowed for the regulation and supervision of credit unions at the federal level. Most deposit insurance, if any, was provided by state insurance funds. Federal deposit (share) insurance became available only in 1970. At that time the **National Credit Union Administration (NCUA)** was established to regulate federally chartered credit unions and the new **National Credit Union Share Insurance Fund (NCUSIF)**. The NCUSIF provided federal insurance to members who owned shares (had deposits) in federally chartered credit unions and in qualifying state-chartered credit unions that elected to obtain federal insurance for their shareholders. The coverage of NCUSIF insurance was similar to that of FDIC and FSLIC insurance. Presently, NCUSIF insurance insures members' shares in a credit union up to $100,000, just like the FDIC. The NCUSIF also uses a CAMELS (capital adequacy, asset quality, management, earnings, liquidity and sensitivity to market risk) rating system, adapted from the FDIC, when examining credit unions to determine their soundness.

Credit union share insurance is funded by one-time contributions of assets, plus annual contributions if NCUSIF balances fall below 1.25 percent of insured shares. In 1985 credit unions recapitalized the NCUSIF by pledging 1 percent of their insured deposits. They also paid a share (deposit) insurance premium of 0.083 percent in years when the fund held an amount of assets less than 1.25 percent of insured shares (deposits). After 1985, that premium was levied only in 1992, for in most years the NCUSIF earns a sufficient amount on its assets to pay all its costs, including the losses incurred in liquidating failed credit unions. Thus, for the last decade, the annual insurance premium for credit unions has been among the lowest among all federally insured depository institutions.

Because federal share insurance is relatively inexpensive and state insurance plans may be unsound (many credit unions in Rhode Island lost their insurance when the Rhode Island state insurance fund failed at the start of 1991), almost all credit unions now are insured by the NCUSIF. The NCUSIF, in turn, is overseen by the NCUA.

Thus, the NCUA is the most important credit union regulator. It not only charters federal credit unions, it also regulates the NCUSIF, which oversees all federally insured credit unions, including state-chartered credit unions that have federal share insurance. In addition, it oversees the **Central Liquidity Facility (CLF)** for credit unions.

The CLF is empowered to make loans to credit unions that have a liquidity need. The Central Liquidity Facility can borrow funds through the Federal Financing Bank, which helps finance government agencies' funding needs, and lends the funds either directly to credit unions or indirectly, through credit unions' privately run **central credit union** system. While the CLF rarely uses its lending authority, it was authorized by Congress in 1978 so credit unions could be assured that they would always have access to funds, if necessary, in the event of a liquidity crisis.

CREDIT UNIONS' OPERATIONS AND BALANCE SHEETS

Credit unions have grown substantially in recent decades, particularly since they have had access to federal share (deposit) insurance since 1970. Thus, by the end of 2003, 9,529 federally insured credit unions had almost $600 billion in total assets, 82 million members, and $354 billion in loans outstanding (see Exhibit 17.11).

The amount of credit union shares and assets outstanding has grown rapidly even though the number of credit unions has shrunk by more than 20 percent since 1988. The number of credit unions has declined, while their assets expanded, because many credit unions have merged with others and the surviving ones have grown rapidly because they have exploited their access to new powers, such as the issuance of checkable (**share-draft**) accounts and credit card loans, and have expanded their common bonds so each credit union can serve more members. Credit unions can often allow retirees in the area they serve to join even if they do not meet the credit union's common bond. In addition, they can stretch their common bonds by allowing family members of those that meet the common bond to join and by letting people retain their membership even if they move or change jobs and no longer meet the common bond requirement. Credit unions can also extend their common bonds through mergers and by extending their common bond requirement to additional groups that could not muster more than 3,000 members if they were to charter a separate credit union.

Exhibit 17.12 shows selected ratios for the credit union industry as a whole and for the smallest and largest credit unions. As you might expect, the smallest credit unions have higher operating costs, as a percentage of assets, than larger credit unions. The smallest ones have operating expenses that nearly equal 4 percent of assets each year, while the largest credit unions' operating expenses are less than 3 percent of assets. Because of their high operating costs, the smallest credit unions pay lower rates of return to their members who hold shares. Because of

EXHIBIT 17.11

Trends in Credit Union Assets, Members, Loans, Investments, and Profits

Year	1993	1997	2001	2003
Credit union trends				
Numbers	12,317	11,238	9,984	9,529
Members (million)	63.5	71.4	79.4	81.8
Assets (billion $)	277.1	351.2	501.6	599.2
Share growth (%)	11.8	7.1	15.3	10.7
Loan growth (%)	9.2	8.6	7.0	6.0
Key ratios (% of assets)				
Loans	55.0	66.1	64.3	59.0
Investments	40.7	28.5	22.3	26.2
Capital (reserves)	9.0	11.1	10.8	10.3
Return (ROAA)	1.4	1.03	0.96	1.06
Memo: Loan delinquency rate				
Delinquency (%)	1.00	1.01	0.84	0.74

Credit unions have experienced constant growth in assets and membership even though the number of credit unions has consistently fallen in recent years. Since credit unions try to accommodate members' financial needs, they reduce their investments when loan demand exceeds share growth and increase their investments when share growth exceeds member loan growth.

Source: National Credit Union Administration, *2003 Mid-Year Statistics for Federally Insured Credit Unions,* Washington, D.C., 2003.

low rates paid to savers, the smallest credit unions have net margins (of income minus the cost of funds) similar to those of larger credit unions. However, because of higher operating costs and lower fee income, they still have substantially lower returns on average assets than larger credit unions. They also offer their members fewer liability services as almost all of their savings shares are in traditional (passbook-type) regular share accounts (Exhibit 17.13). Thus, members of small credit unions have a strong incentive to merge or otherwise expand their common bonds so they can gain economies of scale and more services. If they reduce their costs by increasing their size, credit unions can pay higher dividend rates on their shares and/or charge lower loan rates to their members.

CREDIT UNION ASSETS

Credit unions have relatively simple balance sheets. Their assets primarily consist of loans to members. At year-end 2003, almost 60 percent of their assets consisted of loans (see Exhibits 17.11 and 17.13). Since their members are consumers, their loans are consumer and mortgage loans. Exhibit 17.13 shows that the most important type of credit union lending consists of first and second-mortgage loans

EXHIBIT 17.12

Selected Ratios by Asset Size for Federally Insured Credit Unions (June 30, 2003)

	All Credit Unions	Small CUs (Less Than $2 m)	Large CUs (Greater Than $500 m)
Number of credit unions	9,529	1,803	226
Profitability (%):			
Return on average assets	1.04%	0.30%	1.24%
Cost of funds to average assets	1.77	1.34	1.98
Operating expenses to average assets	3.18	3.66	2.78
Provision for loan losses to average assets	0.32	0.38	0.36
Net operating expenses to average assets	2.45	3.44	2.10
Capital adequacy:			
Capital to total assets	10.46	15.86	9.86
Asset quality:			
Delinquent loans to assets	0.44	2.25	0.50
Asset/liability management:			
Net long-term assets to total assets	23.71	3.35	25.47
As a percentage of total gross income:			
Interest on loans (net of interest refunds)	67.50	81.56	66.36
Income from investments	15.01	12.92	15.36
Fee income	11.52	3.94	10.92

Source: National Credit Union Administration, *2003 Mid-Year Statistics for Federally Insured Credit Unions,* Washington, D.C., 2003.

(26 percent of assets), followed closely by new- and used-auto loans (23 percent of assets). For many years credit unions did not make many mortgage loans, but they have increasingly done so to accommodate members' needs and to try to take advantage of an upward-sloping yield curve to earn extra income. Because many of their real estate–secured loans consist of first or second mortgages, credit unions are exposed to interest rate risk as many of their liabilities are of shorter maturity than their assets. Additional assets of credit unions consist of unsecured personal loans, credit card loans (at larger and more sophisticated credit unions), and investments. Credit unions held 26 percent of their assets in the form of investments at the end of 2003.

Credit union investments can take a variety of forms. Most invest in relatively safe government or government agency securities. Other credit union investments include bank or savings institution CDs and mutual fund shares. In addition, many credit unions invest large portions of their excess funds with one of the 33 "corporate central credit unions" that serve credit unions (credit unions in each state can join the appropriate corporate "central" credit union that serves credit unions in that state). The central credit unions issue certificates of deposit or sav-

EXHIBIT 17.13
Credit Union Assets and Liabilities (June 30, 2003)

	All Credit Unions Millions	%	Small CUs (Less Than $2 m) %	Large CUs (Greater Than $500 m) %
Assets				
Cash & equivalents	$55,933	11	25	9
Total investments	157,193	26	23	22
U.S. government obligations	3,531	1	0	1
Federal agency securities	84,734	14	0	14
Other investments	68,928	12	22	8
Total loans outstanding	353,785	59	52	60
Unsecured credit card loans	20,481	3	0	4
All other unsecured loans	20,416	3	13	3
New-vehicle loans	60,263	10	13	10
Used-vehicle loans	77,222	13	18	11
First-mortgage real estate loans	107,911	18	1	22
Other real estate loans	46,762	8	1	8
Other loans	20,730	3	6	3
Allowance for loan losses	2,886	0	1	0
Other assets	22,315	4	0	4
Total Assets	$599,226	100	100	100
Liabilities/equity/savings				
Total liabilities	$14,645	2	1	4
Total savings	521,182	87	84	86
Share drafts	64,013	11	1	11
Regular shares	189,030	32	73	26
Money market shares	94,728	16	1	19
Share certificates/CDs	120,344	20	6	21
IRA/Keogh accounts	45,315	8	1	8
All other shares and deposits	6,555	1	3	1
Total Equity	63,398	11	16	10
Reserves	24,483	4	5	4
Undivided earnings	38,915	6	11	6
Total Liabilities/Equity/Savings	$599,226	100	100	100

Source: National Credit Union Administration, *2003 Mid-Year Statistics for Federally Insured Credit Unions,* Washington, D.C., 2003.

ings accounts to their member credit unions and utilize their acquired funds by making loans to credit unions that need additional liquidity or by investing their excess funds. In effect, the corporate central credit unions are the credit unions for credit unions.

The central credit unions are members of the **U.S. Central Credit Union**, the nation's only wholesale corporate credit union. The U.S. Central Credit Union has a commercial bank charter in the state of Kansas, so it has access to the nation's check payment system and can invest in a variety of ways—in the securities repo market or in the Eurodollar deposit market, for instance. The U.S. Central Credit Union can also lend money to credit unions, or their centrals, in the event they need excess liquidity, and it is empowered to borrow from the Central Liquidity Facility operated by the NCUA on behalf of its members. Thus, by investing idle funds in the credit union central system, credit unions can channel their funds across their state or across the nation to fill the liquidity needs of other credit unions. In a sense, credit unions in general operate like a giant branch bank through their network of central credit unions. They can also borrow from government agencies if necessary, through their centrals, and can use their centrals as intermediaries that help them clear checks and maintain any required reserves on their checkable (share-draft) deposits with the Federal Reserve.

While most credit unions do not have to maintain reserve deposits, those that hold a large enough quantity of transactions deposits are subject to the same reserve requirements as commercial banks. However, unlike banks, they can deposit their required reserves with their central credit unions, which in turn can maintain reserve accounts with the Federal Reserve.

CREDIT UNION LIABILITIES

Credit unions' liabilities consist primarily of member savings share accounts. Originally, shares were in the form of passbook savings accounts. However, since the 1970s and particularly since the DIDMCA was passed in 1980, credit unions have offered a variety of savings vehicles. Exhibit 17.13 shows that while regular savings shares are still the largest source of credit union funds, they now account for only 32 percent of all member savings. Checkable share-draft accounts (credit unions' version of interest-paying NOW accounts), money market shares (which allow limited numbers of checks to be written and pay higher rates of interest, like MMDA), share certificates (similar to certificates of deposit at banks), and IRA or Keogh retirement savings accounts together account for a larger portion of credit unions' total liabilities than regular savings shares.

CREDIT UNION CAPITAL

Credit unions are mutual institutions that do not hold shareholders' equity. Instead, their net worth account consists of reserves and surplus and **undivided earnings**. They must set aside a portion of their earnings as reserves, until their reserves are sufficiently large relative to their assets. In addition, they may retain additional "undivided earnings" similar to retained earnings if their dividend payments and additions to reserves are less than their total net earnings.

Credit union capital requirements are similar to those of other thrift institutions at the national level. Because of the general national emphasis on improved capital holdings, credit unions have increased their capital in recent years. By year-end 2003, they held equity capital equal to 11 percent of their assets.

CREDIT UNION TRADE AND SERVICE ASSOCIATIONS

Because they are exempt from antitrust restrictions due to their nonoverlapping common bonds, credit unions have developed a large number of service organizations that allow them to cooperate greatly. Their major trade associations are the **Credit Union National Association (CUNA)**, which serves all credit unions, and the **National Federal Credit Union Association (NAFCU)**, which serves the interests of the generally larger, federally chartered credit unions. Both associations have considerable influence with Congress because credit unions, in total, have more than 82 million members in the United States. That is one reason they may continue to receive more favorable tax and regulatory treatment than other depository institutions.

In addition to lobbying, however, their trade associations, particularly CUNA, have developed additional services for credit unions. For instance, CUNA has supported the development of the central credit unions and the U.S. Central Credit Union, which help credit unions manage their liquidity, clear their checks, and obtain various investment and funds-management services. It has also developed CUNA Mortgage to serve as a mortgage bank to pool and resell mortgages originated by credit unions, CUNA Mutual to provide deposit and credit insurance to credit union members, CUNA Strategic Services, Inc. to provide data-processing services to credit unions that are members, and a variety of other services. By providing services that can be used by many credit unions at low cost, CUNA has helped credit unions overcome the disadvantages of small individual size that otherwise might make it impossible for them to afford sophisticated services for their members.

CREDIT UNION FAILURES AND LOSSES

Due to their common bond requirement, credit unions may be undiversified and, thus, subject to failure if, for instance, a large employer of their members goes out of business. Thus, they are somewhat vulnerable in recessions, which is another reason they have tried to expand and diversify their common bonds through merger or other common bond extensions (taking in retiree groups, for instance) in recent years.

As credit unions and their regulators have become more sophisticated, credit union failures have declined sharply. Credit union failures peaked at 164 in 1990 and NCUSIF losses peaked at $163 million in 1991, while the number of credit unions with poor (4 or 5) CAMELS examination ratings peaked at 1,022 in 1988. However, with the adoption of strict examination policies and a strong economy, credit union failures fell sharply. In 2003, only 13 credit unions failed, with a cost to the NCUSIF of only $9.7 million. Thus, in general, credit union failures have not caused severe losses, and their insurance fund has been very sound. As a result, they have had to pay a share insurance premium to the NCUSIF only in 1992; in all the other years since NCUSIF was recapitalized in 1986, the premium has been waived.

Credit unions have historically recorded low credit losses, but they carry delinquent loans on their books for long periods. There are several reasons for

Commercial Banks vs. Credit Unions

As credit unions have gained more powers, banks have increasingly come to view them as competitors that they wish to discourage. When credit unions developed share-draft—that is, checkable savings—accounts that paid interest in the late 1970s, banks sued to prevent them from offering checkable accounts. A federal judge found that checkable accounts other than bank demand deposits were not legal but allowed that Congress could pass a law making them legal. Congress did so in the DIDMCA of 1980.

Later, as credit unions tried to expand their common bonds to obtain larger memberships and economies of scale, banks sued to try to limit their ability to extend their common bonds. They won a case against an ATT credit union in North Carolina that had aggressively expanded its membership criteria. However, Congress quickly passed the Credit Union Membership Access Act in 1998, empowering the NCUA to expand the common bond requirement for credit unions starting in 1999. However, as soon as the NCUA proposed its new credit union membership rules, the American Bankers Association sued again to prevent them from becoming effective immediately. That suit did not get very far because, as in the case of share-draft accounts, Congress typically has been very friendly to credit unions.

Credit unions have over 82 million members and are well organized in letting Congress know their wishes. In addition, they are nonprofit institutions with a good public image as service organizations, so Congress usually supports their endeavors. Congress had already relaxed common bond requirements when it allowed "residential" credit union common bonds to be used in areas that served low-income customers and customers who were not adequately serviced by more profit-oriented institutions. Thus, in general, Congress has supported the interests of credit unions over the interests of commercial banks even when the banks succeed in winning court cases against credit unions.

However, banks are not done with their efforts to hamstring their potential competitors. They have consistently advocated that Congress take away credit unions' federal income tax exemption. Congress may eventually be sympathetic to the banks' argument on taxes, since it is always on the lookout for ways to obtain more tax revenues. In defense, credit unions need to emphasize the following points: (1) Unlike stockholder-owned institutions like commercial banks, they cannot sell stock to expand or acquire additional capital when needed and they cannot merge freely with other publicly traded firms; (2) Unlike profit-oriented institutions, their main goal is to provide service to the public at low cost, and thus they do not raise prices when able just to make the maximum possible profit; (3) They frequently provide financial services to people who otherwise might not have access to them, since credit unions' common bond requirements and membership knowledge may allow them to make loans or issue checking accounts to people that other institutions might consider to be too risky.

this phenomenon: (1) Credit unions often serve members with stable incomes (teachers, government employees, military people, and so forth); (2) Credit unions often have payroll deductions, so they get paid as soon as the borrower's paycheck is deposited—unless the borrower rescinds the agreement; (3) Credit unions often have a "clublike" atmosphere in which members realize that their loan performance will affect their peers' welfare, so members strive hard to repay their debts so other members of the group will not be exposed to losses; (4) The widespread use of credit life insurance, coupled with their willingness to carry delinquent loans for long periods, may marginally reduce loan losses at credit unions. Nonetheless, because credit unions' common bonds limit their loan portfolio diversification, they have strong incentives to hold high capital to absorb cyclical losses, to hold high liquidity in case losses slow cash inflows, and to merge or otherwise relax their common bonds to achieve greater diversification.

The United States is not alone in having thrift institutions. Many foreign countries also have thrift institutions similar to those found in the United States. The United States, in fact, has often copied the form of financial institutions that were first developed in other countries. England, for instance, has "building and loan" societies that provide real estate finance much like U.S. savings and loan associations. In recent years, just like the United States, the British institutions have developed more retail banking powers and have become somewhat more like commercial banks—some have even converted from mutual to stock ownership.

The first credit union was developed in Germany, and mutual savings banks also developed in Europe before they were copied in the United States. While commercial banks play a dominant role in banking in most European countries, many of the European savings banks also are large and economically quite important institutions, as some of them make a wide variety of loans and employ large numbers of people. Savings banks are quite popular in Scandinavia and other countries that favor mutual ownership forms for financial organizations. The International Savings Bank Association, headquartered in Finland, has member institutions in Norway, Sweden, Austria, Germany, Italy, Spain, the United Kingdom (building societies), the United States, and other countries. While many savings banks make a broad range of loans, in many countries, including the United States, building societies, savings and loans, and other specialized mortgage lenders have been popular because construction interests, potential borrowers, and their political friends have perceived a need to make mortgage credit more readily available to a broader range of borrowers than might otherwise be the case.

THRIFT INSTITUTIONS AROUND THE GLOBE

DO YOU UNDERSTAND?

1. What are credit unions' most important assets and liabilities?
2. Why is the credit union common bond requirement changing? How and why is it changing?
3. How does the common bond requirement affect credit unions' credit risk?

FINANCE COMPANIES

Compared to thrift institutions, which tend to specialize in making certain types of loans (mortgages for savings institutions and consumer loans for credit unions), finance companies are more diverse. Many specialize in consumer finance, particularly small loans; others specialize in business loans, purchasing business accounts receivable (factoring), or leasing. Their business structure includes partnerships, privately owned corporations, publicly owned independent corporations, and wholly owned subsidiaries of manufacturers, commercial bank holding companies, life insurance companies, or other corporate entities.

"Captive" sales finance companies help finance goods sold by their parent companies. Other finance companies, such as GE Capital, finance goods sold by their parent company and a wide variety of other goods and services as well. Among the largest finance companies are **sales finance companies** that are "captives" of major retailers and auto manufacturers that help finance sales of their parents' goods. Examples are Ford Credit, Chrysler Financial, General Motors Acceptance Corporation (GMAC), and Sears Roebuck Acceptance Corporation.

Other large finance companies are large factoring finance companies (such as CIT Group) that are subsidiaries of commercial bank holding companies and "lend" to their clients by buying and collecting their accounts receivable. Some large finance companies, such as GE Capital or IBM Global Financing, are owned by nonfinancial firms. Some of these finance companies started by financing goods sold by their parent organization, then broadened their lending and leasing activities. Other finance companies are independent lenders, which largely make personal loans to consumers and are known as **consumer finance companies**. Still other finance companies are diversified lending and leasing subsidiaries of major commercial bank holding companies. Thus, finance companies come in many varieties and are owned by many different types of parent organizations.

In contrast to depository institutions, finance companies obtain most of their funds in large amounts by borrowing from banks or selling securities in the capital markets rather than by issuing many small deposits. In addition, they often make many small loans rather than a few large ones. A few finance companies have industrial bank charters that allow them to accept deposits from the public. Others have started consumer banks, which accept deposits from the public and make loans to consumers but not to businesses.

Traditionally, finance companies have lent to consumers. However, such lending is strictly regulated by state loan rate ceilings, debt collection restrictions, and many other consumer protection or credit control regulations. This strict regulation has caused severe operating problems, especially for small finance companies. Thus, in recent years, finance companies have increasingly consolidated; as a result of their consolidation, the number of finance companies has declined sharply and their average size has increased. They have also shifted their portfolios toward business lending, leasing, and second-mortgage credit, where regulations are less burdensome.

ASSETS OF FINANCE COMPANIES

Although some finance companies make only business loans or leases, and others make only consumer loans or leases, overall, finance companies divide their lending between consumer and business lending. Exhibit 17.14 shows that after

EXHIBIT 17.14
Assets and Securitized Receivables of Finance Companies by Size of Finance Company, 2000

	All Finance Companies		Small Finance Companies (Under $10 m)		Large Finance Companies (Over $20 b)	
	$ in Millions	%	$ in Millions	%	$ in Millions	%
Number of firms	984		670		11	
Assets						
Total assets	1,259,039	100.00	1,526	100.00	841,995	100.00
Consumer receivables	321,389	25.53	603	39.52	249,854	29.67
Motor vehicle fin.	252,256	20.04	205	13.43	214,330	25.46
Revolving credit	31,142	2.47	8	0.52	20,034	2.38
Other	38,441	3.05	390	25.56	15,490	1.84
Real estate secured	157,745	12.53	120	7.86	108,988	12.94
Business receivables	441,876	35.10	691	45.28	179,403	21.31
All other assets	419,440	33.31	238	15.60	341,287	40.53
Gross assets	1,340,901	106.50	1,651	108.19	879,532	104.46
Less unearned income	66,147	5.25	89	5.83	29,807	3.54
Less loss reserve	15,715	1.25	36	2.36	7,730	0.92
Memo: Securitized receivables						
Consumer, total	109,959	8.73	8	0.52	102,465	12.17
Real estate secured	27,543	2.19	0	0.00	26,166	3.11
Business, total	60,589	4.81	10	0.66	41,207	4.89
Total securitized	198,091	15.73	18	1.18	169,838	20.17

Source: Federal Reserve *Bulletin,* "2000 Survey of Finance Companies," January 2002, Table B.1, p.14.

adjusting for unearned income and loss reserves, finance companies' loan and lease receivables usually amount to over 70 percent of their net assets. Other assets consist of cash, time deposits, investment securities, buildings, and computers. Cash and deposits account for only about 2 percent of finance companies' assets. Some of those deposits may be held as compensating balances for bank loans; the rest provide liquidity. Investment securities, which provide both a secondary source of liquidity and direct earnings, usually account for less than 10 percent of assets. Real assets, such as real estate, computers, and equipment, and loans made to foreign borrowers account for the remainder of finance companies' assets.

Types of receivables held by finance companies vary greatly. Some companies, such as GE Capital, make all types of loans to all types of borrowers. Others, such as factors or local consumer loan companies, specialize in only a few types of loans.

CONSUMER RECEIVABLES

Personal Loans.   Traditionally, consumer-oriented finance companies have attempted to serve consumers by extending credit with more lenient terms, making smaller loans, taking more risk, and providing more personal service than other lenders. Consequently, they make many **personal loans**. Consumer finance companies, in fact, usually specialize in personal loans. Personal loans are the largest single category of finance company receivables at smaller finance companies; they are also important at large companies. Because of rising risks and costs of funds, in recent years many finance companies have increasingly made personal loans secured with second mortgages on home equity. Some home equity loans provide a revolving line of credit that can be used many times and often can be accessed with a credit card. However, most second-mortgage consumer loans are for a fixed term and must be renegotiated if the customer wishes to borrow more. Because of the growing importance of home equity–secured loans, finance companies' real estate–secured loans have grown rapidly in recent years.

Automobile Credit.   Finance company subsidiaries of the major automobile manufacturers make a large number of loans to finance the new and used automobiles their dealers sell. Because the business of auto manufacturers' finance company subsidiaries is to help manufacturers profit by selling cars, they can often provide credit on more favorable terms (with 2.9 or even 0 percent financing) than consumers can find elsewhere. Smaller finance companies do little new-car financing since they do not profit from auto sales per se. However, they often finance consumers' used-car purchases. Increasingly, finance companies have provided lease financing for new-car acquisitions.

Mobile Home Credit.   Finance companies expanded rapidly in the mobile home credit market in the early 1970s because such credit was relatively profitable. However, in the mid-1970s many finance companies experienced substantial losses from defaults on their mobile home loans. Meanwhile, their costs of funds rose. As a result, many finance companies slowed their rate of expansion of mobile home lending and others abandoned the field entirely. However, some companies with a large stake in business credit financing for mobile home dealers continued to make such loans. Therefore, mobile home loans continue to provide an important use of assets for some finance companies. This credit is classed with other consumer loans in Exhibit 17.14.

Revolving Consumer Installment Credit.   Revolving credit has become increasingly important to finance companies. Once a finance company extends credit on a revolving basis, a consumer can borrow up to his or her credit limit many times. Revolving credit origination costs are less costly per dollar of credit extended than small loans. It also may be offered through electronic funds transfer systems and can be secured through home equity lines of credit. Many finance companies also offer revolving credit to serve retailers' needs.

Several major finance companies operate **private-label credit** plans for retailers. Here all correspondence with the consumer is carried on using the retailer's name. However, the finance company is responsible for approving all credit card applications. In addition, the finance company bills the customers, receives all interest revenues, and incurs all losses (above a predetermined amount) applicable to credit card purchases made at the retailer's store. Thus, under such plans, the consumer who uses a credit card appears to borrow from the retailer but actually borrows from the finance company.

By offering a private-label credit plan, the retailer is able to gain customer loyalty by offering his or her "own" credit card plan. In return for providing the expertise and personnel needed to run the credit operations, the finance company usually receives a fee equal to a stated percentage of credit sales, compensation for some losses, and interest revenues on credit balances extended under the plan.

Revolving credit has been one of the most rapidly growing areas of finance company lending in recent years. Finance companies have developed dealer plans, offered credit cards directly to their customers, and offered revolving credit lines tied to second mortgages. Because such credit is compatible with electronic funds transfer systems and reduces the overhead costs of lending, it is likely to continue to grow. If revolving credit is secured with a second mortgage, it is a **home equity loan** and is included with **real estate–secured** credit in Exhibit 17.14.

Other Consumer Installment Loans.   Many consumer loans are used to finance purchases of retail goods other than automobiles and mobile homes. Many finance companies obtain potential personal loan customers and solidify dealer relationships by buying consumer receivables from furniture and appliance dealers. Customers who have to borrow to finance a furniture or appliance purchase may also need to borrow to finance other consumer expenditures. Many such borrowers are in the stage of their life cycle where they are fairly heavily indebted. In particular, they may be young people who anticipate rising incomes in the future and have strong needs to buy particular goods (houses, cars, washers and dryers, furniture, and so on) now. Such customers may be prime candidates for finance company personal loans in the near future. Thus, finance companies buy retail credit contracts and later usually try to make the borrowers aware that they can obtain additional cash credit if they need it. Because of the growth of revolving credit plans at retailers and the fact that consumer installment loans of other types are relatively small and, thus, not very profitable, these loans have declined at finance companies in recent years. Thus, personal loans, mobile home credit, and other consumer installment credit are all clustered in one category in Exhibit 17.14.

REAL ESTATE LENDING

In recent years, the fastest-growing area of finance company lending has been real estate lending secured by second mortgages. Finance companies have rapidly expanded their **second-mortgage lending** for several reasons. First, inflation increased both consumers' demands for credit and the equity value of people's homes. For many people, home equity became their largest single asset. The only way they could tap that asset, however, was either to sell their homes or to borrow against their equity with second mortgages. This phenomenon increased the demand for second mortgages. Second, revisions in consumer protection laws, particularly the Federal Bankruptcy Reform Act of 1978, made it difficult to collect defaulted debts if the debts were unsecured. Thus, bankruptcy filings increased greatly. While personal loans often are discharged in bankruptcy and are hard to collect in general, second mortgages provided excellent security for finance company loans in the event of default. As a result, losses on such loans were very low compared to those on unsecured personal loans. Consequently, many finance companies converted much of their personal lending to second-mortgage lending. Third, by making larger, longer-maturity loans, finance companies could obtain a higher rate of return (net of costs) on their loans. At the same time, they could offer lower rates and larger amounts of credit to consumers and thereby attract more customers. Finally, second mortgages have substantial tax advantages relative to other consumer credit. The 1986 income tax reforms phased out consumers' ability to deduct consumer credit interest payments from their federal income tax; however, mortgage interest, including limited amounts of interest paid on second mortgages, retained its tax-deductible status.

BUSINESS CREDIT

Business financing activities of finance companies include the wholesale financing of inventories held by businesses prior to sale, the retail financing of durable goods purchased by firms, lease financing, and other business financing—including the financing of customer receivables held by firms or factored (sold) to the finance company. Business credit in general has expanded much more rapidly than consumer lending in recent years. Consumer lending is highly regulated whereas business lending is not. As a result, business lending has been more profitable than consumer lending. The various types of business lending by finance companies are described in the following sections.

Wholesale Paper.   **Wholesale paper** is generated when a finance company helps a dealer finance the purchase of goods. For instance, retail dealers must pay for the automobiles or washers and dryers kept in stock. Dealers need the stock for display purposes and to guarantee prompt delivery, yet they receive no cash for the goods until they are sold.

A finance company may provide a dealer with interim financing called **wholesale** or **floor-plan financing**. A floor-plan financing arrangement is one in which the finance company pays the manufacturer when the goods are delivered to the dealer. The finance company then holds a lien on the goods as long as the dealer keeps them in inventory. The dealer pays interest on the value of goods financed by floor-plan financing, and when the goods are sold, the dealer uses the proceeds of the sale to repay the finance company.

Because finance companies have close ties with auto or retail goods dealers for whom they provide floor-plan financing, they may also provide retail financing for the consumers who buy the dealers' goods. In that way, their wholesale financing activities help generate retail financing business and vice versa because a dealer is more likely to do business with a finance company that will also provide retail financing for his or her customers.

Retail Paper.   Sales of goods used for business purposes may be financed with installment sales contracts (such as auto credit contracts) provided by finance companies. Business purchases of vans, light or heavy trucks, and other commercial vehicles are often financed this way. In addition, retail sales of industrial and farm equipment to businesses and farmers may be financed with installment contracts.

Lease Paper.   In recent years, leasing of durable goods has been popular for a number of reasons. First, accelerated depreciation and investment tax credits make it profitable for a firm in a high tax bracket to buy and lease durable investment goods at favorable rates compared to firms in low or zero tax brackets, which cannot profit as much from possible tax savings. Second, an institution that leases a durable good need not borrow the funds required to buy it outright. Third, a lessor retains an equity interest in the good and can regain possession of it more easily and cheaply if the lessee defaults on payments than would be possible if the good were sold under an installment sales contract. This advantage is particularly valuable because consumer protection and bankruptcy laws have given far greater protection to consumers and businesses that fall behind on their debt payments. Fourth, leases can be written so that the good is available when desired, and the good need not be disposed of by a purchaser who is relatively unsophisticated in the marketing of used durable goods. Finally, the lessor can maintain the good under an "operating lease," which provides valuable time and cost savings for the lessee.

In summary, leasing often provides greater tax advantages, protection of ownership rights, and financial flexibility or convenience. Consequently, many finance companies have rapidly expanded their leasing activities in recent years.

Other Business Credit.   Other business credit makes up a substantial portion of finance companies' total assets. Two forms of that credit are particularly interesting because they illustrate the long and close relationship that many finance companies maintain with business firms.

First, the largest single source of other business credit is loans on commercial accounts receivable. These are secured by the accounts receivable of the business firm to which the finance company extends credit. In many cases, a finance company will take possession of the accounts receivable as collateral for its loan and collect payments on them as they come due. As it collects payments, it reduces the loan balance its business customer owes.

Second, factored accounts receivable are accounts due that are directly purchased from the business firm by the finance company. The purchase price is discounted to allow for potential losses and also to allow for the fact that the finance company will not receive full payment until some time in the future. To make an adequate assessment of potential losses and repayment lags, a finance company dealing in **factoring** must have a close working knowledge of the operations of a business firm and the nature of its customers.

Once factored, the accounts receivable become the property of the finance company. It is its responsibility to collect all remaining balances due on factored accounts receivable. In return for selling its accounts receivable at a discount, the selling business firm immediately obtains cash from the finance company. Most of the largest factoring firms are owned by commercial bank holding companies because banks have considerable expertise in evaluating accounts receivable.

SECURITIZATION OF RECEIVABLES

In recent years finance companies have securitized an increasing portion of their receivables. Recall from Chapter 13 that by securitizing assets, loan originators can reduce financing costs, reduce their interest rate risk, and earn servicing fee income. As asset-backed securities have become more popular in financial markets, finance companies have securitized leases as well as credit card loans, automobile loans, and automobile leases. Larger finance companies may securitize as much as 25 percent or more of some types of receivables. Shorter-term and non-standard loans are less frequently securitized than longer-term standardized loans (like real estate, automobile, mobile home, or business equipment loans and leases). Small business loans and small personal installment loans are less likely to be securitized than larger and more standardized types of loans and leases.

LIABILITIES AND NET WORTH OF FINANCE COMPANIES

Net Worth.   One of the most striking aspects of finance company balance sheets, as shown in Exhibit 17.15, is that their overall net worth is very small relative to their total assets. Their total capital, surplus, and undivided profits account for around 11 percent of total assets. Thus finance companies are highly leveraged institutions. Consequently, their income can fluctuate substantially if they experience loan losses or if interest rate changes have different effects on their assets and liabilities. However, Exhibit 17.15 also shows that the 11 largest firms dominate the aggregate finance company statistics and that each holds more than $20 billion in assets.

Since finance companies need to have adequate capital so they can maintain their credit ratings and borrow easily from banks, many smaller finance companies back their asset holdings with much higher capital ratios than large finance companies. Only those with strong parent companies (such as GM, GE, Ford, or IBM) are likely to have capital ratios below 10 percent of assets. Smaller finance companies may hold capital equal to 25 percent or more of their total assets (see Exhibit 17.15).

EXHIBIT 17.15
Liabilities and Capital of Finance Companies by Size of Finance Company, 2000

	All Finance Companies		Small Finance Companies (Under $10 m)		Large Finance Companies (Over $20 b)	
	$ in Millions	%	$ in Millions	%	$ in Millions	%
Number of firms	984		670		11	
Liabilities						
Bank loans	32,847	2.61	621	40.69	4,680	0.56
Commercial paper	224,256	17.81	14	0.92	166,480	19.77
Debt owed parent	95,087	7.55	24	1.57	36,718	4.36
Debt owed mkt, n.e.c.	483,703	38.42	333	21.82	334,251	39.70
All other liabilities	277,488	22.04	87	5.70	212,482	25.24
Capital						
Capital and ret. earn.	145,657	11.57	441	28.90	87,384	10.38
Total liabilities and capital	1,259,039	100.00	1,526	100.00	841,995	100.00

Source: Federal Reserve *Bulletin,* "2000 Survey of Finance Companies," January 2002, Table B.1, p.14.

Finance Company Debt. Even though most finance company assets are relatively short term, some, such as leases and certain installment credit contracts, are long-term assets. On the liability side of the balance sheet, finance companies hold a mixture of both short-term and long-term debt. However, the major portion of their liabilities, like the major portions of their assets, usually consists of short-term obligations. These may take several forms.

Many small finance companies that do not have access to national capital markets borrow from banks to obtain a reliable and relatively low-cost source of funds. Large finance companies often use bank lines of credit to back up their commercial paper and thereby obtain higher ratings on their commercial paper. Others may borrow seasonally from banks or even obtain long-term loans. Overall, bank loans are less than 3 percent of liabilities of finance companies, but they amount to more than 40 percent of assets for small finance companies.

Finance companies obtain almost 18 percent of their funds by issuing **commercial paper**. Because commercial paper is unsecured, only large, top-rated borrowers have direct access to that market. Less well-known issuers must either place their commercial paper through dealers for a small fee or obtain their short-term financing from other sources. Commercial paper has been one of the most rapidly growing sources of finance company funds since 1980. However, 75 percent of the commercial paper issued by finance companies is issued by the 11 largest firms, while practically none is issued by the 670 finance companies with less than $10 million in assets each.

In total, there are only about 70 finance companies that regularly place their commercial paper directly with ultimate lenders. However, directly placed commercial paper accounts for most finance company commercial paper outstanding, because the borrowers are very large. They include General Motors Acceptance Corporation, Ford Motor Credit Corporation, and GE Capital—each of which has billions of dollars in debt outstanding.

One valuable source of credit for smaller companies is **transfer credit** in the form of funding provided by their larger parent companies. Exhibit 17.15 shows that transfer credit from finance companies' parents accounted for 7 to 8 percent of their total liabilities.

A few finance companies have outstanding deposit liabilities and thrift certificates among their "other liabilities." Finance companies may sell debt obligations directly to the public, provided that those debt issues are approved by securities regulators. In the past, finance companies often have had difficulty getting small-denomination debt issues approved, because such debt certificates would compete with savings certificates issued by depository institutions. However, limited amounts of small-denomination debt have been sold to the public by finance companies as thrift certificates.

In about 20 states, finance companies can, if they meet certain requirements, obtain charters as **industrial banks**. Industrial banks can accept savings deposits and make loans for specified purposes, such as consumer loans. By obtaining charters as industrial banks, finance companies are better able to compete for the relatively low-cost sources of funds that are available to banks, credit unions, and savings institutions. Nonetheless, because the largest finance companies primarily obtain their funds from other sources, deposit liabilities and thrift certificates outstanding account for a very small percentage of liabilities for all finance companies combined.

Long-term debt is one of the largest liabilities of large finance companies. However, long-term debt waxes and wanes in relative importance as a source of finance company funds. When interest rates are low, finance companies may issue more long-term debt. By doing so, they hope to hold down future increases in their costs of funds if interest rates should rise. They may also sell long-term debt to reduce their interest rate risk when they acquire long-term loans or lease contracts. By the end of 2000, finance companies' capital market debts ("debt owed mkt., n.e.c.") amounted to nearly 40 percent of their assets.

REGULATION OF FINANCE COMPANIES

Finance company consumer lending is heavily regulated, although finance company business lending generally is not. The reason is that businesspeople are presumed to be better able to act in their own interest than consumers. However, finance company business and consumer lending can both be affected by regulations affecting mergers, branching, and market entry.

Rate Ceilings.   The most influential regulations on finance company operations are those affecting rates that can be charged on loans of different types, sizes, and maturities. Most states have regulations that limit rates charged by consumer or sales finance companies. Frequently, higher rates are permitted on small loans and short-maturity loans. In addition, **rate ceilings** may vary with the type of loan or type of lender. Finance companies often are allowed to charge higher rates than other lenders. However, they also are frequently allowed to make only small loans. If the rate ceilings are too restrictive, consumer finance companies will leave the market, as they have in several states.

Sales finance companies, however, can continue to operate in states with low rate ceilings. They can compensate for losses in interest revenues by discounting the consumer finance paper they buy from retail sales outlets. By paying less than face value for consumer credit contracts, sales finance companies can earn a profitable rate of return on their invested funds.

Creditor Remedy Regulation.   States or the federal government impose various restrictions on finance companies' abilities to collect on delinquent or defaulted debts. These restrictions include limitations on creditors' abilities to charge late fees or to garnishee (i.e., to collect a portion of an employee's wages from an employer) a borrower who falls behind on payments. They also may require that certain legal processes be followed and that the lender bear the full expense of collecting on the bad debts.

Creditor remedy restrictions are of particular importance to finance companies that serve customers who are likely to default or fall behind in their payments. If finance companies have few remedies to induce customers to pay their debts (or few remedies to recover the money if a customer stops paying entirely), they will lose more whenever a customer defaults. This means that they will either have to stop serving high-risk borrowers or charge higher rates to make up for increased operating expenses and losses.

Branching, Chartering, and Merger Restrictions.   State departments of financial institutions and banks are responsible for enforcing restrictions on finance company chartering and branching within their states. Convenience and advantage restrictions require a finance company that wishes to organize or form a new office to show that the office will offer a convenience to the local community and will be to the community's advantage. Often such restrictions reduce competition by preventing new entrants from establishing offices in a market if that market is already served by an existing finance company. Although local market entry can be restricted by antitrust or convenience and advantage regulations, no federal regulations prevent finance companies from operating in many states. Thus, the major finance companies have a nationwide presence. Because of this, in the past many bank holding companies acquired finance companies to gain access to interstate markets.

Consumer Protection Regulations. Since 1968, Congress and various state legislatures have passed a large number of consumer protection bills. Many of the regulations in these bills have had a considerable impact on the costs and operations of consumer finance companies. The most important regulations include Regulation Z (truth-in-lending) and the 1978 revisions in the bankruptcy laws. Regulation Z made finance companies disclose their annual percentage rates rather than "add-on" or "discount" loan rates that understated the true rates charged. Subsequently, finance companies lost some of their market share in the consumer credit markets to banks and credit unions. Nonetheless, even though many consumers acknowledge that finance companies are not the cheapest place to borrow, many still patronize them. Because many finance companies offer fast, convenient, and personal service and grant loans on lenient terms, they attract loyal customers who are not highly sensitive to interest rate differences.

The liberalization of federal consumer bankruptcy laws in October 1979 gave increased protection to consumers who declared bankruptcy. Under the law, consumers who declared bankruptcy could eliminate their debts and still retain many thousands of dollars of their assets. Unsecured creditors, such as finance companies, rarely were able to collect their debts once an insolvent debtor declared bankruptcy under the new law. Consequently, the law substantially increased potential finance company losses.

Because of the liberalization of bankruptcy law, finance companies could not afford to take as many risks as before without raising their loan rates, which they often could not do because of rate ceilings. As a result, many finance companies switched to second-mortgage lending, since larger loans allowed them to increase their returns, net of operating costs, without raising their loan rates. Further, the security provided by second mortgages reduced the finance companies' losses substantially.

DO YOU UNDERSTAND?

1. What types of finance companies exist and what does each do?
2. How do finance companies fund their operations?
3. Why are good credit ratings important to finance companies?
4. What regulations have caused finance companies to de-emphasize their unsecured personal lending?

CHAPTER TAKE-AWAYS

1 Thrift institutions were established to serve the needs of savers who had relatively small deposits.

2 Savings institutions (savings associations and savings banks) are the mortgage-oriented "thrifts" that hold a large portion of their assets in mortgage loans or mortgage-backed securities.

3 After suffering many losses in the 1980s due to excessive interest rate risk, savings associations received new regulators, had to comply with stricter accounting and capital requirements, and reduced their risk taking. As a result, the industry is financially much stronger than it was

in the 1980s, when many institutions were weakened because they took too much interest rate risk or credit risk.

4 Credit unions make consumer loans to their members, each of which must have a savings deposit at the credit union and share a "common bond." All credit unions and many savings institutions are "mutual" institutions that are technically owned by their depositors or members rather than stockholders.

5 Finance companies are highly diverse institutions. They can be consumer finance companies, sales finance companies, factors, or leasing companies.

KEY TERMS

Building societies
Thrift institutions
Finance companies
Mutual institution
Savings and loan associations (SLAs)
Stock association
Federal Home Loan Bank Board (FHLBB)
Office of Thrift Supervision (OTS)
FDIC-SAIF
FDIC-BIF
Federal Home Loan Bank
Advances
Federal Savings and Loan Insurance Corporation (FSLIC)
Resolution Trust Corporation (RTC)
Bad-debt deduction

Other real estate owned (OREO)
Contra-asset
Reverse repos
Common bond requirement
National Credit Union Administration (NCUA)
National Credit Union Share Insurance Fund (NCUSIF)
Central Liquidity Facility (CLF)
Central credit union
Share-draft
U.S. Central Credit Union
Undivided earnings
Credit Union National Association (CUNA)
National Federal Credit Union Association (NAFCU)
Captive sales finance company

Sales finance company
Consumer finance company
Personal loans
Private-label credit
Home equity loan
Real estate–secured lending
Second-mortgage lending
Wholesale paper
Wholesale financing
Floor-plan financing
Factoring
Commercial paper
Transfer credit
Industrial bank
Rate ceilings

QUESTIONS AND PROBLEMS

1. Why were each of the U.S. thrift institutions started, and when? Why are they now greater competitors with commercial banks than they were originally?

2. What were the two major types of problems that caused savings institution failures during the 1980s?

3. How did regulatory weakness contribute to some of the savings institutions' problems?

4. What changes in market interest rates can hurt savings institutions? Why? What can savings institutions do to minimize their problems? Explain the kind of market interest rate changes that might help savings institutions.

5. What are (a) the major regulations and (b) the major regulatory bodies that affect savings institution operations? How do these regulations and regulatory bodies affect them?

6. How have savings institutions altered their deposit and liability structures to reduce their interest rate risk exposure in recent years? Would you say they have totally eliminated their interest rate risk? Why or why not?

7. How do finance companies differ from banks and thrift institutions?

8. Why have finance companies shifted from consumer to real estate and business lending in recent years?

9. Why have second mortgages grown in popularity with finance company consumer lenders?

10. What effect have growing consumer credit regulations had on finance companies' lines of business? What about their future opportunities?

11. How can finance companies manage their interest rate, liquidity, and credit risks? What are their advantages or disadvantages vis-à-vis depository institutions?

12. What are the major asset and liability accounts for credit unions?

13. What are share-drafts? Why are they important to credit unions?

14. What are the advantages and disadvantages of the credit union common bond requirement?

15. Compare and contrast the retail operations of a commercial bank with those of a typical credit union in operation today. Taking into account the expanded powers of credit unions, how will they compare in the future?

16. Individual credit unions are very small in size. If there is going to be increased competition in the consumer credit market and greater regulatory equalization among competing institutions, how do you expect credit unions to survive?

17. What is the U.S. Central Credit Union? Why is it important to the future development of the credit union industry?

INTERNET EXERCISE

The major U.S. regulators compile extensive information on the thrift industry. The FDIC http://www.fdic.gov/ site is the primary source of information, since it collects detailed statistics on all federally insured thrift institutions, while the Treasury Office of Thrift Supervision (OTS), http://www.ots.treas.gov, is the primary regulator for federally chartered savings institutions. The main source of information on finance companies is the Federal Reserve. Every month it publishes information on finance companies in the Federal Reserve *Bulletin* and a G.20 statistical release, which is available through the Fed's Web site on the Internet, http://www.federalreserve.gov. The main source of information on credit unions is the National Credit Union Administration, which is their primary regulator and supervises their insurer. The NCUA Web site can be found at http://www.ncua.gov. It publishes regular NEWS items on current events as well as historical data on credit union balance sheets and income, based on call report data.

1. Go to the FDIC Web site, access its databank (www.fdic.gov/databank/index.html) and find the most recent quarterly data on savings institutions. Find out how many savings institutions were insured by the FDIC in the last reporting period and how many assets they held.

2. Go to the OTS Web site listed above and find the most recent quarterly data for OTS-regulated thrift institutions. Find the average ROA and net interest margin for savings associations in the most recent quarter for which the data was compiled. How did the numbers change over the last year? Why do you think they changed?

3. Go to the Federal Reserve Web site, access its statistical releases, find the latest G.20 release, and find information on the terms of auto loans. Find the latest interest rate, maturity, loan-to-value ratios, and average loan sizes for new- and used-auto loans. Which has the highest loan rate, which has the longest maturity, which has the lowest average balance, and which has the highest loan size? Given what you know, explain why the loan rate is higher on used- than on new-auto loans.

4. Access the NCUA Web site and find the most recent NCUA NEWS or Quick Facts publication that provides information from the latest credit union call reports. How many credit unions are there, and how have their numbers changed in the last year? How many members and assets do they have, and how have their members and assets changed in the last year? If the number of credit unions, members, and assets are not all changing in the same manner (i.e., all increasing or all decreasing by about the same percentage amounts), how do you explain the disparity?

CHAPTER 18

Insurance Companies and Pension Funds

CHAPTER PREVIEW

Insurance has been described as "the product everyone buys, but no one wants to use." In the same vein, insurance contracts are often described as "least-read best sellers." Everybody buys insurance, but few people ever take the time to read their contract unless, of course, a loss occurs.

While insurance is often taken for granted, try to imagine a world without it. The death of the family breadwinner might condemn a family to poverty without life insurance pro-

ceeds to replace the lost income. Want to buy a new car or a home? Then you better have enough cash to pay the full purchase price because there's no property insurance available for the car or home, which usually serves as collateral for the loan. What about the risk of being sued? Are you willing to operate a motor vehicle knowing that if you are negligent and injure or kill someone you don't have liability insurance to protect against a lawsuit?

Insurance is a necessity for individuals, small businesses, and large cor-

porations. The terrorist attacks of September 11, 2001, put insurance in the spotlight. A recent estimate of insured losses arising out of the 9/11 attacks is $40 billion. Many types of insured losses occurred: loss of life, medical expenses and disability payable under private insurance and workers compensation, direct loss of property (buildings, business personal property, and aircraft), indirect loss of profits, general liability, aircraft liability, and others. ■

Insurance companies protect people and companies from the financial consequences of events whose risks are actuarially determinable. For those buying insurance, the financial health of the insurance company is the single most important purchase criterion because an insurance contract is just a promise by the insurance company to pay the insured if a defined event occurs. Examples of such events include the unexpected death of a family member, an automobile accident, or the crash of an airship.

Insurance and retirement plans play an important role in providing economic security. They are also important in the capital formation and financial intermediation process. The purposes of this chapter include: (1) to explain how the insurance mechanism works; (2) to provide an overview of the insurance industry, including the market structure, organizational structures, types of coverages sold, and asset holdings; (3) to discuss the role and importance of insurers as financial intermediaries; (4) to provide an overview of the field of retirement plans, including Social Security and private pensions; and (5) to discuss the role and importance of pension funds as financial intermediaries. ■

 LEARNING **O**BJECTIVES

The objectives of this chapter are to:

1 Explain how the insurance mechanism works, including the concepts of pooling and risk transfer, and the requisites of privately insurable risks.

2 Define objective risk and explain the ways in which insurers can reduce the objective risk of their operations.

3 Discuss the economic structure of the insurance industry, the various forms of organizations that operate in the insurance industry, and how and why the insurance industry is regulated.

4 Describe the major products marketed by life and health insurers.

5 Describe the major products marketed by property and liability insurers.

6 Describe the balance sheet of life and health insurers and property and liability insurers, and explain the differences in their asset holdings.

7 Discuss the pension industry, including the various types of pension plans and the regulation of the industry.

INSURANCE

Individuals and businesses face **risk**, which is uncertainty concerning the occurrence of loss. Risk takes many forms, including the risk of premature death or poor health, the risk of damage to property, the risk of legal liability, and the risk of individuals outliving their accumulated assets. Certain risks can simply be avoided. Other risks, however, must be effectively managed. Methods of dealing with these risks include retention, loss control, and risk transfer.

Use of retention means that the individual or business is responsible for the loss. An uninsured risk and the physical damage deductible on your automobile collision insurance are examples of retention. Loss control includes any effort to reduce the frequency and severity of loss. Loss control can take many forms. Some examples include seat belts, sprinkler systems, smoke detectors, nonflammable building materials and fabrics, and ergonomically designed workstations. Finally, risk may be transferred to another party through a contract. The most widely used form of contractual risk transfer is insurance.

THE INSURANCE MECHANISM

Insurance is the transfer of a pure risk to an entity that pools the risk of loss and provides payment if a loss occurs. **Risk transfer** means shifting the responsibility of bearing the risk from one party to another party. **Pooling** means that losses suffered by a small number of insured are spread over the entire group so insurance purchasers substitute the average loss (a small amount) in place of the uncertainty that they might suffer a large loss. **Pure risks** are situations in which two outcomes are possible, loss or no loss. Examples of pure risk include the risk of poor health, the risk of premature death, the risk of legal liability, and the risk of damage to property. **Speculative risks** provide three possible outcomes; loss, no loss, or gain. The "entity" that pools the risk and provides indemnification is usually a private insurance company; however, for some risks, government involvement is necessary to insure the risks.

Insurance benefits society in several important ways. First, it reduces fear and worry because if a loss occurs, the insurer provides a payment to mitigate the loss. Insurance also provides an incentive for loss control because insurance premiums are determined by the chance of loss, and loss control reduces the chance of loss. Insurance helps to facilitate credit by protecting collateral pledged to secure loans. This benefit is especially important in commerce because it helps to facilitate the shipment of raw materials and finished goods. Finally, the insurance industry plays an important role in capital formation. Insurance companies collect small amounts of money from many insurance purchasers. They pool these funds and then make large blocks of funds available in the capital markets.

INSURERS AND OBJECTIVE RISK

If individuals and businesses are unable to bear individual pure risk exposures and transfer them away, how can insurance companies bear the risk of hundreds or thousands of pure risk exposures? The risk that an insurer faces once it has accepted the transfer of risk from insurance purchasers is called objective risk. **Objective risk** is the deviation between actual losses and expected losses. Insurance is priced to cover the cost of expected losses and expenses. If loss levels are as predicted, the insurance mechanism works well. If loss levels are greater than expected, the insurer will lose money. If catastrophic losses occur, the solvency of the insurer may be threatened.

METHODS OF REDUCING OBJECTIVE RISK

Insurance companies use an important mathematical principle, the law of large numbers, to reduce the objective risk of their operations. The **law of large numbers** states that as the number of insured risks increases, the deviation between actual and expected results will decline. A simple coin-flipping example will demonstrate this mathematical principle. If you flip a fair coin twice, you might get two "heads" or two "tails." However, if you continue flipping the coin, the result will grow closer to 50 percent "heads" and 50 percent "tails" as the number of repetitions increases. While an insurance company's underwriting risk increases as more units are insured (there are more potential claims to pay), objective risk declines as the sample size increases.

A second way in which insurance companies reduce objective risk is through careful underwriting. **Underwriting** is the selection and classification of insurable risks. While insurance agents and brokers solicit applications and coverages for prospective insureds, there is no guarantee that the insurer will agree to insure the risk. Insurance underwriters review applications and decide which applicants are acceptable. Underwriters also assign acceptable risks to underwriting classes. For example, an auto insurer may have three categories: superior, average, and substandard. Based upon underwriting information, the applicant may be assigned to one of these categories or the application may be rejected.

Another way of reducing objective risk is to make the insured pay a portion of any loss that occurs. Insurers use a variety of approaches to make the insured participate in the loss. The most common loss-sharing provision is a deductible. **Deductibles** make the insured responsible for the first portion of any loss that

IN PRACTICE

Credit History and Personal Lines Underwriting

Proper use of credit will help you avoid paying late fees and a high rate of interest on the outstanding balance. It might also help you save money on auto insurance and homeowner's insurance as well.

Insurers operate in a competitive environment and are always searching for valid predictors of the cost of future claims. Some rating factors are obvious. In auto insurance, for example, more expensive vehicles cost more to repair. Living in an urban area increases the likelihood of being involved in an accident, as does driving the vehicle more miles annually. An individual's motor vehicle record (charged accidents and traffic violations) is also an obvious predictor of future loss experience.

Many insurers have added a controversial rating factor to their underwriting criteria: an applicant's credit history. The theory is that individuals who better manage their credit (e.g., consistently make payments on time, avoid late fees, etc.) will better manage other aspect of their life, such as operation of a motor vehicle. The relationship is not only theoretical, according to insurers. They claim that studies have shown that individuals who have better credit records file fewer and less costly claims, on average.

Credit organizations, such as ChoicePoint and Fair Isaac, calculate "insurance scores" for insurance applicants. An insurance score is a credit-based score that the credit organization believes is a good predictor of future loss experience.

But is the correlation between credit history and future loss experience enough to justify charging specific applicants more or less for their insurance? Use of credit history as a rating factor is controversial. Proponents argue that rating factors that best predict loss experience should be utilized and that the high degree of correlation between a good credit history and fewer claims filed should not be ignored. Critics argue that using credit history as a rating factor unfairly discriminates against certain groups of individuals (e.g., lower-income applicants and individuals who do not use credit). They further argue that credit reports often contain errors and that general correlation does not imply specific cause-and-effect relationships.

As insurance is regulated primarily at the state level, insurance companies' use of credit history as an underwriting factor varies by state. Many states have enacted legislation limiting the extent to which insurers can use credit history as an underwriting factor.

It's estimated that the terrorist attacks of September 11, 2001, created insured losses exceeding $40 billion. These losses, the largest insured losses attributable to a single event, occurred in many lines of insurance. Insurers that wrote life insurance, health insurance, workers' compensation insurance, disability insurance, building and personal property coverage, aircraft insurance (hull and liability), business interruption insurance, and other lines were called upon to pay the claims.

Through reinsurance, many of the primary insurers that originally insured the 9/11-related loss exposures passed the risk on to reinsurers. It's estimated that Lloyd's of London, Munich Re, Swiss Re, and Berkshire-Hathaway had the greatest liability for 9/11 claims.

Omaha-based Berkshire-Hathaway is headed by billionaire CEO Warren Buffett. Buffett is one the wealthiest people in the world, and Berkshire-Hathaway is an interesting company. Its largest insurance subsidiaries, GEICO and General Re, are household names. In addition, the company owns jewelry and furniture retailers, carpet and apparel manufacturers, an energy company, Dairy Queen, a home builder, newspapers, and several other businesses. The company also makes large investments in the common stock of other companies. For example, at year-end 2003, the company had a $10.98 billion position in Wells Fargo and a $10.15 billion position in Coca-Cola.

If you'd like to invest in Berkshire-Hathaway common stock, you better have a large bankroll! You see, Buffett does not believe in stock splits. At the time of writing, Berkshire-Hathaway Class A shares were selling for about $88,000 per share! If that's too much for you, consider a Class B share, which sells for about one-thirtieth of the price of a Class A share.

---

occurs and are used in property insurance, health insurance, and disability income insurance. Another loss-sharing provision is called **coinsurance**. In the case of health insurance, coinsurance is simple loss sharing after the deductible has been satisfied. In the case of property insurance, if the insured does not carry adequate insurance, coinsurance requires the insured to pay a portion of the loss. Insurance policy exclusions and limits on certain types of losses also make the insured bear some or all of the loss.

A final way in which insurers reduce objective risk is through the use of **reinsurance**. Just as individuals and businesses purchase insurance, insurers can also shift some of the risk that they have insured to another insurance company. This process, called reinsurance, is crucial for some insurers and in certain lines of insurance where objective risk is greater. Reinsurance can be arranged in several ways. For example, an insurer and a reinsurer may share premiums and losses based on a predetermined percentage basis, such as 50–50 or 25–75. Alternatively, the original insurer may place a limit on losses and the reinsurer is only required to pay losses that exceed that limit. While the primary insurer is ultimately responsible for losses, reinsurance recoveries help to mitigate the fear of greater-than-expected losses. Reinsurers were crucial in paying for losses from the 9/11 terrorist attacks.

REQUIREMENTS OF PRIVATELY INSURABLE RISKS

Certain conditions must be present before a private company can insure a risk. First, there must be a large number of similar exposure units. This requirement is necessary so that similar exposures can be placed in the same underwriting category and losses can be predicted based on the law of large numbers. Second, losses that occur should be accidental and unintentional. As the law of large numbers assumes random events, this condition is important. Third, the losses must not be catastrophic. Fourth, losses should be determinable and measurable. Fifth, the chance of loss must be calculable. Finally, the premium for insurance must be affordable.

A review of insurer practices and contractual provisions demonstrates how these requirements are satisfied. Insurers use underwriting categories to group similar risks. For example, one underwriting category might be wood-frame dwellings, while another may be masonry homes. The underwriting category for an auto insurer may be female drivers age 30–40, while a life insurer may group all standard male applicants age 25 in one underwriting class. Heterogeneous loss exposures must seek specialty insurers. For example, a famous racehorse or a professional quarterback's arm may be insured through Lloyd's of London.

Losses that are intentionally caused and perils where the intent is to destroy property (e.g., war) are usually excluded from coverage under insurance contracts. To help assure that only fortuitous losses are covered, insurers often require the insured to bear a portion of any loss through a deductible or other loss-sharing provision. Catastrophic losses are also usually excluded. Floods and earthquakes could simultaneously impact thousands of insureds. Compounding the problem is the fact that only insureds susceptible to these risks (e.g., insureds who live in floodplains or near fault lines) will purchase the insurance. Insureds are often required to pay additional premiums and assume responsibility for more of the loss to obtain coverage for earthquakes. The federal government assists in making flood insurance available to the general public.

To make sure a covered loss has occurred, insurers employ workers called adjusters. It is the adjuster's job to verify that an insured loss has occurred and to try to set a value upon the amount of the loss. Credible data are necessary to determine insurance premiums, and unless the premiums are affordable, no one will purchase insurance.

PRICING INSURANCE

The goal of the insurer when developing an insurance rate is to charge enough to cover claims and administrative expenses and still make a profit. Insurers participate in competitive markets, so the rate must be competitive with other insurers and satisfy any rate regulation. Ordinarily, the states do not regulate life insurance rates, but automobile insurance and workers' compensation rates are often regulated. Health insurance rates often must be "filed" with the department of insurance and approved by the state insurance commissioner. Insurance regulators require that rates be adequate to pay losses, with the goal of insurer solvency in mind. The insurance code also requires that rates not be "unfairly discriminatory."

Actuaries who work for insurance companies and rating bureaus that provide rates to insurance companies develop statistics used in rate making. For life and health insurance, for example, to determine the probable number of people in a group who will die or become disabled at any age, statistics on large numbers of people are collected and developed into mortality and morbidity tables. For property and liability insurance, past losses, premiums, and expense statistics are furnished to rating bureaus, and the bureau furnishes advisory rates based on the statistics. When pricing insurance, actuaries take into consideration investment income that will be earned on premium dollars received. Thus if interest rates are expected to be high and investment income is expected to be large, a lower rate will be charged. If interest rates are expected to decline and investment income is expected to be less, rates charged will be higher.

INTEREST RATE RISK AND INSURANCE COMPANIES

Interest rates are an important consideration in insurance pricing, especially in commercial property and liability insurance. For many years, a cyclical pattern, called the **underwriting cycle**, has been observed in commercial property and liability insurance. Property and liability insurance markets fluctuate between periods of high premiums and tight underwriting standards (called a "hard" insurance market) and periods of low premiums and loose underwriting standards (called a "soft" insurance market). Interest rates and return on invested assets help determine the state of the insurance market.

During the early 1980s, many insurers expected interest rates to continue rising as sharply as they had in the late 1970s, and the companies charged much lower premiums than they should have for certain lines of insurance, especially commercial liability insurance. In addition, because interest rates were high, it was attractive to the companies to take in as many premium dollars as possible for investment purposes. Insurers wrote some exposures that were not good risks from an underwriting standpoint. These companies were engaging in **cash-flow underwriting**, in other words, writing insurance on just about any risk in order to get the premium dollars to invest at high interest rates.

The commercial property and liability insurance markets were "soft" throughout most of the 1990s. Insurers could charge lower premiums and rely on investment income, especially returns on the equity portion of the portfolio, to offset underwriting losses. The market was hardening in the late 1990s due to low rates of return on newly invested funds and adverse equity returns. The terrorist attacks on September 11, 2001, accelerated the hardening of the market because the surplus of the industry was used to pay the large, unanticipated losses. While reinsurers paid most of these losses, the reinsurers increased the price of reinsurance to primary companies. The primary companies, in turn, passed along these rate increases to insurance purchasers.

Life insurance contracts are long term in nature, and the assets backing these products are also long term. Insurers protect themselves from interest rate risk through the large spread between the rate of return earned on invested assets and the guaranteed rate of interest credited to the cash value. It is when insurers assume that high interest rates will continue and guarantee high interest rates for long periods that they can get into trouble. Executive Life Insurance Company of California and Baldwin United are two examples of insolvencies that occurred because of interest rate guarantees that could not be met by the insurer.

THE INSURANCE INDUSTRY

MARKET STRUCTURE OF THE INSURANCE INDUSTRY

The insurance industry approximates a model of pure competition. There are a large number of buyers and sellers, individual buyers and sellers cannot exert pricing pressure, the commodity bought and sold is rather homogeneous, and the barriers to entry are not severe. The first two of these points are self-explanatory, but the latter two points deserve additional explanation. While it is true that there are many different types of insurance products available, there are great similarities between the contracts used to insure specific risks. States, for example, have adopted sets of mandatory provisions that must appear in each life insurance contract. While insurers are free to develop their own forms, many companies simply use forms developed by organizations such as the Insurance Services Office (ISO). With regard to barriers to entry, it is important to remember that the insurance industry is based on financial capital (money) rather than physical capital (e.g., bricks and mortar). While it might take General Motors 2 years to build a $100 million production facility, $100 million in new capital may be added to the insurance industry overnight.

ORGANIZATIONAL FORMS

It's difficult to name an industry in which there are more types of business organizations. Insurers may be organized as stock companies, mutual companies, reciprocals, and Lloyd's associations.

Stock Companies.   A **stock insurance company** is a corporation owned by its shareholders. This form of organization is the most popular one used in the insurance industry in the United States. The oldest U.S. stock insurer is the Insurance Company of North America (INA), which began operations in Philadelphia in 1792. The objective of a stock insurer is to maximize the value of the firm, which will produce positive returns for stockholders. The shareholders elect a board, and the board appoints a management team. Note that at stock companies the owners and customers (policyowners) are separate groups of claim holders.

The types of insurance that a stock insurer may sell depend on the company's charter. A stock insurer must meet minimum capital and surplus requirements of the state in which it is domiciled. Stock insurers dominate in the property and liability insurance industry, especially in the commercial lines market. Some stock companies write only nonparticipating, or "nonpar," policies, while others issue "par" and "nonpar" policies. **Participating policies** are those that pay dividends to policyowners. Dividends to policyowners are not guaranteed and depend on the profitability of the insurer.

Mutual Companies.   A **mutual insurance company** is an insurer that is owned by its policyowners—there are no stockholders. The owner and customer functions are merged into a single group of claim holders. The objective of this type of organization is to minimize the cost of insurance to the policyowners. The oldest mutual insurer in the United States is The Philadelphia Contributionship for the Insurance of Houses from Loss by Fire, which began in 1752 and continues to operate to this day.

Mutual insurers issue participating policies and pay policyowners' dividends if their operations are profitable. The ability to pay dividends is determined by a mutual insurer's loss expense, expenses, and investment returns. Unlike dividends paid to stockholders, policyowner dividends are not considered taxable income. Under the Internal Revenue Code, policyowner dividends are considered a refund of overcharged premiums. While there are many large mutual companies marketing property and liability insurance, mutual insurers account for a disproportionately large (compared to the number and percentage of all organizations) amount of life and health insurance in force.

Several large mutual life insurance companies have "gone public" in recent years, converting to stock organizations through a process called **demutualization**. The primary motivation for these companies is better access to capital. The stock form of organization permits insurers to offer additional shares of stock if capital is needed. John Hancock, Metropolitan, and Prudential are among insurers that have demutualized in the last decade.

Reciprocals. Another type of insurance organization is a **reciprocal or reciprocal exchange**. These organizations operate like unincorporated mutuals, and their objective is to minimize the cost of the insurance. Each member of a reciprocal insures the other members and in return is insured by the other members. Reciprocals are managed by an attorney-in-fact, which is usually a corporation authorized to collect premiums, pay losses, invent premiums, and arrange reinsurance. Most of the remaining pure reciprocals now operating are found in the automobile insurance market. Farmers Insurance Exchange is the largest reciprocal. Most reciprocal business is now written by interinsurance associations, which are more like mutuals than the pure reciprocals. Separate accounts are not kept for each member, and insureds do not have a claim to any portion of surplus funds. Also, expenses and losses are not prorated among insureds. USAA is an example of an interinsurance association.

Lloyd's Associations. **Lloyd's associations** are organizations that do not directly write insurance, but instead provide a marketplace and services to members of an association who write insurance as individuals. In this respect, Lloyd's is similar to the New York Stock Exchange, which does not buy or sell securities but provides a trading floor and services to stock traders.

The most famous Lloyd's association is **Lloyd's of London**, where the members (called "names") have unlimited liability for the risks they underwrite. In England, unlimited liability means one stands to lose everything but "his bed linens and the tools of his trade." Groups of names are organized into "syndicates," and what insurance the syndicate writes and how much premium is charged are determined by the syndicate's underwriters. While Lloyd's of London is well known for writing high-profile risks (e.g., a star quarterback's arm, a diva's voice), the organization is an important player in international insurance and reinsurance markets, insuring space ventures, oil tankers, and many other risks.

Lloyd's of London is admitted to do business as a primary insurer in the United States only in Kentucky and Illinois. Lloyd's was admitted first in Kentucky because of its long association with the Thoroughbred horse industry. Illinois is the "backup" state for Lloyd's, in case for some reason the organization is no longer permitted to write business in Kentucky. In other states, Lloyd's may be used only when a particular coverage is not available from any insurer admitted in the state. In those states, Lloyd's is a surplus lines insurer.

Because it experienced underwriting losses beginning in the mid-1980s, Lloyd's of London instituted a "corporate membership" in 1994. This membership allows for limited liability, has attracted capital, and has changed the makeup of the underwriters and syndicates at Lloyd's of London.

Private underwriters in the United States have formed associations similar to Lloyd's of London over the years. However, several American Lloyd's associations have failed, and some states, including New York, forbid the formation of new American Lloyd's associations.

THE SIZE AND NUMBER OF INSURANCE COMPANIES

At the end of 2002 there were 1,171 life and health insurers operating in the United States. Most life and health insurers are organized as stock companies. Approximately 1,076 of the 1,171 life and health insurance companies were stock companies and 83 were mutuals. Even though the relative number of mutuals is small, they account for 12.9 percent of the total assets of American life and health insurers and 10.9 percent of all life insurance in force. Exhibit 18.1 shows the 10 largest life and health insurance companies in 2002, ranked by total assets.

In 2001, about 3,163 property and casualty insurers were doing business in the United States. The bulk of these organizations were stock companies, although there were some large mutuals (e.g., State Farm Insurance, Nationwide, and Liberty Mutual). Although the number of firms is large, many companies specialize in such areas as personal lines, commercial property or liability coverages, professional liability, aviation, or transportation insurance. Exhibit 18.2 shows the 10 largest property and liability insurers in the United States in 2002, ranked by total assets.

REGULATION OF THE INSURANCE INDUSTRY

Insurance companies are regulated by the states in which they do business. Legislation enacted in 1945, the **McCarran-Ferguson Act (Public Law 15)**, stated that the continued regulation of insurers at the state level was in the best interest of the public and that federal law applies only to the extent that state law does not apply. The debate over whether insurance should be regulated at the state or federal level continues to this day.

Insurance is regulated for several reasons. Regulation is designed to help assure the solvency of insurers, to protect consumers who may have inadequate knowledge of insurance, to make sure that rates charged are reasonable, and to help make sure that needed insurance coverages are available.

The three main sources of insurance regulation are legislation, court decisions, and state insurance departments. State legislatures pass laws that regulate the operations of insurers. Such laws address a number of factors, including surplus and capital requirements, licensing of agents, taxation of insurers, insurance rate regulations, and sales and claims practices. In addition to rules passed by state legislatures, insurers are also subject to regulation by certain federal agencies and are required to follow certain federal acts. For example, the Civil Rights Act bars discrimination on the basis of race, religion, or national origin. Insurers that market products with an investment element (e.g., variable life insurance and variable annuities) are subject to rules of the Securities and Exchange Commission. Insurers must follow the guidelines for private pensions detailed in the Employee Retirement Income Security Act of 1974 (ERISA) and subsequent acts.

EXHIBIT 18.1
10 Largest Life/Health Insurance Companies, 2002

Company	Assets ($ in Billions)
1. Metropolitan Life Insurance Company New York, New York	200.5
2. Prudential Insurance Co. of America Newark, New Jersey	186.6
3. Teachers Insurance and Annuity Association New York, New York	142.2
4. Northwestern Mutual Life Insurance Company Milwaukee, Wisconsin	102.9
5. Hartford Life Insurance Company Hartford, Connecticut	87.1
6. New York Life Insurance Company New York, New York	82.0
7. Equitable Life Assurance Society of the U.S. New York, New York	78.3
8. Principal Life Insurance Company Des Moines, Iowa	78.0
9. Massachusetts Mutual Life Insurance Company Springfield, Massachusetts	74.8
10. Nationwide Life Insurance Company Columbus, Ohio	73.7

Metropolitan Life is the largest life/health insurance company in the United States. Most life/health insurance companies are stock companies.

Source: Best's Key Ratings Guide, Life/Health, 2003, p. A64.

The second method of regulating the industry is through the courts. When a court decision is rendered in a case relating to insurance, a legal precedent is established that can be cited and relied upon in future litigation. If the court decision is adverse to the interests of insurers, exclusions are added when new policies are issued and when contracts are renewed. A 1980s court decision illustrates this point. In this case, two perils jointly brought about a loss. One peril was excluded and the other peril was not excluded. The insurer denied the claim and the policyowner filed suit. When the court ruled that in such cases losses are covered, insurers added an exclusion designed to address this issue.

All states have an agency charged with the regulation of insurance. The first state to establish a separate insurance department was New Hampshire in 1841. This state regulatory agency is headed by the insurance commissioner, who is either appointed by the governor or elected. Insurance commissioners have considerable power. They can issue, revoke, or deny licenses; hold hearings; and place insurers in rehabilitation or liquidation.

EXHIBIT 18.2
10 Largest Property/Casualty Insurance Companies, 2002

Company	Assets ($ in Billions)
1. State Farm Group, Bloomington, Illinois	84.3
2. Berkshire Hathaway Insurance Group, Omaha, Nebraska	78.8
3. American International Group, Inc., New York, New York	59.7
4. Travelers Property Casualty Group[a], Hartford, Connecticut	43.4
5. Allstate Insurance Group, Northbrook, Illinois	40.9
6. Zurich/Farmers Group, Los Angeles, California	33.7
7. Liberty Mutual Insurance Companies, Boston, Massachusetts	31.8
8. CNA Insurance Companies, Chicago, Illinois	30.9
9. Nationwide Group, Columbus, Ohio	26.8
10. Hartford Insurance Group, Hartford, Connecticut	25.8

State Farm is the largest property/liability insurance company in the United States. In recent years, property/liability companies have suffered large underwriting losses.

[a] In 2004, Travelers Property Casualty Group merged with St. Paul Insurance, the eleventh-largest property/casualty company in 2002. The merged company, St. Paul Travelers, is now the third-largest property/casualty insurer.

Source: Best's Key Ratings Guide, Property/Casualty, p. A102.

State insurance commissioners are members of the **National Association of Insurance Commissioners (NAIC)**. This organization was founded in 1871 to help set uniform regulatory standards among the states. The NAIC is not a statutory body but an organization of insurance commissioners who meet regularly to discuss regulatory issues and to prepare model legislation for recommendation to their state legislatures. The commissioners have developed systems for cooperative company audits, simultaneous investigations of interstate problems, and information exchanges that increase efficiency in the regulatory process. By virtue of its high degree of cooperation, the NAIC has overcome much of the burden of conflicting regulation in the different states.

Several important aspects of insurance companies and insurance operations are regulated. After formation, an insurer must be licensed before it can do business in a state. Insurers must meet minimum capital and surplus requirements to obtain a license if they are stock insurers and minimum surplus requirements if they are mutuals.

Every year, insurers must file a series of financial statements called a "Convention Blank" with the commissioner's office in every state in which they operate. An insurer must have sufficient assets to offset its liabilities. Reserves must be shown on the balance sheet, and states regulate the methods that may be used to calculate the reserves. The surplus position of each company is also regulated. Policyholders' surplus is the difference between the insurer's assets and liabilities. This surplus is especially important in property and liability insurance. The amount of new business an insurer is allowed to write is limited by its policyholders' surplus. For example, a conservative rule is that an insurer can write only $2 of net new premiums for each $1 of policyholders' surplus. Also, surplus is necessary to offset any underwriting or investment losses or deficiencies in loss reserves over time.

States regulate the types and quality of investments that insurers make and also establish the maximum percentage of total assets that can be invested in certain instruments. Life insurers, for example, are limited in the percentage of total assets that can be invested in common stocks. In New York, for example, common stock investments are limited to 10 percent of total assets or 100 percent of surplus, whichever is lower. Property and liability insurers are subject to fewer investment restrictions.

Also regulated are expenses of insurers: commission rates that can be paid to agents, bonuses, acquisition fees, and so forth. The New York Insurance Code is particularly limiting. For example, a life insurer licensed to do business in New York may pay no more than a 55 percent first-year commission rate to its agents.

Liquidation of insurers is also regulated, and if a company becomes technically insolvent, the state insurance commissioner assumes control of the company with the intent of rehabilitating it. If it cannot be saved, it is liquidated according to the code. All states have "guaranty funds" that pay the claims of insolvent property and liability insurers. Some states have guaranty funds for insolvent life and health insurers. Often the commissioner can find another insurer to buy a troubled company to avoid liquidation.

Rates, policy forms, sales practices, and claims practices are also regulated in varying degrees among the states. In some states rates must be filed and approved before the insurer can use them; in others they must just be filed. The commissioner must also approve some policy forms before they can be used. All states regulate the licensing of agents and brokers, requiring the agent to pass a license exam before selling insurance. All states have a complaint division to handle consumer complaints about unfair treatment by insurers.

GLOBALIZATION OF INSURANCE

There is a continuing trend toward globalization in insurance company operations. U.S.-based insurance companies often enter foreign markets. For example, Georgia-based AFLAC earns the majority of its revenues by selling insurance in Japan, and a New England–based insurer writes disability coverage in England. Foreign insurers may also enter the U.S. market, as evidenced by Sun Life Insurance Company of Canada marketing coverages in the United States. Foreign ownership of U.S. insurance companies is not uncommon, and mergers and acquisitions often occur across borders. In 2003, for example, Toronto-based Manulife acquired Boston-based John Hancock, creating the second-largest insurance company in North America by market capitalization. Reinsurance markets are truly global in nature. Indeed, three of the reinsurers with the greatest liability for claims arising out of the 9/11 terrorist attacks were from Europe (Lloyd's of London, Munich Re, and Swiss Re).

One other international aspect of insurance deserves mention. Most of the Fortune 500 companies have formed a subsidiary called a **captive insurance company**. Captive insurers are formed for the purpose of insuring the parent company's loss exposures and provide direct access to the reinsurance market.

Captive insurers are often domiciled offshore to avoid domestic surplus and capital requirements and other regulations. The Bahamas and Cayman Islands in the Caribbean are popular domiciles for captive insurers.

SECURITIZATION OF RISK

A recent development likely to have an increasing impact on the insurance industry is the securitization of risk. **Securitization of risk** means that insurable risk is transferred to the capital markets through the creation of a financial instrument, such as a catastrophe bond, futures contract, or options contract. Securitization of risk increases the capacity of the industry. Rather than simply relying on insurers and reinsurers to bear risk, securitization opens the door for other capital market participants to share risk.

Securitization is especially important in addressing potentially catastrophic losses (earthquakes, hurricanes, etc.). An example will demonstrate how securitization works. Assume that a property insurer has concentrated its underwriting efforts in an area where hurricanes are likely to occur. The insurer is concerned about the financial impact of a large hurricane. The insurer could issue catastrophe bonds, borrowing money from a group of investors. The promise to repay principal and interest, however, may be contingent upon catastrophic hurricane losses not occurring. If hurricane losses exceed a specified amount, some or all of the principal and interest payments would be waived, and the insurer could use the funds saved by not having to repay the bondholders to pay the catastrophic losses. USAA Insurance Company issued catastrophe bonds through a subsidiary in 1997 to protect the company from catastrophic hurricane losses.

DO YOU UNDERSTAND?

1. Define insurance. What are the requirements for privately insurable risks?
2. What is meant by the term "objective risk" and why is it so important to insurers?
3. What are the various types of insurance organizations?
4. What are the sources of regulation for the insurance industry and what areas are regulated?
5. How does securitization of risk increase insurance industry capacity?

LIFE AND HEALTH INSURANCE

Life and health insurers offer a wide variety of financial services products, including life insurance, health insurance, annuities, IRAs, mutual funds, and money market accounts. A few traditional products, however, account for a substantial portion of life insurer revenues. These products are life insurance, health insurance, and annuities. These products are designed to protect against the economic risk of premature death, poor health, and living "too long."

The primary purpose of life insurance is to provide financial support to dependents in the case of premature death. While all deaths may seem premature, from an economic standpoint, **premature death** means loss of life while others are financially dependent on you. Life insurance proceeds replace the lost income and cover expenses that may coincide with death (e.g., uninsured medical bills, the cost of funeral, estate/probate costs).

TERM INSURANCE

Term insurance is pure life insurance for a specified period of time, less than all of life. If the insured dies while the policy is in force, the insurer pays the face value of the policy to the beneficiary. If the insured survives the coverage period, the policy expires and there are no further benefit rights. Term insurance is the purest form of life insurance as it provides death protection only and does not develop a savings reserve or "cash value." The premiums for term insurance track the probability of death, so they are low at younger ages but increase, at an increasing rate, as the insured grows older.

Term insurance policies may be classified broadly by the duration of coverage, whether the face value varies, and expiration protection. Straight term insurance is written for a certain time period and then terminates. Popular policy durations are 1-year, 5-year, and 10-year terms. Most term insurance polices have a face value that remains constant during the duration of the coverage. Decreasing term has a face amount that decreases yearly or monthly while the premium stays level. This type of term insurance is often used to cover the outstanding mortgage if the insured dies. Some insurers market increasing term, which provides coverage that increases monthly or yearly. This type of coverage may be used to maintain the purchasing power of the death benefit for the beneficiary. Two provisions are often included in term insurance policies to address the problem of continuing life insurance after the period of coverage expires. They are the renewability and convertibility provisions.

Renewable term insurance policies may be placed back in force again at the end of the coverage period. The insured does not have to provide evidence that he or she is still insurable. The premium increases at the time the policy is renewed, reflecting the increase in mortality risk to the insurer. The number of renewals permitted is usually limited so that the coverage cannot be renewed beyond a specified age, such as 65 or 70. This limitation is designed to protect against adverse selection. **Adverse selection** occurs when those most likely to suffer a loss seek to purchase insurance. Because term insurance premiums increase with the insured's age, by the time the insured reaches age 65 or 70, premiums may have become prohibitively expensive. For that reason, many policyowners who are in bad health or who believe they will not live long will keep their policies in force. Limiting the number of renewals reduces the risk of adverse claims experience for the insurer.

Convertible term insurance permits the term coverage to be switched to whole life insurance without providing evidence of insurability. Conversion must be done within some given time period, such as the first 5 years. This is an attractive provision, since often those who purchase term insurance do so because of the low cost at younger ages. As the insured ages, his or her income may increase and the need for permanent life insurance may develop.

WHOLE LIFE INSURANCE

Some individuals would like to have permanent life insurance protection. **Whole life insurance** provides coverage for all of life, up to and in some cases beyond age 100. Several premium payment plans are available. Under the most popular, continuous premium whole life, a premium is paid each year for the duration of the coverage. Some policyowners would prefer to limit premiums to a specified period, such as 20 years or until they reach age 65. These limited-payment options permit policyowners to pay the entire cost of the coverage earlier, while enjoying the protection until they die.

How can an insurer offer coverage for all of life under a level-premium policy? Simply put, policyowners "overpay" the cost of mortality in early years and "underpay" in later years. Life insurance actuaries first calculate the net single premium for the coverage (the present value of the death benefit payable) and then level the premium by amortizing it over the premium payment period. Leveling the premium makes the policy affordable. As the policyowner overpays the cost of mortality in early years, a saving reserve called the **cash value** develops.

Insurers pay interest on the cash value. The cash value also increases because of a survivorship benefit that is added each year. When members of the insured's "pool" of insureds die, their cash values are divided among the insureds who are still surviving. Every year, a mortality charge is deducted from the cash value to pay the claims of those insureds who died. Then the cash value in the policies of deceased insureds is distributed to those who are still alive, along with interest income. The sum of interest income and the survivorship benefit is greater than the mortality charge, so the savings element increases each year. Interestingly, the interest accumulated on the cash values is not taxed as income unless the cash value is taken out of the policy. This tax benefit, along with the idea of "forced savings," makes whole life insurance attractive to consumers. The cash value serves as a sort of savings account for the policyowner. He or she may borrow the cash value at reasonable interest rates (traditionally around 5 to 8 percent), or the insured may surrender the policy and receive the entire cash value.

Often people purchase whole life insurance with the idea that if they survive until retirement age, they can use the accumulated cash value to purchase a retirement annuity. In these situations, life insurance protects against the peril of premature death during the income-earning years and against the risk of **superannuation** (that is, living too long) after retirement.

Whole life insurance has historically been a popular form of life insurance. Whole life premiums are a large source of funds for life insurers because of the long-term nature of the product and the cash values that accumulate. As with banks, life insurance companies can make money on the difference between the guaranteed fixed rate of return paid on whole life insurance and the rate of return the insurer can earn by investing the funds. While whole life insurance does not provide a high rate of interest, the cash value accumulates tax free and is guaranteed by the insurer.

UNIVERSAL LIFE INSURANCE

In the late 1970s and early 1980s, short-term interest rates were quite high. Many life insurance policyowners looked at the low rate of return they were earning on their whole life policies and compared it to the rate of return on CDs, money market mutual funds, and other money market alternatives. Many policyowners questioned why they should accept a 5 percent rate of return on their whole life insurance cash value when they could earn a 15 percent return in the money market. Many policyowners either surrendered their cash value policies or borrowed the cash value and invested in money market alternatives. This flow of funds away from the life insurance industry, financial disintermediation, led to the introduction and success of a number of products touted as "interest-sensitive" life insurance.

Universal life insurance was the most successful interest-sensitive product during the 1980s. **Universal life insurance** is flexible-premium, nonparticipating life insurance that provides a market-based rate of return on the savings or cash value account. Policyowners pay premiums at their discretion, and each month the insurer deducts a mortality charge from the cash value and adds an interest credit. A minimum interest rate is guaranteed, but the rate credited is pegged to some observable market interest rate. Thus the interest rate paid by the insurer fluctuates with changing interest rates. As with traditional life insurance, interest credited to the cash value is not currently taxable provided the policy satisfies IRS requirements to qualify as life insurance.

Universal life insurance offers lifetime protection, competitive interest rates, and deferred taxation. The product was so successful that by 1984, universal life accounted for 32 percent of the life insurance sold. When interest rates began to fall, the product became less attractive. By 1990, universal life accounted for 20 percent of all life insurance sold, and by 1997, new universal life sales accounted for only 10.5 percent of sales.

Some insurers that marketed universal life insurance became the targets of Policyowner litigation. As only a minimum interest rate was guaranteed and the actual rate paid was determined by market rates, life insurance agents could illustrate universal life policies using alternative interest rate assumptions. Agents wishing to make sales often did not illustrate the impact that low interest rates would have on the cash value element, instead illustrating unreasonably high interest rates. Some policyowners sued life insurers, alleging that the policies failed to perform as illustrated when interest rates declined.

VARIABLE LIFE INSURANCE

The low interest rates of the 1990s helped to fuel the bull market. Facing declining universal life sales and superior equity returns, some insurers began offering another form of interest-sensitive life insurance called variable life insurance. **Variable life insurance** is fixed-premium life insurance that permits the policyowner to select where the cash value is invested. Variable life insurance guarantees a minimum death benefit, but the death benefit can be higher if investment returns are favorable. Insurers offering variable life insurance offer a number of mutual fund alternatives for the cash value. Under this type of life insurance, there are no cash value guarantees. Some insurers offer variable–universal life or universal–variable life, which offers all the characteristics of variable life along with the premium payment flexibility of universal life.

ANNUITIES

Annuities are products sold by life insurers that can be thought of as the opposite of life insurance. Life insurance creates an immediate estate and protects against the economic consequences of premature death. Life annuities are a means of systematically liquidating an accumulated estate and protecting the annuitant against the economic consequences of living too long. Annuities are nice companion products for life insurance insurers. Both products, life insurance and annuities, address personal risks, there are great similarities in premium calculations (e.g., one minus the probability of death equals the probability of survival), and life annuities are sometimes used as a means of paying the death benefit to the beneficiary after the insured has died.

A life annuity purchaser pays the insurer a sum of money for the annuity. In return, the insurer promises to make periodic payments to the annuitant until he or she dies. The annuity income the insurer pays is made up of three components: return of the annuity purchaser's money, interest income, and a survivorship benefit (from those in the pool who die during the year). Each year, the interest income becomes a smaller portion of the annuity payment and the survivorship benefit and liquidation proportion increase while the total payment to the annuitant is level. As annuities are purchased with after-tax dollars, only the portion of payment received that is attributable to investment income is taxable. Once the annuitant has recouped his or her entire investment in the annuity, then the entire annuity payment is taxable. Obviously some annuitants will die before receiving back what they paid for the annuity, while others will live far beyond life expectancy and collect far more than what they paid for the annuity.

Annuities offer great flexibility. They can be purchased through installment premiums or through a lump-sum purchase. The benefit payments can begin immediately or can be deferred to a later date. The purchaser may also add some type of guarantee feature to the annuity. For example, the annuitant may select a "life income with 10 years for certain" option. Under this option, annuity payments are made for life. If the annuitant dies before receiving payments for 10 years, the remaining payments are made to a beneficiary. Finally, an annuity can be purchased on more than one life. A retired husband and wife, for example, may purchase a joint-and-survivor annuity. This type of annuity provides payments until the last of the two annuitants has died.

Annuities are big business for insurers, especially as baby boomers approach retirement age. In 1986, premiums and annuity considerations for individual annuities were $26.1 billion; in 1990 they were $49.0 billion; in 1997 they were $88.7 billion, and in 2002 they were $168.4 billion.

HEALTH INSURANCE

Medical expenses can be catastrophic. The perils insured against in **health insurance** are the medical costs associated with illness and injury and the loss of income. Specific medical costs include the costs of a hospital room, surgical procedures, miscellaneous expenses (e.g., lab tests and X-rays), nonsurgical care, and long-term care. These expenses can be paid through hospital–surgical expense policies, major medical insurance, and long-term care insurance.

Often overlooked in a personal risk management program is the risk of disability. The economic consequences of a long-term, permanent disability can be greater than the economic consequences of premature death. Disability income insurance replaces lost income during a period of temporary or permanent disability caused by illness or injury.

Health insurance can be purchased individually or made available through a group insurance plan. Health insurance providers include insurance companies, Blue Cross–Blue Shield organizations (the Blues), and health maintenance organizations (HMOs). Some group health plans have entered into agreements with care providers through which the care provider offers its services at a discount. Members of the group health plan are given a financial incentive to use the preferred provider organization (PPO) for their care. PPOs and other forms of managed care plans are popular because of continued health-care-sector inflation.

THE BALANCE SHEET OF LIFE INSURANCE COMPANIES

Life insurance company funds originate primarily from the sale of life insurance policies, annuities, and pension plans that have a savings feature as part of the contract. Selling these products creates liabilities, similar to accounts payments for other types of businesses. These liabilities are called reserves. Exhibit 18.3 shows the composite balance sheet for life insurers in 2002.

One is struck immediately by the magnitude of the assets. In 2002, life insurers had assets of $3.37 trillion dollars. Notice that the bulk of the assets are financial assets—$1.70 trillion in bonds, $77.4 billion in corporate stock, $242.9 billion in mortgages, and $21.7 billion in real estate. Clearly life insurers are important financial intermediaries. They collect small amounts of money from millions of policyowners, package the premiums, and make large blocks of funds available in the capital markets.

Several important points deserve mention. First, the long-term nature of life insurance contracts and the steady cash flows they generate motivate insurers toward long-term investments. As Exhibit 18.3 shows, corporate bonds and mortgages are the most important investments backing traditional life insurance products. The second largest asset holding is "separate account assets." This category of assets is segregated from general assets and is exempt from most investment rules. Separate account assets back life insurer products that have an investment nature—variable life insurance, variable annuities, and pension plans.

One item listed as an asset that you may find surprising is "policy loans." Recall that a cash value policy (e.g., whole life insurance) permits the policyowner to borrow the cash value from the policy. So why are policy loans an asset? Policy loans are analogous to accounts receivable. If the insurer had not loaned the money to the policyowner, it would have invested the funds elsewhere in an interest-earning assets. As interest is payable on policy loans, and loans must either be repaid or the outstanding balance is deducted from the death benefit when it is payable, policy loans are interest-earning assets for life insurers.

Exhibit 18.3 shows that policy loans were 3.1 percent of total assets in 2002. Policy loans vary with economic conditions. During the Great Depression, policy loans reached 18 percent of company assets. In 1981, when interest rates in the market were high, policy loans accounted for 9 percent of insurer assets. Policy loans have historically been made at low rates of interest, usually 5 to 8 percent. In 1981, market interest rates greatly exceeded the low interest rates on policy loans, so insureds borrowed their cash values to reinvest in higher-yielding instruments. Since then, all states have enacted insurance legislation called the Model Bill on Policy Loan Rates, or a similar law, that allows life insurers to use a variable policy loan rate tied to a market interest rate.

EXHIBIT 18.3
Life Insurance Companies' Balance Sheet, 2002

Type of Account	Amount ($ in Billions)	Percentage
Assets		
Bonds	1,703.2	50.6
Corporate stock	77.4	2.3
Mortgages	242.9	7.2
Real estate	21.7	0.6
Policy loans	104.3	3.1
Cash & short-term investments	83.4	2.5
Other assets	177.4	5.3
Separate account assets	958.4	28.5
Total	3,368.7	100.0
Liabilities and net worth		
Policy reserves liability	1,691.9	50.2
Policy claims	34.4	1.0
Deposit-type contracts	256.3	7.6
Other liabilities	235.7	7.0
Separate account business	955.8	28.4
Surplus and net worth	194.6	5.8
Total	3,368.7	100.0

Source: Best's Aggregates and Averages, Life/Health, 2003 Edition; Comparative Balance Sheet—Total Industry, p. 1.

The tendency of life insurers to make long-term investments can create some problems. When interest rates increase, the value of outstanding bonds and mortgages drops. In the event of a liquidity crunch, if an above-average number of policyowners request policy loans or surrender their policies, for example, insurers may be required to liquidate long-term investments at substantially depressed prices, resulting in losses. With this contingency in mind, insurance regulation permits insurers to include a **deferment clause** in life insurance policies that accumulate a cash value. This clause permits an insurer to delay payment of the cash value for up to 6 months from the date of the request. In some clauses, the right also applies to withdrawal of the proceeds that are being held by the company at interest. The clause is similar to a provision introduced for bank accounts as a result of the run on banks during the 1930s. Some insurers could become technically insolvent if these long-term assets had to be liquidated or marked to current market values.

DO YOU UNDERSTAND?

1. How do term life insurance and whole life insurance differ with respect to the duration of coverage and savings accumulation?
2. Why was universal life insurance popular in the 1980s but not in the 1990s? What made variable life insurance popular in the 1990s?
3. Why are life insurance and life annuities often described as opposites?
4. What are the largest asset categories on a life insurance company balance sheet?

Property and liability insurers sell policies that offer protection from direct and indirect loss caused by **perils**. Some perils that could cause direct loss to property include a fire, windstorm, explosion, flood, or earthquake. Some indirect losses are also insurable. For example, a successful restaurant that is damaged by a fire may be forced to close while repairs are made. The profits that could have been earned if the restaurant was operating are an indirect loss that could be covered by business income insurance. Property insurance indemnifies policyowners for the financial loss associated with the destruction and loss of use of their property. Liability insurance protects against the peril of legal liability. An insured that is negligent and causes bodily injury, property damage, or personal injury (such as libel or slander) may be called upon to pay damages to the injured party. Liability insurance will pay such awards on the behalf of the insured.

**PROPERTY
AND
LIABILITY
INSURANCE**

PROPERTY INSURANCE

Property insurance is purchased by individuals and organizations to protect against direct or indirect loss to property they own. Perils, causes of loss, are insured against under property insurance policies. Some property insurance policies provide **named-perils coverage**. These policies provide a listing of perils that are covered. If a loss is caused by a peril not listed, the loss is not covered. An alternative to naming perils is to provide **all-risk coverage** (also called "open perils"). This type of coverage insures against all losses except those that are excluded. So if a loss is not excluded, it is covered. An insurer's loss exposure in property insurance is easier to predict than liability loss exposures because it is generally not difficult to determine the value of the property damaged or destroyed.

LIABILITY INSURANCE

Liability insurance is purchased by individuals and businesses to protect against financial loss because of legal responsibility for bodily injury, property damage, and personal injury. Insurers selling liability insurance also agree to defend the insured against suits of negligence and to pay damages awarded by the court for bodily injury, property damage, and sometimes personal injury such as libel or slander. The liability exposure is much more difficult to gauge as there is no upper limit on the damages that may be awarded. Liability claims often take years to settle. Some states have enacted tort reform statutes that may limit punitive damages, but special damages and general damages are not limited. A liability loss, therefore, is one that can be catastrophic in nature.

MARINE INSURANCE

Marine insurance is a special classification of property and liability insurance. Marine contracts, which cover losses related to transportation exposures, are divided into two categories: ocean marine and inland marine. Ocean marine policies include hull coverage for damage to the vessel and indemnity (liability) coverage. The policies can be endorsed to provide cargo coverage, longshore and harbor worker coverage, and other supplemental coverages. Inland marine policies include coverage for such exposures as goods transported by rail, motor vehicles, and armored cars, as well as "instrumentalities of transportation" such as bridges, tunnels, and pipelines. Floater policies that cover scheduled items of high value such as fine arts, jewelry, furs, and antiques also fall under the classification of inland marine.

MULTIPLE LINE POLICIES

Multiple line policies, frequently written by property and liability insurers, combine property and liability insurance coverage in a single contract. The homeowner's policy is an excellent example. This policy was developed in the 1950s and continues to be widely popular. The homeowner's form provides six coverages: damage to the dwelling, damage to other structures, damage to personal property, loss of use, personal liability, and medical payments to others. Like the homeowner's policy, the personal auto policy (PAP) combines several coverages, including bodily injury and property damage liability, medical payments coverage, uninsured motorists coverage, and physical damage coverage for the insured auto.

Some forms used to insure businesses also combine property and liability insurance coverage. The business owner's policy (BOP) used by small businesses provides coverage for building, business personal property, and general liability insurance in one contract. The commercial package policy (CPP) used by large businesses insures the plant, equipment, other property, as well as general liability loss exposures of the organization.

Multiple line policies offer a number of advantages. Purchasing coverages combined in a single policy is less expensive than purchasing the coverages separately. A multiple line policy is underwritten once, whereas separate policies require individual underwriting and individual issue costs. Multiple line policies provide more complete coverage, have a common expiration date, and are convenient for the insured, who faces only one common policy expiration date and has to deal with only one agent and one insurer.

THE BALANCE SHEET OF PROPERTY AND LIABILITY INSURANCE COMPANIES

The operations and investment practices of property and liability insurers differ from those of life insurers for several reasons. First, property and liability insurance policies have a much shorter duration than life insurance policies. Typically, property and liability policies are written for 6 months or a year. Second, the probability of loss is higher under these policies, and property claims are often paid during the policy period. Thus, the insurer can invest premium revenue for a shorter period of time. Finally, the objective risk of the property and liability insurer is greater than that faced by life insurers. Claims against property and liability insurers are greatly affected by economic conditions and are often much greater than predicted. For example, inflation affects workers' compensation losses, the cost of replacing property, and amounts awarded in liability suits. Property and liability insurers invest a larger proportion of their funds in corporate stocks for high yield and in municipal bonds for tax advantages. The balance sheet for all property and liability insurers for 2002 is shown in Exhibit 18.4.

Just as in the case of the balance sheet for life insurance companies, you are immediately struck by the magnitude of the funds. In 2002, U.S. property and liability insurance companies controlled $1.04 trillion in assets. Again, note the financial nature of the assets that appear on the balance sheet. Property and liability insurers held $570.3 billion in bonds and $111.1 billion in common and preferred stock. Also note the higher relative position in cash and short-term investments

EXHIBIT 18.4
Property/Liability Companies' Balance Sheet, 2002

Type of Account	Amount ($ in Billions)	Percentage
Bonds	1,703.2	50.6
Assets		
Bonds	570.3	54.7
Corporate stock	111.1	10.6
Mortgages	2.0	0.2
Real estate investment	1.4	0.1
Cash & short-term investments	72.4	6.9
Investments in affiliates	50.5	4.8
Premium balances	98.6	9.5
Other assets	136.7	13.1
Total	1,042.9	100.0
Liabilities and net worth		
Losses	345.2	33.1
Loss adjustment expenses	67.3	6.5
Unearned premiums	158.6	15.2
Other liabilities	180.9	17.3
Surplus and net worth	290.9	27.9
Total	1042.9	100.0

Source: Best's Aggregates and Averages, Property/Casualty, 2003 Edition; Consolidated Industry Totals, p. 1.

(6.9 percent of total assets) as compared to life insurance companies (2.5 percent of total assets), demonstrating the desire for liquidity.

The liabilities of property and liability insurers are quite logical. They consist of reserves for losses, for loss adjustment expenses, and for unearned premiums. Also of interest is the relatively larger surplus position of property and liability insurers (27.9 percent) as compared to life insurers (5.8 percent). Surplus represents a cushion that can be drawn upon if losses are higher than anticipated. Property and liability insurers must maintain larger relative surplus positions because of objective risk and the higher frequency of loss.

DO YOU UNDERSTAND?

1. Property insurance is available for both direct and indirect losses. Differentiate between these two types of losses.
2. Why is the liability loss exposure more difficult to gauge than the property loss exposure?
3. What are major benefits of purchasing coverage through a multiple line policy as opposed to purchasing the same coverage separately?
4. What are the major classes of asset holdings on a property and liability insurance company balance sheet? How do the asset holdings of property and liability insurance companies differ from the holdings of life and health insurance companies?

PENSIONS

Pensions are used to protect against the peril of superannuation, which can be defined as outliving your ability to earn a living to support yourself. Most individuals do not save enough for retirement, relying on Social Security old-age benefits for the bulk of their retirement income. Social Security was never meant to be the sole source of retirement income. Numerous tax advantages have been made available under the tax code to encourage retirement savings.

Several problems currently exist with retirement savings. Many individuals delay retirement saving, spending financial resources today for current consumption rather than saving for retirement. Some individuals do not earn enough to be able to afford retirement savings. Finally, the period of retirement saving is shortening while the period that the funds are required to last is lengthening. Many individuals delay entry to the workforce until completing college. These same individuals may elect to retire early, shortening the period over which retirement savings can be set aside and earn investment income. Americans, on average, are living longer. Therefore, retirement funds that have been accumulated must last, on average, a longer period of time.

Even with these problems, pension plans have been among the fastest-growing financial intermediaries in the last 25 years. Like insurance companies, pension plans collect small contributions from many employees or larger contributions from employers. The plan pools these contributions and makes large blocks of funds available to purchase stocks, bonds, real estate–related investments, and other securities. The pension fund uses the funds plus investment income to make retirement benefits available.

A BRIEF HISTORY OF PENSIONS

The earliest pension programs were established by the railroads, the first in the United States in 1875 by the American Express Company and the second by the Baltimore and Ohio Railroad in 1880. Railroads were the first to establish pensions because they were the first business organizations to become large enough and, more importantly, because the work was hazardous and some type of relief was needed, particularly for the disabled. By 1929, there were only 400 assorted pension funds in operation with pension assets of less than $500 million, covering fewer than 4 million workers and their families.

During the Great Depression many business firms went bankrupt. Their pension funds often failed, too, because pension benefits were frequently paid out of current income. These nonfunded, pay-as-you-go plans operated without regulation, and participants had few, if any, rights. Pension plans underwritten by insurance companies, however, were actuarially funded and were far superior in weathering the rough financial times of the 1930s.

The financial hardships of the Great Depression underscored the need for some type of universal retirement and disability program, and the passage of the Social Security Act in 1935 helped meet the need for financial security. The program's purpose was to provide a minimum floor of retirement income, with the balance supplied through private savings. It wasn't until World War II that private pension plans became an important factor in the economy. By 1945, private pension plans covered 6.4 million workers, up 50 percent from the number that had been covered 5 years earlier. The number of Americans covered by pension plans continued to grow, with 9.8 million covered in 1950 and 21 million by 1960. More recently, there were 99.5 million active participants in private pension plans in 1998. Private pension fund assets totaled $5.2 trillion in 2002.

Various laws have addressed specific provisions of pension plans and attempted to safeguard pension benefits. Some of these include the Self-Employed Individuals Tax Retirement Act of 1962, the Employee Retirement Income Security Act of 1974 (ERISA), the Pension Reform Act of 1978, the Economic Recovery Tax Act of 1981 (ERTA), the Tax Equity and Fiscal Responsibility Act of 1982 (TEFRA), and the Tax Reform Act of 1986. Recently, the Economic Growth and Tax Relief Reconciliation Act of 2001 increased the tax advantages of private pension plans for employers and employees.

GOVERNMENT PENSION PLANS

State and local government employee pension plans are designed to cover teachers, police officers, firefighters, and other employees of states, counties, and cities. Tax deductibility of pension contributions is not an issue for government entities, so such plans are typically exempt from ERISA and other rules that apply to private pensions. The federal government operates a number of pension funds. Some are large retirement funds of civil service and military employees; others are small separate funds for employees of the foreign service, the federal judiciary, the Tennessee Valley Authority, and the Board of Governors of the Federal Reserve System.

The largest government retirement plan is Social Security, formally referred to as Old Age, Survivors, and Disability Insurance (OASDI). **Social Security old-age benefits** are financed through a payroll tax on employers, employees, and the self-employed. Retirement benefits are paid to those workers who have earned enough credits under the system through paying the payroll tax. Social Security retirement benefits were paid to 34.4 million retired workers and dependents in 2002. The benefits totaled $304.0 billion, with an average monthly benefit of $895.

Social Security old-age benefits are intended to provide a minimum floor of retirement income for those covered by the plan. Participants do not contribute directly to their own benefits; instead, retirement benefits are paid from the Social Security taxes of those currently working. Under the current system, individuals may elect to retire at age 65 and receive full retirement benefits. Retirement benefits are available as early as age 62, but the benefit is permanently reduced to 80 percent of the full retirement benefit. For those born after 1960, the age for full retirement benefits is 67. Retirement benefits are available at age 62, but the benefit is permanently reduced to 70 percent of the full benefit.

Social Security is a social insurance program. Social insurance programs combine elements of private insurance and welfare. Social Security benefits stress **social adequacy**, slanting benefits in favor of certain groups (e.g., lower-paid workers) in order to achieve a broader social goal, a minimum floor of income for everyone. Private pension plans and insurance plans stress **individual equity**, paying benefits in direct relation to contributions.

PRIVATE PENSION PLANS

Private pension plans are those established by private-sector groups, such as industrial, commercial, union, or service organizations, as well as those established by individuals that are not employment related. Private pension plans are afforded significant tax advantages if they satisfy a number of rules. Plans may be organized in a number of ways, depending on how the plan is funded, on benefit or contribution guarantees, and on whether the plan is insured.

Significant tax advantages are available to employers and employees through private pension plans. However, to enjoy these tax advantages the plan must satisfy a lengthy list of rules. **Qualified plans** are plans that satisfy the rules and are therefore granted favorable tax treatment. Employers are permitted to deduct pension contributions as a business expense. Employees do not have to pay tax currently on employer contributions. If the employee contributes to the plan, pre-tax dollars as opposed to after-tax dollars are used. The employee's pension benefit accumulates on a tax-deferred basis, with distributions not taxed until the money is distributed.

Another characteristic of private pension plans is how the plans are funded. **Noncontributory plans** are funded through employer contributions only. **Contributory plans** use employer and employee contributions. A 401(k) plan in which an employee makes a contribution and the employer matches the contribution is an example of a contributory plan. Some plans are fully contributory. Under a **fully contributory plan**, only the employee makes contributions to the plan.

An important consideration in a private pension plan is the promise made by the employer. Older, larger plans tend to be defined benefit plans. Under a **defined benefit plan**, the employer states the benefit that the employee will receive at retirement. The benefit may be a flat dollar amount, a percentage of average salary over a specified period, or a unit benefit formula based on period of employment and salary. An example of a unit benefit plan would be an employer who awards 2.5 percent per year of service, with the total multiplied by average salary during the three highest consecutive years. So an employee who worked for the company for 20 years would receive 50 percent (20 × 2.5 percent) of the average salary for his or her pension benefit.

Defined benefit plans are difficult to administer and place the investment risk squarely on the employer. Consider determining the appropriate pension contribution of the employee in the previous unit benefit example. How long will the employee be with the company? What will his or her average salary be? How long will he or she live after employment with the company terminates? Under a defined benefit plan, the employer promises a benefit and then must fund the plan so that the benefit can be paid.

Defined contribution plans have increased in importance in recent years. Indeed, most of the new plans being started today are defined contribution plans. Employers like these plans because they are easy to administer and shift the investment risk to the employee/retiree. Under a defined contribution plan, all the employer states is what will be set aside for the employee. For example, an employer may promise to contribute 4 percent of an employee's salary to the employee's pension account. For an employee who earns $50,000 per year, the employer will contribute $2,000. No guarantees are offered about the actual benefit payable at retirement. If the investment performance is favorable, a larger benefit will be payable. If the performance is not favorable, a smaller benefit will be payable. Defined contribution plans often permit the employee to decide where to invest, and several funds are often provided for this purpose.

Another way in which pension funds can be characterized is whether the plan is insured or noninsured. An **insured pension plan** is established with a life insurance company. A **noninsured pension plan** is managed by a trustee appointed by the sponsoring organization, such as a business or union. The trustee is usually a commercial bank or trust company, which holds and invests the contributions and pays retirement benefits in accordance with the terms of the trust. In some instances, the investment procedure is handled directly by the sponsoring organization, as in the case with large companies or unions. Pension funds constitute more than one-third of the assets of commercial banks' trust departments, and there is intense competition among financial institutions for the business of managing these large sums of money. Total assets held by all private and government-administered pension funds exceed $7 trillion. Private pension funds accounted for the majority of this total.

PROVISIONS OF ERISA AND SUBSEQUENT LEGISLATION

The **Employee Retirement Income Security Act (ERISA)** was signed into law on Labor Day, 1974. The law does not require employers to establish a pension program for their employees; it does, however, require that certain standards be observed if the plan is to receive favorable tax treatment. ERISA was passed because Congress had become concerned that many workers with long years of service were failing to receive pension benefits. In some instances, workers were forced out of work before retirement age. In other situations, pension funds failed in their fiduciary responsibilities to their participants because the firms failed, pension plans were inadequately funded, or investment funds were mismanaged.

Some of ERISA's more important provisions attempted to (1) strengthen the fiduciary responsibilities of a pension fund's trustees, (2) establish reporting and disclosure requirements, (3) provide for insurance of the retirees' pension benefits in event of default or termination of the plan, and (4) allow self-employed persons to make tax-deferred pension contributions. Because of the importance of ERISA and its far-reaching implications for pension fund operations, we shall discuss some of its more important provisions.

To prevent employers from designing plans that cover only highly compensated employees, certain minimum coverage rules must be observed to receive favorable tax treatment. ERISA also established **minimum funding standards** for the funding of benefits under qualified plans. Funding refers to employers' advance preparation for setting aside money to pay pension benefits. To remain qualified, contributions to pension plans must be sufficient both to meet current costs and to amortize past service liabilities and payments over not more than 40 years. Employers who fail to meet the funding requirements are subject to substantial tax penalties.

Portability is the workers' right to take pension benefits with them when changing jobs. Workers changing jobs may defer taxes on a lump-sum distribution of vested credits from their employers by investing them in a tax-qualified individual retirement account (IRA) or by depositing them in the new employer's plan. The law does not require any specific portability provisions from plan to plan.

Vesting refers to an employee's right to employer-promised pension benefits or employer contributions. To remain qualified under the tax code, defined benefit plans and some defined contribution plans must satisfy one of two standards: complete vesting after 5 years (called cliff vesting, as it is all-or-nothing) or 20 percent vesting after 3 years, with an additional 20 percent per year vested over the next 4 years so vesting is complete after 7 years (graduated vesting). The Economic Growth and Tax Relief Reconciliation Act of 2001 tightens the vesting standards for defined contribution plans in which employers match employee contributions. Such plans must be fully vested after 3 years (cliff vesting) or achieve full vesting under a graduated schedule after 6 years. It's important to recall that these standards are minimums—employers are free to be more generous with vesting if they prefer.

A federal insurance agency, the **Pension Benefit Guarantee Corporation (PBGC)**, was established under ERISA. The PBGC insures defined benefit plans up to a specified amount per month. Only benefits that were vested under the plan prior to termination are guaranteed by the PBGC. If a plan is overfunded when it is terminated, the employer is entitled to receive a reversion of surplus assets. The Tax Reform Act of 1986 imposed a 10 percent tax on reversions to reduce the incentive for terminating such plans.

A **plan fiduciary** is any trustee, investment adviser, or other person who has discretionary authority or responsibility in the management of the plan or its assets. Fiduciaries are required to perform their duties solely in the interest of plan participants and beneficiaries as defined in the pension law. ERISA imposes personal liability on plan fiduciaries who do not render the standard of care required.

All plans are required to file a report (Form 5500) with the Department of Labor annually. This report discloses information about pension and welfare plans, their operations, and their financial conditions to the Secretary of Labor and to plan participants and their beneficiaries.

Overall, ERISA is viewed as a milestone in pension fund legislation. The creation of the PBGC was particularly important from the employee's standpoint. Before ERISA, when an employer went bankrupt, the employee could not collect anything beyond what was in the pension fund. The PBGC relieves employees of the risk of losing pension benefits up to the established maximum amount per month. ERISA's provisions have been strengthened by subsequent legislation, including ERTA, TEFRA, the Tax Reform Act of 1986, and most recently the Economic Growth and Tax Relief Reconciliation Act of 2001. This legislation tightens vesting standards, penalizes companies for reverting assets, and reduces the discrimination favoring highly compensated employees.

DO YOU UNDERSTAND?

1. How are Social Security old-age benefits funded? Are these benefits based on social adequacy or individual equity?
2. What are the tax advantages of qualified private pension plans?
3. Explain the difference between contributory and noncontributory pension plans. Differentiate between defined benefit and defined contribution pension plans.
4. ERISA and subsequent acts regulate several features of qualified private pensions. What is meant by portability, vesting, and fiduciary standards?

CHAPTER TAKE-AWAYS

1 Insurance involves the transfer of a pure risk from one party to an entity that pools the risk and provides payment if a loss occurs. Risk is transferred and the party accepting the risk becomes responsible for payment should a loss occur. The risk is pooled in that the party transferring risk bears the average loss of the group of insureds instead of a large uncertain loss. Not all risks are privately insurable. For a risk to be privately insurable, the following conditions must be met: (1) there must be a large number of similar exposure units; (2) losses should be accidental and unintentional; (3) losses must not be catastrophic; (4) losses should be determinable and measurable; (5) chance of loss must be calculable; and (6) the premium for the coverage must be affordable.

2 Objective risk is the variation between expected losses and actual losses. An insurance company does not know up-front what its loss experience will be. There are several ways in which insurers reduce objective risk: (1) insuring many risks, thereby applying the law of large numbers; (2) carefully underwriting the risks; (3) making the insured pay a portion of the loss through deductibles, co-payments, internal policy limits, and exclusions; and (4) reinsuring some or all of the business written.

3 The market structure of the insurance industry is a pure competition model. There are a large number of buyers and sellers, no buyers and sellers are dominant, the product bought and sold is relatively homogeneous, and the barriers to entry (financial capital rather than physical capital) are not severe. The insurance industry is characterized by the presence of many diverse forms of organizations. There are stock companies, mutual companies that are owned by their policyowners, reciprocals, and Lloyd's associations. The insurance industry is regulated primarily at the state level. The sources of regulation include legislation, court decisions, and state insurance departments. The industry is regulated to protect against the insolvency of insurers, to protect consumers who may have inadequate knowledge, to make sure that insurance rates are not excessive, and to make insurance available.

4 Life and health insurance companies market a number of financial services products to protect purchasers and their dependents from financial loss. Life insurance products marketed include term insurance, whole life insurance, universal life insurance, variable life insurance, medical expense coverage, disability income insurance, and annuities.

5 Property and liability insurance companies market a wide array of products for individuals, small businesses, and large corporations. These products protect against direct loss (damage, destruction, or theft of property), indirect loss (loss of profits or increased expenses after a direct loss has occurred) and the consequences of legal liability. If an insured is alleged to be responsible for bodily injury, property damage, or personal injury, the insurer provides for the cost of a legal defense and pays up to the limit of liability if the insured is judged responsible.

6 The balance sheet of life and health insurance companies and property and liability insurance companies is very different from the balance sheet of nonfinancial organizations. The assets listed are various holdings of financial assets as opposed to plant and equipment. Life and health insurers invest in longer-term assets, matching asset duration with the contracts issued. Property and liability insurance companies invest in shorter-duration assets. They have a much larger relative position in corporate stocks and much smaller holdings in real estate and mortgages. Life insurers list loans to policyowners as an interest-bearing asset. Property and liability insurers have larger relative positions in cash and short-term investments, providing necessary liquidity, and a large surplus position reflecting the riskiness of their operations.

7 Both government and private-sector pension plans are available. Social Security is the largest government plan, and it is designed to provide a minimum floor of income that should be supplemented with a private pension. Private pensions offer significant tax advantages to employers and employees. Private pension plans may be contributory or noncontributory and defined benefit or defined contribution. Significant assets accumulate in government and private pension plans. The assets are used to purchase a variety of financial assets, including stocks and bonds.

KEY TERMS

Risk
Insurance
Risk transfer
Pooling
Pure risk
Speculative risk
Objective risk
Law of large numbers
Underwriting
Deductable
Coinsurance
Reinsurance

Underwriting cycle
Cash-flow underwriting
Stock insurance company
Participating policy
Mutual insurance
  company
Demutualization
Reciprocal or reciprocal
  exchange
Lloyd's association
Lloyd's of London

McCarran-Ferguson Act
  (Public Law 15)
National Association of
  Insurance
  Commissioners (NAIC)
Captive insurance
  company
Securitization of risk
Premature death
Term insurance
Renewable term insurance

Adverse selection
Convertible term
  insurance
Whole life insurance
Cash value
Superannuation
Universal life insurance
Variable life insurance
Annuities
Health insurance
Deferment clause

Perils
Property insurance
Named-perils coverage
All-risk coverage
Liability insurance
Marine insurance
Multiple line policy
Social Security old-age
benefits

Social adequacy
Individual equity
Private pension plan
Qualified plan
Noncontributory plan
Contributory plan
Fully contributory plan
Defined benefit plan
Defined contribution plan

Insured pension plan
Noninsured pension plan
Employee Retirement
Income Security Act
(ERISA)
Minimum funding
standards
Portability
Vesting

Pension Benefit
Guarantee Corporation
(PBGC)
Plan fiduciary

QUESTIONS AND PROBLEMS

1. Throughout this chapter, the role of insurance companies and pension funds as financial intermediaries was stressed. Discuss the financial intermediation process as it applies to insurance companies and pension funds.

2. What is the difference between a pure risk and speculative risk? Provide an example of each of these types of risk.

3. According to the law of large numbers, as the number of insureds increases, risk is reduced. However, as an insurance company writes more policies, it exposes itself to the potential for greater insured losses, which is riskier. Explain this apparent contradiction.

4. To what extent do (a) the risk of unemployment and (b) the risk of war satisfy the requirements of privately insurable risks?

5. What problem is likely to develop for a stock life insurance company that issues participating policies?

6. What are the primary sources of insurance regulation? What are the areas that are regulated?

7. What is meant by the phrase "adverse selection" in insurance? Although discussed in this chapter in connection with term insurance, adverse selection is a problem in all insurance markets. What is the adverse selection risk for insurers marketing life annuities?

8. Term insurance becomes cost prohibitive for aged individuals. However, the same insurance companies that do not offer term policies at advanced ages sell whole life insurance. How are these insurers able to offer life insurance for all of life under whole life insurance but not under term insurance?

9. Why did universal life decrease in popularity from the 1980s to the 1990s? What explains the popularity of variable life insurance in the 1990s?

10. Why are annuities and life insurance often described as opposites? If they are opposites, then why do insurance companies marketing life insurance also commonly market life annuities?

11. What is the relationship between the level of policy loans taken by policyowners and the level of interest rates in the general economy?

12. Why is the liability risk much more difficult to gauge than the property risk?

13. What are the advantages of purchasing a package policy versus purchasing the same coverages included in a package policy separately?

14. What are the major similarities between the balance sheets of life insurance companies and property and liability insurance companies? What are the major differences?

15. How are Social Security old-age benefits funded? What is the age for full retirement benefits for those retiring under Social Security today? What will be the age under current law for full retirement benefits when someone who is 20 years old today retires?

16. Differentiate between defined benefit and defined contribution pension plans. Who bears the investment risk under each of these alternatives? Which type of plan is easier to fund and manage?

INTERNET EXERCISE

There are many useful Web sites that have information about insurers and insurance products. However, many of these sites are marketing tools designed to interest you in purchasing financial services products from the site sponsor. An excellent site for objective information about insurance is provided by the Insurance Information Institute (http://iii.org/). Although the institute's primary concern is property and liability insurance, some excellent information about life insurance, health insurance, and annuities is also provided. Access the site, and use the links provided in the left margin of the homepage to answer the following questions.

1. Click on the "Auto" link in the left margin of the homepage.
   a. What six coverages may an auto insurance policy include? (Click on the link for "What is in a basic auto policy?")
   b. The average American spends about $700 per year on auto insurance. How can you lower your auto insurance premium? (Click on the "How can I save money" link.)
2. Click on the "Home" link in the left margin of the homepage.
   a. What four essential coverages are found in a standard homeowner's policy? (See the "What is in a standard homeowner's insurance policy?" link.)
   b. A homeowner should purchase enough insurance to cover the cost of rebuilding the home. What factors determine the cost to rebuild? (See the "How much homeowner's insurance do I need?" link.)
3. Click on the "Life" link in the left margin of the homepage.
   a. What are four good reasons for purchasing life insurance? (See the "Why buy life insurance" link.)
   b. What are some factors that you should take into consideration when deciding on the amount of life insurance to purchase? (See the "How much life insurance do I need?" link.)
4. Click on the "Disability" link in the left margin of the homepage.
   a. What are three important sources of income replacement for those who experience a nonoccupational disability? (See the "How can I insure against loss of income?" link.)
   b. Using the same link, what are some key factors that you should look for when shopping for a disability income insurance policy?
5. Click on the "Business" link in the left margin of the homepage.
   a. Small businesses, just like large corporations, need property and liability insurance. Small businesses usually obtain this coverage through a business owner's policy (BOP). What coverage is provided through a BOP? (See the "What does a business owner's policy cover?" link.)
   b. Using the same link, what does a BOP not cover?

Investment Banking

Investment banking has the allure of allowing one to make lots of money. How would you like to make $100,000 two years out of college or $5 million a year or more as a partner in a prestigious Wall Street firm? Where else can you even come close to making that much money? Glamorous profession? Well, the job can have its downside.

"Put the handcuffs on them." These words were not spoken to common criminals but to senior executives of Goldman Sachs & Co. and Kidder Peabody & Co., two of Wall Street's classiest old-line investment-banking firms. The two princi-

pals were arrested at their desks and taken out through a trading room full of open-mouthed colleagues! The scene was just part of the ongoing insider-trading bombshell that may be the Wall Street scandal of the century. The scandal involved Wall Street luminaries and some of its brightest and best-educated young stars.

The tragedy for Wall Street is that it cannot explain away the scandals as an outcropping of abnormal behavior or a temporary aberration limited to a few insulated cases. A lack of ethical values, blind ambition, and greed continue as an integral part of Wall Street's cultural fabric. As

an example, on May 22, 2002, Merrill Lynch agreed to a $100 million settlement with New York and other states because its investment analysts gave its customers overly rosy research reports about the stocks that the firm's investment banking division was underwriting. In addition, a dozen other brokerages that are household names are also under investigation, such as Morgan Stanley, Bear Stearns, Goldman Sachs, Credit Suisse, and Salomon Smith Barney. Overall, since 1990, 10 large Wall Street firms have been fined $40 million or more, with an average fine of nearly $200 million. ∎

All investment bankers wear red suspenders. They really do! But, we have no idea why. The core business activities of investment banks are bringing new securities to the market and participating in secondary markets for those securities. Investment banks also innovate cutting-edge financial products for corporations.

This chapter is about Wall Street firms and highlights investment banks, which are the premier players in the capital markets. We discuss investment banks' primary business activities of underwriting new securities sold in the primary markets and their role as dealers and brokers in the secondary markets. We also discuss other services they provide, such as merger and acquisition advising and private placement financing. Our story is also about large money-center banks and their head-to-head struggle with investment banks for products and customers. Commercial banks can now freely engage in investment banking with the relaxation of the Depression-era legislation during the 1990s. Finally, we discuss the role of venture capitalists, who are at the heart of the new business formation process. They supply the capital for these high-risk investments in exchange for a share of the ownership. These fledgling businesses are too risky to receive financing through traditional funding sources. Most of these new business firms are in high-technology areas such medical devices, telecommunications, biotechnology, or nanotechnology. ∎

LEARNING OBJECTIVES

The objectives of this chapter are to:

1 Explain the core business activities of investment banks.

2 Explain the reasons for the enactment of the Glass-Steagall Act of 1933 and discuss its impact on commercial and investment banking.

3 Explain the Gramm-Leach-Bliley Act of 1999 and discuss how it is likely to affect the structure of the financial services industry.

4 Explain why investment banks typically underprice new securities when they are sold in the primary markets.

5 Explain what shelf registration is and why it is important.

6 Describe what venture capitalists do and why they are important to economic growth.

THE RELATIONSHIP BETWEEN COMMERCIAL AND INVESTMENT BANKING

As we discussed in Chapter 1, there are two basic ways in which new financial claims can be brought to market: direct or indirect (intermediation) financing. In the indirect credit market, **commercial banks** are the most important participants; in the direct market, **investment banks** are the most important participants. Investment banks are firms that specialize in helping businesses and governments sell their new security issues (debt or equity) in the primary markets to finance capital expenditures. In addition, after the securities are sold, investment bankers make secondary markets for the securities as brokers and dealers.

The term "investment bank" is somewhat misleading, because those involved have little to do with *commercial banking* (accepting deposits and making commercial loans). The Banking Act of 1933, or the Glass-Steagall Act as it is more com-

The Fall of the House that Junk Built

At 11:07 P.M. on February 13, 1990, Wall Street's most lavish party ended and the host was left with a lot more to clear up than just a hangover. Drexel Burnham Lambert, Inc., filed for Chapter 11 bankruptcy protection. That action brought an end to what some have called the Roaring Eighties, an era of hostile takeovers, leveraged buyouts, high living, and a disregard for huge amounts of debt.

The 55-year-old investment-banking firm rose from Wall Street also-ran in the 1970s to be the extremely profitable and prominent pioneer of what are known as junk bonds: high-yield, high-risk bonds that back ventures with less than investment-grade credit. By becoming the primary player in the junk bond market under the direction of Michael R. Milken, Drexel could take part in the takeover wars that ruled Wall Street in the 1980s. Because of Drexel's ability to raise capital for all types of firms, even very small companies could bid for and sometimes win America's largest firms. Armed with Drexel's bonds, corporate raiders swiftly made some of the largest deals the financial world had ever witnessed.

Investment bankers made billions in fees by advising both the raiders and the takeover targets. One takeover contender explained that all a raider needed to launch a bid was Milken's signature on one of Drexel's letters stating that the firm was "highly confident" of obtaining financing. At the height of his reign as king of junk bonds, Milken could charge as much as $3.5 million for such a letter.

In late 1986 things started to get sticky as Drexel became entangled in the insider dealings of convicted arbitrageur Ivan Boesky. When the smoke cleared, the Securities and Exchange Commission demanded $650 million in fines from Drexel and the ousting of Michael Milken.

Because of the scandal, Milken faced a 98-count indictment, including charges of racketeering and insider trading. In April 1990, he pled guilty to six felonies and was sentenced to 10 years in a federal prison. Milken spent 22 months in a four-man cell at a minimum-security prison before he was released to a halfway house in January 1993. Ironically, he is also one of the first in line as a Drexel creditor, being owed more than $200 million in unpaid compensation from 1987. Banned from the securities industry for life because of his guilty pleas, Milken founded Knowledge Universe, an educational software company that had revenues over $1 billion in 1998.

What could have caused one of Wall Street's largest investment houses to topple? While the hefty SEC fine certainly sapped Drexel's strength, the death blow came as the $200 billion junk bond market slumped. Rising default rates, a slow economy, and regulations that forced S&Ls to divest junk bonds all contributed to a fall in value of almost 50 percent. Because it was holding junk bonds with a face value of nearly $1 billion, Drexel's credit rating began to slide. In an industry where trust and good faith are the stock in trade, any question about a firm's creditworthiness can cause disaster.

Disaster came calling on Drexel. Drexel's parent company could no longer use double leverage to finance its investment subsidiary. It had to buy back the stock of hundreds of laid-off employees and found itself strapped for cash. Drexel tried to arrange bank loans to no avail, as the rate at which banks would lend on junk bond collateral fell from 85 cents on the dollar to less than 50 cents. Drexel even sought a merger candidate that could infuse some cash. No one was willing to deal. The firm discovered only too quickly that confidence can vaporize when it defaulted for want of a mere $150 million, a fraction of what it could have raised only months before.

monly known, separated the investment-banking and commercial-banking industries. The act, however, did allow commercial banks some securities activities, such as underwriting and trading in U.S. government securities and some state and local government bonds. Thus, in the area of public securities, investment banks and commercial banks do compete.

The legislated separation of commercial banking and investment banking in the United States was somewhat unusual. In countries where there is no legislation, commercial banks provide investment-banking services as part of their normal range of business activities. The notable exception to this rule is Japan, which has securities laws that closely resemble those of the United States. Countries where investment banking and commercial banking are combined have what is called a universal-banking system. **Universal banks** are institutions that can accept deposits, make loans, underwrite securities, engage in brokerage activities, and sell and manufacture other financial services such as insurance. Most European countries allow universal banks.

During the 1980s and 1990s, commercial banks and investment banks came into competitive conflict. Large money-center and regional commercial banks saw their largest and most profitable customers increasingly switching from intermediation services, such as bank loans, to direct credit-market transactions, such as commercial paper. As a result, large commercial banks in the United States sought to break down the legal barrier to investment banking established by Glass-Steagall. Ultimately, they were successful in breaking down the barriers, but the barriers worked both ways. Now investment banks also have the opportunity to engage in commercial banking activities. As we shall see, the story of investment banking is inextricably interwined with that of commercial banking.

STRUCTURE OF THE INDUSTRY

There are over 1,400 investment-banking firms doing some underwriting business in the United States. However, the industry is dominated by the 50 largest firms, most of which have their head offices located in New York City. The balance are headquartered in major regional financial centers such as Chicago and Los Angeles.

Exhibit 19.1 lists the 10 largest investment banks ranked by the dollar amount of domestic securities (debt and equity) underwritten. The largest investment-banking firm is Citigroup, which in 2003 underwrote 847 issues totaling more than $200 billion. The next four largest firms underwrote more than 500 issues each, and the total amount underwritten ranged between $112 and $138 billion. It is important to note that in recent years, many investment-banking firms have merged with other financial firms or commercial banks to become full-service financial firms while others have divested subsidiaries to concentrate on their core business.

EARLY HISTORY

Investment banks in the United States trace their origins to the prominent investment houses in Europe, and many early investment banks were branches or affiliates of European firms. Early investment banks in the United States differed from commercial banks. Commercial banks were corporations that were chartered exclusively to issue banknotes (money) and make short-term business loans;

EXHIBIT 19.1
Ten Largest Investment Banks (2003)

Rank	Underwriter	Underwritings ($ millions)			Total Number of Offerings
		U.S. Equity Offerings	U.S. Debt Offerings	Total	
1	Citigroup	9,120	192,921	202,041	847
2	JP Morgan	5,467	132,124	137,591	696
3	Morgan Stanley	11,873	121,445	133,318	1,339
4	Lehman Brothers	6,212	118,095	124,307	518
5	Merrill Lynch	6,730	105,720	112,450	605
6	Deutsche Bank	961	97,962	98,923	403
7	Goldman Sachs	11,818	83,085	94,903	362
8	Credit Suisse First Boston	6,613	83,951	90,564	465
9	Bank of America	2,982	69,503	72,485	1,286
10	UBS	4,682	53,316	57,998	43

In 2003, Citigroup was the top dog among investment bankers. However, competition is fierce and positions can change substantially from year to year.

Source: Bloomberg Terminal.

early investment banks were partnerships and, therefore, were not subject to the regulations that apply to corporations. As such, investment banks, referred to as **private banks** at the time, could engage in any business activity they wished and could have offices in any location. Though investment banks could not issue banknotes, they could accept deposits as well as underwrite and trade in securities.

The golden era of investment banking began after the Civil War. Following the war, America began to build a railroad system that linked the country together and provided the infrastructure for industrialization. Modern investment-banking houses acted as intermediaries between the railroad firms—which needed massive amounts of capital to finance roadbeds, track, bridges, and rolling stock—and investors located primarily on the East Coast and in Europe. Because of the distance between investors and the investment project, investors found it difficult to estimate the value of the securities offered. The reputation of investment bankers to price securities fairly made these transactions possible.

With the rapid industrialization of America, companies began selling new securities publicly, and outstanding securities were traded on organized exchanges. The demand for financial services led to the growth of powerful investment-banking firms like those led by Jay Cooke, J. Pierpont Morgan, Marcus Goldman, and Solomon Loeb. These organizations created some of the giant businesses of the 20th century, such as United States Steel.

As it turned out, investment banking was a very profitable business. Firms discovered innumerable ways to make money, such as charging fees for underwriting, for financial consulting, for trading securities, for redeployment of a client's deposited funds, for private placements, for doing mergers and acquisitions, and so on. Early commercial banks, which were chartered exclusively to issue banknotes and make short-term loans, soon began to covet a wider range of financial activities, especially those that were highly profitable. Over time, because of competitive pressures, states began to permit their state-chartered commercial banks to engage in selected investment-banking activities.

National banks, which were regulated by the Comptroller of the Currency, began pressuring the comptroller for expanded powers. At first, national banks could underwrite and trade only in securities that they were permitted to invest in, which were primarily federal and municipal securities. With time, competitive pressure from state banks, which gained expanded powers more quickly, forced the comptroller to grant national banks the authority to underwrite and trade in corporate bonds and equities. Finally, national banks were allowed to organize state-chartered security affiliates that could engage in full-service investment banking. Thus, by 1930, commercial banks and investment banks were almost fully integrated, and they or their security affiliates were underwriting more than 50 percent of all new bond issues sold.

THE GLASS-STEAGALL ACT AND ITS AFTERMATH

In the 1930s, the long history of suspicion and questionable practices caught up with the investment-banking industry. On October 28, 1929, the stock market declined 12.8 percent, signaling the "crash of 1929" and the beginning of the Great Depression. During the Great Depression (1929–1933), output declined 30.5 percent compared to the beginning of 1929 and unemployment rose to over 20 percent of the workforce. More than 9,000 commercial banks failed. The country and the financial system were devastated. To deal with the crisis at hand, Congress enacted legislation. To regulate investment banks and Wall Street, Congress enacted the Securities Act of 1933, the Securities Exchange Act of 1934, and, of course, the Glass-Steagall Act of 1933 to regulate the banking system. Thus, after years of functioning with little regulation, the financial sector—the securities industry and commercial banking system—became one of the most heavily regulated sectors in the economy.

The Glass-Steagall Act of 1933 effectively separated commercial banking from investment banking.[1] The act did the following:

- It prohibited commercial banks from underwriting or trading (for their own account) stocks, bonds, or other securities. The major exceptions were U.S. government securities, general obligation bonds of state and local governments, and bank securities such as CDs.

- It limited the debt securities that commercial banks could purchase for their own account to those approved by bank regulatory authorities.

- It prohibited individuals and firms engaged in investment banking from simultaneously engaging in commercial banking.

---

[1] The Glass-Steagall Act is technically known as the Banking Act of 1933. The act's popular name comes from its major sponsors, Senator Carter Glass, who sponsored the Senate bill on commercial and investment banking, and Representative Henry Steagall, who sponsored the House bill on federal deposit insurance. The Banking Act of 1933 combined the two bills.

Thus commercial banks and investment banks were given a choice of being one or the other, but not both. Most firms elected to stay in their primary line of business and divested themselves of the prohibited activity. But not all firms did this. For example, Citibank, Chase Manhattan Bank, and Harris Trust took the most common route and dissolved their security affiliates. The investment-banking firm of J.P. Morgan decided to maintain a position as a commercial bank through its subsidiary, Morgan Guaranty and Trust Co. However, some senior partners left the firm to form the investment house of Morgan Stanley. The First Boston Corporation was patched together out of the cast-off security affiliates of several commercial banks, one of which was the affiliate of the First National Bank of Boston.

The Glass-Steagall Act, when passed, had three basic objectives: (1) to discourage speculation in financial markets, (2) to prevent conflict of interest and self-dealing, and (3) to restore confidence in the safety and soundness of the banking system. Regarding speculation, the Act's proponents argued that if banks were affiliated with securities dealers, banks would have incentives to lend to customers of the security affiliates, who would use the money to buy stock on credit. Thus, banks engaged in investment banking were channeling money into "speculative" investment rather than into what was believed to be more productive investments. The conflict-of-interest rationale hinged on the fear that commercial banks might make imprudent loans to firms it had underwritten securities for in order to gain additional securities business. Thus, the quality of the bank's loan portfolio could be compromised by the bank's dual role of lender and investment banker.

Perhaps the most important reason for the Glass-Steagall Act was the fear over bank safety and the desire to prevent bank failures. Simply stated, investment banking is a risky business. Debt and equity markets are inherently subject to large price fluctuations, with the risk of such fluctuations being borne by security dealers and underwriters. The Act insulated commercial banks from that risk by prohibiting them from acting as dealers, underwriters of securities, and investors in private-sector companies.

THE COMPETITION BETWEEN COMMERCIAL AND INVESTMENT BANKING

Beginning in the 1980s, large U.S. commercial banks increasingly pursued their desire to engage in investment banking. These banks discovered that commercial banking was not as profitable as it once was, whereas some investment-banking activities were becoming extremely profitable. At the same time, many of their best customers were turning to investment banks for short-term financing, the traditional business of commercial banks. Commercial banks wanted the flexibility, as other financial firms have, to shift to other more profitable product lines as business conditions change. Because of the lack of flexibility, some large commercial banks in New York City, most notably Chase Manhattan (now J.P. Morgan Chase), threatened to give up their banking charters so that they could operate as investment banks.

The primary factors changing the relationship between commercial and investment banking were (1) the interaction between economic and technological forces and (2) regulatory constraints. First, economic and technological forces comprised the development and merging of electronic computers and telecommunications. With the new technology, electronic information processing is reducing the cost of gathering data, manufacturing, and transmitting financial products to the ultimate user. The technology not only makes it possible to provide traditional financial services at reduced cost but also makes the creation of new financial products feasible. Lower transaction costs favor direct-credit-market rather than intermediation transactions.

A second reason working against intermediation financing is the regulatory taxes that commercial banks must pay relative to other financial firms. Most important are the requirement to hold non-interest-earning reserves against deposits and the mandatory capital requirements that exceed those that would exist in the absence of regulation. Banks find that they are at a disadvantage in financing and keeping loans on their books, although they still have a comparative advantage in analyzing credit risk and originating transactions. As a result of these forces (economic, technological, and regulatory), there is a trend for borrowers to place debt directly with investors and, correspondingly, to do fewer transactions with intermediaries such as commercial banks. Evidence of declining information costs is found in the shrinking amount of bank borrowing by large and middle-market corporate companies that once relied on banks as their primary source of funds.

SECURITIES ACTIVITIES OF COMMERCIAL BANKS

For many years, banks have been able to underwrite and trade (dealer and broker) U.S. government securities and general obligation bonds, to trade financial futures, to do private placement deals, and to do merger and acquisition work. The securities activities denied commercial banks under the Glass-Steagall Act were underwriting and trading corporate bonds, equities, and commercial paper; underwriting and selling mutual funds; and being a full-service broker and investment adviser.

The 1980s, however, marked the beginning of the crumbling of Glass-Steagall's power to limit banks' securities activities. The most important action of the decade may be the U.S. Supreme Court decision on July 13, 1988, to let stand the Federal Reserve Board's approval for commercial banks to underwrite three new kinds of securities: commercial paper, municipal revenue bonds, and securities backed by mortgages or consumer debt. The new securities activities had to be handled through a separate subsidiary of a bank holding company, and underwriting activities could not account for more than 5 percent of the subsidiary's gross revenues. The Fed's approval of the new powers was based on its interpretation that the percentage limit on underwriting would keep the bank affiliate from being "engaged principally" in securities, which was barred by the Glass-Steagall Act. In addition, on June 20, 1989, the Federal Reserve Board allowed J.P. Morgan to underwrite and deal in corporate debt in the United States through its security affiliate, and on September 20, 1990, the Fed allowed J.P. Morgan to underwrite corporate equity in the United States.

At the same time, investment banks began encroaching on activities that were traditionally the preserves of commercial banks. For example, one of the most damaging moves into retail banking was the introduction of money market mutual funds that drew billions of dollars away from commercial banks during the high-interest-rate periods of the late 1970s and early 1980s. It was not until banks were allowed to offer money market deposit accounts that banks regained a portion of their customers. At the commercial level, investment banks moved into short-term business financing with commercial paper, which drew corporate borrowers away from banks to the securities houses that marketed the paper. Finally, investment banks entered the foreign exchange market, which was traditionally a bank activity.

BANKS ENTER INVESTMENT BANKING

By the late 1990s, commercial banks became free to acquire investment banks in spite of the Glass-Steagall Act because of various rulings by regulators and the passage of the Financial Services Modernization Act of 1999 (the Gramm-Leach-Bliley Act). Recall from Chapter 16 that the Gramm-Leach-Bliley Act allows commercial banks, investment banks, and insurance companies to affiliate with each other as part of a "financial holding company" organizational structure. The first acquisition of a major investment bank by a commercial bank occurred in 1997, when Bankers Trust of New York, now part of Deutsche Bank, bought Alex Brown for $2.1 billion. This acquisition, for practical purposes, signaled the end of the Depression-era legislation, the Glass-Steagall Act. Large commercial banks are now able to freely enter into investment banking. Today, nearly every large commercial bank has a significant investment-banking affiliate. Likewise, investment banks (and insurance companies) are able to acquire commercial-banking affiliates and form financial holding companies.

The lure for commercial banks to enter investment banking was that the return on equity for investment banks was substantially higher than for commercial banks during the bull market of the 1990s. The large profits for investment banks came from equity offerings and advising on mergers and acquisitions, not on the debt-offering side of the business, which is the side of the business that commercial banks entered into in the early 1990s. During the 1990s, commercial banks spent more than $40 billion acquiring investment banks.

So far, commercial banks have little to show for these high-stake investments, and some have considered selling their investment-banking subsidiaries. There are a number of problems that have emerged. First and most immediate, beginning with the 2001 recession, investment-banking business profits are down substantially, depressing investment bank stocks. The very profitable merger and acquisition (M&A) activity has declined sharply as have equity offerings. For example, J.P. Morgan Chase, whose stock price declined 20 percent during the 2001–2002 recession, fired its highest-profile investment banker, Geoffrey Boisi. Mr. Boisi was the cohead of the firm's investment-banking division, which had performed below expectations. Second, commercial banks have had difficulty retaining the top investment bankers, whose talents drive the business and made the acquisitions originally enticing. For example, Nationsbank, now Bank of America, acquired Montgomery Securities in 1997, and today there are only 9 out of the 68 original partners left. Third, cultural clashes have been a major problem. Commercial lenders are very good at focusing on downside risk—credit risk—and lending as a relationship business. In contrast, investment banks are deal makers; they take fees for arranging mergers or security offerings and move to the next deal. They are not long-term oriented. Citicorp recognized early on the sharp cultural difference between deal makers and bankers and has kept the two groups separated.

Are large commercial banks going to exit investment banking? A few may, but most will stay the course. Those who persevere will ultimately be able to build strong businesses when the market improves. What is true, however, is that integrating these two dissimilar businesses and cultures is difficult and firms will have to figure out the right structure to get the maximum synergy. Furthermore, all of the investment-banking acquisitions so far by commercial banks have involved smaller investment-banking firms. This suggests, at least for now, that the investment-banking firms, like Merrill Lynch, Morgan Stanley Dean Witter, and Goldman Sachs, will remain independent.

LOOKING AHEAD

Looking ahead, what appears likely to emerge are a core of 15 to 20 large U.S. financial institutions—commercial banks, investment banks, and perhaps some insurance companies that will dominate this country's financial system. These firms are not following a one-size-fits-all business model. Rather, they have different strategies that will allow them to differentiate themselves in the marketplace. These firms will operate in major financial centers throughout the United States as well as in major international financial centers, such as London, Tokyo, Hong Kong, and Frankfurt. They will compete head-to-head to do business with the world's major corporations and investors; will have the capability to underwrite and trade a wide range of financial securities; and will be the flagship financial firms for the U.S. economy in the battle for world economic dominance.

PRIMARY SERVICES OF AN INVESTMENT BANK

Unlike commercial banks, investment banks are not restricted in the range of business activities in which they can engage. The following section describes the major business activities of investment-banking firms.

BRINGING NEW SECURITIES TO MARKET

One of the basic services offered by an investment-banking firm is to bring to market new debt and equity securities issued by private firms or governmental units that require funds. New issues of stocks or bonds are called **primary offerings**. If the company has never before offered securities to the public, the primary offering is called an **unseasoned offering** or an **initial public offering (IPO)**. Otherwise, if the firm already has similar securities trading in the market, the primary issue is called a **seasoned offering**.

An offering can be either a **public offering** or a **private placement**. If a company decides to make a public offering, it must then decide whether to have the issue **underwritten** or sold on a **best-efforts basis**. As the terms imply, in an underwritten issue the investment banker will guarantee (underwrite) that the issuer will receive a fixed amount of money whether the securities are all sold to investors or not. In a best-efforts issue the investment banker makes no such guarantee and instead promises only to make its best sales effort. In this case, the investment banker does not take on the risk associated with underwriting, and compensation is based on the number of securities sold. Not surprisingly, most issuing corporations prefer underwritten to best-efforts contracts, so the actual decision on issue type falls to the investment banker, who usually only forces the smallest and riskiest issues to be handled on a best-efforts basis.

Another decision that must be made by a corporation wishing to make an underwritten security is whether to solicit investment-banking services through

competitive bidding. With competitive bidding, the issuer publicly announces a desire to sell securities and solicits offers from several investment-banking firms. The alternative is direct negotiation with a single investment banker. Virtually all corporations that have a real choice (utilities frequently are legally required to use competitive bidding) choose **negotiated offering** procedures.

The seemingly irrational choice of negotiated offerings can be explained by the fact that investment bankers must invest in performing **due diligence** examinations of potential security issuers. This means that they are legally required to diligently search out and disclose all relevant information about an issuer before securities are sold to the public or the underwriter can be held legally responsible for investor losses that occur after the issue is sold. Since investors understand that the most prestigious investment bankers have the most to lose from inadequate due diligence, the mere fact that these firms are willing to underwrite an issue provides valuable certification that the issuing company is in fact disclosing all material information. With so much to lose, top-tier investment bankers are unlikely to be enticed by competitive bid issues that entail the same risk, but far less profit, as negotiated bids. Thus, issuing firms are willing to pay the higher direct issuance costs of a negotiated bid to obtain the services of a prestigious underwriter.

One of the problems investment bankers face with IPOs is how to price them, since they are securities that have never been traded. The price a security is sold for is important to the issuer because it sets the firm's cost of capital. However, the price must be set "right" to be fair to both the issuing firm and the investment banker. For example, if a firm is selling stock and a new issue is priced too low, more shares are sold than necessary to raise the needed funds, which dilutes the firm's earnings. If the price is too high, the underwriter cannot sell the issue at the proposed offering price, and the investment banker suffers a loss.

The average IPO suffers from **underpricing**. Shares are typically sold to investors at an offering price that is, on average, about 15 percent below the closing price of the shares after the first day of trading. This implies that underwriters deliberately (and consistently) sell shares to investors for only six-sevenths of their value. Exhibit 19.2 gives information on the number of IPOs per year since 1980, the average initial return to investors, and the gross proceeds raised.

In bringing securities to market, investment bankers take clients through three steps: origination, underwriting (risk bearing), and distribution. Depending on the method of sale and the client's needs, an investment banker may provide these services.

Origination. During the origination of a new security issue, the investment banker can help the issuer analyze the feasibility of the project and determine the amount of money to raise; decide on the type of financing needed (debt, equity); design the characteristics of securities to be issued, such as maturity, coupon rate, and the presence of a call provision and/or sinking fund for debt issues; and provide advice on the best sale date so that the issuer can get the highest possible price.

Once the decision to issue the securities is made, the investment banker can help the client prepare the official sale documents. If the securities are to be sold publicly, security laws require that a **registration statement** be filed with the Securities and Exchange Commission (SEC). A portion of this statement, called the **preliminary prospectus**, contains detailed information about the issuer's financial condition, business activities, industry competition, management and

EXHIBIT 19.2
Initial Public Offerings, Gross Proceeds, and Returns

Year	Number of Offerings	Average First Day Return (%)	Gross Proceeds ($ in Millions)
1980	70	14.5	$2,020
1981	191	5.9	4,613
1982	77	11.4	1,839
1983	442	10.1	15,348
1984	172	3.6	3,543
1985	179	6.3	6,963
1986	378	6.3	19,653
1987	271	6.0	16,299
1988	97	5.4	5,324
1989	105	8.1	6,773
1990	104	10.8	5,611
1991	273	12.1	15,923
1992	385	10.2	26,373
1993	483	12.8	34,422
1994	387	9.8	19,323
1995	432	21.5	28,347
1996	621	16.7	45,940
1997	432	13.8	31,701
1998	267	22.3	34,628
1999	457	71.7	66,770
2000	346	56.1	62,593
2001	80	14.0	34,344

Initial public offerings consistently earn large, positive initial returns for investors that are allocated shares. Note that this table excludes offerings with an initial price below $5 per share.

Source: J. Ritter and I. Welch, "A Review of IPO Activity, Pricing, and Allocations," *Journal of Finance,* pp. 1795–1828, LVII, No. 4 (August 2002).

their experience, the project for which the funds will be used, the characteristics of the securities to be issued, and the risks of the securities. After approval by the SEC, the **final prospectus** is reproduced in quantity and distributed to all potential investors. By law, investors must have a final prospectus before they can invest. The information in the prospectus allows investors to make intelligent decisions about the proposed project and its risk. SEC approval only implies that the information presented is timely and fair; approval is not an endorsement by the SEC as to investment quality. Exhibit 19.3 shows the front page of a final prospectus.

During the registration process for a debt issue, the investment banker can also help secure a credit rating; coordinate the activities of a bond counsel, who

EXHIBIT 19.3
The Front Page of a Final Prospectus

Filed Pursuant to Rule 424(b)(4)
Registration No. 333-114442-01,
333-117324

Prospectus

24,221,929 shares

Domino's Pizza, Inc.

Common stock

Domino's Pizza, Inc., the parent company of Domino's, Inc., is selling 9,375,000 shares of common stock, and the selling stockholders identified in this prospectus are selling an additional 14,846,929 shares. We will not receive any of the proceeds from the sale of the shares by the selling stockholders. This is the initial public offering of our common stock.

Prior to this offering, there has been no public market for our common stock. Our common stock has been approved for listing on the New York Stock Exchange under the symbol "DPZ."

	Per share	Total
Initial public offering price	$ 14.00	$339,107,006
Underwriting discount	$ 0.96	$ 23,253,052
Proceeds to Domino's Pizza, Inc., before expenses	$ 13.04	$122,250,000
Proceeds to selling stockholders, before expenses	$ 13.04	$193,603,954

The selling stockholders have granted the underwriters an option for a period of 30 days to purchase up to 3,633,289 additional shares of our common stock on the same terms and conditions set forth above to cover overallotments, if any.

Investing in our common stock involves a high degree of risk. See "Risk factors" beginning on page 9.

Neither the Securities and Exchange Commission nor any state securities commission has approved or disapproved of these securities or passed upon the adequacy or accuracy of this prospectus. Any representation to the contrary is a criminal offense.

The offering is being made on a firm commitment basis, and the underwriters expect to deliver the shares of common stock to investors on July 16, 2004.

JPMorgan   Citigroup

Bear, Stearns & Co. Inc.

Credit Suisse First Boston

Lehman Brothers

July 12, 2004

The prospectus provides full disclosure of relevant information to prospective investors in compliance with U.S. securities laws.

passes an opinion about the legality of the security issue; select a transfer agent for secondary market sales; select a trustee, who sees that the issuer fulfills its obligation under the security contract; and arrange for printing of the securities so that they can be distributed to investors. For an equity issue, the investment banker can arrange for the securities to be listed on a stock exchange or traded in the over-the-counter market.

Underwriting.   Underwriting, or bearing price risk, is what most people think that investment bankers do in a firm-commitment offering. Underwriting is the process whereby the investment banker guarantees to buy the new securities for a fixed price. The risk exists between the time the investment banker purchases the securities from the issuer and the time they are resold to the public. The risk (inventory risk) is that the securities may be sold for less than the **underwriting syndicate** purchased them. In seasoned offerings, there is a risk of unforeseen price changes as a result of changes in market conditions. For example, in October 1979, IBM issued $1 billion in bonds through a syndicate of underwriters. As the issue was coming to market, interest rates suddenly jumped upward, causing bond prices to tumble, and the underwriters lost in excess of $10 million. In unseasoned offerings, there is no prior market price on which to base the offering price.

To decrease the price risk of any one primary issue, underwriters form syndicates comprising other investment-banking firms. Each member of the syndicate is responsible for its pro rata share of the securities being issued. By participating in the syndicate, each underwriter receives a portion of the underwriting fee as well as an allocation of the securities being sold that it can sell to its own customers. In addition, other investment-banking firms, known as the selling group, can be enlisted to assist in the sale of the securities being issued. Members of the selling group bear no underwriting responsibility but receive a commission for whatever securities they sell.

Distribution.   Once the investment banker purchases the securities, they must be resold to investors. The syndicate's primary concern is to sell the securities as quickly as possible at the offering price. If the securities are not sold within a few days, the underwriting syndicate disbands, and members sell the securities at whatever price they can get.

The sales function is divided into institutional sales and retail sales. Retail sales involve selling the securities to individual investors and firms that purchase in small quantities. Examples of national investment-banking firms with a strong retail presence are Merrill Lynch, with an extensive network of 565 branches, and Morgan Stanley Dean Witter, with 448 offices. Most regional investment-banking firms specialize in retail sales. Institutional sales involve the sale of a large block of securities to institutional purchasers, such as pension funds, insurance companies, endowment trusts, or mutual funds. Included among the well-known institutional firms are Goldman Sachs, First Boston, and Salomon Smith Barney.

TRADING AND BROKERAGE

In addition to underwriting and selling newly issued securities, investment banks also provide services as **brokers** or **dealers** for existing securities in the aftermarket; that is, they facilitate secondary offerings for existing securities. Aftermarket

A Loose E-mail Clogs the IPO Money Machine

Frank Quattrone was considered the most powerful investment banker in the dot-com era, handling many prominent high tech IPOs, including Silicon Graphics, Cisco, VA Linux, Netscape, and Amazon.com. During the 1990s high tech stock market bubble, he raised billions of dollars in capital for high tech firms and made hundreds of millions in investment banking fees, profits for entrepreneurs, and bonuses for his employees. He didn't do too badly for himself, either. During the period 1998-2000 alone, Quattrone is reported to have earned $200 million while managing 138 tech IPOs for Credit Suisse First Boston (CSFB). In the backlash following the bursting of the high tech bubble, he now faces an 18-month prison sentence thanks to hitting "Reply All" on an e-mail he received and adding 22 words that encouraged the recipients to heed the first e-mail.

Growing up in a working class family in Philadelphia, Quattrone was fascinated with risk taking from an early age. He finished his MBA at Stanford in the early 1980s and became obsessed with Silicon Valley at a time when the Wall Street establishment largely ignored high tech enterpreneurs. He joined Morgan Stanley, which subsequently became the first Wall Street firm to put an investment banking office in Silicon Valley. In 1996 he moved to Deutsche Bank Securities, finally landing at CSFB in 1998.

Quattrone embraced the entrepreneurs of Silicon Valley. With ski trips, golf outings, and late night karaoke sessions, Quattrone developed a network of strong relationships with entrepreneurs and venture capitalists, ultimately bringing them together to fuel the growth of Silicon Valley. As these firms grew and required more capital, they turned to Quattrone to handle their IPOs. Ultimately, Quattrone became the king of dot-com investment bankers.

Along the way, some questionable practices evolved in the IPO market that came under the scrutiny of securities regulators and prosecutors. One practice, called "spinning" involved investment banks allocating shares in hot IPOs to favored clients in exchange for future business. Another practice involved investment bankers urging stock analysts in their firms to issue glowing reports on the prospects of current and future IPO clients. Quattrone and CSFB came under investigation for these practices, both of which violate securities regulations. CSFB ultimately paid $100 million to settle the cases without admitting any liability.

Ironically, Quattrone has not been indicted for either questionable practice. He was, however, tried and found guilty of obstructing the Federal government's investigation of these practices. The "smoking gun" in the case against him was a 22-word e-mail that he forwarded to his coworkers in which he encouraged everyone to comply with CSFB's standard "document retention" policy. In most businesses, any documents not required to be retained under such a policy are destroyed. The jury in his case, therefore, interpreted his e-mail as tantamount to encouraging employees to destroy potentially incriminating documents, thereby keeping them from the eyes of Federal investigators. On September 8, 2004, Quattrone was sentenced to 18 months in Federal prison, two years of probation, and a fine of $90,300.

A former Quattrone coworker says that Quattrone, who had to deal with hundreds of e-mails daily, had a habit of adding "color commentary" to e-mails as a way of reinforcing messages to employees. Ironically, the "deadly" 22-words Quattrone added to the e-mail were superfluous with the comments of an attached e-mail, apparently meant to encourage employees to read and comply with the firm's standard policy. Questioning whether Quattrone had any criminal intent, this former coworker characterized the government's case as trying to make a jury "simultaneously believe in two impossible contrasts of the same man: on [sic] the one hand, Frank is the wildly successful, Wharton-educated, Wall Street power broker at the top of his game, while on the other side he is the complete idiot who risked his entire position in life on a blatantly incriminating e-mail that he didn't need even [sic] to send in the first place."

activities may involve a simple brokerage function, in which the firm earns a commission for bringing buyer and seller together; or it may involve a dealer function, in which the investment bank carries an inventory of securities from which it executes buy and sell orders and trades for its own account. When an investment bank acts as a dealer for a security, it is said to be "making a market" in the security and is known as a "market maker." The **market maker** is willing to buy the security at one price, known as the bid price, and sell it at a higher price, the ask price. The market maker makes a profit based on the difference between the bid and the ask prices. The price difference is known as the **bid–ask spread**. Of course, with the ownership of the asset comes the risk of price fluctuations caused by changes in economic and market conditions. Because securities firms operate with a small capital base, small declines in the price of securities held can result in insolvency.

Exhibit 19.4 shows the financial assets and liabilities for security brokers and dealers. As can be seen, their largest single asset is security credit. This represents funds that brokerage firms have loaned to their customers for the purchase of securities with margin accounts. **Margin trading** simply means that the investor can buy securities partly with borrowed money. For example, if a customer uses a 40 percent margin, it means that 40 percent of the investment is being financed with the investor's own money and the balance, 60 percent, is financed with money borrowed from the brokerage house. Most types of securities can be purchased on margin—for example, common and preferred stock, corporate and Treasury bonds, convertible bonds, warrants, commodities, financial futures, and mutual funds. Margin requirements are set by the Board of Governors of the Federal Reserve System, and they currently are 50 percent for both equity and debt securities. The other principal assets of brokers and dealers are securities held as dealers' inventories or inventories held from underwriting activities.

The largest source of funds for dealers and brokers is customer credit balances. Customer credit balances represent funds owed by brokers and dealers to

EXHIBIT 19.4
Financial Assets and Liabilities of Security Brokers and Dealers (June 2004)

Financial Assets	($ in Billions)	Financial Liabilities	($ in Billions)
Checkable deposits and currency	52.4	Repurchase agreements	498.8
Open-market paper	48.6	Corporate bonds	60.0
U.S. government securities	113.4	Trade payables	34.5
Municipal securities	25.3	Customer credit balances	507.2
Corporate and foreign bonds	225.6	Security credit from banks	239.2
Corporate equities	113.7	Taxes payable	1.9
Security credit	199.1	Miscellaneous liabilities	290.3
Miscellaneous assets	946.5		
Total assets	1724.6	Total liabilities	1631.9

Source: Board of Governors, Federal Reserve System, *Flow of Funds Accounts.*

their customers following the sale of the customer's securities, as well as customers' funds held in cash management accounts. Security credit from banks is short-term financing in the form of **call loans**, which are collateralized by the securities being financed. **Repurchase agreements** involve the actual sale of the securities to the lender by the borrower, who then commits to repurchase the securities at a higher price. Call loans and repurchase agreements are usually arranged on a daily basis.

Full-Service Brokerage Firms. Brokerage houses compete for investors' business by offering a variety of services that are sold by stockbrokers or account executives. Stockbrokers must be licensed by the National Association of Securities Dealers (NASD), and they must abide by the ethical guidelines of the NASD and the exchanges on which they place orders. The NASD is a self-regulating body comprising brokerage houses. For their services, stockbrokers receive commission rates that vary with the service provided. The basic services provided by a full-service brokerage firm are described next.

Storage of Securities. Investors can leave securities with a broker for safekeeping; thus the investor does not have to rent a safety-deposit box or physically transfer securities to and from the broker's office when a transaction is made. Investors are protected against loss of the securities or cash held by brokers by the Security Investor Protection Corporation (SIPC). The SIPC insures each customer's account up to $500,000 in securities and up to $100,000 in cash balances. Note, however, that the SIPC does not guarantee the dollar value of securities but guarantees only that the securities themselves will be returned.

Execution of Trades. A broker earns a commission by buying or selling all types of financial securities, from U.S. Treasury securities to speculative instruments such as futures and options. Brokers transact on all the major exchanges, such as the New York Stock Exchange; on any of the regional exchanges, such as the Pacific Stock Exchange; and in the over-the-counter market, where most debt instruments, such as U.S. Treasury bonds and more speculative common stocks, are traded.

Investment Advice. Brokerage firms provide a wide range of investment information and advice to their clients, ranging from simple stock and bond guides to detailed research reports written by a security analyst on a particular investment. In addition, some firms publish periodic publications or newsletters that analyze economic, market, and industry conditions and provide lists of securities or investments that the firm's analyst recommends investors buy or sell.

Margin Credit. Brokerage-firm customers can obtain either a cash or margin account. Cash customers must pay cash for the security when it is purchased. Or the client can apply for a margin account, which allows the investor to borrow part of the money from the brokerage firm to pay for the security purchased. The rate of interest charged is usually marked up 1 to 2 percent above the broker's call loan rate (the rate at which brokers borrow from commercial banks), which is usually slightly below the commercial bank prime rate.

Cash Management Services. In recent years, the major brokerage houses have offered investors a variety of cash management account (CMA) programs.

Although the services may vary from firm to firm, a typical CMA allows investors to write checks against credit balances and the value of securities they hold in their brokerage account. The brokerage firm may also broker savings deposits from depository institutions (commercial banks and thrifts); that is, the brokerage house sells federally insured savings deposits to investors who want to hold long-term insured deposits but do not want to bear the prepayment penalty for possible early withdrawal. Finally, some brokerage firms issue credit cards (such as Visa) to their CMA customers, which allows them to obtain funds by drawing down their credit balances or borrowing against the securities in their accounts. Thus, CMAs allow brokerage houses to provide many of the services provided by commercial banks, but at the same time they are not subject to restrictive bank regulations.

Discount Brokerage Firms.   In recent years, a new type of brokerage firm has emerged to compete against full-service brokerage firms—the so-called **discount broker**. Discount brokerage firms compete against full-service brokerage firms by offering fewer brokerage services and passing the savings on to the investors. Specifically, most discount brokerage firms do not have a highly paid research staff producing research reports or account executives soliciting business based on the firm's current recommendations to buy and sell. Instead, they hire telephone clerks to take customers' orders. These clerks do not sell, do not offer any investment advice, and work for modest salaries. These and other savings are passed along to the investor in the form of lower commissions.

Banks as Brokers.   It is important to note that the Glass-Steagall Act does not preclude commercial banks from acting as brokers on behalf of their customers. Recall that brokers, unlike dealers, do not take title to securities but only bring buyer and seller together, an activity that is legal for commercial banks. Until the 1980s, however, commercial banks did not emphasize their brokerage powers or solicit business, except to serve a few large accounts in their trust departments. Beginning in the 1980s, commercial banks began to offer trading services to retail customers, usually in the form of discount brokerage.

Some banks started their own brokerage operations from scratch and others entered into joint-venture arrangements, whereby the bank purchases broker services from an established securities firm and markets the services under the name of the bank. To date, more than 2,000 banks are providing active brokerage services to their customers. Even though the numbers of banks selling brokerage services is impressive, in most cases the operations have not been as profitable as expected.

Arbitrage Activities.   Closely associated with the market-making activities of investment-banking firms are **arbitrage** activities. The essential difference between market making as a dealer or as an arbitrageur is that a risk-free arbitrage transaction involves the simultaneous buying and selling of a security to take advantage of a price anomaly that may exist between two markets. For example, if GMC stock is trading for $35 per share on the New York Stock Exchange (NYSE) and $34 per share on the Pacific Stock Exchange (PSE), an arbitrageur at an investment bank would buy GMC stock on the PSE at $34 per share and immediately sell it for $35 per share on the NYSE. The process would continue until the price differential between the two exchanges was closed so that no arbitrage profits remained after transaction costs. Because investment banks have low costs for their own trades, their arbitrageurs can usually spot and exploit arbitrage opportunities before they are large enough to be profitable to the general public. Investment banks find that arbitrage activities are not only profitable but that they also serve the useful purpose of making financial markets more efficient.

PRIVATE PLACEMENTS

For many businesses, the sale of securities (debt or equity) to the public is not feasible. A private placement is a method of issuing securities in which the issuer sells the securities directly to the ultimate investors. Because there is no underwriting in a private placement deal, the investment banker's role is to bring buyer and seller together, to help determine a fair price for the securities, and to execute the transaction. For these services, the investment banker earns a fee. Firms choose between a private placement and public sale, depending on which method of sale offers to the issuer the highest possible price for the securities after transaction costs.

To qualify for a private placement exemption, the sale of the securities must be restricted to a small group of **accredited investors**. To qualify as an accredited investor, the individual or institution must meet certain income and wealth requirements. The reasoning for the private placement exemption is that accredited investors are financially sophisticated and do not need the protection afforded by the registration process. Typical institutional accredited investors include insurance companies, pension funds, mutual funds, and venture capitalists.

Private placements have several advantages over public securities offerings. They are less costly in terms of time and money than registering with the SEC, and the issuers do not have to reveal confidential information. Also, because there typically are far fewer investors, the terms of a private placement are easier to renegotiate, if necessary. The disadvantage of private placements is that the securities have no readily available market price, they are less liquid, and there is a smaller group of potential investors compared to the public market.

One of the restrictions that the Securities Act of 1933 imposed on buyers of private placements was that they hold the securities for at least 2 years. At the time, it was feared that firms would sell their new securities issues through the private placement market as a means to circumvent the new regulations requiring that securities sold in the public markets be registered through the SEC. The legislation was designed to protect less sophisticated investors with small portfolios from being duped to purchase risky or fraudulent unregistered securities. Rule 144A removes this restriction and allows large institutions to trade private placements among themselves without having to hold the securities for 2 years or register them with the SEC. Large institutions are defined as firms that hold a security portfolio of at least $100 million. The rule significantly improves the liquidity of private placements and, hence, reduces the cost of raising funds.

MERGERS AND ACQUISITIONS

Beginning in the 1980s, mergers and acquisitions (M&As) have become an important and high-profit business activity for investment-banking firms. The reason for the growth in the M&A market is the large number of business consolidations driven by technology and the globalization of business. Though the level of M&A

activity ebbs and flows with economic conditions, M&A work will continue to be an important part of investment banks' business mix into the future, especially in restructuring activities in Europe.

Investment banks provide four categories of M&A services for which they earn fees. First, investment bankers can help firms identify M&A candidates that match the acquiring firm's needs. Large investment banks have a global network of industry and regional contacts that can quickly identify potential acquisition candidates and assess their interest in being acquired.

Second, once an acquisition candidate firm is located, the investment bank can do all of the analysis necessary to price the deal. These activities include reviewing the target firm's financial statements and financial projections, estimating the expected future cash flows, evaluating the firm's management team, doing the due diligence, and, finally, determining the estimated value (price) of the firm. Due diligence is checking the validity of all of the important information the firm has provided the potential buyers. The potential buyers want to make sure that if a firm is purchased, they get what they are promised. The expected cash flows are the heart of the valuation process. There are two cash flows that must be estimated: (1) the cash flows of the acquired firm as a stand-alone business and (2) the additional cash flow that the acquiring firm can generate if it purchases the business. For example, if you're a food-processing firm such as Kraft foods and you buy a regional firm that manufactures egg rolls, you may be able to generate significant additional sales (and cash flows) by selling the egg rolls through your national distribution system. In theory, the acquiring firm that can generate the largest net cash flow should be the firm willing to pay the highest price for the firm.

Third, the investment bankers will work with the acquiring firm management, provide advice, and help them negotiate the deal. Finally, once the deal is complete, investment banks can assist the acquiring firm in obtaining the funds to finance the purchase. These activities range anywhere from arranging bank loans to arranging bridge financing, underwriting the sale of equity or debt, or arranging a leveraged buyout (LBO) deal. Bridge financing is just a temporary loan until permanent financing is obtained. An LBO is where a firm is acquired by issuing debt and then taken private. Both buying and selling firms may seek the services of investment bankers because for most firms, M&As are occasional or intermittent events; thus, hiring expert counsel is good business practice.

The fee charged by investment-banking firms depends on the extent of the work they perform and the complexity of the tasks they are asked to perform. In some cases, the investment banker may simply receive an advisory fee or retainer. In most cases, however, the banker will receive a fee based on the percentage of the selling price. One fee structure used by investment bankers, called the 5-4-3-2-1 formula, is where the investment banker receives 5 percent on the first $1 million, 4 percent on the second $1 million, 3 percent of the third $1 million, 2 percent of the fourth $1 million, and 1 percent on the remaining amount. The flat rate for investment banks' sales is typically 2 to 3 percent of the selling price.

OTHER BUSINESS ACTIVITIES

Investment-banking firms are extremely flexible organizations and will provide virtually any financial service if the firm can earn a satisfactory return. For example, given the high degree of expertise among investment bank personnel, financial consulting is a natural service for them to offer their clients. Financial consulting services include assisting clients in financial planning, determining a firm's optimal financial structure or dividend policy, and providing feasibility studies for major capital projects. The consulting reputation of some investment banks has reached the point where financial consulting is a major source of income and competitive advantage for these firms in competing for other types of business.

Another important business activity for investment banks has been real estate investment and brokerage. Beginning in the 1970s, large institutional investors became increasingly interested in purchasing real estate for investment purposes. Realizing the opportunity, investment banks established real estate departments or subsidiaries that represent clients in the sale or purchase of large commercial properties, such as office buildings, shopping centers, and agricultural land. In the 1980s real estate departments generated substantial profits for investment banks as their activities were fueled by petrodollars from oil-rich countries and from Japanese investors' interest in U.S. real estate because of the dollar's low value relative to the yen.

DO YOU UNDERSTAND?

1. What was the purpose of the Glass-Steagall Act?
2. Describe the steps entailed in underwriting a new security issue.
3. In what activities other than underwriting new securities are investment banks involved?

VENTURE CAPITAL

A relatively new financial intermediary, the **venture capital** firm, has emerged in the last 20 years. Venture capital firms managed investments totaling less than $3 billion in the 1970s. Today they manage over $100 billion. The term "venture capitalist" is usually used to denote institutional investors that provide equity financing to young businesses and play an active role in advising their management. These funds have been a major source of equity capital for new businesses, especially in technology-based industries. Other types of venture capital funds invest in leveraged buyouts and turnaround situations.

WHAT IS VENTURE CAPITAL?

New corporations raise funds from a variety of sources. Initial financing typically is provided by the firm's founders and their friends, and later financing often comes from individuals and perhaps banks. Eventually, a successful venture may raise funds from a public offering of its stock or be acquired by a larger corporation. Venture capital is yet another source of funds to finance growth. Venture capitalists are equity-oriented investors who also provide management expertise to the company. They are most likely to invest after the enterprise has exhausted capital provided by its founders but before it is merged into a larger firm or makes an initial public offering of its stock.

WHO ARE VENTURE CAPITALISTS?

Venture capital firms fall primarily into three categories: private funds, corporate subsidiaries, and publicly funded small business investment corporations. Private funds, typically organized as limited partnerships, are by far the largest. The typical fund manages about $50 million to $100 million, and nearly three-quarters of all venture capital funds manage between $25 and $250 million. The largest funds manage over $1 billion of capital.

Private venture capital funds raise capital from a variety of sources, but over half comes from other financial intermediaries such as pension funds and insurance companies. Private venture capitalists are compensated in two ways, with a management fee and a **carried interest** in the fund. The management fee typically is 1 or 2 percent of the value of the fund. The management fee covers the cost of operating the venture capital fund. It pays for salaries, offices, and travel to investigate potential investments. The carried interest represents the incentive portion of the venture capitalist's compensation. Typically, the venture capitalist receives 20 percent of the profits the fund generates. In some cases the venture capitalist gets 20 percent of the profits only after the investors have received some nominal rate of return on their investment, 8 percent per year, for example.

Corporate subsidiaries specializing in venture capital make investments to diversify the parent companies' activities and to gain knowledge about new technologies that may have applications in their existing businesses. Corporate venture capitalists typically prefer to invest in more mature companies, and if the company is successful, they tend to acquire the entire venture rather than take it public.

Small business investment companies (SBICs) provide the least amount of venture capital. Authorized under the Small Business Investment Company Act of 1958, they operate as closed-end investment trusts licensed and regulated by the Small Business Administration. Many are subsidiaries of banks and insurance companies. The role of SBICs has varied; the federal government has sometimes used them aggressively to fill a perceived need for equity capital for small businesses, but at other times, when small businesses' need for access to the capital markets has not been large, they have played a minor role.

There are also several informal sources of venture capital. Some new businesses receive funds from large corporations not operating through a formal venture capital subsidiary. Many new ventures continue to obtain financing from individual investors known as **angels**. Sometimes these individuals are friends and relatives of the founders, but in many cases they are successful entrepreneurs themselves who are knowledgeable about the particular industry and have special insights into the company's chances for success.

IN WHAT TYPES OF BUSINESSES DO VENTURE CAPITALISTS INVEST?

Venture capitalists typically prefer to invest in technology-based businesses in such areas as electronics, computer software and services, biotechnology, medical care, and industrial products. For several reasons manufacturing businesses are more intense users of venture capital than most service businesses. The lag between formation of a business and initial sales is usually longer in manufacturing than in services. This development cycle is especially long for innovative products and those manufactured with high-technology processes. Also, the minimum efficient scale is typically larger in a manufacturing business. These factors increase the required level of financing and decrease the liquidity of the invest-ment, thus increasing the need for outside equity financing.

WHAT ARE THE STAGES OF VENTURE CAPITAL INVESTMENTS?

There are three early stages of financing. (1) **Seed financing** is capital provided at the "idea" stage. The capital, which generally is less than $100,000, goes for product development and market research and typically is provided by individu-als. (2) **Start-up financing** is capital used in product development and initial mar-keting. This is generally for companies that have been in operation for under a year but have not sold their products or services. (3) **First-stage financing** is cap-ital provided to initiate manufacturing and sales.

There are also three stages of expansion financing. (1) **Second-stage financ-ing** is capital used for initial expansion of a company that has already been pro-ducing and selling a product. The company has revenues but may not be profitable at this time. (2) **Third-stage financing** is capital provided to fund major expansion such as plant expansion, product improvement, or marketing. Companies receiving financing at this stage typically are profitable. (3) **Mezza-nine** or **bridge financing** is capital provided for a company that expects to go public within a year or so.

THE STRUCTURE OF VENTURE CAPITAL INVESTMENTS

The form of investment varies from company to company, but investments tend to feature three characteristics: substantial control over management decisions, some protection against downside risks, and a share in capital appreciation. Typ-ically, venture capitalists have a seat on the board of directors. A popular vehicle for investing in start-up companies is preferred stock that carries the right to pur-chase or convert into common stock. Preferred stockholders have priority over common stockholders in liquidation proceedings.

The convertibility feature enables venture capitalists to participate in the high gains associated with successful ventures that go public or are acquired. In gen-eral, venture capitalists are less likely to provide debt financing. If they do, how-ever, they usually combine the debt with an instrument with equity features such as warrants or convertibility into common stock at a later date.

WHAT RATES OF RETURN DO VENTURE CAPITALISTS REQUIRE?

Venture capitalists often think of their required rate of return in terms of multi-ples of the amount of money they invest in a company. For example, a venture capitalist might expect to receive a return of 10 times the money invested in a start-up company over a 6-year investment horizon, which equals a rate of return of 47 percent per year. A less risky third-stage investment in a profitable company might be expected to return five times the money invested over a 4-year invest-ment horizon, which equals a rate of return of 41 percent per year.

This does not mean that venture capital funds generate returns for their investors in the 40 percent range. Some of the companies in which the venture capitalist invests will fail and will generate a rate of return of zero. Others will be moderately successful and may only double the venture capitalist's investment over a 4- to 7-year investment horizon. For example, at the start-up, for every four companies the venture capitalist invests in with the expectation of a return of 10 times the amount invested in 6 years, two may generate the expected return and two may fail entirely. Thus, the rate of return of the portfolio of four start-up companies would be only 31 percent per year.

HOW ARE VENTURE CAPITAL INVESTMENTS VALUED?

The most important aspect of the venture capital process is the valuation of the company. Various valuation methods can be used to price the transaction, with the two most common methods being comparable companies and multiple scenarios.

Many issues are inherent in the valuation process. First, return expectations typically are defined by the internal rate of return based on the return objectives of the portfolio and the risk expected to be assumed. Risks that affect valuation might not be easily quantified, for example, the risk of poor management. Other issues that affect valuation are: (1) the development stage of the company, that is, whether it is an early or an expansion-stage investment; (2) the valuation of industry comparables; (3) the financial history of the company, its growth rate, and its profitability; (4) the amount of influence that can be exercised by the venture capitalist; and (5) the amount of future dilution expected if additional venture capital financing is required.

Industry multiples typically create a backdrop for the valuation process. The commonly used multiples are based on revenue and earnings. Valuations of companies in an early stage of development are more likely to be based on revenue, and valuations for companies in later stages of development are more likely to be based on earnings and cash flow. These multiples are influenced by the attractiveness of the market in which the company operates, competition among other investors to be part of this financing, the stage of the company's development, and how other relevant or comparable public companies are valued.

An example of the multiple-scenario valuation technique is given in Exhibit 19.5. Assume that a company is seeking $1 million in venture capital financing. Three possible outcomes or scenarios—pessimistic, expected, and optimistic—represent different growth and profitability expectations. In the expected scenario, this company's revenues are expected to be $25 million in 6 years with a net income margin of 8 percent and the potential exit being a sale of the company to a strategic competitor. At a price/earnings ratio of 10, the value of the company is $20 million.

These calculations are repeated for the optimistic and pessimistic cases. Multiplying the company value for each outcome with the probability of the outcome and adding gives the weighted value of the company. Using the numbers given in Exhibit 19.5, the weighted value is $22.9 million. Over a 6-year period and using a rate of return of 45 percent per year, the present value of the company after the financing is $2.5 million. Based on that value today, the venture capitalist ends up with about 40 percent ownership for a $1 million investment. This calculation could also include the expectation for additional financing, which would lead to diluting the initial investment and require additional ownership to meet the return objective.

EXHIBIT 19.5
Calculating the Rate of Return a Venture Capitalist Requires

	Pessimistic	Expected	Optimistic
Probability of outcome	30%	50%	20%
Revenue in year 6 (millions)	$10	$25	$40
Profit margin	5%	8%	10%
Price/earnings ratio at sale	6	10	15
Company valuation (millions)	$3	$20	$60
Weighted valuation (millions)		$22.9	
Annual required rate of return		45%	
Current valuation (millions)		$2.5	

The current valuation of a company depends on its prospects and the venture capitalist's required rate of return.

OBTAINING VENTURE CAPITAL FINANCING

A business makes an application for financial assistance from a venture capital firm by submitting a business plan. The business plan describes the product or service the company produces, the industry in which the company operates, information on the company's management, detailed financial projections, and a description of how the funds will be used. If the business plan interests the venture capitalist, and typically only 10 out of 100 do, the company receives a rigorous examination. Some venture capitalists use their own staffs for this investigation, while others depend on a board of advisers acting in a consulting capacity. Even after being investigated, a high percentage of applications are rejected, with typically only 1 out of 10 companies actually receiving funding. Thus, venture capital is not easy to obtain; out of every 100 business plans received, only 10 companies will receive serious consideration and only 1 of those will receive equity capital.

DO YOU UNDERSTAND?

1. Why would an investor want to invest in a venture capital fund?
2. What are the advantages and disadvantages of venture capital to an entrepreneur?
3. Why do venture capital fund managers follow such specialized strategies?

CHAPTER TAKE-AWAYS

1 The primary business activities of investment banks are underwriting and raising capital for the primary markets, and the trading of securities (dealer/broker) in the secondary market.

2 The Glass-Steagall Act of 1933 separated commercial banking from investment banking and said that financial institutions can do one or the other, but not both. At the time, it was thought that the stock market crash of 1929 and the subsequent collapse of the banking system led to the Great Depression in the 1930s. The reason the Glass-Steagall Act was passed was the belief that investment banking was too risky for banks to engage in and, in part, commercial bank and investment-banking activities of the times contributed to the collapse of the banking system.

3 The Gramm-Leach-Bliley Act of 1999 repealed much of the Glass-Steagall Act by allowing commercial banks, investment banks, and insurance companies to affiliate with each other as part of a financial holding company structure. As a consequence, we can expect to see more mergers across industry sectors.

4 Most new securities issues sold in the primary market are underpriced, meaning that their new offer price is below their closing price after the first day of trading. Investment bankers do this to ensure that the issues sell "quickly," ensuring the issuing firm of a successful issue and reducing its underwriting risk.

5 Prior to shelf registration or Rule 144A, buyers of private placement securities were required to hold the securities for 2 years before they could be resold. This situation reduced the liquidity of private placements and, hence, raised the issuers' borrowing cost. Rule 144A now eliminates the 2-year holding period by allowing large institutions (sophisticated investors) to trade private placements among themselves without having to register the securities with the SEC.

6 Venture capitalists provide new and emerging firms with initial or early financing. For taking this risk, they receive an equity stake in the firm and usually have some say in the management of the firm. Venture capitalists are important because they stimulate the growth of small innovative firms, usually high-technology companies that make significant contributions to economic growth.

KEY TERMS

Commercial bank	Underwritten	Dealers	Angels
Investment bank	Best-efforts basis	Market maker	Seed financing
Universal bank	Competitive bidding	Bid–ask spread	Start-up financing
Private bank	Negotiated offering	Margin trading	First-stage financing
Primary offering	Due diligence	Call loan	Second-stage financing
Unseasoned offering	Underpricing	Repurchase agreement	Third-stage financing
Initial public offering (IPO)	Registration statement	Discount broker	Mezzanine financing
Seasoned offering	Preliminary prospectus	Arbitrage	Bridge financing
Public offering	Final prospectus	Accredited investor	
Private placement	Underwriting syndicate	Venture capital	
	Brokers	Carried interest	

QUESTIONS AND PROBLEMS

1. Explain how investment banks and large money-center banks are similar and how they are different.

2. What are the major business activities of investment banks?

3. Why do commercial banks want to get into investment banking?

4. Explain why issuing new securities can be a risky business.

5. What is a private placement? How does it differ from a deal underwritten by an investment bank?

6. In what ways do some securities dealers and stockbrokers serve as financial intermediaries?

7. Give examples from this chapter to illustrate how different forms of financial institutions may either grow

rapidly or decline as economic and regulatory conditions change.

8. What is venture capital? What types of companies seek venture capital?

9. Assume a venture capitalist requires a 40 percent rate of return per year. If the venture capitalist thinks that a company will be worth $50 million in 5 years, what percentage of ownership in the company will the venture capitalist require today in exchange for a $3 million investment?

10. Explain what impact Rule 144A may have on the private placement market.

INTERNET EXERCISE

1. Go to one of the Internet sites that focus on initial public offerings. A good example is www.123jump.com. Go to the section titled "Latest IPO Pricings" and pick two or three companies that look interesting. What were the offer prices? Click on the ticker symbol. What kind of price movements do you see in the week following the IPO?

2. Pick a recent IPO from the list on www.123jump.com and go to the Securities and Exchange Commission's Internet site at www.sec.gov. Find the company in the SEC's Edgar database and view the final prospectus for the company you chose. What kinds of information do you find in the prospectus?

20

Investment Companies

In 2003 approximately 48 percent of the households in America owned mutual funds, according to the Investment Company Institute (ICI). The median age of a mutual fund owner is 48. Their average household income is $68,700. Seventy-one percent are married or living with a partner, and 57 percent have at least a 4-year college degree. And 99 percent wish they would have saved or invested more.

Okay, so we made up the last statistic, but just about everyone wishes they had saved or invested more when they were younger. As a college student, you are probably relatively young (or certainly young at heart!) and will be faced with decisions about consumption, savings, and investing soon. As we will learn in this chapter, mutual funds hold more assets than any other type of financial institution in the United States. Therefore, if you don't already own any shares of mutual funds, it is probably just a matter of time. In fact, the sooner you begin learning about and using mutual funds, the sooner you will accumulate wealth in them.

For example, if you begin investing $300 a month (what amounts to a car payment these days) in a mutual fund that earns 8 percent per year, compounded monthly, after 5 years, you will have accumulated $22,043. After 10 years, $54,884. After 20 years, $176,706. After 30 years, $447,108. Clearly, the sooner you invest and the more you invest, the more money you will have when it comes time to retire.

Mutual funds are attractive investment vehicles for small investors because they offer the benefits of diversification, professional management, and small denominations. Money market mutual funds are attractive to small savers that are risk averse or need to maintain a source of liquid funds. Other types of investment companies offer specialized investment products targeted to particular investors. For example, hedge funds are targeted at wealthy, sophisticated investors. ∎

If Wall Street were the Wild West, then Eliot Spitzer would be Clint Eastwood, riding in to town and shooting up the bad guys. As the Attorney General of New York State, Mr. Spitzer has aggressively cleaned up abuses on Wall Street by investment banks and mutual funds. He believes these institutions gave preferential treatment in securities transactions to big clients at the expense of small investors.

In this chapter, we first describe the functions of various types of investment funds: closed-end investment companies, mutual funds, exchange-traded funds, money market mutual funds, unit investment trusts, and real estate investment trusts (REITs). We explain the portfolio characteristics of each and note how these institutions have waxed or waned as market conditions, the regulatory environment, or competitive conditions have changed. We also explain the fee structures employed by mutual funds to provide funding for their operations. ■

 ## LEARNING OBJECTIVES

The objectives of this chapter are to:

1 Explain the functions of investment companies.

2 Describe the features of closed-end investment companies.

3 Explain open-end investment companies, or mutual funds, and how they differ from closed-end investment companies.

4 Discuss how hedge funds differ from mutual funds.

5 Explain the development and the role of money market mutual funds.

6 Describe the operations of real estate investment trusts.

INVESTMENT COMPANIES

Investment funds gather funds from savers for investment in capital and money market instruments or investment in specialized assets, such as real estate. Most specialize in long-term investments. They provide investors with risk intermediation by investing in a diversified portfolio of assets. They also provide denomination intermediation, investing in large blocks of securities and typically selling shares to consumers in smaller denominations. They issue liabilities in a wide variety of denominations, and they provide marketability by either issuing liabilities for which a ready market exists or standing ready to repurchase their liabilities at their current asset value. In addition, investment funds offer economies of scale in investment management and transaction costs by spreading the costs of security evaluation over a large number of investors and by taking advantage of lower costs on large-scale transactions.

Investment companies were first started in Belgium in 1822 and in the United States toward the end of the nineteenth century. Initially, all investment companies were closed-end investment companies.

CLOSED-END INVESTMENT COMPANIES

A **closed-end investment company** is a fund that initially sells its shares to the public to obtain cash to invest and then operates with a fixed number of shares outstanding. Once their stock is sold, there is typically no provision for redemption by the issuing company. In effect, the fund operates like any other business that has its stock publicly traded, except that the fund invests in marketable securities rather than real assets. Once a closed-end fund sells its shares, it typically does not offer additional shares to investors. Any investor who wishes to buy or sell shares in the fund does so by purchasing them in the secondary market. Thus, the price of a share of the fund is determined by supply and demand.

There are two important values for shares in a closed-end investment fund. The first is the **net asset value (NAV)** per share. The NAV per share is calculated by summing up the total current value of a fund's assets, subtracting the value of any debts (liabilities) owed by the fund, and dividing by the number of fund shares outstanding.

The second important value is the price at which the fund's shares can be bought or sold in the stock market. The market price for closed-end investment companies often varies from 10 percent above to 20 percent below their NAVs—with even more extreme movements for individual funds. The size of the **premium or discount to NAV** varies with market conditions and the type of fund. Closed-end bond funds, for example, tend to sell at smaller discounts than equity funds. Domestic equity funds tend to sell for smaller discounts than equity funds invested in other countries. Exhibit 20.1 shows premiums or discounts from net asset values of selected closed-end U.S. investment companies on August 5, 2004.

Some people think that the fact that a fund's NAV does not equal its market price may indicate that market "inefficiencies" exist, since the value of the whole should equal the value of the sum of its parts. Others maintain that there are rational explanations for the price discrepancies. For instance, in some foreign countries, investment funds are allowed to invest in shares but individuals are not. Thus, individuals who want to invest in that country may be willing to pay a premium to obtain assets in that country by buying shares in the fund. Also, people may be able to buy stocks, but they don't know when to sell the stocks and alter their investments. Consequently, they may be willing to pay a premium price to obtain shares in a fund that is thought to have a superior manager who can make such decisions for them. On the other side of the ledger, people may not be willing to pay full NAV for a fund with poor managers that cannot be easily replaced or for a fund that has high management costs and fees relative to its expected returns, or for a fund that has unrecognized tax liabilities that will be incurred if assets held by the fund are sold and capital-gains taxes must be paid before the shareholders earn a return. In all those cases, a fund may sell at a discount to its NAV for good reasons, not because of market inefficiencies.

However, if people aggressively sell or buy closed-end funds just because they are in a hurry to get into or out of the fund, it is possible that the price at which they buy or sell may reflect market moods more than market values, and possible temporary mispricings of fund shares relative to their NAVs may result.

OPEN-END INVESTMENT COMPANIES: MUTUAL FUNDS

While closed-end investment companies are popular because they let people obtain professional investment management, diversification, and variable denominations (investment commitment levels) at low cost, the fact that their market price can vary widely from their net asset values is a drawback. An investor never knows for sure what price he or she will receive when the investor sells shares in

EXHIBIT 20.1

Data on Selected Closed-End Funds (August 5, 2004)

Fund	Ticker Symbol/ Exchange	Fund Category	Net Asset Value (NAV)	Market Price	Outstanding Shares	Total Net Assets ($ Millions)	Premium/ Discount	1-Year NAV Return	1-Year Market Return
Adams Express Company	ADX/NYSE	Equity income	$14.23	$12.31	84,886,412	$1,218.86	−13.49%	20.57%	14.67%
Bancroft Convertible Fund	BCV/AMEX	Growth and income	19.95	17.78	5,557,138	115.55	−10.88	9.39	−3.33
Germany Fund	GER/NYSE	Non-US equity	7.53	6.52	15,573,281	130.44	−13.41	28.77	30.42
ACM Income Fund	ACG/NYSE	Government bond	7.89	8.13	227,073,766	1,904.85	3.04	0.79	−7.77
BlackRock Income Trust	BKT/NYSE	General mortgage	7.03	7.19	63,569,490	444.52	2.28	3.73	−5.74
Debt Strategies Fund I Inc.	DSU/NYSE	High-yield corporate	6.70	6.74	105,196,007	975.34	0.60	19.94	6.87
Dreyfus Strategic Municipals	LEO/NYSE	Municipal securities	9.00	8.53	60,588,631	566.36	−5.22	2.60	−12.50

Source: Closed-End Fund Association, http://www.cefa.com.

the fund, because the market price received would depend on both market conditions and the fund's premium or discount from NAV on the day the shares were sold.

Open-end investment companies (now called **mutual funds**) were started in the United States in 1924 to alleviate the redemption problem. Mutual funds typically guarantee that investors in the fund can redeem some or all of their fund shares at their NAV on any given day, provided that the fund shareholder notifies the fund of his or her intention to redeem shares by the cutoff time for redemptions on that day.

Open-end investment companies stand ready to buy or sell their shares based on the current NAV at any time. When an investor buys shares in an open-end fund, the fund fills the purchase order by issuing new shares in the fund. There is no limit to the number of shares, other than the market demand for the shares. Both buy and sell transactions are carried out at a price based on the current market value (NAV) of all securities held in the fund's portfolio, which is calculated daily. Shares are typically redeemed at the fund's NAV. Net redemptions (i.e., redemptions minus purchases greater than zero) will reduce the total number of shares outstanding.

Mutual funds quickly became popular because they guaranteed that investors could always redeem their shares for their NAVs. In contrast, closed-end funds did not guarantee redemptions, and market prices for fund shares might diverge widely from fund NAV. As a result, mutual funds are now the most common type of investment company. Because mutual funds promise to redeem shares on demand, they invest only in highly marketable assets, such as U.S. stocks and bonds, that can be sold quickly if the funds need cash to meet redemptions. Closed-end funds, in contrast, are still popular for investments in illiquid assets that cannot be sold quickly and easily, such as stocks in foreign markets with limited trading, venture capital shares in companies that cannot be easily traded, or bonds (such as municipal, foreign, high-yield, and illiquid corporate bond issues) that cannot be bought or sold quickly and easily without incurring high transactions costs. As can be seen in Exhibit 20.2, most closed-end funds are bond funds or international equity funds.

EXCHANGE-TRADED FUNDS

First introduced in 1989 by the Toronto Stock Exchange (TSE), **exchange-traded funds (ETFs)** are investment companies whose shares are traded on organized exchanges at market-determined prices, similar to closed-end funds. Unlike closed-end funds, however, ETFs have a unique creation and redemption feature that prevents large premiums or discounts from the NAV. ETF shares are created when an authorized participant deposits a specified portfolio of stocks with the ETF trustee. Redemptions are the same, but in reverse—in exchange for a large number of ETF shares (generally 50,000), the participant receives a specified portfolio of stocks.

This creation and redemption mechanism allows large investors to earn arbitrage profits if the price of the ETF differs from its NAV. For instance, if the market price of the ETF is $120 and its NAV is $130, a large investor will buy 50,000 ETF shares for $6,000,000 ($120 times 50,000), exchange the ETF shares for the underlying portfolio of stocks, and immediately sell the portfolio of stocks for $6,500,000 ($130 times 50,000). Assuming no change in the price of the ETF

Until recently, mutual funds had been untouched by the scandals that have rocked Wall Street and corporate America. Now Eliot Spitzer, the New York State Attorney General, who has been compared to Batman trying to "save a sordid Gotham City," is taking on the mutual fund industry. It started in 2003 with an investigation of a small hedge fund, Canary Capital Partners. The investigation uncovered the fact that several mutual funds had allowed Canary Capital and other favored clients to engage in some unsavory trading practices.

One such practice is called "late trading." By convention, most U.S.-based mutual funds calculate NAV once per day at 4:00 P.M. Eastern time. Regulations require that mutual fund trades be priced at the next NAV, calculated after a buy or sell order is received. Late trading involves purchasing mutual fund shares at the 4:00 P.M. price (NAV) after 4:00 P.M. Mutual funds have allowed favored clients to engage in late trading, thus allowing them to take advantage of any information coming out after 4:00 P.M. that would affect the fund's price. This practice allows the favored clients to make a profit at the expense of the other investors in the fund. Eliot Spitzer characterizes late trading as "allowing betting on a horse race after the horses have crossed the finish line." A similar practice, called "market timing," allows favored mutual fund investors to profit from time zone differences across securities markets, particularly international markets.

Here is an example of the type of irregularity uncovered by Spitzer. Suppose that a domestic equity mutual fund calculates the NAV to be $47 at 4:00 P.M. on August 13. Now imagine that at 4:15 P.M. the Fed announces that the economy is doing much better than expected, information that presumably would cause stock prices to increase. Further, because you are a favored client, the mutual fund manager arranges for you to buy 1,000 additional shares at 4:30 P.M. at the 4:00 P.M. price of $47.

On August 14, the stock market reacts favorably to the economic news and, as expected, stock prices generally increase. More importantly, your mutual fund shares increase in price (NAV) to $52—an increase of $5 per share—as calculated at 4:00 P.M. on August 14. At 4:15 P.M. on August 14, you are then allowed to sell your shares at the $52 price. Because you were

Company	Financial Penalties
Bank of America/FleetBoston Financial	$675 million
Alliance Capital Management	$600 million
MFS Investment Management	$350 million
Janus Capital Group	$225 million
Strong Capital Management	$175 million
Putnam Investments	$110 million
BancOne Investment Advisors	$90 million

allowed to "late trade," you made a profit of $5 per share × 1,000 shares = $5,000. Had the mutual fund treated you like the "average Joe" and followed the regulations, your purchase would have been made at the *next* day's price (NAV), which would have been $52, and you would have made no profit from the late release of information.

Listed in the table above are some of the firms that have settled late-trading and market-timing cases with Spitzer, the Securities and Exchange Commission (SEC), and other states' attorneys general. These firms have paid billions of dollars in penalties.

In addition, a number of CEOs and fund managers have been fired or banned from the securities industry for their involvement in late trading and market timing.

Beyond the financial penalties is the longer-run impact of reputational damage on such esteemed firms as Putnam, Janus, Bank of America, and Alliance. Investors are pulling assets out of the funds involved in a big way. For example, Putnam has lost more than $50 billion in assets since being caught up in the scandal, and Janus has lost over $8 billion. The industry as a whole is suffering from a loss of confidence in its integrity.

To repair the damage, mutual fund companies are owning up to their involvement in late trading and market timing and are making highly visible changes in governance structure, fee structure, and managerial incentives to make sure that the practices don't happen again.

EXHIBIT 20.2
Assets and Number of Closed-End Funds by Type of Fund *(End of Year)*

		Equity Funds			Bond Funds			
Year	Total	Total Equity	Domestic	Global/ International	Total Bond	Domestic Taxable	Domestic Municipal	Global/ International
Assets								
(millions of dollars)								
1996	$146,991	$46,987	$19,830	$27,157	$100,004	$28,418	$59,540	$12,046
1997	151,845	49,625	20,536	29,089	102,220	28,315	61,992	11,912
1998	155,814	47,606	22,529	25,077	108,208	34,127	63,628	10,454
1999	147,016	41,267	24,696	16,571	105,749	30,888	64,513	10,348
2000	143,134	36,611	24,557	12,054	106,523	28,581	68,266	9,676
2001	141,251	31,075	22,261	8,814	110,176	26,606	74,467	9,102
2002	158,805	33,724	26,596	7,128	125,081	25,643	90,024	9,414
2003	213,973	51,863	41,835	10,028	162,110	56,438	94,133	11,539
Number of Funds								
1996	498	142	50	92	356	118	205	33
1997	488	135	45	90	353	115	205	33
1998	493	128	44	84	365	123	211	31
1999	512	124	49	75	388	117	241	30
2000	482	123	53	70	359	109	220	30
2001	493	116	51	65	377	109	240	28
2002	545	123	63	60	422	105	292	25
2003	586	130	74	56	456	131	298	27

The majority of closed-end funds are bond funds. Second in importance are world equity funds. Closed-end funds are most useful for buying assets that are infrequently traded or hard to price. Thus, very few closed-end funds specialize in U.S. equities.

Note: Components may not add to the total because of rounding.

Source: Investment Company Institute, *Mutual Fund Fact Book,* 2004.

or its NAV in the short time it takes to do this, the investor will earn a profit of $500,000 less transaction costs. Since large investors are constantly looking for opportunities to earn a quick profit, ETF share values stay pretty close to their NAVs.

Most ETFs are designed to track a domestic stock index, an international index, or an industry sector. For example, there are ETFs designed to track the S&P 500, Nasdaq 100, Fortune 500, S&P 500 financials, Dow Jones Industrial Average, Russell 3000, S&P Europe 350, S&P Latin America 40, and countless others. For example, the first ETFs were Toronto Index Participation Units (TIPs) based on the TSE 35 index. In 1993, the American Stock Exchange

EXHIBIT 20.3

Assets and Number of Exchange-Traded Index Funds (ETFs) by Type of Fund

Year	Total	Domestic Equity	Global/International Equity	Bond
Assets				
(millions of dollars, end of year)				
1993	$464	$464	—	—
1994	424	424	—	—
1995	1,052	1,052	—	—
1996	2,411	2,159	$252	—
1997	6,707	6,200	506	—
1998	15,568	14,542	1,026	—
1999	33,873	31,881	1,992	—
2000	65,585	63,544	2,041	—
2001	82,993	79,977	3,016	—
2002	102,143	92,904	5,324	$3,915
2003	150,983	132,332	13,984	4,667
Number of Funds				
(end of year)				
1993	1	1	—	—
1994	1	1	—	—
1995	2	2	—	—
1996	19	2	17	—
1997	19	2	17	—
1998	29	12	17	—
1999	30	13	17	—
2000	80	55	25	—
2001	102	68	34	—
2002	113	66	39	8
2003	119	72	41	6

There has been explosive growth in ETFs since they appeared in the early 1990s. Most of the growth has been in domestic equity ETFs.

Note: Components may not add to the total because of rounding.

Source: Investment Company Institute, *Mutual Fund Facts Book,* 2004.

(AMEX) introduced Standard & Poor's Depository Receipts (SPDRs), which track the S&P 500. At the end of June 2004, there were over 140 ETFs holding over $175 billion in assets. As you can see from Exhibit 20.3, the growth in ETFs has been explosive since they appeared on the scene in the early 1990s. Just a few of the ETFs traded on the AMEX are listed in Exhibit 20.4.

EXHIBIT 20.4
Selected Exchange-Traded Funds on the American Stock Exchange (August 9, 2004)

Name of Fund	Ticker Symbol	Index or Top 3 Investment Holdings	Market Price	Volume Traded
DIAMONDS	DIA	Tracks the Dow Jones Industrial Average	$98.42	5,095,100
iShares MSCI-Japan	EWJ	Tracks the MSCI (Morgan Stanley Capital International) Japan Index	9.54	3,072,400
FORTUNE 500 Index Tracking Stock	FFF	Tracks the Fortune 500	76.15	12,200
iShares Nasdaq Biotechnology	IBB	Amgen, Biogen, Teva Pharmaceuticals	61.25	388,600
iShares Dow Jones US Healthcare	IYH	Pfizer, Johnson & Johnson, Merck	53.23	47,000
SPDRS (S&P 500)	SPY	Tracks the Standard & Poor's 500 Composite Stock Price Index	107.00	37,481,100

At the end of June 2004, there were over 140 ETFs holding over $175 billion in assets. Unlike closed-end funds, ETFs trade close to NAV.

Source: American Stock Exchange, http://www.amex.com.

Although ETFs have been around since the early 1990s, it has only been in recent years that their popularity has increased dramatically. The reasons for the growth in the market for ETFs are their tax advantages, low expense ratios, ease of buying and selling, and ease of tracking prices. Unlike actively managed mutual funds, ETFs generate fewer capital gains because they usually only sell securities in the portfolio to adjust to changes in the underlying index. They have low expense ratios because they are not actively managed. They are as easy to buy or sell as a share of stock and, like shares of stock, their prices are easy to determine at any time during the day.

UNIT INVESTMENT TRUSTS

Investment trusts are often used to invest in assets, such as municipal bonds, that cannot be bought or sold easily in the market. An investment trust (or **unit investment trust**) consists of pro rata interests in an unmanaged pool of assets. More specifically, shares or "units" in a trust are sold to the public to obtain the funds needed to invest in a portfolio of securities. The securities are held in safekeeping in accordance with a set of conditions spelled out in a trust agreement. The securities purchased are typically government notes and bonds, corporate and municipal bonds, and, on occasion, preferred stock and money market instruments. Once the securities are purchased, no new securities are added and, with rare exceptions, no securities are sold. Because there is no trading of securities by the trustee and most securities purchased have a fixed return, the return (or yield) on an investment trust is fairly predictable. For instance, each unit in a trust with 100,000 units has a 1/100,000th interest in each security owned by the trust and is entitled to receive 1/100,000th of the income generated by that security.

Unit investment trusts may have advantages over mutual funds in some instances. For instance, if interest rates rise, the value of a bond mutual fund will decline. If people then sell shares in the bond mutual fund, some bonds may have to be sold at prices less than their face values to obtain cash to meet the redemption demands. Thus, the remaining shareholders will have a claim on fewer bonds than before. However, with a unit investment trust, no units are redeemed before maturity. Thus, an investor in the fund will be assured that the number of bonds in the fund will remain the same until the trust expires or until the bonds are called or default. If the bonds are called, each investor will receive a pro rata share of the proceeds from the call (including a share of any call premium, as well as the principal repaid by the bond issuer). In the unlikely event that a bond defaults, investors will lose an amount equal to a pro rata share of the loss when the trust terminates. Overall, in most cases, bond mutual funds and unit investment trusts will perform similarly, but the bond mutual fund will suffer if it has to sell bonds at low prices to meet redemption needs before the bonds mature, while unit investment trusts do not have similar problems. In addition, because most bonds in a unit investment trust are purchased at par and redeemed at par, they generally will not expose a buyer to capital-gains tax liabilities, unlike a bond mutual fund that may incur gains or losses on various transactions as it buys or sells bonds. This can be important to buyers of municipal bond funds who buy shares in the trust in order to avoid potential tax liabilities.

Unit trusts are usually formed and sold by brokerage houses to investors with limited resources who want to acquire a diversified portfolio of fixed-income securities and to earn a monthly income. Although there is no active secondary market for trust shares, investors can usually sell them back to the sponsor at a price equal to the prevailing net asset value per unit minus a sales commission if the sponsor can find another buyer.

IMPORTANCE OF INVESTMENT COMPANIES

Public interest in investment companies and mutual funds literally exploded in the decade of the 1990s. By the end of 2003, there were 8,126 mutual funds and over 600 investment companies operating in the United States. Collectively, they owned over $7.0 trillion in assets, more than any other type of financial institution. Assets owned by mutual funds increased more than sixfold from the end of 1990 to the end of 2003. There are a number of reasons for the explosive growth: (1) the many new types of mutual funds and investment companies, (2) the development of Individual Retirement Accounts, (3) the shift of many corporate pension plans from defined benefit to defined contribution plans in the 1980s and 1990s, (4) increased interest in investments by aging baby boomers in the 1990s, and (5) the high rates of return available on common stocks recorded in the 1990s as inflation diminished and the economy recovered from the 1990–1991 recession. Exhibit 20.5 shows how the number of investment funds and the assets under their management have increased. Investment companies are important because they are the primary retirement savings vehicle in the United States. The bulk of the assets held by mutual funds are held for retirement accounts.

EXHIBIT 20.5
Assets of Major Institutions and Financial Intermediaries ($ Millions)

	1996	1997	1998	1999	2000	2001	2002
Depository institutions	$6,072,189	$6,557,007	$7,108,638	$7,547,502	$8,127,399	$8,635,302	$9,277,826
Commercial banks	4,710,397	5,174,550	5,628,599	5,982,499	6,468,674	6,830,725	7,356,976
Credit unions	330,114	353,831	391,483	414,527	441,066	505,501	563,323
Savings institutions	1,031,678	1,028,626	1,088,556	1,150,476	1,217,659	1,299,076	1,357,527
Life insurance companies	2,246,289	2,514,802	2,769,522	3,067,922	3,135,664	3,224,567	3,365,952
Investment institutions	6,357,184	7,988,239	9,693,060	11,403,817	11,603,045	10,973,368	10,228,825
Bank-administered trusts	2,684,453	3,364,447	3,999,321	4,380,798	4,435,911	3,775,697	3,578,717
Closed-end investment companies	144,519	148,885	152,962	142,807	136,882	139,702	156,394
Exchange-traded funds	2,411	6,707	15,568	33,873	65,585	82,993	102,143
Mutual funds	3,525,801	4,468,201	5,525,209	6,846,339	6,964,667	6,974,976	6,391,571

Mutual fund asset holdings grew rapidly during the 1990s. By 1999, mutual funds had more assets than commercial banks and far surpassed life insurance companies in total asset holdings.

Source: Investment Company Institute, *Mutual Fund Fact Book,* 2003.

There now are many types of mutual funds, and they own diverse portfolios. At year-end 2003, mutual funds, in total, held assets worth over 7 trillion. Equity mutual funds owned over 49 percent of those assets, bond and hybrid funds owned over 22 percent, and money market funds owned over 27 percent.

Exhibit 20.6 presents data on the asset holdings of non–money market mutual funds. The historical data illustrate the dramatic rate of growth in mutual fund assets that occurred from 1950 to 1970 and the subsequent slackening in growth that occurred during the 1970s. Mutual funds again experienced rapid growth, beginning during the early 1980s. After the stock market crash of October 1987, the growth of mutual funds has continued, accelerating sharply in the 1990s. The exhibit also reveals the considerable change in asset holdings that occurred from 1965 onward as mutual funds shifted away from common and preferred stock, which accounted for 88 percent of their assets in 1965, only 39 percent of their assets in 1990, and 73 percent of their assets by the end of 2001. This shift reflects

COMPO-SITION OF MUTUAL FUNDS

EXHIBIT 20.6
Assets Held by Equity, Hybrid, and Bond Mutual Funds

Year	Total Assets ($ Billions)	Percentage Distribution of Key Assets						
		Cash and Equivalent	Corporate Bonds	Preferred Stock	Common Stock	Municipal Bonds	Government Securities Long Term	Other
1945	$1.3							
1950	2.5							
1955	7.8	5.6	6.0	6.3	82.1	NA	NA	NA
1960	17.0	5.7	7.3	4.2	82.8	NA	NA	NA
1965	35.2	5.1	7.3	1.7	85.9	NA	NA	NA
1970	47.6	6.6	9.0	2.4	80.9	NA	NA	1.1
1975	42.2	7.6	11.3	1.2	78.6	NA	NA	1.3
1980	58.4	9.1	11.3	0.9	71.2	4.9	2.4	0.2
1985	251.6	8.2	9.9	1.5	47.6	15.2	17.3	0.3
1990	566.8	8.5	7.8	0.5	38.1	20.9	22.6	1.6
1995	2,058.3	6.9	9.3	0.8	58.2	11.9	12.6	0.3
1996	2,624.0	5.8	9.1	0.8	64.7	9.3	10.1	0.2
1997	3,409.3	5.8	3.6	0.9	68.3	7.8	8.3	0.3
1998	4,173.5	4.6	9.3	0.6	71.4	7.0	6.9	0.2
1999	5,233.2	4.2	7.4	0.6	77.0	5.1	5.6	0.1
2000	5,119.4	5.4	6.8	0.5	75.9	5.3	6.0	0.1
2001	4,689.6	4.7	8.0	0.5	72.6	6.2	8.0	<0.1
2002	4,119.6	5.1	10.1	0.4	65.9	7.8	11.7	<0.1

Over time, mutual funds' stock and bond holdings have varied widely in relative importance.

Source: Investment Company Institute, *Mutual Fund Fact Book,* 2003.

that as investors' enthusiasm for stock-oriented funds cooled in the 1970s and 1980s, mutual fund managers shifted to new and more popular investment media, such as municipal, government, or corporate bonds. Then, as investors became enamored of the stock market as a retirement savings vehicle, by the late 1990s, mutual funds held substantially more equities once again. Since 1999, however, there has been a shift toward bonds.

MUTUAL FUND CASH HOLDINGS AND REDEMPTION POLICIES

Conventional mutual funds' holdings of cash and equivalent items can vary, ranging from 4 percent to 10 percent of total asset holdings. Some cash holdings are needed to redeem shares turned in for redemption. However, cash holdings may also represent liquid assets (such as bank CDs) held for later investment.

In general, stock- and bond-oriented mutual funds typically hold more liquid assets when market interest rates are relatively high. Then the yield on liquid assets is high and stock prices may be expected to fall. Therefore, some cash items may be held for investment at lower prices. When interest rates start to fall, however, the return on cash and equivalent holdings falls at the same time that stock prices are expected to rise. Hence, many stock-oriented mutual funds may readjust their portfolios by reducing their cash holdings and buying stocks. When they do, they can cause temporary buying panics as many buyers simultaneously bid up the prices of stocks in order to acquire more shares before their prices rise further.

Because of this phenomenon, many securities analysts monitor mutual fund cash and equivalent holdings closely. They try to determine if the funds (and other investors) have sufficient liquid asset holdings to fuel a buying panic if short-term interest rates fall. Analysts also attempt to identify periods when mutual funds may wish to acquire larger cash holdings, as that means their demand for stocks will be reduced.

In recent years, mutual funds' cash holdings have declined and stayed low. Many funds have credit lines from banks, so they won't have to sell stocks during a market crash to obtain the cash needed to meet redemption demands from their shareholders. Other funds have policies permitting them to distribute stocks in lieu of cash or delay redemption payments under some circumstances. Mutual fund investors must read their fund's prospectus to see if it has credit lines or can delay redemptions, or can redeem shares by paying with stocks instead of cash. These provisions may affect investors in a fund adversely under certain conditions. However, because they reduce funds' need to hold cash, they have allowed funds to hold smaller amounts of cash and invest a higher proportion of their assets in recent years.

TYPES OF MUTUAL FUNDS

Many types of mutual funds exist. The driving force that determines the types of fund offered is investor demand. Some of the major types of funds are described below.

Growth and Income Funds.   Growth and income funds seek a balanced return consisting of both capital gains and current income. These funds place most of their assets in high-quality common stocks. Such funds would be appropriate for investors who need some current income but want the opportunity to participate in the growth of the economy.

Growth Funds. The investment goal of a growth fund is capital appreciation. Such funds invest primarily in common stocks that are judged to have above-average growth potential. Growth funds are most suitable for aggressive investors with long-term investment horizons. The stocks in a growth fund usually pay no dividends, and thus a growth fund would not be suitable for investors who need current income.

Aggressive Growth Funds. Aggressive growth funds are extremely speculative investments that strive for big profits from capital gains. Their portfolios typically consist of the stocks of small companies with high price/earnings ratios or companies whose stock prices are highly volatile. These funds are most appropriate for sophisticated investors.

Balanced Funds. Balanced funds hold a balanced portfolio of both stocks and bonds. They do so to generate both current income and capital appreciation. Typically, a balanced fund will generate a higher level of income than a growth and income fund and be less volatile. However, the opportunity for capital gains will be less.

International and Global Equity Funds. International and global funds are useful for investors who wish to diversify their asset holdings internationally. Global funds can invest anywhere in the world, while international funds tend to invest outside the United States. An international fund can diversify broadly across countries or invest only in a specific country or group of countries. Potential investors need to read the fund's prospectus to determine where it is likely to invest and how its current investments are distributed.

Income-Equity Funds. These funds seek to obtain higher equity income by investing in stocks with relatively high dividend yields and prospects.

Bond Funds. Bond funds invest exclusively in various types and grades of bonds—as specified in their prospectuses. The types of bond funds include U.S. government income funds that buy U.S. Treasury and agency securities; Ginnie Mae funds and other funds that invest in mortgage-backed securities; corporate bond funds; high-yield (higher risk) corporate bond funds; strategic income funds, which invest in a variety of fixed-income securities to generate a high level of current income; municipal security funds; and bonds issued by foreign companies and governments.

Specialty Funds. Some investment funds are managed to achieve specialized objectives. **Index funds** are managed to match the return from a particular market index such as the S&P 500. Sector funds restrict their investments to a single segment of the market, such as precious metals funds. Sector funds may concentrate on special industries, such as telecommunications, oil, oil drilling, biotechnology, health care, and electric utilities. Specialty funds are like international funds in that they are created in response to the demands of investors who want to concentrate their investments in particular areas but do not want to acquire the expertise or the amount of funds needed to do so themselves.

MUTUAL FUND FAMILIES

Mutual funds proliferated in the 1990s, in part, because of the creation of **mutual fund families**. Part of the motivation for creating mutual fund families is to service retirement accounts, particularly 401-k, 403b, IRA, and Keogh accounts that are self-directed by the employee or employer. Mutual fund families, or groups of mutual funds with similar names but different investment philosophies, appeal to people who may want to change the distribution of their assets from domestic to foreign stocks, or from stocks to bonds to cash, or from long-term bonds to short-term bonds or back, and so on. By allowing people to shift their assets around within the fund family, fund families reduce transactions costs and hassles for their customers, particularly for customers who hold their assets in retirement accounts that are subject to extensive governmental regulation and restriction.

Some of the major mutual fund families include the Fidelity funds, which are so numerous that they include funds specializing in all individual sectors of the stock market, such as biotechnology, oil, and small companies; the T. Rowe Price group of funds, which is similar but has fewer highly specialized funds; and the Vanguard group of funds, which has low-cost "index funds" (which try to match the performance of stock market indexes) as well as more specialized funds. Fund management families are growing in size and number because they offer a variety of investment services and choices that consumers desire. By keeping many assets in one fund family, a customer can easily change his or her investment objectives and holdings with a single phone call. Some funds allow cash to be transferred automatically between various funds electronically. Thus, it is very easy for consumers to change the nature of their investments as they see fit. In addition, by dealing with only one fund family, a person can comply with all applicable retirement account regulations more easily as assets are shifted from one fund to another.

Fund families have developed and offer a wide variety of financial services under one roof to attract customers' assets. The fund family assesses different management fees for each of its financial services. Thus, when a customer shifts assets from one fund in the group to another, the fund family will continue to earn management fees on it. By offering many related services and allowing low-cost internal transfers of funds, a fund family can assure itself that it will obtain a more dependable flow of management fees in the long run.

Because of the value of management fee income, fund groups are often sold to other groups at premium prices. The premium is paid in the expectation that the fund's customers will leave their assets in the fund and pay management fees to the fund manager even if the management company changes. Thus, it is not uncommon for mutual funds to be sold and consolidated with other funds under the auspices of one fund management company. As commercial banks have been allowed to enter more investment-banking-related businesses, they have acquired mutual fund groups so they can offer a wider variety of services to their customers.

REGULATION AND TAXATION OF INVESTMENT COMPANIES

Investment companies are regulated by the Securities and Exchange Commission and are subject to state securities regulations. Regulations require that funds provide full and honest disclosure to actual and potential customers, diversify their portfolios, avoid questionable sales compensation or kickback schemes, and avoid conflicts of interest between advisers or management companies and fund shareholders. Federal regulations are embodied in the Investment Company Act of 1940 as subsequently amended. More recently, the National Securities Markets Improvement Act of 1996 assigned federal regulators the sole jurisdiction over the structure and operations of mutual funds and over mutual fund prospectuses and advertising. State regulators retained their ability to prosecute fraud and sales practice abuses.

Under the "conduit" theory of taxation, mutual funds are not subject to direct taxes on their income provided that they distribute to their shareholders at least 90 percent of all income received. Most distribute 100 percent minus expenses. The fund investor must then pay tax on the capital-gains, interest, and dividend income that is distributed to the investor by the fund each year.

MUTUAL FUND FEE STRUCTURES

Mutual funds assess a wide variety of fees, and the nature of their fees sometimes determines their classification. While mutual funds traditionally have redeemed their shares for their full net asset values, some funds sell their shares for more than their net asset values. These funds are called **load funds**. Such a fund may assess a front-end charge, or **front-end load**, of up to 8.5 percent of their net asset value to be paid by purchasers in addition to the NAV of the shares purchased. The "load" is used to compensate the people who recommend or sell the fund on the companies' behalf. Most "loads" are now less than the full 8.5 percent of NAV permitted by regulation because of competition. Many funds levy no front-end load at all and are denoted **no-load funds**.

No-load funds may still incur sales costs and have to pay salespeople, however. Thus, many of them have imposed a **back-end load**, **contingent deferred sales charge**, or **redemption fee** that must be paid by investors who redeem their shares in the fund. The back-end load (or redemption fee) is subtracted from the net asset value of the redeemed shares before payment is made to the shareholder who redeems shares. Contingent deferred sales charges are temporary, however, and may diminish or disappear over time. For instance, a fund may levy a 5 percent contingent deferred sales charge if shares are redeemed within a year of purchase, with the charge falling by 1 percent per year until no charge is levied on people who have held their shares in the fund for over 5 years. Redemption fees may be levied regardless of how long a fund is held and may be stated either as a percentage of assets or in dollar terms. Since redemption fees may not exist, but, if they do, can vary with each fund (even with "no-load" funds), it is essential that investors read the fund prospectus to learn about such fees and charges.

If a fund is a no-load fund that has no redemption fee or contingent deferred sales charges, it may have a problem obtaining the funds needed to compensate outsiders who help sell shares in the fund. Mutual funds have found a way to get around this problem, however, by levying **12b-1 fees**. Such fees are permitted by statute. They let a fund assess current shareholders to help pay for a fund's marketing expenses. Such fees are subtracted from a fund's assets each year. By law, the fee cannot exceed 1 percent of average net assets per year. The 12b-1 fee may contain a service charge of up to 0.25 percent of assets per year to help compensate salespeople or professionals (such as brokerage firms or independent financial advisers) for providing services or maintaining shareholder accounts. Such charges can be levied by any fund, even if it already charges front-end loads or back-end loads (i.e., redemption fees or deferred sales charges).

The 12b-1 fee is an annual fee, but not all funds assess such fees. However, all mutual funds assess annual **management fees** or **advisory fees** that are paid to the company that manages the fund's portfolio. Such fees may amount to 1 percent or more of the fund's annual average net assets. They can be as low as 0.2 percent for index funds that do not have to make portfolio decisions or trade actively or as high as 2 or 3 percent or more for funds that operate in markets where information is costly to obtain and considerable expertise is needed to invest wisely.

Sometimes it is worth paying a high management fee to obtain access to particular markets and superior investment management skills, but the payment of a high management fee doesn't guarantee superior performance. Some of the worst-performing mutual funds levy the highest fees. That result is not totally unexpected since the return to the investor is reduced by the amount of the management fees paid. Once again, it is important for a potential fund investor to read the fund prospectus to see how high its fees are and how well it is likely to perform—remembering that past performance does not necessarily predict future performance.

One reason many academics advocate investment in index funds where fees are low and the fund's performance is approximately equal to the stock index being matched is that the low management fees for such funds do not have much of a negative effect on the investor's returns. While the investor in an index fund will not do much or any better than the market index the fund is matching, he or she may still outperform actively managed funds that only do marginally better than the index. After the discretionary funds that barely beat the index levy their fund management fees, an investor may do less well, on balance, than he or she would do in an index fund that subtracted much lower management fees before calculating the investor's net returns.

There are additional fees that a potential mutual fund investor should be aware of and will be informed of if he or she reads a mutual fund's prospectus. One such fee is an **exchange fee** that may be levied by funds in a mutual fund family or group when shares are redeemed in one fund and exchanged for shares in another fund in the same mutual fund group. In addition, some funds may levy **account maintenance fees** on low-balance accounts. Mutual funds are likely to try to levy fees whenever they incur costs. The only way an investor knows which fees are likely to be levied by each individual fund is to read the fund's prospectus carefully. Some funds levy all fees permitted; others levy very few.

DETERMINING MUTUAL FUND VALUES

The key to determining a mutual fund's value lies in determining its net asset value. Since most mutual funds own actively traded assets, they can determine their assets' values by using end-of-day closing market prices. If an asset is not traded actively, a mutual fund will have to have an objective way to determine the asset's fair market value each day. Once the net asset value is determined, the sales price of the fund can be determined by adding the load charge. The redemption value of the fund is usually the NAV but may be less if redemption fees or contingent deferred sales charges are levied. Much of the information needed to determine a fund's current buying and selling prices is contained in newspaper quotations. Exhibit 20.7 explains how to read mutual fund price quotations in newspapers and determine the basic types of charges levied by each fund. Note that the "r," "p," and "t" footnotes indicate which funds charge redemption fees and/or 12b-1 fees.

EXHIBIT 20.7
How to Read Mutual Fund Quotes in Newspapers

How to Read Newspaper Fund Quotes

The following is an example of how mutual fund tables appear in many newspapers.

The first column is the abbreviated fund's name. Several funds listed under a single heading indicate a family of funds.

The second column is the Net Asset Value (NAV) per share as of the close of the preceding business day. In some newspapers, the NAV is identified as the sell or bid price—the amount per share you would receive if you sold your shares (less the deferred sales charge, if any). Each mutual fund determines its net asset value every business day by dividing the market value of its total net assets, less liabilities, by the number of shares outstanding. On any given day you can determine the value of your holdings by multiplying the NAV by the number of shares you own.

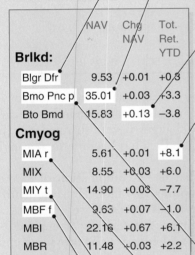

	NAV	Chg NAV	Tot. Ret. YTD
Brlkd:			
Blgr Dfr	9.53	+0.01	+0.3
Bmo Pnc p	35.01	+0.03	+3.3
Bto Bmd	15.83	+0.13	−3.8
Cmyog			
MIA r	5.61	+0.01	+8.1
MIX	8.55	+0.03	+6.0
MIY t	14.90	+0.03	−7.7
MBF f	9.63	+0.07	−1.0
MBI	22.16	+0.67	+6.1
MBR	11.48	+0.03	+2.2

The third column is the change if any, in net asset value from the preceding day's quotation—in other words, the change over the most recent one-day trading period. This fund, for example, gained $0.13 per share.

The fourth column is the fund's year-to-date (YTD) return expressed as a percentage of the NAV at the beginning of the year. The YTD return assumes the reinvestment of all distributions and subtracts annual expenses. The YTD return, however, does not reflect sales charges ("loads") or redemption fees. This fund, for example, gained 8.1 percent per share since the beginning of the year.

A "p" following the abbreviated name of the fund denotes a fund that charges an annual fee from assets for marketing and distribution costs, also known as a 12b-1 fee (named after the 1980 U.S Securities and Exchange Commission rule that permits them).

If the fund name is followed by an "r" the fund has either a contingent deferred sales charge (CDSC) or a redemption fee. A CDSC is a charge if shares are sold within a certain period; a redemption charge is a fee applied whenever shares are sold.

A "t" designates a fund that has both a CDSC or a redemption fee and a 12b-1 fee.

An "f" indicates a fund that reports the previous day's prices instead of the current day's.

Other footnotes may apply to a fund listing, and the meaning of footnotes may differ among newspapers. Please see the explanatory notes that accompany mutual fund tables in your newspaper.

Source: Investment Company Institute, *Mutual Fund Fact Book,* May 2001.

DO YOU UNDERSTAND?

1. What type of investment company is more likely to sell at a price that diverges the most or the least from its net asset value—a mutual fund with a load, a no-load fund, or a closed-end fund? Explain why each type of fund might or might not sell at a price that diverges from its net asset value.

2. What are the pros and cons on investments in mutual funds that try to match a general market index?

3. What are the various types of fees and charges that may be levied by different mutual funds?

4. Why is it essential that potential investors thoroughly read the prospectus for any mutual fund they are considering as an investment?

HEDGE FUNDS

The **hedge fund** industry has been experiencing tremendous change and growth recently. New funds are being formed and there has been a massive inflow of capital from investors. Legislative and regulatory changes have also impacted the industry, and the definition of what a "hedge fund" is has become increasingly uncertain.

Hedge funds comprise investment pools that use a combination of market philosophies and analytical techniques to develop financial models that indentify, evaluate, and execute trading decisions. Hedge funds typically are organized as limited partnerships with the fund manager serving as the general partner and the investors serving as limited partners. The goal of a hedge fund is providing consistent, above-market rates of return while substantially reducing the risk of loss.

The definition of hedge fund has become increasingly unclear. Traditionally, a hedge fund was a manager investing in both long and short positions, buying stocks (long) and selling borrowed shares (short). The definition has since slipped to include almost any fund manager charging an incentive-based fee. However, this broad definition is becoming dramatically less meaningful as traditional money managers have launched limited partnerships in an attempt to tap into the higher fees paid to hedge funds.

In 2004, over $795 billion was under management in hedge funds. The estimated amount in 1994 was only $100 billion. This growth is due to the same factors that drive all business decisions: fear and greed. Hedge funds provide diversification and attractive absolute rates of return. Diversification is a function of the correlations among investment returns. Hedge funds have historically had a very low correlation to traditional investments. Therefore, hedge funds can help to lower the total risk of a portfolio of investments. Furthermore, hedge funds target absolute, not relative, rates of return. The performance of a hedge fund, therefore, depends more on the investment skills of the manager than the movements of the stock market.

HOW DO HEDGE FUNDS DIFFER FROM MUTUAL FUNDS?

Hedge funds differ from mutual funds in a number of ways. Mutual funds are heavily regulated, are required to be registered with the SEC, and are open to all investors. In contrast, a hedge fund is a private, unregistered investment pool open to a limited number of accredited investors. An accredited investor is an individual who has at least $1 million in net worth or an income in excess of $200,000 in each of the past 2 years, with reasonable expectation of making that much in the current year. An accredited institutional investor is one with a net worth of at least $5 million.

Hedge funds used to be limited to 99 investors. But a new type of fund may have up to 500 "super-accredited" investors, who as individuals or family groups must have at least $5 million in net worth. Other accredited investors are institutions with at least $25 million in net worth and "knowledgeable employees" of the investment adviser. Considering that most hedge funds require a minimum investment of $1 million and that investment typically represents a small portion of the investor's portfolio, hedge fund investors are much more wealthy than the typical mutual fund investor.

Hedge funds have great latitude in setting and shifting investment strategies and few constraints on how they pursue those strategies. Hedge funds are extremely flexible investment vehicles that can use financial instruments that fall beyond the reach of mutual funds. Mutual funds are subject to SEC regulations and disclosure requirements that generally prevent them from using short selling, leverage, investments concentrated in only a few securities, and derivatives.

Hedge fund managers, like mutual fund managers, receive management fees usually equal to 1 percent to 2 percent of the assets under management. However, unlike a mutual fund manager, a hedge fund manager can receive an incentive fee that may run as high as 20 percent of the fund's profits. Mutual funds are barred from charging incentive fees. As a result of the ability to charge incentive fees, mutual fund managers have been drawn to hedge funds. They see the opportunity to diversify their business risk and to receive the higher fees.

HEDGE FUND INVESTMENT STRATEGIES

Domestic Hedge Strategies. As in traditional investment management, two basic styles of investing are found among domestic hedge fund managers. They are "value" and "growth." Investment time horizons tend to be short term, and portfolios are usually composed of a relatively small number of concentrated positions. Managers select long positions through fundamental, quantitative, and technical research. Allocations are made based on potential returns without regard to relative index weightings. Short-sale candidates are selected using the same research techniques, but with added emphasis on identifying potential events that can force a revaluation of the security.

Global Hedge Strategies. Global hedge fund managers specialize in specific geographic regions. Areas of geographic specialization include: global; international (non-U.S.); emerging markets; regions such as Europe, Asia, or Africa; or specific countries such as Japan, Russia, or China. Managers using a geographic focus rely on both a global view of world markets and individual stock selection skills to uncover pricing inefficiencies.

PEOPLE & EVENTS

The Demise of Long-Term Capital Management

Long-Term Capital Management (LTCM), like the *Titanic*, was supposed to be unsinkable. After all, the hedge fund had two Nobel Prize winners, Myron Scholes and Robert Merton, working for it, as well as David Mullins, former vice chairman of the Federal Reserve Board and many other experts with Ph.D.s in math and finance. Formed in 1994, LTCM had generated returns for its investors of 43 percent in 1995, 41 percent in 1996, and 17 percent in 1997. However, events in Russia in August 1998 set off a chain of events that led to the downfall of LTCM.

LTCM's strategy called for few trades that carried "directional" risk or depended on which way the markets moved. Instead, LTCM's main strategy was to make hedged trades that it thought could succeed regardless of the general trend of the markets. The fund put its talent to work, for example, at identifying sectors of the bond market in which yields had gotten out of line with yields in other sectors. It would then buy the securities it thought were undervalued and short the securities that it thought were overvalued. For example, it had done trades that in essence bet on a narrowing of the spread between AA-rated corporate bonds and comparable U.S. Treasuries. The bet had looked good because the spread was relatively wide compared with historical levels. A trade of this type can deliver a profit regardless of whether interest rates increase, decrease, or do not change. What matters is that the yields on the securities in the portfolio eventually converge.

However, in August 1998, Russia's financial system crumbled, the country defaulted on $40 billion of debt, and the world's investors fled to quality. That was not what LTCM had been expecting. U.S. Treasury yields declined sharply, and the spread between government and corporate yields suddenly widened even more. The outcome was disastrous for LTCM, and the heavily leveraged hedge fund lost 40 percent of its capital in August alone.

LTCM was brought down by a problem known to every trader—liquidity risk, or the inability to close positions at prevailing prices. LTCM's problem was that as the value of its portfolio declined, it could not close its positions and reduce its risks as fast as it had expected. So its debt–equity ratio increased to levels that made its lenders nervous, and there was a risk that the lenders might seize its assets.

The fund's managers went in search of investors who might contribute new capital to strengthen the firm's balance sheet, but without success. One investor they approached, Warren Buffett, was quoted as saying that the problem with hedge funds is that "You never know who's swimming naked until the tide goes out."

Finally, on September 23, 1998, the Fed stepped in to rescue the firm. LTCM's equity capital, $4.5 billion at the beginning of the year, had almost been wiped out. Alan Greenspan, Chairman of the Federal Reserve Board, summoned the heads of the major banks to a meeting in New York the next day. They met until 3:00 A.M. the following morning, when they finally agreed to an injection of $3.7 billion to keep LTCM alive.

Why did the Fed intervene? Because it thought that LTCM was too big to fail, and without the Fed there would have been no deal. The Fed believed that if LTCM had been pushed into bankruptcy and its net positions, estimated at $200 billion, been liquidated quickly, the financial markets would have panicked.

In retrospect, the ability of LTCM to leverage its $4.5 billion equity base into securities positions of more than $200 billion has shocked many observers who have questioned how banks and securities firms could have extended that much credit. As a result of the LTCM debacle, banks have begun demanding more information from hedge funds before they extend credit to them.

Global Macro Strategies. The strategy of macro fund managers is based on shifts in global economies. Macro managers speculate on changes in countries' economic policies and shifts in currency and interest rates by the use of derivatives and leverage. Portfolios tend to be concentrated in a small number of investment positions. The investments are often specifically designed to take advantage of artificial imbalances in the marketplace brought on by central bank activities.

Market-Neutral Strategies. A market-neutral strategy seeks to eliminate market risk by equally balancing long and short positions. Exposure to the market is reduced because short and long portfolio losses and gains due to market fluctuations typically offset one another. If the longs selected are undervalued and the shorts are overvalued, a profit will result when the market recognizes the mispricing.

Sector Strategies. Sector funds invest long and short in specific sectors of the economy. Examples of such sector specialization include technology companies, financial institutions, health care, utilities, real estate investment trusts, and energy companies. Managers construct portfolios of long and short positions based on intensive research.

Short Selling. This strategy is based on the sale of securities that are overvalued from either a technical or fundamental viewpoint. The investor does not own the shares sold, but instead borrows them from a broker in anticipation that the share price will fall and the shares may be bought later at a lower price to replace those borrowed from the broker earlier. Short sellers typically focus on situations in which they believe stock prices are being supported by unrealistic expectations.

Fixed-Income Arbitrage. This strategy involves taking long and short positions in bonds with the expectation that the yield spreads between them will return to historical levels. When combined, these positions approximate one another in terms of rate and maturity but suffer from price inefficiencies. Risk varies with the level of leverage employed and the types of trades.

Index Arbitrage. Index arbitrage involves buying and selling a "basket" of stocks or other securities and taking a counterposition in index futures contracts to capture differences due to inefficiencies in the market. This process is also known as program trading.

Closed-End Fund Arbitrage. In closed-end fund arbitrage, like stock index arbitrage, the fund manager buys or sells a basket of stocks. In this case, the basket replicates the holding of a closed-end mutual fund. The manager seeks to identify closed-end mutual funds that are trading at prices substantially different from their net asset value.

Convertible Arbitrage. In convertible arbitrage, the fund manager simultaneously goes long in the convertible securities and short in the underlying equities of the same issuers, thereby working the spread between the two types of securities. Returns result from the convergence of valuations between the two securities.

Event-Driven Investing. Event-driven investing is a strategy that seeks to profit from price imbalances or fluctuations. The event-driven investing strategies are risk arbitrage, distressed securities, and special situations.

Risk Arbitrage.   In risk arbitrage, fund managers take a long position in the stock of a company being acquired in a merger, leveraged buyout, or takeover and a simultaneous short position in the stock of the acquiring firm. If the takeover fails, this strategy may result in large losses because the target company's stock price likely will return to its previous price.

Distressed Securities.   In this strategy, fund managers, sometimes referred to as "vulture capitalists," typically invest in the securities of companies undergoing bankruptcy or reorganization. Managers tend to focus on companies that are undergoing financial rather than operational distress.

Special Situations.   Special-situation managers attempt to take advantage of unusual events with a significant position in the equity or debt of a firm. Special-situation managers tend to focus on areas such as depressed stocks, impending mergers or acquisitions, or emerging bad news that may temporarily cause a company's stock or bond prices to decline.

HEDGE FUND PERFORMANCE

The performance of the various hedge fund strategies varies from year to year. Exhibit 20.8 shows the performance of hedge funds for the years 1987 through

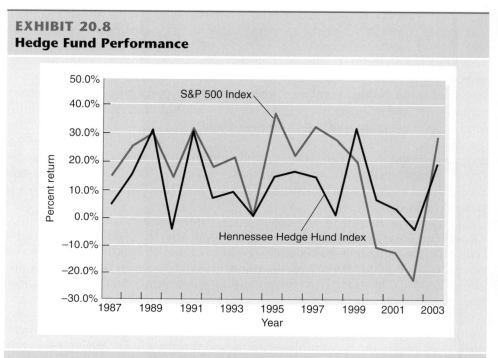

EXHIBIT 20.8
Hedge Fund Performance

Generally, hedge funds did not perform well in the 1990s. Beginning in the late 1990s, however, international and event-driven hedge funds performed well enough to push hedge fund returns higher than the S&P 500. Most recently, the S&P 500 has had higher average returns than hedge funds.

Source: Hennessee Group, LLC.

2003. During the mid-1990s, hedge funds did not perform as well as the S&P 500. In the late 1990s and early 2000s, however, international and event-driven hedge funds performed well enough to push the returns for hedge funds as a group above the S&P 500. Most recently, the S&P 500 has had higher average returns than hedge funds.

DO YOU UNDERSTAND?

1. Why would an investor want to invest in a hedge fund?
2. How are hedge funds different from closed-end funds and mutual funds?
3. Why do hedge fund managers follow such specialized strategies?

Money market mutual funds (MMMFs) invest in very liquid short-term assets (under 120 days) whose prices are not significantly affected by changes in market interest rates and which have little credit risk. In addition, they provide shareholders with ready access to their funds via wire transfers, transfers among stock and bond accounts, check writing, or credit card capabilities.

Money market mutual funds were started in the early 1970s. They grew very rapidly in the late 1970s and early 1980s, from $3.7 billion in total assets in 1976 to $232.3 billion in total assets on December 1, 1982. At that point, competition from financial institutions' newly authorized money market deposit accounts (MMDAs) and Super NOW accounts terminated their rapid growth. Subsequently, their asset holdings fell by more than $60 billion in less than 6 months.

The initial rapid growth of money market mutual funds depended on the existence of Regulation Q, which imposed binding deposit rate ceilings on banks and savings institutions in high-interest-rate periods. In the 1970s, as interest rates rose above Regulation Q rate ceilings on deposits at commercial banks and thrifts, their depositors had powerful incentives to withdraw funds and place them in MMMFs to earn a higher return. After Regulation Q was relaxed in late 1982, MMMFs lost market share, as can be seen in Exhibit 20.9. It was only after financial institutions cut their initially high payout rates on their MMDAs that MMMFs were able to grow once again.

Subsequently, MMMFs have continued to play a major role in the economy. They often pay higher interest rates than banks, and they have developed relationships with banks and their parent organizations that allow them to offer checking accounts, electronic funds transfers, debit cards, and other transactional conveniences to their shareholders. In addition, many MMMFs have been formed that now invest only in securities issued by state and local governments that produce interest income that is exempt from federal income tax and (for residents of the states where the securities are issued) state income tax as well. Consequently, money market funds now contribute substantially to the M2 and M3 money supplies. At year-end 2003, they had well over $1.5 trillion worth of shares outstanding, as you can see in Exhibit 20.9. Net assets of MMMFs have been steadily declining since 2001.

MONEY MARKET MUTUAL FUNDS

EXHIBIT 20.9
Money Market Mutual Fund Asset Holdings (1974–2001)

Year	Total Assets ($ in Billions)	Distribution of Assets (%)			
		Bank CDs and Eurodollar CDs	U.S. Government Securities and RPs	Commercial Paper and Banker's Acceptances	Cash and Miscellaneous
1974	2.4	67	4	25	4
1976	3.7	38	28	23	1
1978	10.9	49	14	34	3
1979	45.2	40	10	43	7
1980	74.4	37	19	42	2
1981	181.9	34	26	39	2
1982	206.6	31	34	33	2
1983	162.5	28	30	41	1
1984	209.7	21	31	47	1
1985	207.5	17	33	48	2
1990	414.7	12	34	50	4
1995	629.7	10	40	38	12
2000	1,607.2	13	29	42	16
2001	2,012.9	16	35	34	15
2002	1,997.2	15	31	30	16
2003	1,763.3	12	34	27	19

In the MMMFs' early years, their assets grew slowly. However, when interest rates rose above depository institutions' Regulation Q ceilings in the late 1970s and early 1980s, their growth exploded. In late 1982, however, depository institutions were allowed to offer unregulated deposit rates on some accounts, and MMMFs' growth reversed in 1982. After bank deposit rates fell and MMMFs' developed new services and tax-exempt accounts, their growth resumed. Net assets of MMMFs have been steadily declining since 2001.

Source: Investment Company Institute, *Mutual Fund Fact Book*, various issues.

TRANSACTIONAL CONVENIENCES OFFERED BY MMMFS

Money market mutual funds have posed formidable competition for banks. While they cannot pay out higher rates of interest than they earn on their holdings of money market instruments, they have been able to offer a variety of transactional conveniences. First, by cooperating with banks, many allow people to write checks on their MMMF accounts that are cleared though the banking system. Second, by cooperating with card-issuing organizations, many have been able to allow their customers to use debit cards (and even credit cards, for customers who hold cash management accounts with brokerage firms) to access the funds in their accounts for transactions purposes. Third, many funds allow customers to obtain wire transfers to designated parties from the balances in their MMMF accounts. Fourth, customers who hold other assets with the parent company of the MMMF may be allowed to "sweep" excess cash balances into their MMMF (if, for instance, they sell stock at the parent brokerage firm). Conversely, the parent firm may also make automatic transfers of funds out of the MMMF on the day that payment is needed for stock market transactions or when funds are needed for transfer into another mutual fund managed by the same fund family. These features allow investors to earn the maximum possible interest on their cash balances by ensuring that their idle cash will always be invested in their MMMF until it is needed. Because of these transactional features, plus the fact that consumers will ordinarily consider balances in their MMMFs when they determine how much money they have available to spend, since 1980 the Fed has included MMMF balances in its definitions of the M2 and M3 money supplies.

COMPETITION BETWEEN MMMFS AND BANKS

Initially, MMMFs had a large advantage relative to depository institutions. They could pass through almost all the interest they earned to shareholders, while depository institutions could pay no more than Regulation Q allowed, and could pay no interest on demand deposits. Because interest rates were high throughout the 1970s, the rapid growth of MMMFs in that decade created so much competitive pressure for depository institutions that the 1980 Depository Institutions Deregulation and Monetary Control Act and the 1982 Depository Institutions Act eventually eliminated Regulation Q and deregulated deposit rate ceilings. Banks were no longer subject to rate ceilings on certain NOW accounts after 1982, so they could offer to pay any interest rate—even rates that were higher than MMMFs could earn on money market assets. Thus, the initial advantage of MMMFs reversed after 1982.

Nonetheless, MMMFs still retained some advantages relative to depository institutions. For instance, if they invested in short-term tax-exempt securities, they could pass through interest payments that were exempt from federal (and possibly state) income taxes. Interest on financial institution deposits, in contrast, was fully taxable. Also, operating costs of MMMFs were typically very low, at about 0.25 percent of assets per year. Thus, MMMFs could afford to pass through a higher portion of their interest earnings than depository institutions—since the MMMFs' main costs were associated with data-processing and communications operations while depository institutions also had to support expensive physical offices and teller operations. In addition, MMMFs that were associated with fund families or brokerage firms often offered transactional conveniences that were not as cheap to obtain or as readily available from most depository institutions. For instance, many money funds augmented their check-writing privileges by letting customers use debit cards, pay bills by phone, obtain cash from banks' ATM networks, transfer funds electronically, and, in conjunction with brokerage accounts, transfer funds automatically between accounts. Even though banks could offer similar transaction services in conjunction with NOW accounts, they were subject to reserve requirements that reduced their net earning power on such accounts. Consequently, MMMFs were able to continue to exist and compete with depository institutions even after bank deposit rates were deregulated.

The main advantage depository institutions had relative to MMMFs was that they could obtain inexpensive federal deposit insurance for their deposit accounts. MMMFs responded by using various strategies to obtain insurance for customers who wanted insured accounts. Some bought or started "nonbank" banks, trust companies, or savings institutions. In that way they could offer federally insured MMDAs. to depositors who desired them. For instance, the Fidelity Investments group started a bank so that it could offer insured accounts to its customers. The Dreyfus Fund acquired a bank so that it could offer MMDAs. Other MMMFs contracted with private insurers to insure their deposits. However, the initial private insurance fee of $3/8$ of 1 percent substantially exceeded federal insurance premiums, so private insurance was not used extensively. Instead, many MMMFs invested only in "risk-free" government securities, and others used the financial support of well-known parent companies to ensure that they would not "break the buck" (i.e., cause their net asset values to fall below their par value of $1 per share) and thereby cause their shareholders to suffer losses. Consequently, the public has retained confidence in the safety of MMMFs even if they don't have federal insurance. Thus, MMMFs have been able to compete effectively with banks to obtain savers' liquid asset holdings and many checkable deposits. Consequently, MMMFs now account for approximately one-third of all assets held by mutual funds and around 25 percent of the M3 money supply.

REAL ESTATE INVESTMENT TRUSTS

A **real estate investment trust (REIT)** is a type of closed-end investment company that invests in real estate. It may hold income-generating properties, acquire mortgages, finance real estate developments, provide interim financing to builders, or acquire and lease property to real estate developers. REITs must abide by the Real Estate Investment Act of 1960, which governs their formation and business operations. REITs are exempt from federal income tax provided that they derive at least three-fourths of their income from operations related to real estate and pass through over 90 percent of their net income to shareholders.

REITs grew slowly until the late 1960s, when their growth exploded. New favorable tax treatment, federal encouragement of real estate investment, a strong economy, and rising real estate prices all contributed to their growth. However, while they were growing rapidly, many REITs took excessive risks, making highly leveraged or speculative investments on the assumption that rising real estate prices would soon increase builders' and owners' equity. Furthermore, REITs that provided construction and interim financing to speculative builders (builders who erected properties without first having firm contracts from end users) took the most risk. Those taking the least risk provided long-term mortgage financing to ultimate users of properties or were "equity trusts" that owned and leased real properties.

When interest rates rose and housing construction sagged during the money crunch of 1973 and 1974, numerous owners could not find permanent tenants for their properties. Many construction and development projects were left uncompleted or deferred as builders saw the market for their project dry up. As a result of these developments, numerous REITs had bad loans and experienced well-publicized financial distress. Many failed. To prevent failure of REITs associated with bank holding companies bearing their names, some commercial banks knowingly purchased bad mortgage loans from their affiliated REITs. This, in turn, jeopardized the banks. Before regulators could stop this practice, several large banks failed.

The bad publicity and financial distress surrounding REITs in the early and mid-1970s halted their rapid growth and started a substantial decline. Many of those that survived the 1973–1974 money crunch were those that held relatively low-risk physical assets. Although most survivors own sound assets, the bad publicity that REITs in general experienced in the mid-1970s made it difficult for them to attract new shareholders and lenders. Starting in the mid-1980s, however, REITs began to play a more important role in the economy once again, in part because tax reforms made other forms of real estate investment less attractive and enhanced the attractiveness of REITs as a source of passive real estate income. Newly formed mortgage REITs bought pools of high-yielding mortgages. In the 1990s, the growth in REITs was fueled by Wall Street's desire to securitize real estate and by favorable changes in the tax laws that allow institutional ownership of REIT shares. As a result, REITs expanded rapidly once again.

Exhibit 20.10 shows that the REIT liabilities increased eightfold from the end of 1990 to 2001, as REITs acquired many more assets. Many of the assets acquired

EXHIBIT 20.10
Financial Assets and Liabilities Held by Real Estate Investment Trusts

	1990	1995	2000	2003
Total financial assets	*28.5*	*33.3*	*62.1*	*114.9*
Mortgages	7.7	14.1	16.3	43.8
Home	0.4	6.9	7.9	35.2
Multifamily residential	2.3	1.6	1.2	0.7
Commercial	5.0	5.6	7.3	7.9
Agency securities	16.5	9.0	14.5	23.2
Miscellaneous assets	4.3	10.2	31.2	47.9
Total liabilities	*28.9*	*62.2*	*217.5*	*289.1*
Security RPs	0.0	10.9	11.9	35.5
Credit-market instruments	27.7	44.6	167.8	213.4
Open-market paper	0.9	0.0	0.2	0.7
Corporate bonds	18.1	15.5	67.0	106.1
Bank loans n.c.c	4.4	5.0	17.7	12.2
Mortgages	4.3	24.1	82.9	94.4
Miscellaneous liabilities	1.2	6.7	37.8	40.3

Financial assets of REITs nearly quadrupled from year-end 1990 through 2003, while their financial liabilities increased tenfold as they borrowed money (with bonds, bank loans, and mortgages) to invest in real assets in the late 1990s and early 2000s.

were real assets that could be leased out to earn rents and could also be used to generate future returns if real estate prices appreciated.

One of the problems that REITs face if they invest in the hope that real estate prices will appreciate in the future is that the properties must be sold before the price appreciation can be realized and passed through as capital-gains income to investors in shares of the REITs. Therefore, some REITs have structured themselves as "finite-life REITs," or **FREITs**, in order to reassure their investors that future property price appreciation will be realized. FREITs have a fixed life, after which they are scheduled to sell their properties and distribute all gains to shareholders. In that way, investors can be reassured that the FREIT will eventually be worth its net asset value and will not sell at a chronic discount to net asset value, like some closed-end funds.

DO YOU UNDERSTAND?

1. Explain the economic and regulatory climate that give rise to MMMFs.
2. What are the competitive advantages and disadvantages that money market mutual funds have relative to depository institutions?
3. In general, why do people often invest in specialized funds like REITs? Why did REITs become more popular during the 1990s, and why do you think they operate like closed-end funds? What problem were FREITs invented to solve?
4. How have money market funds tried to cope with the fact that they do not have federal deposit insurance?

CHAPTER TAKE-AWAYS

1 Mutual funds invest in a wide range of long-term securities (debt or equity) and provide investors with risk, denomination, maturity, and liquidity intermediation as well as access to professional investment management and lower transaction costs.

2 Closed-end investment companies sell stock but don't automatically redeem it. Owners of the shares must sell their shares in the market if they wish to terminate their investment in the fund. The market price of the shares may be at either a premium or a discount to the fund's net asset value.

3 Open-end funds (mutual funds) sell shares at their net asset value, plus a "load" charge or sales fee. Open-end funds promise to redeem their shares for their net asset value unless they have a back-end load, in the form of redemption fees or conditional deferred sales charges, that reduces the net proceeds paid to an investor who redeems shares. No-load funds do not charge a sales fee at the time of purchase but may assess redemption fees or deferred sales charges.

4 Hedge funds differ from mutual funds in three ways. Only accredited investors can participate in hedge funds. Hedge funds can employ investment techniques not available to mutual funds. Hedge fund managers can receive incentive fees but mutual fund managers cannot.

5 Money market mutual funds, which were started in the early 1970s, grew rapidly after the Regulation Q ceiling became binding on commercial banks and other depository institutions. However, they posed such a threat to depository institutions that in 1982, Congress authorized new accounts without rate ceilings for depository institutions.

6 REITs emphasize long-term mortgage or equity forms of real estate asset holdings. Many new ones have finite lives to ensure that they will be valued closer to their net asset (breakup) value.

KEY TERMS

Closed-end investment company
Net asset value (NAV)
Premium or discount to NAV
Open-end investment company
 (mutual fund)
Exchange-traded fund (ETF)
Unit investment trust
Index fund
Mutual fund family

Load fund
Front-end load
No-load fund
Bank-end load
Contingent deferred sales charge
Redemption fee
12b-1 fee
Management fee
Advisory fee

Exchange fee
Account maintenance fee
Hedge fund
Money market mutual fund
 (MMMF)
Real estate investment trust (REIT)
FREIT

QUESTIONS AND PROBLEMS

1. How can the pricing of closed-end funds possibly indicate that market inefficiencies exist? What are the pros and cons of that argument? If market inefficiencies exist, how can they be exploited to make money? Explain, and think of any possible problems that might occur.

2. What type of fund would you want to buy if you believed that stock markets were always fully and completely efficient? Explain why. Why do you think people don't all buy the same kinds of funds?

3. If you invested $10,000 in a mutual fund that charged a 1 percent of net assets management advisory fee and a 1 percent 12b-1 fee, and the fund matched the stock market's returns of 10 percent per year for 10 years, how much would your shares in the fund be worth at the end of that time (assuming no taxes, all income net of fees was reinvested at year-end, and all fund charges were levied at the end of each year)?

4. If you invested $10,000 in a closed-end fund that invested in stocks that matched the market return of 10 percent per year for 10 years, levied a management fee of 2 percent of net assets per year, and sold at a 15 percent discount to its NAV both when you bought it and

when you sold it 10 years later, how much would you have at the end of that time (assuming no taxes, all income was reinvested, and all fund charges were levied at the end of each year)?

5. If you invested $10,000 in an index fund that matched the market return of 10 percent per year for 10 years and levied a 0.25 percent management fee but no other fees, how much would you have at the end of the 10 years (assuming no taxes, all income was reinvested, and all fund charges were levied at the end of each year)?

6. (a) If you earned 3 percent per year in a tax-free money market fund and you were in the 31 percent federal income tax bracket and were fortunate enough to live in a state that had no state income tax, what interest rate would you have to earn in a taxable money market fund or bank account to be equally well-off? (b) What if your state had a 6 percent income tax but did not levy it on interest earned on municipal security obligations issued in your state—which were the only type of securities that your tax-exempt fund bought?

7. What is the major difference between open-end and closed-end investment companies? Why have open-end companies been more popular?

8. Why do you think it is important for a hedge fund manager to focus on a specific investment strategy?

9. How did the regulation of depository institutions contribute to the rapid growth of money market mutual funds?

10. Why are money market fund liabilities included in the broader measures of the money supply that the Federal Reserve introduced in 1980?

11. Give examples from this chapter to illustrate how different forms of financial institutions may either grow rapidly or decline as economic and regulatory conditions change.

12. What is a REIT? What problem did these firms experience during the 1970s?

INTERNET EXERCISE

One of the best sources of information on mutual funds and investment companies is the Investment Company Institute Web site, http://www.ici.org. It contains voluminous data on mutual funds in its annual *Mutual Fund Fact Book*, which is available on its site. It also provides useful data on closed-end investment companies, investment company regulations and pending regulations, and investment companies in general.

1. Go to the Investment Company Institute Web site and find the latest facts and figures on mutual funds. Look for the latest of the current statistical releases.
    a. Find the current asset holdings of all mutual funds.
    b. Calculate the proportion of assets held by (i) taxable money market funds, (ii) tax-free money market funds, (iii) taxable bond funds, (iv) nontaxable bond funds, and (v) all other funds.
    c. Determine the type of fund that experienced the greatest percentage increase or decrease in assets in the last month the data was available.
2. From the same information release you located above, find the ratio of liquid asset holdings to total asset holdings of mutual funds in the last month.
    a. Has it increased or decreased in the last year?
    b. Does it appear to have increased or decreased because mutual fund sales or redemptions have changed, because mutual fund asset prices have changed, or because mutual funds have made a conscious decision to hold more or less cash relative to their assets? You may have to speculate in your answer unless you can see strong evidence that mutual fund net sales or redemptions or asset prices have recently changed dramatically.

Glossary

account maintenance fee A fee levied by some mutual funds on low-balance accounts.

accredited investors Individuals who are considered to be sophisticated investors and who do not need the protection afforded to regular investors by the securities laws.

ACH *See* **automated clearinghouse**

actual reserves The reserve amount computed by a bank by summing its holdings of vault cash with its holdings of reserve deposits at Federal Reserve banks over a 2-week reserve maintenance period.

adjustable-rate mortgages (ARMs) Mortgages on which the contractual interest rate changes when market rates change.

adjustable-rate preferred stock Preferred stock issued with adjustable rates; the dividends are adjusted periodically in response to changing market interest rates.

adjustment credit at discount window Short-term discount window loans that allow financial institutions to meet temporary needs for additional reserves.

ADRs *See* **American Depository Receipts**

advances Loans by Federal Home Loan Bank to its member institutions.

adverse selection The tendency of only the riskiest people or institutions to apply for loans or to buy insurance if rates are high. Thus, institutions making loans or selling insurance must impose strict risk-control criteria to screen out good from bad applicants.

advisory fee *See* **management fee**

agency securities Debt instruments of credit agencies sponsored by the U.S. government.

aggressive stocks Stocks with betas greater than 1.0 that carry greater systematic risk than the market.

agreement corporations Corporations that operate similarly to Edge Act corporations but remain under state charter.

allocational efficiency The capital market is allocationally efficient if funds are channeled to their most productive use.

allocative function of interest rates The function of interest rates in the economy whereby they allocate funds between surplus spending units (SSUs) and deficit spending units (DSUs) in the financial markets.

all-risk coverage Property insurance coverage that insures against all losses except those that are excluded.

American Depository Receipts (ADRs) Dollar-denominated claims issued by U.S. banks representing ownership of shares of a foreign company's stock held on deposit by the U.S. bank in the issuing firm's home country.

American option The right to buy (or sell) and receive (or deliver) the underlying asset at the strike price that exists over time until the option expires.

amortization To pay the principal amount due on a loan in stages over a period of time. When the full amount is repaid, the loan is fully amortized.

amortized loan A loan repaid over the life of the loan, using a contractual rate of interest; each payment includes both interest and principal.

angels Individuals who act as informal venture capitalists.

annuity A product sold by life insurers that can be thought of as the mirror image of life insurance. The function of an annuity is to liquidate an estate.

arbitrage The process of simultaneously selling overvalued assets and buying similar undervalued assets.

ARMs *See* **adjustable-rate mortgages**

ask price The bid price plus a price "spread" that provides the dealer's profit; the lowest price at which the dealer is willing to sell the security.

asset-backed security A security that derives its value from its claim on principal and interest payments made on a pool of underlying assets (such as a pool of mortgage loans or auto loans).

asset-gatherer Financial conglomerate that tries to appeal to people by offering numerous financial services under one roof so people will deposit their money with it to obtain its financial products.

asset management A financial institution's management of its asset structure to provide both liquidity and desirable rates of return.

ATS *See* **automatic transfer of savings service accounts**

auction market A market that provides centralized procedures for the exposure of purchase and sale orders to all market participants simultaneously, thereby eliminating the expense of locating compatible partners and bargaining for a favorable price.

automated clearinghouse (ACH) A clearinghouse for electronic funds transfer (EFT).

automated deposit of payroll Regular payments to the same individuals made through automated clearinghouses; the bank of the paying organization gives the ACH an electronic record of the people to be paid; the clearinghouse then credits the accounts of the receiving banks with the total due and provides data on which depositors' accounts should be credited.

automated teller machine (ATM) A machine that can dispense cash, provide balance information, or accept deposits electronically.

automatic transfer of savings service accounts (ATS) Zero-balance checking accounts fed from savings accounts.

back-end load Fees charged when investors take money out of a mutual fund by redeeming shares; the fees can be either redemption fees or contingent deferred sales charges.

"bad-debt deduction" Federal income tax savings given to savings banks and savings associations after World War II until 1996 that reduced federal income tax obligations of these institutions.

balance of payments A set of accounts that summarizes a country's international balance of trade and the payments to and the receipts from foreigners.

balloon payment mortgages Mortgages on which the final scheduled payment is substantially larger than preceding payments.

banker's acceptance A draft drawn on a bank by a corporation to pay for merchandise. The draft promises payment of a certain sum of money to its holder at some future date. In effect, the bank substitutes its credit standing for that of the issuing corporation.

bank examination A means of ensuring that banks are operated prudently and do not hold too many risky assets relative to their capital.

Bank for International Settlements (BIS) An institution that coordinates international payments and has established certain risk-based capital standards for financial institutions.

bank holding company A major form of organization for banks in the United States in which 25 percent or more of the voting stock of one or more banks is held by a single entity.

Banking Act of 1933 (Glass-Steagall Act) Legislation that barred banks from paying interest on demand deposits, separated commercial banking from investment banking, and restricted the types of assets that banks could own.

bank insolvency A bank is declared insolvent when the value of its liabilities exceeds the value of its assets.

bank liquidity The ability of banks to accommodate depositors' requests for withdrawals, to accommodate borrowers' requests for loans, and to pay other liabilities when they come due.

banknote IOUs issued by a bank; credit money whose value depends on the creditworthiness of the issuing bank.

bank panic. *See* **panic**

bank run. *See* **run**

basis risk A risk that exists because the value of an item being hedged may not always keep the same price relationship to contracts purchased or sold in the futures markets.

Basle Accord Agreement of major industrial countries to adopt the risk-based capital requirements developed by the Bank for International Settlements for financial institutions.

bearer bonds Bonds for which coupons are attached and the holder presents them for payment when they come due.

best-efforts offering The distribution of registered securities in which the investment banker acts only as the company's agent and receives a commission for placing the securities with investors.

beta The measurement of the extent to which a stock's returns are related to general market returns.

bid–ask spread In over-the-counter markets, the difference between the bid price at which a dealer is willing to buy a security and the ask price at which he is willing to sell the security; dealers make a profit by selling at a higher price than the price they paid to buy the security.

bid price The price offered by a dealer to purchase a given security.

bill of lading An international trade document that is a receipt issued to the exporter by a common carrier that acknowledges possession of the goods described on the face of the bill; a contract between the exporter and the shipping company.

BIS *See* **Bank for International Settlements**

Board of Governors The governing body of the Federal Reserve System that sets the nation's monetary policy and is financially and administratively independent of both Congress and the president.

bond A contractual obligation of a borrower to make cash payments to a lender for a fixed number of years; upon maturity, the lender is paid the face value of the security.

bond insurance Municipal bond insurance was developed in the early 1970s as the first financial guarantee product to cover the payment of principal and interest to investors in debt securities in the event of a default.

bond price volatility The percentage change in bond price for a given change in yield.

bond ratings The credit ratings of bonds, principally by Moody's Investors Service and Standard & Poor's, ranked in order of the perceived probability of their default and published as letter grades with the highest-grade bonds being those with the lowest default risk.

bondholder The lender in a bond contract.

borrowed funds (reserves) Short-term funds borrowed by commercial banks from the wholesale money market (or the Federal Reserve).

breadth. *See* **market breadth**

Bretton Woods system Before 1971, a system of fixed currency exchange rates under which a government was obligated to intervene in the foreign exchange markets to keep the value of its currency within a narrow range.

bridge financing *See* **bridge loan**

bridge loan A loan supplying cash for a specific transaction; repayment is made from cash flows from an identifiable source. Usually, the purpose of the loan and the source of repayment are related.

broker One who acts as an intermediary between buyers and sellers but does not take title to the securities traded.

brokerage A function of an investment firm in which the firm earns a commission for bringing a buyer and seller together.

brokered market A market in which trading in an issue becomes sufficiently heavy that brokers begin to offer specialized search services to market participants for a fee (commission); brokers undertake to find compatible trading partners and negotiate acceptable transaction prices for their clients.

building societies The first savings associations.

call An option giving the buyer the right to purchase the underlying security at a predetermined price for a stated period of time.

call feature. *See* **call option (call provision)**

call interest premium The difference in interest rates between callable and comparable noncallable bonds.

call loan Usually, a loan that either the borrower or lender can terminate upon request.

call option (call provision) The option of the bond issuer to buy back the bond at a specified price in advance of the maturity date; the price (call price) is usually set at the bond's par value or slightly above par.

call reports Detailed statements of the operating and financial condition of a bank.

call risk The risk that a callable security will be called.

CAMELS **C**apital adequacy, **A**sset quality, **M**anagement competence and control, **E**arnings, **L**iquidity, and **S**ensitivity to market risk rating system used by financial institution examiners.

cap (on interest rates) A cap on interest rates is created by purchasing a put option (i.e., an option to sell) on a financial futures contract.

capital accounts In the balance of payments accounts, capital accounts measure capital flows into and out of the country.

capital as a deductible If a financial institution incurs losses, its capital will be charged off first, before depositors or their insurer lose money; thus, the value of its capital is "deducted" before the deposit insurer loses money.

capital controls Controls imposed to limit transfers of funds out of a country.

capital flight When owners of capital transfer their wealth out of the country, typically in response to political instability.

capital-gains yield The rate at which the value of the firm is expected to grow.

capital market Financial market in which financial claims with maturities greater than one year are traded. Capital markets channel savings into long-term productive investments.

captive insurance company Insurance company created by a parent company for the purpose of insuring the parent company's loss exposures.

captive sales finance company A sales finance company that is owned by a manufacturer and helps finance the sale of the manufacturer's goods.

carried interest The portion of the profits of a venture capital fund that the manager of the fund earns.

cash-collateral accounts Deposits in accounts whose funds can be used to cover defaults on loans; a credit enhancement for asset-backed securities.

cash drain People's withdrawal of cash from banks, thus depleting actual reserves held by banks.

cash-flow underwriting Writing insurance on just about any risk in order to get the premium dollars to invest at high interest rates.

cash items in the process of collection (CIPC) An account that is the value of checks drawn on other banks but not yet collected.

cash management account An account pioneered by Merrill Lynch, Pierce, Fenner & Smith in the 1970s that offered certain customers the right to buy stocks and bonds from Merrill Lynch brokers and to obtain checking account and debit-card services that would allow them to withdraw cash or make purchases at numerous locations.

cash market Another name for the spot market, which involves the exchange of securities or other financial claims for immediate payment.

cash settled A form of settlement for certain futures and options contracts in which delivery of the underlying asset never takes place. Only the cash value of the contract is transferred between the buyer and seller.

cash value life insurance Because of overpayment of whole life insurance premiums in the early policy years, the premiums paid by the insured earn interest and cash values develop within the policy.

CEBA *See* **Competitive Equality in Banking Act**

central credit union A credit union for credit unions.

Central Liquidity Facility (CLF) An organization empowered to make loans to credit unions that have a liquidity need; the CLF is overseen by the National Credit Union Administration (NCUA).

check clearing and settlement The process through which the transfer of deposit money is made when writing a check.

Check Clearing for the 21st Century (Check 21) Act. Legislation passed in 2003 that rquires banks to accept electronic images for the purpose of interbank check clearing and settling.

checking account Bank demand deposit balances that can be transferred from one person to another on the "demand" of the deposit owner in the form of a written check.

CIPC *See* **cash items in process of collection**

"clean" collection An international collection made without accompanying or attached documentation. Checks, traveler's checks, and money orders are collected cleanly.

clear at par Fed requirement that member banks clear checks at face value, or par.

clearing To settle a transaction by exchanging checking account balances for securities or another checking account balance.

CLF *See* **Central Liquidity Facility**

closed-end fund *See* **investment company**

CMO *See* **collateralized mortgage obligation**

coinsurance Loss-sharing provision in insurance. In health insurance, coinsurance is the loss-sharing percentages after the deductible is satisfied. In property insurance, coinsurance requires the insured to bear a portion of the loss if property is not insured for a specified percentage of value.

collar (on interest rates) By simultaneously buying a cap and selling a floor, a collar is created. Collars limit the movement of a financial institution's interest costs within a specified range.

collateral Assets that are used to secure a loan. Title to them will pass to the lender if the borrower defaults.

collateralized mortgage obligation (CMO) A security issued by a trust or finance subsidiary that promises to pass through specified portions of the principal and interest payments on pools of underlying mortgages.

commercial bank The most important participant in the indirect credit markets. Commercial banks issue checkable demand deposits and make loans.

commercial letter of credit A promise by a bank to pay for goods in a commercial transaction. The letter of credit is written by the bank for a customer that is engaged in commercial transactions. The buyer of the goods arranges for the bank to pay the seller of the goods once the terms of the purchase agreement are satisfied.

commercial paper An unsecured, short-term promissory note issued by a large creditworthy business or financial institution. Commercial paper has maturities ranging from a day to 270 days and is usually issued in denominations of $1 million or more. Direct-placed commercial paper is sold by the seller to the buyer. Terms are negotiable. Dealer-placed commercial paper is sold through dealers with terms similar to those offered on banks' CDs.

commission Compensation for brokers that is usually based on the number of items sold or their value, or else on a share of the profits that their brokerage firm earned on the transaction they helped arrange.

common bond requirement A requirement of a credit union that members share a "common bond" such as an occupational bond, an associational bond, or a residential bond.

common stock Basic ownership claim in a corporation. Stockholders share in the distributed earnings and net worth of a corporation and select its directors.

Community Reinvestment Act (CRA) Legislation created to prevent "redlining," where a lender draws a hypothetical red line on a map around one part of a community and refuses to make loans in that area. Requires that lenders keep records to show they lend in all areas of their community.

compensating balances Minimum average deposit balances that customers must maintain at the bank, usually in the form of non-interest-bearing demand deposits.

competition in laxity Competition between regulators in which some accounting rules and jurisdictions are more lenient than others.

competitive bidding A type of public offering in which the company selects the investment banker who will conduct the offering based on which investment banker offers to pay the highest net proceeds for the securities.

Competitive Equality in Banking Act (CEBA) of 1987 A regulatory act that (1) redefined nonbank banks and (2) provided funding to bail out the failing FSLIC.

competitive sale *See* **competitive bidding**

compounding The calculation of future value based on the assumption that all interest earned will be reinvested to earn additional interest.

computerized exchanges Stock exchanges that use computerized trading and automated exchange facilities.

concentration ratios Concentration ratios measure the percentage of loans or loan commitments allocated to a given geographic location, loan type, or business type by a lender.

constant velocity The idea that if velocity is constant, the annual value of economic activity (GDP) is a constant ratio to the money supply.

Consumer Credit Protection Act of 1969 (Truth-in-Lending Act) Legislation passed with the intent of assuring that every borrower obtained meaningful information about the cost of credit, especially (1) the annual percentage rate and (2) the total finance charges on a loan.

consumer finance company A finance company that specializes in making cash loans to consumers.

contemporaneous reserve accounting system A procedure under which reserves are posted 2 days after a 2-week reserve computational period.

contingent deferred sales charges Fees assessed when people redeem shares in a mutual fund; the fees are usually lower or absent if the money has been in the fund for longer periods of time.

contra-asset Allowances for asset holdings whose value may not subsequently be realized.

contributory plan A pension plan funded by both employer and employee contributions.

conversion option The option allowing the investor to convert a security into another type of security at a predetermined price.

conversion yield discount The difference in yield between convertible bonds with the conversion option and similar bonds without this option.

convertibility A quality of term insurance that permits the insured to convert the term policy to some form of permanent protection, such as whole life insurance.

convertible bonds Bonds that can be exchanged for shares of common stock.

convertible preferred stock Preferred stock that can be converted into common stock at a predetermined ratio.

convertible term insurance Term insurance that may be switched to whole life insurance without providing evidence of insurability.

convexity The curve representing T-bonds' price/yield relationship is convex. Thus, convexity is the adjustment for the shape of the curve in the formula for estimating the percentage change in the price of the bond corresponding to a given change in the market interest rate.

correspondent balances Deposits that banks hold at other banks to clear checks and provide compensation for correspondent services.

correspondent banking A business arrangement between two banks in which one (the correspondent bank) agrees to provide the other (respondent bank) with special services, such as check-clearing or trust department services. International correspondent relationships provide international banking services such as accepting drafts, honoring letters of credit, furnishing credit information, collecting and disbursing international funds, and investing funds in international money markets.

counterparty In a forward market, the contracted party that exchanges one item for another for a predetermined price at a predetermined point in time. Ordinarily, both parties to the contract are bound by the contract.

countertrade In international trade transactions, the practice of accepting locally produced merchandise in lieu of money as payment for goods and services.

country (sovereign) risk The risk tied to political developments in a country that affect the return on loans or investments.

coupon The periodic interest payment in a bond contract.

covered interest rate parity In foreign exchange markets, the difference between current spot exchange rates and forward exchange rates generally reflects the difference in interest rates that can be earned in the two countries over the same period of time.

covered option An option writer's position if they already own the securities that they have agreed to sell or have already sold short the securities that they have agreed to buy.

CRA *See* **Community Reinvestment Act**

credit cards Cards that can be used at the point of sale to pay a merchant; the bank that issued the credit card makes a loan to the customer by adding cash balances to the merchant's account.

credit derivatives A derivative security with a payoff that is tied to credit-related events such as default or bankruptcy.

credit enhancements Provisions of the private sector to reduce the default risk of privately originated asset-backed securities.

credit insurance An insurance policy that pays the holder of a loan in the event the borrower defaults.

credit money Money backed by a promise to pay. In contrast with gold or silver coins, which are worth their face value if sold as a commodity, credit money has little intrinsic value. Paper money is an example.

credit risk (default risk) The possibility that the borrower will not pay back all or part of the interest or principal as promised.

credit swap A swap contract in which the holder of a loan makes periodic payments to the seller of the swap in exchange for a promise to pay the holder of the loan the face amount of the loan in the event the borrower defaults.

credit transfer An electronic funds transfer (EFT) in which the initiating institution sends funds through the system to be deposited in the recipient's account.

Credit Union National Association (CUNA) A major trade and service association of credit unions that lobbies in Congress, supports the development of the central credit unions and the U.S. Central Credit Union, and helps credit unions manage their liquidity, clear their checks, and obtain various investment and funds-management services.

cross-hedging Hedging with a traded futures contract whose characteristics do not exactly match those of the hedger's risk exposure.

cumulative preferred stock The cumulative feature of preferred stock means that the firm cannot pay a dividend on its common stock until it has paid the preferred shareholders the dividends in arrears.

cumulative voting A procedure for electing directors in which all directors are elected at the same time and shareholders are granted a number of votes equal to the number of directors being elected times the number of shares owned.

CUNA *See* **Credit Union National Association**

currency risk Risk resulting from changes in currency exchange values that affect the return on loans or investments denominated in other currencies.

current account The balance of payments account that summarizes foreign trade in goods and services plus investment income and gifts or grants made to other countries.

DACI *See* **deferred availability cash items**

de novo branching Creating a new bank branch.

dealer One who is in the security business acting as a principal rather than an agent. The dealer buys for his or her own account and sells to customers from his or her inventory.

dealer market A market in which trading in an issue is sufficiently active that some market participants maintain bid and offer quotations of their own; such dealers buy for, and sell for, their own inventory at their quoted prices. Dealer markets eliminate the need for searches for trading partners.

debased money Money whose intrinsic value has been lessened by government in order to earn more profit.

debenture bonds Bonds for which no assets have been pledged as collateral. These bonds are secured only by the firm's potential to generate positive cash flows.

debit card Card that allows one to withdraw funds electronically from a bank or security account to obtain cash at an ATM or make payments to a merchant at the point of sale.

debit transfer An electronic funds transfer (EFT) in which the initiating institution withdraws funds from the depositor's account.

deductible Insurance contract provision requiring the insured to bear a portion of an insured loss.

default The failure on the part of the borrower to meet any condition of the bond contract.

default risk (credit risk) See **credit risk (default risk)**

default risk premium The amount of additional compensation investors must receive for purchasing securities that are not free of default risk. The rate on U.S. Treasury securities is used as the default-free rate.

defensive stocks Stocks with betas less than 1 that carry less systematic risk than the market.

deferment clause A clause in all life insurance policies that accumulate cash values; the clause declares the right of the insurer to defer the payment of the cash value for a period not exceeding 6 months from the date of the request.

deferred availability cash items (DACI) Federal Reserve balance-sheet item representing the value of checks deposited at the Fed by depository institutions that have not yet been credited to the institution's accounts.

deficit spending unit (DSU) An economic unit that has expenditures exceeding current income. A DSU sells financial claims on itself (liabilities) or sells equity to obtain needed funds.

defined benefit plan A pension plan in which the employer states the benefit the employee will receive at retirement.

defined contribution plan A pension plan in which the employer offers no guarantees about the actual benefit at retirement, only the periodic contributions that will be made on behalf of the employee.

demand deposit Deposits held at banks that the owner can withdraw instantly upon demand—either with checks or electronically.

demutualization The term applied to the trend in the insurance and thrift industries of large numbers of mutual companies converting to stock companies.

deposit expansion multiplier This multiplier measures the amount that financial institutions' deposits are expected to increase for each $1 increase in the monetary base or, alternatively, banks' reserves.

deposit insurance (state and federal) Funds established with the purpose of protecting depositors in the event of a bank failure.

Depository Institutions Act of 1982 (Garn–St. Germain Bill) Extended the 1980 revisions in banking regulation by authorizing MMDA accounts, accelerating the phaseout of deposit rate ceilings, granting thrift institutions broader powers, and providing for acquisitions of failing institutions by different types of institutions located in different states.

Depository Institutions Deregulation and Monetary Control Act of 1980 (DIDMCA) The first major 1980s banking act. It deregulated financial institution deposit and loan rate ceilings and allowed nonbank institutions to have checking accounts (NOWs) and offer other services in competition with banks. It also extended reserve requirements to all institutions that offered transactions deposits.

depth See **market depth**

direct claim See **direct financing**

direct financing Financing wherein DSUs issue financial claims on themselves and sell them for money directly to SSUs. The SSU's claim is against the DSU, not a financial intermediary.

direct search market Secondary markets in which buyers and sellers must search each other out directly.

discount bond A bond that sells below its par or face value. A bond sells at a discount when the market rate of interest is above the bond's fixed coupon rate.

discount broker Brokerage firms that compete against full-service brokerage firms by offering fewer brokerage services and passing the savings on to investors.

discount rate The interest rate a financial institution must pay to borrow reserve deposits from its regional Federal Reserve bank.

discount window An operation of the Federal Reserve System whereby banks may borrow temporary reserves from the Federal Reserve System as an alternative to selling secondary reserves or borrowing federal funds to cover legal reserve deficiencies; the discount window is part of the mechanism for adjusting short-term required reserve deficiencies.

discount window scrutiny The scrutiny of a financial institution's operations when that institution asks to borrow from the Federal Reserve.

discounting The calculation for finding the present value of some future sum of money.

disintermediation The withdrawal of funds that were previously invested through financial intermediaries so that they can be invested directly in the financial markets.

diversification The process of acquiring a portfolio of securities that have dissimilar risk–return characteristics in order to reduce overall portfolio risk.

dividend yield The expected dividend expressed as a proportion of the price of the stock.

dividends Corporate payments to stockholders.

divisia money Money concept that weights various types of financial assets according to their degree of "moneyness" and sums them up to try to determine how much money people will act like they have when it comes time to spend.

dollarization The practice by some countries of adopting the U.S. currency as a medium of exchange.

domestic market A financial market classification based on where the market is located.

down payment percentage The percentage of the value of a house, car, or other asset that the buyer pays in cash; the remainder can be financed with a loan.

draft In international trade, a request for payment that is drawn up by the exporter (or the exporter's bank) and sent to the bank that drew up a letter of credit for the importer.

DSU *See* **deficit spending unit**

dual banking system A term referring to the fact that U.S. banks can be chartered either by the federal government (national banks) or by state governments—with each system having different laws.

dual-class firms Firms that recapitalize with two classes of stock having different voting rights.

due diligence The process through which an investment banker investigates a company conducting a security offering to ensure that all the information in the prospectus is true.

duration A measure of interest rate risk (or bond price volatility) that considers both coupon rate and maturity; it is the weighted average of the number of years until the present value of each of the bond's cash flows is received.

duration GAP A GAP analysis measure of the sensitivity of a portfolio to interest rate changes.

ECM Electronic commission merchant; electronic brokerage service that uses computers to match buy and sell orders for securities.

economic synergy The primary economic motive for most mergers—the desire to increase the value of the combined firms.

economies of scale Declining long-run average costs of operation as the level of output is increased beyond a certain point.

Edge Act corporation A subsidiary of a U.S. bank formed to engage in international banking and financial activities that domestic banks cannot conduct in the United States.

EFTS *See* **Electronic Funds Transfer System**

elastic money supply A flexible supply of currency that can accommodate changing public demand for cash.

electronic cash Funds withdrawn by a customer from his or her bank account by transferring money from that account to an electronically coded card (purse). The card is loaded with cash and can be taken to a cooperating merchant with an electronic card reader to make a purchase.

Electronic Funds Transfer System (EFTS) A computerized information system that gathers and processes financial information and transfers funds electronically from one financial account to another.

electronic purse An electronic means of storing money withdrawn from a financial institution until it can be spent by transferring it to a merchant.

Employee Retirement Income Security Act (ERISA) A 1974 law that requires employers to observe certain standards if their pension programs are to retain an advantageous tax status. ERISA was passed because Congress became concerned that many workers with long years of service would fail to receive pension benefits.

encrypted cash Cash values that are encoded and transferred by a computer to a recipient who can decode the transfer and claim the money.

Equal Credit Opportunity Act (ECOA) of 1974 Requires that credit be made available to individuals without regard to sex or marital status. In 1976 Congress broadened the scope of the act to forbid discrimination by creditors based on race, age, national origin, or whether credit applicants received part of their income from public assistance benefits. It also requires women's incomes to be treated equally with men's in evaluating credit.

equity   A term implying an ownership claim.

ETFs   *See* **exchange traded funds**

euro   The common currency for the countries that are members of the European Monetary System.

Eurobond   Any bond issued and sold outside of its country of origin.

Eurobond market   The market for long-term borrowing or lending of large amounts of U.S. dollars that have been deposited in overseas banks.

Eurocurrency market   The market for short-term borrowing or lending of large amounts of any currency held in a time deposit account outside its country of origin.

Eurodollar expansion   The expansion of dollar-denominated bank deposits in banks outside the United States.

Eurodollar market   The market for short-term borrowing or lending of large amounts of U.S. dollars that have been deposited in overseas banks.

Eurodollars   U.S. dollar-denominated deposits issued by banks located outside the United States.

European option   An option that can be exercised only at expiration. The buyer of the option pays the seller (writer) a premium. The writer keeps the premium regardless of whether the option is exercised. An option need not be exercised if it is not to the buyer's advantage to do so.

excess reserves   The amount arrived at when required reserves are subtracted from a bank's actual reserves.

exchange fee   In mutual funds, a fee that may be levied by funds in a mutual fund family when shares are redeemed in one fund and exchanged for shares in another fund in the same mutual fund family.

exchange rate   The rate at which one nation's currency can be exchanged for another's at the present time.

exchange traded funds (ETFs)   Investment companies whose shares are traded on organized exchanges at market determined prices. Unlike closed-end funds, however, ETFs have unique creation and redemption features that prevent large premiums or discounts from net asset value.

exercise price (strike price)   The price at which an option allows the buyer to buy an asset (if it is a call option) or sell an asset (if it is a put option).

expected yield   The expected return on a bond at the end of a relevant holding period based on predictions made from interest rate forecasts.

expiration date   The date on which an option expires, and after which it can no longer be used.

export credit insurance   Insurance issued by exporters as an alternative to formal letters of credit (or cash) that enables importers to buy goods essentially on open account without having to acknowledge the indebtedness formally.

Export-Import Bank (Eximbank)   The principal U.S. government agency for subsidizing export activities.

extension risk   The risk that mortgage prepayments are slower than expected.

face value   *See* **par value**

Fair Credit Billing Act (FCBA) of 1974   Requires that creditors provide detailed information to consumers on the method of assessing finance charges and also that billing complaints be processed promptly.

Fannie Mae   *See* **Federal National Mortgage Association**

FDIC   *See* **Federal Deposit Insurance Corporation**

FDIC-BIF   The original bank insurance fund operated by the FDIC that commercial banks and mutual savings banks have long been allowed to join.

FDIC Improvement Act of 1991 (FDICIA)   This act went beyond the FIRRE Act in tightening bank and thrift institutions' capital requirements. It allowed "well-capitalized commercial banks" to enter investment banking in a limited way through subsidiaries.

FDIC-SAIF   A deposit insurance fund run by the FDIC to provide deposit insurance to member savings associations and savings banks.

federal agency   An independent federal department or federally chartered corporation established by Congress and owned or underwritten by the U.S. government.

Federal Deposit Insurance Corporation (FDIC)   A government agency that provides federal insurance for depositors of qualified banks and supervises both the bank insurance fund (BIF) and the savings association insurance fund (SAIF).

federal funds (fed funds)   Immediately available funds that can be lent on an overnight basis to financial institutions. Banks may lend their deposits at the Fed to other financial institutions by transferring them through federal funds market loans.

federal funds market (fed funds market) The market in which banks make short-term unsecured loans to one another. The fed funds market has no connection with the U.S. Treasury.

federal funds rate (fed funds rate) The rate at which banks and other depository institutions lend excess reserves or other immediately available cash deposits to each other overnight; the rate is determined by negotiation between the private borrowers and lenders of reserves.

Federal Home Loan Bank Board (FHLBB) Until 1989, the primary regulatory agency for savings and loan associations. It controlled the Federal Home Loan Bank system, the Federal Home Loan Mortgage Corporation, and the Federal Savings and Loan Insurance Corporation. Its regulations affected all federally chartered and federally insured savings associations.

Federal Home Loan Banks Twelve regional banks empowered to borrow in the national capital markets and make loans, called "advances," to savings and loans in their regions that are members of the Federal Home Loan Bank.

Federal Home Loan Mortgage Corporation (FHLMC—Freddie Mac) A federal agency initially established by Congress in 1970 as a subsidiary of the Federal Home Loan Bank System. Now a quasi-private government agency, it assists savings and loan associations and other mortgage lenders. It provides a secondary market for conventional mortgages and issues mortgage-backed securities.

Federal National Mortgage Association (FNMA—Fannie Mae) An agency that provides a secondary market for insured mortgages by issuing and executing purchase commitments for mortgages.

Federal Open Market Committee (FOMC) A committee that consists of seven members of the Board of Governors of the Federal Reserve System plus five presidents of Federal Reserve banks that determines the nation's monetary policy and financial institutions' reserve balances.

Federal Reserve Act Federal legislation passed in 1913 designed to correct shortcomings in the national banking system by establishing the Federal Reserve System.

Federal Savings and Loan Insurance Corporation (FSLIC) An agency that insured savings association and federal savings bank deposits until 1989,

when deposit insurance responsibilities passed to the Savings Association Insurance Fund supervised by the FDIC.

fed funds *See* **federal funds**

FHA mortgages Mortgages whose ultimate payment is guaranteed by the Federal Housing Administration (FHA).

FHC *See* **financial holding company**

FHLBB *See* **Federal Home Loan Bank Board**

FHLMC *See* **Federal Home Loan Mortgage Corporation**

fiat money Money that has value because the government has decreed that the coinage is "legal tender" that can be legally used to make payments and discharge debts.

final prospectus After approval by the SEC, information provided about a new issue; by law, investors must have a final prospectus before they can invest.

finance company Companies that extend short- and intermediate-term loans and lease credit to individuals and business firms that cannot obtain credit as cheaply or easily elsewhere; nonbank financial institution that makes loans to both consumers and business but is not federally insured.

financial claim A written promise to pay a specific sum of money (the principal) plus interest for the privilege of borrowing money over a period of time. Financial claims are issued by DSUs (liabilities) and purchased by SSUs (assets).

financial guarantee Guarantee by third parties such as commercial banks or insurance companies to cover the payment of interest and principal to investors in debt securities in the event of a default by the borrower.

financial holding company (FHC) A designation applied to bank holding companies that have been approved for "financial holding company" status by the Federal Reserve. FHCs are allowed to own subsidiaries that engage in virtually any financial business.

financial institution Institution that issues deposits and other financial liabilities and invests predominantly in loans and other financial assets.

Financial Institutions Reform, Recovery, and Enforcement Act of 1989 (FIRREA) This act made major changes in the structure of financial regulation. It abolished the FHLBB and FSLIC and established the OTS, FDIC-SAIF, and RTC as their replacements. It required that deposit insurance premiums be raised and that thrift institutions adopt stricter accounting standards. It also imposed "tangible capital" requirements that disallowed the counting of goodwill and various other intangible assets toward a thrift's capital adequacy requirements.

financial intermediaries Institutions that issue liabilities to SSUs and use the funds so obtained to acquire liabilities of DSUs.

financial intermediation The purchase of direct claims (IOUs) with one set of characteristics from DSUs and the transformation of them into indirect claims (IOUs) with a different set of characteristics.

financial markets The markets for buying and selling financial claims.

Financial Services Modernization Act of 1999 (Gramm-Leach-Bliley) Legislation that repealed many of the Glass-Steagall restrictions on commercial banking and investment banking.

finite-life REITs (FREITs) REITs that have a fixed life.

FIRREA *See* **Financial Institutions Reform, Recovery, and Enforcement Act**

First and Second Banks of the United States The central banks chartered by the United States charged with the responsibility of regulating the supply of money in the best interests of the public. The First Bank was chartered from 1791 to 1811; the Second from 1816 to 1836.

first-stage financing Capital provided to initiate manufacturing and sales in a new venture.

Fisher effect The inflation premium component of the nominal rate of interest; it equals the difference between the nominal rate of interest and expected inflation.

fixed exchange rates A constant rate of exchange between currencies. Governments try to fix their exchange rate by buying or selling their currency whenever its exchange value starts to vary.

fixed-rate mortgage (FRM) A standard mortgage agreement in which the lender takes a lien on real property and the borrower agrees to make periodic repayments of the principal amount of money borrowed plus a fixed interest rate on the unpaid balance of the debt for a predetermined period of time.

floor (on interest rates) A floor on interest rates is created by selling a call option (that is, an option to buy) on a financial futures contract.

floor-plan financing Wholesale financing; interim financing provided to a dealer by a finance company.

FNMA *See* **Federal National Mortgage Association**

FOMC *See* **Federal Open Market Committee**

foreign branches A legal and operational part of the parent bank. Creditors of the branch have full legal claims on the bank's assets as a whole and, in turn, creditors of the parent bank have claims on its branches' assets.

foreign currency (exchange) market The market on which foreign currencies are bought and sold.

foreign exchange Markets developed so that people can convert their cash to different currencies as their needs for different currencies vary in their business affairs and operations.

foreign exchange risk The fluctuation in the earnings or value of a financial institution that arises from fluctuations in exchange rates; responsible for gains or losses in the currency positions of financial institutions and changes in U.S. dollar values of non-U.S. financial investments.

foreign market Market located in a different country, typically one that deals in different securities or currencies than domestic markets.

foreign subsidiaries A separately incorporated bank owned entirely or in part by a U.S. Bank, a U.S. bank holding company, or an Edge Act corporation.

fortuitous loss Exposure units used to predict losses must be homogeneous for the law of large numbers to work; the losses that occur must be fortuitous, meaning that the loss is unexpected and happens as a result of chance.

forward contract A contract that guarantees delivery of a certain amount of goods, such as a foreign currency, for exchange into a specific amount of another currency, such as dollars, on a specific day in the future.

forward market A market in which parties agree to exchange a fixed amount of one currency for a fixed amount of a second currency, but actual delivery and exchange of the two currencies occurs at some time "forward."

forward price In a forward contract, the price at which the purchaser will buy a specified amount of an asset from the seller at a fixed date sometime in the future.

forward rate The interest rate that is expected to exist in the future.

fractional reserve banking The banking concept for money creation, in which banks hold only a fraction of their deposits in the form of liquid reserves and invest or loan out the rest to earn interest.

Freddie Mac *See* **Federal Home Loan Mortgage Corporation**

Free Banking era   The period from 1837 to approximately 1862 during which Michigan and other states established uncomplicated systems of chartering banks called free banking; by 1860, 18 states had free banking laws that eliminated some, but not all, banking abuses. The Treasury Department was forced to set up an independent payment system bypassing the banking system.

FREITs *See* **finite-life REITs**

frictional unemployment   A term indicating that a portion of those that are unemployed are in transition between jobs.

FRM *See* **fixed-rate mortgage**

front-end load   Fees paid at the time people invest money in a mutual fund.

FSLIC *See* **Federal Savings and Loan Insurance Corporation**

full-bodied money   Money that is valued not only for its purchasing power but also as commodity. Gold and silver coins are examples.

full employment   Term implying that every person of working age who wishes to work can find employment.

fully contributory plan   A pension plan in which only the employee makes contributions to the plan.

functional regulation   An approach to financial institution regulation in which the Federal Reserve acts as the "umbrella" regulator while the bank and nonbank subsidiaries fall under the supervision of other regulators.

future value   The worth in the future of a currently held amount of money if it is invested and reinvested at known interest rates.

futures contract   A contract to buy (or sell) a particular type of security or commodity from (or to) the futures exchange during a predetermined future time period.

futures exchange   A place where buyers and sellers can exchange futures contracts. The exchange keeps the books for buyers and sellers when contracts are initiated or liquidated.

futures market   A market in which people trade contracts for future delivery of securities, cash goods, or the value of securities sold in the cash market.

GDP *See* **gross domestic product**

GEMs *See* **growing equity mortgages**

general obligation bond   State and local government bonds backed by the "full faith and credit" (the power to tax) of the issuing political entity; they require voter approval.

generally acceptable medium of exchange   One of the functions of money in which it can be easily exchanged to buy goods or services or pay off debts in the economy.

Ginnie Mae *See* **Government National Mortgage Association**

GIRO transfers   A type of payment used in Europe in which an individual instructs a financial institution to make a payment to another individual (or company) who banks with another institution.

Glass-Steagall Act *See* **Banking Act of 1933**

GNMA *See* **Government National Mortgage Association**

goods-related credit   The credit used to finance the purchase of goods with credit contracts.

Government National Mortgage Association (GNMA—Ginnie Mae)   Organized in 1968, a federal agency that helps issuers of mortgages obtain capital market financing to support their mortgage holdings. It does so by creating government-guaranteed securities that pass through all interest and principal repayments from pools of mortgages to purchasers of the pass-through securities.

government note and bond   A debt security issued by the U.S. government with an initial maturity greater than 1 year (note) or 10 years (bond).

GPMs *See* **graduated-payment mortgages**

graduated-payment, adjustable-rate loan (GPAML)   A variant of the GPM where after a few years of low predetermined payments, GPAML payment rates or maturities are adjusted to account for changes in market rates.

graduated-payment mortgages (GPMs)   Mortgages similar to standard fixed-rate mortgages except that instead of having constant repayment streams, they have lower payments in the first few years after which payments start to rise.

Gramm-Leach-Bliley Act *See* **Financial Services Modernization Act of 1999**

Gresham's law   Monetary law from the 1500s that states "bad money drives out good."

gross domestic product (GDP)   The dollar value at current market prices of all final goods and services produced within a country in a given year. Note that the GDP of a country includes the goods and services produced within the geographical boundaries of that country, whereas the gross national product (GNP) includes the goods and services produced by a country's residents regardless of location.

gross interest and fee income The total interest and fee income earned on loans and investment securities.

gross interest expense The total interest paid on deposits and other borrowings.

growing equity mortgages (GEMs) Similar to graduated-payment mortgages, they call for rising payments over time; however, the rising payments allow the loan to be paid off much faster than would otherwise be the case.

G8 policy coordination Meetings by finance ministers representing the eight largest industrial countries, plus associate members (such as Russia) to coordinate economic and financial policies.

hedge fund Pools of investment capital that use a combination of market philosophies and analytical techniques to identify, evaluate, and execute trading decisions.

hedger An individual or firm that engages in financial market transactions to reduce price risk.

home equity loan A personal loan that is secured by a mortgage on the borrower's home.

homogeneous exposure units Units required by insurers so that losses can be predicted based on the law of large numbers.

Humphrey-Hawkins Act Passed in 1978, this legislation specifies the primary objectives of monetary policy—full employment, stable prices, and moderate long-term interest rates. In addition, it requires that the Board of Governors of the Federal Reserve System submit a report on the economy and the conduct of monetary policy to Congress by February 20 and July 20 of each year.

IBF *See* **international banking facilities**

implied forward rate The forward rate of interest implied by the difference in a short-term interest rate and a longer-term interest. The implied forward rate is the rate necessary to make funds invested at the short rate and reinvested at the implied forward rate generate a return equal to that which could be obtained by buying the longer term security.

in-the-money An option contract is said to be in-the-money when its intrinsic value is greater than zero (when the market price of the underlying asset exceeds the strike price for a call option or the market price of the underlying asset is less than the strike price for a put option).

indenture The legal contract that states the rights, privileges, and obligations of the bond issuer and the bondholder.

index fund A mutual fund that tries to match the performance of a specific stock or bond market index, such as the S&P 500 Index, by buying similar or identical securities.

individual equity In a pension plan, the concept of paying benefits in direct relation to contributions.

industrial bank A financial institution chartered under industrial banking laws in a state. Industrial banks make loans and issue savings deposits. Finance companies may obtain charters as industrial banks so that they can issue savings deposits to obtain funds.

industrial development bonds (IDB) Municipal revenue bonds that are issued by private companies. The municipality assumes no legal liability in the event of default.

inelastic currency A supply of national currency that is fixed and does not expand or contract easily as the demand for currency holdings in the economy rises or falls.

inflation The continuous rise in the average price level.

information disclosure Disclosure of corporate information required by the SEC before stocks can be listed on U.S. exchanges.

informational efficiency In an informationally efficient market, prices of securities are the best indicators of the relative values of securities because current market prices reflect all available relevant information.

initial margin A deposit of money or other valuable assets with a futures exchange to guarantee that buyers will keep their part of a bargain.

initial public offering (IPO) The primary offering of a company that has never before offered a particular type of security to the public, meaning the security is not currently trading in the secondary market; an unseasoned offering.

inside information Corporate information that has not yet been disclosed to the public.

insolvent When the value of a firm's liabilities exceeds the value of its assets.

insurance The transfer of pure risk to an entity that pools the risk of loss and provides payment if a loss occurs.

insured pension plan A pension plan established with a life insurance company.

interest The rental price of money usually expressed as an annual percentage of the nominal amount of money borrowed; the price of borrowing money for the use of its purchasing power.

interest rate *See* **interest**

interest rate cap *See* **cap**

interest rate collar *See* **collar**

interest rate floor *See* **floor**

interest rate risk The risk that changes in interest rates will cause an asset's price and realized yield to differ from the purchase price and initially anticipated yield.

interest rates and credit availability When credit becomes more readily available, effective interest rates usually decline, and consumers can borrow more easily to buy durable goods; conversely, when credit becomes less readily available, effective interest rates usually rise, and consumers and businesses can borrow less easily.

interinsurance association A type of reciprocal that functions much like a mutual. They do not keep separate accounts for each member. Losses and expenses are not prorated among insureds, and insureds do not have a claim to any portion of surplus funds.

internal credit risk ratings Internal credit risk ratings are ratings systems that some banks use to identify the credit risk associated with the loans in their portfolios.

international accounting standards Accounting standards that are used in a number of countries so corporate profits, losses, and asset and liability values can be more easily compared.

International Banking Act (IBA) of 1978 Legislation that created a federal regulatory structure for the operation of foreign banks in the United States.

international banking facilities (IBFs) Facilities established by a U.S.-chartered depository institution, a U.S. branch or agency of a foreign bank, or the U.S. office of an Edge Act or agreement bank. IBFs are not institutions in the organizational sense; they are actually a set of asset and liability accounts segregated on the books of the establishing institutions.

international regulatory coordination An effort to obtain standardized international risk-based agreements and to prevent additional regulatory arbitrage.

Interstate Banking and Branching Efficiency Act (IB&BEA) of 1994 Legislation allowing U.S. banks to merge and branch across state lines unless a potential host state "opted out" of interstate branching.

intrinsic value The value that could be realized by exercising an option immediately.

investment bank The most important participant in the direct credit market; firms that specialize in helping businesses and governments sell their new security issues in the primary markets to finance capital expenditures.

investment banker A person who provides financial advice and who underwrites and distributes new investment securities.

investment capital flows Capital flows that are either short-term money market flows motivated by differences in interest rates or long-term capital investments in a nation's real or financial assets.

investment company ("closed-end" fund) A nonbank financial institution that sells stock, then diversifies investors' risk by buying many investments; such funds also provide professional management for investments.

investment-grade bonds The bonds rated in the top four major rating categories by Moody's and Standard & Poor's (i.e., bonds rated Baa or BBB or better).

IPO *See* **initial public offering**

junk (speculative-grade) bonds *See* **speculative-grade (junk) bonds**

Keynesian theory of money and the economy Keynesian theory believes that the velocity of money is unstable and unpredictable, so it is hard to use monetary policy to control the economy directly. Monetary policy mainly affects the economy by changing interest rates, which in turn affect the willingness of both consumers and investor to buy goods.

L The broadest definition of money. L includes all liquid assets in the economy in which people may temporarily store purchasing power before spending.

lagged reserve accounting system A system in which banks know at the beginning of each reserve period exactly the amount of reserves they were required to maintain to back their deposits.

land contract An alternative to a standard mortgage whereby property is sold under a conditional sale agreement. The sale price is agreed upon, along with the interest rate and maturity; the buyer receives use of the property while making payments, but a default nullifies the sale.

law of large numbers A mathematical law that applies to the loss exposures of insurers; the larger the number of loss exposures, the more predictable the average losses become.

leakage The effect caused by cash drains from the banking system that causes changes in banks' holdings of actual reserves to differ from changes in the monetary base.

legal tender Exchange medium decreed by the government to be legal to use for making payments and discharging debts.

lender of last resort The role of the Fed as a lender to banks in difficulty to prevent the banks from failing, due to a lack of liquidity.

less developed country (LDC) loans Countries whose political and financial conditions make loans risky; since most international bank loans are unsecured, business loans are generally made only to large, creditworthy multinationals and are backed by the "full faith and credit" of the borrowing LDC nation.

letter of credit (LC) A financial instrument issued by an importer's bank that obligates the bank to pay the exporter (or other designated beneficiary) a specified amount of money once certain conditions are fulfilled.

liability insurance Insurance against financial loss due to legal responsibility for bodily injury, property damage, or personal injury.

liability management A bank's management of its liability structure to increase or decrease its source of funds as needed.

liability risk The risk incurred when someone is found by a court to be negligent in causing bodily injury, property damage, or personal injury to some person.

LIBOR *See* **London Interbank Offer Rate**

limit order An order to buy or sell at a designated price or at any better price.

limited liability A legal concept meaning that losses of common stockholders are limited to the original amount of their investment; it also implies that the personal assets of a shareholder cannot be obtained to satisfy the obligations of the corporation.

line of credit An agreement under which a bank customer can borrow up to a predetermined limit on a short-term basis.

liquid asset An asset that can be quickly converted to money (M1) with negligible cost or risk of loss. The higher the potential cost of rapidly converting an asset into money, the lower its liquidity.

liquidity Ability of an institution to hold sufficient amounts of cash and liquid assets to allow it to easily meet requests from its liability holders for cash payment.

liquidity premium Additional interest paid by borrowers who issue illiquid securities to obtain long-term funds; the interest premium compensates lenders who acquire a security that cannot be resold easily or quickly at par value.

liquidity risk The risk that a financial institution will be unable to generate sufficient cash inflow to meet required cash outflows.

liquidity trap In Keynesian theory, an occurrence during major depressions when people already have so much money relative to their needs that any extra money is hoarded and will no longer drive down interest rates.

Lloyd's Associations Organizations that do not directly write insurance but that provide services for members of the association who write insurance as individuals.

load fund An investment (mutual) fund that charges a commission when shares in the fund are purchased.

loan rate ceilings Restrictions on the rates that financial institutions can charge on their loans.

loan-to-value (LTV) ratio Ratio of loan amount to the value of the asset that secures the loan; the LTV ratio is important for mortgage loans.

London Interbank Offer Rate (LIBOR) The "prime rate" of international lending and the cheapest rate at which funds flow between international banks.

long position An agreement to buy in the futures market.

long-tail coverages Insurance liability lines in which claims may have to be paid long after the policy expiration; product liability is one such line of insurance.

long-term loan A loan with a term over 1 year.

M1, M2, M3 Alternative definitions of the money supply as designated by the Federal Reserve System.

M1A Components of the M1 money supply that don't pay interest; thus, the primary motive for owning them is to obtain transactional convenience.

M2 multiplier The ratio of M2 money to bank reserves (or the monetary base).

macrohedging Using instruments of risk management, such as financial futures, options on financial futures, and interest rate swaps, to reduce the interest rate risk of the firm's entire balance sheet.

maintenance margin In the futures market, a margin requirement imposed to ensure that people do not default on their contracts if prices move adversely for them.

management fee In mutual funds, the fee paid to the company that manages a fund's portfolio, usually expressed as a percent of the fund's annual average net assets.

margin　In futures markets, money posted to guarantee contracts will be honored and to take account of gains or losses accruing from daily price movements.

margin call　In the futures market, when the funds in an investor's margin account fall below the investor's maintenance margin, the investor is required to add enough funds to the account to get it back up to the initial margin.

margin loans　Loans that brokerage firms extend to their customers to purchase securities.

margin requirement　The amount of money people can borrow so they can buy stocks; this amount is restricted by Federal Reserve Regulations G, T, U, and X in order to prevent excessive speculation in the stock market.

margin trading　Trading in which an investor can buy securities partly with borrowed money.

marine insurance　Insurance against losses related to transportation exposures.

marked to market　In futures markets, a requirement that all gains or losses on futures positions be taken into account in determining the value of all contracts each day.

marketability　The ease with which a financial claim can be resold. The greater the marketability of a financial security, the lower its interest rate.

market breadth　A secondary market is said to have breadth if the orders that give the market depth exist in significant volume.

market depth　A secondary market is said to have depth if there exist orders both above and below the price at which a security is currently trading.

market equilibrium price　The correct price of a stock issue; the highest price that allows all the new securities issued to be sold at the offering price without having unmet demand for the security.

market maker　Term applied to an individual who regularly quotes bid and ask prices in a stock and trades for his or her own account at those prices.

market order　An order to buy or sell at the best price available at the time the order reaches the exchange.

market resilience　A market is resilient if new orders pour in promptly in response to price changes that result from temporary order imbalances.

market risk premium　The risk premium of the market portfolio.

market segmentation　The theory that maintains that market participants have strong preferences for securities of a particular maturity and holds that they buy and sell securities consistent with these maturity preferences, resulting in the yield curve being determined by the supply of and demand for securities at or near a particular maturity.

market value-weighted index　A stock market index that is computed by calculating the total market value of the firms in the index and the total market value of those firms on the previous trading day; the percentage change in the total market value from one day to the next represents the change in the index.

matched funding　A circumstance in which fixed-rate loans are funded with deposits or borrowed funds of the same maturity.

maturity GAP　Interest rate risk measure comparing the value of assets that will either mature or be repriced within a given time interval to the value of liabilities that will either mature or be repriced during the same time period.

McCarran-Ferguson Act (Public Law 15) of 1945　Specifies that insurance companies should be regulated at the state level.

mezzanine or bridge financing　Capital provided to a company that expects to go public within a year or so.

microhedging　Hedging a specific transaction; matched funding is an example.

MMDA　*See* **money market deposit account**

MMMF　*See* **money market mutual funds**

monetarist theory　Theory that when the supply of money is greater than the amount of money people demand, people will spend faster and the level of economic activity in the economy (GDP) will rise. Conversely, if the money supply is low relative to the amount of money demanded, people will spend less in order to accumulate more money and the level of economic activity (GDP) will decline. These effects result from imbalances between the quantity of money supplied to the economy and quantity of money demanded.

monetary base　Currency in circulation plus financial institution reserve deposits at the Federal Reserve. The monetary base consists of all assets that can be used to satisfy legal reserve requirements. Thus, if it grows, financial institution reserves (and financial institution deposits) usually grow as well.

money market　A financial market in which financial claims with maturities of less than a year are sold. The most important money market is that for U.S. Treasury bills.

money market deposit account (MMDA) MMDA consumer deposit accounts at commercial banks originated in 1982. MMDAs are not subject to deposit rate ceilings or reserve requirements. Customers may use them for no more than six withdrawals in a month.

money market mutual funds (MMMF) Funds that issue shares to customers and use the customer's money to invest in interest-bearing assets that are very liquid and have very short maturities.

money multiplier A money multiplier is a variant of the deposit expansion multiplier. It shows how much the money supply changes for every $1 change in a monetary policy instrument (bank reserves or the monetary base). Multiplier values may change over time.

money supply The total value of all assets that are generally acceptable mediums of exchange (M1) or otherwise strongly influence spending decisions (M2, M3, etc.).

moral hazard Excessive risk taking by insured people or institutions, who realize that they will not bear the full costs of any losses they incur as a result of their risk-taking.

mortgage-backed bonds Bonds that can be issued by holders of mortgages; they pay interest semiannually and have a fixed maturity. Examples are FHLMC and FNMA debt, private mortgage-backed debt, and state and local government housing revenue bonds.

mortgage-backed mutual funds Mutual funds established to buy GNMA certificates or other mortgage-backed securities.

mortgage-backed securities (MBSs) Securities such as pass-through securities and "collateralized mortgage obligations," which pass through all or part of the principal and interest payments on "pools" of many mortgages to buyers of the mortgage-backed securities.

mortgage bankers Institutions that originate mortgages and collect payments on them; also called mortgage companies.

mortgages Loans for which the borrower pledges real property as collateral to guarantee that the debt will be repaid.

multiple line policies Insurance policies that combine property and liability coverage in a single contract.

municipal bond Bonds issued by state and local government bodies; they comprise one of the largest fixed-income securities markets.

municipal securities Securities issued by state and local governments that sell for lower market yields than comparable securities issued by the U.S. Treasury and private corporations; exempt from federal taxes.

mutual fund An open-ended investment company; the most common type of investment company that stands ready to buy or sell its shares at the current net asset value at any time.

mutual fund family Cluster of related mutual funds that have similar names, related marketing strategies, and allow funds to be transferred easily between themselves. They facilitate asset gathering by mutual fund management companies.

mutual institution Financial institutions technically owned by their liability holders (depositors) and managed by an elected manager or a public-spirited board of trustees that seek to invest depositors' and liability-holders' funds to earn a safe and secure rate of return.

MZM Zero maturity money; components of the money supply that can be used immediately to conduct transactions; some may pay interest also.

NAFCU *See* **National Association of Federal Credit Unions**

naked option An option writer's position if they do not own the securities that they have agreed to sell or have not sold short the securities that they have agreed to buy.

named-perils coverage Property insurance that provides a specific list of perils that are covered.

NASD *See* **National Association of Securities Dealers**

NASDAQ *See* **National Association of Securities Dealers Automated Quotation System**

National Association of Federal Credit Unions (NAFCU) A credit union trade and service association that serves the interests of the generally larger, federally chartered credit unions.

National Association of Insurance Commissioners (NAIC) An organization founded in 1871 to set uniform regulatory standards among the states.

National Association of Securities Dealers (NASD) Private regulatory authority participating in the determination of rules that financial market participants must follow when they issue and exchange securities.

National Association of Securities Dealers Automated Quotation System (NASDAQ) A computerized communications system that provides continuous bid-and-ask prices on the most actively traded OTC stocks.

National Bank Acts (1863, 1864) Congressional legislation with goals to provide the nation with a safe and uniform currency system and to provide a new source of funds with which to finance the Civil War. The National Bank Acts remain one of the foundations of American banking practice. Important provisions include chartering, capital requirements, asset restrictions, reserve requirements, standardization of banknotes, and bank supervision by the Office of the Comptroller of the Currency.

National Credit Union Administration (NCUA) The regulatory body that sets standards for all federally chartered and federally insured credit unions.

National Credit Union Share Insurance Fund (NCUSIF) An organization providing federal insurance to members who own shares (deposits) in federally chartered credit unions and in qualifying state-chartered credit unions.

natural rate of unemployment Level of unemployment that policy makers are willing to tolerate—a sort of "full employment unemployment rate."

NAV *See* **net asset value**

NCUA *See* **National Credit Union Administration**

NCUSIF *See* **National Credit Union Share Insurance Fund**

near-money Interest-bearing assets that cannot be used as a generally accepted medium of exchange, but can be quickly and easily converted to that form.

negotiable certificate of deposit Unsecured liabilities of banks that can be resold before their maturity in a dealer-operated secondary market.

negotiated offering A type of public offering in which the company selects the investment banker who will conduct the offering and then negotiates the net proceeds that the company will receive for the securities.

negotiated sale *See* **negotiated offering**

net asset value (NAV) A price based on the current market value of all securities held in a mutual fund's portfolio divided by the number of outstanding shares in the fund, and quoted as NAV per share.

net borrowed reserves The borrowed reserves of a bank arrived at by using the equation NBR ∇ BR (borrowed reserves) ER (excess reserves); when a bank has large net borrowed reserves, it will be reluctant to lend or make new investments.

net excess (free) reserves The difference between excess reserves (ER) and borrowed reserves (BR), or ER – BR.

net interest margin The difference between gross interest and fee income and gross interest expense.

no-load fund An investment fund that does not levy a sales charge when the fund is purchased.

nominal income The value of income expressed in current dollars. No adjustment is made for changes in the purchasing power of the dollar.

nominal rate of interest The interest rates that are observed in the marketplace.

nonbank bank A firm that does not simultaneously both make commercial loans and accept federally insured deposits, and thereby escapes regulation as a bank.

noncontributory plans Pension plans funded through employer contributions only.

nonguaranteed agency debt Securities issued by federal agencies that are not guaranteed by the federal government against default.

noninsured pension plan A pension plan managed by a trustee rather than an insurance company.

noninterest expense Salaries, employee benefits, technology-related expenses, and other expenses for a financial institution.

noninterest income Income for a financial institution that consists mainly of fees and service charges.

nonparticipating preferred stock Preferred stock is nonparticipating in that the preferred dividend remains constant regardless of any increase in the firm's earnings.

notional principal The face value amount for which interest payment obligations are computed under a "swap" agreement. Since the principal is never repaid, it is only "notional" for the duration of the swap.

NOW accounts Deposit accounts that pay explicit interest and can be withdrawn by "negotiable orders of withdrawal" (checks) on demand.

objective risk An insurer's risk that is the deviation of actual losses from expected losses; objective risk can be measured statistically.

OCC *See* **Office of the Comptroller of the Currency**

offering price The price of a new issue.

Office of the Comptroller of the Currency (OCC) Created in 1863 by the National Bank Act, the OCC is a subsidiary of the Treasury Department and is responsible for supervising national banks.

Office of Thrift Supervision (OTS) Created in 1989 as a subsidiary of the Treasury Department. Assumed the chartering and many of the supervisory powers of the Federal Home Loan Bank Board, which it replaced.

on-site bank examinations Unannounced visits by bank examiners to a bank or its branches.

open-end fund   *See* **mutual fund**

open interest   The total number of futures contracts for delivery of a specific good at a futures exchange.

open-market operations   The purchase or sale of government securities by the Federal Reserve. Open market operations are used to increase or decrease bank reserves and the monetary base. When the Fed purchases securities, the monetary base expands.

open-market transactions   Money market financial transactions that are impersonal and competitive in nature with no established customer relationships.

operational efficiency   A market is operationally efficient if the costs of conducting transactions are as low as possible. If transactions costs are high, fewer financial transactions will take place, and a greater number of otherwise valuable real investment projects will be passed up.

opportunity cost   The interest rate on the next best alternative investment.

option   A contractual agreement that allows the holder to buy (or sell) a specified asset at a predetermined price prior to its expiration date. The predetermined price is called the strike price. Options to buy assets are call options. Options to sell assets are put options.

option contract   *See* **option**

option premium   The price of the option.

option writer   The party in an option contract that must perform a specific act if called upon by the option buyer or owner. The option writer or seller is "short" the option contract, while the option buyer is "long" the contract.

options market   A market in which options are traded.

OREO   Other real estate owned; asset holdings of thrifts that usually consist of problem assets, such as repossessed properties.

OTC   *See* **over-the-counter market**

OTS   *See* **Office of Thrift Supervision**

out-of-the-money   An option contract is said to be out-of-the-money when the market price of the underlying asset is less than the strike price for a call option or the market price of the underlying asset is greater than the strike price for a put option.

over-the-counter market (OTC)   Primarily a dealer market where securities not sold on one of the organized exchanges are traded.

panic   The event that occurs when depositors lose confidence in banks in general and "run" many banks to redeem their deposits quickly.

par bond   A bond that is selling at its par value.

par value (principal)   The stated or face value of a stock or bond. For debt instruments, the par value is usually the final principal payment.

participating policy   Policies issued by stock companies in which policyholders receive dividends; thus policyholders "participate" in the profitability of the insurance company.

participation loans   A means of reducing international lending risk; an arrangement under which banks participate by joining together so each provides only part of the funds for a loan; the participation thereby reduces the risk exposure for each individual bank.

payoff and liquidate policy   An approach for resolving a bank failure by paying off insured deposits and liquidating the bank's assets.

Pension Benefit Guarantee Corporation (PBGC)   Federal insurance agency that insures defined benefit plans up to a specified amount per month.

peril   Fire, windstorm, theft, explosion, and negligence, conditions against which property and liability insurers offer protection policies.

personal loans   Credit to individuals not related to credit financing of specific assets.

Phoenix merger   Merger of two or more failing thrift institutions to create a new (and, seemingly, sounder) institution.

plan fiduciary   Any trustee, investment adviser, or other person who has discretionary authority or responsibility in the management of a pension plan or its assets.

PMI   *See* **private mortgage insurance**

point-of-sale (POS)   A payment system with a two-stage transfer of information and funds. One transfer requires that information on the status of the customer's account be transferred to the point of sale; the second transfer requires that funds be transferred from that account to the retailer's account.

political capital flows   International capital flows that respond to changed political conditions in a country.

political risk   Country or sovereign risks that can result in financial claims of foreigners being repudiated or becoming unenforceable because of a change of government, or of government policy, in a country.

pooling   Losses suffered by a small number of insureds are spread over the entire group so insurance purchasers substitute the average loss in place of the uncertainty that they might suffer a large loss.

portability In pension plans, workers' right to take pension benefits with them when changing jobs.

positive time preference The preference of people to consume goods today rather than tomorrow.

predictable velocity The monetarist (or quantity theory) view that velocity is predictably stable; thus they advocate changing the money supply to change levels of economic activity.

preferred habitat The theory of the term structure of interest rates that suggests investors leave their preferred maturity range only if adequately compensated for the additional risk of investing in a security whose maturity does not match the investors' investment horizon. This theory is an extension of the market segmentation theory.

preferred stock Corporate stock that has certain "preferences" relative to the interests of common stockholders. Usually, dividend payments are predetermined and must be made before dividends can be distributed to common stockholders.

preliminary prospectus A portion of the registration statement that contains detailed information about the issuer's financial condition, business activities, industry competition, management and their experience, the project for which the funds will be used, the characteristics of the securities to be issued, and the risks of the securities.

premature death In insurance, a death that occurs during a person's income-producing years.

premium bond A bond whose market price is above its par or face value. A bond sells at a premium when the market rate of interest is below the bond's fixed coupon rate.

prepayment risk The risk that a mortgage will be repaid sooner than expected.

present value The value today of a future stream of cash payments discounted at the appropriate discount rate.

price indexes: CPI, PPI, GDP deflator Indexes constructed by selecting a representative group or "basket" of commodities and tracing their price changes from period to period. Price indexes demonstrate whether prices in general are rising or falling.

price risk Interest rate changes can cause the market price of a bond to rise or fall, resulting in gains or losses for an investor.

price stability The stability of the average price of all goods and services in the economy.

price-weighted index A stock market index that is first computed by summing the prices of the individual stocks composing the index; then, the sum of the prices is divided by a "divisor" to yield the chosen base index value.

price-yield profile A plot of a bond's price (y-axis) versus its market yield (x-axis).

primary market Financial market in which financial claims are first sold as new issues. All financial claims have a primary market.

primary offering Offerings of new issues of stocks or bonds.

primary reserves Cash assets on a bank balance sheet that are immediately available to accommodate deposit withdrawals or meet reserve requirements.

prime rate A commercial bank's lowest posted rate.

principal (par value) *See* **par value**

private bank Privately owned investment banks that could at one time engage in any business activity they wished and could have offices at any location.

private-label credit Plans offered by major finance companies for retailers; all correspondence with the consumer is carried on using the retailer's name, but the credit is provided by the finance company.

private mortgage insurance (PMI) Insurance for mortgages not insured by a federal agency; the consumer pays the insurance premium in addition to the loan rate, thus allowing the consumer to buy a house with a lower down payment.

private placements The distribution of some equity securities in which the investment banker acts only as the company's agent and receives a commission for placing the securities with investors.

private-purpose bond Home mortgage bonds, private college and university bonds, and so on are private-purpose bonds and have been restricted under the Tax Reform Act.

promised yield (yield-to-maturity) *See* **yield to maturity**

promissory note Unconditional promise in writing by the borrower to pay the lender a specific amount of money at some specified date.

prompt corrective action A policy of intervening in the management of a financial institution quickly when the institution begins showing signs of financial distress.

prospectus Corporate disclosures required by the SEC for security offerings in which each security and its risks are fully described before the security is sold to the public.

provision for loan losses An expense item that adds to a financial institution's loan loss reserve.

proxy A process in which shareholders vote for the corporation's board of directors by absentee ballot rather than at the annual shareholders' meeting.

public offering The offering of securities publicly in the open market to all interested buyers. Public offerings are usually made through an investment banking firm.

public placement (sale) The offering of a bond issue publicly in the open market to all interested buyers. Public offerings are usually made through an investment banking firm.

purchase and assumption A policy of the deposit insurance fund covering bank failures. The insurance fund can sell the assets of the failed institution to another institution that "purchases" the assets and "assumes" the responsibility for repaying the liabilities of the failed institution.

purchasing power parity An economic concept that says the purchasing power of a currency should be equal in every country if goods, services, labor, capital, and other resources can flow freely between countries. However, because there are impediments to free trade, purchasing power parity conditions often do not hold. Thus, goods often cost more in one country than in another.

pure risk In the language of insurance, a risk in which the outcome is either a loss or no loss; there is no possibility for gain. Pure risks arise from events over which one has little or no control.

put interest discount The difference in interest rates between putable and similar nonputable bonds.

put option The option allowing the investor to sell an asset to the put issuer at a predetermined price.

putable bond An option giving the buyer the right to sell the underlying security at a predetermined price at stated times prior to maturity.

pyramiding of reserves System by which smaller country banks counted their deposits in large city banks as part of their reserves; when the country banks needed currency they exchanged their reserves at larger banks for cash, thus depleting the larger banks' holdings, often leading to a liquidity squeeze and financial panics.

quantity theory of money and the economy The theory that the level of nominal national income is primarily determined by the quantity of money in circulation. People who believe in the quantity theory are called quantity theorists or monetarists.

rate ceilings Regulations limiting the maximum interest rates that can be charged on different types of loans.

rate-sensitive assets Assets that either will mature or can be repriced within a specific period of time (often 1 year).

rate-sensitive liabilities Liabilities that either will mature or be prepriced within a specific period of time (usually one year).

rational expectations theory The theory that the public will correctly anticipate the future; thus a government policy will have an uncertain or negligible effect.

real estate investment trust (REIT) A type of closed-end investment company that invests in real estate.

real estate mortgage investment conduit (REMIC) A legal entity that issues multiple classes of securities that pass through principal and interest payments made on mortgages or CMOs. Like CMOs, most REMIC securities pay structured principal and interest payments.

real estate–secured lending Credit secured with a mortgage on real estate.

real income Income in terms of its purchasing power. (Nominal income adjusted for price level differences.)

real rate of interest The nominal rate of interest prevailing in the marketplace adjusted for the expected rate of inflation; the equilibrium rate of interest if no inflation occurs.

realized real rate of return The nominal rate of return on an investment adjusted for the actual rate of inflation that occurred after the investment was undertaken; the realized real rate can be either negative or positive.

realized yield The rate of return earned on a bond given the price paid and the cash flows actually received by the investor.

reciprocal Reciprocal exchanges; a form of insuring organization that operates like mutuals and whose objective it is to minimize the cost of the insurance product.

redemption fee Fees assessed when an investor cashes in (redeems) shares in a mutual fund.

refinance Obtaining new financing with a lower interest rate and using the proceeds to pay off the balance due on old financing.

registered bonds Bonds for which the bondholder's name is recorded and coupon payments are mailed to the bondholders. No coupons are physically attached to the bond.

registration statement A statement filed with the Securities and Exchange Commission (SEC) when securities are to be sold publicly.

Regulation B—equal credit opportunity Regulation through which the Federal Reserve Board implements the Equal Credit Opportunity Act of 1974.

Regulation E Federal Reserve regulation for electronic funds transfer and payment systems.

Regulation Q (rate ceilings) A historical Federal Reserve regulation that set a maximum interest rate that banks could pay on deposits. All interest rate ceilings on time and savings were phased out on April 1, 1986, by federal law.

Regulation Z—truth-in-lending Regulation requiring disclosures about (1) the annual percentage rate and (2) the total finance charges and other terms of a loan.

regulatory arbitrage The shifting of operations to jurisdictions, regulators, or countries with the least restrictive regulations.

regulatory capture The possibility that industry regulators will represent the interests of the institutions they regulate in order to keep the industry healthy and retain their jobs.

regulatory dialectic The process by which regulations are evaded, new regulations are enacted to close the loopholes, new evasion strategies and products are developed, new regulations are adopted to curb the innovations, and so on.

reinsurance Risk sharing between the original insurer and another insurance company, the reinsurer.

reinvestment risk The risk resulting from market interest rate changes that cause a bond investor to have to reinvest coupon payments at interest rates different from the bond's promised yield.

REITs *See* **real estate investment trusts**

REMIC *See* **real estate mortgage investment conduit**

renegotiated-rate mortgages Mortgages whose rate must be renegotiated periodically. Renewal at the new rate is guaranteed and the maximum rate change is limited.

renewability The ability of term insurance policies to be renewed at the end of the policy term without new evidence of insurability.

repo *See* **repurchase agreement**

representative money Legal tender (such as silver certificates) issued by the government and representing a specified amount of precious metal held on deposit that could be withdrawn on request.

representative offices Offices established in a foreign country primarily to assist the parent bank's customers in that country. Representative offices cannot accept deposits, make loans, transfer funds, accept drafts, transact in the international money market, or commit the parent bank to loans.

repurchase agreement (repo) A form of loan in which the borrower sells securities (usually government securities) and simultaneously contracts to repurchase the same securities, either on call or on a specified date, at a price that will produce a specified yield.

required reserves Financial institutions are required by law to maintain minimum reserves equal to a percentage of specified deposit liabilities. Reserve requirements vary with the deposit size of the institution and the type of deposit. They are held at Federal Reserve banks or as cash in financial institutions' vaults.

reserve requirement changes Requirements established by the Federal Reserve within limits set by Congress; these requirements determine how many funds financial institutions must hold in order to back their deposits. Reductions in reserve requirements can stimulate deposit expansion while an increase can have the opposite effect.

reserves Assets or liabilities held by an institution to provide for future contingencies.

residual claim A feature of common stock that is a claim against the firm's cash flow or assets; in the event of the firm's liquidation, those with prior claims are paid first and the common stockholders are entitled to what is left over, the residual.

Resolution Trust Corporation (RTC) An institution created in 1989 to acquire and liquidate the assets of failed savings associations.

return on average assets (ROAA) An institution's annual net income divided by its average assets during the year.

return on average equity (ROAE) An institution's annual net income divided by its average book value of equity during the year.

return on investment The future additional real output generated by investment in productive capital projects.

revenue bond State and local government bonds sold to finance a specific revenue-producing project; in the event of default, these bonds are backed only by the revenue generated from the project.

reverse annuity mortgages (RAMs) Mortgages designed for older people who own their homes and need additional funds to meet current living expenses but do not want to sell their homes; they allow people to borrow against the equity in their homes at relatively low interest rates. The borrower receives monthly payments.

reverse repurchase agreements (reverse repos) The reverse (lending) side of a repurchase agreement.

reverse repos *See* **reverse repurchase agreements**

revolving credit A formal legal agreement under which a bank agrees to lend up to a certain limit for a period exceeding one year.

rights offering The placement of equity securities directly with the company's existing stockholders; existing stockholders are given "rights" to purchase additional shares at a slightly below-market price in proportion to their current ownership in the company. Stockholders can exercise their rights or sell them.

risk Uncertainty concerning the occurrence of loss.

risk-based capital standards (Established by the Bank for International Settlements, located in Basle, Switzerland, which coordinates international bank payment policies.) Risk-based capital requirements were necessary because many institutions had begun to assume off-balance-sheet risk by obligating themselves in letters of credit, financial guarantees, and other transactions to earn extra fee income from operations that posed risk but did not appear on their balance sheets.

risk premium Required (or expected) return on a risky security minus the return on a similar risk-free security.

risk transfer Shifting the responsibility of bearing risk from one party to another party.

risk-weighted assets Risk-weighted assets is a measure of total assets that weights high-risk assets more heavily than low-risk assets.

ROAA *See* **return on average assets**

ROAE *See* **return on average equity**

rollover mortgages (ROMs) Mortgages that mature before full amortization. At that time the borrower may elect to renew (roll over) the mortgage at the prevailing mortgage rate. Thus the borrower may pay several different rates on the mortgage before it is fully amortized.

rollover pricing Floating-rate loans that allow banks to fund credits in the Eurocurrency market at the beginning of the period and lock in a lending spread for the coming period. At the end of this period, the loan will again "roll over" and be repriced for the subsequent period.

RTC *See* **Resolution Trust Corporation**

Rule 144A SEC rule that allows secondary trading of private securities by large institutional investors.

run Bank runs occur when a large number of depositors simultaneously try to convert a single bank's liabilities into currency. Because banks hold fractional reserves, it is not possible to satisfy all requests immediately. The establishment of the FDIC has eliminated most bank runs.

sales finance company A company that finances the credit sales of retailers and dealers by purchasing the installment credit contracts that they acquire when they sell goods on credit.

Samurai bonds Bonds issued in Japan by foreign companies.

Sarbanes-Oxley Act Legislation passed in 2002 that put in place tougher accounting and auditing standards.

savings accounts Bank accounts in which customers may store idle cash to earn interest before they spend it.

Savings Association Insurance Fund (SAIF) Replaced the FSLIC as the federal insuring agency for savings associations in 1989. SAIF is controlled by the FDIC.

Say's law Law in classical quantity theory that "production creates its own demand."

scalper Traders who follow a strategy of making very quick trades in hopes of making many quick, small profits throughout the day.

seasonal borrowing privilege Fed's borrowing privilege allowing banks with large seasonal fluctuations in loan demand to borrow at the Fed's discount window.

seasonal loan A loan providing term financing to take care of temporary discrepancies between business revenues and expenses that are due to the manufacturing or sales cycle of a business.

seasoned offering The primary issue of securities of a type already trading in the secondary market.

SEC *See* **Securities and Exchange Commission**

second-mortgage lending Mortgage lending in which real estate lending is secured by second mortgages.

second mortgages Loans secured by liens on properties that are already mortgaged; also called junior mortgages.

second-stage financing Capital used for initial expansion of a company that has already been producing and selling a product.

secondary market Financial market in which participants buy or sell previously issued financial claims.

secondary mortgage markets Markets in which mortgage bankers and other mortgage-originating institutions sell the mortgages they originate to both public and private purchasers.

secondary reserves Short-term assets (often Treasury bills) that banks can quickly convert to cash at a price near their purchase price.

secured loan A secured loan is a bank loan guaranteed by collateral consisting of merchandise, inventory, accounts receivable, plant and equipment, real estate, or stocks and bonds.

Securities and Exchange Commission (SEC) A federally established regulator of the financial markets, with enforcement powers and specific corporate disclosure requirements.

Securities Exchange Act of 1934 Congressional legislation that established the Securities and Exchange Commission to regulate the financial markets.

securitization The process of pooling and repackaging loans so they have the characteristics of security instruments, which enables them to be more easily resold.

securitization of risk Transfer of insurable risk to the capital markets through the creation of a financial instrument.

security market line (SML) The linear relationship between systematic risk (beta) and expected return.

seed financing Capital provided to a company at the "idea" stage.

senior debt In the event of liquidation of a firm, senior debt holders must be paid first.

separate trading of registered interest and principal (STRIPs) A Treasury security that has been separated into its component parts: each interest payment and the principal payment become a separate zero-coupon security.

settlement Procedures in a particular market for the exchange of securities or other financial claims for payment in cash, securities, and so on.

settlement date In a forward contract, the future date on which the buyer pays the seller and the seller delivers the assets to the buyer.

share certificates Credit union liabilities similar to certificates of deposit at banks.

share-draft accounts Checking accounts offered by credit unions that pay explicit interest. They are equivalent to NOW accounts.

shelf registration An innovation in the sale of new corporate securities that permits a corporation to register a quantity of securities with the SEC and sell them over a 2-year period rather than all at once.

shell branches A booking office for bank transactions located abroad that has no contact with the public; the easiest and cheapest way to enter international banking.

short position An agreement to sell in the futures market.

short squeeze A circumstance in which an individual or group tries to make it difficult or impossible for short sellers in futures markets to liquidate their contracts through delivery of acceptable commodities.

sight draft A draft that requires the bank to pay on demand, assuming that all documentation is in proper order and that all conditions have been met.

sinking fund A corporate bond provision that requires the bond issuer to provide funds to a trustee to retire a specific dollar amount (face amount) of bonds each year.

social adequacy The concept of slanting pension benefits in favor of certain groups to achieve broader social goals.

specialists Members of the exchange who combine the attributes of both dealers and order clerks; they have an affirmative obligation to maintain both bid and offer quotations at all times for listed securities.

speculative capital flows International capital flows that occur when market forces suggest that the currency's value is incorrect and likely to change soon.

speculative-grade (junk) bonds The bonds rated below Baa (or BBB) by bond rating agencies such as Moody's or Standard & Poor's.

speculative risk In the language of insurance, a risk that can result in either a gain or a loss.

speculator An individual who assumes price risk in the expectation of earning a high return.

spot market The market in which securities are traded for immediate delivery and payment.

spot price An observed price at which current transactions take place.

spot rate An observed interest rate at which current transactions take place.

spread (or straddle) A position in options that combines two or more options (i.e., two or more calls or puts).

SSU *See* **surplus spending unit**

standardized deposit receipt Medium of exchange in early banking in which goldsmiths storing valuables (often gold coins) issued deposit receipts to customers with uniform values. Customers discovered that they could directly exchange such receipts for goods and services provided that the recipient had confidence the receipt would be redeemed by the goldsmith (bank).

standby letter of credit   A guarantee that a financial institution will make a payment (in return for advancing a loan to its customer) if the customer should fail to do so.

start-up financing   Capital used in initial product development and initial marketing.

stock association   A form of savings and loan association that issues common stock to shareholders and is managed by managers appointed by a board of directors elected by profit-seeking shareholders.

stock exchange   An organization established to make purchases and sales of stocks easier. Stock exchanges may either bring buyers and sellers together through the auspices of specialists who trade in each stock, or they may use computer facilities to match buy and sell orders.

stock-index futures contract   A futures contract written on the value of a stock index.

stock-index options   Options contracts written on the value of stock indexes.

stock or bond mutual funds   Funds that take the cash received from customers and invest mainly in stocks or bonds.

store of value   A function of money in which it can be used to store purchasing power between the time it is earned and the time it is spent.

straight voting   A procedure for electing directors in which directors are elected one by one; thus, the maximum number of votes a shareholder has for each director equals the number of shares owned.

strike price   The price at which an option can be exercised.

STRIPs   *See* **separate trading of registered interest and principal**

structural unemployment   Term indicating that a portion of those that are unemployed are unemployed because there is a mismatch between their skill levels and available jobs or that there are jobs in one region of the country but few in another region.

subordinated debt   In the event of default, subordinated debt holders' claims to the company's assets rank behind senior debt; also known as junior debt.

superannuation   Living too long; outliving your income.

surplus   For a mutual institution, net profits that are not distributed as dividends are retained as surplus in the institution's net worth account.

surplus spending unit (SSU)   An economic unit whose income for the period exceeds expenditures. SSUs often purchase financial claims issued by deficit spending units (DSUs).

swap   An exchange of assets or income streams for equivalent assets or income streams with slightly different characteristics.

syndicate   International bank loans in which several banks participate in funding the loans, which are packaged by one or more lead banks.

systematic risk   The risk that tends to affect the entire market in a similar fashion; also known as market risk or nondiversifiable risk.

TBTF   *See* **too big to fail**

technical factors   Factors outside the control of the Federal Reserve (e.g., cash drains, float, and Treasury deposits) that affect the monetary base.

term bonds   A bond issue in which all of the bonds that comprise the issue mature on a single date.

term insurance   A product that provides a death benefit to the beneficiary if the insured dies within a specified time. Such policies provide only death protection and no savings element.

term loan   A loan from a bank with a specific maturity. Typically, term loans have maturities greater than one year.

term structure of interest rates   The relationship between yield and term to maturity on securities that differ only in length of time to maturity; graphically approximated by the yield curve.

term-to-maturity   The length of time until the final payment of a debt security.

thin   A term describing a market where trades are relatively infrequent.

third-stage financing   Capital provided to fund major expansion such as plant expansion, product improvement, or marketing.

Tier 1 capital   A measure of bank capital that includes the sum of common stock, paid-in-surplus, retained earnings, noncumulative perpetual preferred stock, and minority interest in consolidated subsidiaries minus goodwill and other intangible assets. Tier 1 capital is commonly referred to as core capital.

Tier 2 capital   A measure of bank capital that includes cumulative perpetual preferred stock, loan loss reserves, subordinated debt instruments, mandatory convertible debt instruments, and other debt instruments that combine both debt and equity features. Tier 2 capital is commonly referred to as supplemental capital.

time draft   A draft payable at a particular time in the future, as specified in a letter of credit.

time value of money   The concept based on the belief that people have a positive time preference for consumption, preferring to consume goods today rather than consume similar goods in the future; thus a dollar today is worth more than a dollar received at some future date.

TIPS   *See* Treasury Inflation Protection Securities

too big to fail (TBTF)   Policy adopted by federal regulators that the failure of certain financial institutions would have too much of an adverse effect on the economy and so those insitutions will not be allowed to fail.

total reserves   *See* actual reserves

trader   An individual who buys or sells securities in the hope of profiting quickly from expected price movements.

tranche   A specific portion of a security issue; for example, mortgage-backed securities may have interest-only or principal-only tranches.

transaction costs   The costs involved in buying or selling securities.

transfer credit   A source of credit for smaller subsidiaries in a holding company; a form of funding provided by their larger parent companies.

Treasury bill   Direct obligation of the federal government with initial maturities ranging from 3 months to 1 year. They are considered to have no default risk and are the most marketable of any security issued.

Treasury Inflation Protection Securities (TIPS)   Treasury securities that have a fixed coupon rate, but a principal amount that changes in response to changes in the inflation rate.

Treasury note   Similar to Treasury bills in that they are issued by the Treasury and are considered free of default risk; they differ from bills in that they are coupon issues, redeemable at face value upon maturity, and have initial maturities greater than 1 year and no more than 10 years.

Truth-in-Lending Act   *See* **Consumer Credit Protection Act of 1969**

12b-1 fee   Annual fees assessed by a mutual fund, over and above its fund management or advisory fees, specifically to pay for the sales and marketing expenses incurred by the fund.

underpricing   The situation that occurs when securities sold in a public offering immediately begin trading at a price higher than the offering price.

underwriting   The risk-bearing function of the investment banker. Underwriting occurs when the investment banker guarantees fixed proceeds to security issuers while uncertain of the eventual resale price.

underwriting cycle   In insurance, a cyclical pattern in commercial property and liability insurance.

underwriting loss   The amount insurers pay out in claims.

underwriting offering   The most common distribution method for new issues of equity securities in which the investment banker purchases the securities from the company for a guaranteed amount known as the net proceeds and then resells the securities to investors for a greater amount, called the gross proceeds.

underwriting spread   The difference between the fixed price paid for securities and the price at which they are resold, constituting the investment banker's (or underwriter's) gross profit.

underwriting standards   Standards used by mortgage lenders to reduce the chance of default (credit risk) by ensuring that the property, loan amount, and borrower conform to these standards. Conventional lenders may choose their own standards as long as they do not violate laws or regulations; however, since most mortgages are sold to other institutions, national standards are now imposed on most mortgage loans.

underwriting syndicate   A group of investment bankers that underwrite a security issue.

undivided earnings   Part of a credit union's net worth; credit unions must set aside a portion of their earnings as reserves, until their reserves are sufficiently large relative to their assets; similar to retained earnings of a corporation.

USA Patriot Act   Legislation passed in 1991 that, among other thing, requires banks and other financial service providers to establish the identity of new customers

U.S. Central Credit Union   An organization whose members include Central credit unions; the U.S. Central Credit Union has a commercial bank charter in the state of Kansas and has access to the nation's check payment system. The union can invest in a wide variety of assets and can lend money to credit unions or their centrals.

U.S. government agency   An independent federal department or corporation established by Congress and owned or underwritten by the U.S. government.

unit investment trust A group of assets purchased by investment-banking firms and formed into a trust; units in the trust are sold to individual investors. The trust is passively managed, passing through payments of interest and principal on the initial asset pool until all assets are liquidated.

unit of account A function of money in which it can be used to compare costs of production with prices received and to determine whether a firm makes a profit when it sells goods.

universal bank Institutions that can accept deposits, make loans, underwrite securities, engage in brokerage activities, and sell and manufacture other financial services such as insurance.

universal life insurance Flexible-premium, nonparticipating life insurance that provides a market-based rate of return on the savings or cash value account.

unpredictable velocity Keynesian belief that velocity is unstable and unpredictable, and therefore monetary policy does not necessarily work.

unseasoned offering The name for a primary offering if the company has never before offered securities to the public.

unsystematic risk The unique or security-specific risks which tend to partially offset one another in a portfolio.

usury laws State laws that prohibit the charging of interest above a certain limit—the usury ceiling.

value-at-risk (VAR) A method for determining the interest rate risk exposure of a financial institution based on a determination of the amount that the institution might lose if interest rates were to vary by a sufficiently large amount that such a change would occur only about 1 percent of the time; recommended capital requirements to control for interest rate risk are several times VAR.

value exchange system A funds transfer system that allows owners of assets to transfer part of the value of those assets to others in exchange for goods or services.

value of money The value of money is what you can buy with it—its purchasing power. There is an inverse relationship between the value of money and the average level of prices.

VAR *See* **value-at-risk**

variable life insurance Fixed-premium life insurance that permits the policyowner to select where the cash value is invested.

velocity of money Measures of the number of dollars of national income that are supported with each dollar of money in circulation. When velocity rises, more income can be generated with the same amount of money in circulation. The converse holds if velocity declines.

venture capital Funds provided by institutional investors who provide equity financing to young businesses and play an active role in advising their management.

vesting An employee's right to employer-promised pension benefits or employer contributions, usually after a specified period of time.

Veterans Administration (VA) mortgages Mortgages whose payment is guaranteed by the Veterans Administration.

whole life insurance An insurance contract that provides periodic payment of premiums and protection as long as the insured lives. Upon death or a specific age (usually 65), the face amount of the policy is paid to the policyholder or beneficiary.

wholesale financing Interim financing provided to a dealer by a finance company.

wholesale paper Finance company business lending in which a finance company helps a dealer finance the purchase of goods.

Wicksellian theory Theory, developed by Swedish economist Knut Wicksell, used by the Fed to determine whether people are expecting future inflation or deflation to result from present Fed policies; the theory is based on the notion that the economy has two interest rates—the bank rate and natural rate. If the bank rate is below the natural rate, people tend to invest more and inflation may result. If the bank rate is above the natural rate of interest, people borrow and invest less and the demand for goods and investments will fall and commodity prices will fall in the future.

Yankee bonds Bonds issued by foreign entities in the United States.

yield curve The graph of the relationship between interest rates on particular securities and their yield to maturity. To construct yield curves, bonds must be as similar in as many other characteristics as possible.

yield-to-maturity (promised yield) The discount rate that equates the present value of all cash flows from a bond (interest payments plus principal) to the market price of the bond.

zero-coupon securities Securities that have no coupon payment but promise a single payment at maturity.

Credits and Acknowledgments

Part Openers (Left): Shaun Egan/Stone/Getty Images.
(Right): Harald Sund/The Image Bank/Getty Images.

Chapter Openers

Chapter 1	Cyberimage/Taxi/Getty Images.
Chapter 2	Corbis-Bettmann.
Chapter 3	Win McNamee/Corbis Images.
Chapter 4	Gamma Ray Studio /The Image Bank/Getty Images.
Chapter 5	Sandy Shaeffer/Time Life Pictures/Getty Images.
Chapter 6	Anna Clopet/Corbis Images.
Chapter 7	Al Francekevich/Corbis Images.
Chapter 8	James Nielsen/Getty Images News and Sport Services.
Chapter 9	Premium Stock/Corbis Images.
Chapter 10	Stephen Cherin/Getty Images News and Sport Services.
Chapter 11	Newsmakers/Liaison Agency, Inc./Getty Images.
Chapter 12	Travelpix/FPG International/Getty Images.
Chapter 13	Corbis-Bettmann.
Chapter 14	Reuters/Liaison Agency, Inc./Getty Images.
Chapter 15	B.S.P.I./Corbis Images.
Chapter 16	Corbis-Bettmann.
Chapter 17	RKO Pictures/Hulton Archive/Getty Images.
Chapter 18	Alan R. Moller/Stone/Getty Images.
Chapter 19	Chuck Savage/Corbis Images.
Chapter 20	©AP/Wide World Photos.

Exhibit 10.7 *Wall Street Journal*, May 20, 2004. Copyright © 2002 By Dow Jones & Co Inc. Reproduced with Permission of Dow Jones & Co, Inc via Copyright Clearance Center, inc.

Exhibit 18.1 "Ten Largest Life/Health Companies, 2002" from *Best's Key Ratings Guide*, *Life/Health*, 2003 Edition. © A. M. Best Company. Used with permission.

Exhibit 18.2	"Ten Largest Property/Casualty Companies, 2002" from *Best's Key Ratings Guide, Property/Casualty*, 2003 Edition. © A. M. Best Company. Used with permission.
Exhibit 18.3	"Life Insurance Companies' Balance Sheet, 2002" from *Best's Aggregates and Averages, Life/Health*, 2003 Edition. © A. M. Best Company. Used with permission.
Exhibit 18.4	"Propery/Casualty Companies' Balance Sheet, 2002" from *Best's Aggregates and Averages, Property/Casualty*, 2003 Edition. © A. M. Best Company. Used with permission.
Exhibit 20.2	"Assets and Number of Closed-End Funds by Type of Fund," Source: 2004 *Mutual Fund Fact Book*, Copyright © 2004 Investment Company Institute. Reprinted by permission of the Investment Company Institute (www.ici.org).
Exhibit 20.3	"Assets and Number of Exchange-Traded Index Funds (ETFs) by Type of Fund," Source: 2004 *Mutual Fund Fact Book*, Copyright © 2004 Investment Company Institute. Reprinted by permission of the Investment Company Institute (www.ici.org).
Exhibit 20.6	"Assets Held by Equity, Hybrid, and Bond Mutual Funds," Source: Investment Company Institute (www.ici.org). Reprinted with permission.
Exhibit 20.7	"How to Read Mutual Fund Quotes in Newspapers," Source: 2001 *Mutual Fund Fact Book*, Copyright © 2001 Investment Company Institute. Reprinted by permission of the Investment Company Institute (www.ici.org).

Index

Terms in **boldface** are glossary terms.